RABBI JOSEPH DOV SOLOVEITCHIK ON THE EXPERIENCE OF PRAYER

RABBI JOSEPH DOV SOLOVEITCHIK ON THE EXPERIENCE OF PRAYER

Dov
Schwartz

Translated by
Edward Levin

BOSTON
2019

3528   𝑀𝑇

Library of Congress Control Number:2019941908

ISBN 978-1-61811-718-2 (hardcover)
ISBN 978-1-61811-719-9 (paper)
ISBN 978-1-61811-972-8 (electronic)

Cover design by Ivan Grave.
Book design by Kryon Publishing Services Pvt. Ltd.
http://www.kryonpublishing.com

Published by Academic Studies Press in 2019
1577 Beacon Street
Brookline, MA 02446
press@academicstudiespress.com
www.academicstudiespress.com

2/10/20

Table of Contents

Introduction

Any discussion of the relationship between prayer and philosophical, theological, and Kabbalistic thought must go beyond the philological, historical, and halakhic study of prayer. Prayer is an inherent component of the world of the religious individual, and in consequence has always occupied center stage in the intensive research of the history of religions and comparative religion. Prayer is perceived as a defining experience in the relationship between man and the divine, and between man and himself. This experience places man and his initiatives at its center. Man praises, requests, and sings to his God. At times God is seen as a partner to the conversation, and at other times, as a passive listener. On occasion the prayer experience overwhelms the being of the worshiper to the extent that he has no need of any tangible response; it suffices for God to be aware of his prayer. There are times when the worshiper expects that prayer will cause God to actively intervene in his life. Sometimes prayer expresses man's self, and makes him aware of his personality and the deep strata of his soul. The act of prayer and its formulation enable the worshiper to understand his authentic needs, and there are instances in which the worshiper gains insights into the divine by means of his addressing Him. In any event, prayer is humanly-initiated action. It expresses the wealth of a person's expression, progressing from the word and the sound to language and dialogue. Formal dialogue is conducted between man and God, while accompanied by a dialogue between man and himself. The liturgical text became the basis of the experience, and as such, the prayer experience blazed a trail over the course of time to the very heart of religiosity.

These features of the prayer experience are manifest in the Jewish world, as well.[1] It is not surprising that prayer has captivated modern Jewish thought. It is perceived as a subjective act par excellence, which represents

---

1 A detailed list of studies on Jewish prayer was prepared by Joseph Tabory, the indefatigable bibliographer of prayer. See Joseph Tabory, *Jewish Prayer and the Yearly Cycle: A List of Articles*, supplement to *Kiryat Sefer* 64 [Hebrew] (Jerusalem, 1992-1993).

the religious experience of the worshiper. On a parallel track, philosophers such as Hermann Cohen and Franz Rosenzweig highlighted prayer as an expression of the individual, and probed the meaning of the movement from personal to communal, public prayer. Of especial scholarly interest is prayer's median position: on the one hand, it is a product of intimate mental processes, while on the other, it embodies the imperative. Prayer oscillates between the autonomous and the authoritative.

The current book analyzes R. Joseph B. Soloveitchik's writings on prayer. R. Soloveitchik created extensive discussions to this topic, which occupies a prominent place in his legacy. In the current book I will analyze the place of prayer in his writings and the insights regarding prayer that emerge from his writings and thought.

The Study of the Religious Consciousness

R. Soloveitchik did not act in a vacuum. Prayer is an important component of Jewish religiosity in the United States, where R. Soloveitchik was active (as it is in other Diaspora communities), from both the existential-experiential viewpoint and the communal perspective, and its significance will be discussed in the chapters of this book.[2] The centrality of prayer for American Jewry also finds philosophical expression.[3]

The philosophical and theological orientation concerned with the phenomenology of religion occupies an important place in terms of the sources and scholarly methodologies of R. Soloveitchik's thought, as we shall see below. Both the context of the discussion of prayer in R. Soloveitchik's writings and the terminology of this discussion are based on the literature of the phenomenology of religion. I intend to argue that the main goal of R. Soloveitchik's thought on prayer is to offer a phenomenological description of the consciousness of prayer. To this end, we should more sharply define the boundaries of this consciousness.

Phenomenologists of religion generally accepted the principles formulated by Edmund Husserl (1859-1938), viewing religion as a given. Rather than judging the religious phenomenon, the phenomenologist of religion seeks to decipher it and understand its nature. The phenomenologist is occupied with description, and therefore examines the structure of the consciousness, that is, the manner in which objects are perceived by the

---

2 See below, Chapter Twelve.
3 See, for example, Shalom Ratshabi, *Between Destiny and Faith: The Jewish Theological Discourse in the United States* [Hebrew] (Tel Aviv: Am Oved, 2003), 241-242.

consciousness. According to Husserl, consciousness is intentional and relates to objects. For the phenomenologists of religion, the religious individual possesses a distinct consciousness that includes a series of epistemological acts that relate to objects such as God. These phenomenologists examine the various—at times contradictory—appearances of religion in order to isolate the essential elements of the religious consciousness: in this case, the consciousness of prayer. Philosophers and scholars have discussed the nature and definitions of the phenomenology of religion. Eric Sharpe formulated the task of the phenomenology of religion in five stages:

(1) to assign names to groups of phenomena—such as sacrifice, prayer, saviour, myth, etc.;
(2) to interpolate the experiences within one's own life and experience them systematically—a point which seems at the first sight hard to reconcile with the claim that the aim of phenomenology is "pure objectivity";
(3) to exercise *epoche*, that is, to withdraw to one side and observe;
(4) to clarify and comprehend.
(5) to confront chaotic reality and testify to what has been understood.[4]

Sharpe based the work of the phenomenologist on the writings of Gerardus van der Leeuw (1890-1950), Jan Hermelink (1924-1961), and others. Joseph D. Bettis noted that the phenomenology of religion differs from the philosophy of religion in that, inter alia, it is not concerned solely with ideas and doctrines but also studies the diverse forms of religious expression, such as ritual, symbolism, and the like.[5] In other words, phenomenology is also concerned with the epistemological meaning of "objective" acts, and not only with the subjective experience. This distinction is a formative element in the thought of R. Soloveitchik. This forms the background for the phenomenological inquiry into prayer.

The Consciousness of Prayer

The phenomenological discussion of prayer in the scholarly literature of the history of religion in general, and particularly that of the Jewish world, was conducted in at least two planes.

---

4 Eric Sharpe, *Comparative Religion* (London: Duckworth, 1975), 234.
5 Joseph D. Bettis (ed.), *Phenomenology of Religion: Eight Modern Descriptions of the Essence of Religion* (New York: Harper & Row, 1969), 3. See Sharpe, *Comparative Religion*, 248-249.

(1) Prayer by itself. The discussion encompassed various aspects of the virtues, properties, and consequences of prayer. In many instances, the nature of prayer was determined in accordance with its effect and purpose. The aims of prayer are defined as follows:
   (a) influence on divine and cosmic providence;
   (b) influence on the worshiper's moral and religious degree (= education);
   (c) influence on the social fabric (community, public prayer).

(2) Prayer in the context of the worshiper. Prayer is not perceived as an autonomous religious act. Rather, it reflects the worshiper's consciousness and his general relationship to God and the world. In this plane, prayer is not weighed in accordance with its purpose, but by the contribution it makes in the fashioning of the worshiper's religious state and the expressions of this situation. This approach was expressed in three perceptions of prayer:
   (a) as a mirror and symptom of the worshiper's way of life and religious consciousness;[6]
   (b) as standing before God,[7] and as an expression of the relationship with the transcendental dimension of life;
   (c) as an expression of community (public prayer).[8]

The first plane, that of prayer by itself, corresponds to the perception of prayer as an expression of "sacred words," in the terminology of the phenomenologist of religion Edvard Lehmann (1862-1930). According to Lehmann, prayers play a central role in the second of religion's three components ("sacred actions," such as ritual and magic; "sacred words," such as sacred music and ceremonies; and "sacred places," in the sense of

---

6 *Maharal* (R. Judah Loew ben Bezalel) argued that prayer is a component in the definition of the perfect man. According to him, man was created deficient, and he completes himself by means of prayer. *Maharal* used the Aristotelian terminology that refers to man as *medabber* ("rational one"; literally, "the one who speaks"), but while Aristotle referred to inner speech, that is, verbal thought, *Maharal* meant audible speech. Prayer completes speech, and man is a whole "speaking entity" (Judah Loew ben Bezalel, *Netivot Olam, Netiv ha-Avodah* 2 [Jerusalem, 1972], 81a). On speech, see also Karl Erich Grözinger, "Sprache und Identität—Das Hebräische und die Juden," in *Sprache und Identität im Judentum*, ed. K. E. Grözinger (Wiesbaden: Otto Harrassowitz Verlag, 1998), 75-90.

7 Schechter stated that prayer attests to affinity between man and his God. He sharply opposed the view that ascribes a transcendentalist position to the rabbinic literature. See Solomon Schechter, *Aspects of Rabbinic Theology* (New York: Schocken, 1961 [1901]), 22-23.

8 See, for example, Perry D. LeFevre, *Understandings of Prayer* (Philadelphia: The Westminster Press, 1981).

expanse and place in the expanse).[9] Alston listed prayer and "other forms of communication with gods" as one of the "religion-making characteristics."[10]

The second plane, that of prayer as a dynamic reflection of the life of the worshiper, is suitable for the discussion of prayer in the mystic and the phenomenological literatures. Christian spirituality is based in part on the book of Psalms and on the prayers constructed from it. The monastic agenda relies on such prayers as is reflected, for instance, in the writings of Augustine. In the mystical literature, prayer is at times an expression of the aspiration for communion and union with God. For example, Teresa of Avila (1515-1582) called the first stage of such union the "prayer of quiet." Unlike verbal prayer, this is the meditative stage of a sacred ceremony or event from the life of the saints. This results in an experience of proximity to God. She termed the second stage the "prayer of full union," which is marked by the manifestation of the divine presence within the soul. This results in the union of God and the soul in a mutual embrace. The third stage is the ecstatic.[11] According to this depiction, prayer is merely a reflection of the different levels of the mystical experience. An expansive approach of the epistemology of prayer is also to be found among thinkers who are not identified as mystics. For example, Emil Brunner (1889-1966) writes that prayer is a mirror of the worshiper's soul and his relationship to the divine. He argues that prayer proceeds from "profound reflection upon our own lives, as well as from the study of God's Word."[12] R. Judah Halevi's thought, for example, is not mystical—but, nevertheless, views prayer as an expression of the flow of religious life in its entirety.[13]

The Phenomenological Study of Prayer

The academic interest in prayer first arose at the end of the nineteenth century. Scholars who viewed prayer as a central expression of religion

---

9 See Sharpe, *Comparative Religion*, 227.

10 William P. Alston, "Religion," in *The Encyclopedia of Philosophy*, ed. Paul Edwards (New York: Macmillan, 1967), vols. 7-8, 141-142.

11 See Nelson Pike, *Mystic Union: An Essay in the Phenomenology of Mysticism* (Ithaca, NY: Cornell University Press, 1992), 1-11.

12 Emil Brunner, *The Divine Imperative: A Study in Christian Ethics*, trans. Olive Wyon (Cambridge: Lutterworth, 2002]), 314. R. Soloveitchik cited Brunner in *Out of the Whirlwind: Essays on Mourning, Suffering and the Human Condition*, ed. David Schatz, Joel B. Wolowelsky, and Reuven Ziegler (Hoboken, NJ: Toras HoRav Foundation, 2003), 151, 154-155.

13 See below, Chapter Eleven.

began to use critical historical, psychological, and comparative scientific approaches. Many of those who composed studies devoted to prayer were German, such as Eduard von der Goltz (1870-1939), Otto Dibelius (1880-1967), and Paul Drews (1858-1912). Marcel Mauss (1872-1950) from France and Friedrich Heiler (1892-1967) argued that prayer is a universal component of religion and, as such, constitutes man's communion with his God.[14]

The religious phenomenology perceived prayer primarily as a "religious act" or "spiritual act,"[15] which becomes fully significant only in a religious environment. R. Soloveitchik frequently used these expressions, most of which were developed, with thorough argumentation, in the writings of Max Scheler (1874-1928). For Scheler, prayer, as any religious act, could not be fully comprehended unless, as he writes regarding repentance, "one places it within a deeper overall conception of the nature of our temporal life-stream in relation to our permanent personal Self [*feststehender Person hineinzustellen*]."[16] Scheler further argued that the religious act is autonomous, that is, it acquires its meaning only in the context of the religious consciousness. Its psychological, philosophical, and social aspects may be useful in coming to know the standing of prayer, but its full understanding is possible only within the experience of the religious consciousness, the experience of meeting with God.[17] In this respect, Scheler may have been influenced by Rudolf Otto (1869-1937), who stated in his book *The Idea of the Holy* that religiosity cannot be fully translated into other realms (psychology, sociology, philosophy, and the like).[18] The experience of God, or the numinous, is characteristic solely of religion. According to Otto and Scheler's approaches, prayer is considered not as an isolated act, but within the special context of religious life. In any event, prayer is, first and foremost, an act of specific religious consciousness. In many respects, Scheler added depth to Otto's approach.

In R. Soloveitchik's writings, we see direct traces of Scheler and Otto's influence. However, there were also other phenomenologists of religion, who specifically examined the consciousness of prayer (see below), and

---

14 See W. S. F. Pickering, "Introduction" to Marcel Mauss, *On Prayer*, trans. S. Leslie (New York: Durkheim, 2003), 9.

15 Terms "religious act" and "religious action" are both used to denote the act.

16 Max Scheler, *On the Eternal in Man*, trans. B. Noble (Hamden, CT: Archon, 1972), 39.

17 The nature of the religious act will be discussed below, in Chapter Six.

18 R. Soloveitchik was occupied to a great extent in *The Lonely Man of Faith* with the impossibility of translating the religious experience. See Dov Schwartz, *From Phenomenology to Existentialism*, trans. Batya Stein (Leiden: Brill, 2012), 335-339.

we can hardly assume that they had no effect on R. Soloveitchik's discussions. R. Soloveitchik was in Berlin during the time when philosophy written in German was stimulated by these approaches, and he was in close contact with the academic faculty that discussed them and was challenged by them. Indeed, his terminology and the nature of his discussions were fashioned, both directly and collaterally, by the phenomenological approaches, as we shall see below.

Friedrich Heiler's book on prayer, *Das Gebet* (*Prayer*), greatly influenced the early twentieth-century perception of prayer, and in a large degree, also the thought of R. Soloveitchik. His book, in turn, was directly influenced by the conception of Nathan Söderblom (1866-1931) who, alongside Scheler and Otto, argued that the religious act must be understood from within itself, and not in the context of other realms, such as psychology or magic. We will now concisely set forth the phenomenological ideas that appeared in Heiler's work.

Heiler maintained that prayer is a direct expression of the inner religious experience, in contrast to all other ceremonial acts, which are merely indirect expressions.[19] He begins his book with the declaration that religious people, scholars, and theologians all view prayer as "the central phenomenon of religion."[20] He asserts that "prayer is the heart and center of all religion."[21]

Heiler sought to describe the essential nature of prayer and devoted the last chapter of his book specifically to this question. There, he raised a series of arguments concerning the consciousness of prayer. Heiler states that prayer appears in many forms, from spontaneous experience to institutionalized formats. Prayer is the most personal experience, while at the same time it is clearly communal. It ranges from being a product of ecstasy to the fulfillment of institutionalized religious law.[22] The most fundamental psychological motive of prayer is man's primal desire for a higher-quality, powerful, and richer life.[23] Consequently, prayer relates to all aspects of human life, from man's very existence to the loftiest spiritual planes.

---

19 See Ron Margolin, *Inner Religion: The Phenomenology of Inner Religious Life and Its Manifestation in Jewish Sources (from the Bible to Hasidic Texts)* [Hebrew] (Ramat Gan: Bar-Ilan University Press, 2002), 23.

20 Friedrich Heiler, *Prayer: A Study in the History and Psychology of Religion,* trans. S. McComb (New York: Oxford University Press, 1958), xiii.

21 Ibid., xv.

22 Ibid., 353.

23 Ibid., 355.

This motivating factor, however, is not all there is to the consciousness of prayer. Heiler argues that the deep inner structure of the consciousness of prayer is based on three foundations:

(1) the belief in a personal God;
(2) the belief in God's real and immediate presence;
(3) a realistic[24] fellowship between man and God, in which God is conceived as present.

Heiler further maintains that prayer is a personal address by the man's "I" to God's "Thou," and the opening of man's heart before God. In short, prayer is a dialogue with God and the creation of a community with Him. Heiler explains that prayer cannot be summed up as the belief in a personal God and in His presence, but rather described as a process of communication that establishes an inner bond between man and his God. We would not be wrong to state that prayer is communion with God.[25]

Heiler's pioneering discussion was followed by the phenomenologists of religion who analyzed the consciousness of prayer within their studies of religion. William Brede Kristensen (1867-1953), for example, argued that the phenomenology of religion searches for the identical elements in different religions, in order to reveal the nature of man's religious consciousness. Kristensen added that religions do not provide accurate and detailed reports on the nature of the religious need that inspires prayer. He analyzed the conscious expression of prayer and split it in the following two categories:

(1) "magic prayer," which emphasizes prayer's capabilities and influences.
(2) "spiritual prayer," representing submission to God's will, and the spiritual power that ensues from this surrender.[26]

In Kristensen's analysis, these two categories appear from a single conscious element, namely, the act of prayer. His analysis is just one example of the internalization of the categories developed in the late nineteenth and

---

24 Ibid., 356. In the German original: *dramatische* (Friedrich Heiler, *Das Gebet: Eine religionsgeschichtliche und religionspsychologische Untersuchung* [Munich: Verlag von Ernst Reinhardt, 1921], 489).

25 Heiler, *Prayer*, 357.

26 W. Brede Kristensen, "The Phenomenology of Religion," in Bettis, *Phenomenology of Religion*, 36-51, at 39.

early twentieth centuries by the researchers who analyzed the consciousness of prayer.

The Consciousness of Prayer in Judaism

The phenomenological perception of prayer is also to be found in the study of Jewish liturgy and its standing in Jewish law and thought. It was mainly employed by the scholars who went beyond the philological and historical dimension of prayer. The following passage by Uri Ehrlich exemplifies this perception:

> To my mind what is called for is not the restriction of the study of prayer to the prayer-text, but a multifaceted examination of the *act* of prayer. Although undeniably a fundamental component, the text in and of itself gives only partial expression to the full import of the prayer-act. Viewed from this broader perspective, liturgical formulas are not just literary compositions but rather texts placed in the mouths of worshipers standing before their Creator in prayer, aimed at establishing a living dialogue between individuals and their God. Additional factors shape the holistic nature of the prayer-act in conjunction with prayer-formulas: the venue of worship, the number of prayers recited and the time of day, the worshiper's emotional mood, attire, voice, and gestures, and the like.[27]

In a certain sense, the canonical version of the prayers supports the conscious orientation. Prayer arises from a multifaceted reality, but those establishing the prayer texts sought to inculcate a uniform consciousness among the worshipers.[28] In many instances, the prayer text aims to support a universal consciousness, or alternately, a pan-Jewish one.

---

27 Uri Ehrlich, *The Nonverbal Language of Prayer: A New Approach to Jewish Liturgy*, trans. Dena Ordan (Tubingen: Mohr Siebeck, 2004), 3. The use of the term "act of prayer" indirectly reflects phenomenological terminology.

28 An example of this is the prayer for rain, which is adapted to a specific locale (Babylonia or the Land of Israel). On the contrary, those who established the canonical text of prayer sought to compose a formulation suitable for every location. See Arnold A. Lasker and Daniel J. Lasker, "The Jewish Prayer for Rain in Babylonia," *Journal for the Study of Judaism* 15 (1984): 124-44; idem, "The Jewish Prayer for Rain in the Post-Talmudic Diaspora," *AJS Review* 9 (1984), 141-174. On the question of the establishment of the canonical text of the prayers, especially the *Amidah*, see Ismar Elbogen, *Jewish Liturgy: A Comprehensive History*, trans. Raymond P. Scheindlin (Philadelphia: Jewish Publication Society, 1993), 24-37.

The extensive pioneering phenomenological essay on prayer in Jewish thought was written by the scholar of Jewish thought Shalom Rosenberg. In his essay, Rosenberg listed three strata in the study of prayer:

(1) the philological and historical ("formal") analysis of prayer;
(2) revealing the ideas and conceptions in prayer (the "semantic system");[29]
(3) exploring the standing of prayer in religious life and thought (pragmatics").

Rosenberg then offered a number of approaches to prayer.

(1) Simple prayer: the Biblical and midrashic approach to prayer, that is not reflective.
(2) Theurgic prayer: the act of prayer is presented as mending (*tikkun*) of the world and God. This approach finds systematic expression in Kabbalah. Rosenberg includes the discussion of magic prayer in this category.
(3) Mystical prayer: the Kabbalistic approach that presents prayer as communion with God and spiritual elevation.
(4) Didactic prayer: the moral approach that views prayer as educational.
(5) Existential prayer: the communal approach, which holds that prayer expresses communal existence (such as public prayer).[30]

Other approaches could be added to this list, as Rosenberg presents prayer as a system of conscious acts that fully comprises the Jewish religious consciousness. His insights reflect the adaptation of the extensive discussions of prayer in the general literature of religious phenomenology to the analysis of prayer in Jewish tradition. Since then, additional works have been written on Jewish prayer. Lawrence Hoffman, for instance, based on an analysis of specific prayers, viewed the liturgical text as "a source of insight into the way religious consciousness is formed, nurtured,

---

29 On the value of the discussion of meanings in prayer, see, for example, Eliezer Berkovits, "Expectations from Prayer," in *Sefer Aviad: Collection of Articles in Memory of Dr. Isaiah Wolfsberg-Aviad* [Hebrew], ed. Yitzhak Raphael (Jerusalem: Mossad Harav Kook, 1986), 179-184.

30 Shalom Rosenberg, "Prayer and Jewish Thought: Approaches and Problems (A Survey)" in *Prayer in Judaism: Continuity and Change* ed. G. Cohn and H. Fisch (Northvail, NJ: Jason Arondon 1996), 69-107, 89-107.

and lived."[31] It seems that the works by Reuven Kimelman and the book by Stefan Reif contain phenomenological analyses, despite their intent to provide a historical and critical description.[32] Tzvi Zahavy classified prayer by six types of worshipers: performer, mystic, scribe, priest, meditator, and celebrity. I do not intend to discuss the definition of these types or the degree to which they are reflective of all the possible variants. It should be noted, however, that Zahavy assigned the archetype of the performer to R. Soloveitchik.[33] Published works in the religious-Zionist rabbinic world seek mainly to understand the consciousness of prayer.[34] Although the authors from the latter sector almost certainly are not thoroughly familiar with the phenomenological literature, and their approach is not critical, their work, nevertheless, attest to a conceptual climate that finds it important to understand the religious consciousness created and promoted by the act of prayer.

Prayer and Jewish Thought

Jewish thought in the medieval and early modern periods began with the perception of prayer as obligatory and as the fulfillment of the demands of religious law. Jewish thought treats prayer as providing reasons for the commandments and as part of the discussion of man's relationship with his Maker. Taking this as given, Jewish philosophers analyzed a series of theological questions raised by prayer. The place of prayer in Jewish thought is derived from two approaches.

---

31 Lawrence A. Hoffman, *Beyond the Text: A Holistic Approach to Liturgy* (Bloomington: Indiana University Press, 1987), 3.

32 Stefan C. Reif, *Judaism and Hebrew Prayers: New Perspectives on Jewish Liturgical History* (Cambridge: Cambridge University Press, 1993); Reuven Kimelman, "The *Shema'* Liturgy: From Covenant Ceremony to Coronation" [Hebrew], *Kenishta* 1 (2001): 5-109; idem, *Mystical Meaning of Lekha Dodi and Kabbalat Shabbat* [Hebrew] (Jerusalem: Magnes, 2003). Margolin, *Inner Religion*, presents a few phenomenological aspects of prayer.

33 See Tzvi Zahavy, *God's Favorite Prayers* (Teaneck, NJ: Talmudic Books, 2011), 37. R. Aharon Lichtenstein was assigned the archetype of the scribe.

34 A fascinating work in this field was written by Eli Taragin and Michael Rubinstein, *Prayer as Encounter: The Laws of Prayer—A Journey from the Halakhah to the Soul* [Hebrew] (Jerusalem: Merkaz Halakhah and Sifriyat Bet-El, 2011). Also noteworthy is the book by Rabbi Eli Adler, *Tefilat Yesharim* [Hebrew] (Atzmonah: n.p., 2003). The ultra-Orthodox world mainly publishes collections of the laws of prayer and books of ethical teaching of prayer.

(1) Prayer as the observance of a religious commandment or obligation. This sense focuses on prayer itself as everyday obligation and as an ideal. The obligation can be fulfilled in two ways:
    (a) recitation of diverse liturgical texts;
    (b) intent, that is concerned with mental focus and with comprehension of the liturgical texts.
(2) Prayer as the realization or symbol of other religious ideals, besides the fulfilling of the religious obligation. Examples of such ideals are:
    (a) prayer as contemplation.
    (b) prayer as communion with God and as an ecstatic state;
    (c) prayer as influencing heavenly events.

Jewish religious thought in different periods was occupied with the relationship between prayer and theology. This relationship consists of three main parts.

The first important issue is the relationship between prayer and prophecy. Prayer in itself is perceived as speech. The state of prayer refers to a person who verbally addresses his God, with a clear connection to prophecy. In the prophetic state, God and the prophet engage in discourse (with the question of who initiates this discourse). Man and God speak with each other from time to time. Prayer is an event reminiscent of the prophetic dialogue, even though only man speaks, while God is the object of his address. Moreover, institutionalized prayer came after the cessation of documented prophecy. Prayer, accordingly, is discussed in reference to prophecy.[35]

Secondly, prayer is addressed within the context of negative theology. Already in the medieval period, negation of the attributes of God was established as an accepted and semiofficial doctrine. This trend presented God as undescribable in human language, and as absolutely distinct from man. It created an image of immutable God, on whom man's address Him makes no impression. Divine knowledge relates to the rational world that is concerned with universal phenomena, but does not apply to the individual as such and to the stormy events that he experiences. Maimonides systematized this idea, but it was already accepted before his time. Few dared to differ with it, and most did not reject the notion of God's immutability. In light of this theological conception, prayer became sterile. Not only did

---

35 On prophecy and prayer, see *Lonely Man of Faith* (Northvale, NJ: Jason Aronson, 1997 [1965]), 53-66.

prayer alter nothing, but moreover, it was doubtful whether prayer could receive God's attention, coming from a low level in the cosmic structure and the hierarchy of God and His creatures.

Thirdly, the discussion of prayer was linked to understanding of divine perfection. This question stems from that of negative theology. While the preceding section related to the knowledge and attributes of God, here we are concerned with divine providence. If it is observed that prayer alters divine decisions (the healing of the sick, the lifting of harsh laws, and the like), we are left with a contradiction: on the one hand, God is perfect and He and His decisions are immutable, while on the other, prayer has the ability to change the divine decree. However, if, prayer cannot alter the divine decree, then the very benefit of its recitation is called into question. The worshipers feel powerless in the face of the unchanging divine perfection and, as a reaction, they wish to demonstrate the utility of prayer to their society and to themselves.[36]

Jewish thought in the modern world relates to various aspects of prayer, and R. Soloveitchik was one of the leading voices in this discourse.[37] However, the main centers of interest in the contemporary philosophical discussions of prayer are removed from the realm of the theological. Modern Jewish thought is more concerned with the condition of prayer (that is, standing before God) and with the consciousness of prayer than with theological inconsistencies. Unlike medieval thought, in which prayer was anchored in the routine ritual, and, with its symbolism and importance, was one of the spheres requiring reason and clarification, in modern thought prayer has taken on a new and different dimension. It now reflects man's moral existence and his values, consciousness, experiences, and personality: "prayer is not in time but time in prayer."[38] R. Soloveitchik, too, concentrated on the human state of consciousness, which prayer expresses and documents. For modern man, prayer is linked to the phenomenological and the existential dimensions of religious life. R. Soloveitchik undertook a mission that is by no means straightforward. He promoted the approach that prefers the description of the prayer experience to explaining the detailed ritual behavior required by the Torah in the heart of Orthodox thought.

---

36 R. Soloveitchik was not concerned by this theological issue, since his viewpoint was that of the consciousness of prayer, that is, the subject who prays and the human perspective of prayer.

37 Rosenberg, "Prayer and Jewish Thought."

38 Martin Buber, *I and Thou*, trans. Ronald Gregor Smith (New York: Scribner, 2000), 24.

Prayer in the World of R. Soloveitchik

Echoes of philosophical, Kabbalistic, and Hasidic sources clearly resound in R. Soloveitchik's discussions on prayer. Kabbalistic patterns of thought, for example, are obviously present in his writings, even though he generally kept his distance from mysticism. Additionally, his essays contain traces of thought developed by *Maharal* (R. Judah Loew ben Bezalel) in *Netivot Olam* and of other traditional and modern interpretations of the prayer book. But all these sources bubble beneath the surface. R. Soloveitchik's constant "conversants" remain the same: prayer and its texts in themselves, Maimonides (and at times thinkers such as R. Judah Halevi and Nahmanides). The contents of these sources infused his methods of writing and discussion that originated in early twentieth-century philosophy, as we shall see immediately.

R. Soloveitchik was profoundly influenced by the phenomenology of religion, as can be seen in his major works that were composed in the mid-1940s. In these writings, prayer is primarily a "religious act" of the consciousness. In the 1950s R. Soloveitchik began to write existential essays. Religious existentialists argued that prayer is an expression of human existence. Prayer emerges, first and foremost, out of distress and suffering. Accordingly, it addresses the existential rift, and reflects the religious approach to this rift. It is also an expression of discourse and the possibility of elocution. The worshiper has discovered the possibility of intersubjective discourse. At times, therefore, prayer affords existential dignity to the one uttering it.

This said and done, the question of R. Soloveitchik's sources is a complex one. He was unquestionably influenced by the intellectual and theological climate.[39] Moreover, his mastery of various languages is unquestioned: he wrote his doctoral dissertation in German. Nonetheless, the references in his essays usually are to summations in Hebrew, such as articles by Samuel Hugo Bergmann, and works that were translated into English, such as the books of Max Scheler. We may assume that he did not always think it necessary to read these sources in the original and internalized their message from second- and third-hand sources as well. His revitalization of Orthodox Jewish thought

---

39 Relevant in this context are R. Soloveitchik's lectures "On the Religious Definition of Man" delivered in 1957. Recordings of the lectures are available at: (1) https://app.box.com/s/7pxhzhg2ekrid9e5fb4/129360005, (2) torahdownloads.com/shiur_16138.html, (3) on the YUTorah Online site. The printed text appears only in Hebrew: *Ha-Adam ve-Olamo* (Man and His World) [Hebrew] (Jerusalem: Eliner Library, 1998), 9-72.

was based on his internalization of contents and ways of thinking from phenomenological and existential thought, even if he did not spend the effort to delve into the writings of those thinkers.

The shifts in R. Soloveitchik's thought and life are intertwined with the standing of prayer. It has also been suggested that the parameters of a comprehensive educational program are to be sought in R. Soloveitchik's thought on prayer.[40] Notwithstanding the great pains he took to emphasize that there are no degrees in Jewish ritual, prayer occupied him more than many other questions. Needless to say, as an outstanding Torah scholar who was immersed in the world of Torah study and in its teaching, R. Soloveitchik was interested in the formal and halakhic aspects of prayer. This was matched by the considerable extent to which his interest in prayer entered his philosophical writings. As a philosopher, R. Soloveitchik was unquestionably concerned mainly with prayer as reflective of the standing and consciousness of the worshiper, and with prayer as expressing manifold religious ideals. Three different philosophical schools influenced R. Soloveitchik's conception of prayer.

The first school is epistemological idealism: R. Soloveitchik was interested in prayer as a halakhic object, whose foundations are to be uncovered and which is to be constructed as an intellectual product. To this end, he analyzed the components of the halakhic states of prayer. In *Halakhic Man* he grounded this process in post-Kantian epistemological idealism, and mainly in the thought of Hermann Cohen and Paul Natorp. I will discuss this approach mainly in Chapter Ten (below), which examines the conceptions of prayer in Torah scholarship (*lamdanut*).

Secondly, R. Soloveitchik experienced the influence of phenomenology: he examined prayer as an expression of the religious consciousness. Reflected in the act of prayer are the tempestuous processes that characterize the subjective religious consciousness. From this respect, prayer is an objective and practical manifestation of the depths of the dynamic religious consciousness. R. Soloveitchik was influenced mainly by the phenomenological thought of Max Scheler and phenomenological psychotherapy. In practice, revealing the typical structure and processes of the religious consciousness was the primary aim of his works *Worship of the Heart* and *Ra'ayonot al Tefillah* [Thoughts on Prayer]. An analysis of these

---

40 See Moshe Sokolow, *Tefilat Rav: Educating for Prayer, Utilizing the Writings of Rabbi Joseph B. Soloveitchik (the Rav); Curricular and Instructional Guidelines. The Azrieli Papers* (New York: Azrieli Graduate School of Jewish Education & Administration, Yeshiva University, 2006).

works (see the following chapters) seems to indicate that R. Soloveitchik took a greater interest in the structure of the religious consciousness than in the specific act of prayer. On occasion prayer is evidently an excuse to engage in the religious consciousness. Furthermore, other schools of thought, namely, epistemological idealism and existentialism, are casual and episodic in comparison to the intense phenomenological research that R. Soloveitchik presents. His philosophical preferences are beyond doubt: his intellectual curiosity is substantive, and is almost entirely directed to examining the consciousness of (the act of) prayer, specifically, and the religious consciousness in general.

Thirdly, a major trend that influenced R. Soloveitchik's thought is existentialism. R. Soloveitchik focused on prayer as an expression of man's concrete existential conditions. Prayer represents an authentic, unique, and intransitive existence, relates to man's solitude, creates community, and so forth. The central sources of influence were the thought of Kirkegaard and religious existentialist thought (Reinhold Niebuhr, Paul Tillich, and others).[41] R. Soloveitchik was also indirectly moved by the writings of classical existentialist thinkers such as Heidegger, but it should be stressed, once again: it is doubtful whether he troubled himself to read these philosophers in the original, and it is more likely that he read summations.[42] Existentialist psychology, which flourished in the United States in the 1950s and the 1960s, also left its mark on R. Soloveitchik's ideas.

The schools mentioned above molded R. Soloveitchik's thought, and patterns associated with them recur when we analyze his discussions. I extensively clarified the place of these philosophical sources in my previous two volumes on R. Soloveitchik's thought.[43] As I mentioned above, R. Soloveitchik's major works from the 1940s were influenced primarily by

---

41 The circle of Protestant thinkers known as the "theologians of crisis," and especially Karl Barth and Emil Brunner, also significantly influenced R. Soloveitchik's thought. Their thought was close, in some respects, to existentialism. R. Soloveitchik apparently thought highly of them because they provided a basis for Orthodox thought by placing revelation at the center of their theology.

42 At times this presumed reading style adds points of interest and originality, as can be seen in the thought of R. Abraham Isaac Hakohen Kook, who also relied on abstracts and summations. The acquisition of general knowledge that comes from secondary sources might characterize the thought that emerges from the heart of Orthodoxy, for whom historical revelation is the supreme source of knowledge and direction.

43 See Dov Schwartz, *Religion or Halakha*, trans. Batya Stein (Leiden: Brill, 2007); idem, *From Phenomenology to Existentialism* (Leiden: Brill, 2012).

the phenomenology of religion.[44] In any event, R. Soloveitchik did not seek consistency, and at times his thought brought together these three types of sources, often with many additional influences. Still, he did not always mix different types of writing. The topic of prayer is exceptional in this respect, as we shall see in the following chapters of the current work. An examination of the philosophical methods and sources of R. Soloveitchik's discussions of prayer reveals his interest in its anthropological dimension, that is, its contribution to the personality of the worshiper and the environment and community in which he chooses to live his life. For him, the consciousness of prayer is stormy, changes from one person to another, and embodies pure subjectivity and dialectics.[45] Prayer is one of the supreme expressions of religious individualism. Consequently, R. Soloveitchik presented the halakhah as regulating and balancing the subjective consciousness and existence.

R. Soloveitchik's conception of prayer emerged and coalesced from within a wealth of diverse halakhic statements.[46] Stylistically, he incorporated prayer in his oral discourses, in his articles and monographs. In terms of topic, R. Soloveitchik did not limit himself to the *Amidah* prayer. He also analyzed the blessings on pleasures (*birkhot ha-nehanin*), the *Shema*, the chapters of Psalms incorporated in the prayer book, the Yom Kippur prayer of the High Priest, the Torah readings, the penitential *Selichot* prayers, and many additional liturgical texts, which, to his mind, reflected the idea of prayer. He perceived prayer, on the one hand, as a conscious religious act deserving of independent discussion, and on the other, as object-dependent, that is, linked to a specific event (the morning blessings, the blessings of the Torah, the blessing of the new moon, etc.). R. Soloveitchik wrote on prayer in separate articles and monographs, but taken together, his seemingly

---

44 In the meantime, an examination in a Jewish philosophy course taught by R. Soloveitchik in 1936 has been published by Nathaniel Helfgot, on *Tradition*'s site, *Text and Texture*. Its questions directly relate to the phenomenological conception of religion and its consequences for the Jewish consciousness. All the questions concern the religious consciousness, the religious act, object and subject in the religious consciousness, and the like. See http://text.rcarabbis.org/final-exam-in-jewish-philosophy-of-dr-joseph-soloveitchik-1936.

45 See, for example, Evelyn Underhill, *Worship* (New York: Harper, 1957), 171. R. Soloveitchik created complex structures of conscious tensions, which will be analyzed in depth in the current book. The dialectical structure of prayer was already examined by those writing on R. Soloveitchik's thought. See, for example,Yuval Cherlow, *Joined Together in Your Hand: From Dialectics to Harmony in the Thought of Rabbi Joseph Dov Halevi Soloveitchik* [Hebrew] (Alon Shvut: Tevunot, 1999), 99-107.

46 R. Soloveitchik related to "halakhah" in its broad sense; for him, halakhah includes both practice and idea.

casual references to prayer build a rich philosophical construct, that added many valuable insights to twentieth-century Orthodox thought.

The Sources

In my two previous volumes I examined the development of R. Soloveitchik's philosophy over the course of years, and in different periods. In the current book we will discuss the diverse treatments of the standing of prayer and the personality of the worshiper in his writings.

In recent years many summaries of R. Soloveitchik's classes and talks were published, both in English and Hebrew. His writings, discourses, and classes are being published in a seemingly unending stream. R. Soloveitchik was fortunate in that the second and third generation of his offspring married outstanding Torah scholars. These scholars characteristically had some connection with academic studies in the humanities at some stage or other in their lives, with their consequent sensitivity to textual accuracy. Some of these writings such as those published in the "Toras HoRav" series, are subject to the discerning eyes of the Soloveitchik family, while others were edited by his students, without the oversight of the family. The latter include conduct literature, commentaries on prayers, and classes on prayer. It is noteworthy that prayer occupies a central place in the extensive hagiographic literature that was published posthumously.[47] There are many testimonies to R. Soloveitchik's detailed prayer practices. At times these testimonies intrude into marginal and even embarrassing details.

In the two preceding books I analyzed writings by R. Soloveitchik himself, including those edited in the "Toras HoRav" series. The ideational spine of the current volume, as well, is enrooted in the writings that R. Soloveitchik published and in those published as part of the "Toras HoRav" series, based on R. Soloveitchik's manuscripts that underwent different levels of editing. The current book will focus on an analysis of two cardinal works by R. Soloveitchik: *Worship of the Heart* (Chapters 1-8) and "Thoughts on Prayer" (Chapters 9-11).

---

47 See, for example, Zvi (Herschel) Schachter, *The Soul of the Rav* [Hebrew] (Jerusalem: Reshit Yerushalayim, 1999); idem, *From the Pearls of the Rav* [Hebrew] (Jerusalem: Beit Midrash of Flatbush, 2001); idem, *The Words of the Rav* [Hebrew] (Jerusalem: Mesorah, 2010); Rabbi Mendi Gopin, *Davening with the Rav: My Rabbi and My Rebbe* (Jersey City, NJ: Ktav, 2006).

I find *Worship of the Heart*[48] to be of great importance, despite the fact that at times the massive editing it underwent impedes its understanding and its coherence with R. Soloveitchik's other writings.[49] "Thoughts on Prayer" is an important phenomenological piece that R. Soloveitchik published in 1978. In that same year and in the same journal (*Ha-Darom*), he also published "And from There You Shall Seek," although the first version of the article had already been written in 1944-1945. It is unclear whether this chronology holds true for "Thoughts on Prayer," as well.

I also examine the books edited by Hershel Schachter and works by others, such as the book by Reuven Grodner.[50] His interpretations of the prayers, published with the everyday and festival prayer books, seem too problematic to serve as a sole source. The source of many of his comments is not stated, and it is unclear whether these are fragments of ideas that were collected by members of his audiences or whether these are original writings by R. Soloveitchik. Because R. Soloveitchik was so enamored of prayer, and related to it on diverse occasions, I therefore attempted to draw firm conclusions only on the basis of R. Soloveitchik's own writings (with or without further editing).

The Topics for Discussion

In the current work I do not presume to analyze the entirety of R. Soloveitchik's thoughts on prayer, some of which continue to be published. My focus is on the conceptual, philosophical, and halakhic framework of his approach to this topic, and if I missed some publication or another, I bear the blame.

The heart of the book consists of discussions of the book *Worship of the Heart* and the article "Thoughts on Prayer." The great amount of material in these two compositions enables us to understand R. Soloveitchik's basic orientations on the question of prayer. For the first time, his texts on prayer were collected in a single book. Furthermore, the chapters of *Worship of the Heart* ground prayer in R. Soloveitchik's general thought, thus enabling us to conduct a philosophical discussion of this topic. The chapters analyzing

---

48 Rabbi Joseph B. Soloveitchik, *Worship of the Heart: Essays on Jewish Prayer*, ed. Shalom Carmy (Hoboken, NJ: Toras HoRav, 2003).

49 See Lawrence Kaplan, "Review Essay: Worship of the Heart," *Hakirah: The Flatbush Journal of Jewish Law and Thought* 5 (2007): 1-36.

50 Reuven Grodner, *On Prayer: The Classes of Rabbi Joseph Dov Soloveitchik* [Hebrew] (Jerusalem: OU Press, 2011).

Worship of the Heart accordingly begin my book, taking note of the heavy editing it underwent. The following chapters are mostly devoted to "Thoughts on Prayer" and its reflections in R. Soloveitchik's other writings. The last chapter discusses his treatment of prayer in the articles "The Synagogue as an Institution and as an Idea" and "The Lonely Man of Faith."

My central assumption is that the first five chapters of *Worship of the Heart* (the first section of his book) are constructed in accordance with the style of his phenomenological writing: in the first stage, he presents an outline of the consciousness of prayer (chapters 1-2), and in the second stage, the construction of the different phases of the consciousness of prayer, from the consciousness of distress to that of communion with God (chapters 2-4). He then wrote of the evolution of the consciousness to the consciousness of communion (chapter 5). The second section, constructed in similar fashion, consists of a phenomenological analysis of the *Shema*. R. Soloveitchik first compares the consciousness of prayer with that of the *Shema* (chapter 6), and then analyzes the consciousness of God's unity (chapters 6-8) and that of our love of Him (chapter 9). I further assume that his discussion of prayer in *Worship of the Heart* exceeds the methodical frameworks of his other writings. His basic discussion is plainly phenomenological, that is, it examines the consciousness of prayer. He includes in this discussion existentialist writing that depicts existential states of crisis and distress. This in itself to some extent reflects the centrality and importance of prayer for R. Soloveitchik.

I wish to thank a number of colleagues for their assistance: Prof. Avi Sagi, whose guidance was important for finding my way through the winding paths of phenomenological and existentialist thought, for which I am grateful; Profs. Moshe Idel, Meir Bar-Ilan, Ron Margolin, Gideon Freudenthal, Joseph Schwartz, Dr. Gabriel Birenbaum, and my son-in-law Rabbi Baruch Weintraub all helped me with various questions. My special thanks to Rabbi Reuven Ziegler, the research director of Toras HoRav. Last but not least, thanks to Prof. Lawrence Kaplan, who is among the most distinguished authorities on R. Soloveitchik's thought and honored me by reading and commenting on the entire manuscript.

Part I

Worship of the Heart:
The Consciousness of Prayer

Chapter 1

Nature and Purpose

Worship of the Heart is R. Soloveitchik's most focused and important publication on the theoretical aspects of prayer. In this chapter I shall explore the declarations and interpretations of the work's nature and goal, both those by its author and those by the scholars who have written about it. Following a short survey of the book's structure, I will discuss R. Soloveitchik's own statement on its nature, one that he sets forth at the beginning of the book. And finally, I will critically examine a few interpretations of the book's goals and nature.

1. *Worship of the Heat*: Structure

Worship of the Heart is a clearly phenomenological work. It is not concerned with prayer itself, but with the consciousness of prayer. It does not touch upon the address to God, but rather the consciousness of such an address. Prayer is perceived as a plainly intentional act, and we will examine the meaning of this conception in depth in the following chapters of the current book. It is only at times that *Worship of the Heart* digresses from phenomenological writing and enters the realm of existentialist thought. The beginning of R. Soloveitchik's work is an example of such a divergence. The framework of the book as a whole is phenomenological, with clear consequences for the structure of its chapters, as we shall see below.

Writing and Editing

Worship of the Heart outlines the religious consciousness on two topics: prayer (mainly the *Amidah* prayer) and *Shema*. R. Soloveitchik argues that these two liturgical topics establish two different phases or characteristics of consciousness that are presumably in a constant state of tension but, in the final analysis, are complementary. At times the book seems to project the message that R. Soloveitchik's main goal was to determine the structure of the Jewish religious consciousness, and that prayer and *Shema* are only a means to this end. In other words, prayer and *Shema* are echoes and impressions of stormy cognitive, emotional, mental, and experiential processes. R. Soloveitchik chose these two because he felt that they are an expression or traces of a lively religious experience that partially exceeds the restraint, gestures, and limitations of the other commandments. The liturgy occupies a special and exceptional place in R. Soloveitchik's thought. In any event, the entire discussion focuses on the consciousness of prayer, the consciousness of *Shema*, and the differences between them.

The following eight chapters will be devoted to a detailed analysis of *Worship of the Heart*, placing special emphasis on its patently phenomenological methodology. The editor, R. Shalom Carmy, who was a student of R. Soloveitchik and is on the faculty of Yeshiva University, has been the editor of *Tradition* magazine for a number of years. He mentioned in his introduction that R. Soloveitchik entrusted him with the manuscripts. We may therefore assume that R. Soloveitchik was a participant in this project, at least in its beginnings, or laid the groundwork for it. Nonetheless, the book obviously underwent comprehensive and significant editing, and signs of the editor's intervention are visible. Moreover, it seems that the editor undertook an extremely arduous task: uniting a series of documents from different periods to produce an orderly composition. Consequently, I will not relate to the chronological dimension of the book's contents and their place in the evolutionary development of his thought. I will rather restrict myself to an examination of their meaning and contribution to R. Soloveitchik's conception of prayer.

The Structure of the Book

According to the editor's testimony, *Worship of the Heart* is divided into two parts.[1]

(1) "The general theory of prayer": this part is formulated in the first five chapters. The central topic of this part is the consciousness of prayer.

(2) "[T]he liturgy of *Shema*": this part encompasses four chapters (6-9), and is mainly devoted to *Shema*, followed by its comparison with prayer.

Carmy's statement implies that the first part was written as a single unit, "as the basis for a course at Yeshiva University's Bernard Revel

---

1 *Worship of the Heart*, xxix.

Graduate School." The series of notebooks from which chapters 1-5 were taken is labeled "*Seder ha-Tefillot*" (Order of Prayer; in Hebrew transliteration in the original). The second part, as well, is written as a group of notebooks entitled "The Fundamentals of Prayer."[2] The two parts are based on notebooks written in R. Soloveitchik's hand. The English edition contains a tenth chapter, a translation to English of the article "*Ra'ayanot al Tefillah*."

The division of the book into two sections is undeniable. The inner division of the sections, however, seems problematic. In light of my analysis (in the following chapters) of the ideas in the book, I believe that the chapters should be divided differently, in a structure that ensues from the flow of the book's ideas.

The following is an outline of the proposed division, into six instead of the first nine chapters in the English edition:

Current Chapter Division	Proposed Chapter Division	Phenomenological Topic	Liturgical Topic
first: "Prayer and the Media of Religious Experience" second: "Prayer, Petition and Crisis"	(1) first-second (first half) pp. 3-27	the structure of the religious consciousness: (a) the consciousness media for seeking God (b) the subjective dimension and the objective dimension	prayer: its place in the religious consciousness
third: "The Human Condition and Prayer"	(2) second (second half)	the phases of the religious consciousness: (a) existential distress	prayer: (a) petition
fourth: "Exaltation of God and Redeeming the Aesthetic"	- fourth pp. 27-72	(b) numinous (*hadar*) (c) kerigmatic (*hesed*)	(b) hymn (c) thanksgiving
fifth: "The Absence of God and the Community of Prayer"	(3) fifth pp. 73-86	the consciousness process: transition from the numinous stage to the kerigmatic stage	the blessing of the *Avot*

(*Continued*)

---

2 *Worship of the Heart*, xxviii-xxix. R. Carmy wrote to me on September 6, 2012 that in the manuscript the groups of chapters 1-2 and 6-9 appear to be R. Soloveitchik's division (according either to his division into notebooks or markers, such as an empty page, and the like). Carmy wrote me, regarding chapters 3-5: "The Rav [= R. Soloveitchik] did not make a decision about how to split up the material." In his Introduction, Carmy wrote that he "determined the order of the chapters in this volume and added chapter subheadings" (p. xxix).

Current Chapter Division	Proposed Chapter Division	Phenomenological Topic	Liturgical Topic
sixth: "Intention (*Kavvanah*) in Reading *Shema* and in Prayer"	(4) sixth (most of the chapter) pp. 87-103	the consciousness process: alternative model	the differences between reading *Shema* and the *Amidah*
seventh: "The Essence of *Shema*: Unity of God, Love of God, and the Study of His Law" eighth: "Immanence and Transcendence: Comments on *Birkat Yotzer Or*"	(5) sixth (end)-eighth pp. 103-132	discussion of the consciousness of the unity of God according to the sources: (a) halakhah (b) aggadah (c) the liturgical text	the interpretation of reading *Shema* (1) "One" (2) *Birkat Yotzer Or*
ninth: "Accepting the Yoke of Heaven"	(6) ninth pp. 133-143	discussion of the consciousness of love of God	The interpretation of reading *Shema*: "And thou shalt love thy God"

According to the division that I explain below, each of the two sections of *Worship of the Heart* should contain three chapters. The current division interrupts topics in the middle and, in my opinion, also poses obstacles for their understanding. R. Soloveitchik might have made this division in accordance with the material he included in his lectures and classes, which were bound by time restraints.

I will now seek to explore the flow of ideas in *Worship of the Heart* and their meaning. The following chapters will then examine R. Soloveitchik's systematic thought on prayer, as revealed in his book.

2. The Author on the Nature of His Work

Before turning to the approaches offered for the aim and nature of *Worship of the Heart*,[3] we should listen to what R. Soloveitchik says in the beginning of the book. These introductory remarks assume greater force in light of the fact that the book is composed of more or less sequential sections and our assumption that this passage too has its place in this sequence. Indeed,

---

3 R. Soloveitchik might have had his reservations concerning this title. In his classes he insisted on translating *avodah she-be-lev* as "sacrifice of the heart," following Maimonides. That is, *avodah* is understood as the offering of a sacrifice. See Grodner, *On Prayer*, 15.

a perusal of this passage ("When I Speak about the Philosophy of Prayer") reveals that it eloquently sets forth the work's purpose and content.

Personal Experience

The book opens with a partly methodical and partly autobiographical statement by R. Soloveitchik declaring that the religious experience cannot be fully transmitted because of its personal nature. He expressly bases this notion on the ideas of John Henry Newman (1801-1890), the colorful Oxford academic, initially evangelical and later Anglican, who studied the religious experience. Newman was definitely a particularist and spoke of an essential disparity between universal principles and the reality. In his early thought Newman liked the Kierkegaardian approach that problems of faith are to be resolved by means of commitment and decision, and not by rational thought.[4] There is certainly some affinity between such approaches and the conceptual directions of R. Soloveitchik's thought.

Let us return to R. Soloveitchik's reliance upon what Newman wrote at the end of his *An Essay in the Aid of a Grammar of Ascent*.[5] Does R. Soloveitchik's interpretation really suit Cardinal Newman's orientation? Newman argued that as regards the "Evidences of Religion [...] egotism is true modesty."[6] In order, however, to form an opinion regarding the transitivity of the religious experience, we should compare the writings of the two:

Rabbi Soloveitchik	Newman
He may hope that by formulating his own experiences in clear language, others may benefit from this self-revelation and enrich their own religious life. However the latter, being the most subjective and intimate of all modes of existence, is many a time inseparable from the individual personality—its character, temper, moods, and susceptibilities.[7]	He knows what has satisfied and satisfies himself; if it satisfies himself, it is likely to satisfy others; if, as he believes and is sure, it is true, it will approve itself to others also, for there is but one truth.[8]

---

4 See, for example, James M. Cameron, "John Henry Newman and the Tractarian Movement," in *Nineteenth Century Religious Thought in the West*, ed. Ninian Smart et al. (Cambridge: Cambridge University Press, 1985), 69-109.
5 In the sense of unconditional acceptance, out of absolute certainty.
6 John Henry Newman, *An Essay in the Aid of a Grammar of Assent* (London: Longmans, Green, and Co., 1903), 384.
7 *Worship of the Heart*, 1.
8 Newman, *Grammar of Assent*, 385.

Newman argued that a person who attests to a religious experience speaks solely for himself. As soon as it becomes evident that his experience contributes to others and joins with their truth, however, this experience becomes common knowledge. Even if the one undergoing the experience does not aim for scientific truth, he is convinced that what he says will benefit others.[9] For him, his experiences constitute absolute certainty. Newman maintains that ascent and certainty are based on comprehension, and not mere nonrational mysticism. R. Soloveitchik took a different path. In three matters, however, he did agree with Newman:

(1) he, too, sensed the value and positive qualities of religious certainty;
(2) he refrained from characterizing certainty as nonverbal mysticism;
(3) he believed that self-exposure would also enrich the "religious life" of others, as each personal experience painted the experiences of the (religious) others in new colors.

On the other hand, however, R. Soloveitchik asserted that "to say that my feeling of certitude carries universal significance would be sheer ignorance."[10] He definitely did not agree with Newman on this point; at the very least, he had his doubts concerning such universality. This encounter with Newman's approach expresses the dialectical element in R. Soloveitchik's thought.[11]

We further learn that R. Soloveitchik's opening remarks in *Worship of the Heart* reveal two not easily reconcilable orientations:

(1) doubting the transitive capacity of the existential experiential situation that he takes pains to describe: "Whether [...] my experiences can be detached from my idiosyncrasies and transferred to others, I do not know";[12]
(2) despair of effecting such a transfer: "Yet, at times, my feelings and convictions are exclusively my own and I have no way to pass them on to others."[13]

---

9 Ibid., 386.
10 *Worship of the Heart*, 2.
11 See Ehud Luz, "The Dialectic Element in R. Soloveitchik's Works" [Hebrew], *Daat* 9 (1982): 75-89.
12 *Worship of the Heart*, 2.
13 Ibid., 1.

In any event, R. Soloveitchik tended toward extreme individualism and fluctuated between these two options. The conclusion to be drawn from his stance is that he gave his own existentialist interpretation to Newman's approach, thereby adapting it to meet his own needs.

This, however, does not mark the end of the dialectic elements of his discussion. R. Soloveitchik himself was apprehensive of the extreme individualism that he presented. In other words, he revealed to the reader his uncertainty regarding the very possibility of any transmission of the religious experience. In this introductory passage he writes:

> Therefore, when I speak about the philosophy of prayer or *Shema*,[14] I do not claim universal validity for my conclusions. I am not lecturing on philosophy of prayer as such, but on prayer as understood, experienced and enjoyed by an individual.[15]

Thus, R. Soloveitchik used a term perceived as transitive (philosophy of prayer), but immediately retreated from his use of it. He employs a tortuous and tense formulation: he speaks of the philosophy of prayer, but refrains from categorizing prayer as philosophy. Regardless of his formulation, he is concerned with the philosophy of prayer. A personal and unique experience that does not bear within it any comprehensible or transmittable message does not fall within the bounds of philosophy. R. Soloveitchik therefore wavered between the possibility of interpersonal communication and its negation.[16] Such a dialectic recurs in his writings, and in many respects becomes a cognitive and existential value in its own right. R. Soloveitchik elected to begin his book with this fundamental oscillation, thereby attesting to the dialectic character of *Worship of the Heart*.

In practice, R. Soloveitchik's writing is paradoxical. He questions the very worth of his book. At first glance, we have difficulty understanding his doubts. As we shall see below, *Worship of the Heart* is well thought-out and programmatic. It considers structural and analytical questions. It devotes extensive effort to isolating the substantive experiential elements of prayer and of the liturgical text. Why, then, is R. Soloveitchik of two minds regarding the worth of his writing? Since prayer is such an important experience, some will see it as an impulse, one that cannot be analyzed.

---

14 On this addition (i.e., *Shema*), see Lawrence Kaplan, "Review Essay: Worship of the Heart," *Ḥakirah: The Flatbush Journal of Jewish Law and Thought* 5 (2007): 106.

15 *Worship of the Heart*, 2.

16 See Jeffrey R. Woolf, "In Search of the Rav: The Life and Thought of Rabbi Joseph Soloveitchik in Recent Scholarship," *BDD: Journal of Torah and Scholarship* 18 (2007): 18-19.

In Hasidic thought, for example, prayer is frequently perceived as a powerful intuitive and instinctive expression. R. Soloveitchik was well aware of trends in Jewish thought that rejected contemplative prayer and found his phenomenological analysis incomprehensible.

Thus, the centrality of prayer as worship of the heart makes it absurd. As always, R. Soloveitchik's writing is calculated and gradual. Each of the three paragraphs in his introductory passage adds a new dimension to the absurd.

In the first paragraph he presents the tension between the possibility of passing on one's impressions to others and the negation of the transitivity of experience. On the one hand, he argues that "what satisfies me is likely to please others as well," and on the other, he immediately determines that "I have no way to pass them [his feelings and convictions] on to others." In other words, the absurd contradiction is evident.

In the second paragraph R. Soloveitchik once again formulates the contradiction, but this time with the addition of skepticism. "Whether [...] my experiences can be detached from my idiosyncrasies [...] I do not know."

In the third paragraph he deepens the contrast by bolstering the transitive stance. Hoe does he do this? Presumably, it would be possible to find a common denominator for all the individuals who experience prayer:

(1) religious experience (the negation of the "pride and audacity" of scholars of religion who have not undergone such an experience);
(2) reliance on seminal texts (coordinating one's convictions and feelings "with the great disciplines of Halakhah and Aggadah").

R. Soloveitchik, nonetheless, ends this paragraph by declaring that it is impossible "to ascribe to my remarks more veracity" beyond subjective impressions. Thus, the third paragraph intensifies the absurdity in the contrast between the shared basis and the individualism that cannot be transmitted.

R. Soloveitchik begins his book *The Lonely Man of Faith* in a similar manner, but with a difference: in this work he despairs, from the outset, of influencing the religious community at large, and the aim of his writing is therefore solely therapeutic. In *The Lonely Man of Faith* he declares: "I do not intend to suggest a new method of remedying the human situation which I am about to describe; neither do I believe that it can be remedied at all."[17] Accordingly, he writes that "a tormented soul finds peace

---

17 *Lonely Man of Faith*, 2.

in confessing."[18] As we saw above, at least one pole in *Worship of the Heart* casts doubt on the ability of influencing the many, but does not totally rule it out. He believes in the value of the impressions left on others by the description of the personal religious experience. Consequently, *Worship of the Heart* is not limited to therapeutic writing, although part of it might answer to such a definition. Dialecticism as a value, however, recurs in this work. For R. Soloveitchik, the key to understanding the standing and worth of prayer lies in the documentation, balancing, and regulation of the given fluctuations of the religious person.

The Nature of the Work

The introduction to *Worship of the Heart* should be understood on the background of a subjective existential conception. In *The Lonely Man of Faith*, R. Soloveitchik explained that every man is a subject, in the sense that he is individual and unique. Since this is so, the central question for this composition is communication between subjects. Adam and Eve are two subjects for whom no connection is possible. R. Soloveitchik resolved the problem of the possibility of connection between subjects by means of divine grace. Only God's intervention enables the two subjects, Adam and Eve, to communicate with each other.[19] In his lecture "*Al Hagdarato ha-Datit shel ha-Adam*" (On the Religious Definition of Man), published in *Ha-Adam ve-Olamo* (Man and His World), R. Soloveitchik also viewed singularity as a problem. This starting point, of individualism, guided R. Soloveitchik in the opening paragraph of his introduction to *Worship of the Heart*. The prayer experience is an expression of the existential singularity of each subject. The prayer experience of one worshiper does not resemble that of another. This led R. Soloveitchik to have doubts regarding the possibility of a "philosophy of prayer." The very fact that he committed his thoughts to writing teaches that he deemed this question to be of interest. His formulation is not merely therapeutic writing, it also is of value for delineating a substantive outline of the religious experience, no matter how subjective. Moreover, *Worship of the Heart* is a philosophical and interpretive analysis of the religious consciousness that employs descriptive philosophical tools. The book almost entirely lacks the exegetical and personal narratives characteristic of, for example, *The Lonely Man of Faith*. Such narratives are

---

18 *Lonely Man of Faith*, 2.
19 See Schwartz, *From Phenomenology to Existentialism*, chapter 11.

suitable for therapeutic writing. The writing style of *Worship of the Heart*, in contrast, is unsuitable for nontransitive individualism.

The introduction to *Worship of the Heart* is not typical of R. Soloveitchik's phenomenological writings. The two major phenomenological works that he wrote in the mid-1940s, *And from There You Shall Seek* and *The Halakhic Mind*, seek to provide a substantive description of the religious experience in the world of Judaism. With this goal, the description abandons individualism and nontransitive experience, and focuses on general consciousness. Max Scheler wrote in the first introduction to his outstanding work on the phenomenology of religion that he "is consciously anxious to lift up his thought above the storm and turmoil of the age and into a pure atmosphere [*reinere Atmosphere*]."[20] That is, the phenomenological approach is detached from the sensual reality (placing the world in brackets) and aims for scientific, substantive, and comprehensive truth. R. Soloveitchik, especially in his early writings, also sought to describe the general Jewish religious consciousness and based its esoteric nature in revelation. In the Jewish tradition, revelation includes the broad framework of nation, whether with a hierarchy, as rational approaches maintained, or identical for all who share it. Experiences of hidden and revealed are characteristic of any Jewish religious consciousness.[21] Existentialist thought, in contrast, appears in R. Soloveitchik's works as personal, or perhaps even therapeutic, writing that does not necessarily intend to be definitive and make general assumptions.

One thing is clear: *Worship of the Heart* proclaims, from the outset, that phenomenological methodology does not have a monopoly, and the book also contains existentialist ideas. Disregard for the distinction between phenomenological and existentialist notions in R. Soloveitchik's writings will, in the final analysis, influence the understanding of his thought. We may already state that R. Soloveitchik's existentialist ideas in this work (excluding the introduction) are expressed in a description of the state of distress and crisis, which causes the religious consciousness to seek the hidden and revealed God.[22] This is quite understandable: in other writings R. Soloveitchik expressed his view that prayer is a result of distress. In other words, the context of *Worship of the Heart* and the heart of its discussion are clearly, and unquestionably, phenomenological. R. Soloveitchik, however, felt it necessary to argue that prayer is an alluring and comprehensive issue,

---

20 Scheler, *On the Eternal in Man*, 11.
21 See Schwartz, *From Phenomenology to Existentialism*, 83-87.
22 See below, Chapter Four.

and philosophical methodologies and scholastic formulations are capable of revealing only a bit of its experiential nature. The individualistic declaration at the beginning of *Worship of the Heart* (if R. Soloveitchik did indeed decide to place it there) comes to balance the analytic impression that we gain from the book.

3. Scholars on the Nature of the Book

Scholars and writers were aware of the importance of *Worship of the Heart* for understanding the thought of R. Soloveitchik, which explains the numerous articles written on it and the many references to it. It seems to have attracted greater attention than *Out of the Whirlwind*, for example, even though I think that the latter is no less important, and possibly even more so, for understanding the dynamics of R. Soloveitchik's thought. The scholars' fondness for the topic of prayer apparently contributed significantly to their acceptance of the work.

Center and Periphery

Lawrence Kaplan wrote a learned and sweeping review article divided into two parts. In the first section he wrote of the central ideas in *Worship of the Heart* and in the second he criticized the editing of the book. According to Kaplan, the key to understanding the prayer experience is to be found mainly in analytic distinctions. The following are two examples of such distinctions.

(1) The division between *ma'aseh ha-mitzvah* and *kiyyum ha-mitzvah*. The inner dimension of most commandments is included in their fulfillment. Kaplan wrote of the connection between *The Halakhic Mind* and the way to reveal this inner dimension.[23]

(2) The division between the general intent to fulfill the commandment and the special intent of accepting the yoke of Heaven (*Shema*).[24] R. Soloveitchik wrote that Maimonides' approach is not unequivocal, while according to Kaplan, R. Soloveitchik wanted to count Maimonides among those requiring only the general intent of standing before God.

---

23 See Kaplan, "Review Essay," 82.
24 Ibid., 84, cf. 88.

Kaplan's analysis is mainly concerned with the relationship between *Shema* and the *Amidah*. Among his insights he discusses at length the inclusion of Torah study among the commandments that are the "worship of the heart." Accordingly, prayer is only one expression of such worship. Kaplan consequently argued that, according to its title, the book should have included Torah study, and not limited itself to prayer. Love of God, as well, could be added to this argument. Kaplan took note of the different directions of "the dialogical relationship between God and man."[25] Torah is God's message to man, while prayer is man's speaking to God. Kaplan then returns to the place of Maimonides in the discussion. As he usually did, R. Soloveitchik devoted an extensive interpretive effort to find support for his arguments in the thought of Maimonides. Kaplan was broadly critical of the understanding of Maimonides in R. Soloveitchik's book, which led him to correctly conclude that R. Soloveitchik offered "a creative reinterpretation" of Maimonides.[26]

Kaplan's review article touches many issues, and we will frequently refer to it in the analysis of *Worship of the Heart* in the following chapters. It seems, however, that the main emphasis of the article is on the special subjective dimension of prayer, and that this dimension is directly derived from R. Soloveitchik's halakhic stance. Kaplan attempted to explain that *Worship of the Heart* typically corresponds to R. Soloveitchik's general approach in his various writings. I intend to show in the following chapters that the analysis of prayer as an act of consciousness is of great interest in its own right.

We should make three comments that were not emphasized by Kaplan:

First, R. Soloveitchik placed prayer at the phenomenological center of his thought, even though he continually stressed that this is only one expression of the religious mind. I maintain that R. Soloveitchik thereby struggled with himself, revealing a degree of dialectic. Presumably, he feared he would be swept away by the force of the prayer experience. In any event, the terminology that R. Soloveitchik usually uses clearly comes from the phenomenology of religion, a point that Kaplan did not explore in depth. If R. Soloveitchik himself took pains to translate *kavanah* as "intentional act," and from time to time in the course of the discussion

---

25 Ibid., 93.
26 Ibid., 102. See also Lawrence Kaplan, "Maimonides and Soloveitchik on the Knowledge and Imitation of God," in *Moses Maimonides (1138-1204): His Religious, Scientific and Philosophical Wirkungsgeschichte in Different Cultural Contexts*, ed. Gorge K. Hasselhoff and Otfried Fraisse (Wurzburg: Ergon, 2004), 491-523.

used terms such as "act," "eidetic analysis," "subjective consciousness," and "objectivization," then religious phenomenological thought is not merely an additional dimension or possible variation; it is necessary for understanding his arguments.

Secondly, in his phenomenological discussion of prayer, R. Soloveitchik digressed from the model that he put forth in his other writings, and especially from those of the mid-1940s. While in the latter he vigorously advanced the need for reconstruction, that is, the perception of the (objective) halakhic dimension as a given, one not amenable to fashioning, in his discussion of prayer he maintained that the subjective dimension molds the halakhah. Despite this argument's limitation to the "worship of the heart" commandments, it is highly significant.[27]

Third, his giving pride of place to prayer caused R. Soloveitchik to adopt additional, and unconventional, ideas (tolerance for sensual perceptions of God, the lonely God model, the notion of all-encompassing unity, and others), and to use equally unconventional methods (combining phenomenological and existential styles, such as establishing the existential crisis as the first phase in the formation of the religious consciousness as a whole, and specifically, the consciousness of prayer).

It therefore seems that *Worship of the Heart* is more innovative than Kaplan is willing to admit. Not only does it demonstrate new developments in R. Soloveitchik's thought, but also contains syncretic thought patterns seldom found in his other works. Moreover, these three comments, whose depth will be explored below, aid us in understanding the dynamics of his thought in *Worship of the Heart* and possibly also deflect part of the criticism that Kaplan leveled at the book.

On Methodology

Joshua Amaru's article focuses on the aesthetic dimension of *Worship of the Heart* and offers a detailed description of the ideas in its first five chapters, accompanied by a few critical comments. Amaru begins by presenting two general approaches to prayer: the anthropocentric approach, stating that prayer is for man's benefit, and the theurgic approach, stating that prayer is meant to influence God. He argues that R. Soloveitchik's approach is dialectic: on the one hand, prayer is a real dialogue with God, while on the other,

---

27 As we shall see (below), Daniel Rynhold stressed this matter.

the question of influence upon Him is of no concern to us. The very fact of dialogue is "an end in itself."[28]

Understanding the religious phenomenological methodology character-istic of *Worship of the Heart* will likely release this tension. R. Soloveitchik's conceptual interest is primarily essentialist, that is, it seeks to describe the religious consciousness. The dialogic "media" that he portrays[29] is not an actual conversation, but a dimension of consciousness: the manner in which the consciousness perceives standing before God. Just as R. Soloveitchik was not concerned with the question of prayer's influence upon God, he was similarly uninterested in the question of whether a true dialogue actually takes place.[30] The dialogue that he depicts is directed to the worshiper's self, and not to divine feedback. Kaplan already noted the connection between *The Halakhic Mind* and *Worship of the Heart*, and a short perusal of the former teaches that R. Soloveitchik's thought is firmly grounded in the study of the consciousness. Religious phenomenological methodology is not characteristic only of the second chapter of *Worship of the Heart*,[31] it is present throughout the entire book, as I shall demonstrate below. At times R. Soloveitchik employs an existentialist approach,[32] with some degree of tension with the phenomenology of religion. The anthro-pological shift, however, is absolute, and ensues from the methodology of R. Soloveitchik's thought.

Consequently, Amaru's criticism, stating that R. Soloveitchik's teachings are more appropriate for outstanding individuals (esoterism or elitism),[33] could be realistic, but is unsuited to R. Soloveitchik's original conceptual intention. As far as R. Soloveitchik is concerned, he is reveal-ing the consciousness and existential underpinning of every individual. The two proofs of this are actually one:

---

28 See Joshua Amaru, "Prayer and the Beauty of God: Rav Soloveitchik on Prayer and Aesthetics," *The Torah u-Madda Journal* 13 (2005): 151.

29 Cf. Amaru, "Prayer," 153

30 In his halakhic lessons, R. Soloveitchik frequently related to God as a personal God who hears and accepts prayer. See, for example, *Lessons in Memory of Father, My Teacher... R. Moses Halevi Soloveitchik* [Hebrew], vol. 2 (Jerusalem: Mossad Harav Kook, 2002), 38-39.The goal in the halakhic lesson, however, was not to make an ontological state-ment, but to create a halakhic object free of difficulties and questions. Additionally, this relation also exists in the worshiper's consciousness, and therefore, the author does not presume here to present an existential statement (see below, Chapter Ten).

31 Cf. Amaru, "Prayer," 154.

32 Ibid., 155 and ff.

33 Ibid., 162. We will examine the educational aspect of this argument below, in the discussion of the article by Rabbi Elyakim Krumbein.

(1) R. Soloveitchik objects to religious esoterism and mysticism;[34]
(2) he constantly emphasizes the presence of the halakhah, whose authority is all-inclusive.

Nor should we fear the personification of God in these aesthetic discussions, presuming that knowledge of God is effected also by sensual means. R. Soloveitchik, rather than in theology, is interested in existentialism or in the phenomenology of religion. His statements relate to consciousness, and are not ontic. Phenomenology and existentialism are primarily interested in man's perspective, and not in a reality that lies beyond the consciousness and the human. Once again, we must conclude that an awareness of R. Soloveitchik's methodology would change the scholarly perspective on this point.

Prayer as a Mirror of R. Soloveitchik's Thought as a Whole

Daniel Rynhold attempted to place R. Soloveitchik's attitude to prayer within a two-directional theoretical context, and show that, along with R. Soloveitchik's assertion that the act (halakhah) fashions the subjective and philosophical dimension, the opposite direction, too, is correct: the conceptional dimension molds the act (that is, the ruling of the halakhah). He analyzed *Worship of the Heart* in this light, based on R. Soloveitchik's statement at the beginning of the book that prayer is an expression or objectivization of the human experience.[35] Rynhold correctly interprets objectivization in accordance with *The Halakhic Mind*,[36] that is, from a phenomenological perspective. In the latter work R. Soloveitchik lists the three dimensions of the religious consciousness: the subjective, the objective-normative, and the objective-actual (action).[37] Rynhold ignores the threefold division found in *The Halakhic Mind* passage he cites and uses a simpler subjective-objective division. Similarly, he refrains from focusing on the methodology of revealing the subjective, known as reconstruction (a term clearly defined in R. Soloveitchik's writings from the 1940s), and uses

---

34 On the rejection of esotericism in R. Soloveitchik's writings, see, for example, Schwartz, *Religion or Halakha*, 155-162; idem, *From Phenomenology to Existentialism*, 83-87.
35 Daniel Rynhold, "Letting the Facts Get in the Way of a Good Thesis: On Interpreting Rabbi Soloveitchik's Philosophical Method," *Torah u-Madda Journal* 16 (2012-13): 60.
36 Ibid., 62.
37 See Schwartz, *Religion or Halakha*, 64-67.

this term for other purposes.[38] Rynhold then turns to prayer, as expressing the distinction between surface and deep crisis, which is characteristic of R. Soloveitchik's existential thought, but has no presence in *The Halakhic Mind*.[39] This being the case, we must give two reasons for R. Soloveitchik's determination, based on Maimonides, that prayer is a Torah commandment: one, the human condition. "First, according to R. Soloveitchik, it is presumably because the human condition is tragic and conflicted in this manner that the commandment to pray on a daily basis as an expression of this inner experience has to be biblical."[40] The second reason is of a theological nature, that is, the very idea of daring to pray.[41]

To this point Rynhold based his discussion solely on *Worship of the Heart*. He then turned to other works by R. Soloveitchik and David Hartman's interpretation of them, relating mainly to R. Soloveitchik's banning of voluntary prayer. He concludes:

> This suddenly casts a rather different light on the process through which R. Soloveitchik arrives at his view of prayer. We now see that while it is true that the philosophical picture of prayer is built up out of the texts, at the same time, there is a primary philosophical stance that lies deep in the background, and that itself pushes the principled decision on the *de-Oraita* status of prayer.[42]

In other words, just as the halakhah fashions "subjective" notions, such notions also have a place in the fashioning of the halakhah.

---

38 Rynhold, "Letting the Facts," 60. Rynhold argues that the term "reconstruction" (*shihzur*) is inspired mainly by Dilthey, and incidentally mentions Natorp. See Daniel Rynhold, *Two Models of Jewish Philosophy: Justifying One's Practices* (Oxford: Oxford University Press, 2004), 50-57. R. Soloveitchik himself, however, used this term in his Hebrew compositions, as in *And from There You Shall Seek*. Rynhold mentions the rejection of phenomenology, and its connection with Nazi ideology, of which R. Soloveitchik speaks in a lengthy note at the beginning of *Halakhic Man*. See Schwartz, *Religion or Halakha*, 19-29. This, however, is precisely what R. Soloveitchik maintains: Husserl and his school distorted the phenomenological conception because they did not consider the methodology of reconstruction, that is, they ignored the practical objective dimension of the consciousness. This explains why their approach became the basis of the Nazi ideology. R. Soloveitchik, however, presented a clearly phenomenological approach in *The Halakhic Mind*. On reconstruction, see also below, Chapter Two.
39 Rynhold, "Letting the Facts," 64-65.
40 Ibid., 65.
41 This led R. Soloveitchik to develop the idea of *mattir* (the permission needed to pray, that is, giving the finite man the ability to pray before the infinite God); see below, Chapter Ten.
42 Rynhold, "Letting the Facts," 70.

Rynhold bases his interpretation of *Worship of the Heart* on R. Soloveitchik's works taken as a whole, without considering the fine details of changing periods and philosophical styles. From this respect, he sought to attain a comprehensive overview, which is legitimate in its own right. Rynhold's methods of argumentation and the philosophical and legal models that he applied to R. Soloveitchik's thought are similarly impressive. It seems, nevertheless, that such a methodology does not allow him to listen to the messages and interests in R. Soloveitchik's thought as is was formulated during his lifetime. We should not disregard the chronological developments in R. Soloveitchik's thought, which may be roughly divided into two periods.

The first period lasted until the mid-1940s and encompassed R. Soloveitchik's thought in his major works from the middle of that decade, which focused exclusively on consciousness. He adopted Natorp's concept of reconstruction,[43] because he did not doubt that the objective dimension of the consciousness, that is, observance of the commandments and the halakhic norms, is a primary and unquestionable given. Such certitude leaves little room for exceptions. He went to great pains in *The Halakhic Mind* to explain the absence of any causal linkages between the subjective and the objective consciousness. All this in order to present the halakhah as a primal and obligatory revelational given and in order to provide a profound philosophical basis for Orthodoxy. In this period his thought showed no flexibility regarding the primal, strong standing of halakhic practice, either regarding ritual minutiae or when we speak of halakhot with a strong cognitive and experiential context, such as the laws of mourning. In this respect, R. Soloveitchik's thought is indeed "one-directional." His thought on the study of consciousness was undoubtedly meant to present the halakhah as the most certain given of the consciousness. The reconstruction of the subjective stratum reveals a liquid world of consciousness, with only the objective anchor to enable the proper activity of the religious consciousness.

The second period began in the 1950s. It was only in this period that R. Soloveitchik detached a defined group of a few halakhot, which he entitled "worship of the heart," from the reconstruction model. He usually included prayer, Torah study, and communion with God (*devekut*) in this group. Only this group led R. Soloveitchik to be somewhat flexible in his positions. This issue is exceptional in his writings, because it gives substantive weight to the subjective experience, and does not demand full reconstruction from

---

43 See below, Chapter Three.

within the objective. In retrospective, however, R. Soloveitchik declared unequivocally: "*Kavanah* (intention), related to prayer, is, unlike the *kavanah* concerning other *mitzvah* (good-deed) performances, not an extraneous addendum but the very core of prayer."[44] Consequently, intent is only an "addendum" to the objective dimension of the commandments regulating everyday life, and prayer is an exceptional case. He further made an important statement regarding the Days of Awe, as he focused mainly on repentance and the special prayers and *piyyutim* (liturgical hymns) for this period:

> I always stress that there are two sides to the religious coin: objective and abstract halakhah,[45] on the one hand, and, on the other, subjective existence. At times objectivity is preferable to subjectivity, the formal to the vision, halakhah to sentiment, thought to feeling, and thus it seems to us at times as if the transcendental consciousness, with all its indecision, pains, and holy fire, with all the warmth and flame within it, are all embodied and solidified within obligatory halakhic molds, that impart a fixed nature to streaming and ongoing subjective life. This is exemplified by the Sabbath, in which the halakhah is greater than aggadah, stability, more than the dynamic, and strict law, more than the experience.
>
> Sometimes, however, the parallel between formality and the full inner nature of the experience is evident. From within the halakhah a fountain of stormy religiosity gushes and seeks to ascend, as if the halakhah itself did not conceal the transcendental dimension [in the Hebrew: *tevusah*, defeat] within the quantitative that it created. To the contrary, it emphasized the hint that is concealed within it and that is directed to new and invigorating experiential domains.
>
> Actually, the days of *din* [strict judgment] and *rahamim* [mercy] are noted for such a striking parallel. The halakhah admits that it is nourished from the hiding places of the great mysterium, and does not deny the value of the experience that lacks form or order and that sweeps man's being into its expanses.[46]

---

44 *Lonely Man of Faith*, 74 n. 1.

45 R. Soloveitchik's use of this expression is unclear, which may possibly be explained by the material having been transcribed from a recording.

46 The passage was rendered into English from the text in "Prayer, Confession, and Repentance," in Joseph Dov Soloveitchik, *Divrei Hashkafah* [On Worldview], trans. Moshe Kroneh (Jerusalem: Eliner Library, 1994), 114-115.

The Days of Awe are portrayed as a sort of "breach"[47] of subjectivity into the objective plane, or even blurring the dividing line between the two consciousness planes. The presumably "quantitative" halakhah is shaped by subjectivity, which somewhat moderates the reconstruction conception of the earlier period. It should not be forgotten, however, that the Days of Awe are a defined and limited period lasting only ten days, the "Ten Days of Repentance"—and reflect a high point. The Jew's usual daily routine is mainly subordinate to what has been fashioned by the concrete and quantitative halakhah. In this respect, R. Soloveitchik did not retreat from the theses of And from There You Shall Seek and The Halakhic Mind. In the current work I will show in additional ways how R. Soloveitchik became more flexible, and thought that there is a direct commandment regarding the subjective consciousness, and that this consciousness contributes to the fashioning of the objective consciousness. He also revealed new insights on prayer, and gave himself the image of one who placed prayer at the center of halakhic worship of God. Prayer, however, like the other "worship of the heart" commandments, is exceptional. This atypical issue does not undermine the stability of the halakhah as a given objective system that is not influenced by the subjective and existential dimensions.

Clearly, in all the periods of R. Soloveitchik's thought, the existential dialectic could be balanced and regulated only thanks to the unshakable standing of the halakhah. First, the halakhah documents existential states, and makes them habitual. Second, the halakhah modulates the tempestuous oscillations of existence. It is the immutable revelational anchor that remains in place. This is R. Soloveitchik's most important contribution, as a Jewish philosopher, to religious phenomenological and existentialist philosophies. The halakhah shapes abstract thought, and not vice versa. Returning to R. Soloveitchik's opening comments in Worship of the Heart, we find that he himself wanted to emphasize this, specifically in regard to prayer:

> The pride and audacity which usually mark the philosophical pronounce-
> ments in the field of Jewish religion by secular scholars who have never had

---

47 This is R. Soloveitchik's own wording: "During the days of din [strict judgment] and rahamim [mercy] subjectivity breaches the bounds of objectivity and is revealed in all its formative and amorphous might. The subjective motifs are pronounced in the halakhot themselves to the extent that halakhic formality cannot cover them. If I may use the accepted term, I would say that the aggadic tendency of the halakhot is actually exposed to the critical eye" ("Prayer, Confession, and Repentance," 120; rendered into English from Kroneh's translation into Hebrew).

the opportunity to live through great religious experiences must be done away with.[48]

That is, even if we thought for a moment that the existential dimension projects upon the halakhah, it is halakhic activity that is the starting point. Jewish religious life is the starting point for any possible discussion of the experiential. The halakhah is a given and completely autonomous system of laws. R. Soloveitchik says, "Of course, I try to corroborate my own convictions and feelings by coordinating them with the great disciplines of Halakhah and Aggadah."[49] Read closely, this means: the halakhah comes before aggadah. R. Soloveitchik does not walk in the opposite lane, in which the halakhah corresponds to the idea. Talk of prayer "as understood [...] by an individual"[50] is possible only upon the assumption of the primacy of the halakhah.

For the reasons I mentioned, I find problematic the conclusion that Rynhold draws from prayer regarding R. Soloveitchik's thought as a whole. Rynhold is correct, specifically, in his analysis of R. Soloveitchik's attitude to prayer and the other "worship of the heart" commandments, which is brilliant. Prayer, however, is not an example for other topics, except for Torah study and communion with God.[51] R. Soloveitchik was steadfast in his insistence on the reconstruction of the subjective dimension, and nothing else, in order to maintain the stability of the objective dimension (namely, the halakhah). Nonetheless, when he discussed prayer, the underpinnings of the reconstruction were weakened, with a rise in the proximity between the subjective and the objective (see below, the following chapters). To some degree, the subjective consciousness "invades" the objective, as is reflected in the notion of intent. In the end, the experiential nature of prayer and the solemn standing of a person praying to his Creator overcame the clear inclination to isolate the objective dimension of the consciousness and grant it absolute autonomy. In other words, prayer is more closely related to the subjective consciousness than are other halakhic topics. Rynhold therefore justly felt that R. Soloveitchik showed greater flexibility in his consciousness models of prayer than he did regarding other issues; we will

---

48 *Worship of the Heart*, 2.
49 *Worship of the Heart*, 2.
50 *Worship of the Heart*, 2.
51 In popular homiletics, R. Soloveitchik extended this exception to the Days of Awe; he most likely referred mainly to repentance, the holiday prayers, and the blowing of the *shofar* (ram's horn)—that, in addition to being a mechanical act, is also, in halakhic terminology, the *kiyyum* of song and outcry.

discuss this question at length.[52] However, prayer and the other obligations connected to the "worship of the heart" (Torah study and communion with God) are exceptions, and are not generally representative. In my estimation, Rynhold's imprecision can be traced to his viewing prayer as expressive of the entirety of R. Soloveitchik's thought. At times, the application of external models is liable to blur our understanding of the development and internal cohesiveness of R. Soloveitchik's thought, even if prayer is not an outstanding example of this.

The Educational Aspect

R. Elyakim Krumbein argues, sensitively and at length, that *Worship of the Heart* marks a turning point in the development of the educational aspect in R. Soloveitchik's writings.[53] He acknowledges the multifaceted nature of R. Soloveitchik's teachings, but "it seems that education was of prime interest for him."[54] He claims that R. Soloveitchik's other essays are characterized by a personal writing style reflective of his own specific personal state, but not that of his readers. He believes that the oscillations and anguish depicted by R. Soloveitchik were not representative of his time. This is because R. Soloveitchik's dialectic is typical of a genius, who stands far above all others, but is not suitable for the average person. *Worship of the Heart*, in contrast, is directed to the public at large.[55] To a certain degree, this argument contradicts Amaru's statement that this is a somewhat esoteric composition.

I assume that Krumbein's argument is realistic, that is, he does not claim that this was R. Soloveitchik's intent from the outset. R. Soloveitchik, on his part, was interested in educating the entire generation, and, from the outset, wanted to address his writings to the broad public; otherwise, he would not have published them, and in rabbinical venues.[56] The tragic result—for Krumbein—is that "R. Soloveitchik's writings allow a breathtaking glimpse, and open a window to the mysteries of a great soul, but,

---

52 See below, Chapter Five.
53 See Elyakim Krumbein, "The Importance of the Book *Avodah She-ba-Lev* by R. J. B. Soloveitchik" [Hebrew], *Akdamot* 18 (2007): 141-163.
54 Ibid., 142.
55 Krumbein might have seen the discussion of the existential crisis in *Worship of the Heart* as being exceptional. See below, Chapter Four, section 1.
56 The *Talpioth* journal, in which "*Ish ha-Halakhah*" was published, edited by Samuel K. Mirsky, published articles on halakhah, aggadah, and scholarly research. *Hadorom*, in which *And from There You Shall Seek* was published, is the journal of the Rabbinical Council of America.

this said and done, they do not necessarily provide balm for the soul of the individual, or teach of a tangible experiential way of life for the masses."[57] If I correctly understand what Krumbein wrote, then he meant that R. Soloveitchik was in the heights of his sublime experiences, and did not think about the disparity between them and those of his followers and readers. Amaru joins him on this point, and argues that the experiences depicted in *Worship of the Heart* belong to "the Rav's personal psychology."[58]

We therefore may state decisively (as was noted above), that R. Soloveitchik himself undoubtedly believed that his thought and works accomplished the following:

(1) revealed the existential consciousness infrastructure common to every man as such;
(2) expressed the idea that Judaism directs Halakhah, its eternal creation, to that same consciousness and existential infrastructure.

R. Soloveitchik's clearly existential ideas were first formulated, forcefully and in concentrated fashion, in a series of lectures that he gave at the National Institute of Mental Health in New York. He was also influenced by the existentialist psychology that gained in standing in the United States in the 1950s and 1960s.[59] This psychological school maintained that the fundamental tensions characteristic of self-esteem, anxieties relating to nothingness, finitude, and other distressing issues, existential assurance, communicating with others, existential dialogue, and the respect characteristic of human existence are at the basis of human personality and behavior. They pointed to those fundamental tensions and the existential structure as the source of personality and behavioral disturbances. Whether or not these tensions speak to the broad public, for R. Soloveitchik they are a fact of personality and consciousness.

Just as the therapist cannot reach the patient without an awareness of the basic structures and tensions of existence, so too, the rabbi cannot educate and fashion the character of his students without knowledge of their mental framework, which must be addressed. R. Soloveitchik found great worth in revealing the existential structure of the personality. He wrote:

> Man is surely aware of many needs, but the needs he is aware of are not always his own. At the very root of this failure to recognize one's truly

---

57 Krumbein, "Importance," 143.
58 Amaru, "Prayer," 163.
59 See Schwartz, *From Phenomenology to Existentialism*, 228-230.

worthwhile needs lies man's ability to misunderstand and misidentify
himself, i.e. to lose himself.[60]

He defined modern man's real needs as coming to know the experiences
of suffering and dialogue. He viewed himself as a "therapist" and educator,
and he was convinced that existentialist psychotherapy, for example, is the
way to arrive at modern man's true needs. Obviously, according to his conceptual approach, he himself possessed the capabilities of a therapist, in the
sense that the halakhah addresses the existential structure, which it reveals
and balances—and he was the "halakhic man."

For his part, therefore, R. Soloveitchik spoke to a broad public. He
was convinced that the tensions he felt were shared by his students and his
readers. Without an awareness of these tensions, the educational process
could not take place, and psychological theories would remain fruitless.
As was mentioned above, R. Soloveitchik objected to mysticism whenever he had any contact with it, since he vigorously opposed any approach
not intended for the public at large. The halakhah, by its very nature, is
meant for a broad audience, and any attempt to limit part of it to select
individuals is doomed to failure.[61] At least in terms of the meaning of
R. Soloveitchik's writings themselves, there is no difference between
Worship of the Heart and existential works such as *The Lonely Man of Faith*
or some of the essays in *Out of the Whirlwind*. Admittedly, modern man—
as Krumbein portrays this[62]—is subject to the pressures of economic
security and social status, and not the anguish of being and nothingness.
The tragedy, however, of modern man, according to R. Soloveitchik, is
his unawareness of the superficiality of these pressures, which conceal a
world of existential tensions in ferment. In the terminology of *The Lonely
Man of Faith*, Adam the first seeks to dominate Adam the second, and he
refuses to believe that existence means every man's oscillating between the
two types. He writes:

> Majestic Adam has developed a demonic quality: laying claim to unlimited
> power—alas, to infinity itself. [...] I am thinking of man's attempt to dominate
> himself, or, to be more precise, of Adam the first's desire to identify himself
> with the total human personality, declaring his creative talents as ultimate,
> ignoring completely Adam the second and his preoccupation with the

---

60 Joseph B. Soloveitchik, "Redemption, Prayer, Talmud Torah," *Tradition* 17, no. 2 (1978):
     62.
61 See below, Chapter Three.
62 Krumbein, "Importance," 145.

unique and strange transcendental experience which resists subservience to the cultural interests of majestic man.[63]

The primary goal of education, as formulated by R. Soloveitchik, is to recognize the deep experiences of existence. Such an awareness will also cast the surface experiences (that include economic pressure and social standing) in the correct light.

Krumbein did not explore R. Soloveitchik's educational efforts and assumed an impermeable barrier between the personality of the genius and that of any man. Out of his great esteem for R. Soloveitchik, Krumbein's analysis was actually counterproductive, and voided his teacher's words of any relevancy. According to Krumbein, R. Soloveitchik's doubts do not pertain to the average person. I wish to argue that, from R. Soloveitchik's perspective, Krumbein's article constituted a failure of his educational approach. R. Soloveitchik found supreme value in man's conflict with his self. The ideas set forth in *Worship of the Heart* somewhat express his religious existentialist approach, and most particularly, his phenomenological methodology. This is a direct continuation of R. Soloveitchik's thought as expressed in his other works. Although the individualistic preface to *Worship of the Heart* could have suggested he is addressing the modern Orthodox public with its typically individualistic lifestyle, this is the same individualism that appears in his other writings as well.

To some extent Krumbein is correct, and in this *Worship of the Heart* breaks new ground. For the first time, R. Soloveitchik implies that the phenomenological approach that he adopted in many of his writings might not be appropriate for a broad audience.[64] But even in such statements he modestly included himself among the broad public, and removed himself from the elitist community. Methodologically, the centrality of the halakhah in his writings led him to oppose elitism, and in terms of his personality, he was revolted by such thought. The halakhah essentially encompasses all strata of the Jewish people, and cannot be delegated solely for certain groups. The central, subjective experience of prayer, specifically, is liable to result in religious elitism. In any event, R. Soloveitchik wanted to emphasize the popular dimension of the prayer experience. Failing in this attempt, he then turned to existentialist thought so that this experience would be accessible to all. Prayer is an expression of a person in distress, and

63 *Lonely Man of Faith*, 102-103.
64 See below, Chapter Three.

existentialist thought finely depicts existential suffering. The educational orientation of R. Soloveitchik's thought is evident.

Momentum

The publication of *Worship of the Heart* energized the study of R. Soloveitchik's philosophy of prayer. It would no longer be possible to remain indifferent to the standing of prayer in his thought. Recently, additional researches have been published, such as the book by Reuven Ziegler, who devoted two chapters to prayer.[65] Unlike the essays by Kaplan and Amaru, who focused on the analysis of a single work by R. Soloveitchik, Ziegler's methodology is comparative. His comparison of different compositions by R. Soloveitchik compelled him to concentrate on one or two central ideas in each composition, at the expense of the rich nuances in R. Soloveitchik's writings. This methodology cannot examine the inner tensions typical of R. Soloveitchik's conceptions and style. His comparative perspective, however, adds to our understanding of the ideational flow of R. Soloveitchik's thought. In my analysis in the current book, I attempt to clarify why a composition such as *Worship of the Heart*, with its lack of inner cohesion and flawed editing, so fascinates the world of thought and scholarship.

4. Summary

In this chapter we engaged in general assessments of the nature and aims of *Worship of the Heart*, and we saw that its author himself viewed it as a personal composition that, paradoxically, seeks to explore the systematic sides of his private, intimate experience. R. Soloveitchik took pains to commit to writing what could be formulated from that personal experience, and to share these formulations with the public. The dense dialectic in the declaration of intent at the beginning of the book reveals R. Soloveitchik's typical style in his theoretical works.

R. Soloveitchik's public declaration of his modesty is not without reason. He does not presume to forge ironclad rules for all, for two reasons, one obvious and the other covert. The obvious reason is that *Worship of the Heart* presents a personal experience, that is, characteristic of a single individual, and therefore, its aspirations for acceptance among the public at large are

---

65 Reuven Ziegler, *Majesty and Humility: The Thought of Rabbi Joseph B. Soloveitchik* (Jerusalem: Urim Publications, 2012), 213-33.

limited from the outset. There is also, however, an additional reason. The book's discussions encircle a defined legal frame, whose boundaries have been firmly set by the halakhah. The assumed immutability of the halakhic system is the basis of any discussion of its meanings. A conceptual discussion of prayer goes no further than reconstruction or speculations concerning the subjective motives of the religious act. Accordingly, the goals of *Worship of the Heart*, as those in R. Soloveitchik's other conceptual works, are modest and relate to the subjective cognitive dimension and the impression it leaves. The tempest remains behind the scenes in the determination of the links between the subjective consciousness and the objective, but the result can only be one: the preservation of the halakhah within defined bounds. To restate this: unlike the halakhic lesson, that contributes to an awareness of halakhic reasoning in its own right, but nonetheless dismantles the halakhah into its components and reconstructs it, the theoretical essay can only surmise its subjective dimension. With the given halakhic system, together with R. Soloveitchik's personal character (that is not fully transitive), the author felt that he could not diverge into the realm of universal statements.

A comparison of *Worship of the Heart* with R. Soloveitchik's other writings shows its fidelity to the spirit and style of the latter. At times, the complex messages that appear in the other works are formulated more simply here, as we shall see below. From this aspect alone we may concur that *Worship of the Heart* was directed to a broader audience. R. Soloveitchik believed that the prayer experience could be placed within the context of the study of the consciousness, together with an awareness of the actual existence. Just as the act of prayer is an expression of a lively and rich subjective consciousness, prayer has man face his actual existence, and causes him to gain an awareness of the fundamental characteristics of existence. Just as prayer is the objectivization of the deep dimensions of knowledge, it also is an expression of dialogue, existential dignity, existential distresses, and the like.

Most of the Torah authorities and modern scholars who related to *Worship of the Heart* sensed R. Soloveitchik's singular attitude to the prayer experience. They noted the singular weight of the subjective experience in this halakhic realm, which is understandable on the background of R. Soloveitchik's writings taken as a whole. In other words, we cannot ignore the philosophical methodologies characteristic of R. Soloveitchik's thought in general. Generally speaking, the flaws in some of these scholarly articles are the result of partial or insufficient consideration of these methodologies. We will now turn to an analysis of the insights that *Worship of the Heart* offers.

Chapter 2

The Consciousness of Prayer: An Outline

The first five chapters of *Worship of the Heart* focus on the consciousness of prayer. R. Soloveitchik defined this consciousness, considered its uniqueness, and analyzed in great detail the processes of its development. In the following discussion, I will examine the religious phenomenological conception of prayer as it assumed shape in *Worship of the Heart*, and the models of religious consciousness that emerge from prayer or have some connection to it. The first chapter of *Worship of the Heart* offers what is in essence a classification, locating prayer as a significant act among the various expressions of religious consciousness. In a preface to this discussion, R. Soloveitchik presented a series of broad insights on the standing of prayer and on the methodology for reconstructing its passionate subjective dimension. One of these dimensions, which assumes a unique role, is dialogue. We will begin, then, with some general remarks about the standing of prayer in worship, move on to an analysis of its place in prayer, and conclude with the dialogical conception of prayer.

1. Objectification

Layers of Consciousness

The preface to the first chapter of *Worship of the Heart*, which deals with the standing of prayer, is independent.[1] Its style differs from that typical of the first five chapters, and its independence is indicated by the fact that the entire chapter—except for the preface—appeared in another book with many omissions and in a different style, as a reconstruction of a self-standing lecture.[2]

---

1 The preface was printed in *Worship of the Heart*, 3.
2 "Prayer as Dialogue," in Joseph B. Soloveitchik, *Reflections of the Rav: Lessons in Jewish Thought Adapted from Lectures of Rabbi Joseph B. Soloveitchik*, ed. Abraham R. Besdin

In the preface, R. Soloveitchik discusses prayer's standing in consciousness and its nature as an objective dimension of the subjective consciousness. In what follows, we will attempt to locate this preface within R. Soloveitchik's general phenomenological philosophy.

In our Introduction we already spoke of the important place that the phenomenology of religion occupies in R. Soloveitchik's discussions of prayer. He looked at prayer in an attempt to understand its expressions as a distinct act of consciousness. He examined his own personal experience and sought to set up general structural constructs concerning prayer. He then endeavored to understand the borders of subjective experience and of ritual in the consciousness of prayer. R. Soloveitchik viewed the setting of these subtle borders as the mission of Judaism, and it is in this light that the main body of *Worship of the Heart* should be understood.

Status and Value

In the preface to the first chapter, R. Soloveitchik presents a series of general assumptions and assessments on the status of prayer. I will first cite him at length, and examine this passage's meaning regarding the characteristics of the consciousness of prayer. I will then discuss the key terms used by R. Soloveitchik. He writes:

> Prayer (*Tefillah*) is one of the media through which man communicates with the Almighty God. I purposely say "one of the media" in order to refute the doctrine advanced by the mystics,[3] and accepted by the advocates of religious

---

(Jerusalem: World Zionist Organization, 1979), 71-88. This work is heavily edited, and the editor notes in the introduction that it is not a literal transcript, and includes also his own impressions. Note that while Carmy indicated in his introduction (xxviii) that the notebooks from which the chapter was taken had been written in 1956-1957, Besdin dates the writing to 1950. This may be an earlier version that R. Soloveitchik polished at a later stage. In any event, the independent lesson includes additional sections of *Worship of the Heart* (see below).

3 R. Soloveitchik referred to Christian mysticism, which used the term "prayer" to express different states of consciousness (see above, Introduction). Although he repeatedly rejected mysticism, in his discussion of prayer he was actually ready to accept several of its aspects (see below, Chapter Three). He emphasized that, contrary to the situation that prevails regarding other commandments, the subjective dimension is the very reason for prayer, to which I refer several times in the current work. The reason for this tension is that the present context is controversial. R. Soloveitchik related to the trends that harmed or threatened to erode the validity of halakhah. By contrast, in a substantive discussion, he did affirm the mystical and subjective dimensions prominent in prayer.

subjectivism,[4] that prayer is the only means leading to the successful realization of our blind intent[5] of reaching out to Him. Judaism has not subscribed
to the idea of the centrality of prayer, even though it has not underestimated
the importance of prayer as regards our God-searching and God-pursuing.[6]
Basically prayer is a mode of expression or objectification[7] of our inner
experience, of a state of mind, of a subjective religious act, of the adventur-
ous and bold attempt of self-transcendence[8] on the part of the human being,
and of his incessant drive toward the infinite and eternal. [...]

Prayer designates certain aspects of *avodah she-ba-lev*, the intimate and
silent worship of God by the heart. Worship of the heart actually embraces
the total commitment of man to the Creator, his being rooted in, close to
and at the same time infinitely far from God, his fear and his love of God, his
anxiety and security, despair and hope, his certainty and doubts, his awareness of Being and non-being, of rationality and purposiveness, and, simultaneously, of the absurdity and meaninglessness of the human performance.
Prayer is one aspect of *avodah she-ba-lev*, but worship is not confined in its
process of objectification to prayer; worship expresses itself in a variety of
ways, since it is the sum total of man's relationship to God.[9]

This prefatory passage to the first chapter contains three important statements of the place of prayer in consciousness.

The first statement concerns the standing of prayer. R. Soloveitchik's
objection to overemphasizing the importance of prayer is not difficult to
understand, since the entire book is devoted to prayer; additionally, prayer
was a central act in R. Soloveitchik's conception of consciousness. His res-
ervation is twofold:

(1) prayer is not the only means of reaching God;
(2) prayer is not a discrete type of consciousness, but rather belongs to
    a broader sort of consciousness, *avodah she-ba-lev*.

---

4 That is, the phenomenologists and pragmatists who rejected the objective and rational
    dimension of religion.
5 Kaplan maintains that this should read "bold." See Kaplan, "Review Essay," 104.
6 Such an assertion is repeated in *Worship of the Heart*, 25. I will observe below that the
    consciousness of prayer focuses on man and his relationship to God.
7 On this concept, see below.
8 On this concept, see below.
9 *Worship of the Heart*, 4. This statement resembles the model of R. Bahya in *Duties of
    the Heart*. R. Bahya determined that some commandments are imposed on the heart
    and, furthermore, every practical commandment is accompanied by a duty of the heart,
    which is intent. The worship of the heart thus exhausts subjective religious consciousness
    in R. Soloveitchik's thought. See below, Chapter Three.

Thus, R. Soloveitchik was apparently apprehensive about two things:

(1) he was concerned about the central standing mysticism assigned to prayer, which was liable to overshadow the preservation of the halakhah;[10]

(2) he feared the centrality of prayer to the same extent in his life, his personality, and his thought. Such a cardinal status could also harm the philosophical and halakhic balance that he sought to achieve in his phenomenological thought.

R. Soloveitchik clarified in the course of this work that "worship of the heart" as an element of consciousness includes other expressions besides prayer, such as the obsessive pursuit of the experience of communion with God[11] and Torah study.[12] Furthermore, prayer is perceived not only as a specific act ("liturgic performance") but also as a generic name for all the activities through which "man expresses his inner religious self."[13] R. Soloveitchik thereby prepared the reader for the fact that the goal of the first part of *Worship of the Heart* is to sketch the basic lines of religious consciousness, while prayer is only a means toward this end. That is, through knowledge of the cognitive component (prayer) the reader comes to understand the entire structure of consciousness. Only the second part of the book, which deals with the reciting of *Shema*, concentrates exclusively on the consciousness of prayer. The reader, as it were, is not ready to grasp

---

10 See, for example, *The Lonely Man of Faith*, p. 65-66.

11 *Worship of the Heart*, 24.

12 *Worship of the Heart*, 25.

13 *Worship of the Heart*, 26. On prayer as the manifestation of the self, see also below, Chapter Twelve. Here we have an important dialectic characteristic of the consciousness of prayer. One of R. Soloveitchik's substantive statements on prayer is that it is based on the negation of the self. For example, "First and foremost, prayer represents humility. An insolent person does not know what prayer is. The negation of the self and submission are at the basis of prayer" (*Festival of Freedom* [Alon Shvut, Toras HoRav Foundation, 2006], 111 [published only in Hebrew]); "*Talmud Torah* requires self-affirmation and self-appreciation, confidence in one's ability to understand and judge, to discriminate and equate. *Tefillah* demands self-negation, just the opposite approach. The mood that generates a desire for prayer is one of hopelessness and bankruptcy. To pray means to surrender one's pride and self-confidence, to put aside any awareness of greatness, freedom, and independence" (Joseph B. Soloveitchik, *Abraham's Journey: Reflections of the Life of the Founding Patriarch*, ed. David Shatz, Joel B. Wolowelsky, and Reuven Ziegler [Jersey City, NJ: Toras HoRav Foundation, 2008], 188). Thus, R. Soloveitchik alternated between the perception of prayer as the negation of the self and as the revealing and empowering of the self.

the consciousness of prayer before understanding the structure of religious consciousness. Possibly, this is also an indication of the issues that most intrigued R. Soloveitchik, above all, the foundations of consciousness.

The second statement describes prayer as a component of consciousness: prayer is an objective expression of the subjective religious consciousness. Objectification has two meanings in R. Soloveitchik's thought. One is the construction of the cognitive object within thought (*Denken*), in accordance with the approach of Hermann Cohen. The second meaning, that is relevant for our purposes, is phenomenological. R. Soloveitchik adopted Max Scheler's view, arguing that objectivity relates to the cognitive dimension of consciousness linking us to our surroundings. Scheler argued that, contrary to the animal necessarily involved in its environment and unable to confront it, humans can turn their surroundings into an object. Objectification, claimed Scheler, is "most formal category of the logical aspect of spirit [*Geist*]."[14] Humans can rise above themselves as organic beings operating in a given and transitory time and place and transform what is around them and even themselves into objects of knowledge and consciousness.[15] This ability is evident in humans' perception of the objective aspect of objects, which Scheler defined in phenomenological terms: we are liberated from the local and temporal surroundings of the object we seek to know, and know it as an "object."[16] Although R. Soloveitchik adopted Scheler's terminology, instead of identifying the objective with the conscious, he rather equated it with action. In lieu of relating solely to a "conscious" environment, he placed the environment beyond the consciousness together with elements to which the consciousness relates. Objectification, for Scheler, means placing the world in brackets and exposing the object's essential

---

14 Max Scheler, *Man's Place in Nature* (Boston: Beacon Press, 1961), 39. Scheler applied the term *Geist* to the array of factors that differentiate man from animals. R. Soloveitchik endorsed this approach. See, for example, Joseph B. Soloveitchik, *The Emergence of Ethical Man*, ed. Michael S. Berger (Jersey City, NJ: Toras HoRav Foundation, 2005), 8. In the essay "Reflections on the *Amidah*," R. Soloveitchik described objectivization in relation to prayer as follows: "The service of the heart gained a foothold in the world of forms and facts" (*Worship of the Heart*, 147). He apparently referred to Scheler's style; otherwise, his use of the term "forms" in this context is unclear.

15 *Man's Place in Nature*, 46.

16 Scheler, *Man's Place in Nature*, 37. Scheler referred to this as man's "freeing himself from the environment." Human consciousness replaces fixed correlation to local and temporal surroundings with "openness to the world." R. Soloveitchik indirectly confronts this approach in the first essay in *The Emergence of Ethical Man*.

nature. For R. Soloveitchik, objectivization is the connection between the consciousness and the external surroundings, that is, action.

Scheler's religious phenomenological thought required him to objectify feeling. In the objectification he intended, however, prayer and knowledge are replaced by faith and grace.[17] R. Soloveitchik, however, took the meaning that Scheler had suggested in *Man's Place in Nature*—confronting the external surroundings and revealing the essential dimension of its components—while adopting the religious meaning only in the formal sense, that is, as the need for an objectification process. Prayer belongs to the practical realm, involving recitation and gestures, and is thus, above all, an objective expression. From the act of prayer—the series of practical commands related to it—we can reconstruct its subjective dimension. This dimension is indeed vibrant and passionate, but prayer is bound by the defined and rigorous rules of halakhah.

The third statement concerns intention: the objectification of the religious act does not exhaust the meaning of prayer, which is first and foremost a practical (halakhic) expression of subjective consciousness. The halakhic command regarding prayer relates, first and foremost, to its practice. The fundamental construct in R. Soloveitchik's writings is that the command relates primarily to the practical aspect, while the subjective side is reconstructed from within the act, or is correlated to it. Even if R. Soloveitchik does not explicitly declare this, his discussions are built in this manner.[18] *Worship of the Heart* teaches that the subjective consciousness itself is included in the divine command. That is to say, R. Soloveitchik will argue in *Worship of the Heart* that prayer is a command imposed directly on man's soul. He thereby strove to spiritualize religious life through prayer.[19]

R. Soloveitchik resorts in these assertions to phenomenological terms and concepts that recur in several works that he published in his lifetime

---

17 Scheler, *On the Eternal*, 288.
18 See below, Chapter Three.
19 To some extent, the last two assumptions convey the same approach. R. Soloveitchik formulated the spiritual approach when he determined that the worship of the heart is "the quintessence of Judaism" (*Worship of the Heart*, 4). This approach, as was mentioned above, resembles spiritualizing trends in Jewish thought, such as that of R. Bahya in *Duties of the Heart*, which R. Soloveitchik explicitly mentions in the second chapter of *Worship of the Heart* (see below, Chapter Three). Finally, it is noteworthy that this assumption indicates that, for R. Soloveitchik, the spiritualization of religious life fitted the subjective religious consciousness of religious phenomenology. On the types of intent in *Worship of the Heart*, see Kaplan, "Review Essay," 88-89.

after they were subject to his thorough and meticulous review. This use clarifies the course that he also follows in *Worship of the Heart*.

Basic Terms

The preface to the first chapter of *Worship of the Heart* sets guidelines for the first five chapters of the book. As we saw above, R. Soloveitchik uses this preface to present prayer as the key to processes that religious consciousness undergoes and includes the concepts underlying his discussion of consciousness. Following are the concepts and ideas on the standing of prayer detailed in this preface:

(1) "Self-transcendence." This term reflects how consciousness strives for the divine on the one hand and, on the other, the ability of consciousness to transcend itself and place its objective dimension vis-à-vis the subjective one. Both these meanings are present in the religious phenomenological literature and I have already discussed them at length elsewhere.[20] R. Soloveitchik viewed prayer as an expression of self-transcendence.

(2) The consciousness of opposites. Following Rudolf Otto and others (see below), R. Soloveitchik infused the subjective dimension of the consciousness of prayer with the notion of antitheses in religious consciousness vis-à-vis God. The fundamental paradox of consciousness, which yearns to become close to God while flinching at God's otherness and sublimity, is reflected in prayer. According to R. Soloveitchik, prayer records the love-awe and closeness-distance relationships between man and God.[21] In *And from There You Shall Seek* and in *The Halakhic Mind*, R. Soloveitchik presented a hierarchical and intricate structure

---

20 See Schwartz, *From Phenomenology to Existentialism*, 2-4. On the Kantian and Hegelian sources of the term, see Joseph Dov Soloveitchik, *The Halakhic Mind: An Essay on Jewish Tradition and Modern Thought* (New York: Seth Press, 1986), 126-127 n. 78. Emil Brunner viewed self-transcendence as an expression of inner conflict. See Emil Brunner, *Man in Revolt: A Christian Anthropology*, trans. Olive Wyon (New York: Scribner's, 1939), 20. See also Avi Sagi, *Prayer after "The Death of God": A Phenomenological Study of Hebrew Literature* [Hebrew] (Ramat Gan and Jerusalem: Bar-Ilan University Press and Shalom Hartman Institute, 2011), 178.

21 These relationships validate the inclusion of prayer in the category of "worship of the heart." The fact that R. Soloveitchik was forced to justify the categorization of prayer teaches of his desire to put prayer in its proper place and to avoid exaggeration.

of the external and internal tensions typical of subjective consciousness;[22] as in these essays, in *Worship of the Heart* this consciousness is based on two polarities: closeness-distance and awe-love. In the first two essays, however, religious consciousness refers to the mutuality in the man-God relationship. At times we seek God, while at other times God seeks us. Hence, R. Soloveitchik opens his comprehensive phenomenological treatise, *And from There You Shall Seek*, with metaphors from the Song of Songs where the lover and the beloved seek each other. In *Worship of the Heart*, focused mainly on the consciousness of prayer and only marginally on the consciousness of prophecy and revelation, it is man who seeks God.

(3) The revealing of subjective religious consciousness: R. Soloveitchik argued that prayer is a medium—emphasizing that, though important, it is only one of the means—for the "objectification" of consciousness. Particularly in *The Halakhic Mind*, he focused on the objective dimension of consciousness, that is, on religious norms and actions. Just as the consciousness addresses God subjectively, that is, with feeling, the soul, understanding, and reason, it similarly seeks Him with action. An intentional act also includes action directed to the object, that is, God. In *The Halakhic Mind* R. Soloveitchik referred to the objective and practical intentional act as a "psycho-physical religious" one.[23] He thereby anchored the halakhah in his phenomenological thought and found a philosophical basis for Orthodoxy. In that work, he further argued that the philosophical aim of religion is to understand the subjective dimension of consciousness that underlies its objective dimension. For him, the religious consciousness is built of layer upon layer: the subjective dimension of the consciousness is vibrant and fluid, and contains understandings, feelings, and dispositions. These enter the objective strata of the consciousness as the system of commandments. R. Soloveitchik maintains that the philosophy of religion is to examine the process of the subjectivization of religion's objective dimension and to document it, and, alternately, to describe the process of the objectivization of the subjective dimension. In this manner, Judaism is seen to possess a balanced and regulated religious consciousness.

---

22 See, for example, Jonathan Sacks, "Rabbi J. B. Soloveitchik's Early Epistemology: A Review of *The Halakhic Mind*," *Tradition* 23, no. 3 (1988): 75-87; Schwartz, *From Phenomenology to Existentialism*, 123.

23 *The Halakhic Mind*, 81.

We learn that the discussion of the value of religion and the ways of revealing its consciousness is well-grounded in R. Soloveitchik's thought. We may, therefore, conclude that the preface to the first chapter of *Worship of the Heart* aims to present the phenomenological framework of the discussion and to connect it with other discussions that R. Soloveitchik devoted to the religious consciousness.

2. Objectivization

The Dimensions of the Subjective Consciousness

What, then, is the place of prayer in religious consciousness? In *Reflections of the Rav* and in *Worship of the Heart*, R. Soloveitchik related similarly to the structure of religious consciousness in general, and to the consciousness of prayer in particular. These two works are not of equal weight, since the former was compiled by a listener, while the latter is based on the edited notes of R. Soloveitchik's lectures. Yet, they definitely shared a common source: R. Soloveitchik's notes, which he probably relied on in his lecture. Following is a description of the dimensions of consciousness according to these works.

The Nature of Religious Consciousness

In these two works, R. Soloveitchik notes four media, expressions, or dimensions of religious consciousness: intellectual, emotional, volitional, and dialogical.[24] He thereby endorses a schematic and simplistic division of consciousness. These four dimensions denote the modes of the actions through which consciousness strives for God. Prayer definitely attains full expression through the dialogical dimension. Between *Reflections of the Rav* and *Worship of the Heart*, two differences come to the fore.

The first concerns the independence of consciousness: in *Reflections of the Rav*, prayer determines an independent expression of consciousness. Consciousness, then, is made up of reason, feeling, and volition, and prayer creates a new "autonomous realm"—dialogue.[25] In *Worship of the Heart*, in contrast, R. Soloveitchik presents the dialogical dimension of consciousness as a given realm, where we locate not only prayer but also prophecy. Here we have prayer as consciousness, contrary to prayer as an element

---

24 Both *Reflections of the Rav* and *Worship of the Heart* refer to the dimensions of consciousness as "media." On the historical appearance of the dialogical dimension of prayer, see, for example, Ehrlich, *The Nonverbal Language*, chapter 11.

25 *Reflections of the Rav*, 77.

of consciousness in the "worship of the heart" or, alternatively, prayer as dialogical consciousness vis-à-vis prayer as intimate consciousness. In a sense, the difference between the two versions is merely a question of precedence: in R. Besdin's version in *Reflections of the Rav*, prayer creates dialogical consciousness, whereas in *Worship of the Heart*, this consciousness is an *a priori* given, and prayer assumes its place within it. Both perceive prayer as dialogical consciousness, but the modes of presenting this consciousness are different. Perhaps we have a retreat here: from prayer as religious consciousness to prayer as a component of this consciousness.

The second difference is in the relations between matter and form: in *Reflections of the Rav*, the first three realms are not significantly related to prayer, because they entail neither mutuality nor dialogue. R. Soloveitchik split off the content or the "matter" of prayer (wording, gestures, halakhah) from its form or essence (dialogue). The three realms of consciousness connect to prayer solely on the level of content, but only dialogue ("form")—speaking to the Holy One, blessed be He, characterizes prayer properly, as experience.

In *Worship of the Heart*, however, the media of consciousness are connected in all of prayer's manifestations. R. Soloveitchik poured the patterns of prayer in all its dimensions into the intellectual, emotional, and volitional media, with the fourth, dialogical dimension of consciousness being the peak of the consciousness of prayer. The connection of the first three media to prayer is sometimes clear and emphasized, and concealed in other instances. Prayer, then, gradually and latently takes shape in the first three media of consciousness and erupts in all its power in the fourth (dialogical) dimension. These dimensions denote acts and experiences of consciousness, each reflecting another of its aspects. Furthermore, the first realms are expressed through prayer as dialogue. R. Soloveitchik writes in *Reflections of the Rav*:

> The material content of prayer is not unique; it partakes of elements of the first three media, primarily of the emotional. What is unique is its form,[26] its dialogue aspect. Prayer may be defined as the objectivating agency or medium of expression for the other three media.[27]

In other words, prayer is an objective stratum of the subjective media of consciousness. The first three (the intellectual, emotional, and volitional) are elements of the subjective consciousness, while dialogue is the objective component. Dialogue is perceived as the praxis of prayer. Standing before

---

26 By "form," R. Soloveitchik referred to both the technical manifestation of prayer (that is, speech) and its essence, hinting at the Aristotelian sense of the term. We could say that he draws a distinction between dialogue as speech and dialogue as relation

27 *Reflections of the Rav*, 79.

God is simply a mutual conversation. R. Soloveitchik linked the discussion of prayer with those of consciousness that appear in his early writings.

Some scholars have already indicated the threefold structure that describes the subjective-objective hierarchy as elements of the religious consciousness in R. Soloveitchik's thought. In *The Halakhic Mind* R. Soloveitchik presented the following model of consciousness:

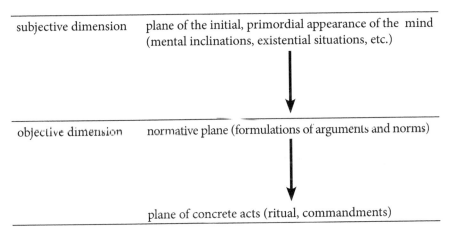

subjective dimension — plane of the initial, primordial appearance of the mind (mental inclinations, existential situations, etc.)

objective dimension — normative plane (formulations of arguments and norms)

plane of concrete acts (ritual, commandments)

We can offer a model of the consciousness of prayer based on the description in *Reflections of the Rav* and the structure of consciousness in *The Halakhic Mind*[28]:

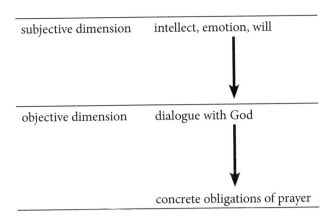

subjective dimension — intellect, emotion, will

objective dimension — dialogue with God

concrete obligations of prayer

In this model, the first three dimensions of consciousness in *Reflections of the Rav* (intellect, emotion, and will) are perceived as the subjective realm, while the act of prayer is their objective dimension, in accordance with the

---

28 I will discuss the expressions of the consciousness model in *Worship of the Heart* in Chapter Three, below.

model of consciousness mentioned above. The recitation of prayer is the dialogue (the norm), while the system of gestures and halakhot associated with prayer constitutes the praxis.

Mention should also be made of the parallel presentation in *Reflections of the Rav* of another model, in which the consciousness of prayer stands alongside other consciousnesses, as an equal:

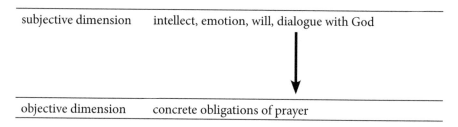

subjective dimension	intellect, emotion, will, dialogue with God
objective dimension	concrete obligations of prayer

By contrast, in the first chapter of *Worship of the Heart*, R. Soloveitchik does not make such a sharp division between the (subjective) content and (objective) essence of prayer. We can speak of a progression from *Reflections of the Rav* to *Worship of the Heart* as the movement from the objective to the subjective. In the early recording of the lecture, prayer is focused wholly in the objective plane. Dialogue expresses the subjective dimensions of consciousness. In *Worship of the Heart*, on the other hand, the essence of prayer is mainly in the subjective, while its expressions are in the objective.

Intellectual Experience

I will now present the different dimensions of religious consciousness, and offer a few observations on the conscious structure they represent.

The intellectual is the first dimension of consciousness. As R. Soloveitchik presents it:

> Man must serve God at the intellectual level. Judaism believes that human thinking is only a reflex of the infinite mind and that knowledge and cognition are basically Divine possessions. Man is only allowed to share these treasures with their real Master—with God.[29]

Consciousness strives for God through knowledge and through the acquisition of knowledge. It is only the intellectual worship of Him that R. Soloveitchik presents in the language of obligation and command.

---

29 *Worship of the Heart*, 4.

The other media of consciousness are set forth as tools for the one who wishes to approach God:

> The Emotional Medium: Man is also able to approach God through his great and passionate love for Him.[30]
> The Volitional Medium: Man also approaches God through a third medium, the volitional sphere.[31]
> The Dialogical Medium: The fourth medium through which communication of man with God is accomplished is dialogue.[32]

To some extent, R. Soloveitchik follows Maimonides, who regarded the acquisition of knowledge as necessarily deriving from man's definition as possessing intellectual apprehension (*Mishneh Torah, Hilkhot Yesodei ha-Torah* [Laws of the Fundamentals of the Torah] 2:2; *Guide of the Perplexed* 1:1). The acquisition of wisdom is not merely a question of religious perfection or approaching God; it is obligatory. R. Soloveitchik, apparently, thought that basic axioms of consciousness could not be established without the intellectual medium.

Moreover, between the lines, R. Soloveitchik adopted the Aristotelian approach that identifies God as the thought that thinks itself, that is, as infinite thought.[33] Acquiring knowledge means drawing closer to the infinite divine intellect, and hence also to God's worship. R. Soloveitchik included two realms within the intellectual worship of God, and claimed he was thereby following Maimonides:

(1) scientific-metaphysical knowledge;
(2) Torah study, which R. Soloveitchik included in the category of "ethical truths."[34]

---

30 *Worship of the Heart*, 5.
31 *Worship of the Heart*, 9.
32 *Worship of the Heart*, 10.
33 According to *Reflections of the Rav* (71), R. Soloveitchik added the unity of knowledge model (cognition, cognizing subject, and cognized object), thus clearly formulating the Aristotelian model. On this model in R. Soloveitchik's thought, see Dov Schwartz, "R. Soloveitchik as a Maimonidean: The Unity of Cognition," in *Maimonides and Mysticism: Presented to Moshe Hallamish on the Occasion of His Retirement*, ed. Abraham Elqayam and Dov Schwartz [Hebrew] (Ramat Gan: Bar-Ilan University Press, 2009), 301-321.
34 See, e.g., *Sefer ha-Mitzvoth of Maimonides*, Positive Commandment 3 (English edition: *The Commandments: Sefer Ha-Mitzvoth of Maimonides*, trans. Charles B. Chavel [London and New York: Soncino, 1967], vol. 1: *The Positive Commandments*, 4), in which Maimonides included contemplation within the commandment to love the Lord

In his description of the intellectual dimension, R. Soloveitchik writes:

> Maimonides considers this thesis [the acquisition of knowledge as "sharing" in the divine intellect] as the crux of his religious philosophy. The intellectual approach to God is closely bound up either with scientific-metaphysical research and knowledge or with the study of the Torah. Maimonides considered both of these cognitive performances to be an expression of man's clinging to God. Thinking in terms of eternal truths, whether theoretical or ethical, is an act of love, of craving for God. In theory and ethos we give ourselves to Him.[35]

R. Soloveitchik included Torah study in the intellectual dimension of consciousness, a seemingly logical move because Torah study requires intellectual energies. Relying on Maimonides in this regard, however, is problematic, for two reasons.

(1) The analytical ability required by Torah study is an important tool, but still not the sole one. Maimonides finds value in the acquisition of knowledge, and not in honing one's ability to think.

(2) The acquisition of scientific and metaphysical knowledge is necessary for the sake of human perfection, that is, for the purpose of communion with the Active Intellect.

On these grounds, R. Soloveitchik gave precedence to scientific-metaphysical knowledge over Torah knowledge. Torah study functions as the preparation for the acquisition of knowledge. In Maimonides' view, the commandments of the Torah were designed to create the social and political foundation for the improvement of the wise man.[36] R. Soloveitchik sensed the problematic nature in of Maimonides' view, and therefore included Torah study in the realm of ethics. He thereby also deferred to modern philosophical trends that included religion in this realm (Kant and Cohen). By making it part of ethics, R. Soloveitchik turned Torah study into a philosophical endeavor, and he sought to present it as such in Maimonides' approach as well.

The intellectual dimension set up intellectual communion as a purpose and a goal. The intellectual experience includes two dimensions: (1) the acquisition of

---

35 *Worship of the Heart*, 4. See *Guide of the Perplexed* 3:54 (end).

36 Maimonidean scholars throughout history have endeavored to compare observance of the commandments to philosophical inquiry. See Menachem M. Kellner, *Maimonides on Human Perfection* (Atlanta: Scholars Press, 1990).

knowledge; (2) devotion to attaining it. Given that phenomenological language speaks of a rational act, this act is intentional, that is, it is meant to acquire knowledge of God. R. Soloveitchik presented this rational act as an experience, and it is no wonder that he mentions in this context the issue that concludes the *Guide of the Perplexed*—the divine worship of the perfect individuals.

Now, for a characterization of the intellectual experience. Since wisdom is a characteristic of God, this conjunction is "a sort of identification with Divine thought,"[37] and thus also a *unio mystica* of the cognizing intellect and the cognized object. R. Soloveitchik, then, refrains from confining himself to rationalist trends and sets forth the ideal of intellectual communion as characterizing "leaders of both Hasidut and Lithuanian halakhic rationalism."[38] He concludes his discussion of the intellectual medium with the term *unio mystica*. In the description of the intellectual dimension of consciousness in *Worship of the Heart*, R. Soloveitchik laid the foundations for the dialogue that would characterize prayer. In his view, "in the intellectual gesture, there is a human turning towards God, a silent communication, a speechless dialogue with the Creator, Artist and Lover."[39] His description of the intellectual experience explicitly mentions Torah study as dialogue, which is one of the modes of "worship of the heart," while prayer, as dialogue, appears indirectly, in allusion. Prayer is verbal dialogue with the Creator, although only man speaks.

Emotional Experience

The second dimension of consciousness is emotional and intuitive. The consciousness strives for its God out of love and yearning, happiness and joy, distress and despair. This dimension of consciousness includes

---

37 *Worship of the Heart*, 5. See Schwartz, "R. Soloveitchik as a Maimonidean."

38 Once again, R. Soloveitchik adopted the phenomenological approach, which seeks the essential component generic to all religious phenomena. From this respect, the intellectual element is common to both Hasidism and Lithuanian rationalists. Moreover, R. Soloveitchik apparently referred to the Habad conception that elevates Torah study to the metaphysical value of mysticism and magic. Indeed, the dialogue that he conducts in his various writings with Hasidism is usually directed to Habad Hasidism. From this respect, what he says applies to both the *Tanya* and *Nefesh ha-Hayyim* by R. Hayyim of Volozhyn. Each of these works viewed Torah study as a way for connecting to the godly.

39 *Worship of the Heart*, 5. R. Soloveitchik thereby alluded to the connection of intellectual consciousness to the three key realms of knowledge: the metaphysical ("Creator"), the aesthetic ("Artist"), and the ethical ("Lover").

the experience of the divine presence, which is not effected by means of reason. R. Soloveitchik writes:

> Man, many Jewish philosophers and mystics maintained, may reach God not only through the intellect but also through the "heart," through a pure and serene mind, however naive and simple; through a passionate, sincere, though not intellectually enlightened love; through craving for God, even when the heart which craves has not been illuminated by Divine knowledge and wisdom; in loneliness and despair, even if the lonely and despairing soul cannot interpret its own misery; or through joy and jubilation, notwithstanding the fact that the heart which is filled with gratitude and happiness is too ignorant to analyze its aroused emotions.[40]

R. Soloveitchik spoke of an emotional and psychological deposition, which a person cannot fully know or analyze. In the article "A Theory of Emotions," which appears in the collection of essays *Out of the Whirlwind*, he adopts Freudian principles, while being critical of psychoanalysis. In an analysis of this essay, I showed that R. Soloveitchik made use of the criticism leveled at psychoanalysis by phenomenologists.[41] He nonetheless adopted the psychoanalytical principle that the roots of the emotions are latent and repressed.[42] R. Soloveitchik maintained in the above passage that the emotional experience is immediate, albeit not aware of its sources.

The question of the relationship between emotion and reason and intellectual analysis continued to intrigue R. Soloveitchik. In *Reflections of the Rav*, he relied on R. Judah Halevi's approach, which held that sensual impressions affect one's love of God as emotion more than abstract reason.[43] In *Worship of the Heart*, he identified the approach of Judah Halevi with that of Maimonides, and argued that they differ only in their point of origin. Judah Halevi proceeds from the emotional, sensual experience to reason,[44] while Maimonides moves from the rationality of the emotional experience

---

40 *Worship of the Heart*, 6.

41 See Schwartz, *From Phenomenology to Existentialism*, 277-88.

42 Ibid., 278.

43 *Reflections of the Rav*, 72. On traces of this approach in prophecy and epistemology, see Warren Zev Harvey, "Judah Halevi's Synthaesthetic Theory of Prophecy and a Note on the *Zohar*," in *Rivka Shatz-Uffenheimer Memorial Volume* [Hebrew], ed. Rachel Elior and Joseph Dan, 141-155 (*Jerusalem Studies in Jewish Thought* 12-13 [1996]).

44 According to R. Soloveitchik, Judah Halevi interpreted "the emotional experience in rational terms" (*Worship of the Heart*, 8). That is, the experience begins as emotional, and its continuation is "interpreted" rationally. R. Soloveitchik most likely referred to

to the love of God. In the end, however, both describe the experience of perfection as including all the mental capabilities. Such an argument is characteristic of the religious phenomenological view that the various approaches are merely expressions of the same religious consciousness.

And now, for the place of prayer: the difference between the parallel discussions in *Reflections of the Rav* and *Worship of the Heart* pertains also to the mention of prayer as an emotional experience. In the latter, R. Soloveitchik not only mentioned Judah Halevi's approach but also added a quote from the *Kuzari* applying the principle directly to prayer: "Do you not see that you cannot arrange all your prayers in thought alone without speech."[45] Verbal prayer, as opposed to prayer in thought, deepens the experience. Obviously, the description of the emotional and experiential second dimension cannot ignore the gestures of prayer. Hannah's prayer is thus also briefly mentioned in *Reflections of the Rav*, which then adds: "*Teshuvah* means return to one's metaphysical origin, and *tefillah*, too, means a return to one's wellspring."[46] By contrast, in *Worship of the Heart*, R. Soloveitchik writes explicitly:

> The craving for closeness to Being as such, with the origin and root of everything, is an *avodah she-ba-lev*. *Avodah she-ba-lev* is realized in the misery of humiliation, when the soul cries out "My God, my God, why hast Thou forsaken me" (Ps. 22:2), in the bliss of beholding His glory, when man sings out: "Raise O gates your heads… and let enter the King of glory" (Ps. 24:7) […].[47]

In this passage, R. Soloveitchik already presented prayer as one of the key expressions of "religious emotionality," as he defines it.[48] This time, he explicitly uses the term *avodah she-ba-lev* and offers by way of illustration the spontaneous prayer bursting forth from the passionate heart of the psalmist, on the one hand, and on the other, well thought-out hymns. In his view, prayer is an emotional and experiential shift of the personality toward God. Clearly, then, R. Soloveitchik founded the second dimension of consciousness directly on prayer.

---

the discussion in the first part of the Fourth Article and the entire Fifth Article. His definition of this approach as "rational" is forced, albeit phenomenologically.

45 *Kuzari* 4:5, as quoted in *Worship of the Heart*, 6. R. Soloveitchik presented this doctrine as an expression of "religious emotionality," although Halevi was referring to concrete tools that help us to focus on the abstract.

46 *Reflections of the Rav*, 73.

47 *Worship of the Heart*, 7.

48 *Worship of the Heart*, 6.

Moral Experience

The third dimension of consciousness is volition. Consciousness strives for God through self-control and moral behavior. Indirectly, R. Soloveitchik censures the rationalist tradition in medieval and modern Jewish thought, which views the moral realm as a means for rational attainments rather than as an end in itself: "Important is the deed, not the theory."[49] In *Reflections of the Rav*, the description translates into a twofold controversy with the Christian flesh-spirit dichotomy and with Schopenhauer's conception of blind will, but without mentioning prayer.[50] In *Worship of the Heart*, R. Soloveitchik does not engage in a dispute with Christianity, but hints at prayer. He writes:

> The Torah did not distinguish in this respect between cult and ethos. One worships God not only by approaching Him directly through cultic ceremonial, by which man addresses himself to God, and which are supposed to serve as a sign-language expressing man's anxiety and longing for the Creator, but also (and perhaps mainly) through moral self-realization and activation. The Decalogue contains nothing cultic. It is throughout an ethical code; its realization constitutes the basic relationship between God and Israel as a nation, as a community of the committed.[51]

R. Soloveitchik adopted the position that the Torah does not distinguish, in terms of worth, between cultic and moral activity. No distinction is drawn between prayer or the ritual purity laws and the Ten Commandments, which express a universal ethos. The discussion of the ceremonial and the Ten Commandments is ethical and normative. In *Reflections of the Rav*, in contrast, the discussion focuses on the rationality of the command. The text distinguishes between idolatry, which is an irrational rite, and the Ten Commandments, which are subject to common sense:

> Pagans invented mechanical, irrational cults to placate their deities, because their gods were irrational. Thus, the Grecian cults were devoid of ethical content; their gods had no concern with morality. In the Torah, God speaks to man in rational terms about the moral life. The Decalogue is devoid of ritual prescriptions. Even the *hukkim* are not rites, but rather acts of submission and compliance, involving the concept of total surrender to God.

---

49 *Worship of the Heart*, 9.
50 *Reflections of the Rav*, 76.
51 *Worship of the Heart*, 10.

This is rational, as with a son who complies with his father's behest in the performance of an act which is incomprehensible to him.[52]

This is influenced by R. Saadiah Gaon's discussion in the third treatise of *Beliefs and Opinions* in two ways:

(1) as regards terminology: R. Saadiah Gaon draws a distinction between "rational precepts" and "revealed laws";
(2) contentually: R. Saadiah Gaon argues that the revealed laws (*hukim*), too, are not irrational, they rather have a logical aim: to create discipline. That is, a person undertakes to do things that are not consistent with logic, in order to be obedient.

Moreover, in *Worship of the Heart* R. Soloveitchik differentiated between two strata in the commands of the Torah, the ritual and the rational, while in *Reflections of the Rav* the distinction is between idolatry and the mandates of the Torah. We then could say that over the course of time R. Soloveitchik became convinced that the Torah's commandments relate also to the irrational aspect.

A careful reading of the above passage from *Worship of the Heart* reveals that rite and ethos are related realms. The ceremonial commandment and the ritual act give substance to the moral will, just as the rational act. R. Soloveitchik stated this outright: "[…] the deed is the powerful expression of an active moral will."[53]

To return to the place of prayer in the description of the religious consciousness in *Worship of the Heart*. It is present latently in the rational and emotional dimensions of consciousness, while in the volitional dimension it has no special presence beyond being a ritual-practical medium, like the other commandments. These facts can be viewed as a continuation of the withdrawal from the central standing of prayer. As we wrote, in *Reflections of the Rav*, prayer was an independent means of consciousness. Now, in *Worship of the Heart*, it is merely one expression of the dialogical medium, and also appears in other aspects of consciousness. R. Soloveitchik seemingly "scattered" the consciousness of prayer among the various media of consciousness.

The overt and oblique mention of prayer in the description of the two dimensions of consciousness (the rational and the emotional) in

---

52 *Reflections of the Rav*, 9.
53 *Worship of the Heart*, 9.

Worship of the Heart presents these dimensions as preparation for, and direction to, the fourth dimension, the dialogical. The conception of consciousness in this work aims for as unified a structure as possible. In R. Soloveitchik's phenomenology, the more homogeneous the consciousness, the more tempestuous its subterranean dimensions, that produce a union of opposites.

3. Prayer as Dialogue

The connection between prayer and dialogue is at once natural and profound. It is natural, because prayer is essentially speech, and speech has at least two partners. Petitioners assume that God listens to them, even when no evident response is forthcoming. The dialogical connection indeed rests on the depths of the individual's consciousness, because dialogical ability—the capability of expressing oneself verbally—is an important characteristic of humans as such. R. Soloveitchik relates to prayer as dialogue in several works, and sheds new light on this issue on virtually every occasion. I will begin my analysis of prayer as dialogue with the relevant discussion in the first chapter of *Worship of the Heart*, and compare it with R. Soloveitchik's words on the topic in his other writings.

The Nature of Dialogue

In order to understand the characteristics of dialogical consciousness, which, according to *Worship of the Heart* and *Reflections of the Rav*, is the consciousness of prayer, we must examine two issues: the character of the dialogue, and the connection between prophecy and prayer in the dialogical context.

At least two conceptions of dialogue appear in R. Soloveitchik's writings.[54] The first regards dialogue as exposure. At times, dialogue is perceived as a feature of the self, that is, as a characteristic of the personality. Dialogue is an aptitude of the subject as such. According to this notion, dialogue is the very addressing of another subject.[55] This addressing is perceived as expressive ability: a person expresses himself, abandons silence for speech, and is also aware of his self and is capable of expressing his

---

54 On the sources of this division, see below, Chapter Nine.
55 Husserl himself pondered the question of whether one can progress from the constitution and the presence of the other in the consciousness (dialogue as an expression of the self) to the actual presence of the other (intersubjective communication).

desires. Dialogue is the exposure of the self, and its opposite is alienation, in the sense of distance and lack of self-awareness.[56] One who is alienated is unaware of the basic characteristics of existence and of his own self; he removes himself from his self and from his authentic existence. Dialogue as exposure generally emerges in our union with God. When we stand before Him, in this case in prayer and supplication, we also discover ourselves.

The second treats dialogue as an intersubjective connection, that is, as a possibility of communication between two subjects, each of them unique. Dialogue focuses here on connection and knowledge of the other. The subject is unique, and its characteristics are therefore not transferable to another subject who, by definition, is also different from all others. In a sense, we are speaking of an aspect of existential loneliness. Meaningful communication with another is not self-evident.[57] Subjects face problems connecting with one another and, were it not for God's involvement in the community, such communication would be impossible.[58] A meaningful existence is therefore one characterized by intersubjective communication or dialogue. A meaningful existence is also an active one, wherein subjects are aware of their surroundings and leave their mark on them, by contrast with an objective existence that is marked by passivity and that follows the crowd. Discovery of and knowledge of another is at the focus of intersubjective dialogue. Dialogue redeems us from loneliness in regard to another. This is the type of dialogue that takes place, above all, between man and God, but sometimes another subject joins in. At times, a "Thou" joins the "I" and the "It."

R. Soloveitchik, then, viewed dialogue as redeeming us from loneliness. Irwin Yalom, who engaged in group therapy, argued that both types of loneliness derive from a single source. Dialogue as a discovery of the self derives from intersubjective dialogue. Yalom writes:

> Individuals are often isolated from others and from parts of themselves, but underlying these splits is an even more basic isolation that belongs to existence—an isolation that persists despite the most gratifying engagement with other individuals and despite consummate self-knowledge and integration. Existential isolation refers to an unbridgeable gulf between oneself

---

56 It is noteworthy that in *The Emergence of Ethical Man*, R. Soloveitchik speaks of a new kind of loneliness typical of the charismatic individual. Abraham, who was forced to leave Ur, is a paradigm of this sort of loneliness. The charismatic individual knows that God is his only friend. See *The Emergence of Ethical Man*, 150-152.

57 See Avi Sagi, "The Loneliness of the Man of Faith in the Philosophy of Soloveitchik" [Hebrew], *Daat* 2-3 (1978): 253.

58 See Schwartz, *From Phenomenology to Existentialism*, chapter 11; see below, Chapter Four.

and any other being. It refers, too, to an isolation even more fundamental—a separation between the individual and the world.[59]

Both conceptions of dialogue as redemption from loneliness appear in R. Soloveitchik's writings, but separately. In the article "Redemption, Prayer, and Talmud Torah" and in the first chapter of *Worship of the Heart*, only the first conception appears, that is, dialogue as the discovery of the self. By contrast, in the parallel discussions in *Reflections of the Rav* and in *The Lonely Man of Faith*, we find the second conception, which views dialogue as the discovery of the other, that is, as intersubjective communication.

Changing Directions

Let us return now to the first chapter of *Worship of the Heart*. The connection between prayer and prophecy follows directly from the standing and the nature of dialogue, and was a recurrent concern for R. Soloveitchik. He repeatedly emphasizes the distinction whereby, in prophecy, God speaks and man listens, while in prayer the roles are reversed: man speaks and God listens. God initiates prophecy and humans are passive, whereas in prayer, it is humans who take the initiative while God is passive. From this reversal of directions, we may conclude that true dialogue, that is, a dialogue in which two partners speak, usually combines prophecy and prayer.[60]

In the first chapter of *Worship of the Heart*, R. Soloveitchik presents the bidirectional dialogical dimension through the opposite connection, that between prophecy and prayer:

> The fourth medium through which communication of man with God is accomplished is dialogue. Both prayer and prophecy are basically dialogues between finitude and infinity. They differ only as to the respective roles assigned to creature and Creator. In prophecy God is the active partner of the dialogue community and man is happy being just a listener, an onlooker, watchful and vigilant; in prayer the roles are reversed. God is the listener and man is the speaker.[61]

Both in prayer and in prophecy there is an active and a passive party—the actor and the recipient of the action. From the outset, one of the parties

59 Irvin D. Yalom, *Existential Psychotherapy* (New York: Basic Books, 1980), 355.
60 Cf. Eliezer Schweid, *The Siddur: Philosophy, Poetry and Mystery* [Hebrew] (Tel Aviv: Miskal, 2009), 28-29.
61 *Worship of the Heart*, 10.

is passive. R. Soloveitchik's formulation suggests that passivity is not forced, as it were, on one of the parties, but is rather passivity out of choice. Obviously, one cannot change the very fact that God does not answer one's prayer. Indirectly, however, we might conclude that, as the prophet is "happy" being a passive listener, the praying man might also be content with his absolutely active standing before God. One of the tensions present in R. Soloveitchik's discussions of prayer lies between prayer out of self-affirmation and that which comes forth from distress.

By contrast, in *Reflections of the Rav* and in *The Lonely Man of Faith*, both man and God are active in prophecy as well as in prayer. These works speak of true dialogue, and not of a merely formal statement. *Reflections of the Rav* states that the silence of humans or of God in prophecy and in prayer is "temporary."[62] Ultimately, dialogue is mutual. In *The Lonely Man of Faith*, R. Soloveitchik explicitly argues that the distinction between prophecy and prayer is only one of "order," that is, it hinges on the question of who initiates and opens the dialogue: "The difference between prayer and prophecy is [...] related not to the substance of the dialogue but rather to the order in which it is conducted."[63] But prophetic and liturgical dialogue is, as such, bilateral, hence the "sameness" between the community of prophecy and the community of prayer.[64] R. Soloveitchik thus fluctuated between the conception of prayer as mutual dialogue and the preservation of the passive-active model

The Consciousness of Dialogue: (1) Worship of the Heart

"The Dialogical Medium" section, which closes the first chapter of *Worship of the Heart*, deals entirely—except for the preface which I discussed above—with a subject that, ostensibly, is not directly related to the dialogical dimension of prayer: petition. The first chapter concludes with a long apology of petition prayers. Against the view of petitions for human needs as belittling the prayer experience of standing before God, R. Soloveitchik argued that Judaism "considered such prayer ['selfish' prayer] the central theme of the service."[65] He also added that in the Bible, too, "petition is

---

62 *Reflections of the Rav*, 78.
63 *The Lonely Man of Faith*, 57.
64 *The Lonely Man of Faith*, 57. For a discussion of the communal nature of prayer, see below.
65 *Worship of the Heart*, 10. R. Soloveitchik reiterated this approach in *Worship of the Heart*, 29. Kierkegaard argued that prayer changes man in that, through it, he abandons

the main form of human prayer."[66] The crux of the daily *Amidah* prayer is petitions. The blessings of petitions are perceived as "*avodah she-ba-lev* in action."[67] The selfishness motif—asking for knowledge, health, rain, and so forth—is actually the central feature of inner worship ("worship of the heart"). R. Soloveitchik discussed this at length, with examples of petition prayers in the Bible and the halakhah.

Why the sharp thematic shift from, at the beginning of the section, dialogue of opposing directions—prophecy and prayer—to petition prayers? R. Soloveitchik digresses to petition prayers and no longer returns to consider dialogue, not even in the chapter's closing lines. This literary development demands an explanation.[68] Apparently, R. Soloveitchik sought to correct a weakness in his argument. We know that many prophecies include an actual discourse between the prophet and God. The prophet is indeed passive and God is the speaker, but at times this situation develops into a dialogue. In prayer, however, God is altogether passive. The petition prayer suggests an image of an active party, since God is to listen and respond to the petition. The discussion of petitions would appear to support a dialogical conception of prayer.

But this conception is progressively undermined as the discussion develops, and ends up collapsing entirely. How so? In the course of his

---

his personal requests and gains freedom from his individual desires. Through prayer, he is "conquered" by God. Paradoxically, man who initiate prayer retreat through it from the presence of God. See Gregor Malantschuk, *Kirkegaard's Thought*, trans. Howard V. Hong and Edna H. Hong (Princeton, NJ: Princeton University Press, 1971), 314. R. Soloveitchik indeed notes that philosophers assigned no importance to petitionary prayers.

66 *Worship of the Heart*, 10-11. See, for example, Moshe Greenberg, *Lectures about Prayer* [Hebrew] (Jerusalem: Akademon, 1985), 6-25. Most of the examples of Biblical prayers cited by R. Soloveitchik were uttered out of distress. Hence, he almost never speaks of prayer in a joyful context, such as that of King Solomon (II Kings 8:23-52).

67 *Worship of the Heart*, 11.

68 Kaplan argued (in his letter to me) that the text is lacking. He maintains that we should have here a text concerned with the communal dimension of prayer (see below, Chapter Four), that is supported by the blessings of praise and thanksgiving. Kaplan finds backing for his assertion in what R. Soloveitchik writes in the continuation of *Worship of the Heart*: "prayer, which is basically a dialogue between God and man, thus supplanting prophecy, attains communal relationship between Creator and creation" (62). Kaplan accordingly assumes that the discussion on 62-63 regarding the communal nature of prayer, that is, the community of man and God, in actuality belongs to the current discussion in the book (10). This argument has a firm basis, mainly when the discussion is compared to Besdin's version. Nonetheless, I intend to present an alternative explanation for the text as it stands.

discussion, R. Soloveitchik cites a consciousness argument for the superiority of petition prayers: they reflect a feeling of unqualified dependence on God. A petition prayer does not comprise self-affirmation, it rather is an expression of unreserved dependence. He writes:

> The reason for the centrality that Judaism has given to the element of petition in the service lies in our philosophy of prayer. *Avodah she-ba-lev*, for all its tendency to express the religious experience as a whole, and particularly its emotional aspect, does also tend to single out a particular state of mind.[69] For when we view the noetic content of prayer we must admit that one emotion is central as far as prayer is concerned—the feeling of unqualified dependence.[70]

The concept of prayer as reflective of dependence appears in the Jewish tradition in, for example, in the thought of *Maharal*, who writes:

> For the prayer that a person directs to the Lord, may He be blessed, teaches that man is dependent upon Him, may He be blessed, needs Him, and has no existence without Him. This is [the meaning of] His godliness, may He be blessed, that all beings need Him and are dependent upon Him, so that all is [directed to] the Lord, may He be blessed.[71]

For him, prayer expresses absolute "subjugation."[72] *Maharal* used the term "dependence" in reference to prayer in additional places.[73] He formulated

---

69 In light of the phenomenological background, this can also be understood as "state of consciousness."

70 *Worship of the Heart*, 12. At the beginning of the first chapter of the book, R. Soloveitchik speaks of "the total commitment of man to his Creator" (4). In other words, he began with dependence and ended with commitment.

71 Judah Loew ben Bezalel (*Maharal*), *Netivot Olam* (Jerusalem, 1972), *Netiv ha-Avodah* 3, 82a. Dependence is perceived here as existential dependence, as was already observed by R. Aharon Lichtenstein; see Haim Sabato, *Seeking His Presence: Conversations with Rabbi Aharon Lichtenstein*, trans. Binyamin Shalom (Tel Aviv: Yedioth Books, 2016), 126-127. In his master's thesis ("'Avodat HaBitul' in Rabbi Schneur Zalman of Liadi's *Sefer Shel Benonim*—Its Nature and Sources: A Comparative Study in the Thought of the Maharal of Prague, the Maggid of Mezeritsch and Rabbi Schneur Zalman of Liadi"), my student Avinoam Bir viewed this approach as the anticipation of Hasidic self-negation.

72 *Netivot Olam*, *Netiv ha-Avodah* 3, 82b-83a.

73 *Maharal* thereby explained the need to keep one's feet together during the *Amidah* prayer, which symbolizes man's immobility and passivity when facing God. He wrote: "And one of the implications of the perfect service is that a person will be cognizant and know that He, may He be blessed, is his Cause, and the effect receives from the Cause to the extent that his soul is dependent upon the Cause, who is the Lord, may He be blessed. From Him is his vitality and all that he needs" (*Netivot Olam*, *Netiv ha-Avodah* 6, 90a).

the principle of ontological dependence, that is, dependence as fact, and not merely as feeling.

R. Soloveitchik was directly influenced in this regard by Friedrich Schleiermacher, and not in vain did he endorse the "feeling of dependence" or "absolute dependence,"[74] a concept characteristic of this influential Protestant thinker. Schleiermacher adopted the Kantian approach that renounces pure reason, meaning the scientific knowledge of the absolute ("the-thing-in-itself") that cannot be apprehended through forms of sensibility and categories. The existence of the divine as an absolute is therefore not discussed through epistemic categories. Contrary, however, to Kant, who located certainty about the existence of God in moral knowledge, Schleiermacher situated it in feeling—the feeling of dependence. This feeling is concerned with "the immediate self-consciousness underlying all our knowing and doing."[75] The feeling of dependence is immediate and intuitive, in the sense that it does not become reflective, an object of analysis and observation. It is noteworthy that Schleiermacher distinguished between the receptive and active facets of self-consciousness. He called the element that unites all the aspects of external dependence the "feeling of dependence," and that which underlies the aspects of self-consciousness, the "feeling of freedom." These elements do not exist in a pure state, rather, every act combines the two in some manner or other. God, as an idea, reflects the pole of the "feeling of absolute dependence."[76]

R. Soloveitchik adopted the feeling of dependence as a clarification of prayer because he held that the gist of prayer does not lie in reason (the contemplative prayer), social rectification (public prayer), or other dimensions of consciousness. He finds that prayer is fundamentally an entirely unconditioned experience of dependence on God, and petition is therefore its

---

74 R. Soloveitchik mentioned this term once again in his essay "Reflections on the *Amidah*." See below, Chapter Nine.

75 See, for example, Brian A. Gerrish, "Friedrich Schleiermacher," in *Nineteenth Century Religious Thought in the West*, edited by Ninian Smart et al. (Cambridge: Cambridge University Press, 1985), 135-136. Scheler, Tillich, and others called for a reexamination of Schleiermacher's dependence conception. Scheler argued for binding the object of religion to the intentional or the cognitive, rather than to the emotional; see Scheler, *On the Eternal in Man*, 285. Against those who criticize the emotion of dependence as "subjective sentimentality," Tillich asserted that the "feeling of dependence" is actually consciousness with a cognitive dimension. See John Macquarrie, *Studies in Christian Existentialism* (Montreal: McGill University Press, 1965), 31.

76 Friedrich Schleiermacher, *The Christian Faith*, ed. H. R. Mackintosh and James S. Stewart (London: T & T Clark, 1999), 17.

main feature, just as distress is its starting point. Self-awareness, according to Schleiermacher, does include a connection with people and with the world, but this consciousness is, above all, a consciousness of self.

Schleiermacher's approach precludes the mutuality required for the existence of dialogue. The feeling of unqualified dependence, by definition, sets the human partner in a position of passivity that is essentially antidialogical. R. Soloveitchik articulated the collapse of dialogue in a situation of unqualified dependence in the words of the psalmist:

> David expressed this experience of complete, absolute, unconditional dependence upon God in his beautiful verses: "If I did not quiet myself like a weaned child upon his mother, verily my soul is like one weaned. Let Israel hope in God now and forever" (Ps. 131:2-3).[77]

The child's dependence on the mother presents him as quiet, in striking opposition to dialogue. Paradoxically, then, prayer leads to human muteness.

The thematic structure of the discussion, then, is the following:

(1) dialogue (preface): R. Soloveitchik begins with dialogue in prayer (man speaks and God listens);
(2) petition (the body of the discussion): from dialogue, R. Soloveitchik shifts to the prayer of petition;
(3) unqualified dependence (end): R. Soloveitchik concludes with antidialogical quietness.

The unique structure of this discussion reflects the dialectic of prayer. The petitioner wavers between a situation of self-affirmation (dialogue) and one of unqualified dependence (muteness). This dependence is articulated in a monologue of supplication that, given dependence, ends in quietness. The prayer of petition has a dual structure. On the one hand, it reflects a dialogue in which God responds to the petition; on the other, it reflects a dependence that precludes genuine dialogue. Petition includes a dimension that turns to discourse, and another that turns to quietness. The petitional prayer is, thus, an interim link between two dialectical poles. Prayer fluctuates between initiative and passivity, between taking a stand before God and absolute submission before God's infinity. The worshiper shifts between petition and quietness, and between dialogue and monologue.

---

77 *Worship of the Heart*, 12.

What is clear is that the dialogue of prayer, according to the first chapter of *Worship of the Heart*, does not entail the mutual commitment of partners to a dialogue. The intersubjective connection is nowhere mentioned in this discussion. In *Worship of the Heart*, the dialogue exposes a person to his own self and to his own personal needs ("petition"),[78] and he turns to God in prayer in order to fulfill these needs. Moreover, the dialogue reflects the conscious fluctuations of the prayer experience.

The Consciousness of Dialogue: (2) Reflections of the Rav

In *Reflections of the Rav*, in contrast, R. Soloveitchik discusses the dialogical aspect as an intersubjective relationship. The essence of prayer is no longer based on utilitarianism. Human needs are not "our primary motivation."[79] The petition prayer, central in *Worship of the Heart*, is now pushed to the margins of consciousness, and prayer becomes mainly a discourse with God.

R. Soloveitchik argued in *Reflections of the Rav* that dialogue involves "engagement and interaction," and takes place "even if the other is temporarily silent."[80] Although man is the initiator and speaker in prayer, from a consciousness perspective he expects an answer from the listening God. We should not think that prayer is a dialogue involving only knowledge of self. Quite the contrary, consciousness in prayer is an act involving at least two players. Thus he mentioned two quite close points:

> Dialogue means communication, engagement, and interaction. When we pray, God emerges out of His transcendence and forms a companionship with us; the Infinite and finite meet and the vast chasm is bridged [...] The ideal communion in prayer is signified by the word *adekha* (unto you) as in *shome'a tefillah, adekha kol basar yavo'u*. "O, You who hear prayer, to You does all flesh come" (Ps. 65:3). The word *el* (to) connotes direction and distance; the word *ad* (unto), however, suggests that the distance has been covered and the gap bridged.[81]

The commitment created by prayer, according to *Reflections of the Rav*, eventually transforms it into a dialogue. But this commitment is not only the petitioner's—prayer requires God to be revealed and create a dialogue.

---

78 See below, Chapter Nine.
79 *Reflections of the Rav*, 78.
80 *Reflections of the Rav*, 78.
81 *Reflections of the Rav*, 78-79.

God, as it were, is dragged into such a discourse against His will. And yet, we do not find here even a hint of a magical approach to prayer suggesting that, through it, the magician imposes his will on the supernal world. The consciousness of discourse in *Reflections of the Rav* is essentially bidirectional. We cannot think of dialogue without knowledge of the other, and dialogue is therefore accompanied by revelation.

The view of dialogue in *Reflections of the Rav* is thus entirely different from the one that emerges in *Worship of the Heart*. In the former, the main foundation of the dialogue is mutuality and intersubjectivity;[82] in the latter, dialogue is one of the dialectical poles between which the petitioner fluctuates, the other being unqualified dependence and quietness. Furthermore, the dialogue itself is the consciousness of self through the petition prayer. The true drama unfolds at the level of the self, through a penetrating examination of its boundaries and options. R. Soloveitchik seems to have changed his view after his public lecture, and when he wrote down this account in an orderly fashion at a later stage he decided to consider selfhood rather than mutual commitment. Possibly, the preaching style meant for a broad public presents mutuality as the most important message, whereas writing fits the consciousness experience more adequately. As R. Soloveitchik noted at the opening of the work, he confesses his personal experiences, without any hope of turning them into a general rule.

4. Summary

R. Soloveitchik ascribed the power of Jewish religious consciousness to its sharp and radical dialectic. In *And From There You Shall Seek*, the dialectic becomes an apologetic element: Jewish consciousness is evident in its antitheses, that are more pronounced than in the consciousness of other religions.[83] The dialectic that characterizes R. Soloveitchik's writings is well reflected in the conscious and dialogical standing of prayer. R. Soloveitchik pondered the nature of prayer's subjective consciousness. The objective, practical dimension of prayer is a subject for legal governance. The praxis records and regulates the dialectic, but does not itself fluctuate. Practical behavior is black-and-white. By contrast, the structure of subjective consciousness is a matter for discussion and analysis. At times

---

82 On intersubjectivity, see this recent study: Doron Nachum, "The Social Constitution of the Selfhood: The Theory of Intersubjectivity in Alfred Schutz's Thought (1899-1959)" [Hebrew], PhD diss., Bar-Ilan University, 2011.

83 See, for example, Schwartz, *From Phenomenology to Existentialism*, 145-46.

R. Soloveitchik maintained that prayer determines an entirely independent act of consciousness and, in other instances, he held that the act of prayer is structured by other acts of consciousness.

The dialectic applies to the dialogical dimension of prayer, as well. At times this dimension is turned inward, to the individual and the world, while on other occasions it is directed outward, to the other. Sometimes prayer means a confrontation with the self, and at other times, prayer has the petitioner confronting God. Prayer is an experience that cannot be exclusively reduced to only one pole. In Chapter Four of *Worship of the Heart*, R. Soloveitchik intensifies this dialectical dimension.[84] Hence, he does not limit the discussion of prayer to phenomenological or existentialist dimensions, and expands it to include features from other realms, as well.

The dialectic emerges in a comparison between the two versions of the structure of consciousness in R. Soloveitchik's writings from the 1950s (*Worship of the Heart*, *Reflections of the Rav*), and even intensifies in light of developments in his philosophy in the decade that followed. The dialectical understanding only increases the centrality of prayer in R. Soloveitchik's thought.

---

84 See below, Chapter Four.

Chapter 3

The Consciousness of Prayer: The Subjective and the Objective

In the previous chapter we examined the structure of the consciousness of prayer. This structure, based on the subjective and objective dimensions of consciousness, presents the halakhic act in two planes. On the one hand, it is independent. Halakhah is autonomous in the sense that it is not contingent, for its very existence, on any extra-halakhic factor. Its existence is unfettered by emotions and moods. Nor is praxis dependent upon consciousness or either rational or mystical perception. On the other hand, the halakhic act stands at the end and bottom, of a series of subjective and normative conscious acts, and is thereby their direct continuation. From this aspect, consciousness and divine worship are built as a three-storey structure (following *The Halakhic Mind*): the upper storey is the subjective, the middle floor is the normative, and the bottom, the praxis. To be precise: the subjective floor is the most profound, while the praxis is superficial, forming a sort of funnel whose narrow mouth is the act. The halakhic act therefore reflects tempestuous worlds of subjective consciousness, and is defined, in R. Soloveitchik's terminology, as the objectivization of the subjective consciousness. The phenomenological analysis in *Worship of the Heart* thus closely corresponds to *And From There You Shall Seek* and *The Halakhic Mind*.

The phenomenological description of prayer in the first section of chapters in *Worship of the Heart* gradually grows deeper. In the second chapter of the book, we take another step, and uncover another layer in the depth of the analysis of the structure of religious consciousness. In this chapter, R. Soloveitchik once again examined the relation between the objective and subjective dimensions of consciousness. He opened the chapter by setting forth the two dimensions of the halakhic act and ended with the existential perception of depth crisis. As in the first chapter of *Worship of the Heart*, parts of the second chapter also appear, even if in a different style, in *Reflections of the Rav*, edited by Abraham Besdin. In the second chapter, R. Soloveitchik diverged from his original approach regarding the relation between the dimensions of consciousness, as it was formulated in his writings from the 1940s, and saw much closer ties between the subjective and the objective. In other words, he wanted to present prayer as exceptional halakhah, in terms of its consciousness element.

1. More on the Relations between the Dimensions of Consciousness

R. Soloveitchik prefaced his discussion of the consciousness of prayer in the second chapter of *Worship of the Heart* with a description of the general structure of consciousness. The picture he paints here is not congruous with his other discussions of the religious consciousness. Although I find this portrayal to be exceptional in the landscape of R. Soloveitchik's thought, and perhaps for this very reason, it is worthy of our attention.

The Scope of Halakhah

The term "halakhah" assumes different meanings in R. Soloveitchik's thought. As I have shown at length in *Halakhic Man* halakhah is mainly given a scholarly, erudite meaning, in the Brisk style.[1] In many works R. Soloveitchik voiced his opinion that halakhah does not refer solely to action, but also encompasses the world of inner intent, consciousness, and the mysterious.[2] We saw in the preceding chapter that the very "expansion" of the halakhah to man's inner world is a sort of norm, one based on commandment, without any practical possibility of examining whether man fulfills this mission.

In the beginning of the second chapter of *Worship of the Heart*, R. Soloveitchik presented an extensive general consciousness model of the halakhah that is portrayed in the following sketch:

---

1   See Schwartz, *Religion or Halakha*, 1-2. R. Soloveitchik also used the term "theoretical halakhah" with the same meaning (see, for example, *Halakhic Man*, trans. Lawrence Kaplan [Philadelphia: Jewish Publication Society of America, 1983], 24; cited in *Religion or Halakha*, 117).

2   See Schwartz, *From Phenomenology to Existentialism*, 234-35.

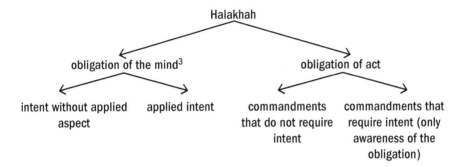

R. Soloveitchik made two basic assumptions regarding the halakhah, as a given system of acts and implementation:

(1) the implementation of the halakhah is "a meaningful performance endowed with significance",[4]

(2) the implementation of the halakhah has "idealizing and purifying power."[5]

The act possesses intrinsic value. In other words, the observance of the halakhah has immanent justification, even without any considerations of consciousness. The question then is: whether, and to what degree, the act expresses consciousness beyond the actual performance. The above diagram formulates doctrines of halakhah that relate to this question. At times, R. Soloveitchik's formulations range between differing and complementary positions. If these are four different stances, then they relate to the commandments as a whole; and if these are four complementary views, then each refers to a different group of commandments, that is, this is a quadrate classification of the commandments. The list of positions, apparently, includes both possibilities. I will present each position and briefly locate it in terms of consciousness.

(1) Reductionist position (a): extreme objectivity. This position posits the "actional" nature of the praxis, and is completely indifferent to the subjective dimension of consciousness. It bases the halakhic mandate entirely on the act (commandments do not require intent [kavanah]). According to this limiting position, the connection between the subjective and objective dimensions of consciousness

_____

3 R. Soloveitchik defined these as "experiential mitzvot"; see Worship of the Heart, 15.

4 R. Soloveitchik might have wanted to combine the meanings of intent and significance.

5 Worship of the Heart, 14.

is irrelevant. In his phenomenological writings R. Soloveitchik emphasized nondependence between these two dimensions. This stance deepens this nondependence, which it turns into an actual break. R. Soloveitchik writes: "The actional *mitzvot* form a halakhic objective order which is not correlated with a parallel subjective one. The objective action does not point to a corresponding experience, mental attitude, or inner activity."[6] The act is complete in itself.

(2) Reductionist position (b): minimalist subjectivity. This position limits the consciousness solely to an awareness of the obligation. For it, commandments require intent in the sense of the consciousness of command. That is, the one observing the commandment must be aware of the authoritative source of the commandment.

> The pious Jew pronounces a similar *hinnei mukhan* [I hereby ready myself to fulfill the *mitzvah*][7] prior to both eating *matzah* and blowing the *shofar* [ram's horn], notwithstanding that in terms of symbolic interpretation the two *mitzvot* represent opposite attitudes.[8]

R. Soloveitchik probably meant that eating *matzah* is an expression of freedom and independence, while blowing the *shofar* represents submission, a broken heart, and asking for forgiveness. Nevertheless, the halakhic intent of the two commandments, according to the minimalist approach, is the same: the observance of the command, that is, the consciousness of obligation.

(3) Maximalist subjective position: this view argues for the existence of a system of commands imposed on the subjective dimension of consciousness, with no operative expression. This approach teaches that belief, thought, emotion, and the like may be directly commanded. The spiritual experience ("apprehending something that is at an endless distance from actuality and definiteness")[9] can be subject to command. Significantly, R. Soloveitchik mentioned R. Bahya, whose book *Duties of the Heart* promotes the commanding of man's thought and feelings.[10] R. Bahya famously advocated

---

6 *Worship of the Heart*, 14.
7 See Moshe Hallamish, *Kabbalah in Liturgy, Halakhah, and Customs* [Hebrew] (Ramat Gan: Bar-Ilan University Press, 2000), 45-70.
8 *Worship of the Heart*, 14-15. See Kaplan, "Review Essay, 84".
9 *Worship of the Heart*, 15.
10 "These precepts, using Rabbi Bahya's phrase in the eleventh-century work, *Duties of the Heart*, are concerned with the *hovot ha-levavot* (duties of the hearts), not with those of

the primacy and dominance of the inner dimension of the divine service in the halakhah and the divine command, and argued that the system of actional commandments receives its meaning and validity from inner mandates. R. Soloveitchik also recruited Maimonides in support of this stance. He mentioned the *"mitzvot kelaliyot* [that] lean upon the whole body of the law,"[11] which were presented in the fourth principle at the beginning of *Sefer ha-Mitzvot*. Maimonides himself did not include such mandates in his enumeration of the commandments, and vigorously argued against their inclusion. In R. Soloveitchik's formulation, man's inner subjective consciousness is subordinate to explicit commandments.

(4) A moderate subjective position, which maintains that the objective act manifests the subjective experience and constitutes an "external symbol."[12] The act is an expression of profound inner moods. The significance of the halakhic act, from this aspect, is that it "tells a tale of the human mind and heart."[13] R. Soloveitchik also applied the scholarly distinction between *ma'aseh ha-mitzvah* and *kiyyum ha-mitzvah* to this model. *Ma'aseh ha-mitzvah* is the execution, that is, the actual act of the commandment, while

---

the limbs" (*Worship of the Heart*, 16). On the sources of R. Bahya's spiritual approach, see, for example, Diana Lobel, *A Sufi-Jewish Dialogue: Philosophy and Mysticism in Bahya Ibn Paquda's "Duties of the Heart"* (Philadelphia: University of Pennsylvania Press, 2007). See also the discussion by Gerald Blidstein, who finds traces of R. Bahya in Maimonides' perception of intent (Gerald J. Blidstein, *Prayer in Maimonidean Halakha* [Hebrew] [Jerusalem: Bialik Institute, 1994], 88-92). Cf. Shalom Rosenberg, "Prayer and Jewish Thought: Approaches and Problems (A Survey)" in *Prayer in Judaism: Continuity and Change*, ed. G. Cohn and H. Fisch (Northvail, NJ: Jason Arondon, 1996), 69-107.

11 *Worship of the Heart*, p. 16; the term appears in transliteration. The term *"mitzvot ha-kelalot"* or *"ha-kolelot"* appears in critical annotations of Nachmanides on *Sefer ha-Mitzvot*, *Sefer ha-Hinukh* (Commandment 433), and elsewhere. Maimonides himself uses the wording *amr*, that is, command, and for commandment, the Hebrew term itself (*mitzvah*). R. Moses ibn Tibbon accordingly rendered this as "charges which cover the whole body of the Torah" (as translated by Chavel, *The Commandments*, part 2: *The Negative Commandments*, 380). The statement by R. Soloveitchik accords with the ninth principle (*shoresh*), in which Maimonides argues that the Torah's commandments and prohibitions relate to four realms, the first of which is "opinions," concerning beliefs such as the belief in the unity of God (Chavel, *The Commandments*, part 2: *The Negative Commandments*, 397). The fourth principle refers to the commandments as a whole, such as "You shall observe My laws" (Lev. 19:19).

12 *Worship of the Heart*, 17.

13 *Worship of the Heart*, 17.

kiyyum ha-mitzvah refers to the subjective stratum, the inner mental disposition manifest in its execution. The model that presents this position and its meaning was discussed extensively in the preceding chapter.

The portrayal of the last position is the most interesting, in terms of its presence in R. Soloveitchik's thought. The moderate subjective approach, which correctly describes the conscious standing of prayer, was R. Soloveitchik's message in his writings from the middle of the 1940s. In these works he sought to present, for the first time in Orthodox thought, a phenomenological description of the Jewish religious consciousness. And now, the moderate subjective position reveals a picture different from what R. Soloveitchik had set forth about a decade preceding *Worship of the Heart*. In this presentation, he retreated from the important, and fateful, characteristic of the relationship between the subjective and objective consciousness, that is, he drew back from the concept of reconstruction. We will now examine the concept of reconstruction in R. Soloveitchik's writings, along with the alternative conception set forth in the second chapter of *Worship of the Heart*.

The Rejection of Reconstruction

In *The Halakhic Mind* R. Soloveitchik discussed the relationship between the subjective and objective dimensions of consciousness. Reconstruction is one of the important concepts in this relationship. It has its roots in the philosophy of epistemological idealism, phenomenology, and the conventionalist approach in the philosophy of science.[14] Here is a concise review of the principles of reconstruction in the realm of religious consciousness.

(1) The objective dimension of consciousness has its most reliable standard of reference in the canonized Scriptures.[15] In the case of Judaism, the canon is the Bible and the Oral Law; consequently, the subjective dimension in the Jewish religious consciousness is reconstructed within the halakhic texts.

(2) The subjective dimension of consciousness may be revealed most reliably only from within its objective dimension. "There is no direct approach to pure religious subjectivity. Objective forms

---

14 See Schwartz, *Religion or Halakha*, Index, s.v. "Reconstruction." See also the detailed presentation of the reconstruction of the consciousness of prayer in Chapter Two, above.

15 *The Halakhic Mind*, 81.

must be postulated as a point of departure, and by moving in the minus direction, one may gradually reconstruct underlying subjective aspects."[16]

(3) The objective dimension of consciousness does not clearly ensue by causality from its subjective dimension.[17] The subjective and objective components do not have a cause-and-effect relationship, in the strict sense. The relation between these components is rather one of representation[18] and correlation.[19] Consequently, reconstruction is the only means of revealing the subjective dimension.

(4) This conception of reconstruction enriches the religious consciousness, since it makes it pluralistic and multidimensional. That is, the fact that the relationship between the subjective and objective dimensions of consciousness are not bound by strict causality means that some subjective acts of consciousness may be reconstructed from a single objective component.[20]

R. Soloveitchik characterized modern philosophy and phenomenology in particular as ignoring the principle of reconstruction. These approaches immediately turn to the subjective, that is, to "wholeness and totality" and inclusive "metaphysical" explanations, while disregarding their components.[21] In his writings from the middle of the 1940s he was often a severe critic of the modern conceptions in the philosophy of religion that focuses on the subjective, while neglecting objectivity. In his Ph.D. dissertation he discussed at length Paul Natorp's conception of reconstruction, this time from the perspective of epistemological idealism. He wrote:

> The difference between Natorp and Cohen regarding the principle of origin [*Ursprung*] lies in their differing attitudes to the structure of logic.[22]

---

16 *The Halakhic Mind*, 81.
17 See Schwartz, *Religion or Halakha*, 74.
18 *The Halakhic Mind*, 72. R. Soloveitchik clarified the lack of a precise cause-and-effect relationship with a psychological example: at times marginal events leave a marked impression on the consciousness, while weighty ones remain without any influence. Accordingly, there is no necessary relationship between the assemblage of the subjective components of the consciousness and the objective element
19 *The Halakhic Mind*, 67.
20 *The Halakhic Mind*, 88. And in another place: "There is no difference between a shoemaker and the Vilna Gaon in the *kiyyum* of the act of taking the *lulav* [that is, the Four Species]. Both perform the same action. Although their subjective experience is different, both are nevertheless equal in the observance of *ma'aseh ha-mitzvah*" (Grodner, *On Prayer*, 25).
21 *The Halakhic Mind*, 61.
22 That is, epistemology.

The unification of thought [*Denken*],[23] its principles, and rules can be established in two ways: either we begin from the numerous scientific objects [*wissenschaftlische Gegenstande*] (that unite into a single object), which move toward the center, that is, from the periphery to the unity of thought; or, we begin with thought, and follow its development and constitution. By having resolved in our mind the process of thought and its development, we perceive the unifying nature of this process. While the first methodology (the reconstructionist) observes the thought process from the viewpoint of periphery and center (the periphery includes the many scientific directions that converge in the center), the second, that comes from the thought to the object, presents the thought process as a mathematical series. If, however, the process is depicted as a series, it thereby includes the concept of anticipation.[24] The opening of the series also means relating to what will develop from it. The first ideal order precedes the infinite series. Thus, Cohen's category of origin [*Ursprungkategorie*] is fully justified. We do not come to the origin, we rather set forth from it. The fact that the way is infinite does not pose an obstacle.[25]

In this passage R. Soloveitchik contrasted the approaches of Hermann Cohen and Natorp. While Cohen began by building the foundations of cognition from the origin (the small to the infinite), with the cognition using these foundations to create its (scientific) objects, Natorp started with the objects, from which he constructed the cognition of the origin. R. Soloveitchik characterized Natorp's view as seeking the epistemological center in the periphery of a multiplicity of objects. Natorp called this approach "reconstruction." *The Halakhic Mind* similarly presents reconstruction as stripping "our experience of all objective elements like time, space, intensity, quality, etc."[26] One view presents all epistemological idealism, that is, the thought of Cohen, Ernst Cassirer, and others, as

---

23 "Thought" is concerned with the perception of an object without inner contradiction. As we will see below, Cohen argued that thought creates the objects of the mathematical sciences.

24 That is, anticipation of perception, meaning the inner size of the sensation. In other words, Kant argued that the maximal reduction of sensation exposes an epistemic inner size. Cohen applied this principle to his entire idealistic thought: quantitative reduction (to the infinitesimal) will lead to a new epistemological structure.

25 Josef Solowiejczyk, *Das reine Denken und die Seinskonsitutierung bei Hermann Cohen* (Berlin: Reither & Reichard, 1933), 49.

26 *The Halakhic Mind*, 66.

"reconstruction," since the philosophical aim of this school was to reconstruct the scientific foundations and objects from within experience.[27]

Reconstruction is a founding principle in the epistemological idealistic thought of R. Soloveitchik, as well, as is expressed in *Halakhic Man* and other compositions. In other words, the concept of reconstruction in R. Soloveitchik's thought is the junction where epistemological idealism meets the phenomenology of religion. In *And From There You Shall Seek* and *The Halakhic Mind*, the subjective consciousness is revealed by reconstruction, which appears at the seam line between the objective and subjective dimensions.[28]

I maintain that in *Worship of the Heart* prayer, specifically, and the manifestations of worship of the heart (repentance, mourning, rejoicing on holidays, Torah study and communion) as a whole breach the framework of reconstruction, and that their subjective dimension (intent) is a part of the act of the commandment. The subjective dimension of prayer is a given, just like the objective dimension. That is to say, the divine commandment concerning prayer also pertains to its subjective dimension.[29] R. Soloveitchik was a man of deep inner conviction, that a person may be commanded regarding his faith and his character, although there is no unequivocal way to examine whether he has answered the call.[30] In many instances R. Soloveitchik called this obligatory address to the consciousness "halakhah." Reconstruction disappeared, with causality appearing in its stead.

The idea of reconstruction seeks to firmly set the conceptual and processive differentiation between the objective and subjective dimensions of consciousness. The objective stratum, the praxis of halakhah, is unequivocal, while the subjective stratum is variegated. The relationship between the two strata is therefore not causal in the strict sense. Reconstruction indirectly aided R. Soloveitchik to maintain the stability

---

27 Fritz Kaufmann, "Cassirer, Neo-Kantianism, and Phenomenology," in *The Philosophy of Ernst Cassirer*, ed. Paul Arthur Schilpp (Evanston, IL: Library of Living Philosophers, 1949), 812-813.

28 See Reinier Munk, *The Rationale of Halakhic Man: Joseph B. Soloveitchik's Conception of Jewish Thought* (Amsterdam: Gieben, 1996), 63; Eliezer Goldman, "Religion and Halakha in the Teaching of Rabbi J. B. Soloveitchik" [Hebrew], *Daat* 42 (1999): 126-127; Schwartz, *Religion or Halakha*, 63-66, where I showed how the tripartite consciousness model explains other commandments discussed by R. Soloveitchik.

29 See below, Chapter Six.

30 See, for example, Menachem M. Kellner, *Must a Jew Believe Anything?* (London: Littman Library, 1999).

of the halakhah.[31] In his discussion in the second chapter of *Worship of the Heart* he explained that the two dimensions of consciousness, the subjective and the objective, are included in the term "halakhah." That is, he showed no propensity for the reductionist approaches that base the halakhah solely on the act or on the consciousness of obligation. Mourning is a fine example of this:

> A mourner who has complied scrupulously with the ritual of *avelut* but remained unresponsive to and unaffected by his encounter with death—if the passing of his next of kin did not fill him with gloom—has failed to fulfill the precept of mourning.[32]

This raises the question: what relationship is charted in *Worship of the Heart* between these subjective and objective dimensions? R. Soloveitchik gives a cogent reply:

> The Halakhah enters a new dimension of human life, that of subjectivity and inwardness. In contrast to actional *mitzvot*, the experiential *mitzvot* postulate a way not only of doing but of experiencing as well. The halakhah attempts to regulate not only the body but also the soul.[33]

R. Soloveitchik used two metaphors that illustrate the connection between the two dimensions of consciousness:

(1) the technique of painting (objective) and skill and creativity (subjective);[34]

(2) the extent of the periphery (objective) and the center (subjective).[35]

We already mentioned the distinction between the objective *ma'aseh ha-mitzvah* and the subjective *kiyyum ha-mitzvah*. Thus, the subjective dimension imparts meaning and content to its objective counterpart.

---

31 Lawrence Kaplan, "Rabbi Joseph B. Soloveitchik's Philosophy of Halakha," *The Jewish Law Annual* 7 (1987): 144-145.

32 *Worship of the Heart*, 17. R. Soloveitchik devotes extensive discussions to the tension between holiday rejoicing and mourning in some of his writings. See *And From There You Shall Seek*, trans. Naomi Goldblum (Jersey City, NJ: Toras HoRav Foundation, 2008), 195-197 n. 19; "Catharsis," *Tradition* 17, no. 2 (Spring 1978): 48-49; "Mourning" [Hebrew], in *Lessons*, vol. 2, 197-212.

33 *Worship of the Heart*, 16.

34 *Worship of the Heart*, 18.

35 *Worship of the Heart*, 19.

"The action is kerygmatic, message-bearing."[36] From a certain aspect, the subjective dimension is the form, in the Aristotelian sense, for the objective one, since it gives the latter dimension its essence and real substance. The subjective dimension reflects "structural wholeness" and an "axiological category."[37] R. Soloveitchik concluded his discussion by stating:

> Thus, the parallelism of act and fulfillment is not to be equated with duplication or replication. The objective and subjective orders represent two aspects, technique and accomplishment, respectively, the preliminary process and fulfillment itself.[38]

The boundaries that R. Soloveitchik erected in his writings from the mid-1940s between subjective and objective consciousness fell on the issue of prayer. The methodology of reconstruction was meant to break the undivided relationship between the two dimensions of consciousness. But now, in this discussion reconstruction is shunted aside, to be replaced by a one-directional relationship. From then on, the relationship between the subjective and objective dimensions of consciousness can be defined in two ways:

(1) the two sides of the same coin;
(2) a preliminary process and its realization.

Adopting R. Soloveitchik's metaphor, the circle has only a single center, one that is stable and firm, just as its circumference is fixed. The reconstruction methodology posited the existence of many subjective possibilities, and the impossibility of determining one as the motive for and cause of the objective dimension. Now, the subjective dimension is clearly delineated (intent and dialogue), with no alternatives. Despite its personal and intimate nature, it is subject to the divine fiat, which is the cause of the act. The experiential nature of prayer, which, in effect, was the broad context of his discussion, resulted in a new conception of the inner relations within the consciousness. We will see below that intent in prayer and in *Shema* means that the subjective stratum fashions the objective one. *Kavvanah*,

---

36 Ibid., 17. R. Soloveitchik frequently used the term "kerygmatic" to denote the normative message, that is, the message which contains command and law. See, for example, *The Lonely Man of Faith*, 61-62.
37 *Worship of the Heart*, 18.
38 *Worship of the Heart*, 18-19.

which R. Soloveitchik defined as an intentional act and as an expression of the subjective dimension of consciousness, is part of *kiyyum ha-mitzvah*.[39]

One fact is incontrovertible: the discussion of prayer was the direct cause for relegating reconstruction to the sidelines. The import of the subjective dimensions of prayer, that is, pouring out one's soul and standing before the Creator, led R. Soloveitchik to relax his rigid reconstructive conception, as regarding the absolute separation of the parts of the consciousness. This teaches of a continuum in prayer between the subjective and the objective in the consciousness.

2. An Eidetic Analysis

Why did prayer cause R. Soloveitchik to adopt a different model of the contexts of consciousness? Or, in even stronger language: how did prayer undermine the firm model that R. Soloveitchik had gone to such pains to set forth in his lengthy compositions from the mid-1940s? He obviously felt that prayer was exceptional in the halakhic landscape. In this section, we will examine the nature of his discussion of the consciousness of prayer.

Between the Phenomenological and the Theological

While in all other commandments the subjective and objective dimensions are two sides of the same coin, in prayer the subjective is the dominant and perhaps the authentic component. R. Soloveitchik writes:

> We must discriminate between two aspects of *tefillah*: the external one, constituting the formal act of prayer, and the inner experience, which expresses the very essence of the mitzvah. The physical deed of reciting a fixed text serves only as a medium through which the experience finds its objectification and concretion. It is not to be identified with the genuine act of praying, which is to be found in an entirely different dimension, namely, in the great, wondrous God-experience.[40]

R. Soloveitchik asserts here that the subjective dimension of consciousness is the "genuine" one. In compositions that were written before his discussion of prayer, only the objective dimension, that is, the actual observance of the halakhah, was stable and authentic, while the subjective dimension

---

39 See below, Chapter Six.
40 *Worship of the Heart*, 20.

was fluid and offered many choices. Prayer, however, was a game changer. From then on, the inner experience was the stable element, and it alone imparted meaning to the recitation of the sacred text. In prayer, as for any other halakhah, the act is "objectification," a term that R. Soloveitchik frequently used in *The Halakhic Mind*. Furthermore, he stressed a number of times in *Worship of the Heart* that the act is a necessary condition for the actualization of the prayer experience. Still, "[t]he Halakhah is distrustful of the genuineness and depth of our inner life."[41] In another passage he similarly defined the subjective dimension of consciousness as "the inner experience, the subject correlate of prayer."[42] The true arena in which prayer takes place, however, is the "God-experience," that is, the state of standing before God.

R. Soloveitchik had no qualms about asserting the exceptional nature of prayer in the halakhic system as a whole. He was aware that the adoption of the second reductionist approach (= minimalist subjectivity) sufficed for the needs of the halakhah. As we saw, in this approach the consciousness of the commandment suffices to fulfill one's obligation, that is, the observance of the commandment with an awareness of its source in the authority of the written Torah or the Oral Law. This is not the case as regards prayer. He writes:

> The controversy about *mitzvot tzerikhot kavvanah*, whether *mitzvot* require
> intention,[43] is confined to the class of objective norms. As far as *tefillah* is

---

41 *Worship of the Heart*, 16.
42 *Worship of the Heart*, 28. Correlation somewhat allays the relation of dependence between the objective and the subjective dimensions of consciousness.
43 In another place R. Soloveitchik wrote that *kavvanah* is an "intentional act" (*Worship of the Heart*, 88). Husserl's formulation of this phenomenological term was influenced by Brentano. R. Soloveitchik's translation of *mitzvot tzerikhot kavvanah* ("*mitzvah*-performance must be an intentional act"—88) enables us to understand the phenomenological framework of the discussion, which we shall clarify in brief:
    Husserl maintains that consciousness is the consciousness of objects. Intentionality separates the "stream of consciousness" into objects that the consciousness recognizes ("intentional") objects. The stream of consciousness usually includes the data received from the senses. An intentional object, or an "intentional unit," is the object recognized by the consciousness, to which the sensory data relate. An intentional act relates the sensory impressions to the content of consciousness or, in other words, to objects. Such an act infuses the objects of the consciousness with intuitive content. The object has many aspects, and Husserl explained that sensory perception does not capture all of them. Looking at a person's head from the front, we miss his image in profile. Consequently, the intentional act combines the images seen from different angles, so that the consciousness recognizes a person's head. The act directs the different aspects, and the consciousness turns their combination into an object. Husserl was much more interested in the eidetic structure of the intentional act than in the object to which the act is directed. The process

concerned, all agree that the physical performance divorced from the inner experience is worthless. Maimonides writes: "Prayer without *kavvanah* is no prayer at all. The man who has prayed without *kavvanah* is duty bound to recite his prayer over again" (*Hilkhot Tefillah* [Laws of Prayer] 4:15).[44] For *kavvanah* with respect to *tefillah* forms the very core of the act; without it prayer would become a meaningless and stereotyped ceremonial.[45]

[…] the very essence of *tefillah* expresses itself in a romance rather than in disciplined action, in a great passionate yearning rather than a limited cold achievement, in a movement of the soul rather than performance of the lips, in an awareness rather than in action, in an inner longing rather than a tangible performance, in silence rather than loud speech.[46]

In the sixth chapter of *Worship of the Heart*, R. Soloveitchik discussed the reading of the *Shema* and summarized the approach presented in the second chapter. He distinguished between two phenomenological models of the connection between subjective and objective consciousness. One is the standard model pertinent to most commandments, when subjective consciousness is not a central component and the commandment is reconstructed from objective consciousness, as noted above. The other

---

of relating the sensory data to the cognitive object may be called "objectification," a term that R. Soloveitchik used a few times. On objectification in Husserl's thought, see, for example, Rudolf Bernet, Iso Kern, and Eduard Marbach, *An Introduction to Husserlian Phenomenology* (Evanston, IL: Northwestern University Press, 1993), 88-101.

This obviously explains the phenomenological identification of halakhic *kavvanah* with the intentional act. The commandments are the practical sensory data. They express outside action and implementation. Moreover, they can be perceived by the senses. *Kavvanah* relates the flow of sensory data to the object, which the consciousness recognizes, and reveals the connection between praxis and consciousness. It imparts meaning to the commandments. This understanding enables us to overlay the practical dimension with subjective cognitive layers. This is an additional unequivocal testimony to the phenomenological nature of the terminological system with which R. Soloveitchik expressed his thought regarding the religious consciousness. I will further examine the intentional act and its expressions in the realm of the religious consciousness in Chapter Six, below.

44 In this context we should also mention the well-known interpretation by R. Hayyim of Brisk (on *Mishneh Torah, Hilkhot Tefillah* 4:11) that intent as standing before God is part of the act of prayer. R. Soloveitchik mentioned this understanding in his writings: "Reflections on the *Amidah*" (*Worship of the Heart*, 182 n. 4); *Lonely Man of Faith*, 74 n. 1. See also George Foot Moore, *Judaism in the First Centuries of the Christian Era: The Age of the Tannaim* (New York: Schocken, 1971 [1927]), vol. 2, 223-226; Tzvi Zahavy, "*Kavvanah* (Concentration) for Prayer in the Mishnah and Talmud," in *New Perspectives on Ancient Judaism*, ed. Jacob Neusner et al. (Lanham, MD: University Press of America, 1987), vol. 1, 37-48.

45 *Worship of the Heart*, 20-21.

46 *Worship of the Heart*, 21.

grants primacy to subjective consciousness within the commandment. R. Soloveitchik places prayer within this model:

> A subjective halakhic norm, in contradistinction to the objective, signifies *mitzvot* realized through an inner experience, in a state of mind, in a spiritual act, in a thought, a feeling, or a volition. Although the Halakhah, being very distrustful of human subjective life because of its vagueness, transcience and volatility, has introduced, even in the realm of subjective norms, concrete media through which an inward religious experience manifests itself, the real essence of the subjective *mitzvah* is confined to the spiritual element.[47]

We learn that for R. Soloveitchik prayer is a conscious act that ensues from the experience of the presence of God. The worshiper stands before God, and his subjective experience is of crucial importance. The path taken by R. Soloveitchik from the middle of the 1940s to the following decade is noteworthy. The term "act" that he used in *The Halakhic Mind* and in other works from that period, points to a noetic rather than a psychological state. Phenomenologists of religion emphasized that the religious act is autonomous and explained from within, that is, within the unique religious cognition irreducible to other realms such as science, sociology, or psychology. R. Soloveitchik adopted this position as the starting point of his discussion in *The Halakhic Mind*. The application of this stance to prayer is rooted in the phenomenological literature. Rudolf Otto took note of the aspects of prayer that reflect the "wholly other." He explained that the feeling of the wholly other, the numinous, is clearly a religious feeling (*mysterium tremendum*) untransferable to other realms, such as the rational, and is expressed in prayer through a series of not fully comprehensible terms (Hallelujah, Amen, and the like).[48] Max Scheler wrote: "The act of prayer [*Gebetsakt*] can be defined only from the *meaning* of prayer."[49] Scheler argued that the combination of diverse emotions, imaginings, and gestures that accompany prayer are totally separate from its being a religious act.

The discussions of prayer in *And from There You Shall Seek*, a work meant to describe the Jewish religious consciousness, are devoted to seeking God. They perceive prayer as an expression of the relationship between man and God, that is, the experience of God. R. Soloveitchik stressed there that the initial appearance of divine revelation is chaotic, is not subject to

---

47 *Worship of the Heart*, 88
48 Rudolph Otto, *The Idea of the Holy*, trans. John W. Harvey (New York: Oxford University Press, 1970), 64–65.
49 Scheler, *On the Eternal in Man*, 155. Scheler's book probably had the greatest influence on R. Soloveitchik's choice of terminology.

any regularity, and thus is independent of prayer.[50] Consequently, according to *And from There You Shall Seek*, the central aim of prayer is the quest for the presence of God.[51] The poetical style of this composition does not overshadow the conception of prayer as an act of the consciousness of the human-God relationship, nor does it leave prayer exclusively in the realm of emotion and temperament. In *Worship of the Heart* R. Soloveitchik maintained the pure phenomenological sense of his vigorous assertion that prayer is the experience of God. In addition, he clearly declared his phenomenological intent in the following passage:

> Our next task is to analyze the general precept *avodah she-ba-lev* with, on the one hand, its purely subjective elements, and, on the other hand, the specific aspect of *avodah she-ba-lev* that relates to the rituals of prayer. We must pose two questions: First, what does the norm of *avodah she-ba-lev* contain in its universal form; to what kind of state of mind is it related? Second, what does the *kavvanah* associated with the specific experience of prayer mean in philosophical, analytical terms? What are its basic motifs?[52]

R. Soloveitchik sought to explore the "universal form" and the subjective and objective aspects of the consciousness of prayer. As in *The Halakhic Mind*, R. Soloveitchik declared in the second chapter of *Worship of the Heart* his intent to engage in an "eidetic (structural) analysis" of prayer.[53] Eidetic reduction is meant to separate the nonessential elements of events and objects from their essential components, with the aim of exposing their fundamental structure. This is typically phenomenological language. Already, however, in the preceding passages on prayer, both as regards its subjective standing and in the personal introduction to *Worship of the Heart*, R. Soloveitchik entered psychological and emotional realms that were not typical of his rigorous phenomenological discussion of a decade earlier. One of the characteristics of phenomenology is restraint and noninvolvement. The phenomenologist observes from the side and tries to understand. It is precisely this noninvolvement that separates the phenomenologist of religion from the theologian.[54]

---

50 See Schwartz, *From Phenomenology to Existentialism*, 39.
51 Ibid., 27-28.
52 *Worship of the Heart*, 22.
53 *Worship of the Heart*, 23; *The Halakhic Mind*, 41. On this approach, see Schwartz, *Religion or Halakha*, 44-45.
54 See Eric J. Sharpe, *Comparative Religion: A History* (London: Duckworth, 1975), 233.

Methodologically, then, R. Soloveitchik shifts between an essentially phenomenological description of prayer that views the religious act as autonomous and precluding any outside involvement and a psychological and emotional description. Such a depiction does not always maintain the autonomous framework of religion, and encroaches on contiguous realms. R. Soloveitchik's formulations fluctuate between personal involvement in the experience of prayer and the phenomenological analysis of such an experience.

Worship of the Heart: A Phenomenological Analysis

Now, for an examination of the elements of the eidetic analysis of prayer in the second chapter of *Worship of the Heart*. R. Soloveitchik presented prayer as one of the paradigms of "worship of the heart," that is, of the spiritual worship of God. As we noted earlier, R. Soloveitchik was seemingly apprehensive of the central, and exceptional, pride of place given to prayer, and wrote in the first pages of *Worship of the Heart* that prayer is only one of the acts of the religious consciousness.[55] Accordingly, he began his presentation of the consciousness of prayer with another paradigm of "worship of the heart": the intellectual worship in the thought of Maimonides, to teach us that prayer is not the sole component of such worship. To this end he quoted from Maimonides' description in the closing chapters of *Guide of the Perplexed* of the worship of those who have "acquired a knowledge of the high truths."[56] His analysis of the Maimonidean text is patently phenomenological. In those chapters Maimonides depicts the ethos of the perfect man: the intellectual. He extensively discusses the way of life of the individual who has attained perfection. In the cited passage Maimonides defined worship of the heart to mean: "this man concentrates all his thoughts on the First Intellect (God) and is absorbed in these thoughts as much as possible."[57] The thought of the perfect man is directed to Heaven,

---

55 See above, Chapter Two.
56 The quotation is from *Guide of the Perplexed* 3:51. See, for example, Eliezer Goldman, *Expositions and Inquiries: Jewish Thought in Past and Present*, ed. Daniel Statman and Abraham Sagi [Hebrew] (Jerusalem: Magnes, 1997), 60-86; see Kaplan, "Review Essay," 85-86; Steven Harvey, "Avicenna and Maimonides on Prayer and Intellectual Worship," in *Exchange and Transmission across Cultural Boundaries*, ed. Haggai Ben-Shammai, Shaul Shaked, and Sarah Stroumsa (Jerusalem: Israel Academy of Sciences and Humanities, 2013), 82-105.
57 *Guide of the Perplexed* 3:51. On this tradition in the medieval period, see, for example, Moshe Idel, "*Hitbodedut* as Concentration in Jewish Philosophy" [Hebrew], in *Shlomo*

and he engages in metaphysical conceptions even when he interacts with other people.

In R. Soloveitchik's interpretation of Maimonides, the perfect man has the experience of God even within everyday life. As we saw above, phenomenological analysis shunts aside nonessential elements. R. Soloveitchik decided to subject the experience of the perfect man to eidetic analysis, with emphasis placed on spiritual worship in its Maimonidean formulation, and therefore removed the nonessential components. At least two such elements can be listed, one overt, and the other implicit.

(1) Ascetic overtones: the Maimonidean intellectual approach required asceticism, since total dedication to the intellective means detachment from material life.[58] The substantial dimension, however, is the experience itself, and therefore asceticism is not perceived as essential.

(2) The intellectualist component: in the Maimonidean approach, the experience of God must come from within the acquisition of knowledge. Even the approaches that ascribe a certain degree of mysticism to Maimonides[59] link it to intellectual perfection. Since the essential dimension is the experience itself, rationalism is not perceived as an essential element.

Phenomenology is not interested in the elements characteristic of the approach of Maimonides, as a twelfth-century rationalist thinker, it rather seeks examine the testimony of the Maimonidean approach regarding the

---

Pines Jubilee Volume, ed. Moshe Idel, Warren Zev Harvey, and Eliezer Schweid, vol. 7 of *Jerusalem Studies in Jewish Thought* (1988), 39-60.

58   See Dov Schwartz, "Ethics and Asceticism in the Neoplatonic School of the Fourteenth Century" [Hebrew], in *Between Religion and Ethics*, ed. Avi Sagi and Daniel Statman (Ramat Gan: Bar-Ilan University Press, 1993), 185-208, at 192-196.

59   On the traditional and scholarly approaches that establish the Maimonidean doctrine on the mystical element, see, for example, Moshe Idel, *Maimonide et la mystique juive*, trans. Charles Mopsik (Paris: Cerf, 1991); David R. Blumenthal, *Philosophic Mysticism* (Ramat Gan: Bar-Ilan University, 2006); Menachem Kellner, *Maimonides' Confrontation with Mysticism* (Portland, OR: The Littman Library of Jewish Civilization, 2006). See also Raphael Jospe, "Maimonides and *Shi'ur Komah*" [Hebrew], in *Tribute to Sara: Studies in Jewish Philosophy and Kabbala Presented to Professor Sara O. Heller Wilensky*, ed. Moshe Idel, Devora Dimant, and Shalom Rosenberg (Jerusalem: Magnes, 1994), 195-209; Dov Schwartz, "R. Soloveitchik as a Maimonidean: The Unity of Cognization" [Hebrew], in *Maimonides and Mysticism*, ed. Abraham Elqayam and Dov Schwartz (Ramat Gan: Bar-Ilan University Press, 2009), 301-321.

structure of the religious consciousness. After having removed the nonessential elements, namely, those that especially describe the Maimonidean doctrine in its local historical context, we are left with the task of determining: what are the essential components of the worship of the perfect individuals, according to Maimonides' depiction? R. Soloveitchik specified two such elements.

(1) The psychological element deals with the entire personality fixating on the experience of God. "It is a love that transcends the bounds of reasonableness and sense, and reaches into the paradoxical and the absurd."[60]

(2) The mystical element, that seeks communion with God ("sharing infinity itself").[61] R. Soloveitchik called this an "ecstatic act," in which consciousness seeks to breach its boundaries and merge with God.[62] R. Soloveitchik alludes to the term Ein-Sof (literally, the Infinite), although he does not mention it explicitly. Communion with God is "the transcendence of finitude; it is the extension of the existential experience into the boundlessness of the beyond in the direction of the supreme Being."[63]

We should add a clarification regarding the mystical element of experience: in this instance, R. Soloveitchik's eidetic analysis relates specifically to the Maimonidean notion of the structure of the consciousness. R. Soloveitchik himself generally objected to mysticism, whether overt or implicit. The esoteric nature of mysticism, that is, its being limited to individuals who undergo a mystical experience, evoked his opposition. Since the halakhah is at the center of his thought, and, by its very nature, is directed to the entire community, mysticism is shunted aside, to the fringes of the consciousness. R. Soloveitchik states this outright: "Hence, *avodah*

---

60 *Worship of the Heart*, 24.

61 *Worship of the Heart*, 24.

62 It is noteworthy that Paul Tillich, as well, presented prayer as an "ecstatic act," but in a completely different existential sense. Tillich defined "ecstasy" as a state in which the object and the subject do not merge, rather, their unity transcends what he called the "subject-object structure." For him, prayer is an ecstatic state, because addressing God in prayer as an object causes one to experience Him as a subject. See Robert P. Scharlemann, *Reflection and Doubt in the Thought of Paul Tillich* (New Haven, CT: Yale University Press, 1969), 161. In this passage R. Soloveitchik retained the classic mystical sense, claiming that ecstasy is a departure from the self.

63 *Worship of the Heart*, 24.

she-ba-lev, in the Maimonidean description, is an esoteric adventure, one that is not understandable to the average person."[64] R. Soloveitchik excluded himself from such a goal: "But we may not be able to do so." *Guide of the Perplexed* is definitely the work of an esoteric.[65] R. Soloveitchik devoted a lengthy explanation to show that Maimonides' position is opposed to the nature of the halakhah.

The eidetic analysis of the Maimonidean view demonstrated that "worship of the heart" is the indefatigable quest for the experience of God, and that prayer, too, is an expression of this search. Simply put, prayer is the total dedication of the consciousness in search of conjunction with God. Following the eidetic analysis of spiritual worship, we can now examine the substantial aspect of the experience of God itself. R. Soloveitchik writes:

> Through *avodah she-ba-lev* the soul longs to recover its resemblance to God, even while it is aware of the dissimilitude that separates the creation from the Creator. Through the medium of *avodah she-ba-lev*, man tries to express his closeness to and endless remoteness from God, his love and his fear, his anguish and his serenity, his unshakable faith and his satanic doubts, his joy and his sorrow, his being and his non-being, his capacity both for achieving greatness and for falling into the abyss of smallness.[66]

Before this, R. Soloveitchik presented the "paradoxical" and the "absurd" as the aim of spiritual worship. He noted that this "transcends the bounds of reasonableness and sense."[67] Now he presents the meaning of these terms in detail. The experience of God is dialectical, and is concerned with the fluctuation between the high and low points of this experience. The concurrent sensation of closeness and remoteness, the longing for God together with aversion for Him, are not logical. Reason cannot absorb the unity of contrasts. These elements, typical of the classical description of the religious experience in Kierkegaard's thought, Otto's *The Idea of the Holy*, and other phenomenological works,[68] find expression in prayer. From this aspect, the description of the experience of prayer does not differ from, for

---

64 *Worship of the Heart*, 26.

65 In another place R. Soloveitchik spoke of Maimonides' discoursing in *Guide of the Perplexed* "on the devotional and mystical goal of all religious actions, a state of mind characteristic only of the great geniuses of religion" (*Worship of the Heart*, 93).

66 *Worship of the Heart*, 25.

67 *Worship of the Heart*, 24.

68 R. Soloveitchik even uses Otto's expression, *mysterium tremendum* (*Worship of the Heart*, 25).

example, the depiction of the religious experience in *Worship of the Heart*. R. Soloveitchik's eidetic analysis teaches that the prayer experience is an indefatigable and uncompromising search for the presence of God. The eidetic analysis of the Maimonidean text leads to an eidetic analysis of the religious consciousness as a whole: prayer as seeking God. The Maimonidean consciousness of prayer is an individual case of the religious individual's consciousness of prayer. The eidetic analysis is therefore twofold:

(1) removing the Maimonidean historical and philosophical garb (placing the world in brackets) leads to prayer as focusing on God and as mystical communion;

(2) removing the specific garb of esoteric focus and communion leads to the general nucleus of prayer as seeking God.

3. The Transition to Existence

The preceding discussion taught that prayer is the thirst for communion and the presence of God, and it itself reflects the dialectical religious experience. This is the conclusion of the eidetic analysis of the religious experience. From this point on, R. Soloveitchik's discussion somewhat exceeds the religious phenomenological analysis, and enters the realm of existentialism (the description of profound crisis and prayer as a cry from the depths of existential distress). R. Soloveitchik maintained that the religious consciousness is built of stages and layers. One of these strata is explained by means of such distress. The existential discussion therefore is combined with the comprehensive phenomenological description of the stages of consciousness reflected in prayer. Since the general context of R. Soloveitchik's discussion in *Worship of the Heart* is distinctly phenomenological, we must ask why this change occurred.

The Problem

R. Soloveitchik presented the quest for the experience of God as a problem to be solved. The consciousness of prayer is constructed from the Maimonidean element, as well. The Maimonidean conception of its psychological and mystical aspects cannot be presented as the only key to understanding the religious experience, and the experience of prayer cannot be explained in a psychological and mystical experiential manner. This approach is elitist, and is limited to exceptional individuals, and therefore is not compatible with the spirit of the exoteric halakhah. Only individuals obsessively live their life with total dedication to God, to love of Him and the quest for communion with Him. Basing the experience of prayer on the experiences of the elect perfect individuals removes it from its halakhic meaning. The halakhah inherently addresses the people as a whole. R. Soloveitchik termed the contrast between the experience of prayer according to the Maimonidean interpretation of "worship of the heart" and the nature of the halakhah a "problem" and an "absurdity." He wrote explicitly: "However embarrassing the problem is, it should not be considered insoluble. I dare say there is a solution that might save *tefillah* from becoming a Halakhic absurdity."[69]

R. Soloveitchik accordingly wanted to reveal an experiential dimension that, on the one hand, is not mystical and esoteric, but, on the other, explains the consciousness of prayer as the experience of God. He found such an experiential dimension, first of all, in existentialist thought, that is, in prayer's addressing man's existential crisis structure. Such an address is relevant for the public as a whole, and therefore is not the exclusive province of elitist individuals. The existential crisis will be revealed within petitionary prayer. The discovery of prayer leads the worshiper, who finds a voice for his distresses, to the religious experience. For R. Soloveitchik, an additional experiential dimension is contingent on the aesthetic aspect of religious life. Aesthetic regard for the experience of God—connected with sensory impression—is the province of the public as a whole, by its very definition. As we will see below in Chapter Four, this dimension is fully revealed within laudatory prayers.

Structure

The second chapter of *Worship of the Heart* is divided, philosophically, into two parts: the first is devoted to a clearly phenomenological analysis,[70] and the second, to an existentialist analysis.[71] Additionally, the essay "Prayer as Dialogue" in *Reflections of the Rav* does not contain the consciousness analysis that we surveyed above in the current chapter; in other words, the first part of the second chapter in *Worship of the Heart* is completely omitted.

---

69 *Worship of the Heart*, 27. See Amaru, "Prayer and the Beauty of God," 155.
70 *Worship of the Heart*, 13-27.
71 *Worship of the Heart*, 27-36. A similar structure appears in a few expositions in *Out of the Whirlwind* and *Family Redeemed*.

The existentialist analysis, in contrast, appears in a different and abbreviated style, as a continuation of our discussion above.[72]

In the beginning of the second part of the chapter, R. Soloveitchik presents the answer to the problem of elitism as the plan of the discussions in the succeeding chapters, which are divided in accordance with the basic structure of man's consciousness, that prayer addresses. The consciousness structure is based on a tripartite process that constructs the consciousness of prayer:

(1) "the conception of *mi-ma'amakim* (*de profundis*), the crisis cry from the depths" (the second half of chapter 2);
(2) "the concept of *kevod Elokim* (*majestas Dei*), the majesty of God" (the first aesthetic experience; chapters 3 and 4);
(3) "the concept of *hesed Elokim* (*caritas Dei*), the grace of God" (the second aesthetic experience;[73] the end of chapter 4).[74]

The first stage expresses the situation of the religious individual as such, with no distinction by intellectual or spiritual standing. The second and third stages represent the religious man who is dedicated to the religious experience that culminates in the quest for communion. Chapter 5 of *Worship of the Heart* is devoted to the idea that the structure of the consciousness is dialectical. That is, after attaining the third stage, man once again retreats to the second, and back again. The process in which the consciousness is completed pendulates. The structure of the *Amidah* prayer also alludes to these three stages of consciousness, which describe the religious man's personality, existence, and experiences[75]:

(1) petitionary blessings: the crisis of mortality, alienation, and boredom that are characteristic of human existence;

---

72 See above, Chapter Two.
73 *Worship of the Heart*, 28.
74 The structure of the discussion seems reasonable, although the chapters should have been divided by specific topic (existential crisis; the first aesthetic experience; the second aesthetic experience), instead of presenting this discussion at the end of the second chapter, while different experiences are included in the same chapter. See Kaplan, "Review Essay," 107-108.
75 On the divisions of the *Amidah* prayer, see Aaron Mirsky, "The Origin of 'The Eighteen Benedictions' of the Daily Prayer" [Hebrew], *Tarbiz* 33 (1963): 28-39 (reprinted in *Studies in Jewish Liturgy*, ed. Hananel Mack [Jerusalem: Magnes, 2003], 64-73); Ezra Fleischer, "The *Shemone Esre*—Its Character, Internal Order, Content and Goals" [Hebrew], *Tarbiz* 62 (1993): 179-223, at 192-195 (reprinted in Mack, *Studies*, 170-173)

(2) laudatory blessings: the divine majesty and splendor as aesthetic religious experience; standing before God, the foreign and the Other (the numinous);

(3) thanksgiving blessings: the divine good and lovingkindness as aesthetic religious experience: standing before the nearby and loving God.

The common denominator of these three ideas of consciousness, then, is their inclusion in Halakhah, which relates to them explicitly, documents them, refines them, and even balances them. In this manner these human conditions, whether of distress or of self-affirmation and authenticity, are redeemed. And redemption relates to every man. R. Soloveitchik accordingly began with distress and crisis, which characterize human existence. The experiential stages (2-3) are contingent upon the religious consciousness, which is not necessarily a given. The prayer experience therefore offers "remedial and inspiring energy for everybody."[76] The structure of the discussion ensues from R. Soloveitchik's three answers to the problem that he set forth at the beginning of his discussion.

4. Summary

From the end of Chapter 2 to Chapter 5, *Worship of the Heart* moves from a phenomenological examination of the general outline of the consciousness of prayer to a detailed analysis of the stages of this consciousness and the transition from one stage to the next (the process of the perfection of the consciousness). The reader descends from the heights of the religious experience and the total dedication of the consciousness to this experience (communion with God) to the detailed states of consciousness and the process of transition between them. We therefore should take a brief look at the phenomenological conception as formulated in the first two chapters of *Worship of the Heart*. Like most of the book's other chapters, these two chapters should be read as the uninterrupted and direct continuation of R. Soloveitchik's works from the mid-1940s (*The Halakhic Mind, And from There You Shall Seek*). Moreover, without prior familiarity with these works, it would be difficult to understand the nature and meanings of the terminology that he uses in presenting prayer as a clearly intentional act of consciousness. Just as *Halakhic Man* cannot

---

76 *Worship of the Heart*, 28.

be properly understood without R. Soloveitchik's Ph.D. dissertation,[77] where this terminology originates, *Worship of the Heart* cannot be comprehended without the phenomenological directions in 1940s works. Ignoring these trends, results in the loss of historical and methodological aspects of his thought.

R. Soloveitchik presented two models of an eidetic analysis of the consciousness of prayer or of the prayer experience. The first model places prayer on the map of consciousness alongside intentional acts or other dimensions of the consciousness. Prayer is set forth as dialogical consciousness, alongside intellect, emotion, and will as other dimensions of the consciousness. This model enhances the quality of the consciousness standing of prayer, and presents it as fashioning an independent realm. Furthermore, R. Soloveitchik thoroughly investigated the question of the links between those subjective part of the consciousness, and offered various ways of understanding them.[78] The second model views prayer as one of the branches of a single act of consciousness, namely the spiritual worship of God ("worship of the heart").

The oscillations between the two models expresses R. Soloveitchik's indecision regarding the subjective standing of prayer. On the one hand, prayer is a substantial component of the subjective consciousness, while on the other, its centrality is somewhat blurred. R. Soloveitchik always feared the strengthening of the subjective dimension of consciousness and its entailing temptation.

In either event, prayer reveals the dialogical dimensions of the consciousness. The two models can be depicted in the following diagram:

Model A

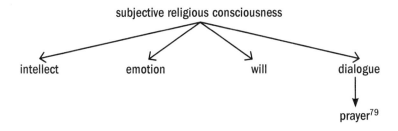

---

77 See Schwartz, *Religion or Halakha.*

78 We examined this model in the preceding chapter.

79 In one possibility, prayer is identified with dialogue, and in the other, the dialogue includes other religious expressions, such as prophecy.

Model B

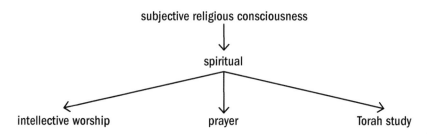

Although both models portray prayer as one of the expressions of the consciousness, R. Soloveitchik placed it in the center of the consciousness. This placement has two important aspects that are especially characteristic of the consciousness of prayer.

(1) Rejection of reconstruction: this, accordingly, fashions the relationship between the subjective and objective dimensions of prayer. R. Soloveitchik retreated in great degree from the careful reconstructive conception that typified his thought in the 1940s, and indicated the strong linkage between these two dimensions. From this point on, the practice of prayer, that is, its formulation and the gestures characteristic of the practical mandate, directly express the subjective experience of the pouring out of one's soul and standing before God.

(2) Tempering the methodology: the meticulous eidetic phenomenological analysis of prayer became more fluid. Although the phenomenology of religion takes the religious consciousness as a given, along with its demand to refrain from including personal experience in the concrete world, R. Soloveitchik did not succeed in maintaining complete detachment from his personal prayer experiences. This moderation is twofold:

(a) a personal complexion in prayer, as is evident in the Introduction to the book;

(b) a concrete existential crisis, which becomes a component of the structure of the consciousness.

To a certain degree, the transition to existentialist conceptions was due to the failure of the phenomenonalist approach, which was unable to contend with its characteristic problem of esotericism. That is, the depictions of the religious life as longing for communion, and even for assimilation within the divine entity, and the dialectic of closeness and distance, are seen as the ways of the perfect individual. The halakhah, in contrast, is founded on its addressing the public at large. This led R. Soloveitchik to think that the phenomenological explanation of the prayer experience cannot be complete without the existential dimensions. Knowledge of the tangible reality and God's place in relation to it allows us to fully understand prayer.

Worship of the Heart, then, presents the methodologies at the basis of R. Soloveitchik's thought in a new light. Before this volume, he had viewed phenomenology and existentialism as two important alternatives, but not as competing approaches. For him, each was a proper methodology for exposing man's stance when facing God's truth. We see this in his continued use of both approaches until his later years. *Worship of the Heart*, however, shows that the phenomenological approach alone is insufficient, although it is by far the greatest part of the book; additionally, his existentialist writing is set within a plainly phenomenological framework. Thus, R. Soloveitchik saw the two approaches as complementary. In other words, the full possibility of clarifying the standing of halakhah in concrete life is dependent on conceptual mobility. We see, therefore, that the prayer experience crosses the boundaries of the carefully charted frameworks. In the beginning of the next chapter we will analyze the existential ideas regarding prayer.

Chapter 4

The Consciousness of Prayer: The Process of Consolidation

We have so far analyzed the consciousness of prayer as outlined in the first chapters of *Worship of the Heart*. We will now turn to an exploration of the ways in which the consciousness of prayer develops, from the concrete reality to the heights of the religious experience. How does R. Soloveitchik's discussion until the middle of chapter 2 of *Worship of the Heart* (which we examined in the preceding chapter) differ from the discussion that extends from the middle of chapter 2 to the end of chapter 4? As far as the order of his discussion is concerned, the answer is clear: until this juncture, R. Soloveitchik focused on the consciousness itself, and did not emphasize the dimensions that transform prayer into an experience of the broad public. The methodological picture is similarly straightforward: until then, R. Soloveitchik defined the subjective consciousness of prayer, and examined its relationship with the objective consciousness. Now, he seeks to describe the manner in which the stages of consciousness come into being. He portrays how the consciousness is devised, from its beginning to the uppermost stage of the consciousness, and exposes the reader to the process. His basic assumption is that the blessings of the *Amidah* prayer (petitional, hymnal, and thanksgiving) reflects the stages of the consolidation of the religious consciousness (crisis, dialectical experience, and the unified experience, respectively). From this respect, *Worship of the Heart* applies R. Soloveitchik's phenomenological methodology as it was formulated in his writings from the mid-1940s:

(1) in *The Halakhic Mind* R. Soloveitchik defined the religious consciousness and its basic structure, and in the beginning of *Worship of the Heart*, he defined the consciousness of prayer and its fundamental structure;

(2) in *And from There You Shall Seek* he discussed in detail the process of the formulation of the different stages of the consciousness, while from the middle of chapter 2 to the end of chapter 4 of *Worship of the Heart* he clarified the forging of the consciousness of prayer.

R. Soloveitchik described at length the stages of the subjective and existential consciousness of prayer in the unit combining chapters 2-4 of *Worship of the Heart*. He began with distress (crisis), continued with the dialectical religious experience of consciousness that is anchored in aesthetic existence (aesthetic redemption), and concluded with the blissful religious experience (the aesthetic stage of communion). We will further examine the parallelism between these stages and those of consciousness depicted in *And from There You Shall Seek*. The three stages of crisis existence and the aesthetic consciousness share their being given meaning by prayer, which redeems them. Prayer records man's existential situations and states of consciousness. Moreover, prayer is a popular religious phenomenon because the command to pray encompasses all strata of the people, and each community has a single basic prayer version. Therefore, prayer redeems human consciousness and existence as such.

1. Crisis Prayer

Prayer is rooted in man's fundamental intuitions. The immediate and most primal motive for prayer is distress. The man in torment calls out to his God. Distress, the most basic framework of existence, is reflected in petitional prayers that, to a large extent, constitute the backbone of the *Amidah* prayer.[1] R. Soloveitchik, accordingly, began with an analysis of crisis prayer, even though the *Amidah* prayer, for instance, opens with the hymnal blessings. The starting point of the consciousness of prayer is crisis.

---

1 See, for example, Naomi Cohen, "On the Original Nature of the Prayerbook of Rabbi Saadia Gaon" [Hebrew], *Sinai* 95 (1984): 350-360. In "On the Religious Definition of Man," R. Soloveitchik argued that "the essence of prayer in Judaism does not lie mainly in the utterance of hymns and words of exaltation, although such elements are unquestionably to be found in it. Mainly, however, it is a petition for aid from Heaven in time of distress. Prayer in Judaism is usually connected with the word 'tzarah,' distress. *Tzarah* expresses disaster, danger, and the like—man is in distress—and *min ha-meitzar karati Yah* ['In distress I called on the Lord'; Ps. 118:5]. This human situation arouses the man in Israel to arise and pray. Not a hymn, rather the seeking of divine mercy. A person beset by distress sees himself cast low and dejected, threatened and fearful, and he asks of his Creator to provide him with refuge and relief" (*Ha-Adam ve-Olamo*, 23).

Crisis

There are two phases to R. Soloveitchik's discussion of crisis prayer. In the first phase, he presented crisis as the almost necessary cause of prayer. Although there are hymnal and thanksgiving prayers that do not necessarily ensue from the depths of crisis (see below), the first—and perhaps fundamental—appearance of prayer is in response to distress. The basis of prayer is, naturally, petition, which rises from the depth of suffering. In the second phase, R. Soloveitchik analyzed the state of crisis, and found two types of crisis: surface and depth crisis.

Turning now to the first phase, that is, the conception of prayer as a response to states of crisis, distress, and anxiety. R. Soloveitchik writes in his various works:

> *Tefillah*, according to Halakhah, is closely knit with the experience of *tzarah*, distress,[2] or—to be more loyal to the literal semantics—constriction; it means finding oneself in distressingly narrow straits.[3]
>
> Prayer is warranted and meaningful only when one realizes that all hope is gone, that there is no other friend besides God from whom one may expect assistance and comfort, when the soul feels its bleak despair, loneliness and helplessness. However, if one is not haunted by anxiety and brute fear, if one does not look upon his existence as a heap of debris, if his self-confidence and arrogance have not been undermined, if neither doubt nor anguish assails his mind—then prayer is alien to him and any recital of a fixed prayer-text is meaningless. Success and prayer, impudence and prayer, are mutually exclusive.
>
> Prayer as a personal experience, as a creative gesture, is possible only if and when man discovers himself in crisis or in need.[4]

R. Soloveitchik makes two claims:

(1) the main concern of prayer is to respond to distress;
(2) distress is the reason and justification for prayer.[5]

Prayer is anchored in the nadir. In order to express this principle, R. Soloveitchik used various wordings that, in the existentialist literature,

---

2 R. Soloveitchik apparently referred to texts such as Jer. 30:7; Ps. 20:2.
3 *Worship of the Heart*, 29.
4 *Out of the Whirlwind*, 161.
5 R. Soloveitchik devoted much attention to the question of the legitimacy of prayer; see below, Chapter Ten.

reflect a condition of crisis (terror, anxiety, crisis). Two observations must be made: first, *Reflections of the Rav* emphasizes the "feeling of dependence."[6] The dependence expressed by prayer is existential and not that of the consciousness. A person prays out of his precarious existence, exposed to external, unfamiliar, and threatening factors. Second, all three works contain veiled, or even open, criticism of mystics. This time, the criticism is directed to their focus on praise of God while ignoring human distress. For them, petitional prayer is unworthy.[7] In *Reflections of the Rav*, mystics are lumped together with Christians in their rejection of prayer that relates to human needs.

Patently, then, R. Soloveitchik viewed prayer, first and foremost, as an expression of the human condition. In a large degree, this is an anthropological modification of prayer. The prayer experience places man at its center. Although prayer is perceived as a human initiative and as a response to profound human need, this is not self-affirming for man. To the contrary: the anthropological shift comes into being because prayer is a consequence of underlying existential crisis. This is not a person who confronts God, and bravely stands before Him. The worshiper is a dejected and broken person whose existence is conflicted and flimsy. Prayer is an expression of man embracing his mortality and realizing the meanings of this.

The Types of Crisis

The dimensions of the crisis existence constantly occupied R. Soloveitchik. He discussed two types of crisis in the essay "The Crisis of Human Finitude" in *Out of the Whirlwind* and at the end of chapter 2 of *Worship of the Heart*. A summary of these discussions already appeared in the chapter "Prayer as Dialogue" in *Reflections of the Rav*. In short, he distinguished an external, "surface crisis" contingent on the surroundings ("illness, famine, war, poverty…")[8] from an inner, "depth crisis" that characterizes the basis of concrete existence. The differences between the two types are the following:

(1) Causes: a surface crisis is the result of external factors that are imposed on man (danger, illness, and the like). A depth crisis ensues from the anxiety over the inherent finitude and limitations

---

6 "Prayer as Dialogue," in *Reflections of the Rav*, 84. On the feeling of dependence, see above, the end of Chapter Two.
7 *Out of the Whirlwind*, 161; *Worship of the Heart*, 28-29; *Reflections of the Rav*, 84.
8 *Worship of the Heart*, 30.

of human existence ("the paradoxical concept of [man's] being born out of nothingness and running down to nothingness").[9] In Heideggerian style, R. Soloveitchik declares that man is "thrown into" this crisis.[10]

(2) Nature: the surface crisis is tangible and immediate, while the depth crisis is reflective, and deliberation and contemplation are needed to reveal it.

(3) A person must struggle with and overcome the surface crisis, while the existential depth crisis should usually be embraced and consciously chosen ("This type of crisis is searched out and discovered by man and accepted by him freely").[11]

The third distinction is not unequivocal. R. Soloveitchik stated that the existential crisis (the "depth crisis"), as well, has a tragic element.[12] It is bound up with suffering and afflictions, since it ensues from man's existential finitude and cessation. At times he argued that authentic existence means acknowledging the crisis and accepting it out of choice. The hero struggles against the surface crisis. It is incumbent upon man to fight against the ravages of nature. No such struggle, however, is to be waged against inner crisis. To the contrary, it is to be freely accepted. "With respect to the inner crisis, however, which is rooted in depth-experience, man was told not only that he should not try to disengage himself from his involvement in it but, on the contrary, that he should deepen and accept it."[13] At times, however, the picture that emerges from R. Soloveitchik's portrayal of the depth crisis is that of a Romantic hero who struggles against his fate. Man seeks to combat suffering, but since the definition of his personality is anchored in suffering, such a contest is paradoxical. Man cannot extricate

---

9 *Worship of the Heart*, 32. On the conception of crisis and its sources, see Schwartz, *From Phenomenology to Existentialism*, 247-249. I noted elsewhere that R. Soloveitchik himself was occupied with psychology and offered insights about his own personality: see Dov Schwartz, "Personality and Psychology," *Review of Rabbinic Judaism* 12 (2009): 273.

10 *Worship of the Heart*, 78. R. Soloveitchik expressly mentioned Heidegger as the source of the wording "thrown into the world" ("On the Religious Definition of Man," in *Ha-Adam ve-Olamo*, 62). Kaplan already noted the problem of editing in the discussion of depth crisis; see Kaplan, "Review Essay," 108-109. It should be mentioned that the loneliness discussed here, and that in chapter 5 (78-80) are different. Here, this is loneliness regarding the other, and in chapter 5, in relation to God; see below.

11 *Worship of the Heart*, 31; *Out of the Whirlwind*, 163 (in an almost identical version).

12 *Worship of the Heart*, 32; *Out of the Whirlwind*, 164.

13 *Worship of the Heart*, 32.

himself from the depth crisis, and the struggle against suffering is doomed to fail. Original sin, that fashioned the "human condition,"[14] does not allow a person to overcome existential suffering. R. Soloveitchik presents

> one unalterably cruel reality, It is that man never emerges victorious from his combat; total triumph is not his destiny. Even when he seems to win the engagement, he is defeated in the very moment that triumph is within his reach. This paradox of our existence manifests itself in this strange experience: at the very instant we complete the conquest of a point of vantage we are tossed back onto the base from where we began our drive. The Divine curse pronounced at the dawn of human experience hovers over all human endeavor.[15]

Two observations should be made regarding the tension between the two approaches: the adoption of the crisis and the heroic struggle against it.

(1) The given situation: the depth crisis is a fact, and is characterized by a state of suffering. Whether it is embraced intentionally, from the outset, or only after conflict, man returns to his original starting point.

(2) The uncertainty regarding the response to the existential crisis is reflective, in great degree, of the dialectical dimension that typifies this crisis. Accordingly, R. Soloveitchik frequently used the words "paradox" and "absurd" in this context.[16] The depth crisis relates "to an experience in which the affirmation is indissolubly bound up with the negation, the thesis with the antithesis."[17]

Crisis and Prayer

R. Soloveitchik's message is that prayer relates to the depth crisis. Before discussing the meaning of this, it should be noted that R. Soloveitchik used the two types of crisis to explain the well-known disagreement between Maimonides and Nachmanides on the source of the obligation to pray. He maintains that the two great decisors of Jewish law concur that in a time of trouble for the public, there is a Torah obligation to

---

14 See Karl Barth, *The Doctrine of Reconciliation*, vol. IV, part 1 of *Church Dogmatics* (London: SCM Press, 1965), 358.
15 *Worship of the Heart*, 33.
16 See *Worship of the Heart*, 32; *Out of the Whirlwind*, 166.
17 *Out of the Whirlwind*, 167.

cry out in prayer. Consequently, both connect prayer with distress. However, while Nachmanides limits the Torah obligation of prayer to external crisis (such as fear of enemies and war), Maimonides expands the obligation to the inner crisis, as well. Since the latter is characteristic of the human condition, then it is constant. Maimonides accordingly rules that the obligation for routine prayer comes from the Torah.[18] Maimonides' reasoning is that "[m]an is always in need because he is always in crisis and distress."[19]

For R. Soloveitchik, the connection between crisis and prayer is threefold:

(1) awareness: prayer is an expression of awareness of and embracing of the depth crisis;
(2) source: prayer sprouts from the distress and suffering that are inherent in the depth crisis (petition);[20]
(3) relief: prayer is also the ability to express, which enables a person to bear the crisis and live a balanced, honorable life with it.

R. Soloveitchik was, undoubtedly, aware of the reservations in Hasidic teachings regarding petitions and prayers of distress. For the most part, the early Hasidic masters rejected petition per se. No one need trouble God for his personal needs. Some interpreted petition as relating to divine needs, as it were, namely, the suffering of the *Shekhinah* (Divine Presence) and theurgic activity.[21] Hasidic masters directed their attention mainly to contemplative

---

18 *Worship of the Heart*, 29; *Reflections of the Rav*, 79-82; Grodner, *On Prayer*, 13. Besdin's edition states outright that Nachmanides referred to surface crisis, and Maimonides, to depth crisis, that is, their disagreement revolves around *tzarah*, distress. *Worship of the Heart*, however, does not make such a conclusion, and lets the reader reach it. The text is therefore lacking in some degree, as Kaplan already noted in "Review Essay," 106-107.
19 *Worship of the Heart*, 35. R. Soloveitchik did not offer such an explanation in "Reflections on the *Amidah*," and merely stated that the obligation to cry out in time of trouble is "a sort of waiving of the absolute stance that prayer is not a Torah obligation" (*Ra'ayanot al Tefillah*, in *Ish ha-Halakhah: Galui ve-Nistar* [Halakhic Man: Revealed and Concealed] [Jerusalem: World Zionist Organization, 1979], 241; a direct translation from the Hebrew was more suitable in this context than the published translation: "Reflections on the *Amidah*," in *Worship of the Heart*, 144-182, at 146). This might indicate that the article was written before the 1950s, since we may reasonably assume that if R. Soloveitchik had embraced an existentialist approach then, he would have mentioned this.
20 Amaru called the first two sections "circular movement." See Amaru, "Prayer and the Beauty of God," 156.
21 See, for example, Rivka Schatz-Uffenheimer, *Hasidism as Mysticism: Quietist Elements in Eighteenth-Century Hasidic Thought*, trans. Jonathan Chipman (Princeton: Princeton

prayer as conveyed, for example, in the intents attached to the letters of the alphabet.[22] Notwithstanding the Hasidic sources from which R. Soloveitchik drew, he viewed prayer as an expression of man's actual situation and his distresses. For him, the aim of prayer is awareness and expression of these troubles. His stance is diametrically opposed to the Hasidic position, at least as the latter was formulated in the early days of the movement. Prayer, in R. Soloveitchik's understanding, is a manifestation of the self and reveals basic existential needs. Not only need man not negate himself, he is exposed to his own existence by means of prayer. Consequently, the conception of crisis prayer rejected the quietist Hasidic stance, from the outset. The latter position appears in the threatening side of the sublime divine experience (the numinous), that is, in the fear and trembling in the face of the awesome and hidden God, the halakhic expression of which will be hymnal prayer.

Prayer and Loneliness

We will now return to the prayer of crisis. In order to understand the foundations of the connection between crisis and prayer, we must examine the individualistic and nontransitive dimension of the experience of crisis. R. Soloveitchik writes:

> Out of the depths in which the individual finds himself, one calls upon God in seclusion and loneliness. The existential, passional experience is not shared by the thou, however close he is to the I, since it is an integral part of the existential awareness, which is singular, and hence inexpressible in the universal terms through which we communicate our standardized experiences. No one but the sufferer himself is involved in this deeply human anguish and conflict. [...] The prayer echoing the depth crisis of a questing soul emerges from seclusion, from out of the loneliness of the individual whom everybody save God has abandoned: "For my father and mother have abandoned me and God will take me in" (Ps. 27:10). The psalmist speaks of such suffering—the situation of the afflicted person, overwhelmed by his pain, who pours out his complaint before the Lord.[23]

Before clarifying the standing of prayer according to this passage, we should mention an additional principle formulated here: the crisis experience entails

---

University Press, 1993), 144-167; Louis Jacobs, *Hasidic Prayer* (New York: Schocken, 1973), 23-32; Ron Margolin, *Inner Temple: Religious Interiorization and the Structuring of Inner Life in Early Hasidism* [Hebrew] (Jerusalem: Magnes, 2005), 302-307.

22 See Moshe Idel, *Hasidism: Between Ecstasy and Magic* (Albany: SUNY Press, 1995), 149-170.

23 *Worship of the Heart*, 33. Such loneliness is portrayed also in *Out of the Whirlwind*, 171.

existential solitude. Such loneliness appears in R. Soloveitchik's writings with at least three meanings. The first two are mainly directed to the other, that is, the intersubjective relation, while the third refers directly to God.

(1) Structure: the characteristics of man's existence are personal, and therefore nontransitive. The depth experiences of anxiety, fear, finitude, and the like are anchored in man's existential structure. At the same time, each person experiences them in a unique fashion, so that these experiences are not transitive.[24]

(2) Values and goals: people who live in an authentic existence,[25] that is, who are aware of their deep existential frame, are also characterized by a system of values, the most striking of which is the quest for existential redemption. Being redeemed means a life with dignity, with an awareness of the existential depth structure. The loneliness linked to the authentic state is twofold:

   (a) Values of redemption and dignity are unique to such a degree that each individual experiences them in a special, nontransitive manner.

   (b) Such values are foreign to modern and postmodern society, each of which is driven by utility and control.

     Clearly, then, the social loneliness of the individual is a direct consequence of existential moral loneliness.[26]

(3) Religious experience: man experiences God as a "mystery of the numen" (R. Soloveitchik frequently uses Otto's term: numinous). Man's existence is detached as a result of the encounter with the exalting transcendental, which generates fear and anxiety. Such a situation is defined, in R. Soloveitchik's vocabulary, as "loneliness." Man feels separated and distanced from God.[27]

Returning to the passage cited above: the existential crisis bound up in petitional prayer is related to loneliness of the first sort. Prayer presumably documents the depth crisis inherent in human existence. This crisis

---

24 See above, the discussion on dialogue in Chapter Two.

25 In the existentialist literature they are also called "subjects" or are said to exist in a subjective existence. The meaning of the Heideggerian term in an existentialist context naturally differs from the phenomenological meaning that appears in section 3, below.

26 Such a type of loneliness appears in *The Lonely Man of Faith*. See Schwartz, *From Phenomenology to Existentialism*, 332-333.

27 *Worship of the Heart*, 78-80. See below, Chapter Five.

"echoes" in prayer. Intersubjective communication with another is doomed to failure; all have forsaken the worshiper. Man feels existential loneliness, and prayer is intended for the only One with whom communication exists (at least on the part of the worshiper): God.

Prayer also causes a person to become aware of his inner existence. To a great degree, prayer confronts a person with his self. Since each individual encounters a unique self, crisis, too, is experienced in singular fashion. This existential fact is a source of suffering and anguish, since this singularity does not enable comprehensible expression. Here prayer comes to the fore. Because structural-existential loneliness is not transitive in the language of communication, only prayer enables proper expression. Like the palmist mentioned in the end of the above passage, the worshiper, too, makes three discoveries about the qualities of prayer:

(1) prayer enables awareness of self (the individual finds himself in the depths);
(2) prayer makes it possible to turn to God (pouring out one's complaint before the Lord);
(3) prayer enables expression (to speak of tribulations).

In other works, R. Soloveitchik's formulation of the power of prayer is poetic. Prayer "consecrates the defeat, redeems the misery and elevates it to the level of sacrifice."[28] Prayer enables man to bear the existential crisis, which is a given "[T]he existential crisis can only be met by prayer."[29] Prayer affords a life of courage. The sufferer endures his travail in loneliness, but with dignity, by means of prayer. We learn that the petitional blessings of the *Amidah* prayer reveal the existential crisis and enable a life with dignity in its shadow. Petition is, in essence, an awareness of distress. Man contends with the crisis by the expressive ability that these blessings impart. Thus, prayer records the existential crisis and makes it possible for man to fittingly engage it.

2. Aesthetic Prayer: (1) Hymn

Chapters 3 and 4 of *Worship of the Heart* are, in fact, a single unit. The truth be told, the title of chapter 3, "The Human Condition and Prayer," is not

---

28 *Out of the Whirlwind*, 167.
29 *Reflections of the Rav*, 82.

reflective of its content, which has nothing to do with prayer. It rather discusses the problematic standing of the aesthetic, while chapter 4 considers the ways of remedying this, namely, by the redemption of the aesthetic. Prayer appears only at the end of the sweeping discussion of the aesthetic gesture. Upon reflection, however, we learn that prayer depicts the entire drama of consciousness, including the aesthetic realm. Prayer is present between the lines in R. Soloveitchik's discussion, even when not mentioned explicitly. The care taken by R. Soloveitchik in planning the structure of *Worship of the Heart* is evident, even though, in the end, he was not successful in writing as precisely as he had wished. Indeed, it is only in the middle of chapter 4 that the reader comes to realize the place of prayer in the aesthetic redemption. To begin, then, with definitions: the aesthetic gesture in comparison with other gestures, and a description of the problematic nature of this gesture; we will follow this with a discussion of the redemption of the aesthetic and its relation to prayer.

Aesthetic Theory

What are the foundations of R. Soloveitchik's aesthetic approach, in light of its possible sources? Chapter 3 of *Worship of the Heart* is mainly concerned with the presentation of the aesthetic dimension as a clearly existential and experiential characteristic. R. Soloveitchik's analysis, therefore, will address mainly the standing and worth of the aesthetic approach. He discussed aesthetics in two stages: in the first, he defined and evaluated aesthetics per se, that is, without the mending offered by the religious experience, and in the second, he was concerned with what he called the "redemption of the aesthetic." Consequently, his discussion begins with the assumption that the aesthetic is inherently negative. Aesthetics, by its very existence, is in need of mending and redemption. Presumably, the starting point of R. Soloveitchik's thought is that of conservative religious thought, which objects to the aesthetic as such. Possibly, however, R. Soloveitchik shared the distinct tendency in twentieth-century philosophy, beginning with the "Viennese Circle," to depreciate the worth of the aesthetic in science.[30] R. Soloveitchik was not noticeably influenced by the philosophy of language but indeed quite the contrary. He was affected by the rationalist tradition of Descartes and Kant that, in Hermann Cohen's analysis, had failed to free itself from observation, meaning sensory perception. Cohen wrote that, in

---

30 See, for example, Ruth Lorand, *Philosophical Reflection on Beauty* [Hebrew] (Haifa: Haifa University Press, 2007), 32-46.

the rationalist philosophical tradition, "every thought remains contingent upon intuition [*Anschauung*], in its simple meaning, although pure intuition is distinct from sensual intuition."[31] He argued that the rationalist tradition had failed to isolate the sensual element of intuition from intuition. Romanticism, by contrast, had sought to strengthen the antilogical (meaning the antiepistemic) dimension of intuition. Accordingly, the realm of aesthetics, as a product of sensory perception, is inherent in the rationalist tradition and R. Soloveitchik understood this as detrimental. In any event, his discussion of aesthetics does not distinguish between the moral and the descriptive. He presented the aesthetic as a realm that is inherently sinful, born of a curse, and narcissistic.

R. Soloveitchik identified aesthetic activity with sensory perception. For him, aesthetics is "an immediate, constant contact with reality at the qualitative, sensible level."[32] Almost all aesthetes agree that such activity originates in the senses; the painting and the sculpture are seen, one listens to a musical piece, and so on. Aesthetics is primarily concerned with what is apprehended by the senses, that is, the external dimension of the world. Many, however, included the reflective activity relating to aesthetic activity within the latter.[33] R. Soloveitchik, on the other hand, wanted to sharply delineate between the aesthetic experience and the cognitive and the moral. He maintained that reason plays no part in aesthetic activity, and he drew the following two distinctions.

(1) Between the Heraclitic and Parmenidian approaches: R. Soloveitchik connected the emotional and ontological aspects[34] in his description of the two approaches; he chose to employ pre-Socratian approaches: Heraclitus argued that the essence of being lies in change (movement), while Parmenides championed total stability and the absence of change. These approaches have a personality and behavioral aspect. The Heraclitic approach seeks constant change, volatile adventurism, and the indefatigable quest for new experiences. Parmenides, in contrast, remains steadfast to unchanging principles, moderation and consistency, and persistence.

---

31 Hermann Cohen, *Aesthetik des Reinen Gefuhls* (Berlin: Bruno Kassirer, 1922), vol. 1, 24.
32 *Worship of the Heart*, 51.
33 See, for example, Eugene F. Kaelin, *An Existentialist Aesthetic: The Theories of Sartre and Merleau-Ponty* (Madison, WI: University of Wisconsin Press, 1962), 10; Diane Collinson, "Aesthetic Experience," in *Philosophical Aesthetics: An Introduction*, ed. Oswald Hanfling (Oxford: Blackwell, 1992), 112-113.
34 *Worship of the Heart*, 39.

(2) "Cognitive and ethical experience" vs. "aesthetic experience": R. Soloveitchik spoke of three types of experience that follow from these two approaches.

(a) Epistemological experience—pertinent to the seeker of truth. As usual, R. Soloveitchik used the conventionalist view of science to describe the cognitive experience. The "cosmic drama"[35] causes the scientist to engage in mathematical ratios and arithmetical models that lack any substantial connection to the real world.

(b) Moral experience—pertinent to one who desires to impose justice. R. Soloveitchik argues that moral principles are immutable, and are not dependent upon environment or society. "The infinite moral will"[36] is expressed in a series of fixed rules. A moral stumbling block results in shame, which is a "metaphysical experience,"[37] and as such is independent of society.

(c) Aesthetic experience—pertinent to the person who desires to interact with tangible beauty (poetry, literature, and the arts) and to fulfill hedonistic sensory needs. The aesthetic experience is sensual, lacking any purpose other than the aesthetic act itself; nor is it rational. The aesthetic experience knows no doubts; the aesthete possesses overwhelming self-confidence. This experience is detached from the basic features of existence. It "does not promote the idea of self-discovery, self-realization and self-redemption."[38] An aesthetic impropriety (such as nudity) causes embarrassment, which is a "relational experience," that is, it occurs only in a social environment.[39]

---

35 *Worship of the Heart*, 41.

36 *Worship of the Heart*, 41.

37 *Worship of the Heart*, 49. I already noted the problematic usage of the term. See Schwartz, *From Phenomenology to Existentialism*, 89. Besides this, the term was commonly used by phenomenologists, together with the adjective "religious"; see Scheler, *On the Eternal*, 360.

38 *Worship of the Heart*, 50.

39 *Worship of the Heart*, 48-49; *Family Redeemed*, ed. David Schatz and Joel B. Wolowelsky (n.p.: Toras HoRav Foundation, 2000), 82. In the latter, the word " embarrassment" is analogous to "shyness," while "shame" is the existential condition of guilt and finitude. Here, too, Brunner's influence is evident. See Schwartz, *From Phenomenology to Existentialism*, 297. In the continuation of the discussion we learn that R. Soloveitchik added a fourth experience, the religious one. This experience is paradoxical, since it is defined as possessing aesthetic aspects, but characterized by cognitive and ethical traits.

The two cognitive-ethical experiences are Parmenidian in nature: abstract, purposeful, the product of reason ("pure" and practical, respectively); the aesthetic experience, in contrast, is clearly Heraclitic: tangible and lacking purpose or rationality.[40] The two cognitive-ethical experiences are, typically, constantly skeptical, and incessantly seek transcendental values. These experiences search for metaphysical goals that are beyond everyday existence. These aims are unattainable, at least fully; the closer their attainment, the more distant they appear.[41] The aesthetic experience, on the other hand, does not go beyond itself, and in this respect, it is immanent.

This description of such experiences shows the constant inner confrontation and struggle waged within man between the cognitive-ethical and the aesthetic experiences. "The aesthetic orientation, when it overcomes the ethical, is at the root of sin, with all of its distressful features."[42] This inner conflict has ethical and religious meanings: sin means preferring a pleasurable, beautiful experience to one that is cognitive and ethical, while proper and moral behavior means balancing the aesthetic and subordinating it to the cognitive and the ethical.

In this manner R. Soloveitchik interpreted Maimonides' well-known explanation of the original sin and the distinction he drew between *muskalot* ("things cognized by the intellect") and *mefursamot* ("things generally accepted as known") (*Guide of the Perplexed* 1:2). According to R. Soloveitchik, before the sin, Adam engaged only in the cognitive and ethical realms (the distinction between truth and falsehood),

---

40 On the Kantian model in this division, see Amaru, "Prayer and the Beauty of God," 164.
41 *Worship of the Heart*, 52. R. Soloveitchik illustrated this with Moses, who did not enter the Land of Israel, and concluded there: "The goal, both the cognitive and the moral, is always beyond the reach of the human being; it transcends endeavor. The impossibility of attainment is required to render an activity teleological." This argument regarding purposefulness is reminiscent of the approach of Paul Natorp, that the solution of a problem raises new problems, as in the ratio between the radius of a circle and its area. See *Halakhic Man*, 8-9.
42 *Worship of the Heart*, 37. The term "conflict" in reference to experiences appears also in the version in *Reflections of the Rav*, 86-87. There, however, the Parmenidian represents only the cognitive, that is, the ethical experience is absent in the *Reflections of the Rav* version. On the conflict between aesthetic and other norms, see, for example, Jan Mukarovsky, *Aesthetic Function, Norm and Value as Social Facts*, trans. Mark E. Suino (Ann Arbor, MI: University of Michigan, 1970), 55-57. R. Soloveitchik wrote in *Lonely Man of Faith*, 18-19, that the esthete, too, makes laws for himself, since he perceives disorder and chaos as the opposite of the aesthetic. According to this, the aesthetic law is in conflict with the ethical one.

that is, *muskalot*.[43] He sought abstract and purposeful ("Parmenidian") experiences. The sin was committed because man wished to engage in the aesthetic, the *mefursamot* (the distinction between good and evil).[44] R. Soloveitchik, therefore, understood the Maimonidean approach as follows: Adam preferred the aesthetic experience to the cognitive-ethical, and thereby committed his fateful sin. The aesthetic as experience and as a "philosophy of life on the part of man,"[45] and not necessarily as sexual desire or norms in general, is the source of sin.

Now we can clearly formulate the qualities and characteristics of the three experiences (the cognitive, the ethical, and the aesthetic), and examine the terminology used by R. Soloveitchik to elucidate them, in the following table:

	cognitive-ethical gesture	aesthetic gesture
Nature	1. abstract 2. purposeful 3. directed to the infinite and the eternal 4. transcendental 5. altruistic	1. tangible 2. not purposeful 3. directed to the finite and temporal 4. immanent 5. narcissistic
Result	1. truth 2. righteousness	1. satisfaction 2. boredom
Assessment	1. value 2. positive action	1. experience 2. sin
Impression (affect)	shame	embarrassment

43 *Worship of the Heart*, 45-48. R. Soloveitchik criticized those who distinguish between truth and falsehood based solely on the cognitive experience, and between good and evil, exclusively on the ethical experience. For him, good and evil relate only to the aesthetic experience. Significantly, Maimonides included both the moral and the aesthetic realms among the *mefursamot* (*Milot ha-Higayon, Shaar* 8), which many scholars have examined. On the discussions of this question, see the Hebrew edition: Michael Schwarz (ed.), *The Guide of the Perplexed* (Tel Aviv: Tel Aviv University Press, 2002), vol. 1, 32, 33 n. 16.

44 R. Soloveitchik defined *mefursamot* as "superficial nature" (*Worship of the Heart*, 50).

45 *Worship of the Heart*, 48. R. Soloveitchik emphasized the scholastic approach that finds concupiscence at the root of the sin, which he rejected as a possible explanation for Maimonides' approach. See, for example, Shlomo Pines, "Nachmanides on Adam in the Garden of Eden in the Context of Other Interpretations of Genesis, Chapters 2 and 3" [Hebrew], in *Exile and Diaspora: Studies in the History of the Jewish People Presented to Professor Haim Beinart*, ed. Aharon Mirsky, Avraham Grossman, and Yosef Kaplan (Jerusalem: Ben-Zvi Institute, 1988), 159-164.

We will now examine the sources of the aesthetic gesture for R. Soloveitchik. His aesthetic starting point is Kantian. He adopted the approach that scientific reason, by its very existence, acts by classifying objects into general categories, while the nature of the aesthetic experience is opposed to this. Reason strives to rise above the individual sensory event to the general rule, while aesthetics focuses on the event itself. The ethical, too, desires to rise above all the specific instances, and apply general ethical principles. The categorical imperative expresses the quest for the general rule. As was noted above, aesthetics is founded on sensory experience. The aesthetic object is perceived by sense, and not by abstraction. Kant writes: "In order to find anything good, I must always know what sort of a thing the object ought to be, i.e. I must have a concept [*Begriff*] of it. But there is no need of this to find a thing beautiful."[46] In contrast with the classical and neoclassical theories that identified the beautiful with the good, or at least saw a connection between them, R. Soloveitchik rigorously distinguished between them and argued for the autonomy of the aesthetic. In this, he was close to Oscar Wilde and Nietzsche.[47]

The claim that aesthetic acts lack purposefulness is also Kantian. R. Soloveitchik wrote that the aesthetic "does not search for a good which is transcendent to the aesthetic occupation itself."[48] Kant distinguished between outer purpose, which denotes the utility,[49] in moral and concrete terms, of the beautiful, and inner purpose, which is concerned with aesthetic activity itself. Kant called this inner teleology "purposiveness without purpose" or "formal purposiveness." He denied the aesthetic object any objective purposefulness, and wrote that "the satisfaction in an object, on account of which we call it beautiful, cannot rest on the representation of its utility."

We should beware of the temptation to find the basis for R. Soloveitchik's distinctions in Kierkegaard. The distinction between the aesthetic and the ethical already appears in Kierkegaard's early work *Either-Or*. Kierkegaard divided this composition into two parts, with the first presumably written

---

46 Immanuel Kant, *Critique of Judgment*, trans. J. H. Bernard (New York: Hafner, 1972), 41. The critics of the Kantian conception argued, for instance, that general terms are present in an analysis of aesthetic creations, as well. On the topic of "concept" and purposefulness in this work, see the first two chapters of Aaron Kolender, *Transcendental Beauty* [Hebrew] (Jerusalem: Bialik Institute, 2001), 25-54.

47 See Friedrich Kainz, *Aesthetics the Science*, trans. Herbert M. Schueller (Detroit: Wayne State University, 1962), 87.

48 *Worship of the Heart*, 42.

49 Kant, *Critique of Judgment*, 62.

by an aesthete, and the second, by an ethicist. The former becomes addicted to his pleasures, while the ethicist seeks a life of responsibility and seriousness. The aesthete chooses indecision, while the ethicist draws conclusions. The aesthete is divorced from concrete life, and his existence is momentary and fragmented, while the ethicist chooses concrete life.[50] For Kierkegaard, the choice between the two types reveals the responsibility and anxiety characteristic of concrete existence. In *Either-Or* he drew a sharp distinction between the aesthetic and the ethical. In other works he added a third dimension, the religious. The cognitive intellectual personality of the scientist and the philosopher is not an independent type for Kierkegaard. The scientific personality in the thought of R. Soloveitchik, in the sense of building abstract models, is for Kierkegaard synonimous with the aesthetic personality. Kierkegaard characterized Hegel's synthesis of history as aesthetic. Hegelian philosophy is patently abstract, and the ethical is opposed to abstraction.[51] Kierkegaard argued that it is the ethical, specifically, that addresses concrete existence, while the aesthetic disregards the concrete subject that knows. The Hegelian unification of opposites is, therefore, abstract, while for Kierkegaard this is the activity of the aesthete. While Kierkegaard identified the abstract with the aesthetic, R. Soloveitchik contrasted the two approaches. The cognitive-ethical propensity is occupied with abstractions and universal rules, while the aesthete holds fast to the concrete reality. Thus, even if R. Soloveitchik was influenced, formally, by the division between the aesthetic and the ethical, contentually, his approach was completely different, and was firmly grounded in Kantian and theological thought, as we shall see below.

R. Soloveitchik directly adopted the characterization of the aesthetic of Emil Brunner, an important thinker of the "theology of crisis" school. R. Soloveitchik's discussion is grounded, in both content and terminology, in Brunner's book *The Divine Imperative*. Brunner presented the aesthetic as lacking purpose. When reason turns to the aesthetic, Brunner argued, it no longer is a means to attain an external end; now, man himself becomes the aim. Reason derives pleasure from self-focus. He added that subjective existence focuses on man himself, who creates beauty.[52] Brunner connected Kantian thought with the theological sphere. Following Brunner,

---

50 See Abraham Sagi, *Kierkegaard, Religion and Existence: The Voyage of the Self*, trans. Batya Stein (Amsterdam: Rodopi, 2000), 75-76.

51 See, for example, Robert Cumming, "Existence and Communication," *Ethics* 65 (1955): 83.

52 Emil Brunner, *The Divine Imperative: A Study in Christian Ethics,* translated by Olive Wyon (Cambridge: Lutterworth Press, 2002), 24-25.

R. Soloveitchik rejected the purposefulness of the aesthetic gesture, which he presented as fixated on itself.

Now, for a new difference between the various approaches-gestures that, too, follows from Brunner's analysis. While R. Soloveitchik presented the cognitive-ethical by means of a disciplinary description of relational realms, he set forth the aesthetic in plainly typological fashion, namely, presenting the aesthetic type.[53] Just as he called the religious individual *homo religiosus*, he referred to the aesthete as *homo aesthesis*.[54] He characterized the latter as follows:

> The aesthete, however, when he indulges in self-reflection and self-gazing, does not make the effort of objectification and self-projection into an outside world of thinghood, but rather reflects more and more into himself. He refuses to estrange himself from the very self with whom he was united. Therefore, when the aesthete, the artist, speaks of himself he does so in terms of pure subjectivity. He does not try to recognize himself in an objective manner, but intoxicates himself with self-admiration and adoration, gazing into himself with the candor and detachment of the scholar examining a strange object, since his self has been, in the expression coined by one theologian, expanded to "a world self."[55] Nothing else exists; there is one world, which reflects himself.[56]

The scientific and ethical types devote intellectual effort to understanding themselves. Self-understanding is an act of alienation, because in order to comprehend oneself, a person must relate to himself as an object, that is, to be estranged from himself. The subject goes out from himself, as it were, and contemplates himself as an object. This act of alienation is a necessary concession by the scientific-ethical type in order to properly assess himself.[57] By contrast, the aesthetic type is self-centered and unwilling to pay the price of objectification. He has no need for alienation,

---

53 Cognitive and ethical gestures or approaches are contrasted with the aesthetic type in *Worship of the Heart*, 42-45, 51-52.
54 *Worship of the Heart*, 64-65.
55 Referring to Emil Brunner (see below).
56 *Worship of the Heart*, 44.
57 *Worship of the Heart*, 58. R. Soloveitchik is not unequivocal in his assessment of alienation. On the one hand, he regards objectivization as a negative process, in which a person loses his individuality; while, on the other, he presents this process as necessary for the ethical-cognitive type, without which this type loses the possibility of sober self-evaluation and knowledge of one's self. As regards the perception of rationality and abstraction as alienation, R. Soloveitchik echoes Kierkegaard.

since he is totally absorbed in his self-admiration. Brunner mentions two varieties of cultural existence that are connected with culture: one tends to the objective and is interested in the artistic process; while the other is inclined to the subjective and focuses on man, on the creative genius. The objective type takes an interest in humankind and its values. The subjective type, representative of the pure aesthetic type, is concerned solely with himself. His self expands to a "world-self."[58] Put differently, his self is everything. R. Soloveitchik characterized only the second aesthetic type, and contrasted the ethical-cognitive type with the subjective aesthetic one. Similarly, the characterization of sin as self-love frequently appears in the theological literature.[59]

R. Soloveitchik chose to present the aesthete as a type, with the idea undergoing a process of personification. The cognitive and the ethical, however, are presented only as ideas. Patently, then, in both stylistic and methodological terms, he does not place the aesthetic on the same plane as the cognitive and the ethical. The typological methodology in *Worship of the Heart* draws the aesthetic closer to the tangible dimension of life, to concrete sensual activity, and distances it from the abstract concept. The aesthetic replaces the spiritual experience with the material, and the idea with sensory activity. Additionally, the focus upon the self, too, is understandable: the human genius that concentrates on itself is the object of the discussion, and the use of the type further emphasizes the narcissistic aspect of the aesthetic approach. Clearly, then, typology is the best method for depicting the aesthetic.

Boredom

R. Soloveitchik opened the presentation of his aesthetic theory with a discussion of boredom, which results from a Heraclitic personality, whose activity is based on constant change. Boredom has its roots in the absence of purposefulness and meaning, and therefore belongs to the realm of the aesthetic. R. Soloveitchik contrasted the bored type with the lonesome one, whom he mentioned above in his discussion of crisis. The bored individual is unaware of the future, as a goal and purpose, while the lonely one loses contact with the past, in terms of causality. The lonely person

---

58 Brunner, *Divine Imperative*, 25.
59 See, for example, Reinhold Niebuhr, *The Nature and Destiny of Man: A Christian Interpretation* (Louisville, KY: Westminster John Knox, 1996), 228-240.

leads a detached existence.[60] R. Soloveitchik vividly portrayed the lack of satisfaction in the bored individual's everyday routine, and his adventurousness and quest for experience. He likewise mentioned the fall and melancholy when the adventurer and conqueror realizes his lack of success in overcoming the routine.[61] R. Soloveitchik further argued that boredom came into existence following the original sin, He then writes:

> The awareness of a stable, persistent Parmenidean existence is supplanted
> by a daemonic, manic craving for vanities and unreal boundlessness. In this
> imagination, fixed persistent forms and desires disappear into a hyletic mass
> of experience. [...] Fantasy surrounds the experience of man with the halo
> of change, and man rides upon the crest of a tide that rolls on and on until it
> breaks down at the immovable shore.[62]

We may surmise that boredom is the basest expression of the demonic personality. This very term—the demonic personality— was fashioned in the wake of Brunner's terminology, as R. Soloveitchik states outright in *Out of the Whirlwind*.[63] The discussion in *Worship of the Heart*, likewise, is fashioned around Brunner's terminology. Brunner, for instance, mentions that the demonic element seeks "boundless fantasy" and "infinity."[64] Moreover, in *Out of the Whirlwind* R. Soloveitchik characterized Ecclesiastes as a demonic type in his adventuresomeness, search for the aesthetic experience, and propensity for self-love. Ecclesiastes' character clarifies an additional dimension in the struggle against boredom: conquest. The demonic personality wants to use its achievements to conquer the realms of science, finance, and so on.[65] Ecclesiastes is mentioned in *Worship of the Heart*, as well, albeit briefly, but its connection to the aesthetic is evident:

> Boredom is the wages of sin, of an existence overcome by aesthetic enthu-
> siasm or trance. The heroic-adventurous attempt to adore existence as
> something delightful and great, and to surrender completely to beauty, is
> followed by the hollow feeling of bankruptcy and discouragement, a feeling
> that borders on morbidity. This state of affairs was brilliantly dramatized in

---

60 *Worship of the Heart*, 78-79.
61 *Worship of the Heart*, 38; Brunner, *Divine Imperative*, 26-27.
62 *Worship of the Heart*, 40. For a phenomenological analysis of boredom, see, for example, Lars Svendsen, *A Philosophy of Boredom*, trans. John Irons (London: Reaktion Books, 2005).
63 *Out of the Whirlwind*, 154-155.
64 Brunner, *Divine Imperative*, 24.
65 *Out of the Whirlwind*, 154-155. Elsewhere R. Soloveitchik observed that Kohelet attempts to escape "from this existential emptiness" ("Prayer as Dialogue," in *Reflections of the Rav*, 86).

> Koheleth: "All is vanity" (Ecclesiastes 1:2). Boredom does not characterize the ethical experience but the aesthetic. This is what Adam and Eve found out after they ate from the Tree of Knowledge: "they opened their eyes and knew that they were naked" (Gen. 3:7), that their nude and senseless lives were full of absurdity and worthless.[66]

R. Soloveitchik linked boredom with the aesthetic personality. Boredom accompanies the blossoming of the aesthetic type, who struggles against boredom his entire life. The intellectual and the ethical man are not bored. For Kierkegaard, the aesthetic type is a hedonist, who seeks his experiences in art, music, and erotica, on the one hand, while on the other, the philosophical type does not make the decision to choose concrete life. Kierkegaard also spoke of the aesthetic type's constant conflict with boredom.[67] R. Soloveitchik, too, wrote that boredom "is thus an aesthetic phenomenon. The aesthetic man is resentful of identity and uniformity."[68] Once again, we are confronted by the fact that Kierkegaard's discussion might be in the general background of R. Soloveitchik's interest in the significance of boredom, but as we have already seen, it was Brunner's terminology that fashioned the dynamics of its description. The beginning of the above passage teaches that R. Soloveitchik was no less interested in the theological aspect than in the existential and typological meaning of boredom. Put succinctly, boredom is a result of sin.

An additional comment on R. Soloveitchik's sources is necessary here. He mentioned in the beginning of the third chapter of *Worship of the Heart* that the experiences with which the chapter is concerned, including boredom, are an expression of distress and deep crisis.[69] It is noteworthy that the influential philosopher Arthur Schopenhauer connected the crisis of human finitude with boredom. Finitude and boredom are elements of a deep crisis, and Schopenhauer indeed presented them as such. He discussed the meaning of death at length in his writings. Schopenhauer argued that

---

66 *Worship of the Heart*, 49.
67 See, for example, Shmuel Hugo Bergman, *Dialogical Philosophy: From Kierkegaard to Buber*, trans. Arnold A. Gerstain (Albany: SUNY Press, 1991), 53-55. Kierkegaard's conceptual starting point completely differed from that of R. Soloveitchik. Kierkegaard viewed boredom as a necessary consequence of anthropocentric Romantic subjectivity. He then connected boredom with pantheism, in the sense that the presence former's inherent emptiness is symmetric to pantheistic fullness. See, for example, Soren Kierkegaard, *Either/Or: A Fragment of Life*, vol. 1, trans. David F. Swenson and Lillian Marvin Swenson (Princeton: Princeton University Press, 1949), 239.
68 *Worship of the Heart*, 45.
69 *Worship of the Heart*, 37, 78-79.

man, as a finite and limited creature, is cast into infinite space and time. Man lives only in the present, and, to a certain extent, his life is a process of dying. Physical life is a (temporary) impediment to death, and intellectual activity is an incessant struggle against boredom.[70] Additionally, the essence of man, and in this sense of the animal, as well, is volition. When the object of desire is not attained, this results in pain; and when such an object does not exist, because man has attained his goals, then the result is emptiness and boredom. Life "swings like a pendulum to and from between pain and boredom."[71] Boredom appears when existence itself is assured, and it is then that man seeks to escape his ennui. Man seeks constant change in order to be rid of and repress the burden of existence ("to kill time").[72] R. Soloveitchik tended toward such a line of thought, and wrote that the aesthetic type "would like to liberate himself from all the restrictions of a Parmenidean existence."[73]

Schopenhauer anchored boredom in existence and, in his pessimistic manner, presented it in terms of crisis. In a certain sense, this is a modern version of the approach of Blaise Pascal, who cast boredom as "distress" and as a feeling of insignificance and emptiness.[74] Conceptually, Schopenhauer's systematic approach is the closest to the range of meanings that R. Soloveitchik imparted to boredom. R. Soloveitchik, however, chose not to use Schopenhauer's terminology. He rather relied mainly, and declaratively, on the terminology and ideas of theologians such as Brunner, whom he apparently thought to be aware of the existential problems of the religious man in the modern world. The unyielding and nonrational dogmatic image of the "theologians of crisis" did not deter R. Soloveitchik. To the contrary: belief in the absolute authority of revelation and the word of God suited his philosophical and Orthodox interests. Barth's approach, stating that the discourse on God is dialectic,

---

70 Arnold Schopenhauer, *The World as Will and Representation*, trans. E. F. J. Payne (New York: Dover, 1969), vol. 1, 311.

71 Schopenhauer, *World as Will*, 312. Schopenhauer wrote in his *Aphorismen zur Lebensweisheit* [*Wisdom of Life*] that refraining from desires leads to boredom, and that addiction to them causes pain and tribulations. Only a life of contemplation enables one to overcome this oscillation. See Arnold Schopenhauer, *Wisdom of Life*, in *Complete Essays of Schopenhauer*, trans. T. Bailey Saunders (New York: Willey, 1942), 35-36.

72 Schopenhauer, *World as Will*, 313.

73 *Worship of the Heart*, 39.

74 See, for example, Blaise Pascal, *Pensees* 2:131, accessed August 17, 2018, www.ccel. org/ccel/pascal/pensees.pdf (in English translation, Blaise Pascal, *Thoughts and Minor Works*, trans. W. F. Trotter [New York: Collier, 1910], 51.

since human language is limited and restricted, profoundly influenced R. Soloveitchik. The fluctuating between the merciful and the detached God characterizes R. Soloveitchik's thought. Moreover, he had no qualms about indicating Brunner's thought as a source of his ideas. The theological discourse in the United States in the 1960s included the worldviews expressed by thinkers such as Karl Barth, Emil Brunner, Paul Tillich, and Reinhold Niebuhr, and R. Soloveitchik wanted to awaken a similar discourse in the Jewish world. To this end, he added the notion of the original sin as the source of boredom.

The Complex Personality

After defining the characteristics of cognitive-ethical and aesthetic gestures, R. Soloveitchik turned to their interpretive consequences. We saw that the significance of the original sin lies in the aesthetic approach's surmounting of the cognitive-ethical worldview. R. Soloveitchik's interpretation of the consequence of the original sin has man oscillating between the different gestures. He writes:

> Until the fall, man was a cognitive-ethical being: his aesthetic cravings were apparently subordinated to these basic drives in him. Upon eating from the Tree of Knowledge, man chose the aesthetic way of life and departed from that of abstract thought and unqualified imperative. The magnitude of the loss was tremendous, since he forfeited the ability of thinking in purely abstract terms, and became, even in his cognitive processes, a slave to sensibility.[75]

The end of the passage shows R. Soloveitchik's seemingly Kantian interpretation of the original sin. Before man's fall, he possessed pure thought. Presumably, things-in-themselves, that is to say, beings that exist beyond cognition, can be conceived.[76] Man was capable of perception without the participation of the senses and feelings. The aesthetic faculty and its instruments (the senses) had no place in the thought process. Seemingly, the ideal cognitive-creative process, the possibility and existence of which Hermann Cohen strived so mightily to prove, was realized in the Garden of Eden.

---

75 *Worship of the Heart*, 49.
76 R. Soloveitchik used the terms "abstract" and "pure" to denote the cognitive state that preceded man's fall. Many contemporary Kant researchers maintain that the thing-in-itself defines the boundaries of cognition, and not objects. Numerous theologians, however, attribute a concrete ontic dimension to the thing-in-itself. That is, the objects of cognition exist in space and time; however, the thing-in-itself exists beyond the forms of sensibility.

After the sin, however, it is impossible to know the thing-in-itself, but only its phenomena. The only possible cognition is by means of the forms of intuition (space and time), that are representations of sensibility.

Between the lines, we gather that R. Soloveitchik had despaired of Cohen's idealistic cognitive model, which presumed to allow for thought completely divorced from the senses. This thought was to be creative, in that it creates its objects and does not receive them from the outside. Cohen maintained that it was possible to reduce quantity to the infinitesimal in order to attain pure quality, according to the Kantian principle of anticipation of perception, that is, the inner size of the perception. Cohen argued that cognition creates its objects within itself, namely, from the pure quality. R. Soloveitchik studied this approach in his youth, and based the halakhic man's cognition on it.[77] Now, in *Worship of the Heart*, he presented the great punishment for the original sin as negating the possibility of pure understanding. Sensibility penetrates the cognition to the extent that consciousness without sensory perception is impossible.

The distinction between the pre-fall state and that reigning after it can be condensed in the following statements, anchored within each other:

(1) before the original sin, the cognitive and ethical sphere was balanced with the aesthetic, while this balance was undermined after the fall;

(2) before the original sin, the aesthetic realm was totally dominated by the cognitive and ethical, while it became dominant following the sin;

(3) before the fall, pure thought was possible without aesthetic-sensory frameworks, while such a possibility completely ceased afterwards.

We understand from this that the various gestures that accompany human existence are poles between which man oscillates. Before the original sin, the choice was clear: cognitive-ethical, on the one side, and the aesthetic, on the other. The former was dominant, and the latter was subservient to it. After the sin, the aesthetic infiltrated the cognitive, as well, thus complicating human existence. Now, the boundaries of the realms and gestures would no longer be distinct and unequivocal, and single-dimensional life became to a great extent dialectical. The chaotic dimension generally characteristic of kabbalistic explanations joined this complexity. Before

---

77 See Schwartz, *Religion or Halakha*. In that period, as well, R. Soloveitchik was aware of the problem of sense perception, which Cohen tried to dismiss, but without total success.

the fall, the human structure had been ordered according to a hierarchy of values; after it, chaos emerged and the aesthetic mingled with the cognitive, upsetting the entire natural order. The future of the aesthetic will thus be restorative, reinstating the balanced and pure pre-fall state.

The Redemption of the Aesthetic

After R. Soloveitchik defined the aesthetic and presented it as the source of sin and emptiness, he argued unequivocally: the value of the aesthetic relates to the aesthetic gesture per se, divorced from Judaism and from the singular religious consciousness that it brought forth. When, however, this gesture is cast in the light of Judaism, its value will likely change. "Judaism attempted a revolutionary undertaking: to ethicize the aesthetic experience, to raise it to a teleological level."[78] This seems paradoxical: if the aesthetic gesture is inherently purposeless, and is directed solely to itself, how can it be given purpose? R. Soloveitchik answers this as follows:

> If the aesthetic experience is to be cleansed and redeemed, it must express the transcendental yearning in man. Hence, it must always be encountered as a reflection of Divine beauty. It must direct the human eye toward the remote, infinite and exalted, suggest to the human being a nobler and sacred world, another order of existence. There is an eternal vision that beckons to the aesthete, which fascinates and pulls him towards unknown distances and uncharted lands. There is an ideal in the world of beauty as there is in the realm of ethics, an ideal that will never be completely attained. At this point we arrive at religious experience.[79]

In other words, R. Soloveitchik argued that the aesthetic itself lacks purpose, while the divinely aesthetic is purposeful. Transferring the aesthetic to the divine realm redeems it. The religious experience, in which man experiences God, enables one to come to know teleological beauty. R. Soloveitchik raises the possibility of purposeful aesthetic experience based on a few underlying assumptions:

(1) divine beauty: aesthetic existence in the divine world is dialectical: the purposeless becomes the purposeful;

---

78 *Worship of the Heart*, 50.
79 *Worship of the Heart*, 52-53.

(2) *imitatio Dei*: human beauty can imitate the divine beauty;[80]
(3) experience: the religious experience enables the acquisition of the divine aesthetic consciousness.

Thus, R. Soloveitchik believed that the religious consciousness was capable of elevating the aesthetic, which in itself constitutes conquest, unbridled and brutal existence, one of "savagery,"[81] of self-focus to the point of narcissism. The religious consciousness forces the aesthete to confront abstract questions, despite his ingrained opposition to abstract thought. R. Soloveitchik writes:

> [...] the aesthete will have to contend with the problem of the ultimate worth of his experience. He will be compelled to wonder about the nature of beauty. In order to safeguard the unique character of his experience, he will be induced to seek the origin and the meaning of the beautiful He will finally have to find the link between the sensuous experience and a supra-sensory world. In other words: there will arise in his mind an aesthetic skepticism in the manner of epistemological and ethical skepticism.[82]

The religious consciousness forces the aesthete to doubt the aesthetic path. The aesthete is exposed to a reflective experience; from a certain aspect, he confronts himself. A skeptical aesthetical type is an oxymoron. Dialectical religious existence, however, is capable of creating such a tension-laden type, and to compel the skeptic to face his self.

Such an approach, presuming to refine the aesthete, has a stylistic aspect as well. We explained that typology is the best way of explaining the aesthetic approach according to R. Soloveitchik. The aesthete's divorce from abstraction makes him a living, active creature, and therefore his description as a type allows us to understand the aesthetic experience. But now, the refinement of the aesthetic leads R. Soloveitchik in the opposite direction: now the aesthetic is depicted as an experience and realm. Not only is the aesthetic type close to the religious one, "[t]he aesthetic experience has an affinity with the religious emotion."[83] R. Soloveitchik assumed

---

80 "The aesthetic is raised to a world of eternal beauty in God [...] God is extolled and adored because He is beautiful" (*Worship of the Heart*, 65). See Shalom Rosenberg, "And Walk in His Ways," in *Israeli Philosophy* [Hebrew], edited by Moshe Hallamish and Asa Kasher (Tel Aviv: Papyrus, 1983), 72-91.
81 *Worship of the Heart*, 53.
82 *Worship of the Heart*, 54.
83 *Worship of the Heart*, 54.

the presence of an aesthetic dimension in the religious experience, just as there a religious dimension to art. That is, he did not doubt for a moment the intermingling of the two realms.

The Exalted: (1) The Process

I mentioned before that the consciousness of God and its reflections facilitate a refined perception of the aesthetic. Elevating beauty to an expression of the divine enables us to cast the aesthetic in a new light. But we must ask: just what turns the aesthetic experience into a religious-aesthetic one? What is the link in the chain that transforms the features of the aesthetic, which it redefines by the process of refinement? R. Soloveitchik mentioned two such connections: the conception of exaltation and the experience of the heroic.[84]

Exaltedness is an attribute of God, to be more precise, it is an emotional way for man's consciousness to experience God as exalted and sublime. Exaltedness is a means of consciousness to depict God, because it expresses the infinite and absolute perfection that transcends man's capabilities. Exaltedness presumably voids the personality of the person who stands in its presence, rendering it worthless and detached. The regular aesthetic experience facilitates a sense of "worth and self-respect." The aesthetic experience of the divine, however, is completely different. As R. Soloveitchik writes:

> Exaltedness, by way of contrast, suggests to man the vision of something unique and great that is connected to witnessing the beautiful. It is basically a religious emotion. Exalted[85] is God and exaltedness has the connotation of transcendence, being superior to, and elevated beyond and outside the human reach. In a word, it denotes infinity [...] Truly, only God is exalted since only He is outside finite existence.[86]

Friedrich Kainz situated the exalted and the elevated among the "aesthetically basic forms," that is, modifications of the aesthetic objects. Other such forms

---

84 Kaplan, "Review Essay," 108, correctly observes that the heroic is not mentioned in the continuation of the chapter. R. Soloveitchik might have referred to the struggle in the absence of God, that is discussed in chapter 5; see also Kaplan, 109.

85 Afterwards R. Soloveitchik cited the verse "on an exalted and high throne" (Isaiah 6:1) as proving the exaltedness of God.

86 *Worship of the Heart*, 55.

are the graceful, the tragic, and the comic.[87] Affinity to the experiential religious perception of the exalted could be found in the early thought of Edmund Burke, who viewed the exalted as an aesthetic quality that challenges beauty as the sole or most important aesthetic property. While beauty is related to the feeling of pleasure, exaltedness causes dismay and tension.[88] Rudolf Otto defined the numinous, as well, in distinctly aesthetic terms. In this manner, aesthetic conceptions such as Burke's entered the religious world. Otto argued that "[i]n the arts nearly everywhere the most effective means of representing the numinous is 'the sublime.'"[89] R. Soloveitchik, on his part, frequently used Otto's terminology ("the numinous") for exalted-ness. We stated above that, for R. Soloveitchik, the consciousness of God includes a clearly aesthetic element. God is the absolute Other, who is exalted and elevated above the reality. R. Soloveitchik maintained that this exaltedness, too, contains a decidedly aesthetic dimension. Unlike Burke, however, R. Soloveitchik's religious aesthetic conception did not distinguish between the sublime and the beautiful. For him, each reflects the aesthetic component of the divine. That is, standing opposite the Other—who is also the absolute elevated and beautiful—causes the one experiencing this to doubt the fullness of his aesthetic urge. Absolute beauty leads to doubting the relatively beautiful. Conversely, questioning relative beauty leads to standing before absolute beauty. The aesthete becomes aware of critical and reflective thought.

> What is required is the awakening of the skeptic, the rise of a critique of the aesthetic judgment and beauty-appreciation. Through the emergence of doubt—the thought that everything experienced as beautiful is perhaps not beautiful at all—the catharsis of beauty is made possible.[90]

Aesthetic redemption is the last of the four stages in the following process.

(1) Starting point: the aesthetic experience is characterized by self-focus. The aesthete is engrossed with himself.
(2) Becoming aware of the religious experience: standing opposite the divine neutralizes self-focus in two stages.

---

87 Kainz, *Aesthetics the Science*, 503.
88 Edmund Burke, *A Philosophical Enquiry into the Origin of Our Ideas of the Sublime and the Beautiful* (Oxford: Oxford University Press, 1990).
89 Otto, *The Idea of the Holy*, 65.
90 *Worship of the Heart*, 56.

(a) It causes skepticism ("whether everything which is apprehended as beauty and as pleasant expresses indeed genuine
beauty").[91]

(b) It causes the one undergoing such an experience to lose his
self-respect.[92]

(3) Coming to know the aesthetic component of the consciousness
of God: He is the absolute aesthetic ("the origin of beauty, of the
delightful and the pleasant").[93] Therefore, standing before Him
exposes this individual to a new aesthetics.

(4) The redemption of the aesthetic: now the aesthetic experience
undergoes a transformation, and characteristically is directed outward, that is, to God. The one undergoing the experience imitates
the aesthetic dimension of the divine.

Thus, R. Soloveitchik added a fourth experience, the religious, to the
three other experiences: the cognitive, the ethical, and the aesthetic. The
religious experience knowingly embraces the aesthetic, but paradoxically
defines it in terms that typically belong to the cognitive and ethical realms.
The religious experience—to be precise, its aesthetic dimension—redeems
the aesthetic dimension. It does so by substituting the heavenly experience
for the earthly. The aesthetic experience becomes transcendental, turning
to what is beyond the transient and fleeting. This experience is directed to
the heavens, and in another place R. Soloveitchik called this "relating the
aesthetic to the numinous."[94] Additionally, the religious aesthetic experience is two-directional: earthly beauty is connected with the divine, and the
divine beauty, on its part, is present within the worldly, which it motivates
and redefines: "the feeling of the sublime and the lofty (exalted) is an inner
motif of aesthetic experience."[95]

Clearly, then, R. Soloveitchik preserved the paradoxical and dialectical
characteristics of the religious experience, but used aesthetics to express
them. The religious experience is tense, and the impression it makes on
the experiencer entails anxiety and self-effacement, on the one hand, and
spiritual elevation, on the other. The aesthetic is the source of both terror

---

91 *Worship of the Heart*, 56.
92 *Worship of the Heart*, 55.
93 *Worship of the Heart*, 57.
94 *Worship of the Heart*, 97.
95 *Worship of the Heart*, 56.

and excitement. Such a religious experience effects a balance in man's inner struggle between the cognitive-ethical and aesthetic experiences.

The Exalted: (2) Characteristics

Now for an examination of the characteristics of the religious aesthetic experience, to which prayer is central. This experience is characterized, first and foremost, by glory and majesty. In contrast with the crisis existence and existential loneliness of the aesthetic experience, it offers an existence of fullness and conquest. R. Soloveitchik writes:

> This direct revelation of the Creator has always been explained by Judaism as a result of *kevod Elokim* (*majestas Dei*, the glory of God). Isaiah says "His glory fills the whole universe" (Isaiah 6:3). Glory of God expresses the aspect of revelation to sensuous man: "The glory of God filled the tabernacle" (Ex. 40:34). "Blessed is the name of the *kavod* of His majesty forever and ever," as we recite immediately after the first verse of *Shema* (based on Ps. 72:19). While Judaism alludes to the cosmic-dynamic role of God as creator and originator of the universe, the addition of *kavod* stresses the majesty element, a pure aesthetic phenomenon which fascinates and frightens man. *Majestas Dei* conveys the thought that absolute beauty rests in God, and that only He is the fountainhead out of which pulchritude, grace and loveliness flow into the world [...] "You are enthroned in *hod* and *hadar*, splendor and majesty" (Ps. 104:1). The God experience can also be immersed in aesthetic enthusiasm when man faces the grandeur.[96]

This teaches that the religious aesthetic experience means standing before absolute beauty. One feels as if standing before royalty, in all its power and might. The aesthetic experience enables direct contact with God ("the God experience"). How, then, does the aesthetic experience have man meet his God? The traits of the aesthetic experience provide the explanation.

(1) The experience of opposites: the first response to standing before grandeur is fear and trembling, to the extent of losing one's self-worth or engaging in self-abrogation.[97] R. Soloveitchik defined this as fear. Since, however, this is an aesthetic experience, he also

---

96 *Worship of the Heart*, 59-60.
97 This is how Otto described the element of "overpowering" (*majestas*) of the numinous. See Otto, *Idea of the Holy*, 19-23.

added fascination and enthusiasm: "Man is fascinated by infinity."[98] Standing before splendor and beauty is also an expression of self-affirmation. We have seen that the worldly aesthetic experience is totally self-focused. A remnant of this narcissism has also penetrated the religious aesthetic experience, which is the refined expression of the earthly aesthetic experience. The aesthetic personality is absolutely fascinated by the beauty of the universe and its Sovereign.

(2)   The experience of imitation: the individual undergoing a religious aesthetic experience exerts himself to imitate the absolute divine beauty. Such an experience necessitates man to assume a confident stance. The aesthetic experience of the majestic individual means resembling the divine majesty and splendor. Accordingly, such an experience borders on the conquest of the reality, together with its concurrent fear and fascination. There is an element of self-affirmation in resembling God, especially as regards the aspect of majesty and splendor.

(3)   The experience of love and communion: the religious aesthetic experience contains a dimension of endless love, which borders on madness and ecstasy. Standing before God does not only kindle fear and fascination, it also arouses longing and love. The aesthetic dimension is reflected in love and in the aspiration for total intercourse (in the non-physical sense), not only in appreciation of absolute beauty. R. Soloveitchik observed that Judaism used many modes of expression to denote man's love of God, including that of erotic love.[99] For him, earthly love and heavenly love are not homonyms. Erotic worldly love is an actual "model" for love of God.[100]

(4)   Sensuous experience: the aesthetic experience is patently sensuous. It is here that R. Soloveitchik clarified the place of the aesthetic experience, as the missing link necessary for communion. Cognitive and ethical perfection elevates man to a sublime level, but is not capable of effecting communion with God. This is

---

98 *Worship of the Heart*, 60.

99 *Worship of the Heart*, 61.

100 An extreme expression of this is to be found in the literature of medieval German pietists. See, for example, Gershom Scholem, *Major Trends in Jewish Mysticism* (New York: Schocken, 1961), 95-96.

because communion is made possible only by means of the senses (the realization of love and longing). There are two reasons for this:
(a) both psychologically and physiologically, great desire and love originate in sensuality;
(b) for the communion to be complete, dismissing the senses would be inconceivable.

Consequently, without the participation of the senses, an abyss opens between the perfect man and God. The aesthetic experience, that joins the cognitive and ethical experiences, creates the basis for the actualization of love of God, that is, communion. "This ecstatic love is born not out of a philosophical abstraction or ethical excellence but out of aesthetic beholding and apprehension."[101] Only the senses are capable of intoxicating man to such an extent; neither logos nor ethos can do so. The aesthetic experience bridges the gap between the cognitive and the ethical and communion.

---

101 *Worship of the Heart*, 73. In this manner R. Soloveitchik resolved a contradiction in what Maimonides wrote in *Hilchot Yesodei ha-Torah* [Laws of the Fundamentals of the Torah] 2:2: "And what is the way that will lead to the love of Him and the fear of Him? When a person contemplates His great and wondrous works and creatures and from them obtains a glimpse of His wisdom which is incomparable and infinite, he will straightway love Him, praise Him, glorify Him, and long with an exceeding longing to know His great Name; even as David said 'My soul thirsteth for God, for the living God' (Ps. 42:3). And when he ponders these matters, he will recoil affrighted, and realize that he is a small creature, lowly and obscure, endowed with slight and slender intelligence, standing in the presence of Him who is perfect in knowledge. And as David said 'When I consider Thy heavens, the work of Thy fin gers... what is man that Thou art mindful of him?' (Ps. 8:4-5). In harmony with these sentiments, I shall explain some large, general aspects of the Works of the Sovereign of the Universe, that they may serve the intelligent individual as a door to the love of God, even as our sages have remarked in connection with the theme of the love of God, 'Observe the Universe and hence, you will realize Him who spake and the world was' [*Sifrei* on Deuteronomy, *Va'ethanan* 33:6; *Ekev* 49:22, and more]" (*Mishneh Torah: The Book of Knowledge by Maimonides*, trans. Moses Hyamson [Jerusalem: Boys' Town Jerusalem, 1962], 35b). R. Soloveitchik, apparently, indicated two contradictions. First, he found an inner contradiction within halakhah 2: on the one hand, Maimonides defined love as the result of contemplation and knowledge of nature, while, on the other, love results from an emotional and sensory experience (desire and thirst). Secondly, a contradiction is discovered between two *halakhahot* in *Hilchot Yesodei ha-Torah* and *Hilchot Teshuvah* [Laws of Repentance] 10:3. Each of the two *halakhot* define love of God. In the former, however, love is a result of cognition, and contemplative activity has substantive place in the love of God. The latter, in contrast, states that love is only the product of emotions and senses. Both contradictions have a single resolution, namely, cognition provides the basis and the disposition for love of God, which can be realized only in the aesthetic realm.

Thus, the aesthetic experience enables the realization of human perfection. The sensuous characteristic of the aesthetic experience connects it at last to prayer, as we shall see below.

It would be hard to overstate the importance of the fourth characteristic, namely, the sensuous basis of the aesthetic experience, and we shall therefore clarify its standing in R. Soloveitchik's thought. The transition from the aesthetic experience to the religious aesthetic one means a metamorphosis of the aesthetic. From this point on, the aesthetic oscillates between lack of purpose to purposefulness and from lack of doubt to the cause of questioning. The typical movement of the aesthetic that is directed inward (narcissism) is henceforth directed outwards, toward the transcendental divine. Another factor, however, remains stable in both the worldly and the divine experiences: the central standing of the senses. The aesthetic experience was, and remains, a sensuous experience. R. Soloveitchik's advice to the aesthete is the following: "experience God not through your facilities of abstracting conceptualization, which dismiss the immediate reality, but by tasting Him, as it were, by feeling Him right here and now."[102] The mind experiences the divine by means of the senses: man sees and hears God.

Medieval philosophers did not reach a consensus on the issue of the sensory addressing of God, its limits, and its very possibility. R. Soloveitchik favored the opinion of R. Judah Halevi, and not that of Maimonides. He based the former's view on two ideas.[103]

(1) Prophecy as experience and as vision: fundamentally, prophecy is not detached from the senses. The prophet has his experience in a vision and hears the word of God. Not a few thinkers limited the sensual dimension of prophecy to the symbolic realm. R. Judah Halevi, however, focuses, at length, on the sensual experience of the prophet itself. He asserted that

---

102 *Worship of the Heart*, 58.

103 In a letter to Simon Rawidowicz, R. Soloveitchik writes: "I am inclined to accept the perspective of Rabbi Yehudah ha-Levi regarding the [issue] of the intellectual religious experience in contrast to the 'concrete' transcendental religious experience. However, our great teacher [Maimonides] was dedicated to his perspective with all his heart and soul, though it cannot be maintained in day-to-day religious life" (58. "On the Love of God in Maimonidean Thought," in *Community, Covenant and Commitment: Selected Letters and Communications*, ed. Nathaniel Helfgot [Jersey City, NJ: Toras HoRav Foundation, 2005], 286-87). See Israel M. Ta-Shma, *Talmudic Commentary in Europe and North Africa: Literary History*, part 2: *1200-1400* [Hebrew] (Jerusalem, Magnes, 2000), 193-94; see also Ephraim Kanarfogel, "Did the Tosafists Embrace the Concept of Anthropomorphism?," in *Ta Shma: Studies in Judaica in Memory of Israel M. Ta-Shma* [Hebrew], ed. Avraham Reiner et al. (Alon Shevut: Tevunot, 2011), 671-703.

the prophet sees and senses God in his vision ("inner eye"). The divine majesty becomes the basis of the divine revelation to the prophet. R. Judah Halevi also mentioned man's psychological need to rely upon the tangible in order to understand the abstract and to focus on its cognition.[104]

(2) Revelation: R. Judah Halevi remained faithful to the notion of factual revelation. R. Soloveitchik mentioned the distinction between "the God of Abraham and the god of Aristotle."[105] "The God of Abraham" was revealed to the first monotheist and spoke in his ears. Furthermore, in R. Judah Halevi's thought, revelation became a principle of authentification. While the reality of the philosophical god is confirmed by reason ("an abstraction and a metaphysical idea"), the reality of the God of the Bible is certified by means of actual experience, namely, revelation ("His presence felt"). While the rational philosophical position is prone to doubts, revelation (to the masses) is an unquestionable fact. The realm in which God is revealed is patently sensual.

Here R. Soloveitchik inserted into R. Judah Halevi's thought the principle of "religious sensuousness." He argued that, according to the great philosopher-poet: "Only such a full, sensuous experience of God gratifies the God-thirsty soul and arouses passion and ecstatic love in man for the living God, for whom one is willing to incur martyrdom."[106] Halevi is perceived as an aesthete par excellence.

On the other hand, R. Soloveitchik objected to the Maimonidean view, attesting about himself: "I could never feel sympathy for Maimonides' horror at religious-sensual portrayal."[107] Maimonides was a fierce opponent of personification, and devoted most of the chapters of the first part of *Guide of the Perplexed* to the struggle against it. In those chapters he took pains to give a nonliteral interpretation of many examples of divine personification in the Bible. Additionally, the standing of the imagination in prophecy aids in acquiring scientific intelligibles or is a vehicle for translating abstract messages for the masses.[108] Maimonides' influence on

---

104 Based on *Kuzari* 4:3-5 (*Worship of the Heart*, 6-7).
105 *Worship of the Heart*, 58.
106 *Worship of the Heart*, 58.
107 *Worship of the Heart*, 63. It is noteworthy that tolerance of personification is to be found, for instance, in the thought of Kaufmann Kohler. See Eliezer Schweid, *A History of Modern Religious Philosophy*, part IV [Hebrew] (Tel Aviv: Am Oved, 2006), 341.
108 See Dov Schwartz, "Psychological Dimensions of Mosaic Prophecy—Imagination and Intellect" [Hebrew], in *Moses the Man—Master of the Prophets: In the Light of*

R. Soloveitchik is well-known.[109] Since, however, R. Soloveitchik's thought is not directed to a factual description of the reality as it is, but seeks to examine the consciousness of the individual who perceives it and examines the existence through this prism,[110] he had no qualms about viewing anthropomorphism as a legitimate aesthetic expression of consciousness, and therefore adopted Halevi's stance.

Prayer and the Aesthetic Experience: (1) Oscillations

Now we can understand the consciousness of hymnal prayer. The lengthy discussion of aesthetics was seemingly meant to comprehend the second stage in the formation of the consciousness of prayer. Basing the aesthetic experience on the senses fashions the character of prayer and sheds new light on its standing. The relationship between the aesthetic and prayer in R. Soloveitchik's writings indirectly leads to a dialectical perception of the prayer experience. This relationship is expressed in two apparently opposing aspects of prayer: on the one hand, prayer reflects the dialogue between God and man, as a continuation of prophecy. R. Soloveitchik usually formulated this assumption in existentialist terms. On the other hand, prayer is an experience of seeking closeness to the transcendent God, who is not limited to the human reality. This assumption is usually worded in terms taken from the phenomenology of religion. Prayer oscillates between dialogue and the quest for communion with the hidden God.

We will begin with the aesthetic aspects of the conception of prayer as dialogue, since prayer is "basically a dialogue between God and man."[111] Dialogue has a range of aspects in R. Soloveitchik's thought, and is recurringly discussed in the context of prayer.[112] Prayer is nothing other than pouring out one's heart before God. First, dialogue is utterance. Second, it enables man to come to know his own self. Third, dialogue facilitates exposure to the other. And fourth, dialogue enables a person to bear his existential loneliness

---

Interpretation throughout the Ages, ed. Moshe Hallamish, Hannah Kaser, and Hanokh Ben-Pazi (Ramat Gan: Bar-Ilan University Press, 2010), 251-283.

109 See, for example, Zeev Harvey, "Notes on Rabbi Soloveitchik and Maimonidean Philosophy," in *Faith in Changing Times: On the Teachings of Rabbi Joseph Dov Soloveitchik* [Hebrew], ed. Avi Sagi (Jerusalem: World Zionist Organization, 1996), 95-107.

110 See Schwartz, *From Phenomenology to Existentialism*, 2-7. Avi Sagi called this trend a "subjective shift." See Avi Sagi, *A Challenge: Returning to Tradition* [Hebrew] (Jerusalem: Shalom Hartman Institute, 2003), 30-34.

111 *Worship of the Heart*, 62.

112 See above, Chapter Two.

with dignity and perhaps even to redeem it.[113] R. Soloveitchik added an additional aspect here: dialogue reveals its participants to be taking part in an aesthetic experience. Dialogue is made possible by seeing and hearing, and the aesthetic consciousness leads to a dialogical existence.

Prayer as dialogue with God has special meaning in a community of concrete individuals. R. Soloveitchik, however, did not develop concrete communality with the other (*minyan*). The only two concrete elements that are examined in *Worship of the Heart* are "I" and "He" (= God). The man-God dialogue has two characteristic features:

(1) it is conducted between concrete subjects;
(2) the address in this dialogue is tangible.

Jewish thought throughout the ages often examined the advantages of public prayer. For R. Soloveitchik, communal dialogic prayer is, primarily, an aesthetic experience. Man perceives the other through his senses and emotions, and his prayer is within the context of an actual community. "A community of existence can only emerge when there is an encounter at the concrete level of sensuous portraiture, realizing the presence of the parties committed to a common destiny."[114] Additionally, the dialogic dimension of prayer mandates a personified attitude to an abstract God. A community welcomes its God in a sensuous experience. The model of a sensuous relationship with the other as a concrete being standing before one was now applied in the relationship with God. The dialogue with Him is derived from the dialogue with the other, and vice versa. Prayer documents dialogic existence.

The aesthetic experience of prayer, however, cannot be reduced to dialogue alone. While dialogic aesthetics is based on the senses (speech, listening), the aesthetics of the God experience is grounded mainly in the emotions. Communion with God results from love, yearning, and infinite pining for the divine. Unlike dialogue, these emotions are one-directional: man seeks contact with the Creator. The divine itself is beyond the concrete human, God is "something supernal, great, awesome and beautiful, although this 'something' is neither seen nor heard."[115] The impact of the transcendent God on man is included in the aesthetic gesture. This impression is both

---

113 See below, Chapter Twelve.
114 *Worship of the Heart*, 62.
115 *Worship of the Heart*, 63.

sensuous and mental, and it causes man to thirst for God. R. Soloveitchik writes on the aesthetic dimension of the experience of God:

> It is impossible to imagine prayer without, at the time, feeling the nearness and greatness of the Creator, His absolute justice, His fatherly concern with human affairs, His anger and wrath caused by unjust deeds. When we bow in prayer, we must experience His soothing hand and the infinite love and mercy for His creatures. We cling to Him as a living God, not as an idea, as abstract Being. We are in His company and are certain of His sympathy. There is in prayer an experience of emotions which can only be produced by direct contact with God.[116]

The anthropomorphic orientation of prayer, that is, the perception of a personal God who acts and responds, arouses man to experience communion with Him. Truth be told, God is beyond feelings and emotions; but the path to communion with the entity beyond passes through the realm of the aesthetic. This is the force of the aesthetic gesture: it skips over the system of indirect circumstances that interpose between man and his God. It interrupts the numerous intermediaries and the ramified hierarchical structure that separates the creature from his Creator. Man "senses" his God in his quest to approach Him. Prayer imparts expression to feelings and emotions. Its aesthetic dimension creates the encounter between the worshiper and his God. Thanks to prayer, God is present as compassionate Father, righteous Judge, wrathful Reproacher, and responsible Leader. R. Soloveitchik writes:

> [...] the aesthetic experience of God, whether constructed of impressions and sensations drawn from our daily life, where man is engrossed in images and psychophysical sensuous processes, or consisting of ecstatic emotions, in the throbbing of the heart and the longing of the soul, is the basis of the community of God and man.[117]

Hymnal prayer confronts man with God and creates a community composed of God and man. There is no place here for the other.

Thus, prayer documents both the consciousness experience of the man-God dialogue and the consciousness experience of contact with the divine. Both experiences are anchored in the aesthetic, in terms of their growth and development, from within the sensuous and emotional dimension,

---

116 *Worship of the Heart*, 63.
117 *Worship of the Heart*, 63.

from dialogue to communion, and from two-directional to one-directional. From this aspect, prayer is no different from other commandments that R. Soloveitchik interprets as reflective of the fundamental tensions of the human experience, which they bring into balance. The fundamental tension in prayer ensues from considerable difficulty in resolving the two experiences, the dialogic and that of the consciousness. Dialogue assumes the tangible response of the "He," that is, God, while the religious experience of conjunction belongs solely to the realm of the consciousness, that is, in the presence of the *mysterum tremendum*. Dialogue also assumes the existence of the other as axiomatic,[118] while communion is based, as a primary given, on the exclusivity of the absolute, divine, Other with which we wish to commune. The aesthetic dimension of prayer presents it as a dialectical action.

Prayer and the Aesthetic Experience: (2) Telos

R. Soloveitchik bound prayer together with the aesthetic gesture. Since the basis of this gesture is negative, it needs fundamental change. The redemption of the aesthetic takes several paths.

(1) *Imitatio Dei*: since God is beautiful, imitating Him elevates the aesthetic to a heavenly level.
(2) Exaltation: the dialectic religious experience has a clearly aesthetic dimension: the religious man stands in the presence of the exalted, which he experiences in the sensual plane.
(3) The possibility of communion: the cognitive and the ethical experience leads one to perfection. Perfection by itself, however, does not constitute communion with the divine. The aesthetic is the link joining these two experiences to communion.

R. Soloveitchik argued that prayer leads to the redemption of the aesthetic. It gives purpose to the aesthetic gesture, and transforms the aesthetic type into the purposeful one. How does prayer contribute to this upheaval in the non-purposeful character of the aesthete? R. Soloveitchik incorporated prayer mainly in the second and third ways of the redemption of the aesthetic. The experience of exaltation is made possible only by the aesthetic factor.

---

118 See, for example, Paul F. Pfuetze, *Self, Society, Existence: Human Nature and Dialogue in the Thought of George Herbert Mead and Martin Buber* (New York: Harper & Row, 1961), 131.

This is the exactly the place of prayer, more precisely, of hymnal prayer. R. Soloveitchik maintains that the hymn is a "purely an aesthetic phenomenon," because it "signifies a rise of religious emotion. When the religious temperament is aroused, the soul is stirred and the experience becomes tempestuous. Under the impact of such an inner wave of rapture, man begins to adore God and to sing a hymn to Him."[119] The hymnal prayer transforms the mute experience of God into a vivid and tempestuous one. Such prayer refines the aesthetic, since it in itself is an aesthetic experience par excellence. "*Birkot ha-shevah*[120] perform the feat of relating the beautiful to the eternal, truthful and good."[121] Hymnal prayer gives balanced and rich expression to the emotions that effervesce within the consciousness. The blessings of praise are the objectivization of the consciousness phase of the redemption of the aesthetic.

3. Aesthetic Prayer: (2) Thanksgiving

Does prayer redeem the aesthetic as a byproduct, or is it destined to effect such redemption? R. Soloveitchik has prayer oscillating between dialogue and the experience of the hidden God (the numinous). His discussion indicates that the oscillations between recoiling and anxiety, on the one hand, and on the other, seeking closeness and communion, is the main dimension of interest to him. For R. Soloveitchik, prayer is, foremost, a dialectical encounter with God in all his "majesty." We have so far been concerned with the "glory of God," that is, the experience of divine splendor and majesty. Hymnal prayer became an aesthetic act, expressing the exaltation of the transcendental and awe at its greatness up to the very intoxication of madness. R. Soloveitchik then addresses the prayer of thanksgiving, which he defined in relation to hymnal prayer. As we will see, thanksgiving prayer reflects the highest stage of the religious consciousness, of the endless love of God.

The Evolution of the Consciousness

R. Soloveitchik distinguished between *kevod Elohim* (*majestas Dei*), meaning the experience of the transcendental God or the experience of the numinous, and *hesed Elohim* (*caritas Dei*), that is, the experience of the beneficent God who shows lovingkindness. While the transcendental

---

119 *Worship of the Heart*, 64.
120 The blessings of praise.
121 *Worship of the Heart*, 65.

experience results in a dialectic of attraction-repulsion, the experience of the divine lovingkindness is exclusively one of attraction. The beneficent God no longer imposes terror. The experience of the divine good is the most sublime and most perfect stage of the religious consciousness. Man connects to his God, and they become fellows. This is the stage of communion, and the divine consciousness model that suits it is that of limitless lovingkindness. R. Soloveitchik explained elsewhere that this is the supreme stage of consciousness, as he mentioned that for Maimonides, such consciousness is characteristic of the perfect individuals. *Guide of the Perplexed* preaches "a moral ideal of continuous fellowship with God," in which such constant cleaving to God is "an esoteric one."[122] While the transcendental experience is expressed in hymns of praise, that of the divine good finds expression in hymns of thanksgiving. R. Soloveitchik writes:

> [   ] in the thanksgiving hymn we sing of God's *hesed* (lovingkindness). Good becomes an aesthetic value; it turns into beauty. We experience the moral law not so much as an imperative but as something beautiful. Its binding power is supplemented with a quality of fascination; the decision, by desire; surrender by merger. Whenever this happens the gratitude, which is, at one level, no more than a feeling of expedience, turns into enthusiasm, and indebtedness into rapturous love. God is good and therefore beautiful. This sort of beauty is not identical with majesty, but it does manifest itself in grandeur and vastness, in the powerful drama of the creation. It emerges as *caritas* or *amor Dei*.[123]

R. Soloveitchik defined "God's lovingkindness" (thanksgiving) in relation to "God's majesty" (praise). The line of thought he embraced here suits the stages of the fashioning of the religious consciousness, as he portrayed them in *And from There You Shall Seek*. These are the stages that he depicted in his composition from the middle of the 1940s.

(1) Crisis: the collapse of the proofs for the existence of God following the Kantian revolution, which means, the bankruptcy of rationalism in the realm of belief.[124]

(2) Dialectic: the consciousness of God that is revealed. This is a consciousness of opposites, such as love and fear. That is, the relation

---

122 *Worship of the Heart*, 93. On the communal dimension of bonding with God, see below, Chapter Five.

123 *Worship of the Heart*, 66-67.

124 See Schwartz, *From Phenomenology to Existentialism*, chapter 2.

of the consciousness to God is characterized both by the aspiration for closeness to Him and by the distance of fear and trembling.

(3) Transformation: in the second phase, the responses of the consciousness become transformed into one another: love becomes fear, and love is revealed in fear.[125]

(4) Unity: in the third phase, only love remains. This is the stage of communion.[126]

This model recurs in a similar discussion in *Worship of the Heart* on the relationship between prayers of praise and of thanksgiving.

(1) Petition: the existential crisis reflects the collapse of the existential and finite systems.[127]

(2) Praise: in this phase, there is the closeness-distance dialectic in the face of the divine splendor and majesty. The cognitive-moral dimension distinctly differs from the aesthetic.

(3) Praise (i): transformation: in this phase the moral dimension becomes the aesthetic. In R. Soloveitchik's wording, the "moral law" becomes "beautiful."

(4) Praise (ii): unity: following the transformation, only love and desire for God's closeness remain.

The consciousness of prayer, as a specific instance of the religious consciousness, is described in accordance with the phenomenological criteria that R. Soloveitchik set forth. The portrayal of the religious consciousness in *And from There You Shall Seek*, however, is not completely identical with that in *Worship of the Heart*. In the former, the transformation of the consciousness occurs when the rational element enters the picture. When the experiencer understands that God's concealment is intentional, then fear becomes endless love. In contrast, in the work devoted to prayer, the moral

---

125 Ibid., 106-109.

126 Ibid., chapters 6 and 7

127 The starting point of the worshiper is not a crisis of faith. Tillich, for example, already argued that the power of prayer ensues from the profound belief in God's activity and His influence on the existential condition. See Paul Tillich, *Systematic Theology* (Chicago: University of Chicago Press, 1951), vol. 1: *Reason and Revelation—Being and God*, 267. Accordingly, R. Soloveitchik set forth the existential crisis, in place of the collapse of the rational proofs for the existence of God. The formal parallelism between *And from There You Shall Seek* and *Worship of the Heart* is complete, but since the latter discusses the consciousness of prayer, their starting points are different.

becomes the aesthetic because the prayer of thanksgiving presents God as absolute good and absolute beauty. It is not the rational element that takes the stage, but that of choice and free will. Man chooses, adopts, and accepts upon himself the numinous God.[128] He thereby elevates worldly beauty to the level of the divine, which turns God into the source of both the moral and the aesthetic. Unlike the prayer of praise, where the consciousness of God is both threatening and attractive, no such dialectic is found in the prayer of praise. The moral becomes the aesthetic not as a result of new conception and insight, but because the consciousness of God has changed: beauty is no longer dialectic. The oscillation between the beautiful and the exalted, according to Edmund Burke's aesthetic model, has vanished; now, the divine is the absolute union of the good and the beautiful, that is, the moral and the aesthetic. "Yet the moral infinity of God, however supra-rational and distant from us, is not frightening or awe-inspiring, but on the contrary, beckons to us and invokes in us the desire for imitation and merger."[129] What was previously perceived as threatening becomes merciful and compassionate. The distant becomes close. Love dominates the experience of God, and the consciousness is solely that of communion. In formal terms, the consciousness of prayer develops in accordance with the model that was assumed in *And from There You Shall Seek*. Contentually, prayer creates a different consciousness. In the consciousness of prayer, aesthetics and free will replace reason.

Prayer and Consciousness

Thus, R. Soloveitchik evidently sought to express a comprehensive phenomenological thesis concerning prayer, that it reflects man's experience of God. From this respect, prayer is the reflection of the religious consciousness as a whole. Initially, man is in a state of crisis. God is concealed from him, and he is thrown into his existential distress. Penitential prayer represents this distress. From within the crisis, man undergoes an elevating experience. Revelation comes in a state of despair, and it is then that man becomes aware of the dialectic in the encounter with the divine. The prayer of praise reflects this experience. Then, the exalting experience becomes the experience of the loving God, who is replete with lovingkindness. The dialectic becomes love. The prayer of thanksgiving expresses this change in

---

128 See the extensive discussion below, Chapter Six.
129 *Worship of the Heart*, 67.

the consciousness process. Prayer, therefore, reflects the various phases that the consciousness undergoes until the supreme stage of communion, which is absolute and unconditional love, of—in the wording of Ezek. 1:14—dashing to, but not back. R. Soloveitchik wrote of this supreme phase:

> What we are aware of is not something uncanny, alien, which is beyond the sphere of the orderly, the lawful and the normal, and which astounds us, but of something close to and intimately related to us, which we try to acquire and take possession, to which our soul responds and clings passionately. This something is not beyond the grasp of order and nomos but on the contrary their full realization and representation.[130]

R. Soloveitchik explained that even when the subjective consciousness reaches the peak of its aspirations, it still is connected to its objective dimension. That is, prayer as halakhic praxis records, not only the primal subjective stage of the consciousness (crisis, exaltation, and the like), it also records its supreme stage (communion). The prayer of thanksgiving is based on the laudatory formulations of the hymns and prayers (the *Kedushah*, the thanksgiving blessings of the *Amidah* prayer, and the like). These formulations are merely expressions of a divine law. In short, the objective divine command accompanies the group of steps in which the subjective religious consciousness is formed.

Prayer of Love

The prayer of praise reflects the love of God, which is two-directional. Such prayer presents God as "a loving Father and Caretaker,"[131] and the worshipers, in response, as having "a feeling of felicity and love."[132] Hermann Cohen presents prayer as love in his *Religion of Reason: Out of the Sources of Judaism*. Scholars disagree concerning the relationship of this book to Cohen's critical works. Some viewed it as an additional volume in his series of critical essays, while others saw in it a change of direction and thought.[133] Cohen made efforts in his Jewish essays to show that the strict scientific cognitive structure and the intuitive religious conception of

---

130   *Worship of the Heart*, 68.
131   *Worship of the Heart*, 69.
132   *Worship of the Heart*, 68.
133   See, for example, the articles in the collection: Helmut Holzhey, Gabriel Motzkin, and Hartwig Wiedebach (eds.), *"Religion der Vernunft aus den Quellen des Judentums": Tradition und Ursprungsdenken in Hermann Cohens Spätwerk* (Hildesheim: Olms, 2000).

the prophets, for example, are likely consistent. He found support in Plato's theory of ideas: for Cohen, the perception of ideas is both discursive and intuitive.[134] The beginning of Cohen's discussion of prayer closely matches the creative model of the cognitive idealism approach that he developed in his philosophical thought. Cohen maintained that prayer is "an original form [*Urform*] of monotheism."[135] Such a claim is anchored in the following argument:

(1) prayer is a rational[136] and moral expression of trust in God;[137]
(2) rationality is reflected in intent, and accompanies, and even preceded, prayer;
(3) morality, too, is evident in intent, because a moral decision is a consequence of psychological concentration and introspection;
(4) trust in God is expressed verbally;
(5) the discourse (the "art of speaking" that develops into poetry) is an original form (*Urform*) of monotheism.[138]

This leads to the conclusion:

(6) prayer is a "monologue" that is actually a dialogue with God.[139]

We should explain the manner in which prayer is indeed an *Urform*, that is, a cornerstone in the cognitive process of creating the object as an object of scientific knowledge and ethical will. As we will see below, the conception of prayer is grounded in the cognitive idealistic notion. Cohen asserted that basic assumptions (*Grundlegungen*) are tested on the basis of their fruitfulness (*Fruchtbarkeit*), that is, the potential for creating the object (the individual or God) from within them by means of the method of thought.[140]

---

134 See Hermann Cohen, *Jüdische Schriften* (Berlin: Schwetschke, 1924), vol. 1, 306-307.
135 Hermann Cohen, *Religion of Reason: Out of the Sources of Judaism*, trans. Simon Kaplan (New York: Ungar, 1972), 371. See Andrea Poma, *Yearning for Form and Other Essays on Hermann Cohen's Thought* (Dordrecht: Springer, 2006), 227-242; Joseph Ballan, "Dialogic Monologue: Hermann Cohen's Philosophy of Prayer," *Toronto Journal of Jewish Thought* 1 (2010): 1-11.
136 Prayer is "an expression of thought" (Cohen, *Religion of Reason*, 372).
137 On prayer as an expression of trust in God, see Poma, *Yearning for Form*, 136-138.
138 Cohen, *Religion of Reason*, 37.
139 Ibid., 373.
140 Ibid., 185.

Now we must clarify: how, and from which basic assumptions, is prayer formed? Before providing a detailed explanation, the processes may be presented in graphic form in the following table:

construction of the relationship[141]	"the fact of prayer" (law)	construction of the rite
(a) longing (*Sehnsucht*)	(a) intent (*Andacht*)[142]	(a) discourse
(b) love (*Liebe*)	(b) prayer (*Gebet*)	(b) psalm
(c) correlation (*Korrelation*)		(c) prayer

In the creative process of the consciousness, it reduces to the infinitesimal the quantitative dimension of the object ("differential"), and thus is left with pure quality. The consciousness then recreates the object in accordance with its judgments, from the origin to the complete object (within the consciousness). This creation follows a system of rules that, within the cognitive context, Cohen referred to as "the fact of science," and which we will call, within the context of the religious process (that is our concern here), "the fact of prayer." R. Soloveitchik subjected the cognitive creative process to thorough and critical analysis in his PhD dissertation. Cohen projected this structure to ethics, with religion being one of its expressions, and to aesthetics. The origin from which the consciousness creates prayer is the "pure" discourse, that is, not actual discourse, but the inner element from which the substantial discourse will likely sprout. When we restrict the mythical and historical contexts of the hymns and psalms, we are eventually left with the pure discourse. Reason creates the religious object—in this case, prayer—from within the pure discourse. The discourse is magnified into a psalm, and the psalm becomes prayer. The creative process also includes the creativity of the bond between man and his God, beginning with the longing for the divine and ending with complete correlation. Cohen argued that (also) from within, the pure prayer discourse, the consciousness creates, in a structured and gradual

---

141 Cohen seemingly describes a psychological process, from longings and desire through love to correlation. This creative process is of interest, because Cohen struggled to escape from psychologism in all his writings. Another possibility is that this refers to intellectual love, which is entirely rational and has no psychological basis. For a discussion of this issue, see Poma, *Yearning for Form*, 140-143.

142 This term relates to intent as a religious-halakhic term, which also reflects solemnity or awe. Cohen wrote on the relationship between intent and development: "What longing is to love, devotion [*Andacht*] is to prayer" (Cohen, *Religion of Reason*, 375).

fashion, the two objects on which religion is based: the individual and God. The objects are formed as follows.

(1) Longing: "Prayer is longing."[143] "[T]he fact of prayer" in a rational-religious process that parallels "the fact of science" in the cognitive process is intent. That is, Halakhah as the Jewish system of laws presents intent as the legal expression of the limitless yearning for God.

(2) Love: "The prayer is love."[144] In this stage, too, intent is the legal expression of the love that is created out of longing.

(3) Correlation: "the correlation of man and God."[145] The correlation between the individual and God results from reason building the object (prayer) from the initial discourse to correlation.

The conception of prayer as love has an additional dimension. Cohen forged a parallelism between prayer and psalm, which is "the original poetic form of the lyric."[146] This parallel is actually more of an analogy, since the Psalms are an integral part of prayer. Cohen's father was a cantor, and this profession was not foreign to Hermann the son, either. Lyricism sprouts from within the inner sentiment of love. "The lyric poem is the confession that the soul itself utters about its innermost and most intimate experience. This most intimate experience is love."[147] The psalm reflects pure love, after the reduction (to the infinitesimal) of the "quantitative" dimensions of Eros and sexuality. After this, the consciousness constructs this love as love of God,[148] which is a correlative bond between the individual and his God. Since this analogy lies beyond two independent realms, prayer may be viewed as an expression of the pure love of God, as Cohen expressly states.

To a certain degree, R. Soloveitchik's perception of the prayer of praise is anchored in Cohen's approach. Since, however, R. Soloveitchik's world is not limited to cognitive idealism, he did not accept Cohen's absolute limitation of the "quantitative" dimensions. Cohen unequivocally asserted

---

143 Cohen, *Religion of Reason*, 374.
144 Ibid., 374.
145 Ibid., 374.
146 Ibid., 373.
147 Ibid., 373.
148 See, for example, Nathan Rotenstreich, *Jewish Thought in the Modern Period* [Hebrew] (Tel Aviv: Am Oved, 1966), vol. 2, 81-82. It should be noted, once again, that the objects that are built by cognition are man as individual and God. Their construction is a correlation of love.

that "[o]ne cannot love God as a man or a woman."[149] His notion of love categorically rejects any tangible expression of Eros and sexuality.[150] In contrast, R. Soloveitchik's religious phenomenology background, with its analysis of religious sentiment and experience, did not shrink from applying various degrees of sentiments and relations to God, and not only as symbolic and allegorical. R. Soloveitchik writes plainly:

> The erotic love fans out in all directions reaching infinity itself. Judaism did not discriminate between *eros* (worldly love) and *agape* (purely spiritual love) as the Christian mystics did, but set up as a model of love of God, the unredeemed passion - not the spiritual, sublimated adoration.[151]

Elevating the aesthetic experience from sensuality to the passionate love of God does not demand the absolute diminution (to the infinitesimal) of sexuality and Eros. We may reasonably assume that Cohen himself would object to such a requirement. In any event, the presentation of the supreme stage of prayer as pure, unreserved love is somewhat reminiscent of Cohen's analysis.

Consciousness and Hermeneutics

R. Soloveitchik concluded the phenomenological discussion that produced the tripartite model of the stages of the consciousness of prayer with an interpretation of Ps. 103-104. His commentary details the experience of the beneficent God in Ps. 103 and the experience of exaltation in Ps. 104. The former psalm mainly expresses serenity, while the latter depicts a tempest of opposites. Actually, already at the end of Ps. 103 the composure of the experience of the beneficent God turns stormy, in light of the divine majesty (the numinous). Since each psalm begins with a call to splendor and majesty, R. Soloveitchik maintains that "the numinous element comes to the fore at the outset and at the conclusion of the hymns."[152] What led R. Soloveitchik to this interpretive direction?

The structural cognitive model is developmental. The consciousness is woven in stages: existential distress leads to the experience of exaltation, which in turn brings about the experience of the divine absolute good. Already, however, in *And from There You Shall Seek* R. Soloveitchik repeatedly

---

149 Cohen, *Religion of Reason*, 373.
150 Poma, *Yearning for Form*, 130. Poma viewed this as an expression of the process of internalization of Cohen's pure sentiment.
151 *Worship of the Heart*, 61. See Schwartz, *From Phenomenology to Existentialism*, 283-286.
152 *Worship of the Heart*, 69.

alluded that the Jewish religious consciousness is more dialectical, with greater tension, than the general religious consciousness. Presumably, when a person comes to experience the good he has attained perfection. Two phenomena, however, pose a threat to the developmental model: one, a person could fall from the perfect level that he has reached; and the other, the dialectic of the tempest is present, albeit in hidden and latent fashion, in the state of perfection, as well. R. Soloveitchik accordingly enters into the details of the experiences in these psalms, and explains that even after the experience of the good a person stands once again in the presence of the hidden and mysterious God. The developmental model is realized fully only when the messianic consideration enters the discussion. R. Soloveitchik writes:

> In Judaism, the numinous experience is a prologue to redemption—man hopes to free himself finally from the dreadful, and to march forward towards beatitude and bliss. Eschatology is the final destination of the religious experience, and an eschatological experience means a redeemed one, when the now unknown will appear in our midst as an old friend and acquaintance, when man will see God, feel His presence, and enjoy Him continuously, when the curtain of the numinous will be raised. Yet, eschatology is placed outside the historic-cosmic circle. As long as our existence is fenced in by the historic and the natural—our experience of God is a dual one.[153]

The experience of the divine good is destined to be dominant in the messianic future. Then, the dialectic experience will give birth to an experience of unity. The consciousness will reach the final stage, of endless love, with no fall to an earlier stage and with no hidden, immanent, and threatening presence of the numinous within this love. The end of this passage clearly teaches that the aesthetic experience (sensual, feeling, pleasure), too, will reach its final redemption. The messianic era, however, is not a historical and natural period. Historical and cosmic regularity will no longer be in force in the fantastic future period.[154] Consequently, R. Soloveitchik does not find a real phenomenological consideration in the messianic idea. In the present (that is, premessianic) time, the model of the concealed and impenetrable God appears even after a person has experienced the God of absolute good.

---

153 *Worship of the Heart*, 78. For the various models in R. Soloveitchik's messianic conception, see Dov Schwartz, *Faith at the Crossroads: A Theological Profile of Religious Zionism*, trans. Batya Stein (Leiden: Brill, 2002), 193-210.

154 On the transformations of the apocalyptic notion, see Dov Schwartz, *Messianism in Medieval Jewish Thought*, trans. Batya Stein (Boston: Academic Studies Press, 2017).

R. Soloveitchik thereby indirectly explained the fact that the recording of the experiences in the *Amidah* prayer does not necessarily follow their conscious order. The *Amidah* begins with praise, proceeds to distress (the petitional blessings), and concludes with thanksgiving. The redactors of the *Amidah* most probably had considerations of their own. Man seeks his God with praise, for it is only polite to do so, even though he is motivated by distress, by the very nature of his existence. R. Soloveitchik, however, might have attributed an additional meaning to this: the religious consciousness is tense and stormy, and at times this fact upsets the developmental model, despite the latter's being the key to understanding the consciousness.

* * *

The aesthetic is elevated and redeemed by two different experiences: the experience of exaltation (the numinous) and that of unlimited love and lovingkindness. The redemption of the aesthetic is effected by its transformation—actually, its elevation—to an act of the religious consciousness. The aesthetic is expressed in two stages of the development of the consciousness: the dialectical phase (closeness-distance) and that of unification (only closeness). Both are realized by sentiment and fervor, and both erupt when the consciousness stands facing the God experience. In each of these two stages, the pure aesthetic sentiment is dominant, in comparison with reason, which is held in check. Presumably, this is the routine and timeworn formulation of the existentialists and the phenomenologists: religion imparts redemption and meaning to life's problems. The aesthetic is redeemed when it becomes an act of the religious consciousness. R. Soloveitchik grounded the aesthetic in both the subjective aspect of the consciousness and its objective aspect, namely, prayer. The act of prayer records the stormy developmental processes of the consciousness. Prayer is one of the expressions of the religious consciousness, and as such reflects both the fundamental structure of the consciousness and the stages of its formation.

4. Summary

A lecture on prayer that R. Soloveitchik delivered ended with the general formulation that prayer, and only prayer, is the fitting and comprehensive response to the existential challenges facing man's consciousness:

> The existential depth crisis and the state of alienation and boredom which ensue are unresolvable except through prayer. Primarily, because prayer is

a dialogue, it differs from the other media of communion. It involves an interrelationship with God which can dispel the existential restlessness and unhappiness of man. In this respect, prayer is a unique experience.[155]

R. Soloveitchik included in this the various aspects of the centrality of prayer in a person's world. The most important aspect of all, however, is the perception of prayer as reflective of the structure of the consciousness and the stages of its formulation (see below). We will conclude with the perception of prayer as a struggle, following which we will draw conclusions regarding the structure of the religious consciousness.

The Worshiper as Hero

Generally speaking, R. Soloveitchik devoted much energy to describing the structure of religious consciousness and its accompanying existential situations. At times, he went considerably beyond his efforts to understand the action of prayer in relation to such situations. Patently, though, prayer represents man's daily existential struggle and his contending with his depth crises. From a certain respect, prayer transforms the worshiper into a hero who struggles with his fate and who courageously bears the burden of crisis. Avi Sagi writes:

> In human life, possibility is the manifestation of self-transcendence: We are not bound to our factual data, and human existence is manifest in the ceaseless rejection of factuality. In this existentialist phenomenology, prayer is a clear alternative, recurrently actualized by people from different cultures at different times. Refusing subservience to factual data, humans return to prayer and thereby open up a horizon of hope and future.[156]

According to Sagi, prayer denotes the possibilities open before a person and his freedom not to accept the given reality. To a certain extent, prayer fashions the hope for change and improvement. It seems that the center of gravity is different for R. Soloveitchik, who lost hope for changing the facts. For R. Soloveitchik, the struggle in prayer is not to be free from existential situations, but to bear them with dignity; that is, to accept and adopt the existential frame out of choice. Prayer occupies a substantial place in the efforts of the religious consciousness to attain communion.

---

155 *Reflections of the Rav*, 87.
156 Avi Sagi, *Prayer After the Death of God: A Phenomenological Study of Hebrew Literature*, translated by Batya Stein (Boston: Academic Studies press, 2016), 149.

Prayer, then, marks the individual's contending with the given existential situation. R. Soloveitchik, however, added a meticulous and expansive phenomenological analysis of the consciousness of prayer as an intentional act of the religious consciousness as a whole. He adopted the prevalent formulation of many phenomenologists and religious existentialist thinkers that religion or the religious act impart meaning to existence. The existential frame becomes authentic in the wake of the religious factor, in this instance, prayer.

The Consciousness Structure

We already spoke at length about the formal and contentual parallel to the structure of the religious consciousness, as R. Soloveitchik described it in his early works. According to this, prayer reveals and records the various stages of the formation of the consciousness:

(1) the state of crisis: the initial datum of distress (petitional prayer);
(2) the discovery of God (exaltation): the dialectic of fear and love, dread and seeking closeness (hymnal prayer);
(3) the love of God: the dialectic situation becomes one of love alone (thanksgiving prayer).

As we already noted, this process is dialectical and not one-directional. Following the state of absolute love of the infinite divine good, man falls back into the numinous state of the hidden and alienated God, and then returns. The following table presents the three stages in the building of the consciousness of prayer, reflecting the phases and processes of religious consciousness as a whole:

Evidently, then, prayer is the record and driving force of the formation of the religious consciousness. The stages of this consciousness are slowly built in accordance with the various prayers. The experience of God, also, develops in accordance with prayer. The attributes of God are constructed from within the act of prayer. In short, the phenomenology of religion passes through the phenomenology of prayer. To a certain degree, the phenomenology of religion *is* the phenomenology of prayer. A person's religious consciousness is formulated and is transformed from the primal state of distress to supreme communion during the course of his daily, Sabbath, monthly, festival, and Days of Awe prayers.

Once again, we see that R. Soloveitchik's portrayal of the development of the consciousness is not free of dialectics. To the contrary: in each stage,

consciousness stage	Gesture	consciousness structure	existential state	consciousness of God	prayer	hymn
First	–	Distress	loneliness	"listening" God	petition	–
Second	ethical and aesthetic (divine beauty and emotions)	Dialectic (oscillation from one gesture to the other)	loneliness	*majestus Dei* ("exalted", "numinous" God)	hymn	Ps. 103
Third	ethical and aesthetic (divine beauty and emotions)	1. transformation of the gestures 2. unity: conjunction and love	community (correlation with God)[157]	absolute good ("kerygmatic")[158]	thanksgiving	Ps. 104

157 The following chapter will discuss this characteristic.
158 This characteristic, too, will be discussed in the following chapter.

the consciousness is stabilized after extreme oscillations. The fashioning of the experience of exaltation follows the oscillation between the perception of prayer as dialogue, on the one hand, and on the other, as a one-directional act of consciousness. The aesthetic itself swings between the infinite freedom of beauty and sensation and its restraining rechanneling to the realm of the divine.

There can be no doubt that R. Soloveitchik's general discussion of prayer is phenomenological. His predilection for intensifying the oscillations enriches this discussion and turns prayer into an event replete with insights based on diverse philosophical sources. Man stands before his God in prayer with his full personality, existence, and consciousness.

Chapter 5

The Path of the Consciousness of Prayer to Perfection

In the fifth chapter of *Worship of the Heart*, which concludes the first group of chapters in the book, R. Soloveitchik presented the ways in which the religious consciousness developed, from the dialectic stage to that of unification, and the parallel transition from the model of the exalted and concealed God to the beneficent God who is connected to man. In this discussion, he methodically and gradually explained that prayer has an important place in these changes of the consciousness. In this chapter we will explore his writing, in which, in his unique style, he instructed the reader, stage after stage, regarding the standing of prayer in religious life.

1. The Framework

The fourth chapter of *Worship of the Heart* presumably should have ended at the highest and most serene stage of the consciousness, in which love of God dominates man, with prayer reflecting the state of communion attained by the consciousness. Instead, however, it concludes with the crisis of the silence of God, and the fifth chapter ("The Absence of God and the Community of Prayer") continues the discussion of this crisis of consciousness and its overcoming. Not only does the discussion return to the dialectic state of numinous exaltation, moreover, it begins with the silence of God and the concealment of His countenance. This phase, which is solely the initial stage in the analysis of the religious consciousness in *And from There You Shall Seek*, now concludes the discussion of the consciousness of prayer.

The Conflicted Consciousness

Why didn't R. Soloveitchik stop at the top? Prayer already reflected the summits of man's religious achievements; then why did the fall have to come?

A few answers may be offered. First, the objective dimension of prayer is concerned with routine everyday activity, that is, at least three daily prayers. Prayer itself reflects the human state of consciousness, and in such a fluid state spiritual elevation cannot long survive. Second, R. Soloveitchik sought to show the way to experience God by means of prayer, and it is the fall that reveals the need for connection to God. Third, about a decade after it had been written,[1] R. Soloveitchik might have already left behind the innocence of *And from There You Shall Seek*, that is, the possibility of attaining cognitive conjunction, which is the religious ideal. He understood that absolute perfection belongs to the eschatological future, but not to the history of human existence. Finally, R. Soloveitchik personally preferred the embroiled to the resolved and oscillation to unity. Quite possibly, R. Soloveitchik's tempestuous personality did not allow him to depict the actual existence of unity and serenity. Whatever the reason, the fact remains that he concluded with the consciousness of the silent God and its redemption, with the cyclic process continuing.

The Religious Consciousness: From Structure to Process

The fifth chapter was written to indicate the manner in which prayer elevates the religious consciousness from the dialectic stage to that of unity. To this point, prayer recorded the cognitive processes and their various stages. Petitional prayer recorded the crisis situation, hymnal prayer, the experience of exaltation, and thanksgiving prayer, the experience of the unlimited good. In this chapter R. Soloveitchik examines the active place of prayer in the process of the consciousness's perfection. The fifth chapter teaches how to make the transition from one state of consciousness to a higher one, and how prayer reflects this process. R. Soloveitchik considered the success and failure of prayer. That is, at times prayer succeeds in conveying a person from one state of consciousness to the next, and at other times it fails. The process of the perfection of the consciousness is dialectical, because man constantly oscillates between the polarized and the unified. We will explore

---

1   The first version of *And from There You Shall Seek* was written ca. 1944. Any of a number of possible reasons might have led to the decision to reprint it in 1978. R. Soloveitchik might have wanted to present his intellectual biography to the reader. Perhaps he was dissatisfied with the first version and improved it over the course of time. Another possibility is that in light of his innovative existentialist writing within the Orthodox context, he wanted to present the opposite phenomenological pole, for the sake of balance.

R. Soloveitchik's exceptional manner of expressing the active place of prayer in the consciousness processes in the following discussion.

2. The Consciousness of the Concealed God

After R. Soloveitchik presented, at the end of the fourth chapter of *Worship of the Heart*, the possibility of attaining the highest stage of the consciousness, he was compelled to explain that this is not an irreversible process. To the contrary, the moment that a person reaches communion and endless love, when he experiences dialogue with the beneficent God, he plummets once again to the crisis situation and crashes in the face of the exalted and sublime God, who is impervious to humans. R. Soloveitchik accordingly clarified, yet again, the tempestuous and oscillating nature of the religious consciousness, in order to place the process of the perfection of the consciousness in its proper light.

The Return to Oscillations

At the beginning of the fifth chapter of *Worship of the Heart*, R. Soloveitchik once again rejected the image of religion as refuge. Such a dismissal already appeared in a lengthy note at the beginning of *Halakhic Man*. The perception of religion as a shelter to which people escape from life's struggles is formulated in *Halakhic Man* in sentences such as "the religious experience is tranquil and neatly ordered, tender and delicate; it is an enchanted stream for embittered souls and still waters for troubled spirits."[2] In both compositions R. Soloveitchik vigorously opposed such an approach. For him, religion is an agonizing and fluctuating experience. The religious consciousness is dialectical, and the movement from one model to another, and from one act of consciousness to another, leads to rupture and a soul at war with itself.

The starting point of the discussion in *Halakhic Man* is clearly polemical, as it contests specific philosophical and religious orientations. In *Halakhic Man*, R. Soloveitchik is critical of those who ascribe the following four proximate characteristics to the religious experience:

(1) subjectivity: the religious experience occurs solely within the personal, inner, and singular sphere;

---

2 *Halakhic Man*, 140. See Schwartz, *Religion or Halakha*, 19.

(2) transcendence: the religious experience relates to what lies beyond mundane existence;

(3) irrationality: the religious experience lacks any rational traits;

(4) a lack of dialectics: the religious experience is simple and arouses serenity.

In *Worship of the Heart* R. Soloveitchik once again leveled criticism at the notion of religion as refuge, employing two arguments:

[1] The religious experience does not always free man from care and pain, as many religious leaders assert [...] To be religious is not to be confused with living at ease, with unruffled calmness and inner peace. On the contrary, the religious life is fraught with emotional strife, intellectual tensions which ravel and fray its harmony.[3]

[2] Halakhah never acquiesced to the subjectivistic interpretation of the religious act.[4] Such an approach sees in man's relationship to his Creator only a subjective performance, exhausting itself in a peculiar state of mind, in a unique inner experience that, in turn, can never be translated into normative pressure and action.[5]

In these arguments he mentioned almost all the characteristics in *Halakhic Man* that were listed above. The motives for rejecting such a view of religion, however, are not identical in these two works. In *Halakhic Man*, R. Soloveitchik contested the transcendental conception of religion holding that religion is not expressed in the realm of action (such as observance of the commandments), but only in the subjective experience beyond it. He attributed this approach to "Protestant groups" and "American Reform and Conservative Judaism"[6] that, in various measures, share a rejection of religious activity and perceive religion as a refuge and as mental tranquility rather than as a way of life. In *Worship of the Heart*, by contrast, R. Soloveitchik seeks to correct this error and contends with the attempt to establish religion exclusively on love and communion.

The consciousness process in which the model of the exalted, numinous God (and as shown below, the concealed God whose attribute is the *majestas Dei* symbolized in the hymnal blessings) leads to the model

---

3 *Worship of the Heart*, 73-74.
4 Here R. Soloveitchik also used clearly phenomenological terminology.
5 *Worship of the Heart*, 83.
6 *Halakhic Man*, 140.

of uniting lovingkindness (*caritas Dei*, the thanksgiving blessings), is itself a dialectic structure. Although the individual attained the level of the absolute love of God, that is, the response by the consciousness to the God of lovingkindness, he once again experiences fear and trembling when facing the concealed God. "The numinous element is important because it lends greatness to the religious experience; it deepens the human awareness of the existential and metaphysical antinomies that his nature involves and brings his historical destiny into a sharp focus."[7]

R. Soloveitchik illustrated the anxiety in the experience of God through the examples of Jacob's and Moses' struggles with the angel.[8] These fathers of the Jewish nation eventually triumphed and reached the level of joy, love, and communion. In religious life, however, the battle is renewed even after the victory. R. Soloveitchik's first argument in *Worship of the Heart* is contentual and not polemical: religious life, rather than soothing, is an ongoing process of polarized and stormy swings.

Loneliness as Concealment of the Divine Countenance

God's silence is the greatest threat to prayer. The experience of prayer as dialogue is challenged by the model of the concealed God. From the aspect of the worshiper, who wishes to pour out his supplication before Him, God's concealment means His absence (*numen absens*). This is the background for the lengthy discussion of the concealed God at the beginning of the fifth chapter of *Worship of the Heart*. R. Soloveitchik declares: just as God is revealed in two planes, the natural and the historical, so too, He is concealed in these two planes. God's concealment means the experience of loneliness.

The experience of "metaphysical solitude and existential void"[9] would not come about unless preceded by the experience of the presence of God. If in an existential solitude context the uniqueness and loneliness of the subject preceded the presence of the other, in the consciousness relationship between man and God, solitude follows revelation. Man feels abandoned after having experienced the divine presence.

How had he experienced this presence? This is a dual experience, in both nature and history. The divine presence in these two realms results in a feeling of both solemnity and significance. R. Soloveitchik writes of the

---

7 *Worship of the Heart*, 74.
8 *Worship of the Heart*, 73.
9 *Worship of the Heart*, 77.

presence of God in nature: "There is solemnity, fullness and overabundance of meaning in nature, when man delights in all the nuances of the tone and tempo of life, when he enjoys the world surrounding him, because wherever he turns he finds God."[10] The presence of God in history is attested by the purposefulness of the historical process. The divine presence is especially evident when man is cognizant of a "distant ultimate end." The teleological interpretation of the twists and turns of history reveals the purposefulness of a process that extends over so many years and leads to "grandeur and magnificence."[11] Towards the end of this chapter, R. Soloveitchik formulated the connection between nature and history as the principle of "the parallelism prevailing between the norm implied in God's encounter with man, and the Divine revelation through the cosmos."[12] For him, natural law and the moral law issue forth from the same source: "the cosmic law itself is an expression of Divine grace and morality."[13]

On a number of occasions R. Soloveitchik adopted the models and styles of religious Zionist thought, examples of which can be found in *Kol Dodi Dofek* (*Listen: My Beloved Knocks*).[14] This trend distinctly tends to equate the attitude to nature with that to history, based on the profound belief in divine providence and divine guidance of the world. R. Isaac Jacob Reines, the founder of the Mizrachi movement, devoted numerous discussions to the emphasis placed on the divine presence in nature and in the historical process.[15] Isaiah Wolfsberg-Aviad, an important Mizrachi

---

10 *Worship of the Heart*, 85. Scheler maintained that life's physiological and psychological processes are identical, in that both are characteristically purposeful and move toward universality. See Scheler, *Man's Place in Nature*, 74.

11 *Worship of the Heart*, 76-77. See Jeffrey Woolf, "Time Awareness as a Source of Spirituality in the Thought of Rabbi Joseph B. Soloveitchik," *Modern Judaism* 32, no. 1 (2012): 54-75. The historical consciousness that Woolf discusses relates mainly to the Biblical and Second Temple periods, which are relevant for the halakhah. Unquestionably, the halakhah fosters the historical memory of these periods. R. Soloveitchik, however, was aware of modern discussions of history, its place in the humanities, and the disputes regarding Jewish history that were engendered by *Wissenschaft des Judentums*. This resulted in a complex analysis regarding the experience of the divine presence in history.

12 *Worship of the Heart*, 83.

13 *Worship of the Heart*, 84.

14 See, for example, Schwartz, *Faith at the Crossroads*, 216

15 See Schwartz, *Faith at the Crossroads*, 54-55. On the divine presence in the historical process in religious Zionist thought, see Schwartz, *Faith at the Crossroads*, chap. 2. Many scholars have discussed the problematic nature of secularized history from a historiographic perspective, following the book *Zakhor: Jewish History and Jewish Memory* by Yosef Hayim Yerushalmi (Tel Aviv: Am Oved, 1988; English edition: Seattle: University of Washington Press, 1996). See, for example, Michael L. Morgan, *Dilemmas in Modern*

leader, identified the accidental and purposefulness in nature, on the one hand, and in history, on the other. Heisenberg's uncertainty principle is one of the arguments advanced for the randomness of the historical process. R. Abraham Isaac Hakohen Kook and his ideological circle sought to view the reality as a unity, and in this respect they did not distinguish between nature and history. By the same coin, religious Zionist thinkers spoke of the purposefulness in the historical process.[16] Wolfsberg-Aviad wrote in his book on the philosophy of history that

> only if we assume that all this abundance of phenomena is not mere chance, but rather among the signs of the tremendous and dramatic struggle whose goal is clear and defined,[17] may we speak of the orders of history and of our being privileged to reveal them.[18]

That is, the very discourse on the philosophy of history is conditional upon historical purposefulness. This approach is an expression of a religious Zionist mode of thought.

Knowledge of the laws of nature and the ways of history imparts the consciousness of God's presence. R. Soloveitchik, however, maintains that the sense of solemnity is replaced by one of smashing against the rocks of life and crisis. When the consciousness of the divine presence fades and vanishes, man experiences the concealed and silent God—or solitude. Many historical events characterized by randomness or evil crush the feeling of purposefulness and of a guiding presence. "The experience of the *numen absens*, of an empty world, at a cosmic and historical level, is shattering."[19]

Solitude arouses struggle. Man fights God's concealment in the cosmic-natural realm. This struggle is expressed in his scientific achievements, in his success in formulating the laws of nature by mathematical and physical means.[20] An orderly and organized universe evinces a directed

---

Jewish Thought: The Dialectics of Revelation and History (Bloomington: Indiana University Press, 1992).

16 Isaiah Wolfsberg-Aviad, *Thoughts on the Philosophy of History* [Hebrew] (Jerusalem: Mossad Harav Kook, 1958), 34.

17 He alludes to the historical process that ends in the messianic era; see Wolfsberg-Aviad, *Thoughts*, chapter 15.

18 Ibid., 38.

19 *Worship of the Heart*, 77.

20 R. Soloveitchik apparently relied, once again, on the definition of scientific activity as creating "mathematical relationships" (*Worship of the Heart*, 84) that not connected to the phenomena. Between the lines, he alludes here to the conventional approach, which separates the sensual phenomenon from the mathematical model that it inspires in the thought of the scientist. See Schwartz, *Religion or Halakha*, 124.

divine plan, and therefore, a divine presence, as well. But this struggle is doomed to failure. The scientific enterprise does not succeed in revealing God within the universe, nor does it quiet the sense of anxiety and dread. An analysis of R. Soloveitchik's discussion teaches of three limitations of scientific achievements that are indicative of the concealment of God:

(1) scientific achievements are unsuccessful in uncovering rationality in the ramified physical laws (the lack of rational causality);[21]
(2) scientific achievements lead to a model of an infinite and meaningless universe (the lack of purposefulness);
(3) scientific achievements have not overcome many natural evils that threaten man's very existence and demonstrate his vulnerability (incurable diseases and the like).

Consequently, the struggle against the concealment of God's countenance in nature has no real chance of success. From the outset, reason is powerless, which prevents any true victory. In parallel, the teleological interpretation of history collapses in the face of chaotic events. "Many a time man wonders whether or not God cares to intervene on his behalf."[22] R. Soloveitchik did not specify which events motivated him to write *Halakhic Man*, namely, the Holocaust and the destruction of Europe's *yeshivot* and other Torah institutions. He did, however, allude to "savagery." Simply put, the course of history is not amenable to the teleological interpretation that reason and religion try to apply to it.

The sense of the divine presence incessantly swings between grandeur and failure. The divine good retreats and disappears, with the (indifferent) infinite and impermeable coming in its stead, and vice versa. Success and failure touch one another. The dynamics of the religious consciousness is an indisputable fact. R. Soloveitchik emphasizes at the end of the chapter that the Torah is concerned with dynamic instruction and guidance. He based this dynamic on the process of the perfection of the consciousness that he described at length in this chapter. The term "Torah," according to R. Soloveitchik, "emphasizes the methodological rather than the static and formulated."[23] In other words, the Torah records the changing and pendulating nature of the religious consciousness. The ascents and

---

21 There is no rational and comprehensible connection between, for example, the hand that throws a weight and the mathematical formula that describes the phenomenon
22 *Worship of the Heart*, 76.
23 *Worship of the Heart*, 85.

descents of the consciousness are recorded in the Torah, which balances and channels them.

3. Failure and Success in Prayer

How does prayer contend with the model of the hidden God that threatens its very existence? R. Soloveitchik mentions two modes of prayer that relate to the crisis in the face of God's silence.[24] The first manner denotes the failed struggle, that is, the lack of dialogue. The second way depicts success, when prayer leads man from the stage of the silence of God to that of dialogue with Him. The first mode is voluntary: a person's moaning from the heart bears his personal stamp, while the other is institutionalized, that is, based on the set prayer formulations. In this section we will examine the portrayals of the two prayer modes and their being reflective of different channels of consciousness, and the factors responsible for the differences between them.

Spontaneous Prayer

For R. Soloveitchik, prayer reflects the desperate struggle with God's concealment. When a person offers a voluntary prayer, he sighs about his condition and seeks to change this state of affairs, which he does not accept. After depicting the concealment of the divine countenance in nature, R. Soloveitchik describes spontaneous prayer:

> Man prays to the hidden God: Please reveal Thyself to me, show me a sign that Thou art here and there, that the universe is not a still desert, where the accidental event reigns supreme.[25] Not always, however, does he receive an answer to his fervent prayers. Man seeks God in nature and he cannot find: "Let me rise and wander in the town; have you seen Him whom my soul loves?" (Song 3:2).[26]

R. Soloveitchik speaks of the experience of solitude in nature, and not in history, and of the silence of the universe. Man utters a prayer from the depths of his soul, while God is silent and concealed. R. Soloveitchik did not write this outright, but there is no response to such a prayer. The divine alienation continues. R. Soloveitchik obliquely mentions that such prayer is destined

---

24 *Worship of the Heart*, 76, 80.
25 R. Soloveitchik referred to "accidental" in the scientific sense, as opposed to law of nature.
26 *Worship of the Heart*, 76.

to failure, in the historical plane as well. He brings a proof for this from the prophets, who were "dismayed by prayers unheard,[27] and sacrifices rejected, and martyrdom incurred seemingly in vain by the just and righteous."[28] The two prayers he mentions are not institutionalized. The first, on the obliviousness of nature, is clearly spontaneous, and is formulated in the worshiper's own words. The prayer on the obliviousness of history is ascribed to the prophets, whose style, too, was personal. These spontaneous prayers are dashed against the silent God. Even though they do battle with this silence, they are unsuccessful in breaching the wall of the hidden God.

We must further ask: what meaning is prayer to reveal ("Please reveal Thyself to me"[29])? R. Soloveitchik states, from the outset, that the dialectical situation will continue as long as nature and history exist. The messianic era, in which only the consciousness models of the beneficent God and the unity of the nonfluctuating religious consciousness will predominate, is beyond this discussion. According to him: "Yet, eschatology is placed outside the historic-cosmic circle. As long as our existence is fenced in by the historic and the natural - our experience of God is a dual one."[30] R. Soloveitchik declares that he is concerned solely with the real existence. If so, then what point is there to seeking revelation, since its attainment is also the starting point of its loss? The dialectic is a given of concrete existence. Consequently, prayer is meant to perpetuate the bond between man and his God, and to internalize its aesthetic and consciousness meanings. Prayer does not alter the state of affairs. It aims to make the worshiper conscious of the dialectical situation.

The Community of Prayer

In the wake of the prayer for God to reveal Himself, which did not yield any significant change, communal prayer successfully brings man to connect with God. In order to understand the distinction between spontaneous prayer and communal prayer, which, as we will see, is institutionalized, we must examine a number of issues:

(1) the meaning of communality (man and God);
(2) the path to the perfection of the consciousness (the transition from one stage to the next, by embracing the crisis);

---

27 Based on the wording from the *Amidah*: "who hears prayers."
28 *Worship of the Heart*, 77.
29 *Worship of the Heart*, 76.
30 *Worship of the Heart*, 78.

(3) the identity of the successful prayer (institutionalized prayer);

(4) the place of prayer in the process of the perfection of the consciousness (recording and reflection of the process).

The editor of *Worship of the Heart* took pains to base the fifth chapter
on the community of prayer, as is also attested by the chapter's title ("The
Absence of God and the Community of Prayer"). A cursory look at the
chapter, however, reveals two facts that are characteristic of the entire first
section (chapters 1-5) of the book as a whole

(1) Prayer itself does not occupy a central place in the chapter. Only
isolated and subtle references uncover its important weight in the
discussion.

(2) Prayer in the traditional sense of community, that is, public prayer
(*tefilah be-tzibbur*), is relegated to a marginal role.

And now, for the discussion itself. Community was an issue that
famously concerned R. Soloveitchik in his various writings.[31] Quite surprisingly, the "community" prayer, in his terminology, does not refer to
public prayer. We will now examine one of R. Soloveitchik's isolated references in this chapter to the hidden God who is revealed by means of prayer.
He writes:

> In prayer, man tries to break through the unknown to the kerygmatic
> and to attain contact with the Creator, to convert tenseness into intimacy,
> strangeness into acquaintance. Judaism wants him to take courage and
> address himself to God, and by boldly approaching Him—the Infallible and
> Unknowable—to lift the veil and dreadful mystery of the numen. When this
> takes place, man finds the unknown to be an old friend; in the numen he dis-
> covers the intimately Unknown, radiating warmth and love. Through prayer,
> man accomplishes the impossible: the transformation of the numinous into
> the kerygmatic, of fear into love and of absence into presence. Thus when
> prayer is born, a community is established and man finds himself no longer
> lonely, forlorn; there are two lonely beings who have sought and found each
> other. This relation is not a functional but an existential one.[32]

---

31 See, for example, "The Community," *Tradition* 17, no. 2 (Spring 1978): 7-24. The
communities of prophecy and prayer were the subject of extensive discussions in
The Lonely Man of Faith, as well.

32 *Worship of the Heart*, 80.

We should clarify the two terms that R. Soloveitchik used in the fifth chapter of *Worship of the Heart*, that also appear in this passage.

The first term is "kerygmatic," refersto the standing before the revealed God who commands or delivers tidings to man. This is the third stage of religious consciousness, as was noted in Chapter Four (above). This phase reflects the phase of the consciousness of the beneficent God (R. Soloveitchik previously called the kerygmatic phase "God's loving-kindness"). At the same time, it reflects the summit of the mutual limitless love between man and God (communion). Kerygma reflects two meanings.

(a) Command: God addresses man, is revealed to him in the course of history, and commands him. That is the experience of historical revelation.
(b) Community: God is connected to man, and is revealed to be good and a friend. Man and God create a community.

The second term, "numinous,"[33] relates to the standing before God, the absolute Other. God is the awful and sublime mystery. Unlike kerygma as revelation, the numinous reflects the hidden God ("the glory of God"). The numinous refers to the second phase of the consciousness, in which it stands before the incomprehensible God. The numinous experience arouses two responses:

(a) anxiety: man feels dread, annihilation, and detachment ("emotional chaos"[34]) in the face of God's absence.
(b) muteness: the response to the God who is absent denies any possibility of revelation and dialogue.[35]

According to R. Soloveitchik, the mission of the consciousness whose realization is aided by prayer is to "translate his numinous experience into a kerygmatic experience."[36] Again, at the end of the chapter he explains that

---

33 At times I will call the numinous the "experience of exaltation," since it refers to standing before the hidden and threatening God. With this experience, man confronts his nullity and rootlessness. See above, Chapter Four.
34 *Worship of the Heart*, 81.
35 The distinction between the kerygmatic type and the numinous, in relation to the other and to society, appears in *Family Redeemed*. See Schwartz, *From Phenomenology to Existentialism*, 305-307.
36 The transition from the second stage of consciousness (the dialectic) to the third (of unity), is described by R. Soloveitchik as the reducing, and actually, the elimination, of "the gap separating the kerygmatic from the numen" (*Worship of the Heart*, 81-82).

prayer is only one of the expressions of this task. The Torah in its entirety is concerned with this movement of the consciousness. "[…] the Torah's main objective is the translation of the numinous into the kerygmatic."[37] God, who before the prayer was as lonesome as man, is connected to the worshiper by prayer. Such a connection is the community, the community of prayer. Thus, prayer is the expression of the process undergone by the consciousness.

It is evident from the end of the passage cited above that R. Soloveitchik adopted the model of the lonely God. Man's solitude is enrooted in that of God.[38] The Talmudic and midrashic sources often declare that God is "unique in His world,"[39] but in most cases this is not said in a negative sense. That is, God's uniqueness does not mean distress; it does not reflect troubling solitude, it rather usually indicates fullness. R. Soloveitchik, however, seems to write of the meeting between God and man as the forging of a community of two lonesome entities. The approach that God, as it were, needs man is deeply enrooted in Jewish tradition. The conception of God as good assumes the need of objects that enable the potential good to be actualized. Consequently, God, as it were, needs the creature.[40] The theurgic principle characteristic of Kabbalah is founded on such an approach. The term *tikkun* (mending) usually refers to a flaw or a non-activated virtue in the divine world that demands human agency, not to the state of consciousness of solitude. R. Soloveitchik might have been influenced by rabbinic depictions of the personification of God, the *Shekhinah*, which possesses human attributes and is a partner to human existence. The *Shekhinah* shares in the suffering of the people and the individual, and will likely accompany them in their solitude. God's dependence upon man was expressed by thinkers with whose philosophy R. Soloveitchik was familiar. One example of such a philosophical direction is Kierkegaard, who argued that just as God loves, so too, He desires to be loved,[41] and who frequently discussed God's need of man. Another example is Abraham

---

He also formulated the transition as aiming "to convert a numinous feeling into a community experience" (*Worship of the Heart*, 80); see below.

37 *Worship of the Heart*, 85.

38 Cf. the end of *The Lonely Man of Faith*, where R. Soloveitchik writes that God "abides in the recesses of transcendental solitude," and that He is "the Lonely One" (*Lonely Man of Faith*, 112).

39 See, for example, JT Rosh Hashanah 1:3, 57b; BT Pesakhim 118a; *Shemot Rabbah* 4:4.

40 Saadia Gaon, *The Book of Beliefs and Opinions*, trans. Samuel Rosenblatt (New Haven: Yale University Press), beginning of Treatise III.

41 See Søren Kierkegaard, *Søren Kierkegaard's Journals and Papers*, ed. Howard V. Hong and Edna H. Hong (Bloomington, IN: Indiana University Press, 1970), vol. 2, 147. See also Sagi, *Kierkegaard, Religion and Existence*, 139.

Joshua Heschel, who entitled one of his books *God in Search of Man*, and who wrote: "It is as if God were unwilling to be alone, and He had chosen man to serve Him."[42] R. Soloveitchik, however, had no qualms about presenting God as lonely. His portrayal of God as suffering from the distress of solitude is not common in Jewish tradition.[43]

We also learn from the passage cited above that "community" does not mean a partnership of "I" and "Thou," that is, man and his fellow, but rather one of "I" and "He"—man and God. The terminology of "community" for connecting between subjects, namely, the link between two human beings, appears in the fifth meditation in Husserl's *Cartesian Meditations*.[44] R. Soloveitchik, however, was not concerned from the outset with the question of the intersubjective relationship with another person and its reflection in prayer. The Other in this discussion is God. R. Soloveitchik adopted the terminology of Friedrich Heiler in his work on prayer. In Heiler's discussion on the essential nature of prayer, he frequently used the term *Verkehr* to describe the standing of man and God in prayer.[45] Heiler maintained that prayer creates a relationship of partnership and connection between man and God. He used additional terms such as *Gemeinschaft* to denote the communal dimension of prayer, that is, the connection between God and man.

For R. Soloveitchik, standing before God "means to experience the dreadful feeling of loneliness, of a solitary and desolate experience, a creature fallen away from the Creator and the Sustainer."[46] Furthermore, loneliness in regard to other humans is perceived as an external expression of the profound loneliness that man feels before God.[47] Prayer makes the

---

42 Abraham Joshua Heschel, *God in Search of Man: A Philosophy of Judaism* (New York: Farrar, Straus and Giroux, 1978), 136.

43 The Christian tradition of the personal suffering God undoubtedly left its mark on the discussion. Such a notion is opposed, in some degree, by theologians of crisis such as Barth and Brunner, who emphasized the absolute perfection of God, not dependent on extradivine factors. For them, the partnership of God and man is not that of equals. God is always superior and sublime. Kierkegaard and other existential thinkers, in contrast, claimed that God relates to man, also as a consequence of His solitude.

44 See David T. Carr, *Phenomenology and the Problem of History: A Study of Husserl's Transcendental Philosophy* (Evanston, IL: Northwestern University Press, 1974), 105; Steven W. Laycock, "God as the Ideal: The All-of-Monads and the All-Consciousness," in *Phenomenology of the Truth Proper to Religion*, ed. Daniel Guerrière (Albany, NY: State University of New York Press, 1990), 256-259.

45 See Heiler, *Das Gebet*, 490; English translation: Heiler, *Prayer*, 357.

46 *Worship of the Heart*, 79.

47 *Worship of the Heart*, 79.

hidden God manifest to such a degree that He becomes man's Colleague and Friend. In *Worship of the Heart*, the community of prayer is therefore the correlation of God and man who, prior to their meeting, had been alone in their respective worlds. The relationship between two lonely subjects, Adam and Eve, which is portrayed in *The Lonely Man of Faith*, is now transformed into the relationship between God and man. The conversion of "a numinous feeling" into "a community experience"[48] is nothing other than the covenantal relationship between man and his God. Again, the social community is an outer expression of the community that is created between God and man. The dialectical experience of the exalted, the hidden, and the silent becomes a connection of joining and friendship. The community of prayer is the direct continuation of the covenant. R. Soloveitchik refrains from digressing to the question of the Other, and remains within the realm of the phenomenological study of the experience of God. Prayer redeems man and God together from the state of loneliness. In order to understand the place of prayer as the consciousness of community, we must, once again, define the condition of human loneliness. R. Soloveitchik defined this situation within his phenomenological discussion of the religious consciousness, that is, the consciousness of God: loneliness means God's concealment, as we saw above.

The Consciousness Process

R. Soloveitchik emphasizes at the beginning of the first chapter of *Worship of the Heart* that prayer is only one medium of religious consciousness. We already noted the weight of this declaration, meant to balance the centrality of prayer in R. Soloveitchik's thought. At times, halakhic authority makes it difficult for us to determine what is central, and what only secondary.[49] In any event, R. Soloveitchik argues here, as well, that prayer is a specific instance of the perfection of the consciousness and one of the expressions of "method."[50] It helps man in developing, in terms

---

48 *Worship of the Heart*, 80. Cf. what R. Soloveitchik wrote in 1954 against mixed seating in the synagogue: "Prayer means communion with the Master of the World, and therefore withdrawal from all and everything. During prayer man must feel alone, removed, isolated. He must then regard the Creator as an only Friend, from whom alone he can hope for support and consolation" ("On Prayer in a Synagogue with Mixed Pews," section 18 in *Community, Covenant and Commitment*, 134-35).
49 See above, Chapter Two.
50 *Worship of the Heart*, 80.

of his consciousness, from the fluctuating to the unified, from loneliness to community (with God), and in R. Soloveitchik's terminology, from the numinous state to the kerygmatic. How does the consciousness pass from one stage to the next? The process has three components.

(1) An awareness of the covenant: the covenantal relationship between the Jewish people and God guarantees that the numinous state of the hidden God cannot be permanent. In a certain stage, God will be revealed as good, and the state of connection with Him ("community") will be possible. The continuity of this state is not assured, and dread may return, with this cycle continuing. The covenantal relationship, however, is recorded, and has legal force. "In spite of His frequent, frightening withdrawals from our midst, He cannot, on juridic grounds, forsake us."[51] The very awareness of the covenant motivates the dialectical consciousness not to despair, and to ascend to its unified phase.

(2) The attitude to the exalted: the consciousness of the concealed God could be sudden and traumatic. The discovery of powerlessness and self-negation in the face of the exalted shocks man when he is least prepared for such an upheaval. If, however, man accepts the exalted voluntarily, then the exalted is seen to be beneficent and loving. In R. Soloveitchik's terminology, when man adopts and responds to the numinous experience, it becomes kerygmatic. The numinous experience is translated to the kerygmatic by "the acceptance of the numinous authority, truly, wholeheartedly and with conviction."[52]

(3) Exposure: at the end of the chapter R. Soloveitchik adds a third component to the process of the perfection of the consciousness. The model of the exalted God is formulated from contemplation of tremendous and impermeable nature. But the infinite divine good is present within this unbending, silent nature. "The numen, in all of its appearances (both presence and absence), at all levels, hides the kerygma within its strange order: *majestas Dei* is the garment

---

51 *Worship of the Heart*, 80. God's commitment as a covenantal relationship now acquires legal force.

52 *Worship of the Heart*, 81. As in *And from There You Shall Seek*, the ascension of the consciousness entails transforming the foreign to the familiar. See, for example, Schwartz, *From Phenomenology to Existentialism*, 126.

covering *caritas Dei*."[53] Like a husk, natural law covers the divine good and is present within it. The model of the beneficent God is present in the exalted model. When man takes note of this, then he ascends from the stage of exaltation to that of communion and connection with the beneficent God. The mechanism of elevation is therefore bound up with the revealing of the divine presence within inanimate nature.

To this point, R. Soloveitchik explained how the consciousness passes from the dialectical stage to the unified. He perceives such perfection of the consciousness as repentance.[54] Thus, the process of repentance explicates the parallel process of the elevation of the consciousness, as follows:

(1) the numinous experience causes suffering (the first stage of consciousness);
(2) the voluntary adoption of suffering leads to catharsis;
(3) the voluntary adoption of the numinous experience, too, leads to catharsis;
(4) this catharsis leads to closeness to God (the second state of consciousness).

The process of the perfection of the consciousness that is depicted here is conceived as repentance, as is depicted in the verse: "When you are in distress because of all these things that have befallen you and, in the end, return to the Lord your God" (Deut. 4:30). According to the verse, repentance is dependent upon distress, that is, suffering.[55] R. Soloveitchik based suffering on the experience of the numinous. The beginning of the verse presents the repentant as passive. For R. Soloveitchik, the events that come to him ("that have befallen you," literally: that have found you) refer to the sudden and shocking experience of the exalted God. In the end of the verse, in contrast, the repentant initiates the response, and is therefore

---

53 *Worship of the Heart*, 85.
54 On the connection between repentance and prayer, see, for example, Jacob Elbaum, *Repentance and Self-Flagellation in the Writings of the Sages of Germany and Poland 1348-1648* [Hebrew] (Jerusalem: Magnes, 1993), 201.
55 Prayer, repentance, and asceticism were bound together mainly in Pharisaic circles. See, for example, Ephraim Kanarfogel, *"Peering through the Lattices": Mystical, Magical, and Pietist Dimensions in the Tosafist Period* (Detroit: Wayne State University Press, 2000), 125-126.

presented as active ("[when you] return," and not "[when] I bring you back"). How does man change from passive to active? R. Soloveitchik supplied the missing link: when the sufferer resolves to adopt the sudden experience, which he chooses of his own volition, then it transforms him to one who is connected to God and with Whom he creates a community: "man subsequently finds it easier to approach God and to be intimate with Him. God does not admit man to Himself unless he has gone through the experience of atonement."[56] The perfection of the consciousness is therefore a process of repentance.

Institutionalized Prayer

Now, to turn to the role of prayer in the development of the consciousness. Prayer is briefly mentioned twice in this discussion, and each instance is meant to explain the second element in the process of the perfection of the consciousness, that is, the change in the attitude to the exalted as the key to attaining the supreme phase of consciousness, that of connection with God ("community"). This phase is based on the divine model of the beneficent God. The change in consciousness comes in the wake of the free and intentional choice of the experience of the exalted.

The first time, the blessing is mentioned: "That is why one recites a blessing for evil occurrences just as one thanks God for good tidings."[57] Thus, the acceptance of the divine judgment enables one to accept the numinous out of choice, voluntarily.

The second instance speaks of the *Amidah* prayer. Here we see prayer that succeeds in elevating the individual to the perfection of the consciousness. R. Soloveitchik writes:

> That is why *tefillah* begins by referring to the God of Abraham, Isaac and Jacob. It is because our fathers displayed the ability to interpret the numinous in terms of a great kerygma. They took the absolute inconceivability (Otto's term[58]) of the great mysterious experience and found in it an inexpressible order, positive and sustaining. Out of utter despair emerges

---

56 *Worship of the Heart*, 90.
57 *Worship of the Heart*, 82.
58 See Otto, *Idea of the Holy*, 13. Interestingly, R. Soloveitchik often used the English version that was readily available in the United States. Otto explained that the use of conceptual styles leads solely to "a merely negative one." He argued that, in this context, the term "mystery" (*mysterium tremendum*) refers to what is "beyond conception or understanding."

the great message. Whenever man is swept into the abyss, whenever meaninglessness seems to have deflated purposiveness and sense, man rises up, striding vigorously over the mystery toward the revelation of a message.[59]

The *Avot* blessing is seen to be the adoption of the experience of the exalted. It records the success of the Patriarchs of the Jewish people in the process of the perfection of the consciousness. Prayer succeeds in expressing an inner process, that itself is verbally inexpressible. The Patriarchs stood before God, who alternately threatens ("the covenant between the pieces") and is silent,[60] and managed to find their way to the experience of community and communion by their acceptance of the experience.

This enables us to understand the paradoxical place of prayer. When a person undergoes a numinous experience he is in distress, and utters a spontaneous prayer in order to be extricated from the crisis, as we saw in the preceding section ("Please reveal Thyself to me"[61]). Man groans under the burden of his tribulations and expresses his suffering in voluntary prayer. This prayer, however, is doomed to fail. It does not elevate him to the supreme phase of consciousness. Why is this so? Because in order to advance from the numinous model to the kerygmatic, one's personality and attitude must undergo wrenching and profound change. Suffering does not necessarily indicate deep change experienced by an individual. Since prayer is an objective expression of consciousness—a religious act—it is reflective of subjective moods. It is not enough that prayer reflects distress. It must express the three following changes, anchored in each other:

(1) embracing dread and anxiety, that is, accepting the experience;
(2) adopting the divine model, that is, accepting the exalted numinous;
(3) changes in personality and in consciousness.

R. Soloveitchik believed that only the institutionalized halakhah is capable of producing a prayer text that reflects the true change in one's personality. The success of prayer cannot be contingent on an individual's personal utterances in time of distress. To a certain respect, voluntary prayer is sterile. It is specifically the text of the first blessing of the *Amidah* prayer: "the God of Abraham, the God of Isaac, and the God of Jacob," which enables the transition to the supreme stage of consciousness.

---

59 *Worship of the Heart*, 83.
60 *Worship of the Heart*, 81.
61 *Worship of the Heart*, 76.

This formulation is the fixed and precise record of the subjective process undergone by the consciousness (the embracing of suffering and divine alienation). Between the lines, R. Soloveitchik sought to explain, once again, that only the objective expression of the consciousness determined by the halakhah is the faithful and effective reflection of the fluid and stormy consciousness. The set prayer text is the trustworthy expression of the passage to the kerygmatic stage, that is, of connection to God and the creation of community with Him. This prayer succeeds where spontaneous prayer has failed.

Nature and History

I explained above that the divine silence is expressed in the universe and in history. Spontaneous prayer did not succeed in breaking this silence, neither in the universe nor in history. Institutionalized prayer, however, the *Amidah* prayer (the *Avot* blessing), did succeed in creating dialogue. This success was expressed in the historical arena more than in the cosmic plane. R. Soloveitchik attributed the events experienced by the Patriarchs and the promises given them to a "numinous historical experience."[62] The acceptance of the numinous as the key to the ascent of the consciousness was on the historical level, and not the cosmic. The community that is built between man and his God—the community of prayer—was forged in the historical plane.

In this context we should mention the disagreement in the Babylonian Talmud regarding the establishment of the prayers: were they initiated by the Patriarchs, or do they correspond to the *tamid*—the daily burnt offering? The former assertion has a cosmic context, and the latter, a historical setting. *Maharal* (R. Judah Loew ben Bezalel) of Prague provides a philosophical basis for this distinction.[63] He explains that the former possibility regards prayer as expressing God's being the beginning of the world, that is, its Cause, while, for the latter, prayer expresses

---

62 *Worship of the Heart*, 81. On prayer in the Bible, see, for example, Sheldon H. Blank, "Some Observations Concerning Biblical Prayer," *HUCA* 32 (1961): 75-90; Moshe Greenberg, "On the Refinement of the Conception of Prayer in Hebrew Scriptures," *AJS Review* 1 (1976): 57-92.

63 BT Berakhot 26b; *Maharal, Netivot Olam, Netivot ha-Avodah,* chap. 3. On prayer in the thought of *Maharal*, see, for example, André Neher, *Le Puits de l'exil: Tradition et modernité: la pensée du Maharal de Prague, 1512-1609* (Paris: Cerf, 1991), 169-172; R. Soloveitchik himself addressed this issue in his article "Reflections on the *Amidah*" (see below, Chapter Ten).

the world's drawing nearer to God. The perfection of the world brings it closer to its Source, that is, God. To a certain degree, the former possibility focuses on God as efficient Cause, and the latter, as final Cause. In either event, the approach of the Patriarchs as the beginning is of historical significance, while that of the world's drawing nearer to its Source tends to cosmic import.

Maharal's explanation might have contributed to fashioning R. Soloveitchik's approach, since he, too, adopted the distinction between the historical and the cosmic. In R. Soloveithik's final analysis, success is achieved by historical prayer, rooted in the halakhah. This prayer breaches the bounds of silence and creates dialogue between man and his God.

5. Summary

The first group of chapters in *Worship of the Heart* teaches that prayer is reflective, not only of the stages of consciousness (the fourth chapter), that is, its anatomy, but also of the way in which the transition from stage to stage is effected (the fifth chapter). We should now address the question of the standing of this fifth chapter, and how it is integrated in the discussion of the consciousness of prayer. This chapter is actually a double journey of the consciousness:

(1) from the solitude caused by the absence of God to the creation of a community with Him;
(2) from communality with God to law, that is, the halakhah.

We will now examine the question: how are we to understand the contribution of this chapter, on the background of the chapters that preceded it?

Ethos and Process

The structure of consciousness, as expressed in the second, third, and fourth chapters of *Worship of the Heart*, lends itself to a two-stage description:

(1) deep crisis (described in the second chapter) leads to petitionary blessings (beginning of the third chapter);

(2) the experience of aesthetic redemption, which leads to guilt and boredom when unredeemed (depicted in the third chapter), results in the numinous consciousness expressed in the blessings of praise and to the kerygmatic consciousness in thanksgiving blessings (fourth chapter).

Two explanations could be offered for the standing of the fifth chapter, each of which is based on the structure of the consciousness, as R. Soloveitchik did in the preceding chapters of *Worship of the Heart*.

(1) From anatomy to ethos. The first chapters of *Worship of the Heart* are concerned with defined stations of the *Amidah* prayer. These chapters discuss the sections and components of the *Amidah*. The fifth chapter is concerned with what Kaplan, following R. Soloveitchik, calls "prayerful life."[64] The description of the consciousness of prayer in this chapter ranges between communal conjunction with God, as was done especially in the time of the Patriarchs, to the beginning of the ethical and commanded norm. By his ending the chapter with the *Amidah*, R. Soloveitchik seemingly sought to clarify that communality with God is expressed in the prayer experience, just as the prayerful life expresses the divine command and Torah study. Kaplan observes that such movement from communality to commitment also appears in the conception of prayer in *The Lonely Man of Faith*.[65]

(2) From anatomy to process. The first chapters of *Worship of the Heart* teach that prayer reflects, not only the phases of the consciousness (fourth chapter), that is, its anatomy, it also represents the transition from phase to phase in the ladder of consciousness (fifth chapter). Prayer denotes a dynamic process, in addition to structure. Between the lines, R. Soloveitchik scattered allusions to the place of prayer in the process of ascent. Thus prayer is the objective expression or reflection of a series of lively processes that mark the perfection of the consciousness and the constant dialectic to which it is subject.

64 In a letter to me. See *Lonely Man of Faith*, 65-66; see also Reuven Ziegler, *Majesty and Humanity: The Thought of Rabbi Joseph B. Soloveitchik* (Jerusalem: Urim, 2012), 223.

65 See *Lonely Man of Faith*, 65. This essay, however, omits Torah study, which appears in *Worship of the Heart*.

Since R. Soloveitchik's preceding discussion was based on the phenom-enological method, and therefore the more coherent explanation describes a process, that is, while the preceding chapters examined the phases of the consciousness, the fifth chapter portrays the transition from one phase to the next. We will now summarize the ways in which prayer records the process of perfection within the consciousness, and their meaning.

Process

The following table reflects the consciousness journey from crisis to the numinous and from the numinous to the kerygmatic, paralleling the types and changing style of the prayers:

stage	feature of consciousness	*Amidah* blessings	prayer content	prayer status	achievement (transition to next stage)
(a)	distress	supplication	outcry over *tzarah*[66]	halakhic	success
(b)	numinous	hymn	1. petition for revelation[67] 2. *Amidah*[68]	1. voluntary 2. halakhic	1. failure 2. success
(c)	kerygmatic	thanksgiving	thanksgiving hymn[69]	halakhic	—

Thus, the transition from a state of crisis to the consciousness of the numinous is effected by the fixed version of the petitional prayers. Prayer reflects the fact that the existential crisis, and in its wake, the crisis of the consciousness, caused man to acknowledge and embrace his existence and its distresses. In the next stage, the numinous progresses to the kerygmatic, too, by means of hymnal prayer. Once again, prayer reflects the embrace and acceptance of the numinous. In this manner, the highest stage is attained,

---

66 *Worship of the Heart*, 29, following *Mishneh Torah, Hilkhot Taanit* [Laws of Fasting] 1:1 ("A positive Scriptural commandment prescribes prayer and the sounding of an alarm with trumpets whenever trouble befalls the community"). See Maimonides, *The Code of Maimonides, book 3: The Book of Seasons*, trans. Solomon Gandz and Hyman Klein (New Haven: Yale University Press, 1961), 432. Individual prayer, too, comes from "the depths," and is anchored in the halakhah.

67 *Worship of the Heart*, 76.

68 That is, the blessing of Avot (*Worship of the Heart*, 83).

69 *Worship of the Heart*, 66-67.

and back again. In other words, when a person has reached the highest stage, he finds himself, once again, facing existential distress, and the crisis threatens to sweep him along to meaningless existence. And then again, the petitional prayer makes him aware of his own self, and the consciousness process continues and advances. The language of prayer, therefore, accompanies the forging of the consciousness. Prayers range from recording the process to a factor that aids, and even determines, the process itself. R. Soloveitchik clarified, between the lines, that only prayers firmly anchored in Halakhah succeed in effecting the ascent of the consciousness. But he did so only gradually, at the end of a journey from voluntary to institutionalized prayer. When the reader comprehends that prayer accompanies his ascent, then he understands that such perfection is made possible, not from within the spontaneous cry out of distress, but from fixed and defined halakhic practice. If a person's cry from the heart does not lead him to the traditional halakhic path, he remains in his solitude facing oblivious nature, and thereby misses the uniting moments of the consciousness.

The Task

We learn that R. Soloveitchik ended the fifth chapter with solitude.[70] This ending is not especially encouraging: loneliness is a harsh experience. R. Soloveitchik again emphasized that the "cosmic" existential solitude is far harsher than social loneliness. "This form of solitude expresses a feeling of having fallen away from being, in transcendental uprootedness in spite of immanent rootedness."[71] R. Soloveitchik evidently wanted to show that the process of perfection of the consciousness is dialectical, as we showed a number of times in the preceding discussion. Additionally, however, he also sought to present the attainment of the supreme stage of consciousness, that of communion with the beneficent God, as a never-ending mission that faces the consciousness. For, communion is not the finish line of the path taken by the consciousness, but a new beginning. Every time that the consciousness ascends to communion, it discovers that there is no perfect communion, and the descent creates a new-renewed state of consciousness of solitude. This state of consciousness advances with hesitant but firm steps to the task of continual communion. The completion of the mission

---

70 As Kaplan mentioned, the paragraph that ends the chapter does not accord with its content and style. See Kaplan, "Review Essay," 105-106. Therefore, I did not relate to it in the current discussion.

71 *Worship of the Heart*, 85.

is not a matter for flesh-and-blood individuals who act in the current finite existence, it rather undoubtedly belongs to the messianic era. But R. Soloveitchik generally shows no interest in such a period and in the belief in the final redemption. Such a pattern of a "defeatist" or dialectical end to the consciousness process frequently recurs in R. Soloveitchik's thought over the course of time.

The consciousness is, therefore, in a constant and tormented process of the battle with loneliness when confronted by the hidden God. The cycle of prayers reflects the constant struggle to forge a community with God, or in other words, a dialogue of communion and even unification. "Prayer is the mirror of the lovesick religious soul."[72] The final conclusion of the first group of chapters in *Worship of the Heart* is that contending with solitude does not end. Religious consciousness ceaselessly endeavors to sustain the endless mission prescribed in the Torah: ascend to the third stage of consciousness and reach communion with the beneficent God.

---

72 *Worship of the Heart*, 86.

Chapter 6

The Dialectic of Consciousness: Between Reading *Shema* and Prayer

The editor of *Worship of the Heart* attests that the book is constructed of two sections (chapters 1-5, 6-9). The distinction between reading *Shema* and "prayer"[1] and an interpretation of reading *Shema* and its blessings are at the heart of the chapters in the second section. To a certain degree, R. Soloveitchik moderated his conception of the religious consciousness in this section; the introduction of reading *Shema* to the discussion altered R. Soloveitchik's perspective regarding the consciousness of prayer as a whole. If it were not for the editorial testimony (the division into two sections), we would have thought that R. Soloveitchik was somewhat deterred by the stormy model that he had presented in the first section, and accordingly wished to mitigate it in the second. We will now examine the contribution of reading *Shema* to our understanding of the structure and processes of the consciousness of prayer.

1. Between Reading *Shema* and Prayer

The connection between prayer and faith and trust in God is self-understood. A person intuitively prays because he believes that his prayer leaves some impression on God. The consciousness of prayer assumes a God who responds and answers needs. Reading *Shema* is not an appeal to God, but a declaration of belief in Him. To a certain degree, reading *Shema* reflects a dogmatic consciousness: it expresses belief, while the *Amidah*

---

1 See the editor's introduction to *Worship of the Heart*, ix: "*Tefillah*—prayer in the narrow sense of the term—refers to the *Amidah* (literally, the prayer recited while standing before God)."

is an expression of petition or hymn. The formal reading *Shema* (*Keri'at Shema*, beginning with the "Hear, O Israel" declaration in Deut. 6:4) was already recited by the priests in the Second Temple, while the fixed version of the *Amidah* prayer was established after the destruction of the Second Temple; the stages of its formulation are the subject of scholarly disagreement. The fact that the *Amidah* immediately follows reading *Shema* in the prayer service serves only to increase our interest in comparing the two. It has been argued that "[e]fforts were being made to ensure a continuity between the *shema* and the *Amidah* by the adoption of passages, with suitable benedictions, expressing faith in God's special relationship with Israel."[2] It is noteworthy that hints of such a comparison are already to be found in the Tannaitic literature.[3] R. Soloveitchik devoted considerable intellectual effort to compare reading *Shema* with the *Amidah*, in which he highlighted the differences between the two. Such a line of thought has deep roots in his sources. After indicating two such sources, we will discuss the elements of a comparison between reading *Shema* and the *Amidah*.

Conceptual Background

R. Soloveitchik's connection to Habad thought is firmly anchored in his personal life.[4] R. Schneur Zalman of Lyady (*ha-Admor ha-Zaken*, the founder of Habad Hasidism) extensively discussed the distinction between reading *Shema* and the *Amidah* prayer. For him, the former reflects the unification of the countenances of *Abba* and *Ima* (literally, "Father" and "Mother"), parallel to the *Sefirot* of *Hokhmah* and *Binah*, while the *Amidah* mirrors the unification of *Zeir Anpin* and *Nukva* (of the world of *Atzilut* [emanation]), parallel to *Tiferet* and *Malkhut*. Reading *Shema* makes visible the primordial creation, namely, the initial manifestation of the light of *Ein-Sof*. Its recitation leads to the appearance of the light of *Ein-Sof* ("and it must be drawn

---

2 Stefan C. Reif, *Judaism and Jewish Prayer: New Perspectives on Jewish Liturgical History* (Cambridge: Cambridge University Press, 1993), 128.

3 See, for example, Kaplan, "Review Essay," 87. On the halakhic distinctions between the reading of *Shema* and the *Amidah*, see, for example, M Berakhot 3:3; BT Berakhot 15a; Shabbat 11a. See also Tzvy Zahavy, *The Mishnaic Law of Blessings and Prayers: Tractate Berakhot* (Atlanta, GA: Scholars Press, 1987).

4 See Dov Schwartz, *Habad's Thought from Beginning to End* [Hebrew] (Ramat Gan: Bar-Ilan University Press, 2010), 367-385. For R. Soloveitchik's views on the Habad *melamed* (private tutor) and the way in which he internalized Habad thought, see his recently published: "Joyfully Shall You Draw Water" [Hebrew], *Ma'ayanotekha: Quarterly for Habad Thought* 30 (2011): 21-24.

down from the initial source, to renew the emanation [*hamshakhah*] from nothingness to being, which is the unification of *Hokhmah* and *Binah*"[5]). The intent in reading *Shema*, too, is directed to the substantiality (*atzmut*) of the light of *Ein-Sof*.[6] Paradoxically, the appearance of the light of *Ein-Sof* is thought to be above time. Reading *Shema* is thereby compared to Torah study, which is also above time. The *Amidah* prayer, in contrast, expresses the drawing down of the divine emanation in time, with the emanation being channeled to different aspects ("such as in the *Atah Honen* [You grace humanity with knowledge] blessing, the aspect of *Hokhmah* is drawn down"[7]). The emanation is received in the *Sefirah* of *Malkhut*. According to R. Schneur Zalman, reading *Shema* is the supreme stage of *Atzilut*, while prayer is an inferior phase. In practice, the order of reading *Shema* and the *Amidah* reflect the order of the descent of the divine emanation. As we shall see, R. Soloveitchik accepted the distinction between these two, but for him, the supreme stage was the *Amidah*, and not reading *Shema*.

Hermann Cohen maintained that the institutionalized prayers are a direct continuation of the prayers of the prophets and the Biblical psalms. "The original spirit (*Urgeist*) and the originality of the Bible are evident in the prayers."[8] He wrote, regarding reading *Shema*: "The stock prayers are grouped about the fundamental forms [*Grundformen*] of faith. Thus, the *Shema* ['Hear, O Israel'] is first taken from Deuteronomy. It is Israel's watchword, the watchword of the unique God."[9] Cohen also indirectly referred to the midrashic tradition that linked *Shema* with self-sacrifice.[10] He did not explain how cognition developed reading *Shema* out of faith, but he vigorously asserted that by means of the Biblical passages of *Shema* the individual worshiper communes with the one God. Reading *Shema* is the key to intellectual, cognitive conjunction. On the other hand, the *Amidah*, the "main prayer,"[11] is devoted to "earthly concern" as such. For Cohen, petition

---

5 *Siddur im DEH* (Prayerbook of the *Admor ha-Zaken*) [Hebrew] (Brooklyn, NY: 2002), 75a.
6 Schwartz, *Habad's Thought*, 117 n. 366.
7 *Siddur im DEH*, 75b. This statement has a magical flavor. See, for example, Moshe Idel, *Hasidism: Between Ecstasy and Magic* (Albany: SUNY Press, 1995).
8 Cohen, *Religion of Reason*, 392.
9 Ibid., 393.
10 "One should reflect upon the regulation of the Talmud, which says that while uttering in the *Shema* the word 'unique' (*Ehad*) the praying one in his thought and feeling should dedicate his entire soul and life to God" (ibid., 393). On the significance of this tradition in Habad thought, see below, Chapter Seven.
11 Cohen, *Religion of Reason*, 394.

is the main concern of the *Amidah*: "It is noteworthy that the main prayer of the *Shemoneh Esreh* unites in the first benediction earthly concern with that of the afterlife."[12] In this respect, reading *Shema* and the *Amidah* lead the worshiper along the same experiential path that was already set forth in the Bible.

Reading Shema *and the* Amidah: *A Comparison*

The sixth chapter of *Worship of the Heart* is devoted mainly to a presentation of the like and the disparate between reading *Shema* and prayer. The chapter begins in a similar way. R. Soloveitchik includes both reading *Shema* and the *Amidah* among those few commandments in which the subjective dimension is dominant.[13] Although they possess an objective dimension (wording, gesture, and the like), the subjective dimension becomes a necessary and central component of the halakhic praxis. For the decisive majority of the commandments, R. Soloveitchik distinguished between the praxis of the commandment and its subjective dimension (intent, rationale, etc.). The reconstruction of the subjective dimension merely presents this dimension as a possibility, while the act is necessary. The observance of the Sabbath, the taking of the Four Species on the Sukkot holiday, the wearing of *tzitzit* (ritual fringes), and so forth, are independent of feelings or their rationales. As a general rule, two people can have completely different subjective consciousnesses, while engaging in identical praxis. One may observe the Sabbath because he thinks that it contributes to social consolidation; another, because he experiences emotional partnership with the Creator, who rests, as it were, from the work of Creation; and a third, because of the great importance he ascribes to a day of rest. Their objective consciousness, however, is identical: all three observe the Sabbath in the same way. There is only one praxis. R. Soloveitchik thereby confirmed the authority of the halakhah, and provided a rationale for the conservative Orthodox approach. In, however, reading *Shema* and the *Amidah*, the

---

12 Ibid., 377. Cohen illustrated this with the blessing of *Gevurot* (divine might), which relates to both life's problems and the resurrection of the dead ("who keeps His faith with those who sleep in the dust").

13 The question of *kavannah* and its meaning for the individual has often been raised in the philosophy of prayer throughout the ages. In this respect, the *Shema* and the *Amidah* have been discussed together. See, for example, Nahem Ilan, "Between Halakhic Codification and Ethical Commentary: Rabbi Israel Israeli of Toledo and Intention in Prayer," in *Esoteric and Exoteric Aspects in Judeo-Arabic Culture*, ed. Benjamin H. Hary and Haggai Ben-Shammai (Leiden: Brill, 2006), 131-173.

subjective stratum is not reconstructed (or is not only reconstructed). It is an inherent component of these commandments. Intent in reading *Shema* and the *Amidah* is obligatory and not optional. R. Soloveitchik writes:

> Thus intention, in these [other] commandments, does not constitute an integral part of the religious gesture. By contrast, the *kavannah* in regard to *Shema* and *tefillah*[14] forms the core of accomplishment, the central idea and the intrinsic content of the *mitzvah*. It is not a mere modality,[15] expressing only the "how" of the *mitzvah*-fulfillment (as it does in other *mitzvot*), but rather is identical with the very substance and essence of the commandment.[16]

In this way, R. Soloveitchik resolved a disagreement among *Rishonim* (medieval authorities). Rashi, the Tosafists, and Nachmanides did not distinguish between reading *Shema* and other commandments, and argued that the intent in the former is to fulfill one's obligation, that is, the consciousness of the very mandated act. *Rashba* (R. Solomon ben Abraham Adret) and the students of R. Jonah Girondi spoke of intent as internalization, that is, the acceptance of the yoke of the kingdom of Heaven.[17] R. Soloveitchik sought to add Maimonides to those who based intent on the individual's internal world, and drew upon the *Mishneh Torah* for support. In the end, however, he admitted that "we lack a clear statement by Maimonides defining the essence and the need of *kavannah* while reading *Shema*."[18]

---

14 In the following paragraph, R. Soloveitchik defined intent as "meditation," "spiritual surrender," and "the turning and directing of the heart unto the Lord," thus drawing *kavannah* away from regular intentionality.

15 That is, the observance of the commandment in a certain manner.

16 *Worship of the Heart*, 89.

17 *Rashba*, for example, writes: "But a person's heart should not be directed to other things, regarding these [commandments], which entail the acceptance of the kingdom of Heaven or the order of praises [i.e, the hymnal blessings in the *Amidah*]" (*Hiddushei Rashba* on BT Berakhot 13b, in Rashba, *Sifrei ha-Rashba*, ed. Menahem Mendel Gerlitz [Jerusalem: Oraysoh, 1986], vol. 1, 27). The commentary of the students of R. Jonah contains the intent for the proclamation of God's kingship in the world (*Rif*, 7b). On the spiritual dimension in the students' commentary to prayer, see Israel M. Ta-Shma, "Ashkenazi Hasidism in Spain: R. Jonah Gerondi—the Man and His Work" [Hebrew], in Mirsky, Grossman, and Kaplan, eds., *Exile and Diaspora*, 177-178.

18 *Worship of the Heart*, 91. See Kaplan, "Review Essay," 83-84; Gerald J. Blidstein, *Prayer in Maimonidean Halakha* [Hebrew] (Jerusalem: Bialik Institute, 1994), 100-103. On intent in prayer for R. Abraham, the son of Maimonides, see Abraham ben Moses ben Maimon, *Sefer ha-Maspik Le'Ovdey Hashem: Kitab Kifayat al-'Abidin* [Hebrew], part 2, vol. 2, ed. Nissim Dana (Ramat Gan: Bar-Ilan University, 1989), 24-25.

Since Maimonides' halakhic work did not provide unequivocal support for the subjectivization of reading *Shema*, R. Soloveitchik was forced to turn to the teaching of *Guide of the Perplexed* on the worship of "those who have apprehended true realities," that is, those who attained intellectual perfection. At the end of the *Guide*, Maimonides described the worship of these perfect individuals, placing emphasis on contemplation.[19] They live a contemplative life (*vita contemplativa*) even when they are involved in the material world. Reading *Shema* is a cardinal expression of a Biblical text with outstanding conceptual meanings ("Hear, O Israel"), and therefore also a rich subjective substrate. The contemplation of these meanings is an integral part of the commandment itself. The addition of the *Guide*, therefore, provides a basis for the cognitive interpretation of reading *Shema*.

At the same time, however, there was a price to pay for referring to the *Guide of the Perplexed*. R. Soloveitchik was aware that this work is clearly esoteric, and its ideal goals are not directed to the masses. Esotericism is plainly contrary to the exoteric nature of the halakhah; R. Soloveitchik himself frequently stressed in his writings that the halakhah is meant for all strata of the public, and is not the sole province of mystics, intellectuals, scholars, or ascetics and exceptional individuals. In the section concluding the original nine chapters of *Worship of the Heart*, he wrote that "Judaism, always impervious to religious esotericism, has made it possible for all to have a full life."[20] R. Soloveitchik did not ignore the harm in referring to an esoteric work that the Jewish world, for many generations, perceived as a paradigm of concealment and masking by various techniques and, therefore, attempted to keep its damage to an absolute minimum. He argued that a general educational message could be derived from the *Guide*, and that such a message was not limited to individuals: Maimonides instructed the public as a whole to attain perfection. He writes:

> Maimonides introduces a halakhic motif which is of utmost importance to all of us. In expounding the way to attain Divine friendship and continual communion, he inserts a parenthetic remark of great relevance. He advises us to proceed gradually. The first mental exercise should consist in expanding the norm of spiritual concentration, or unqualified devotion and surrender, to religious areas where the Halakhah does not require such a meditative

---

19 See, for example, Eliezer Goldman, "The Worship Peculiar to Those Who Have Apprehended True Reality" [Hebrew], *Bar-Ilan* 6 (1968): 287-313; Kaplan, "Review Essay," 85-86; Blidstein, *Prayer in Maimonidean Halakha*, 80-86.
20 *Worship of the Heart*, 142.

devotional attitude. Gradually one learns the practice of employing oneself
entirely, with all one's faculties, in the service of God.[21]

The meditative way of worship is valid for the entire public, for novices
and the public at large, on the one hand, and on the other, for the perfect, although, in the end, only "those who have apprehended true reality"
reach the highest levels of the consciousness. In the *Guide* Maimonides set
forth an educational message valid for all. This educational path meant to
expand the contemplative approach to all spheres of religious life.

Once again, we can appreciate the great and exceptional value that
R. Soloveitchik ascribed to the liturgical realm. He wanted to join reading
Shema to the *Amidah*, in terms of the decisive importance of intent. He
was willing to pay the price of tolerance for the esoteric, a step which was
not to his liking in his other writings, in order to marshal Maimonides in
favor of the subjective perception of reading *Shema*. R. Soloveitchik consequently was of the opinion that Maimonides equated reading *Shema* and
the *Amidah* in terms of the dominance of the subjective consciousness
and its "invasion" of the objective realm.[22]

Reading Shema *and the* Amidah: The Difference

The cognitive proximity of the *Shema* to the *Amidah* is substantive and
structural, but the difference between them, too, is profound. "Reading
Shema does not entail the state of consciousness required for prayer."[23]
Throughout the comparative discussion, R. Soloveitchik drew the following
number of distinctions between prayer and reading *Shema*.

(1) Nature: the *Amidah* is dialogue, while reading *Shema* is an act of
faith and trust in God.[24]

(2) The Other: the *Amidah* addresses "Thou," and the *Shema*, "He."[25]

---

21 *Worship of the Heart*, 93.
22 In R. Soloveitchik's formulation, Maimonides "treats *Shema* and *tefillah* in an identical
manner, implying that he identifies the subjective correlate of both *mitzvot*" (*Worship
of the Heart*, 94). That is, the relation between the subjective consciousness and the
objective consciousness of the act is identical in the *Shema* and in the *Amidah*. The correlative relation between subjective consciousness and the act (= the commandment) is
reconstructive, but the *Shema* and the *Amidah* are exceptional.
23 *Worship of the Heart*, 96.
24 R. Soloveitchik defined it as "declaration" or "profession," but without any connection to
dialogue with God (*Worship of the Heart*, 96).
25 *Worship of the Heart*, 95, 96.

(3) Standing: the *Amidah* is enrooted in the equality of the worshiper and the One who hears prayer, while the *Shema* emphasizes the worshiper's acceptance of authority.[26]

(4) Existentialism: the *Amidah* stretches human finitude to the extreme, that is, until it borders on the infinite, while the experience of reading *Shema* is concerned with the preservation of finitude.[27]

(5) Revelation: the *Amidah* is a mode of man's revelation to God, and the *Shema* is an expression of God's revelation to man.[28]

(6) Rationality: the *Amidah* is not fully subject to rational description ("a mystical experience"), while reading *Shema* is of rational nature and content.[29]

(7) The dimension of "temperament": the *Amidah* is a tempestuous experience, while reading *Shema* is a moderate, restrained, and controlled one.[30]

(8) The individual and the collective: the *Amidah* is a personal experience, conducted between man and his God, while reading *Shema* is a collective experience, which reflects time-honored tradition.[31]

(9) Time: this distinction is derived from the preceding one. The *Amidah* relates solely to the present; reading *Shema* relates both to the past and to the present.[32]

(10) Purpose: the *Amidah* is the goal, while reading *Shema* is the way and means.[33]

(11) Halakhah: the above distinctions have a number of concrete halakhic expressions. For instance, the laws of the *Amidah* are suitable for the encounter with the divine presence, while those of the *Shema* suit rational perception.[34]

---

26 *Worship of the Heart*, 99. In *The Lonely Man of Faith* the distinction is different, and even somewhat the opposite. R. Soloveitchik asserted there that during the *Amidah* the worshiper is exposed in the negation of his standing and authority. This awareness "negates the legitimacy and worth of human existence" (*Lonely Man of Faith*, 75 n. 2). In contrast, when reading *Shema*, the worshiper is conceived as possessing a certain standing: he commits himself before God (*Lonely Man of Faith*, 75 n. 2).

27 *Worship of the Heart*, 95.

28 *Worship of the Heart*, 96. That is, man's exposure before God is what enables dialogue.

29 *Worship of the Heart*, 96.

30 *Worship of the Heart*, 95.

31 *Worship of the Heart*, 111-112. The various meanings of this distinction will be discussed in Chapter Seven, below.

32 *Worship of the Heart*, 111-112.

33 *Worship of the Heart*, 98.

34 *Worship of the Heart*, 99-103.

Now, to clarify the relation between reading *Shema* and prayer. In R. Soloveitchik's understanding, both commandments express subjective conscious acts that fashion the praxis (objective consciousness). In each, intent is a part of the observance of the commandment, that is, the dividing line between the subjective and the objective fades. The subjective consciousness, however, of each of the two differs from the other. The conclusion to be drawn from this series of distinctions is that the *Amidah* and reading *Shema* represent completely different stages of consciousness.

Terminological Clarification

In the preceding chapters of *Worship of the Heart* R. Soloveitchik used the terms "numinous" and "kerygmatic" to denote, respectively, the experience of the God of mystery and exaltation and the experience of God that generates a dialogue of closeness with man. He does not use these terms in chapter 6, but I will continue to use them, in order to create as methodical a continuity as possible.

We, therefore, need to clarify the meaning of the terminological continuity. The *Amidah* represents the kerygmatic cognitive stage, of the beneficent God, who correlates with the human being, and forms a community with him. Reading *Shema* represents the numinous stage of the sublime God who is alien to the human being. We should, however, realize that the meaning of "numinous" in reference to reading *Shema* is not completely identical with its import in the context of the aesthetic experience and the dialectical experience that we discussed in the preceding chapters. The numinous in reading *Shema* is solely transcendental. God is the absolute Stranger, but He is not threatening. In the preceding chapters the numinous was perceived as the cause of the chaotic situation in which the person stands before impermeability and disorder in nature and in history. R. Soloveitchik accordingly mentioned a few times that the goal of the Torah is to bring a person from the numinous stage to the kerygmatic.[35] The threatening and chaotic state pulls man down to a nadir and loneliness, and is not characteristic of reading *Shema*. In terms of the *Amidah*, experiencing the numinous as Therefore, from now on we will use the term kerygmatic experience.

---

35 *Worship of the Heart*, 80, 85.

Therefore, from now on we will use the term "numinous" with the following meanings:

(1) transcendental, that is, the absolute Other;
(2) absolute authority, in terms both of its standing and its commandments.

The response to the numinous with these meanings is rational. A person acknowledges the absolute Other, and declares that he accepts the authority of the absolute.

2. Reading *Shema*: A Phenomenological Analysis

The two commandments of reading *Shema* and the *Amidah* are two different cognitive axes, and the distinctions between them create a lively and multifaceted religious consciousness. We extensively discussed the subjective consciousness of prayer in the opening chapters of the current book, and we will return to it below. Now, we will examine the description of the consciousness of reading *Shema*. For R. Soloveitchik, reading *Shema* is an "act of the acceptance of the kingdom of Heaven," and we will discuss the meaning of an intentional act in the context of the religious consciousness, and then examine its consequences for reading *Shema*.

Intentional Act

R. Soloveitchik frequently uses the terms "act" and "intentional act." I discussed this term in the preceding chapters, and now I wish to subject it to closer scrutiny, and examine its meaning for prayer. Intentionality is a fundamental principle in Husserl's phenomenological thought, and it has been discussed by many scholars. Husserl maintains that the consciousness is a consciousness of objects. Intentionality plays a central role in the objectification process, that is, the process of constituting the object in the consciousness. How does this happen? The "stream of consciousness" includes a series of affections and intuitive experiences, usually of sensual data. These affections and experiences are deemed "matter" or "hylic" (in Husserl's terminology: "hyletic data"). That is, they themselves lack any direction whatsoever. This "matter," however, arouses consciousness to an act of intentionality, namely, to a movement ascribing affections to a cognitive object that is perceived intuitively—an act that is intentional.[36] Examples of such acts are cognition, emotion, casting doubt, imagination, and the like. All such acts are always directed towards an object: it is always cognition of something, for example, a tree, rather than unfocused cognition; the emotion of love for one's spouse, rather than abstract, undirected love; doubting the existence of angels rather than casting doubt in general; imagining a manned spacecraft landing on Mars rather than simple imagination, and so forth. The object, however, rather than being a component of the act is "transcendental" to it. The element that directs the act and connects it with the cognitive object is called "noema." The noema is, primarily, meaning. It is noteworthy that Husserl's "traditional" interpreters view cognitive noema as a type of perception (that relates to material objects), while those belonging to the positivist logical tradition see it as a concept (that relates to meaning).[37] In either event, Husserl conceived of consciousness as the consciousness of beings, and not only of meanings. To a certain extent, the object of the consciousness is constituted by an intentional act, and the process of constituting is defined as objectivization.

This schematic depiction is employed mainly in the study of the religious consciousness. Phenomenologists of religion such as Gerardus van der Leeuw argued that the intentional act also explains the structure and modes of action of the religious consciousness. The religious act is a clearly cognitive intentional act. Max Scheler is an outstanding representative of this approach. He was influenced by Husserl's religious thought in the latter's early "naïve" period in assuming that the cognitive process confirms itself, with no need for the realistic world beyond the consciousness. Herbert Spiegelberg asserted that Scheler's religious phenomenology has three tasks:

(1) to analyze the essential appearances of the divine;
(2) to study the ways in which the divine is revealed (epiphany);

---

36 See above, Chapter Three n. 39. See also Herbert Spiegelberg, *The Phenomenological Movement: A Historical Introduction* (Hague: Martinus Nijhoff, 1965), vol. 1, 108.

37 See, for example, Hubert L. Dreyfus, "Husserl's Perceptual Noema," in *Husserl, Intentionality and Cognitive Science*, ed. Hubert L. Dreyfus and Harrison Hall (Cambridge, MA: MIT Press, 1984), 97-123; Robert C. Solomon, *From Hegel to Existentialism* (Oxford: Oxford University Press, 1987), 223-224.

(3) to explore the religious acts in which the revelation of the divine is reflected.[38]

The religious act thus represents the consciousness of revelation. In his cardinal work on the phenomenology of religion, Scheler wrote:

> For it is from that act and its internal logic that we may most plainly see how there may come into being a religious self-evidence (*Glaubensevidenz*) which, residing in faith, resides in itself and how religion proceeds to unfold and throw out new and higher structures in conformity with its own autonomous laws.[39]

Scheler explained at length that the religious act is not limited to the psychological dimension, for example, and exceeds it. The religious act is not subsumed under other groups of cognitive intentional acts (*noetische intentionale Aktgruppen*[40]), nor is it derived from them. Such an act is explained only from within its own nature, acts in accordance with its characteristic regularity, and is entirely anchored in the religious realm. It is directed to the reality of consciousness that lies beyond the natural. Intentionality is, in whatever way, directed to God.[41] In other words, the direction of the intentional religious act is always transcendental in relation to the world, its content is divine,[42] and it is realized in the consciousness of the revelation of the divine (a mutual relationship between man and God).[43] These meanings of the intentional act in the context of the religious consciousness will facilitate our examination of the meanings of the act of the acceptance of the yoke of Heaven.

---

38 Spiegelberg also mentioned that "revelation" does not necessarily mean a supernatural event. At any rate, this question need not interest the phenomenologist. See Spiegelberg, *The Phenomenological Movement*, 263.

39 Scheler, *On the Eternal in Man*, 162.

40 Ibid., 248.

41 Ibid., 246.

42 The establishment of God as the object of an intentional act is somewhat problematic. The intentional act is constitutive, and plays a central role in the objectivization process. If God is constituted by the consciousness, then He is not really transcendental, and at the least, is not separate from the consciousness. See Laycock, "God as the Ideal," 250.

43 Scheler, *On the Eternal in Man*, 250. Scheler devoted an extensive discussion to the various aspects of the intentional religious act (246-270), that left a serious impression on R. Soloveitchik's thought over the course of time. For example, the classical proofs for the existence of God as ways to reach Him has its source in Scheler, 260. See Schwartz, *From Phenomenology to Existentialism*, 14-18.

Knowledge and Acceptance

R. Soloveitchik maintained that the act of the acceptance of the yoke of Heaven in the intent of reading *Shema* has two aspects: knowledge and assent. He writes:

> The realization of accepting the yoke of Heaven consists in an intellectual as well as a volitional gesture. It asserts itself in an act of comprehension and asserts knowledge of God in the form of creed. Free assent to this creed comprises the inner essence of accepting the yoke of Heaven.[44]

Plainly, then, the cognitive element is contentual and linguistic ("knowledge").[45] This aspect can be linguistically formulated and expressed ("asserts … creed"). The volitional aspect ("assent") is the inner experience of the acceptance of the yoke of Heaven. R. Soloveitchik continued to explain the difference between these aspects:

> Both knowledge and assent must be realized as an immediate awareness, a glowing and vivid experience, something real and dynamic, an ideal effort toward a Divinely organized and morally inspired existence, the adventure of a heroic life. Nevertheless, the quality of this experience is basically intellectual and logical, and it takes place within an imperativistic frame of mind. The very act of accepting the yoke of Heaven manifests itself in lifting intuition to the level of discursive thinking, converting the implicit into the explicit, that is to say, the objectivation of an inner experience via the medium of the religious logos.[46]

The linguistic and cognitive expression is the objectivization of the volitional inner experience. This passage contains a phenomenological analysis of the cognitive element of reading *Shema*, which I will discuss at length. We will see that reading *Shema* represents the numinous stage of

---

44 *Worship of the Heart*, 97. On the basis in the Bible and in the rabbinical literature, see Israel Knohl, "A Parsha Concerned with Accepting the Kingdom of Heaven" [Hebrew], *Tarbiz* 53 (1984): 11-31. R. Samson Raphael Hirsch wrote of "the view of God in world and history" in the reading of *Shema* (Samson Raphael Hirsch, *Horeb: A Philosophy of Jewish Laws and Observances*, trans. I. Grunfeld [New York: Soncino, 1981], 481, sect. 628). I will examine the dogmatic nature of the *Shema* in Chapter Seven, below.

45 On the intellectual aspect of the reading of *Shema*, see the extensive discussion in Chapter Seven, below. Yitzhak Baer argued, as part of his comprehensive theory regarding the early halakhah, that the fashioning of the reading of *Shema* in proximity to the *Tamid* sacrifice drew upon Greek culture. For this approach, see Hayyim Dov Mantel, *The Men of the Great Synagogue* [Hebrew] (Tel Aviv: Dvir, 1981), 177.

46 *Worship of the Heart*, 97.

consciousness, that is, the phase of exaltation. The stream of consciousness contains affections of an orderly and moral universe, organized history, and the existence of absolute truth.[47] Affections (or "matter") arouse the consciousness to an act of intentionality ("toward… existence"), namely, the act of reading *Shema*.

Scheler's approach, as an expression of the phenomenology of religion, is in great degree the connecting link between the (early) classical Husserlian phenomenology and R. Soloveitchik's religious thought. Affections of an orderly universe and history are directed by the consciousness as an act of the acceptance of the yoke of Heaven. This conscious act intuitively ascribes the previously experienced cosmic, moral, and historical order to the numinous divine presence. The object of this intentionality is the exalted (numinous) God.[48] Accordingly, the application of the phases of the objectivization to reading *Shema* will look as follows:

stage/stratum	objectivization in phenomenology	objectivization in reading *Shema*
(a)	stream of consciousness, primal datum (lacking direction)	intuitive cosmic and historical experience
(b)	intentional act	channeling the experience ("acceptance of the yoke of Heaven") to a conscious act
(c)	the object of consciousness (the direction of the intent)	the numinous God

The process of the transition from the first phase to the third is "objectivization." Husserl showed great interest in the structure and process of formulation of the intentional act, and R. Soloveitchik inherited this fascination from him. How does the experience become a cognitive object? In other words: how does the intentional act of the acceptance of the yoke of Heaven work? R. Soloveitchik's answer is grounded in the direction of the process in which experiences and intuitive affections become

---

47 By the same coin, the chaotic features of personal existence and of history gives additional data faced by the consciousness. However, R. Soloveitchik does not relate to this aspect of numinous impressions, because the *Shema* is directed to the rational and orderly side of the consciousness.

48 Again, R. Soloveitchik does not discuss here the sense of insignificance and nonexistence in the presence of the numinous. He patently desired to remain within the realm of the cognitive in this discussion.

a structured rational act.[49] In the act of the acceptance of the yoke of Heaven, the intuitive religious act becomes informative. The rational processing of these affections intensifies the intentional act (the acceptance of the yoke of Heaven) and transforms it into a cognitive object (the numinous presence of God). Reading *Shema* is therefore an intentional act by means of rationality.[50] The commandment to recite the Biblical formulation turns unstable feelings and intuitive sentiment into perception, rational cognition, meaning, and content. The numinous divine is revealed as the content of the rational act, which is the objectivization of the act of reading *Shema*.

3. Reading *Shema* and the Processes of the Consciousness

The phenomenological analysis of reading *Shema* as objectivization enables us to gain a deep understanding of two comparative issues:

(1) the distinction between reading *Shema* and the *Amidah*;
(2) the structure of the religious consciousness and the processes derived from this distinction.

The cognitive process gains in complexity when we take into account the aggregate of processes that the Jewish religious consciousness undergoes. Reading *Shema* is an expression of the cognitive phase that R. Soloveitchik called "numinous," that is, the exalted God. I wish to examine the impact of this claim on the sum of cognitive processes and on the basic structure of the religious consciousness.

The Divine Model of Reading Shema and Its Sources

As we mentioned above, the religious consciousness develops divine models that correspond to its varying conditions and phases. R. Soloveitchik

---

49 See Kaplan, "Review Essay," 89. On the sources in Habad Hasidism, see Schwartz, *Habad's Thought*, 231.

50 As we already explained, R. Soloveitchik viewed reading *Shema* as the rational aspect of the declaration of faith. It is noteworthy that the obligation of reading *Shema* was most likely derived from Torah study. That is, the recitation of *Shema* as a mandate for all strata of the public (and not only for the members of the priestly class [*kohanim*] in the Temple) was established as the minimal observance [*kiyyum*] of Torah study. See Itzchak D. Gilat, *Studies in the Development of the Halakhah* [Hebrew] (Ramat Gan: Bar-Ilan University, 1992), 284. This fact reinforces the rational nature of the *Shema*. See also Moore, *Judaism in the First Centuries*, vol. 1, 291.

writes about the divine consciousness of reading *Shema*, namely, the numinous God:

> God, in the experience of reading *Shema*, is "He," the third person, the remote, transcendent Being Whose yoke we do accept, Whose will we must abide, Whose might we respect and fear, Whose authority we acknowledge, yet into Whose presence we must not venture.[51]

This divine model somewhat draws upon the spirit of crisis theology or dialectic theology. At this point, we should add a few words about this circle's influence on R. Soloveitchik. Barth, Gogarten, Brunner, and their colleagues challenged liberal theology and the Christian historicist conception as it was expressed, for instance, by Troeltsch.[52] For them, God is indescribable, and completely exalted above the human plane. Only divine grace enables revelation, that is antithetical to reason and comprehension. Revelation does not fit into any mold, nor does it have any regularity. As such, the experience of God is chaotic and replete with suffering. Like Bultmann, the dialectical theologians view the sources and their interpretation as a component of the experience of God, and not necessarily as historical knowledge.

R. Soloveitchik was influenced by this circle, both formally and contentually. Kierkegaard's joint influence on him and the dialectical theologians drew him even closer to the latter. The circle's influence on the thought of R. Soloveitchik can be summarized in the following three central issues.

(1) Style: Barth's preaching style left a special mark on R. Soloveitchik, as a number of researchers of *The Lonely Man of Faith*, including myself, have shown at length.[53]

(2) Consciousness (formal) structure: as we see in many places in the current work, R. Soloveitchik placed great importance on the distinction between the objective and the subjective. The dialectical theologians asserted that content and the kerygmatic constitute the objective religious dimension, while one's mental attitude is the subjective.[54] R. Soloveitchik was critical of those theologians'

---

51 *Worship of the Heart*, 96-97.
52 See, for example, Robert Morgan, "Ernst Troeltsch and the Dialectical Theology," in *Ernst Troeltsch and the Future of Theology*, ed. John P. Clayton (Cambridge: Cambridge University Press, 1976), 33-77.
53 See Schwartz, *From Phenomenology to Existentialism*, chapter 11.
54 See, for example, Karl Barth, *Dogmatics in Outline*, trans. G. T. Thomson (New York: Harper & Row, 1959), 15. Barth used the term "subjective faith."

approach, arguing that it was "agnostic" and "skeptical," and sought to divert the faith experience from the mental cognitive dimension,[55] but he frequently drew upon the circle's style and approach in setting the division between the objective and the subjective.

(3) Revelation: the chaotic conception of revelation, at least in the first stages of the religious consciousness, was also one of the ideas that R. Soloveitchik conceived under the influence of dialectical theology.[56]

Returning to our discussion of *Worship of the Heart*, the model of the numinous God is enrooted in crisis theology, but R. Soloveitchik differed from this group in two essential matters:

(a) the model of God of the crisis theologians is not rational, while R. Soloveitchik based reading *Shema* on the rational model;

(b) the numinous model of crisis theology is chaotic and traumatic, while R. Soloveitchik grounded reading *Shema* in the model of the authoritative Other.

The model of Barth and Brunner is more suitable to the God who is revealed in the first phases of the consciousness as set forth in *And from There You Shall Seek*, in which the initial response to the God who reveals Himself is withdrawal and crisis.[57] Reading *Shema*, in contrast, is an intellectual experience, that maintains God's distance and exaltation.

Emotional Processes

Man discovers the divine presence by reading *Shema*. Since this revelation is cognitive and rational, it is one-directional, that is, man discovers God, and the revealed God is numinous and exalted. He does not respond to the

---

55 *The Halakhic Mind*, 129 n. 93.

56 Except for a series of homiletical discussions, R. Soloveitchik's relation to the school of dialectic theology has not been seriously examined. An exception is Alan Brill, who discussed Brunner's ideas and their influence on R. Soloveitchik. See Alan Brill, "Elements of Dialogic Theology in R. Soloveitchik's View of Torah Study," in *Study and Knowledge in Jewish Thought*, ed. Howard Kreisel (Beersheva: Ben-Gurion University of the Negev Press, 2006), 265-296. Notwithstanding this, I am not certain that this school's influence on R. Soloveitchik was as profound as Brill portrays in his important essay.

57 Schwartz, *From Phenomenology to Existentialism*, chapter 2.

act of revelation. Between the lines, R. Soloveitchik portrays the rational nature of reading *Shema* by the process of elimination.

(a) Reading *Shema* is not a dialogue, and certainly exhibits no mutuality beyond dialogue.

(b) There is no aspect of friendship and affinity between man and his God in reading *Shema*.

(c) The pretension of building a community of man and God is completely absent in reading *Shema*.

(d) Reading *Shema* does not express emotion.

These statements clearly lead to a rational conception of God. R. Soloveitchik states unequivocally:

> Yet, since the experience of companionship and intercourse is not required in the state of mind of the reciter, the claim to totality is actually realized in an intellectual act of knowing and assenting, not in feeling.[58]

The *Amidah*, in contrast, has a "feeling of friendship" and ensues mainly from feeling.[59] Now we can lucidly depict the cognitive process: the act of reading *Shema* channels and directs the cosmic experience to a rational model of God, of the sublime and the exalted. This is the God of nature and history, who by nature is concealed and impermeable.

Sensual experiences and impressions are directed to the purely intellectual realm. The act of reading *Shema* is followed by another intentional act, namely, the *Amidah*, directed to the beneficent and infinite God. In the liturgical order, reading *Shema* leads to prayer (the *Amidah*), and in R. Soloveitchik's common terminology, the numinous leads to the kerygmatic.

And now, for a phenomenological analysis of the emotional distinction. The numinous phase characteristically lacks emotion, that is, it is marked solely by rationality, while the kerygmatic phase is characterized by emotion. The cognitive process of climbing from one stage to the next now receives new and intriguing meaning. The following are the phases of the process.

---

58 *Worship of the Heart*, 98. R. Soloveitchik also declares that "the performance of *Shema* [...] is rather a sedate, placid experience. No encounter takes place" (*Worship of the Heart*, 96).

59 *Worship of the Heart*, 98.

(a) Emotion: in the first stage, the consciousness is flooded with data of a cosmic and historical experience, which is emotional and intuitive. The laws of the cosmos are unpredictable and inexplicable, and history does not lend itself to teleological explanation.

(b) Rationality (reading *Shema*); in the second phase, the consciousness directs this experience to the exalted. It does so by elevating the emotional experience to a rational one. The God who is revealed in this stage of the consciousness is the impermeable God. No dialogue develops, and man stands before the cosmic, rational God.

(c) Emotion after reason (the *Amidah*): in the third and highest stage of consciousness, man returns to the emotional experience. This time, however, the feeling of friendship and community replaces the original feeling, the hylic experience. The emotionality that follows the rational phase is no longer the initial fluid feeling. In this phase, God is a friend.

The religious consciousness description of *Worship of the Heart* in great measure parallels the portrayal in *And from There You Shall Seek*: what in the first phase seems traumatic and chaotic (in *And from There You Shall Seek* it is the phase of revelation, while in *Worship of the Heart* it is the experience of cosmic and historical chaos) becomes, in the highest cognitive phase, predictable and an integral part of limitless love.

Reading *Shema* parallels the second phase of the religious consciousness (the exalted and numinous), while the *Amidah* is parallel to its third phase (the kerygmatic unlimited good). R. Soloveitchik compared the consciousness process to the Binding of Isaac. Reading *Shema* is the journey of Abraham and Isaac from Beersheva to Mount Moriah, and the *Amidah* is the binding on the altar, with the father's unsheathed knife. Consequently, the order of institutionalized and objective prayer is also the change in the personal consciousness: reading *Shema* is the way (the second phase of consciousness), and the *Amidah* prayer is the direct contact with God (the third phase of consciousness).[60]

Dialogic Processes

Since reading *Shema* is a cognitive experience of faith, it is not a dialogic experience. An act of cognition does not constitute conversation.

---

60 *Worship of the Heart*, 98.

The *Amidah* prayer, in contrast, is a dialogue between man and his God. R. Soloveitchik writes:

> Speech is not always a colloquy, a conversation that expresses a sympathetic community and a friendship. Many a time we address ourselves to others in the form of a monologue, which the "other" happens to overhear. The addressee never enters our presence as the second person thou does. He remains outside of ourselves as a third party, alien and remote. The crux of prayer manifests itself in a feeling of companionship with Him and mainly in experiencing Him face to face (*panim el panim*)[61]; in having my whole self talk not only towards Him but also *with* Him, confronting Him. The preposition "with" makes all the difference. Hence, the moment of *majestas* which spells strangeness, inapproachability, exclusiveness, and the He "capitalized" is superseded by the motif of the parent who is not only close, but also involved with the fate and destiny of his child. The King is always addressed in the third person; the Father, in the second.[62]

Here, as well, R. Soloveitchik employs a phenomenological style. Husserl addressed the question of the Other, which is a nonroutine object-subject in terms of the consciousness.[63] Husserl used the terminology of the other who enters the realms of the consciousness. He wrote in the fifth meditation of *Cartesian Meditations*:

> Let us assume that another man enters our perceptual sphere. Primordially reduced, that signifies: In the perceptual sphere pertaining to my primordial Nature, a body is presented, which, as primordial, is of course only a determining part of myself; an "immanent transcendency".[64]

The Other is a datum that confronts consciousness, challenges it, and causes it to provide an explanation for its existence. The transition from

---

61 The addition of the Hebrew in transliteration might allude to the Kabbalistic concept of "*panim be-fanim*," which refers to full coupling (*zivug*). This intensifies the dialogic dimension of prayer.

62 *Worship of the Heart*, 99.

63 Avi Sagi writes that, according to Husserl, "I cannot see only my intentional objects in other subjects without harming the basic finds of my experience. On the other hand, in the constitutive conception, they are no more than objects for me. Husserl is faced by a problem here: how to contend, within an intentional conception, with the other, who, too, is a constitutive subject, and not only a constitutive object" (*The Problem of the Other from Hegel to Buber*, [Springer, 2019], chapter 2, forthcoming).

64 Edmund Husserl, *Cartesian Meditations: An Introduction to Phenomenology*, trans. Dorion Cairns (The Hague: Martinus Nijhoff, 1982), 110.

the numinous cognitive stage (reading *Shema*) to the kerygmatic phase (the *Amidah*) is therefore characterized by the Other's entering the consciousness. In the first phase, God is the other (absolute) subject, one that is inexplicable. In the second phase, the consciousness succeeds, by means of projection, analogy, and other methods, to come to know the other as such. The consciousness brings the other into its bounds. Now the intentional act, that until now was inner-oriented, is directed to the other. In this manner Husserl explains the constitution of the Other in the consciousness.

Phenomenologists of religion complete the description of the act with the connection to God. For them, the intentional act of the religious consciousness is, by definition, directed to God. The initial phase of the consciousness consists of standing before the exalted God, who does not relate to man as such. This is a distinctly cognitive phase. The highest phase of the consciousness is concerned with an awareness of God's presence and dialogue with Him. In this phase, the consciousness relates to God as Friend and Comrade within a community.

Halakhic Processes

Finally, R. Soloveitchik discusses the objective dimension of the consciousness: halakhah, which, in reading *Shema* and the *Amidah*, unlike other commandments, ensues directly from the subjective dimension of the consciousness. Accordingly, the reconstruction is marginalized and, in practice, disappears, because the objective and subjective dimensions are substantively intertwined. In reading *Shema* and the *Amidah* "the objective element is closely correlated to the subjective correlate."[65]

R. Soloveitchik begins his discussion of the halakhic distinctions between reading *Shema* and prayer by declaring: "Let us now take a look at the *halakhot* pertaining to *Shema* and *tefillah* (prayer), as codified by Maimonides, to see whether this analysis is valid."[66] That is, the criterion for justifying the phenomenological discussion is its correlation to the halakhah. His analysis indicated various subjective experiences (numinous, kerygmatic), but such an analysis might not, in the final analysis, suit the objective reality. In R. Soloveitchik's thought, the halakhah functions as the objective reality, and confirms the subjective consciousness. Also as regards

---

65 *Worship of the Heart*, 104.
66 *Worship of the Heart*, 99.

the commandments in which the subjective is part of their fulfillment, the halakhic canons (in this instance, Maimonides' *Mishneh Torah*) are the touchstone of subjective confirmation.

As was noted above, the halakhic praxis is seen in R. Soloveitchik's writings, and especially in *The Halakhic Mind*, as the objective dimension of the consciousness. Here R. Soloveitchik is faithful to the position of (early) Husserlian phenomenology, which influenced the phenomenology of religion in Scheler's thought. Husserl maintained that the test of the consciousness is its activity. That is, the criterion for the truth of the phenomenological analysis is evidence. For this reason, Husserl's thought was criticized as naive. At any rate, unlike the epistemological idealism of Hermann Cohen, for whom confirmation lies in the world beyond cognition, that is, in the sensual world, phenomenology places confirmation in evidence. R. Soloveitchik therefore views the objective dimension of the consciousness as confirming its subjective process. The consciousness confirms itself.

Now, to explore the halakhic direction that R. Soloveitchik took. R. Soloveitchik listed a series of halakhot that are more stringent regarding the *Amidah* prayer than as regards reading *Shema*. For him, this stringency means that in the *Amidah*, man stands in the presence of his God and conducts a direct dialogue with Him, while in reading *Shema*, the rational addressing of God is indirect and merely reflective. This series of stringencies relates to the following liturgical aspects of the *Amidah*:

(1) intent: the *Amidah* requires the absolute intent of standing before God ("that he void his mind of all thoughts"—*Mishneh Torah, Hilkhot Tefilah* [Laws of Prayer] 4:16[67]);

(2) gestures: the *Amidah* requires a series of gestures, as follows:
   a. praying in the direction of Jerusalem and the Temple Mount;
   b. fitting posture (hands on one's heart, and not on the hips), and bowing in certain blessings;
   c. proper dress;
   d. a proper location (not on the top of a wall, and the like);
   e. modulation of one's voice;

---

67 On standing for reading *Shema* in comparison with standing during the *Amidah* prayer, see Israel M. Ta-Shma, "Standing and Sitting While Reading the *Shema*'" [Hebrew], *Kenishta: Studies of the Synagogue World* 1 (2001): 53-61.

(3)   awareness: the *Amidah* requires one's full attention, as follows:
a.   distraction, due to intoxication and the like, precludes the fulfillment of one's obligation (*la-tzet yedei hovah*);
b.   interrupting one's prayer due to being addressed by another is forbidden;
c.   a lengthy interruption in prayer, even in time of emergency, requires that the *Amidah* be recited from anew.[68]

For R. Soloveitchik, the halakhah confirms the subjective division between the consciousness of reading *Shema* and that of the *Amidah*. Since the latter is a dialogue with God, that is, standing before Him and forging a community with Him, then it requires solemnity and meticulousness. R. Soloveitchik writes:

> The Halakhah thus depicts *tefillah*, unlike *Shema*, as a singular performance that rules out all distractions and intermissions. At the same time, the Halakhah challenges man to adopt a very solemn and yet a humble mood, to understand that it is a difficult and extremely serious business, requiring attention, discipline, concentration, alertness, tension, humility, and awe.[69]

The rational experience of God, in contrast, has no need of such a rigid atmosphere. The laws of reading *Shema* are lenient in comparison to those governing the *Amidah* prayer. The stringencies for the *Amidah* confirm the emotional, subjective consciousness's analysis of the dialogue and communality, while the leniencies of reading *Shema* validate the rational consciousness of *majestas* and exaltation.

There is a great deal of reason in R. Soloveitchik's thought on this point. If the *Amidah* is a dialogue, in terms of standing in the presence of God and creating a community of man and God, this situation demand the meticulous observance of its ceremonial and praxis components. Such an assumption, however, is not a foregone conclusion. Standing before God in the phase of the *Amidah*—the kerygmatic phase—does not relate to the numinous God.[70] The opposite is the case: man stands before the infinite good and aspires to commune with it, and be absorbed within it.

---

68   *Worship of the Heart*, 100-102. On the halakhic dimension of prayer, see below, Chapter Ten.
69   *Worship of the Heart*, 102-103.
70   R. Soloveitchik generally characterized the *Amidah* prayer as an expression of the limitless divine beneficence. He nonetheless considered that the picture is more complex, since the *Amidah* itself contains blessings that speak of the numinous God. As usual,

R. Soloveitchik toiled to explain that the highest cognitive stage is concerned with a relationship of friendship and fraternity between man and his God. Man should reasonably be at ease in such a relationship. Moreover, R. Soloveitchik had already mentioned in *Worship of the Heart* that prayer is a result of man's infinite love of his God, to the point of madness.[71] Such a feeling of comradeship and madness is not easily reconciled with rigidity and punctiliousness, just as enjoying oneself with friends does not demand unyielding normative rules. We would have expected that the laws of the *Amidah* would actually express the informal atmosphere between man and the God of lovingkindness. From a certain aspect, the feeling that the halakhot impart to prayer suits man's emotions in the numinous experience depicted in the first section of *Worship of the Heart*, that is, standing before the unpredictable, harsh, and impermeable. In the current section, the kerygmatic is depicted as congenial. For R. Soloveitchik, however, the laws of the *Amidah* are meant to detach man from whatever diverts him from the experience of the encounter with the divine. "The cosmos shrinks to just one point— at which God meets man. Everything else is submerged, dismissed, and forgotten."[72]

Thus, R. Soloveitchik presents a complex picture. In order to attain mutuality with God, one must strictly and meticulously observe the halakhah. Tthe *Amidah* as dialogue requires a conservative and reserved mood, despite lovesickness, and possibly just because of the existence of such love.

4. Tensions and Contrasts

The discussion of the consciousness standing of reading *Shema* indicates differences between the two major sections of *Worship of the Heart* (chapters 1-5, 6-9). These distinctions relate to the very structure of the religious consciousness, that is, to the assessment of the two main phases of this consciousness, the numinous and the kerygmatic. The picture that emerges from these disparities is a tension-laden portrayal of the religious consciousness. Moreover, his discussion of reading *Shema* and the *Amidah* led R. Soloveitchik to reexamine the consciousness of the latter. As noted

---

he sought to express, both openly and between the lines, the tensions that typify the religious act.

71　*Worship of the Heart*, 86.
72　*Worship of the Heart*, 103.

above, this distinction focuses on an assessment of the numinous state. We will now detail the elements of this distinction.

Hierarchy vs. Equivalency Experiences

In the first section of *Worship of the Heart*, the numinous phase of the consciousness is perceived as a phase that a person must undergo, overcome, and transcend. In terms of the characteristics of prayer, the model of the concealed and silent God is traumatic, and the encounter with Him is a harsh experience for the worshiper. The *Amidah* as dialogue needs a God who is good and responsive, and completely negates the hidden numinous. It should come as no surprise that R. Soloveitchik concluded this section on a decisive note:

> God Himself appears to us both as *Deus absconditus* and as *Deus revelatus*, as numen and kerygma. Man, however, can establish communion only with God Who reveals Himself, not with God who hides.[73]

Man presumably falls to the numinous state, is thrown into it, but is then elevated to the kerygmatic state of the beneficent God. The dialectic is of falling and rising. The worshiper knows that he has no choice but to experience and adopt the numinous phase, for otherwise he cannot reach the highest phase, the kerygmatic. Furthermore, the attainment of the kerygmatic phase is perceived as repentance.[74] Man aspires to reach the safe haven and realize complete love for his God.

The second section of *Worship of the Heart*, however, presents a different sort of attitude to the divine model. Man relates to the numinous as royal majesty, which, in terms of importance and independent standing, parallels the kerygmatic where one relates to God as friend, partner in community, and so on. Each of the two experiences of God is of independent worth, and man traverses between the two in consequence of his attitude to the divine. Religious consciousness seeks to undergo two different experiences, represented by two different liturgical expressions: reading *Shema* and the *Amidah*. In the second section of his book, R. Soloveitchik refrained from setting forth a hierarchy of the experiences of God in terms of their value and qualities. The majesty of reading *Shema* leads to love, but these two experiences are of equal worth.

---

73 *Worship of the Heart*, 85-86.
74 See above, Chapter Five.

Compulsion or Choice

There is a parallel distinction between the emotional manner in which a person relates to the various experiences. In both sections the way to the kerygmatic phase of the consciousness (= the phase of limitless good) leads through the acceptance of the numinous. The first section, however, clearly teaches that the proper attitude to the numinous as a springboard to the kerygmatic is quite suitable for theodicy. It is not coincidental that in the numinous context R. Soloveitchik mentions the Patriarchs, who justified God's actions,[75] as if they did so out of their free will. Man chooses the collapse of his spiritual systems, and consciously embraces the fear and trembling in the face of the numinous. He knows that only such a choice will lead him upwards on the ladder of consciousness.

By contrast, according to the second section, the numinous ensues from respect and admiration for the important value of divine majesty, and not from mere acceptance. Man chooses the numinous out of his awareness of the greatness of God, and feels exaltation in the face of such greatness. The experience of the numinous is one that the consciousness knowingly desires. Just as the consciousness seeks communion with God (community), it likewise wants the rational experience and experience that is measured by reason. As we have seen, reading *Shema* is an independent exalting experience. In terms of the worshiper's inner world, reading *Shema* is not merely a preface to the *Amidah* prayer; it is an experience in its own right.

The Identity of the Numinous

The difference between the two sections is not limited to the dialectical movement between the phases of the consciousness, that is, it does not lie only in the process, it is also expressed in the very definition of the numinous cognitive phase itself. The first section portrays both the order and lack of order of the numinous, that is, man oscillates between a harmonious universe and a reality that lacks order and direction, between purposeful history and chaotic events. The model of God is constructed in accordance with the experience: God is revealed in His might, but He also is hidden. Man's standing before the numinous is dialectical. Man feels elevation—alongside terror. Attraction and rejection are mingled

---

75 At times the behavior of the Patriarchs is characteristically theodicean (*Worship of the Heart*, 81), and at other times, it exhibits general acceptance of law, and specifically, of moral law (*Worship of the Heart*, 84).

together. The numinous experience is rational, on the one hand, and on the other, irrational.

The second section, in contrast, mainly emphasizes order, and chaos has no real place here. The numinous is evident within the experience of the cosmic and historical harmony, and is distinctly rational. Reading *Shema* reflects boldly facing the numinous, in a stance that is not dialectical. The oscillation is between the numinous to the beneficent God, the Friend, that is, between two different phases of the religious consciousness, but not between the components of the numinous itself. R. Soloveitchik might very well have been deterred by the model of the stormy consciousness, in which the worshiper is seized by fear and trembling in the face of the numinous, while also being drawn to it, all this in tandem with the desire to commune with the limitless good. Chaos, impermeability, and the concealment of God's countenance, that cause the religious consciousness to collapse and obliterate itself, give way to the comfortable model of preprogrammed order and process.

Conclusions

I do not think that these three distinctions between the sections of *Worship of the Heart* are due to the editing of the book. These differences can be resolved by the explanation that the second section describing the mature religious consciousness, after it embraced the numinous. That is, in the first section it appears as a trauma, while after being embraced it is seen, in the second section, to be an experience that could be foreseen. Then the numinous joins the experience of the infinite good, and both together become the basis for communion with God. This explanation also suits R. Soloveitchik's writing style in his other works. But this seems to be too easy a solution.

We cannot deny the tension between the two sections regarding the attitude to the consciousness of the exalted. And this is not all: if *Worship of the Heart* had not been divided into two sections, we could assume that these distinctions were meant to create a dialectical image of the religious consciousness. This might be what R. Soloveitchik intended if he kept his notebooks together, and expected them to be published. Between the lines of his writing, he hints more than once that the Jewish religious consciousness is infinitely more complex and fluctuating than other religious consciousnesses (mainly the Christian). He even alludes in *And from There You Shall Seek* that the highest, uniform cognitive phase is subject to a subterranean dialectic; and in *Worship of the Heart* he explicitly states that the kerygmatic consciousness is not the final word. Man is fated to oscillate between the numinous and the kerygmatic. The question of the consciousness standing of reading *Shema* patently presents R. Soloveitchik's thought in all its characteristic dynamics and ferment.

5. Summary

The distinctions between reading *Shema* and the *Amidah* offer us a comprehensive perspective on the structure of the religious consciousness. When we examine the structure of reading *Shema* and the *Amidah*, we once again come to realize the complexity and winding paths of the religious consciousness. The picture that emerges is quite intricate. We learn from the sixth chapter of *Worship of the Heart* that the numinous phase of the consciousness is acquired in reading *Shema*, and the kerygmatic phase, by the *Amidah*. The earlier chapters, in contrast, teach that the *Amidah* prayer itself includes a numinous phase (the hymnal blessings) and a kerygmatic one (the thanksgiving blessings), in addition to existential distress (the petitionary blessings). That is to say, the highest phase of the religious consciousness, in which man faces the beneficent God and forges a community with Him, is a phase in which the silent, hidden, and impermeable God exists, with a subterranean presence, and even emerges in the hymnal blessings. The general model may be represented graphically as follows:

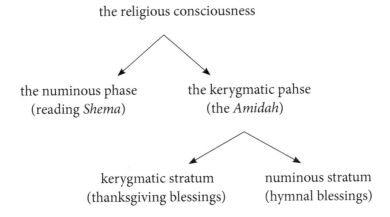

the religious consciousness

the numinous phase   the kerygmatic pahse
(reading *Shema*)   (the *Amidah*)

kerygmatic stratum   numinous stratum
(thanksgiving blessings)   (hymnal blessings)

We need not assume a contradiction here. The kerygmatic encompasses a numinous dimension and a dimension of distress. Man's passionate communion with his God includes a dimension of reserved and moderate rationality. Blazing love or lovesickness do not cause the one in a state of communion to forget the state of crisis of the human condition. Additionally, the *Amidah* prayer, which consists entirely of dialogue, begins with a numinous dimension. It is only at the end of the *Amidah*, in the thanksgiving blessings, that the infinite love "wins" and man communes with God.

In this respect, the consciousness analysis of *Worship of the Heart* does not differ from R. Soloveitchik's other phenomenological writings. *Worship of the Heart*, however, contains intriguing elements, that were not formulated or stressed in his other essays, such as the application of the structure of the religious consciousness to the consciousness of prayer. The aesthetic dimension of the consciousness and existential distress are incorporated in his phenomenological portrait.

Chapter 7

The Interpretation of Reading *Shema* and Its Blessings: (1) Methodology and Sources

After having devoted lengthy and intricate discussions to the structure of the religious consciousness in the first six chapters of *Worship of the Heart*, R. Soloveitchik now turns to another matter of which he was fond: interpretation of the prayers. In his essay "Thoughts on Prayer," he extensively examined the first three blessings of the *Amidah*. *Worship of the Heart* contains a special focus on reading *Shema* and its blessings, and in the last two original chapters he explained the *Yotzer Or* ("who forms light") blessing, and the verse: "Love the Lord your God" (Deut. 6:5). For R. Soloveitchik, interpretation is one of the central keys for unlocking the structure of the religious consciousness. The experience, with its content and boundaries, are defined within foundational texts. The acts of consciousness are distinguished and clarified from within the sources (the prayerbook). In the current chapter, we will explore R. Soloveitchik interpretive principles in *Worship of the Heart* for the prayers, and in the following chapter we will examine the interpretations themselves.

1. On Methodology

R. Soloveitchik's textual interpretation of reading *Shema* is based on the phenomenological principles that guided him in his demarcation of the religious consciousness. He preceded his commentary with a methodological discussion, in which he clarified the types of sources likely to offer a platform for the commentary based on a phenomenological analysis. He then turned to the interpretation of the prayers themselves. This commentary was meant to be a comprehensive undertaking. Apparently, not all of this interpretive enterprise has survived,[1] but the extant parts aid us in understanding his approach as a whole.

Sources

What are the textual and canonic sources the interpretation of which molds our religious experience and its fashioning consciousness? At the end of the sixth chapter of *Worship of the Heart*, R. Soloveitchik indicated three types of foundational sources that are valid for all acts of the Jewish religious consciousness. These types are the content of the remaining chapters of *Worship of the Heart*:

(1) Halakhah (chapter 7);[2]
(2) Aggadah (chapter 7);[3]
(3) Foundational texts of a specific act—in this case, liturgical texts—and the ideas based on them (chapters 7, 8).[4]

We should add a note regarding the third source: in the case under discussion, that of the consciousness of reading *Shema*, the foundational texts are "liturgy."[5] The *Shema* blessings interpret the experience of reading *Shema*. To a certain extent, liturgy is a branch of halakhah, since it is the halakhah that determines the structure and wording of the blessings of the *Shema* and of reading *Shema*. R. Soloveitchik also referred to the meaning that emerges from the liturgical texts. The blessings of *Yotzer Or* and *Ahavah Rabbah* ("great love"; or *Ahavat Olam*, "eternal love," in the *Maariv* evening service) immediately preceding the reading of *Shema*, and the blessing of Israel's redemption and preservation (or the extended version ["lengthy redemption"] recited outside Israel, in the evening) immediately following it, create a textual framework that gives rich interpretation to reading *Shema* itself. We will examine this source and give a phenomenological interpretation in the next chapter.

These three sources paint a broad picture of the experience of reading *Shema*. This portrait contains differing emphases.

---

1 Kaplan, "Review Essay," 95.
2 *Worship of the Heart*, 107-109.
3 *Worship of the Heart*, 110-13.
4 *Worship of the Heart*, 107-32.
5 *Worship of the Heart*, 104.

(1) Authority: the halakhah is seen as the most stable source. This is especially true as regards reading *Shema*, for which the halakhah also establishes the subjective dimension of the commandment. Other sources, such as aggadah, are to be regarded with caution and suspicion, "in order not to fall prey to one's own imagination and read into the texts alien ideas."[6] R. Soloveitchik was especially guarded concerning preachers who insert their personal ideas into the text.[7] In the final analysis, the halakhah is the stable element, and it alone can serve as a firm criterion for the veracity of homily. "From time to time it is good to check aggadic interpretations against halakhic ideas in order to ascertain the adequacy of our approach."[8] In terms of authority, R. Soloveitchik distinguished yet again between the subjective and objective dimensions of the consciousness. Even in places where the two dimensions of consciousness come into contact, as in reading *Shema* and prayer, it is the objective dimension that is stable. R. Soloveitchik's modern Orthodox position shines forth from this emphasis.

(2) Inner and outer dynamics: the first sources that fashioned the reading *Shema* experience are, in great measure, external to it. The halakhah determines the liturgical praxis in terms of times, gestures, and rules of recitation. From a certain aspect, we can say that the halakhah dictates liturgical behavior. It also is a participant in the choice of texts. But these texts, or at least some, are not of halakhic origin. Reading *Shema*, for instance, is a clearly Biblical text with literal meanings and its own philosophical orientation. Aggadah fashions the psychological, emotional, and intellectual structure of the prayer experience.

---

6 *Worship of the Heart*, 104.
7 The debate concerning homily already arose in the late thirteenth century, when rationalists such as R. Levi ben Abraham composed far-reaching allegorical exegeses. See, for example Abraam S. Halkin, "The Ban on the Study of Philosophy" [Hebrew], *P'raqim: Yearbook of the Schocken Institute* 1 (1967-1968): 53-55. See also Dov Schwartz, "On the Study of Jewish Homiletics" [Hebrew], *Peamim* 59 (1994): 149-153. R. Soloveitchik himself was a gifted preacher, and various aspects of his homiletical activity have been discussed by Peli, Fox, and others. See, for example, Pinchas H. Peli, "The Uses of Hermeneutics ('Derush') in the Philosophy of J. B. Soloveitchik—Method or Essence?" [Hebrew], *Daat* 4 (1980): 111-128; Marvin Fox, "The Rav as Maspid," *Tradition* 30 (1996): 164-181.
8 *Worship of the Heart*, 107. For reservations regarding aggadah, see Norman E. Frimer and Dov Schwartz, *The Life and Thought of Shem Tov Ibn Shaprut* [Hebrew] (Jerusalem: Ben-Zvi Institute, 1992), 60-61.

Halakhah and aggadah each has a dynamic of its own that guides its path in many areas, not only in prayer. From this respect, they are heteronomous to the experience itself. Only the liturgical texts fashion the experience from within, and they are the direct expression of this experience. Although the halakhah established some of the texts, from this point on they are the internal expression of the experience.

(3) Interpretation: the first source, the halakhah, interprets the third source, namely, the liturgical texts. "The Halakhah did not add anything new in the *berakhot*, anything that the original text of *Shema* did not contain. Rather, it takes an implicit motif and unfolds its meaning and sense."[9] Between the lines, we learn that the central foundational sources of reading *Shema* are both the halakhah and the liturgy. The halakhah generates the meanings from within the texts and transforms their recitation into an intentional act. The aggadah is shunted aside. It does not have any weight in the interpretive canvas before us. R. Soloveitchik would later use aggadah to develop his ideas on reading *Shema*, but did not ascribe decisive importance to it when developing in fashioning these ideas. Moreover, his use of aggadah was always closely linked to the halakhah. He set for himself an aggadic model that was tested by the touchstone of halakhah. He would do so on two topics: the recitation of *Barukh shem kavod malkhuto* ("Blessed be the name of His glorious kingdom forever and ever") and the laws of *Kiddush Hashem* (martyrdom).[10]

After examining the sources, we will turn to R. Soloveitchik's interpretive methods. R. Soloveitchik set for himself a comprehensive program for the interpretation of the prayers. This plan directly relates to the interpretation of reading *Shema* and its blessings.

The Articles of Faith

The sixth chapter of *Worship of the Heart* outlines the interpretive and cognitive plan for the following chapters of the work. The underlying assumption is that reading the *Shema* is a "creed," that is, it possesses clearly

9 *Worship of the Heart*, 105.
10 See below.

dogmatic standing.[11] Faith is perceived here more as a "cognitive act,"[12] and less as a psychological and conscious state of trust in God or an emotional experience. In other words, reading *Shema* encapsulates a defined list of articles of faith whose content and boundaries are to be explored and analyzed. R. Soloveitchik indicated the correspondence between the blessings accompanying reading *Shema* and the Biblical passages comprising it. The blessings and the passages together set forth a series of articles of faith, which can be summarized as follows:

article of faith[13]	Blessing	section of *Shema*
1. divine unity[14]	*Yotzer Or* (morning)	first (Deut. 6:4-9)
2. divine sovereignty	*Ma'ariv aravim* ("who	
3. (existence of angels and their subordination to God)[15]	brings on evenings"; evening)	

(Continued)

11 This dogmatic standing is attested, to great degree, by the connection between *Shema* and the Decalogue, which has already been discussed in numerous studies. See, for example, Ephraim E. Urbach, "The Role of the Ten Commandments in Jewish Worship," in *Collected Writings in Jewish Studies*, ed. Robert Brody and Moshe D. Herr (Jerusalem: Magness, 1999), 294-296; Moshe Weinfeld, *Decalogue and the Recitation of "Shema": The Development of Confessions* [Hebrew] (Tel Aviv: Hakibbutz Hameuchad, 2001).

12 *Worship of the Heart*, 106.

13 R. Soloveitchik used the terms "idea," "motif," "motto" to denote articles of faith. One opinion views reading *Shema* and its blessings as a model of creation, revelation, and redemption. See, for example, Joseph Heinemann, *Prayer in the Talmud: Forms and Patterns, trans.* Richard S. Sarason, vol. 9 of *Studia Judaica* (Berlin: De Gruyter, 1977), 30-31, 230; idem, *Studies in Jewish Liturgy* [Hebrew], ed. Avigdor Shinan (Jerusalem: Magnes, 1981), 17. For a critical discussion, see Kimelman, "The *Shema* Liturgy," 103-105.

14 Unity is perceived as an intellectual issue. See, for example, Eli Gurfinkel, "The Influence of Ideological Changes on the Text of the Declaration of Faith (*ani maamin*)" [Hebrew], *Kenishta* 4 (2010): 80-81.

15 It is unclear whether R. Soloveitchik viewed the existence of angels, which was of great concern to Christian theology, as having dogmatic standing. See, for example, David Keck, *Angels and Angelology in the Middle Ages* (Oxford: Oxford University Press, 1998). R. Soloveitchik's formulation is equivocal ("The angels are depicted as accepting the yoke of Heaven"—*Worship of the Heart*, 105). The end of chapter 8 implies that the angels manifest the principle of divine unity in that the will of God is present in them (see below). At any rate, one view includes the existence of angels among the fundamental tenets of Judaism. For example, R. David ibn Bilia (early fourteenth century, Portugal) lists the existence of the separate intellects as the first tenet. See Israel Efros, *Medieval Jewish Philosophy: Systems and Problems* [Hebrew] (Tel Aviv: Dvir, 1965), 154; Menachem Kellner, *Dogma in Medieval Jewish Thought: From Maimonides to Abravanel* (Oxford: Littman Library, 1986), 78. See also Dov Schwartz, "*Maamar Magen David* by ibn Bilia" [Hebrew], *Kobez al Yad* 12/22 (1994): 196-197. R. Soloveitchik wrote of the angels' singing in the *Yotzer Or* ("who forms light") blessing in the morning service (see below).

article of faith	Blessing	section of *Shema*
4. revelation 5. giving of the Torah[16]	*Ahavah Rabbah* (morning)[17] *Ahavat Olam* (evening)	second (Deut. 11:13-21)
6. the Exodus[18] 7. redemption	*emet ve-yatziv* ("true and firm"; morning) *emet ve-emunah* ("true and faithful"; evening)	third (Num. 15:37-41)

R. Soloveitchik joins a long list of thinkers in the Jewish world, who toiled to compose lists of the articles of faith, and those who associated these beliefs with prayer. The concluding chapters of *Worship of the Heart*, his book on prayer, should have followed this schema. The published material, however contains only a discussion of the first principle, that of the unity of God,[19] and to a certain degree, that of angels.[20] The book also adds a discussion of the love of God, following the opening verse of the first passage of *Shema* ("You shall love the Lord your God with all your heart and with all your soul and with all your might"—Deut. 6:5).[21] Love of God is the cognitive, moral, and consciousness consequence of belief in the unity of God.

R. Soloveitchik meant to thoroughly examine the cognitive, interpretive, and consciousness meanings of reading *Shema* and its blessings, but succeeded in formulating only their beginning, namely, the unity of God as a liturgical axis. He undertook the comprehensive task of composing a phenomenological

---

16 R. Soloveitchik might have viewed revelation and the giving of the Torah as a single article of faith.

17 In the *nusah Sefarad* prayerbook, the second blessing of *shema* in the morning also begins with *Ahavat olam*.

18 This shows that R. Soloveitchik thought that acknowledgement of historical events in which God was present is perceived as a dogmatic element. He thereby adopted the approach of R. Judah Halevi (*Kuzari* 3:17). See, for example, David Kaufmann, *Mekhkarim ba-Sifrut ha-Ivrit shel Yemei ha-Bainayim* [Studies in Medieval Hebrew Literature] [Hebrew], trans. Ysrael Eldad (Jerusalem: Mossad Harav Kook, 1962), 212-213. R. Judah Halevi's dogmatic list was also formulated within a commentary to the blessing following *Shema*.

19 Chapters 7 and 8 of *Worship of the Heart*. The principle of divine unity as a prayer topic is of Biblical origin. See Moshe Weinfeld, "The Biblical Roots of the Standing Prayer on the Sabbaths and Festivals" [Hebrew], *Tarbiz* 65 (1996): 547-548 (also included in *Studies in Jewish Liturgy: A Reader* [Hebrew], ed. Hananel Mack, vol. 6 of *Likkutei Tarbiz* [Jerusalem: Magnes, 2003], 35-36). On divine unity as a linguistic axis of prayer (*meyahadim*) in the context of reading *Shema*, see José Faur, "Delocutive Expressions in the Hebrew Liturgy," *Journal of the Ancient Near Eastern Society* 16-17 (1984-1985): 45.

20 *Worship of the Heart*, the end of chapter 8, which discusses the *Kedushot* [sanctifications] in the *Yotzer Or* blessing.

21 *Worship of the Heart*, chapter 9.

interpretation of prayer, but he did not complete most of this project. From what he did write, however, we understand the plan of the second half of *Worship of the Heart*: after defining the difference between reading *Shema* and the *Amidah* (prayer), R. Soloveitchik intended to apply the tripartite methodology (halakhah, aggadah, and foundational liturgical texts) to all the articles of faith. Of this great project, he succeeded, mainly, in discussing only the first article of faith, the unity of God. "The principle of the unity of God is the very foundation of our faith, whose witnesses and defenders we all are, even to the end of time."[22] Here, as well, he managed to fully apply only the first two methodological tools (halakhah and aggadah), while the third (liturgical text) was applied only regarding the *Yotzer Or* blessing and the opening verse of the first passage of the *Shema*. The plan of *Worship of the Heart* was ambitious, but R. Soloveitchik did not succeed in completing it. Now we will analyze his discussion of the first article of faith, the unity of God.

2. Halakhah: On Intent

The seventh chapter of *Worship of the Heart* initiates a lively discussion of the article of faith that is contingent on reading *Shema*: the unity of God. The beginning of the discussion is halakhic-interpretive, continues in an exegetical vein, and its end is interpretive-liturgical. Prayer commentary paints an expansive portrait of the consciousness of divine unity. I will first briefly present the principles of the halakhic discussion, which bears an aura of Torah scholarship. At times R. Soloveitchik incorporated short scholarly-halakhic discussions in his writings, and the seventh chapter of *Worship of the Heart* is an example of such an inclusion. As we shall see, the halakhic discussion that R. Soloveitchik offers is of a distinctly analytic nature, and, to an even great extent, exhibits associative thought.

Quantity and Quality

R. Soloveitchik argued that Maimonides divided the contents of the three passages (*parshiyot*) of the *Shema* into two main parts:

(1) the dogmatic part that presents abstract beliefs;
(2) the practical section, concerned with the commandments.[23]

---

22 *Worship of the Heart*, 114.
23 Kaplan, "Review Essay," 95, argues that this is the classical Maimonidean distinction between reason and revelation.

Maimonides wrote in *Hilkhot Keriat Shema* (Laws of Reading *Shema*)
1:2 that the first *Shema* passage (Deut. 6:4-9) contains "the obligation
of acknowledging the unity of God, loving Him, and studying His
[words], which is a great matter on which all depends."[24] The two other
passages ("If you indeed heed"—Deut. 11:13-21; the *tzitzit* passage—
Num. 15:37-41) are concerned with "the obligation to remember all the
commandments."[25] R. Soloveitchik raised three arguments, which border
on associative thinking.

(1) Interpretation: Maimonides mentioned three dogmatic principles
that are formulated in the first passage of *Shema* ("a great matter").
R. Soloveitchik assumed that these principles correspond to the
first three verses of this passage, as follows:
Deut. 6:4: "Hear, O Israel"—(1) "the unity of God";
Deut. 6:5: "Love the Lord your God"—(2) "loving Him";
Deut. 6:6: "These words shall be"—(3) "studying His
[words]" (Torah study);[26]

(2) Halakhah: R. Soloveitchik presumed that the intent of *Shema*
refers to such dogmatic principles. Consequently, he implied that
Maimonides shared the view of R. Eliezer in BT Berakhot 13a:
"'These [words shall be]'—to this point intent is necessary";

(3) Halakhah and interpretation: R. Soloveitchik argued that in order
to adopt (2), we must accept Rashi's view: "'To this point'—to

24 On the correlation to the beginning of *Hilkhot Yesodei ha-Torah*, see Eliezer Hadad,
The Torah and Nature in Maimonides' Writings [Hebrew] (Jerusalem: Magnes, 2011),
308. R. Soloveitchik sidestepped the complex issue of *Shema* in *Guide of the Perplexed.*
See, for example, Leo Strauss, "How to Begin to Study the *Guide of the Perplexed*," introductory essay to *The Guide of the Perplexed*, trans. Shlomo Pines (Chicago: University
of Chicago Press, 1963), xlvii-xlix; Marvin Fox, *Interpreting Maimonides: Studies in
Methodology, Metaphysics, and Moral Philosophy* (Chicago: University of Chicago Press,
1990), 57.
25 See Kimelman, "*Shema* Liturgy," 16-19. For a philosophical comparison between the
three *Shema* passages, see, for example, Assael Ben-Or, *Gershonides' Numeration of
Commandments* [Hebrew] (Jerusalem: Keren Or, 2003), 20-21. The rationalist and
Kabbalistic exegesis also ascribed abstract ideas to *Shema.* See, for example, Dov
Schwartz, "The Sermons of R. Ephraim ben Gershon: Sources and Character" [Hebrew],
in *Alei Sefer* 21 (2010): 91.
26 *Worship of the Heart*, 109. Cf. Jacob S. Levinger, *Maimonides' Techniques of
Codification* [Hebrew] (Jerusalem: Magnes, 1965), 98-99. Kaplan, "Review Essay,"
101, cited the views of scholars who understand the word *talmudo* [studying His
(words)] as commanding to recognize of the Holy One, blessed be He, and not to
study Torah.

[the words] 'on your heart' [Deut. 6:6]."[27] Only Rashi's understanding allows us to match the three principles with the three
verses.

R. Soloveitchik, accordingly, based Maimonides' ruling on Rashi's
commentary on R. Eliezer's dictum, thereby adapting Maimonides' dogmatic principles to the Biblical verses.

R. Soloveitchik then asked[28] whether Maimonides' view could now
be identified with that of R. Eliezer. But R. Meir and R. Akiva, who dis-
agreed with R. Eliezer, were authoritative figures. The Babylonian Talmud
itself offers opinions coinciding with that of R. Meir: that intent for the
first verse (6:4) suffices. We should add to this objection that Maimonides
himself ruled in accordance with R. Meir in *Hilkhot Keriyat Shema* 2:1.
Then how could Maimonides have ruled in accordance with a view that
was not accepted as the halakhah?

R. Soloveitchik's answer distinguished between the two aspects of
intent. The first fundamental aspect is qualitative. The acceptance of
the yoke of Heaven means, in contentual and cognitive terms, the acceptance of the three dogmatic principles (divine unity, love of God, and
Torah study). That is, we extract from R. Eliezer's dictum its substance
and intent, namely, these principles. As regards the "qualitative" dimension, Maimonides ruled in accordance with R. Eliezer. As R. Soloveitchik
writes, "The question about the qualitative content and structure of the
kavvanah is not identical to the whole controversy between R. Eliezer
and the other sages about the extent of the required *kavvanah* [...]
all concurred that the first three verses cover the whole area of that
experience."[29] Moreover, the three principles are not subject to dispute.
All the Tannaim concur regarding the qualitative dimension of intent.
The second aspect is "quantitative" and pertains to the question of how
many verses are necessary to fulfill the qualitative aspect. In a certain

---

27 Rashi included verse 6 as requiring intent, in contrast with the view of the Tosafists. The
    latter (BT Berakhot 13a, s.v. *Ad Kan*) did not include Torah study among the principles.
    Their list is more suitable to the dogmatic aspect of such matters (unity of God, love of
    Him, fear of Him).

28 He used the word "perplexity" in a possible allusion to the *Guide of the Perplexed*. This
    word was already used by Friedlander as the title of his 1881 translation of Maimonides'
    text. Accordingly, R. Soloveitchik wanted to emphasize once again that the discussion of
    the subjective philosophical topic of prayer is an integral part of the observance of the
    commandment itself.

29 *Worship of the Heart*, 109.

sense, this is the practical interpretive aspect, although the question itself is legal, that is: what are the minimal conditions necessary to fulfill the requirement of intent in reading *Shema*. As regards the quantitative issue, Maimonides felt that a single verse ("Hear, O Israel"—Deut. 6:4) suffices to fully cover the acceptance of the yoke of Heaven, thus ruling in accordance with R. Meir. Proper intent for this one verse includes all the elements that are detailed in the three verses. For R. Soloveitchik, these two aspects of intent are clearly halakhic.

A Variegated Act

R. Soloveitchik thus proposed the classic division between various aspects of intent in reading *Shema*. Nonetheless, he was aware of the dogmatic aspect stressed in his writing and, especially, of the contentual "qualitative" aspect. He therefore feared that they could be entirely based on the cognitive dimension. He wrote:

> *Kabbalat ol malkhut Shamayim* [acceptance of the yoke of Heaven] is not exhausted by an abstract cognitive act regarding the principle of unity, but includes also the element of free assent and consecration, exerting a power over the soul and a fascination which no other idea is able to raise.[30]

There are two reasons for R. Soloveitchik's apprehensiveness about basing the articles of faith exclusively on cognition and knowledge.

(1) The question of the articles of faith is usually based on the cognitive dimension. Many authorities have sought to define the meaning of these tenets; in most cases, the very existence of religion is dependent upon such dogma. Such an assumption, in most instances, is cognitive (the existence of God, Divine Providence, His revelation, etc.).

(2) Torah study is included in these three articles of faith, and this is a distinctly cognitive activity. Furthermore, the inclusion of Torah study in this list reveals, to some extent, the cognitive nature of the two other articles of faith.

R. Soloveitchik, therefore, explained that the acceptance of the yoke of Heaven is not limited to abstract cognition and intellectualism, but also

---

30 *Worship of the Heart*, 109.

includes mental perfection. As we noted in the preceding chapter, an intentional act contains feeling. The act of acceptance of the yoke of Heaven is not only cognitive, it is also mental and a function of the individual's personality. The halakhic significance of this intent, therefore, fashions the experience of reading *Shema*, both contentually and emotionally-psychologically.

3. Aggadah: Rationality and Methodology

The discussion of aggadah is limited, as was the halakhic discussion. Two examples sufficed for R. Soloveitchik to show that the interpretation of the aggadah is among the basic sources that fashion the religious consciousness generally, and especially the consciousness of the act of reading *Shema*. The first example explores the midrashic explanation of the source of reading *Shema* ("Blessed be the name of His glorious kingdom"). R. Soloveitchik devoted special attention to the way in which Maimonides read this midrash in his magnum opus *Mishneh Torah* and fully exhausted the consciousness consequences of this reading. In his analysis, R. Soloveitchik spoke of a new dimension of the religious consciousness: the intellectual dimension.

In the second example R. Soloveitchik was concerned with the connection between reading *Shema* and the suffering endured by R. Akiva. In this instance, the aggadah aids in reconstructing and uncovering the halakhic basis of the consciousness of the unity of God. Here, too, a window is opened for us to understand R. Soloveitchik's sources, on whose basis Jewish religious consciousness took shape.

Authority

We will begin with the first usage of aggadah, which is meant to indicate the establishment of the belief in divine unity as a longstanding intellectual tradition. This grounding clarifies the nature of reading *Shema*. As we noted, R. Soloveitchik grounded the dogma that he chose in Maimonides' ruling in *Mishneh Torah*, to teach us, yet again, that caution is required when relating to aggadic teachings and that they are to be viewed within a halakhic context.[31] His dependence upon Maimonides' halakhic authority (since *Mishneh Torah* is fundamentally a halakhic composition) affords

---

31 Maimonides himself had reservations regarding aggadah. See *Mishneh Torah, Hilkhot Melakhim* [Laws of Kings] 12:5.

us a certain degree of confidence in examining the relevant midrashic sources that helped fashion the consciousness.

R. Soloveitchik related to the recitation of "Blessed be the name of His glorious kingdom" after that of the *Shema* verse ("Hear, O Israel"— Deut. 6:4).[32] Numerous *midrashim* attribute this declaration to Jacob before his death,[33] and Maimonides uses this attribution in *Hilkhot Keriyat Shema* 1:4. R. Soloveitchik was greatly interested in the manner in which Maimonides internalized this midrashic teaching, and what he accepted and what he rejected. R. Soloveitchik refers a few times to this passage from *Mishneh Torah*, but chose not to quote it.[34] Maimonides writes:

> Why does one recite in this fashion? We have a tradition to the effect that when our father Jacob's death was nigh he gathered his sons together in Egypt and exhorted them to take particular care concerning correct belief in God's unity and not to stray from the path of God, on which his fathers Abraham and Isaac had walked. He then diligently inquired of them: "My sons, perchance there is among you someone unworthy who does not agree with me on the issue of the unity of the Master of the Universe?"—as Moses our master said to us, "Perchance there is among you some man or woman or some clan or tribe, whose heart is even now turning away from the Lord our God to go and worship the gods of those nations—perchance there is among you a stock sprouting poison weed and wormwood" (Deut. 29:17).[35] They all replied: "Hear, O Israel! The Lord is our God, the Lord alone" (Deut. 6:4), that is to say, "Hear us say, our father Israel, the Lord our God, the Lord alone." The old man responded, "Blessed be the name of His glorious majesty for ever and ever." It is therefore customary among all Jews to recite the praise uttered by the elderly Israel after the first verse of the Shema.[36]

---

32 See Ezra Fleischer, "Towards a Clarification of the Expression 'Poreis 'al Shema'" [Hebrew], *Tarbiz* 41 (1972): 133-144 (also included in Mack, *Studies in Jewish Liturgy*, 79-90).

33 See, for example, Moshe Minkovitz, "Variant Customs and Traditions for the Recitation of *Shema*" [Hebrew], *Sinai* 93 (1983): 119-122.

34 *Worship of the Heart*, 110-112. R. Soloveitchik quoted extensively from the exposition in BT Pesakhim 56a, as if he wanted to explain to the reader that Maimonides' premier authority appears between the lines in the discussion of the aggadah.

35 A reference to idolatry. Maimonides wants to stress that the discussion is based on abstract cognition.

36 The English version of the passage from Maimonides is from *The Code of Maimonides*, book 2: *The Book of Love*, trans. Menachem Kellner (New Haven, Yale University Press, 2004), 3-4.

Isadore Twersky maintains that this passage shows "the way they [midrashic texts] are filtered through Maimonides' intellectualistic-spiritualistic outlook."[37] Twersky probably referred to the fact that Maimonides based the midrashic event on the abstract knowledge of God. R. Soloveitchik, as well, argued that Maimonides "availed himself of a composite version."[38] He stressed a few aspects of Maimonides' use of the midrash.

(1) Dogmatism and rationality: Maimonides selected from the *midrashim* the formulation relating to "the unity of God." This formulation imparts a sense of intellectualism to the event, that is, it bases the midrashic event on knowledge and cognition. The unworthiness of which he speaks, too, refers to a flaw in the knowledge of God.

(2) Tradition: Maimonides presented the principle of the continuity of the Patriarchs. Jacob continues the way of "his fathers Abraham and Isaac."[39] Again, the path taken by the Patriarchs means mainly the knowledge of the abstract truth, namely, divine unity. The unity of God is therefore the key to historical continuity and uniformity.

(3) Omission of the messianic component: Maimonides does not use the wording "Jacob wished to reveal to his sons the end of days,"[40] and he avoided the messianic content in the different versions of the midrash that relate to it.[41]

R. Soloveitchik combined the first two aspects and argued that belief is anchored in tradition. "[…] the creed of *Shema* goes back to the very origin of our history, to the dawn of our collective existence. The solemn declaration is perhaps the first truth, which our great Patriarchs discovered."[42] The phenomenological interpretation of the midrash facilitates

---

37 Isadore Twersky, *Introduction to the Code of Maimonides (Mishneh Torah)* (New Haven: Yale University Press, 1980), 150.

38 *Worship of the Heart*, 111.

39 R. Soloveitchik did not mention Moses, to whom Maimonides does refer. The mention of Moses seemingly intensifies the linkage to the constitutive figures of the Jewish people. Cf. *Worship of the Heart*, 112-13.

40 *Worship of the Heart*, 110.

41 BT Pesakhim 56a. All the many parallels to the opening of the midrash relate to the messianic dimension. See, for example, *Bereshit Rabbah* 99:5; 100:49; *Tankhuma, Vayehi* 8.

42 *Worship of the Heart*, 111.

a new distinction between reading *Shema* and the *Amidah* (prayer). R. Soloveitchik writes:

> In prayer, we experience the presence of God; we stand near and commune with Him. In reading the *Shema*, by contrast, we enter the presence of those persons who walked with Him, we stand in their shadow; we converse with men who, though they died a biological death, have been reincarnated time and again in our historical experience via divergent media and various forms of existence. The great drama of destiny, begun by the Patriarchs, is reenacted again. Searching for and finding God, struggling with fate, absorbing defeat and yet emerging victorious—all these mark continuity of Being amid a changing world. This experience is explicated through this reading of *Shema*. God is one and this spells oneness of historical event.[43]

In his later thought, Scheler characterized human tradition by historical knowledge, which is composed of the conscious memory of symbols, sources of knowledge, and foundational texts. Scheler argued that human intelligence makes the content of the tradition objective, that is, it puts it through a process of objectivization. Human reason is engaged in "throwing it [the content of the tradition] back, as it were, into the past where it belongs and, at the same time, clearing the ground for new discoveries and inventions in the present."[44] Scheler explained that projection to the past and the preparation of a foundation for the present is a cognitive act. As we have seen, the tradition of reading *Shema* is based on rational knowledge and cognitive content. The knowledge of the past is made relevant by tradition.

Now, in light of this perception of tradition, we can reexamine the distinction between prayer and *Shema*. This distinction, as formulated now, is multifaceted: prayer is concerned solely with the present, while reading *Shema* relates to the individual as a representative of the community, with members extending over centuries. Prayer reflects an isolated, single event, while the *Shema* denotes a continuum. Prayer is a dialogue with God, while reading *Shema* is a dialogue with the worshiper's collective identity. Prayer denotes man's natural ascent to his God, and the *Shema*, the tragic struggle typical of the hero in romantic literature. The distinction between praying and reading *Shema* is based on the latter's inclusion within time-honored tradition.

43 *Worship of the Heart*, 112.
44 Scheler, *Man's Place in Nature*, 27.

Rationalist Tradition

The aggadah on "Blessed be the name of His glorious kingdom forever and ever" emphasizes the dimension of tradition. The consciousness of tradition as a connection to the progenitors of the Jewish nation recurs in R. Soloveitchik's writings. This conception is also anchored in his discussions of eternity and time.[45] The current discussion, however, sheds light on a new facet of his perception of tradition. To now, R. Soloveitchik was concerned solely with the halakhic tradition and the transmission of novellae. In *Halakhic Man* and in *And from There You Shall Seek* the tradition that is transmitted is that of Torah study. The tradition begins and ends with the halakhah (in the different senses it acquires in R. Soloveitchik's thought). In contrast, in the discussion in *Worship of the Heart*, the tradition is mainly philosophical and theological. It is concerned with the unity of God and the uniformity of history, to which R. Soloveitchik added the psychological dimension. The belief in one God obviously possesses elements of a mental experience. Moreover, the experience develops from a clearly halakhic foundation, namely, the laws of reading *Shema* and the acceptance of the yoke of Heaven. This experience, however, is primarily intellectual and cognitive.

Now we are to come to terms with the cognitive-intellectual dimension, which up to this point[46] had only briefly been mentioned in the discussions on prayer. R. Soloveitchik formulated his rationalist conception as follows:

> There is, however, a second aspect[47] to the creed proclaimed in *Shema*. The theme of *Shema* has not only been communicated to us through an apocalyptic revelation as a truth that is metaphysical and transcendental. It was also discovered and ascertained by the human mind itself, employing its natural categorical instruments of apprehension and comprehension, Revelation only confirmed what the logos had already attained. Jacob is the representative of a natural ethical system of the charismatic community who went forth to find God and discover His ways, relying on his own wits and talents. Moses, who was found by God and taken prisoner by Him in the great encounter of revelation, proclaimed the same truth—*Shema Yisrael*. The logos is capable of arriving at an apocalyptic truth. Hence, the experience connected with *Shema* is not something mysterious and paradoxical,

---

45 See Schwartz, *Religion or Halakha*, 304; *From Phenomenology to Existentialism*, 183-88.
46 See above, Chapter Six.
47 The first being tradition.

which man can only accept but not comprehend. It is an august truth rooted
in the logos and reaching out to the deepest strata of the human personality. It begins with the awakening of the logical awareness of man, with the
ripening of his thoughts and insights, with the dawning upon him of the
greatest of all questions—the question of origin and root. That occurs with
the advent of the Patriarchs, Hence, the experience is consummated at the
level of naturalness and rationality, when man begins to examine himself
and his surroundings.[48]

R. Soloveitchik presumably discussed the aggadic material from a
Maimonidean perspective, or at least so it would appear from the continuous attention paid to aggadah in Maimonides' writings.[49] The sense we gain
from R. Soloveitchik's works as a whole is that Maimonides' philosophical
impact on R. Soloveitchik's writings cannot be compared to the halakhic
impression that they made. Maimonides the halakhist is frequently present
in R. Soloveitchik's writings, while Maimonides the philosopher does not
appear so regularly. *Sefer ha-Mitzvot* and *Mishneh Torah* are the sources for
a lively and constant discourse, while the *Guide for the Perplexed* appears
only rarely.[50] The discussion of divine unity in Chapter Seven, as well, relies
on Maimonides' halakhic writings.[51] In the current discussion, however,
R. Soloveitchik mentioned Maimonides together with a clearly rationalist conception, and we should examine this. I wish to argue that in this
discussion R. Soloveitchik adopted a naive medieval rationalist approach,
which is not fundamentally Maimonidean. Medieval Jewish thought was
characterized by two main types of rationalism.[52]

(1) Naïve rationalism: the rationalism typical of R. Saadiah Gaon and
     other philosophers whose cultural and conceptual world drew
     mainly upon Islamic theology (*kalām*), and that maintained that
     Judaism could be absolutely confirmed by means of logical and
     scientific thought.

---

48 *Worship of the Heart*, 112-113.
49 *Worship of the Heart*, 110-111. We already noted the Maimonidean version of the aggadah.
50 See Zeev Harvey, "Notes on Rav Soloveitchik and Maimonidean Philsophy," in *Faith
    in Changing Times: On the Teachings of Rav J. B. Soloveitchik* [Hebrew], ed. Avi Sagi
    (Jerusalem: World Zionist Organization, 1996), 95.
51 *Worship of the Heart*, 115-119.
52 Scholars like Leo Strauss and Shlomo Pines suggest additional types, such as agnostic
    rationalism that finds worth exclusively in the political sphere. R. Soloveitchik certainly
    did not take such views into account.

(2) Rationalism as a value: the rationalism characteristic of the thought of Maimonides and his successors, whose ideational and conceptual world was rooted in Islamic philosophy, and that held the acquisition of scientific knowledge as its highest goal. The Jewish sources could be interpreted in accordance with such a value.

To being with a question: how was R. Soloveitchik influenced by intellectual rationalism? Maimonidean rationalism has much in common with the epistemological idealism of Hermann Cohen, although these two approaches have completely different cultural backgrounds. Maimonidean rationalism is completely absorbed in the acquisition of scientific knowledge and the experience that it imparts (communion with God, the immortality of the soul, and the like). The acquisition of scientific knowledge is a goal and value in its own right. Epistemological idealism, as well, viewed scientific knowledge as the backbone of cognitive creativity, and therefore such knowledge possesses intrinsic worth. The creation of cognitive objects in accordance with the rules of (Newtonian) science is a paradigm also for creativity in other cultural fields (ethics and aesthetics). For R. Soloveitchik, science and scientific cognition are a discrete element of the consciousness (*And from There You Shall Seek*) and a distinct approach to the cognitive and extracognitive reality (*Halakhic Man, The Lonely Man of Faith*). Furthermore, in *The Lonely Man of Faith* science is perceived as a legitimate form of worship. Scientific inquiry is "an integral part of religious commitment,"[53] and R. Soloveitchik thought highly of this endeavor.[54]

Science is a tool for reaching important religious achievements.[55] Scientific thought is an important vehicle for understanding the creativity of the halakhic man, and R. Soloveitchik therefore used Maimonidean rationalism to describe such activity.[56] Such a way of thinking would eventually become a distinct personality type.[57] As was noted, Cohen's epistemological idealism became an interpretive tool for R. Soloveitchik. In his view, Cohen's teaching interprets Maimonides; in other words, medieval rationalism and Cohen's thought are identical.

---

53 David Schatz, "Science and Religious Consciousness in Rav Soloveitchik's Thought" [Hebrew], in Sagi, *Faith in Changing Times*, 307-44 See, especially, 307, 310.
54 Ibid., 310.
55 Ibid., 314.
56 See Schwartz, *Religion or Halakha*, 320-328.
57 Dov Schwartz, *Halakhic Man: Religion or Halakha?* [Hebrew] (Ramat Gan: Bar-Ilan University Press, 2008), 8.

The above passage from *Worship of the Heart*, however, does not reflect the intrinsic value of scientific knowledge. Its orientation is more inclined to the "double truth" or the "double faith."[58] Thus, in this passage R. Soloveitchik set forth the notion that both revelation and reason lead to the same truth. He adopted approaches such as that of R. Saadiah Gaon, who was convinced that the faith of Judaism is confirmed by rational thought. Maimonides, too, has been understood in this spirit, although he wrote in a few places of his "perplexity" (the inability to resolve the astronomical models with Aristotelian physics) and reason's inability to reach a conclusion on certain questions (Creation). These issues have been the subject of considerable scholarly interest. At any rate, R. Soloveitchik indirectly interpreted R. Saadiah's teachings in a manner that does not necessarily coincide with medieval "naïve" rationalism. For R. Soloveitchik, rational inquiry results from charisma. Reason strives to reveal itself. Man reveals by vision and inspiration what he already found in himself, in the "deepest strata" of his personality. The discovery is not only a matter of one's personality, it is also intellectual. Man is exposed to his outstanding intellective capabilities, with which he confirms the unity of God. Furthermore, initiative and momentum belong to the human intellect. Inquiry ensues directly from the self's desire to expose the source and reach its roots. Indeed, medieval rationalism was greatly concerned with the question of divine unity,[59] but it did not touch upon the consciousness senses of self-discovery.

Without question, R. Soloveitchik embraces here a "naïve" rationalist approach in the style of the early medieval period, but his style connects the reader to a conception of prayer in general as self-discovery.[60] By reading *Shema*, as well, the worshiper comes to know his own personality—but only its intellectual and rational dimension, not all facets of the personality. Man uncovers his rational abilities when his intellect succeeds in reaching the Source, the one God. This turning point in the discussion of the intent in reading *Shema*, to one's personality, is therefore based in the intellectual dimension of the self, but not in exposure by means of the liturgical process. Once again, the reader faces the fact that R. Soloveitchik was willing to

---

58 See Harry Austryn Wolfson, "The Double Faith Theory in Clement, Saadia, Averroes and St. Thomas, and Its Origin in Aristotle and the Stoics," *JQR* 32 (1942-1943): 213-264.

59 See, for example, Daniel J. Lasker, "Definitions of 'One' and Divine Unity" [Hebrew], in *Studies in Jewish Thought*, ed. Sara O. Heller-Willenski and Moshe Idel (Jerusalem: Magnes, 1989), 51-61.

60 See above, Chapter Two.

embrace unconventional traditions (from his viewpoint) in order to depict the rich and variegated experience of reading *Shema*. From the outset, R. Soloveitchik argued that in his analysis of the idea of divine unity he would employ "the halakhic-midrashic method instead of the scholastic."[61] His aggadic material ("Blessed be the name...") provided a basis for the intellectual tradition of the belief in one God. The style, however, of his portrayal of the intellectual tradition bound up with reading *Shema* is clearly scholastic. Thus, we see that reading *Shema* adds depth, not only to the collective tradition, but also to its charged dialectical dimension.

Two Methodologies

The second use of aggadah is meant to present a distinctly consciousness model of the unity of God as is manifest in reading *Shema*. This is the tripartite model (subjective-norm-praxis) that R. Soloveitchik already used in the earlier chapters of *Worship of the Heart* in his consciousness analysis of prayer, which he now applies to reading *Shema*.[62] In order, however, to examine the use of aggadah in the development of this triple model, we must first present the course of the discussion of the proper methodology for presenting the consciousness structure of reading *Shema* and its accompanying belief in divine unity.[63] R. Soloveitchik lays out two methodologies here: (1) the inductive approach; and (2) what I call "inverse reconstruction."

We shall begin with the first methodology. R. Soloveitchik made a straightforward distinction between two approaches:

(1) an inductive halakhic-midrashic approach, according to which the general is derived from concrete individual situations;
(2) a deductive rationalist approach, which presumes the principle, from which the individual situations are derived.[64]

---

61 *Worship of the Heart*, 113.
62 See above, Chapter Two.
63 *Worship of the Heart*, 113-115.
64 R. Soloveitchik's distinction is general, and is indifferent to the precise logical ways of the halakhic process. At any rate, thinkers of that time, such as Adolf Schwarz and R. David Cohen (the "Nazirite") devoted special attention to the question. See Dov Schwartz, *Religious Zionism between Logic and Messianism* [Hebrew] (Tel Aviv: Am Oved, 1999), part 2.

Halakhah, in most instances, is characteristically inductive, but at times the deductive approach appears, as well (the Decalogue). R. Soloveitchik declares: "Since the inductive method has been so successfully employed by the Halakhah, we shall employ it in our present analysis of the reading of *Shema*."[65]

And now for the second methodology. R. Soloveitchik raised the question whether the belief in the unity of God is the source of the halakhah and the ethos, or perhaps is an abstract idea that is not translated into praxis? He decided in favor of the first possibility, and therefore engaged in reconstruction. The reconstruction here, however, is reversed: the discussions relating to reconstruction in R. Soloveitchik's writings (especially in *The Halakhic Mind* and *And from There You Shall Seek*) engaged in uncovering the subjective from within the objective. The phenomenologist of religion seeks to reconstruct from within the halakhic praxis thoughts, feelings, and ways of relation to God. Here, however, in *Worship of the Heart*, R. Soloveitchik went in the opposite direction: he attempted to examine and derive the practical halakhic dimension from within the mental dimension of the unity of God. R. Soloveitchik aimed "to find the halakhic revelations of this great truth [= the unity of God]."[66] In a certain respect, this action is explicative, since its direction is the opposite of reconstruction. The discussions of reconstruction in R. Soloveitchik's writings (especially *The Halakhic Mind* and *And from There You Shall Seek*) sought to uncover the subjective within the objective. The phenomenologist of religion aims to reconstruct the thoughts, emotions, and methodology within the halakhic praxis. Here, however, in *Worship of the Heart*, R. Soloveitchik reversed direction, as he attempted to examine and detach the applied halakhic dimension from within the consciousness philosophical dimension of the unity of God.

R. Soloveitchik strove, in unconventional fashion, to reconcile revelation and reason within a rationalist context. In an additional matter, as well, he continued the approach of R. Saadiah and of other pre-Maimonidean thinkers. R. Saadiah explains in the introduction to *Emunot ve-Deot* that rational inquiry is desirable only when based on the prophetic sources. That is, the dual truth cannot be attained with certainty by free inquiry, but only when delineated from the outset, beginning in the written sources.[67]

---

65 *Worship of the Heart*, 114.
66 *Worship of the Heart*, 114.
67 See Saadia Gaon, *The Book of Beliefs and Opinions*, 27-31. R. Saadia Gaon recommended such guided inquiry, for if the one conducting the inquiry were to begin from a starting point that is not enrooted in Scripture, he would waste his time, and even reach errone-

Even if R. Saadiah's reasoning is pedagogic and practical, and not essentialist, the demand for guided inquiry still stands. R. Soloveitchik presented the approach that the idea of the unity of God is perceived in man's intellect, and ensues from it. In order, however, to avoid complications and obstacles—that could be aroused by the aggadah—the idea is to be examined from within the halakhic material.

There is tension between the two methodologies offered by R. Soloveitchik. The inductive method is characteristic of most halakhic methodology. The list of exegetical rules (*midot*) by which the Torah is expounded teaches of a distancing from rigorous deduction, toward analogy, induction, and association. R. Soloveitchik, however, intends to describe the halakhah based on the subjective and dogmatic assumption of divine unity. Such an approach is of a more deductive nature, even though reconstruction moderates the necessity of deducing details from the general principle. Did R. Soloveitchik seek to allude, once again, to the prayer experience, that exceeds the consciousness frameworks typical of the other divine commandments? Did he attempt to once more hint at the dialectic principle characteristic of the pace of his teachings? In any event, R. Soloveitchik planned to concentrate on "more practical facets of this idea [that is, divine unity],"[68] meaning the norm and the halakhah. He devoted a quite lengthy discussion to clarify that it is the halakhah that gives meaning and fullness to life.[69] Accordingly, inductive thought suits the nature of his discussions.

The Consciousness of Unity

R. Soloveitchik applied "reverse reconstruction" to the principle of the unity of God, that is, he began by constituting the mandated-practical dimension of this principle. He strove to locate the practical expressions and to reconstruct them from within the subjective dimension. Here, too, he adopted the model of the three dimensions of consciousness that we examined above.

---

ous conclusions, if he were not to conduct his inquiry in proper fashion. On topics such as Creation, Maimonides presented a philosophical inquiry, and only at the end of the discussion he examined the biblical correspondences to it. Such manner of discussion also appears in *Emunah Ramah* by R. Abraham ibn Daud, an elder contemporary of Maimonides.

68 *Worship of the Heart*, 114. R. Soloveitchik referred to the commandment of martyrdom (see below).

69 *Worship of the Heart*, 118-121.

The subjective dimension of divine unity lies in the realm of the theological and metaphysical. The philosophical basis of divine unity boasts a lengthy history. Over the course of time, many philosophers sought to prove and refine this principle by means of profound rational analysis. Medieval rationalism devoted much intellectual effort to the conceptual and abstract discussion of the unity of God. These sources were undoubtedly accessible to R. Soloveitchik, for whom the rationalist foundation was an important component of the subjective religious consciousness. The underlying phenomenological question, however, that concerned him in no small measure was: how do we descend from the subjective level of the consciousness to the normative dimension, and how do we reveal the practical dimension from within the normative?

In order to resolve the question of the structures and processes typical of the religious consciousness, R. Soloveitchik examined two Maimonidean halakhic sources that directly relate to the unity of God: *Mishneh Torah* (*Hilkhot Yesodei Torah* [The Laws of the Fundamentals of the Torah]) and *Sefer ha-Mitzvot* (Positive Commandment 2). He concluded that *Mishneh Torah* is concerned with the metaphysical-rationalist aspect ("God is one. He is not two, nor more than two"), while *Sefer ha-Mitzvot* speaks of the normative historical facet, namely, the covenant between God and Israel ("He indeed took us out of bondage"). He thereby found in the sources of halakhic ruling a movement from abstract faith to norm: from the metaphysical principle of the unity of God to the concrete covenant that was forged between the Holy One, blessed be He, and the people of Israel. The covenant is the source of the norm. Kaplan already directed sweeping, and at times justified, criticism, at this interpretation by R. Soloveitchik.[70] Kaplan, nonetheless, showed that R. Soloveitchik was aware of the weak links in his thought, but still sought to link the subjective dimension to the norm, and he continued by revealing the nature of the act that ensues from the belief in divine unity: martyrdom. "The martyrdom of the Jewish saints, unequaled and unrivaled in the annals of human history, is the most impressive and awesome manifestation of the doctrine of unity as a halakhic-ethical principle to which one is committed and consecrated."[71] *Kiddush Hashem* is a halakhic issue with clearly practical definitions.

---

70 Kaplan, "Review Essay," 96 ff. On the distinction between belief and knowledge, Kaplan referred to the article by Abraham Nuriel, "Maimonides' Concept of Belief," in Nuriel's *Concealed and Revealed in Medieval Jewish Philosophy* [Hebrew] (Jerusalem: Magnes, 2000), 78.

71 *Worship of the Heart*, 117.

Now, we can set forth the structure of the consciousness of divine unity, following the model that R. Soloveitchik presented in *The Halakhic Mind*:

subjective dimension:

unity of God
("The norm enjoins us not only to believe but also to comprehend and interpret this article of faith, as far as the human mind is capable")[72]

objective dimension:
(1) norm
("the original covenant between God and Israel, from which the people of Israel derives charismatic endowment")[73]
(2) act: martyrdom

The subjective dimension of the consciousness is presented in the first verse of *Shema*. R. Soloveitchik argues that the "cognitive origin"[74] derives directly from this wording ("One"). The objective dimension is represented in the second paragraph of *Shema*, "with all your soul" ("an act of consecration and self-dedication")[75]. To firmly ground the model, he brought the "aggadic tradition connecting R. Akiva's martyrdom (with the concept of the unity of God)."[76] This is R. Soloveitchik's second usage of the aggadic-midrashic material that clarifies the subjective consciousness of *Shema*. The Babylonian Talmud (Berakhot 61b) relates that R. Akiva was killed while reciting *Shema*. He "was accepting upon himself the kingship of Heaven" when he underwent his last agonies, and therefore the aggadic tradition is the constitutive text of the consciousness of *Shema*. This tradition mentions two texts that are explicated within the narrative:

(1) "One" (Deut. 6:4);
(2) "with all your soul" (Deut. 6:5).

The act of martyrdom derives from the second text ("All my days I have been troubled by this verse, 'with all your soul'—even if He takes your soul"), and the idea of the unity of God derives from the first

---

72 *Worship of the Heart*, 115.
73 *Worship of the Heart*, 116.
74 *Worship of the Heart*, 118.
75 *Worship of the Heart*, 118.
76 *Worship of the Heart*, 118.

("he prolonged the word 'One' until he expired while [saying] 'One'"). R. Soloveitchik wrote on this:

> We have emphasized that the second verse signifies an act of consecration and self-dedication, while the first verse conveys to us a truth, a noetic message, which finds its realization on a dynamic-ecstatic level of love.[77]

If we set aside for a moment R. Soloveitchik's explanations, we are forced to admit that the first impression gained from the "prolonging" of "One" is that of communion and pouring out one's soul. Furthermore, the parallels of the aggadic tradition in the Ten Martyrs reveal proximity to the early esoteric literature,[78] thus adding a mystic chord that casts R. Akiva's responses in the light of an emotional and ecstatic experience. R. Soloveitchik's explanation, however, of this legend contains a contemplative meaning. The unity of God demands a deepness of intellectual understanding. The intent of the first verse is attained through abstract rational contemplation. This is a rationalist—we might even say Maimonidean—explanation of martyrdom. According to this, when R. Akiva's body was raked by iron combs, he was occupied with perceiving the unity of God. Perhaps then, from this intellectual perception he reached a state of ecstatic love as his soul expired. This is the supreme phase of intellective communion with God.

Now, for a second time, we can present the cognitive structure in accordance with *The Halakhic Mind*, as we emphasize the connection to the recitation of *Shema*, following the aggadic tradition of R. Akiva's anguished death:

subjective dimension

Oneness of God
(the belief in unity according to R. Akiva's intellect and cognition)

objective dimension
(1) [covenant]
("On this condition I brought you out of the land of Egypt, that ye sanctify My name publicly")[79]

---

77 *Worship of the Heart*, 118.

78 See Yoseph Dan, "*Hekhalot Rabbati* and the Legend of the Ten Martyrs" [Hebrew], *Eshel Beer-Sheva* 2 (1980): 63-80; Michal Oron, "*Merkavah* Texts and the Legend of the Ten Martyrs" [Hebrew], *Eshel Beer-Sheva* 2 (1980): 81-95.

79 This conjunction is based on what Maimonides writes in *Sefer ha-Mitzvot*, vol. 1: *The Positive Commandments*, 13 (Positive Commandment 9). R. Soloveitchik bases his

(2) "with all your soul"
(martyrdom, following the exposition of R. Akiva)

R. Soloveitchik illustrated the method of deduction or "reverse reconstruction" in the aggadic account. R. Akiva's cognitive truth is to be found in "One." He prolonged this word until his soul expired, because it is an inherent component in human perception. This is a fundamental cognitive assumption. The intellectual component is the source for deriving the halakhah from the wording "with all your soul." While in R. Soloveitchik's religious phenomenological discussion we would expect a reconstruction of the subjective consciousness of divine unity from within the commandment of martyrdom, here he took the opposite action: he derived the system of halakhot of martyrdom (the praxis) from the unity of God (the theory), and did so as interpretation of the aggadic R. Akiva tradition.

R. Soloveitchik himself might have been aware of the exceptional nature of the reverse move that he made, that digresses from the absolute validity of "objective" halakhic authority. He therefore saw the aggadah as a "fluid" source, and even warned of its excessive flexibility.[80] This discussion, specifically, teaches of the special standing in R. Soloveitchik's thought of prayer, and to be more precise, of *Shema*. He was willing to go beyond the limits of the methodology that supported the absolute authority of the halakhah—and at the very least fracture it—in order to explain the exceptional relationship between the subjective and the objective in the recitation of *Shema*. The aggadah is eminently suited to support such revolutionary moves. To a certain degree, R. Soloveitchik warned of the plasticity of the aggadah, a trap into which he himself eventually fell.

Judaism and Hellenism, or: Values and Science

R. Soloveitchik ended his discussion of the aggadah of R. Akiva with the masked claim that all roads lead to the halakhah. The revolutions of the aggadah are all firmly enveloped within the halakhah. In other words, an

---

thought here on Maimonides's passage on martyrdom, which mentions *Sifra* (cited here, *Emor* 8, end of chapter 9. A similar idea is present in *Pesikta Zutarta*, *Emor*, fol. 62a). That is, the halakhah deduced from the aggadah of R. Akiva's death also connected his martyrdom to the covenant between God and Israel. An examination of the norms derived from the unity of God logically leads to recognizing the divine covenant, and this covenant, when threatened, requires martyrdom.

80 *Worship of the Heart*, 104.

analysis of the Jewish religious consciousness has its roots deep in norm and act. In the final analysis, it is the halakhah that reveals this consciousness. In order to provide a basis for these claims, R. Soloveitchik compared the Greek model with the Jewish one[81] in three main realms: life, morality, and actual existence. This comparison can be outlined as follows:

    (1) Life:
          (i) meaning: Judaism ascribes meaning to life, while Hellenism finds meaning only in reason;
         (ii) nature: Judaism views life as action, while Hellenism regards it as a datum;[82]
    (2) Morality and values:
          (i) value vs. experience: Judaism is a religion of values ("axiological"[83]) whereas Hellenism, which focuses on the "ontic" actual reality,[84] is rational ("theoretical," "noetic"[85]);

---

81 The distinction between Judaism and Hellenism is quite widespread in modern Jewish thought, and R. Soloveitchik was, undoubtedly, exposed to these discussions. See, for example, Joseph Klausner, "Judea and Greece: Two Opposites?," in *Festschrift Armand Kaminka zum siebzigsten Geburtstage*, ed. S. Rappaport and M. Zikier, (Vienna: Verlag des Wiener Maimonides-Instituts, 1937), Hebrew volume, 49-58; Aharon Kaminka, "Judea and Greece in Rhetorical and Ethical Writings" [Hebrew], *Knesset* 4 (1939): 345-364. It is noteworthy that comparisons between Judaism and Hellenism appear in Religious Zionist thought. For R. Ze'ev Jawitz, see Dov Schwartz, *Challenge and Crisis in Rabbi Kook's Circle* [Hebrew] (Tel Aviv: Am Oved, 2001), 226-227. For R. Moshe Avigdor Amiel, see Schwartz, *Faith at the Crossroads*, 56. At the same time, in 1918, Kaufmann Kohler, the ideologue of Reform Judaism in the United States, drew a distinction between the God of morality, righteousness, and holiness, in Jewish belief ("the Biblical belief in God") and the god of Intelligence, who is responsible for the "plan and order" of the universe, in Greek philosophy. Kohler projected these models on martyrdom. He argued that, for the Greeks, truth was "an object of supreme delight" for the thinker. As regards Judaism, in contrast, he wrote: "truth became the holiest aim of life for the entire people, for which all were taught to battle and to die, as did the Maccabean heroes and Daniel and his associates, their prototypes" (Kaufmann Kohler, *Jewish Theology Systematically and Historically Considered* [New York: Macmillan, 1968], 85). See, for example, Schweid, *History of Modern Religious Philosophy* [Hebrew] (Tel Aviv: Am Oved, 2006), part IV, 341. Kohler linked divinity and morality to martyrdom, and saw this connection as the heart of Jewish belief, in contrast to Hellenism. R. Soloveitchik also argued in favor of this approach. Cf. *From Phenomenology to Existentialism*, 329.

82 *Worship of the Heart*, 120. The distinction between action and datum is derived from that between life and reason.

83 In the text: "biological." Kaplan already noted the erroneous replacement of "axiological" by "biological"; see Kaplan, "Review Essay," 104.

84 *Worship of the Heart*, 119.

85 *Worship of the Heart*, 119-20.

(ii) standing: Judaism regards morality and action as a goal in themselves, while Hellenism sees them solely as a means (to the contemplative life).

(3) Existence:

(i) standing: for Judaism, existence is a goal that is not self-understood and as the object of qualification and action, while Hellenism takes is as a fact;

(ii) struggle: Judaism consecrates and elevates the tragic, while Hellenism regards it as absurd.[86]

Hellenism is represented in *Worship of the Heart* by Greek philosophy. The presentation of rationality as a trait of Hellenism is undoubtedly connected to the Nietzschean critique of the Apollonian. In the final analysis, the opposition between Judaism and Hellenism set forth by R. Soloveitchik can be summarized in the contrast between halakhah and philosophy, and concrete existence versus reflection. The former, relating to the concreteness of reality, clarifies R. Soloveitchik's digression from the usual comparisons between Judaism and Hellenism. Unlike Greek culture, he argues, Judaism revealed a lively and changing world (a "new situation"),[87] that of normative and ethical law. The uncovering of the "new" is grounded wholly in the concrete existence. Greek culture did not recognize law as a source of independent interest, and the Jewish corpus was therefore something completely new in its eyes. The halakhic corpus showed that the world of action is rich and diverse. It exposed Greek culture to a new and full way of life, with ramified contents and ways of thinking all its own.

R. Soloveitchik was troubled by the question of whether the tremendous force and presence of the act and existence afford them exclusivity. Did Judaism, in its special way, forego rational truth, abandoning it to Hellenism? Is the aggrandizement of scientific truth foreign to Judaism? He ruled out such a possibility,[88] and wrote:

---

86 *Worship of the Heart*, 120.

87 *Worship of the Heart*, 121.

88 We may reasonably assume that R. Soloveitchik had the medieval rationalist tradition in mind when he wrote this. Although his references to Maimonides of the *Guide of the Perplexed* are few, he never refuted the philosophical side of Maimonides. As we showed above, the intellectual experience is an inherent component of the consciousness. See, however, Lawrence Kaplan (ed.), *Between Philosophy and Halakhah: Rabbi Joseph B. Soloveitchik's Lectures on the "Guide of the Perplexed"* (Jerusalem: Urim, 2016).

Truth, itself, is not only a noetic problem but also an ethical one. There is a truth norm implied in the theoretical awareness. The scientist knows that the attainment of truth is an imperative, not merely a useful performance. People fought for scientific truth even when their championship of it spurred martyrdom and certain death. Thus, there is a normative motif in the ontic awareness as such. "To be" is an ethical goal entailing commitment to something, not only a fact to be accepted, or a theoretical mystery to be unraveled. Being challenges us to pledge ourselves to its realization, instead of surrendering to its factual impact.[89]

According to this, the approach that reveals the rich world of law and being need not be opposed to the method that glorifies the scholastic life, since the scientific way of life itself has an inner dimension of law and norm. Scientific truth has a moral and existential aspect, which is concerned with the uncompromising fidelity to scientific truth, even at personal cost. Consequently, commitment to scientific truth is a sort of martyrdom. For the scientist, this commitment is a matter of values and morality, and is normative. Over the course of history, not inconsiderable numbers of scientists have been willing to sacrifice their membership in the community (such as Spinoza), and at times, even their lives, rather than deny scientific truth (Giordano Bruno). Now we can offer a more precise formulation of the distinction between Judaism and Hellenism: the former is cognizant of the moral, normative, and practical dimension of scientific truth, while the latter does not. Judaism consecrates the struggle for truth.[90] In the following chapter of *Worship of the Heart* (chapter 8), R. Soloveitchik maintains that the unity of God does not allow for any division between cognition and ethics. "The cosmic pattern is identical with the ethical."[91] It is inconceivable to distinguish between God the wise and God the good, because we would then harm His unity. This unity dictates the identification of scientific and moral truth. Consequently, the ethical dimension of scientific cognition is indirectly derived from the conception of divine unity. The ramified branches of the consciousness of divine unity also determine the nature of scientific cognition.

Actually, R. Soloveitchik's discussion of this issue, namely, the relationship between ethico-halakhic thought to scientific thought is not

---

89 *Worship of the Heart*, 120.
90 R. Soloveitchik's argument is problematic in light of the example of Socrates, who is mentioned in another context on 121.
91 *Worship of the Heart*, 123.

sufficiently developed, and moves between the two approaches, without reaching a decisive conclusion. At times these two approaches were even formulated one after the other—in one breath, as it were. For example, he writes on the halakhah:

> Life is considered to be an ethical affair, basically exoteric and simple. The metaphysical dimension has been supplemented by the ethico-halakhic. Being is comprehended not in metaphysical-causal but in ethico-normative categories. As a matter of fact, however, the cognitive method, though very helpful in bettering physical conditions, cannot assist man in his search for the meaningful and for ontic worth.[92]

On the one hand, Judaism offers a conception that complements Greek philosophy. According to this, Judaism embraces the normative element, both on its own and in its presence in scientific thought. It acknowledges the worth both of religious martyrdom and total devotion (to the extent of giving one's life) to scientific truth. The abstract philosophical dimension of Hellenism has been "supplemented" by the halakhic one. On the other hand, Judaism presents an alternative conception to Greek philosophy. The idea of Judaism is indifferent to the scientific ideal for its own sake, that is, science for the sake of science, setting forth a completely different ideal, one that is normative and moral, in its stead. So perhaps the moral dimension of science comes to support Judaism's alternative approach. In either event, the dogmatic subjective principle of divine unity is the source of the halakhic approach of martyrdom, since this is the "Jewish" way to contend with the abstract ideas: to find expressions in real life, and to reveal the teleological meaning in such expressions.

4. Summary: Aggadah and Halakhah

Our analysis of the two *midrashim* (the death of Jacob and R. Akiva's martyrdom) teaches that the aggadah leads man to distant, new, and renewed realms. It is a vital and vibrant source that arouses somnolent cognitive sources in R. Soloveitchik's thought, such as philosophical rationalism and the mystical experience, and the use of unorthodox phenomenological methods, such as deduction, which we called "reverse reconstruction." That is, aggadah is the vehicle for revealing and reconstructing martyrdom (= objective consciousness) as a realistic expression of divine unity

---

92 *Worship of the Heart*, 121.

(= subjective consciousness). Actually, this relationship borders on causality. The objective dimension almost becomes dependent upon the subjective, unlike other cognitive analyses in R. Soloveitchik's writings.

R. Soloveitchik took pains to emphasize that uncovering the halakhah was the main purpose of his occupation with aggadah. In the final analysis, the context of his aggadic discussion is clearly halakhic. "Judaism activates all its abstract ideas and articles of faith in the halakhic-ethical sphere."[93] The halakhah bounds the free flow of the aggadah, and sets cognitive guidelines for it. The halakhah continues its role of constraint and setting boundaries by translating the subjective into praxis.

After having determined the two central sources that produce the prayer experience, R. Soloveitchik then turned to a third source, namely, the interpretation of constitutive texts, which is the subject of the eighth chapter of *Worship of the Heart.*

---

93 *Worship of the Heart,* 117.

Chapter 8

The Interpretation of Reading *Shema* and Its Blessings: (2) Application

This chapter concludes our discussion of the original nine chapters of *Worship of the Heart* (to which "Reflections on the *Amidah*" was added as chapter 10). R. Soloveitchik chose to end his examination of the consciousness of reading *Shema* with interpretations of this "reading." The following discussion will focus on the third constitutive source of the consciousness of prayer, namely, the liturgical texts of Jewish prayer. After R. Soloveitchik used halakhic and aggadic tools to establish the dogmatic principle of divine unity, he then turned to the interpretation of the liturgical text itself, to which he devoted the concluding chapters of this work.

What is religious phenomenological interpretation? R. Soloveitchik, for his part, defined such interpretation as the reading of a text "not as an isolated literary text but as a manifestation of a grand tradition rooted in the very essence of our God-consciousness that transcends the bounds of the standardized and fixed text and fans out into every aspect of our existential existence."[1] Religious phenomenological interpretation views a text as an expression of religious consciousness, the consciousness of God. The text reflects substantive aspects of consciousness that transcend its fleeting and local context. We will examine the phenomenological interpretation that R. Soloveitchik wrote on prayer in light of this interpretive approach.

---

1 Joseph B. Soloveitchik, *The Emergence of Ethical Man*, ed. Michael S. Berger (Jersey City, NJ: Toras HoRav Foundation, 2005), 6.

1. *Shema*—"Hear, O Israel"

Of the far-reaching and methodical interpretive program that R. Soloveitchik planned for reading *Shema* and its blessings, following the consciousness principles of prayer, he completed only his interpretation of three texts:

(1) "Hear, O Israel, the Lord our God, the Lord is One" (Deut. 6:4: the consciousness of unity, corresponding to chapter 7 of the *Worship of the Heart*);

(2) The *Yotzer Or* blessing (the unity of the universe and the angelic sphere—chapter 8);

(3) "And you shall love your God" (Deut. 6:5: the consciousness of love of God—chapter 9).

This shows that R. Soloveitchik interpreted the opening verse of *Shema* even before he offered his consciousness interpretive approach to the *Yotzer Or* blessing and the motif of love of God in the beginning of the *Shema*. In this commentary he laid the phenomenological foundation for the idea of the unity of God. In the following discussion, we will examine the elements of R. Soloveitchik's liturgical interpretation, based on the order he set for himself in the last chapters of *Avodah she-ba-Lev*.

Unity within and beyond the Consciousness

R. Soloveitchik declared in *And from There You Shall Seek* that the question of the transcendence or immanence of God was of no interest for him. His curiosity was aroused by the manner in which man conceives God, that is, by the ways of consciousness. "The question of whether the Deity's connection with the world is transcendent or immanent is irrelevant. Man sometimes attempts to find God within reality, and sometimes beyond it. It all depends on the viewpoint of the individual who searches."[2] His discussion in *Worship of the Heart*, as well, is clearly phenomenological, as I discussed at length in the preceding chapters. R. Soloveitchik continued to examine the human God experience through acts of consciousness. The worshiper's consciousness of God actualizes the divine presence. In the beginning of chapter 8, R. Soloveitchik was concerned with the dynamic

---

2 *And from There You Shall Seek*, 8. See Schwartz, *From Phenomenology to Existentialism*, 4-5.

divine will, which is present in the universe and drives it. He championed the conception of constant creation and revelation. He writes:

> God reveals himself within the cosmos, within the regularity and sequence. He speaks to man both through the abstract scientific cosmos, which is relational, formal and ideal, and through the immediate, living, avid concrete and fleeting world of sense perception and sensation. Being, in all its dimensions, is a revelation. God wills the cosmic process and speaks through it.[3]
>
> The cosmos, in its seemingly mechanical, insensate, repetitious conformity to the mathematical cycle, is not engaged in a monotonous and absurd performance. It is rather committed to a great undertaking, the realization of the Divine will, which in its very essence is ethical. The cosmic event is an ethical event, hidden, of course, from the human eye which stares only upon the surface and is incapable of apprehending and comprehending the mysterious link between the factual and the meaningful. Naked facticity, stripped of meaning and worth, was never created by God.[4]

In the first passage, R. Soloveitchik once again formulated the two stages of the scientific process, in accordance with the conventional conception of science. He was already fascinated by the notion in his writings from the 1940s, but now he reversed the order. In the conventional view, the scientific process begins with impressions from the sensory world influencing the scientist. These impressions stimulate the scientist and lead him to the second phase, in which he develops a series of mathematical relations that are not related to the sensory world.[5] Here, however, R. Soloveitchik began with abstract mathematical relations out of his desire to emphasize the divine presence in scientific thought. The claim of God's presence in the sensory world is understandable. The world of mathematical relations is situated entirely in man's cognition, and R. Soloveitchik sought to stress that God is present there, as well.

R. Soloveitchik indirectly adopted various formulations of the cosmic proof of God's existence.[6] The variegated and harmonious activity in the universe reflects the divine presence. We learn from the

---

3 *Worship of the Heart*, 123.
4 *Worship of the Heart*, 123-124. Incidentally, *Siddur ha-Gra* writes that the divine presence and Providence apply only when the world is in a state of unity (*Siddur ha-Gra* [Prayerbook of the Vilna Gaon], ed. Naphtali Hertz Ha-Levi [Jerusalem, 1895], 83b).
5 See Schwartz, *Religion or Halakha*, 96-98.
6 See, for example, Harry Austryn Wolfson, "Notes on Proofs of the Existence of God in Jewish Philosophy," *HUCA* 1 (1924): 584-596.

second passage that the divine presence in the natural regularity and its mathematical-physical formulations is also of ethical significance. This passage is concerned with divine involvement in the ethical sense of cosmic regularity. Such meaning necessitates deep analysis, but the divine stamp in the meaning of the natural regularity is obvious: the laws of nature reflect the purposeful divine will. R. Soloveitchik emphasizes that the divine is also present in the scientific formula, that is, in the scientist's closed mathematical-physical world. The essence of this presence is the meaning and purposefulness of the natural world.

R. Soloveitchik's discussions are not occupied with the concrete presence of God. He declared at the outset that when speaking of immanence he referred to divine activity, and not to God's actual presence. When he wrote of the divine presence in natural phenomena, he meant that every phenomenon "is born out of a Divine actus that is creative and primordial, willed and filled with meaning."[7] R. Soloveitchik presented nature as testimony—natural, ethical, and meaningful—to divine action. The divine presence is the seal of the natural and ethical divine will. R. Soloveitchik distanced the divine presence from ontological involvement.

The meaning of divine unity can now be defined more precisely. After establishing the definitions of the divine presence, R. Soloveitchik then turned to examine the subjective content of reading *Shema*. He related to the cosmic and ethical experience as the basis for the consciousness of God the Creator, and anchored the experience in the dogmatic foundation of reading *Shema*. He wrote:

> *Kabbalat ol malkhut Shamayim*, accepting the yoke of Heaven, signifies the fulfillment of both the natural law and the moral law. When we pronounce *Ehad* ("One") and affirm the unity of God, we intend to state that God, in his dual role as Creator and legislator, Master of the universe and Teacher, is one. His word made heaven and earth spring into existence, and the same word founded the moral law. Hence, the ontic law is moral. Hermann Cohen was wrong in his theory that Judaism did not discover God in the cosmic process and preferred the ethical approach to the ontic. Judaism found God both in the cosmos and in the conscience, in natural and in moral necessity.[8]

---

7 *Worship of the Heart*, 123.
8 *Worship of the Heart*, 124. R. Soloveitchik's approach unites sensation, thought, and volition in the subject ("I think"). See, for example, Meshullam Groll, *Selected Writings* [Hebrew], vol. 1 (Tel Aviv: Sifriat Poalim, 1956), 158.

Divine unity means the unity of nature and ethics. The same divine will that is the source of the creation of the law of nature is also the source of the moral imperative. R. Soloveitchik was not apprehensive of the consequences of such unity as this had worried many modern Jewish thinkers.[9] Cohen argued that the conception of God in Judaism absolutely rejects any basis in nature. He wrote in his magnum opus on Judaism that "Nature, however, is and remains nothing in comparison with the being of God's I [*göttliche Ich*],"[10] and added: "Knowledge of morality and knowledge of nature do not coincide, as pantheism, which is rooted in this error, thinks."[11] Cohen forcefully explained that nature lacks any inherent moral dimension, and is limited solely to its mathematical and physical one.[12] R. Soloveitchik referred to Cohen as an example, but his intent was uphold the direction in modern Jewish philosophy that constitutes Judaism on the basis of morality. This orientation has clear theological implications. The God of morality is the dominant model in this conception, while the God of the unity of morality and nature leads to pantheism, that is, the identification of God and the world. From many aspects, Hermann Cohen marks the high point of the tendency to identify the Jewish God with the God of morality. Cohen concluded his well-known essay from 1908, *Ethics of Maimonides* (*Charakteristik der Ethik Maimunis*) as follows:

> God is not the God of metaphysics, nor the God of cosmic substance [*Weltsubstanz*], but the God of ethics, that is, the God of humankind. God as the paradigm and ideal for human emulation and for the human Self; solely as this human ethical ideal does God relate to the world and to humanity.[13]

In *Religion of Reason: Out of the Sources of Judaism* Cohen fundamentally assumes the conceptual identification of religion and ethics and maintains that the distinction between the two is merely methodical.[14] Cohen argued: "Religion itself is moral teaching or it is not religion."[15]

Additionally, R. Soloveitchik uses the term "ethical" in his discussion in an extremely broad sense. The unity of nature and the ethical is also the

---

9   On the rejection of pantheism, see below.
10 Cohen, *Religion of Reason*, 47.
11 Ibid., 108-109.
12 Ibid., 323.
13 Hermann Cohen, *Ethics of Maimonides*, trans. Almut Sh. Bruckstein (Madison, WI: University of Wisconsin Press, 2004), 192, para. 179.
14 Cohen, *Religion of Reason*, 32.
15 Ibid., 33.

unity of "the cosmic and the consciousness."[16] That is, the acceptance of the yoke of Heaven means both internal and external unity, the unity of the mental and the outer worlds. R. Soloveitchik used the same terminology employed by Franz Rosenzweig to express the unity of divine revelation, which is "meta-logical and meta-physical."[17] Moreover, by adopting the notion of the unity of nature and ethics as the presence of the divine will, R. Soloveitchik associated himself with the dominant trend in religious Zionist thought, which could be called the orientation of unity.[18]

R. Soloveitchik never strove for a metaphysical conception of divine unity and simply sought the complete harmonization of religious consciousness and the consciousness of nature, that is, between nature and ethics. The person reading *Shema* and its blessings is to be aware that the consciousness of God is not detached from the external and the objective. The objective dimension of consciousness had previously been directed to action, meaning halakhic observance, while now it is also connected to the divine presence beyond consciousness. R. Soloveitchik writes:

> One pattern runs through the whole of Being, concrete and abstract, natural and supernatural, this-worldly and other-worldly, cosmic-causalistic and spiritual-purposive, mechanical and meaningful.[19]

As I explained above, R. Soloveitchik did not examine the world beyond the consciousness, on which he focused exclusively. The acceptance of the yoke of Heaven is an act of faith. Such a fact necessitates all the paths of the

---

16 *Worship of the Heart*, 125.

17 *Worship of the Heart*, 125. Rosenzweig used these terms to express his new conception of God (meta-physical) and the world (meta-logical). R. Soloveitchik adds the cosmic dimension to divine unity. If this is a veiled reference to Rosenzweig, then he chose his language with care.

18 This orientation is pronounced in the thought of R. Abraham Isaac Hakohen Kook and his ideological circle (R. David Ha-Kohen [the "Nazir"], R. Jacob Moses Harlap, R. Zevi Yehudah Kook, and their associates). However, it is also present in other schools within religious Zionist thought, such as the thinkers belonging to the Hasidic branch of Ha-Poel ha-Mizrachi. See Schwartz, *Faith at the Crossroads*, index, s.v. "Unity." The difference between R. Soloveitchik and the religious Zionist ideological circles is that the latter related to the ontological, psychological, aesthetic, and moral realm, while R. Soloveitchik discussed the religious consciousness. These groups spoke of what, for them, is only an objective fact and metaphysical truth; the subjective conception was foreign to them. R. Soloveitchik, in contrast, related to a clearly subjective act and the manner in which it perceives what lies beyond the consciousness. For him, the unity of nature and morality is the content of consciousness as it reflects of the unity of God and experiences reading *Shema*.

19 *Worship of the Heart*, 125.

cognition, including the knowledge of nature. Additionally, the acceptance of the yoke of Heaven assumes that the consciousness of God has a parallel in the world outside the consciousness. The consciousness of unity of *Shema* means full unity, both in and beyond the consciousness. The conception of nature, on the one hand, and, on the other, revelation (beyond nature) are the "reconstruction" of the unified divine will. "Revelation is the supernatural reconstruction."[20] Here we find traces of the conceptions that R. Soloveitchik set forth in his writings from the middle of the 1940s. The subjective consciousness of the divine will is reconstructed both from nature and from revelation. The divine will is one, but it is reconstructed from two different factors. R. Soloveitchik, however, chose not to use the idea of reconstruction to explain the *Amidah* and *Shema*, since these are subjective commandments that do not fit in the time-tested mold. According to that pattern, the commandments apply solely to the realm of the objective.

The Rejection of Pantheism

To now, R. Soloveitchik's discussion concentrated on internal and external unity. He then continues to explore the consciousness of unity in terms of the relationship between divine existence and existence outside God. The fundamental argument that recurs in religious thought is that the existence of God, unlike that of other objects, is absolute. But what is the precise relationship between the two types of existence? R. Soloveitchik alludes to the following possibilities and moves between some of them.

(1) Causality and autonomy: the existence of God is the cause of existence outside Him, but once the extradivine existence (the object) appeared, it is totally independent.

(2) Dependency: the existence of God is the cause of existence outside Him, that is, the object's existence is dependent on the existence of God. This dependence means that if we do not assume the existence of God, existence outside Him is impossible.[21]

(3) "Weak" involvement: in this possibility, related to the reality or existence of objects, the existence of God includes the existence of all

---

20 *Worship of the Heart*, 125.
21 The first two approaches preserve the model of the theist God, who is clearly transcendental. From a certain aspect, dependency is reminiscent of the conception of God as the Form of the world, which appears in the thought of Maimonides (*Mishneh Torah, Hilkhot Yesodei ha-Torah* 1:2; *Guide of the Perplexed* 1:69).

beings. Consequently, the existence of the object—whose existence is distinct and substantive—occurs within the divine existence.[22]

(4) "Strong" involvement: the divine essence includes all objects. Accordingly, the object takes part in the divine essence, which is present in the object (panentheism).[23]

(5) Unification: the divine existence is identical to all. The existence of objects and that of God are one and the same (pantheism).

R. Soloveitchik swung between the second and third possibilities. In the end, the third, which he called "panontic-theism,"[24] proved dominant in his thought. As usual, he relied on Maimonides' approach, this time on the division between essence and existence. In this understanding, existence is an attribute, and, accordingly, it is also accidental. For God, in contrast, essence and existence are one and the same. God "is not accidental or adjectival, but necessary and essential."[25] Existence, then, is not an attribute of God but is identical to His essence. R. Soloveitchik went a step further and wrote:

> Since He is the absolute Being, no other existence is possible without sharing His Being. Every existence is a relative one and as such must be related to the absolute one; otherwise the relative would become absolute. This relatedness is not that of effect to cause, however permanent it is, but of all-inclusiveness. Since God is the only Being and since this excludes all other things from having a reality of their

22 The distinction between 2 and 3 follows from the disparity between analysis and assertion of positive existence. For the second possibility, dependency ensues from hypothetical analysis: if God did not exist, then nothing external to God would exist. In actuality, however, such possibility does not exist. According to the third possibility, all existence external to God is part of the divine existence. Everything "takes part" in the divine existence. R. Soloveitchik argued that with the third possibility, "[t]his relatedness is not that of effect to cause, however permanent it is, but of all-inclusiveness" (*Worship of the Heart*, 126).

23 The difference between 3 and 4 is based in the question of whether the divine presence in the objects is real and substantial (the fourth possibility), or whether God's presence means a source, which gives existence to other objects (the third possibility). The third possibility focuses on the attribute of existence, and is based on the distinction between essence and existence. The fourth possibility focuses on presence.

24 *Worship of the Heart*, 128. He characterized this approach as "mystery."

25 *Worship of the Heart*, 126. Apparently, R. Soloveitchik did not distinguish between essence and existence, on the one hand, and, on the other, between necessity or possibility of existence. For him, both oppositions only prove that existence of all objects is based in the divine reality. On the distinction between essence and reality, see, for example, Alexander Altmann, *Studies in Religious Philosophy and Mysticism* (London: Routledge & Kegan Paul, 1969), 108-127. On modality in relation to the divine existence, see, for example, Aviezer Ravizki, "Possible and Contingent Existence in Exegesis of Maimonides in the 13th Century" [Hebrew], *Daat* 2-3 (1978-79): 67-97.

own, it follows that only in God may one find the completeness of being. "To be" means to participate in the Divine Being; it means "to be in Him."[26]

The divine existence is absolute, while the existence of all other objects is relative. Accordingly, every object exists to the extent that it participates in the absolute divine existence. Participation is not ontic and substantial. The divine presence does not mean involvement in the object's self, but only in its existence. Presumably, the existence of a creature is a part, in small measure, of the infinite divine existence. This portion is present within the whole. This is only an *attribute* of existence, and human existence is only a minuscule part of the divine existence. R. Soloveitchik then called the extradivine reality "finitude"[27] and emphasized that it participates in the one infinite divine Being. He wrote: "Yet shifting the categorical approach from substantia to extentia, from matter and content to ontic modality,[28] the whole perspective changes [from the pantheistic philosophies]."[29] He states, decisively: in terms of existence, the existence of the world is within the existence of God; in terms, however, of substance, there is no commonality between the world and its God. "The world was created as a separate substance, but not, however, as a separate existence."[30]

R. Soloveitchik was troubled by the thought of substantive commonality between God and man. All that is shared is the fact of existence itself. If he rejected substantive immanence of God within the object, then he certainly negated pantheism, which he ascribed to Plotinus, resulting from the notion of the emanation of matter from spirit,[31] and to Spinoza, due

---

26 *Worship of the Heart*, 126. In R. Soloveitchik's writings, he employed the language of Maimonides in *Hilkhot Yesodei ha-Torah* 2:10: "for everything is attached to Him, in His Being" (see Maimonides, *Mishneh Torah: The Book of Knowledge by Maimonides*, 36b). See, for example, *And from There You Shall Seek*, 15.

27 *Worship of the Heart*, 128.

28 It is unclear what R. Soloveitchik meant by "ontic modality". One possibility is that he harnessed two Maimonidean issues—the distinction between essence and existence and the distinction between several modalities of existence (the categories of the necessary, the possible, and the impossible)—to clarify the relation between human and divine existence. God is necessarily existent, and so existence outside Him is only possible, while His existence is necessary. Another possibility is that R. Soloveitchik used the term "ontic modality" for the distinction between relative and absolute existence. If this is the case, then there would be no need to employ Maimonides' modality categories.

29 *Worship of the Heart*, 127.

30 *Worship of the Heart*, 126.

31 *Worship of the Heart*, 128. On the presence of the spiritual element in the material in neo-Platonism, see Jonathan Scott Lee, "Omnipresence and Eidetic Causation in Plotinus," in *The Structure of Being: A Neoplatonic Approach*, ed. R. Baine Harris (Norfolk, VA: International Society for Neoplatonic Studies, 1982), 90-103; Cristina D'Ancona, "Greek into Arabic:

to his definition of materiality as an attribute of the object.[32] At times, Hegel served as a source for pantheistic conceptions in modern Jewish thought. Franz Rosenzweig and others spoke of the pantheistic element that is emphasized in Hegelian thought. While R. Abraham Isaac Kook, for instance, was noticeably influenced by Hegelian idealism, R. Soloveitchik referred specifically to Plotinus and Spinoza.[33] R. Soloveitchik writes:

> Although Judaism admits the immanence of God in His creation and the
> ontic fellowship of the earth with Him, it insists upon the full absolute

---

Neoplatonism in Translation," in *The Cambridge Companion to Arabic Philosophy*, ed. Peter Adamson and Richard C. Taylor (Cambridge: Cambridge University Press, 2005), 24-26. See also Dov Schwartz, *Central Problems in Medieval Philosophy*, (Leiden: Brill, 2005), 2-3. R. Soloveitchik described the Neo-Platonian One, the source of all existence, as "more of a principle than a reality" (*Worship of the Heart*, 128). Obviously, such an approach allows for no transcendental dimension of God. On such distinctions in the thought of Plotinus, see, for example, Reiner Schurmann, "The One: Substance or Function?," in *Neoplatonism and Nature: Studies in Plotinus' Enneads*, ed. Michael E. Wagner (Albany: State University of New York Press, 2002), 157-177. What was the basis of R. Soloveitchik's interpretation of Plotinus? He was almost certainly influenced by the arguments of Hermann Cohen, who viewed emanation as an immanent conception bordering on pantheism. The following passage (Cohen, *Religion of Reason*, 64) exemplifies the pantheistic interpretation of Neo-Platonism:

> The distinction of monotheism from *pantheism* depends on the exact understanding of the term "creation." Immanency is the condition of *emanation*. Becoming, the presumptive being, has to be explained. From what, however, could the origin of becoming be derived if not from true being? That the latter is the unique being cannot exclude the thought that false being can be explained through the true being. If, however, this explanation is understood in a materialistic sense, so that dependence is thought of as emanation, then one acknowledges material immanence and, along with the latter, pantheism.

Cohen noted the vagueness in the meaning of creation, which is perceived both as principle and source. Instead of viewing the creation as the principal origin, Neo-Platonism sees it as the source of materiality. Consequently, the true existence is material, that is, immanence leads to pantheism. R. Soloveitchik termed Spinoza's approach "cosmic" pantheism, and neo-Platonism, "mystical" (*Worship of the Heart*, 127).

32 Numerous scholars have already noted that the infinity of attributes to the substance in Spinoza's philosophy prevents total corporeality and materialization; we need not discuss this further here. In any event, R. Soloveitchik adopted the straightforward understanding of pantheism and stated that "pantheism preached the unity of God and world because of their identity of substance" (*Worship of the Heart*, 134-135).

33 R. David Cohen (the "Nazir"), who received a scientific education, found R. Kook's conception of God close to that of Spinoza. See Benjamin Ish-Shalom, "R. Kook, Spinoza and Goethe: Modern and Traditional Elements in the Thought of R. Kook" [Hebrew], in *Rivkah Shatz-Uffenheimer Memorial Volume*, vol. 2, ed. Rachel Elior and Joseph Dan (vol. 13 of *Jerusalem Studies in Jewish Thought* [Jerusalem: Mandel Institute for Jewish Studies, 1996]), 525-556; Dov Schwartz, *Religious Zionism between Logic and Messianism* [Hebrew] (Tel Aviv: Am Oved, 1999), 201-202.

transcendence of God in His mystic infinity, and on the complete detachment of God from the creation. The world is thus reduced to the state of existential tenancy: it exists in God, by Him, and shares his reality, not claiming any ontic autonomy. God, however, is absolute and unconditioned. He is all-inclusive; yet He is also all-exclusive, remote and inaccessible. Since God and being are synonymous, and the transcendental world is not an exception to this rule, we must assume that both the cosmic and the transcendental existence merge into one ontic order whose abode is God.[34]

If R. Soloveitchik denied substantial divine presence, and limited the participation of the partial and fragmented reality in the infinite reality, why did he find it necessary to separately refute pantheism? The negation of the divine presence undoubtedly includes the rejection of pantheism. In order to understand R. Soloveitchik's thought on this point, we must take account of his background and sources. Scheler's discussion of divine love presents pantheism in the progression that began with Plotinus and continued with Spinoza and Hegel.[35] As we will see below, this discussion influenced R. Soloveitchik. Pantheism concerned modern Jewish thought. Some thinkers viewed pantheism as a characteristic, to a great degree, of Christianity: the Christian God acts in the world and is involved in it.[36] Solomon Formstecher and Samuel Hirsch laid the groundwork for the presentation of pantheism as a pagan conception, or as the philosophical foundation for such a conception, with many thinkers following in their footsteps.[37] R. Nachman Krochmal posited divine immanence.

---

34 *Worship of the Heart*, 128.

35 Scheler, *On the Eternal*, 226. Scheler rejects pantheism on moral grounds. He writes: "If—as in the pantheistic view—God were related to the world only as the whole to its parts or the essence to its phenomenon or the substance to the modes of its attributes, finite minds would be left with only *one* task, to 'think' the world rightly and know it truly. No longer would they have the task of *reshaping* the world, of *freely* making a better world in accordance with a *plan*, under the dominance of norms and ideas of value" (ibid., 226-227). R. Soloveitchik negated pantheism because it does not allow for divine transcendence.

36 See, for example, Yehoyada Amir, *Reason out of Faith: The Philosophy of Franz Rosenzweig* [Hebrew] (Tel Aviv: Am Oved, 2004), 242

37 See Rotenstreich, *Jewish Thought*, vol. 2, 154; Eliezer Schweid, *A History of Modern Jewish Philosophy*, vol. II: *The Birth of Jewish Historical Studies and the Modern Jewish Religious Movements*, trans. Leonard Levin (Leiden: Brill, 2015), 74. Generally speaking, Schweid's pioneering work took note of the innovative dimensions of modern Jewish thought, such as the conception of history and national basis. Less expression was given to metaphysical ideas, such as pantheism, which deserves a discussion of its own.

Again, Hermann Cohen plays a key role here. As we saw, Cohen is a hidden or overt participant in R. Soloveitchik's discussions since his doctoral dissertation on Cohen's epistemological doctrine, that is, epistemological idealism. Cohen devoted strenuous conceptual efforts to reject pantheism. Moreover, the negation of pantheism is one of the motifs that constantly recurs in Cohen's thought. Cohen regarded monism as being an outstanding expression of pantheism. For him, only monotheism is capable of preserving diversity and multiplicity within unity. Cohen explained in the beginning of his *Religion of Reason Out of the Sources of Judaism* that pantheism is religion's greatest enemy. He reasons as follows: we have already seen that religion is substantively connected to ethics, and it is not perceived as an independent realm. When it addresses the individual, religion, in a certain sense, complements ethical teachings. The erroneous identification of religion with pantheism led to the need to undermine the standing of religion. "Only pantheism is responsible for the fact that religion has crept into hiding behind moral teaching [*Sittenlehre*]."[38] Cohen joined the harsh critics of pantheistic morality, with its "instinct for *self-preservation* [*Selbsterhaltungstrieb*]."[39] In this realm, as well, Cohen's thought became one of the premier expressions of modern Jewish philosophy: the negation or acceptance of pantheism became a major epistemological and ethical motif.

This might enable us to relate to "pantheism" as representing all the immanent conceptions of God, that is, notions that posit actual divine presence, or some degree of an actual divine element, in the existence. "Pantheism" is not limited to the absolute identification of God and nature. R. Soloveitchik related to pantheism as representation, and rejected it, even though he had already taken pains to negate the idea of a concrete divine presence ("strong" divine involvement). The reason for this is unmistakable: he advocated divine unity in nature and in ethics, and the commonality of God and the universe in the attributes of the reality, being, and existence. He therefore explained to the reader that he nevertheless did not fall into the trap of paganism, and does not identify God with nature. The unity of nature and ethics is expressed solely in the presence of the divine will. The negation of immanence suffices on logical grounds. R. Soloveitchik, however, hinted at the pantheistic threat against which Cohen warned, as if he wished to say: even though he himself

---

38 Cohen, *Religion of Reason*, 33. See Rotenstreich, *Jewish Thought*, vol. 2, 90-91.
39 Cohen, *Religion of Reason*, 226. Cohen did not necessarily refer to Spinoza, who regarded the instinct for self-preservation as a rational move, and not as an instinctive action (*Trieb*). Cohen's central argument was that naturalism, in its different versions, cannot be a basis for ethics.

diverged from Cohen's thought, and asserted that God is also the cosmic God, and not only the God of ethics, he evades the snare of paganism.

The God Experience

In his discussion of unity, R. Soloveitchik emphasized the dogmatic aspect expressed in the constitutive text of the first verse of *Shema* and the *Yotzer Or* blessing. For the halakhah, divine unity is a central component of the intent (*kavanah*) required of the worshiper in reciting this passage. He writes:

> The first verse of *Shema* proclaims not only a theological principle, but an ontic-metaphysical one as well. God-as-being is one, to the exclusion of any other form of reality. Through the grace bestowed upon finitude, the creation is privileged to possess Him as *Elokim* and by so doing, it may lay claim to existence, to reality. Here are two main phases of the God experience. God is one in the sense of exclusiveness and He is one in the sense of all-inclusiveness.[40]

In the final analysis, the connection between God and existence beyond Him is clearly dialectical. God Himself is transcendent, and is completely distinct from the existence outside Him; but divine lovingkindness enables the creature to take part in the divine reality. That is, God is both distinct and allows the creature to participate in a minuscule part of His infinite existence.

According to what R. Soloveitchik wrote, the first verse of *Shema* contains two clearly rational statements regarding the consciousness of God:

(1) a theological statement (divine attributes), which comprises two principles, namely:
    (a) the unity of God;
    (b) divine transcendentalism;
(2) an ontic-metaphysical statement: objects take part in the divine reality by their very existence.

To be precise: R. Soloveitchik does not speak of God as a reality beyond the consciousness, but of the "God experience." He was not interested in the theories of divine attributes as they had been set forth in religious thought over the course of time. The careful reader will understand that what thinkers such as R. Saadiah Gaon, R. Bahya ibn Pequda, R. Abraham ben David of Posquieres, Maimonides, and their many successors in the tradition of Jewish religious thought deemed sublime did not occupy R. Soloveitchik.

---

40 *Worship of the Heart*, 128-129.

The questions of negative attributes, the nature of divine unity, and its relation to existents outside God become topics in the study of the religious consciousness. Now, the real question becomes: how does man perceive divine unity and presence? Now, experience and subjectivity take center stage. And for them, the textual foundation is of great importance. In this discussion, R. Soloveitchik is concerned with the nature of the subjective consciousness that emerges from reading *Shema*.

Summary

To sum up the meaning of the intent of *Shema*: the elements of the unity of God, which are the basis of R. Soloveitchik's interpretation of the first verse of *Shema*, are therefore:

(1) the conception of unity:
    (a) statement: the unity of nature and ethics;
    (b) explanation: this unity is attained due to the divine will and the divine activity, but not as a result of the divine essence;
    (c) statement: the unity of the (finite) human reality and the (infinite) divine reality;
    (d) explanation: the unity of the reality is not essential unity;
(2) the derived conceptions of God:
    (e) God is transcendental;
    (f) various forms of pantheism are rejected;
    (g) divine lovingkindness facilitates unity.

All this is incorporated in the reading of *Shema*. When the halakhah formulated the requirement of intent for the first verse of *Shema*, it insisted upon the internalization of the concept of the unity of God, if not also the ramified theological and ontological notions derived from this concept. The spiritualization and the rationalization of reading the *Shema* are intermingled in the interpretive and philosophical direction taken by R. Soloveitchik. One who recites *Shema* is immersed in a profound intellectual experience and gives himself over to sublime insights.

Thus, R. Soloveitchik fully explored the dogmatic and rational aspect of prayer in his interpretation of *Shema*, which he presented as a ritual of deep study and of a spiritual and rational experience.[41]

---

41 See Adiel Kadari, "Liturgical Recitation as a Ritual of Study" [Hebrew], in *Study and Knowledge in Jewish Thought*, ed. Howard Kreisel (Beer Sheva: Ben-Gurion University of the Negev Press, 2006), vol. 2, 21-35.

2. The *Yotzer Or* Blessing

After R. Soloveitchik interpreted the verse that begins the first passage of *Shema* and its intent, he then explained the blessing that parallels it conceptually and dogmatically, the *Yotzer Or* blessing.[42] His interpretation presents the blessing as the application of the consciousness of the unity of the universe, on the one hand, and that of the angelic world, on the other. Contentually, he continued his examination of the consciousness of the unity of God, as he had done previously in his explication of the "Hear O Israel" verse. This time, however, theological and philosophical unity is interwoven with the unity of the liturgical text, that is, the inner cohesiveness of the two parts of the *Yotzer Or* blessing.

Contrast

The *Yotzer Or* blessing in *Shaharit* (the morning service) is divided into two units, that include two main topics: the cosmic order that reflects the imprint of God, and the angelic song, in the format of the *Kedushah*. Two tenets of faith meet in this blessing, namely, the unity of God and the existence of angels.

The two parts of the blessing are seemingly not closely related to one another. Both contentually and formally-stylistically, they are totally different. The researchers of prayer disagree regarding the redaction of the blessing. Some argue that its parts were redacted in different periods, while others assign an early dating to both parts.[43] Scholarly research views the song of the angels as a late addition, while R. Soloveitchik supports the affinity of the two thematic motifs and the unity of the blessing.

---

42 See above, Chapter Seven.
43 See, for example, Ismar Elbogen, *Jewish Liturgy: A Comprehensive History*, trans. Raymond P. Scheindlin (Philadelphia: Jewish Publication Society, 1993), 18-19, 59-61 (with Joseph Heinemann's additions); Heinemann, *Prayer in the Talmud*, 232-35; Ezra Fleischer, "The Diffusion of the *Qedushshot* of the *'Amida* and the *Jozer* in the Palestinian Jewish Ritual" [Hebrew], *Tarbiz* 38, no. 3 (1969): 226; I. Gruenwald, "The Song of the Angels, the *Qedushah* and the Composition of the *Hekhalot* Literature" [Hebrew], in *Jerusalem in the Second Temple Period: Abraham Schalit Memorial Volume*, ed. A. Oppenheimer, U. Rappaport, and M. Stern (Jerusalem: Yad Izhak Ben-Zvi and Ministry of Defence, 1980), 476-79; Zeev Zekharya Breuer, "The Structure of the *Yozer* Benediction" [Hebrew], in *Proceedings of the Tenth World Congress of Jewish Studies*, division C, vol. i: *Jewish Thought and Literature* (Jerusalem: World Union of Jewish Studies, 1990), 261-68. R. Isaiah Wohlgemuth, a teacher in the Maimonides School in the Boston area, and the author of *A Guide to Jewish Prayer*, mentioned that R. Soloveitchik highly recommended Elbogen's book.

In order to examine the philosophical direction taken by R. Soloveitchik, we should mention the characteristics of the two parts of the *Yotzer Or* blessing, as set forth in *Worship of the Heart*. R. Soloveitchik described the two parts and the transition between them in the following words:

> In the first part, the central motif is that of the Divine wisdom expressing itself in the cosmic order, particularly in the rising and setting of the sun—to the naked eye of the observer a most outstanding and magnificent cosmic event. Suddenly, this theme is suspended and a new one is introduced—not one of this-worldly orderliness but of otherworldly vision: the angelic choirs, singing numinous hymns at the very throne of glory, are beheld by the worshipper. Only a moment ago the worshipper glorified God in the simple manner of the psalmist, citing the marvels of nature; now he finds himself in the angelic world of bliss immersed in the magnificence and splendor of something mysterious, awe-inspiring and transcendental. The worshipper, overcome by ecstasy, and filled with solemnity[44] and devotion, joins with the angels to chant the praise of God in the *Kedushah* (sanctification).[45]

R. Soloveitchik sought to argue for the unity of *Yotzer Or*. But here, in his clear and informative style he highlighted the differences between its two parts. The poetical intertwined with the informative does not blur the differences, rather, paradoxically, it intensifies them. He draws a sharp and unequivocal distinction between the cosmic event, with the wonder it arouses on the popular and intuitive level, and the transcendental event within the reality beyond the cosmic existence. The cosmic event is formulated in a simplistic style, while the style of the transcendental event is that of the angelic choir (*Kedushah*). These are only a few examples of the wealth of distinctions that R. Soloveitchik draws in the above passage. He apparently thought that emphasizing the differences would facilitate uncovering the various links that connect the two parts of the blessing.

The series of distinctions between the two parts of the *Yotzer Or* blessing that R. Soloveitchik makes in this passage can be summarized as follows:

---

44 On singing as a component of the ecstatic process of the *Kedushah*, see, for example, Daniel Boyarin, "*Ha-Shir ve-ha-Shevah*: Ambiguity and Poetics in the Fixed Prayers" [Hebrew], *Eshel Beer-Sheva* 3 (1986): 91-99.

45 *Worship of the Heart*, 129. Notwithstanding this, the worshipers do not join together with the angels in the *Yotzer Or* blessing, unlike the *Kedushah* in the *Amidah*.

part of *Yotzer Or* blessing	sources of the experience	topic of the experience	nature of the experience	nature of the divine will	effect of the experience	way of cognition
(1) "In compassion He gives light to the earth and its inhabitants, and in His goodness continually renews the work of creation, day after day. 'How many are the things You have made, O Lord; You have made them all with wisdom; the earth is full of Your creations' [Ps. 104:24]"	verses from Psalms ("simple manner")[46]	cosmic worldly order ("this-worldly")	Revealed	concealed and distant	excitement, marvel	sight[47]
(2) "'Holy, holy, holy is the Lord of Hosts; the whole world is filled with His glory' [Isa. 6:3]. Then the Ophanim and the Holy Hayot, with a roar of noise, raise themselves toward the Serafim and, facing them, give praise, saying: 'Blessed be the Lord's glory from His place' [Ezek. 3:12]"	sanctity ("numinous hymns")[48]	transcendental heavenly order ("not one of this-worldly orderliness")	mysterious and mystical	revealed and intimate[49]	solemnity and ecstasy	vision

46 *Worship of the Heart*, 129.

47 R. Soloveitchik defined this as "realistic observation" and as "apprehension."

48 On the connection between the *Kedushah* in reading *Shema* and that in the *Amidah*, see, for example, Joseph Heinemann, "*Qedushah* and Proclamation of 'Kingship' in the Reading of the *Shema*' and in the '*Amidah*'" [Hebrew], in *Studies in Jewisa Liturgy*, ed. Avigdor Shinan (Jerusalem: Magnes, 1981), 12–21.

49 The divine will is not revealed in the cosmic experience, but only following analysis. In the angelic experience, the divine will is revealed and close. In contrast, the impression that this event leaves on the one undergoing the experience is the opposite. The cosmic experience is revealed, while the angelic experience is concealed. See *Worship of the Heart*, 132.

Unity

R. Soloveitchik then sets out to interpret *Yotzer Or* in a manner that will clearly present its thematic unity. His interpretation is concerned with the unity of nature and ethics and the problem of evil; as we shall see, this interpretation is not consistent with what he wrote elsewhere. We will begin with the text of the blessing: "who forms light and creates darkness, makes peace and creates all." R. Soloveitchik noted the differences between the blessing and its Biblical source (Isa. 45:7), that concludes: "creates evil," in place of "creates all."[50] He writes:

> The prayer connects the cosmic order with an ethical category: God is the Creator of light and darkness, the Maker of peace and all things. [...]
>
> *Ra*, evil, is only an illusion, a non-being which one apprehends when beholding only a minute segment of creation. It is a phenomenon isolated from the whole, seen in a limited perspective, which might impress us as impervious to the ethical good. Yet within the greater all-inclusive perspective, embracing the totality of being, it is part of an organic whole. Evil is dissolved into the universal pattern of goodness.[51]

R. Soloveitchik derived two principles from the distinction between the Biblical and liturgical wordings, namely, the substitution of "all" for "evil."

(1) The source of nature and ethics: "evil" reveals the meaning of "all." Although "evil" was omitted from the liturgical version, it teaches, paradoxically, that the Creation relates to both good and evil. This statement has two meanings.

   (a) Regularity: the Creation of the world also encompassed the creation of ethical principles, and natural and ethical causality join together. "The word *ha-kol*, 'all,' means not only the tangible natural phenomena but ethical ideas as well."[52]

   (b) Teleology: the activity of the universe is meant to attain ethical goals. "Ethical-axiological realization is the main affair of the universe."[53] The wording of the blessing accordingly expresses the unity of ethics and nature. We already discussed

---

50 See Kimelman, "The *Shema'* Liturgy," 28-29.
51 *Worship of the Heart*, 130.
52 *Worship of the Heart*, 130.
53 *Worship of the Heart*, 131.

the presence of the divine will in nature that transforms ethics into the principle of natural regularity.

(2) The exclusivity of good: "all" clarifies "evil." Evil is perceived as such only when it is detached from the totality. Evil itself is only an illusion. R. Soloveitchik follows the Maimonidean approach in *Guide of the Perplexed* 3:10, which he later quotes. According to this notion, evil is only the absence of good, and it has no independent existence. Consequently, the blessing version expresses ethical all-inclusiveness.

These two principles teach of the unity of divine will and action. God is the Source of nature and ethics, and His actions are exclusively good. This means that the universe and its activity are based on a unity that is reflective of the divine unity. Although R. Soloveitchik spoke, specifically, only of the natural and ethical branches of this unity, aesthetic unity, too, emerges from his writing: "One must not see the physical universe as separated from the realm of the just, the good, and the beautiful."[54]

Now, to discuss the concept that evil is illusional. The reader who is familiar with R. Soloveitchik's writings will realize that this is an atypical idea. R. Soloveitchik's works characteristically refrain from downplaying suffering, anguish, rifts, and indecision. In both his phenomenological and existential thought, he did not ignore differentiated and partial existence. The consciousness experiences chaos and detachment (for example, the consciousness of the revelation of the God of strict judgment in *And from There You Shall Seek*), existence that is accompanied by fear and trembling (such as the threat to values in "The Crisis of Human Finitude"), and the like. In light of such an orientation, can it be argued that evil is illusionary?[55]

Furthermore, in a well-known essay from the time of the writing of *Worship of the Heart*, R. Soloveitchik forcefully rejected this approach. In *Kol Dodi Dofek* (*Listen: My Beloved Knocks*)[56] he criticized the approach of Maimonides and the rationalists concerning the illusory nature of evil, on

---

54 *Worship of the Heart*, 131.

55 R. Soloveitchik's phenomenological thought, as developed in *And from There You Shall Seek* and other works, presents the model of primordial chaos that, as the consciousness progresses, is seen to be planned from the outset. R. Soloveitchik took pains, however, to note the continuous presence of the oscillations between the initial and advanced stages. See Schwartz, *From Phenomenology to Existentialism*, part 1.

56 The essay is based on an address that he delivered on Israel Independence Day (April 4, 1956).

the one hand, and, on the other, the Kabbalistic concept of the substantiality of evil, that is, its basis in the divine structure (such as the concept of the *kelipah* [husk]).[57] He rejected the harmonistic approaches—such as the one he offers in *Worship of the Heart*—and maintained that they deceive the sufferer "[…] to the point of self-deception—the denial of the existence of evil in the world."[58] Thus, evil as illusion in *Worship of the Heart* becomes self-deception in *Kol Dodi Dofek*.

The undeniable fact is that in *Worship of the Heart* R. Soloveitchik set forth a conception of all-inclusive unity, and differentiation is merely an illusion. I do not have a clear answer to this striking inconsistency in R. Soloveitchik's writings. Nonetheless, I will offer two possibilities:

(1) In *Worship of the Heart* R. Soloveitchik set aside the phenomenological approach to prayer and argued for the possibility of ascending to the transcendental level, when one attains a comprehensive vision that negates evil. The worshiper does, indeed, possess such an all-inclusive perspective.

(2) R. Soloveitchik remained within the boundaries of phenomenological analysis, and drew a distinction between the consciousness of suffering, which he discussed in *Kol Dodi Dofek*, and that of prayer. The former is distant from metaphysics and its inherent consciousness of God. Occupation with the question of the cause of suffering is futile, since man cannot know God's mind. The consciousness of suffering must keep apart from curiosity of a purely informative nature, and turn to the teleological question of the meaning of suffering in terms of the personal and national ethos expressed in the halakhah. In contrast, the consciousness of prayer, in which man stands before his God, forms a conception of God and of all existence. The consciousness of prayer does not fear to engage in what is deemed illusory. Nor does it flinch from presenting insights concerning the divine attributes and the dogmatics of Judaism. In the consciousness of suffering, the negation of evil is an illusion, while in the consciousness of prayer it is a basis for the communion of creature and Creator. *Homo religiosus* oscillates

---

57 See Schwartz, *From Phenomenology to Existentialism*, 198-99.

58 "*Kol Dodi Dofek*: It Is the Voice of My Beloved That Knocketh," trans. Lawrence Kaplan, in *Theological and Halakhic Reflections on the Holocaust*, ed. Bernhard Rosenberg (New York: Ktav, 1992), 53.

between the consciousness of suffering and the consciousness of prayer. Moreover, the consciousness of suffering is described by existentialist criteria, and the consciousness of prayer, by phenomenological ones. Accordingly, *Yotzer Or* faithfully reflects the consciousness of prayer.

Now to return to the association between the liturgical form of *Yotzer Or* and its content. The unified concept of both parts of the blessing clarifies its connection to reading *Shema. Yotzer Or* is meant to emphasize the unity of God. The cosmic experience of sunrise and sunset is not mentioned as an independent value, rather, it reflects the presence of God. The fact that He is present in both the cosmic reality and that of the angelic choir, is what places it in its liturgical context. The divine will that drives the reality of the parts of the universe, both the material and the spiritual, those in the universe and those in the sphere beyond it, is the direct expression of the divine unity. R. Soloveitchik writes:

> God's will includes the entirety of creation. Since it is a creative dynamic will,[59] one that seeks realization and fulfillment through both the kingdom of nature and the kingdom of history, we may say that at this juncture religious thought takes the liberty of transcending the boundary line of theology and entering the epistomologico-metaphysical domain.[60]

Concluding the eighth chapter of *Worship of the Heart*, this passage marks the ontological and epistemological boundaries of R. Soloveitchik's interpretation. In his terminology, theology is concerned with God's direction of the physical world; metaphysics and epistemology relate to the spiritual world of the angels. That is, the ethical divine will is the source of both worlds. The infinite divine good makes possible the natural regularity, and is also its explanation and reason. Creation attests to the merging of divine wisdom and will. "Majesty of God, His glory, wisdom and might, blend perfectly with His grace and kindness."[61]

Just as the problem of uniformity with which R. Soloveitchik opened his discussion was taken from liturgical scholarship, so, too, the content of the resolution he suggests is not original. He adopted the concept of the blessing's unity as it is understood by prayerbook commentaries. We may

---

59 R. Soloveitchik advocated the concept of "the miracle of perennial creation" (*Worship of the Heart*, 132).
60 *Worship of the Heart*, 132.
61 *Worship of the Heart*, 132.

assume that he was familiar with these commentaries, since this is a common literary genre. The prayerbook commentators, too, sensed the weak connection between the parts of the first blessing of *Shema*, leading them to take vigorous efforts in their search for the link between its two topics, the celestial orb of the angels and the lowly human world. Their efforts yielded tortuous connections.[62] R. Soloveitchik's contribution consists mainly of the phenomenological direction he gave to the discussion. The connection between the parts of the blessing is clearly one of consciousness.

The meaning of the first passage of *Shema* already appears in the preliminary *Yotzer Or* blessing, as does the content of the proper intent by the worshiper in this passage. R. Soloveitchik ends his interpretation of the blessing by stating that the unity of its formulation is preparatory for the unity of God.

3. The Verse "And You Shall Love"

The original text of *Worship of the Heart* concludes with a commentary to the second verse of the first passage of *Shema* ("You shall love the Lord your God with all your heart and with all your might"—Deut. 6:4). R. Soloveitchik devoted the ninth chapter, which ends the original Hebrew version of the book and its second section, to this commentary.

R. Soloveitchik first sought to show how the unity of God is the source of His love. In other words, the consciousness of the unity of *Shema* leads

---

62 We may reasonably assume that the interpretive literature that the Soloveitchik family used or held in esteem stood open before R. Soloveitchik when he engaged in phenomenological analysis. The following are a few examples: *Siddur ha-Gra* states in the name of the Vilna Gaon that "even the heavens to their uttermost reaches cannot contain You [following I Kings 8:27], He desires the honor of the lowly in the lowly world, and all the supernal worlds serve and give light and emanation to the earthly world" (*Siddur ha-Gra*, 80a). The connection between the angels and the earthly world consists of ordering the functioning of the levels of reality and the interaction between them. This understanding was recorded in the *Otzar ha-Tefilot* collection. R. Isaac Elijah Landau, who was active in Dubno in the nineteenth century, linked parts of the blessing to God's specific nature as separate from the world. That is, the earthly and the heavenly creation are equivalent in that God is exalted above and distinguished from both: "Even though He, may He be blessed, is holy and differentiated from the lower world, nonetheless, 'the whole world is filled with His glory' [Isa. 6:3; in the *Kedushah*]" (*Dover Shalom*, in *Siddur Otzar ha-Tefilot* [Vilna, 1925], 104a). R. Aryeh Leib Gordon of Kelm, who was later active in Petah Tikvah, saw this unity in the very praise of God. He writes: "After completing the praise of the creation of the luminaries, one begins to bless the Lord, may He be blessed, for the creation of the angels, who were created to tell His greatness" (*Iyyun Tefillah*, in *Siddur Otzar ha-Tefilot*, 132a).

to the consciousness of the love of God, with both being parts of a single structure. He therefore chose to interpret the love in the first passage of *Shema*, and not, for instance, the opening of the second blessing of *Shema* ("great love" [*Ahavah Rabbah*], in *Shaharit*, or "everlasting love" [*Ahavat Olam*] in the evening prayer, *Arvit*). The formal reason, obviously, is that the second blessing is concerned with God's love for man, while the first passage of *Shema* speaks of man's love for God.

R. Soloveitchik thoroughly examined the conscious connection between unity and love. We will see that just as divine unity is anchored in the nature of the human and divine existence, so, too, love of God has an ontological foundation. R. Soloveitchik then entered into a short phenomenological description of love, using this as a basis for his discussion of love of God, which is nothing other than the presence of the lover in God.

The Consciousness of Accepting the Yoke of Heaven

At the beginning of the ninth chapter of *Worship of the Heat*, R. Soloveitchik summarized the structure of "accepting the yoke of Heaven," in terms of the subjective consciousness or the intentional act of reading *Shema*. Such a consciousness model enabled him to analyze the act of loving God. In short, this process contains five components.

The following table presents the components of the consciousness of reading *Shema*, along with their matching phenomenological terminology. We will then explain and analyze the process by which the consciousness of "accepting the yoke of Heaven" is formed.

R. Soloveitchik's wording	phenomenological terminology
"First, one acknowledges God as the highest and greatest worth in his life."	object
"Second, in the axiological awareness, a normative component emerges: that is to say, one experiences normative pressure, one yearns to realize or to possess its value."	intentional act (volitional)
"Third, we have the fulfillment of the norm: the attainment of the value, the experience of benefit, asserts itself in a continuous compresence, and inseparability, of value and valuing object."	subjective consciousness

(Continued)

R. Soloveitchik's wording	phenomenological terminology
"[Fourth,] Divine immanence within the cosmic drama [...] spells the unity of the natural and moral law, of the concrete and transcendental order, the unity of creation expressing the Divine moral will."[63]	intentional act (cognitive)
"Ontic monism constitutes a fifth element [...] There is only one form of reality, God. [...] *Ehad*, unity, signifies that only God exists; nothing else beside Him and besides Him. Only within Him is existence thinkable."[64]	noema

Now, to examine the structure of the consciousness of prayer and its components. The first component is the consciousness object, to which the various acts of consciousness are directed.[65] The second component is the consciousness act itself, which consists of desire and longing for the object, namely, the first component of the consciousness of prayer. Seeking the object is effected by seeking to realize the norm. The third component places the act squarely within the subjective consciousness. Additionally, this consciousness is clearly that of objects (values, in this case). The fourth component is the cognitive act that accompanies the volitional act. The fifth component reveals the meaning of the longing for values. It depicts God as the sole substantiality. Other substantialities participate in the divine reality. The meaning of the act, the noema, is revealed here.

On the one hand, the model proposed by R. Soloveitchik is structural, while on the other, he also describes a process, from setting forth the object to its attainment, at the highest and most mature level. In the first phases, the consciousness internalizes the values, and in the more mature stages it explores their meaning. The internalization of ethical laws leads to the awareness that they are united with the laws of nature, and to the perception of God as the unity of nature and ethics. Returning to the phenomenological system of terminology, we see that the consciousness of *Shema* leads the worshiper from the act and its object to noema, that is, the meaning of the intentionality. The noema is expressed mainly in the fifth component.

63 *Worship of the Heart*, 133.
64 *Worship of the Heart*, 133-134.
65 R. Soloveitchik adopted Scheler's approach (discussed above, in Chapter Five), in which God is the object of the consciousness in the phenomenology of religion.

The absolute divine reality and the participation of the existents are the reason why the act of reading *Shema* is directed to God. The structure of this process is presented below.

(1) Man thirsts to acquire ethical values (volitional act).
(2) Two further acts:
    (a) the acquisition of ethical values enables him to identify them with cosmic values (cognitive act);
    (b) the identification reveals the object of the intentional act, namely, the unity of nature and ethics (cognitive act).
(3) The cognition of unity has the cognizant face its absoluteness (noema, the meaning and purpose of the volitional and cognitive acts).
(4) The volitional and cognitive acts are directed to the absolute divine Object (intentionality).

A person acquires ethical values, with the goal of approaching, at the end of the process, their Source, that is, God. The cause of this approach is the all-encompassing model of the divine. The acceptance of the yoke of Heaven is a volitional and cognitive act that directs the consciousness to the Creator. In other words: reading *Shema* leads the consciousness to the pure and true perception of God. R. Soloveitchik analyzes the path to this end in the model that he proposed.

In the final analysis, the consciousness of *Shema* is one of reason. Its meaning is clearly rational, since this is the proper conception of God. The consciousness of "the yoke of Heaven" includes the unity of ethics and nature, and as such is based, first and foremost, on values, but is primarily cognitive. The correct conception of God is the intent of *Shema*, and focuses on God being the sole reality, the exclusive existence. The internalization of the divine model of the absolute in which all participate by force of their very existence is also the source of the love of God.

Love as Presence

R. Soloveitchik depicted two intentional acts, one normative, and the other, cognitive. Notwithstanding this, the dominant act in reading *Shema* is the cognitive. R. Soloveitchik explained in great detail the meaning of the unity of God, and expects the one reading *Shema* to have the intent of this meaning. For him, the belief in divine unity contains two perceptions:

(1) the unity of ethics and nature, in terms of the presence of the divine will;

(2) the unique existence of the divine reality: other realities exist only to the extent that they participate in it.

This is, obviously, not a simple task for the worshiper. R. Soloveitchik, however, felt that the consciousness of reading *Shema* and that of the *Amidah* were not meant only for the select few. When he discussed the *Amidah*, he portrayed the existential crisis as a factor that unites the entire community of worshipers.[66] Both the simple person and the elitist intellectual share this existential distress. Now, R. Soloveitchik faces a similar problem. The intent that he found in reading *Shema* requires sort of contemplation on the profundities of the divine unity. How can this be demanded of a community of worshipers, that includes both the unlettered and the intellectual? His answer pertains to the general consciousness of prayer. He writes:

> To entreat God is synonymous with apprehending and comprehending the real essence of being. To realize God as the highest value, to attain Him, to possess Him, is to realize one's own being, to possess one's own existence and to reconstitute[67] and reform it. If I possess my own self as a moral being, I am conscious both of my being an integral part of a great process through which the Divine will is realized, in which the cosmic and transcendental order is involved, and I am also conscious of my role as an individual, personal, unique reality, with an intricate task and high meaning; I am then *eo ipso* partaking of God, of *Elokim*, He who, within me, has set a task and it is this task within which I find myself. In short, realization of God as a value is identical with self-realization and self-redemption.[68] The highest norm-realization of the God ideal finds a practical equation; to be.
>
> Under this monistic aspect, we may grasp the great secret of the love of God. Love, which asserts itself in a feeling of possessiveness, of inseparability from the beloved person, is basically an expression of ontic unity, of existential compresence and community.[69]

---

66 See above, the end of Chapter Three.
67 The constitution of the consciousness is a fundamental phenomenological term.
68 R. Soloveitchik portrays a process that clearly belongs to the realm of consciousness: the consciousness of God and the consciousness of the "I" unite (see below).
69 *Worship of the Heart*, 134.

R. Soloveitchik argues that standing before God in prayer and entreaty is perforce equivalent to comprehending divine unity. He depicted this standing before God as a circular situation.

(1) The cognition of God is affirmed as supreme value.
(2) Adopting the consciousness of God (the preceding section) leads to revealing and exposing the selfhood.
    (a) Cognitive explanation: the fragmentary human existence occurs within the eternal and whole divine existence. Coming to know and embracing the full existence leads to the full awareness of the fragmentary existence, and therefore to mastery of the latter.
    (b) Ethical explanation: the personal will participates in the divine will, and thereby man comes to know his task, that is, self-realization.
(3) Mastery of the self leads to a double awareness:
    (a) participation in the (cosmic and ethical) divine unity;
    (b) existence as a task, that is, the value of meaningful existence.

Thus, the meaning of existence is dialectical. The cognition that human existence is a tiny and negligible fraction of the divine existence is what enables man to exist as an independent entity. Paradoxically, immersion within the divine (in terms of the attribute of existence) is also the discovery of selfhood and distinct existence. The awareness of self-annihilation is also the discovery of being. Negation before God makes man a partner with Him, no less. The task is to understand that God's existence and man's independent existence are two sides of the same coin. This is what imparts meaning to human existence. The one who stands before God in prayer and entreaty is equivalent to the person who understands this consciousness dialectic and internalizes it. It is as if the worshiper has found himself within his negation in the face of the divine reality.

The dialectic of commonality and differentiation, immersion and the distinctness of the "I" is also the source of understanding love. At this point, we address the adaptation of the experience of unity for the public at large: just as the lover finds himself in his love for his beloved, man finds himself in his nullity in the divine selfhood. The love of God is reflected in love for another person. The experience of love, which is known to man by his very nature, enables the experience of God. R. Soloveitchik makes three central arguments concerning love.

(1) The lover is present in his beloved. The consciousness of love is concerned with the ontic unity of the lovers.

(2) The consciousness of love is meaningful; thanks to it, the existence of the lovers becomes axiological and just.

(3) Love is the path to self-realization.[70]

R. Soloveitchik chose to exemplify the dialectic of the consciousness of the human and divine existence by means of a mother's love for her child. This love remains constant during different periods of life. During pregnancy, this love is based on organic connection. He writes:

> As long as the fetus forms a part of the mother's body, the awareness of identity of mother and child consists in the feeling of unity connected to the dynamics of organic metabolic processes. These phenomena are classified under the heading of substance and accidents.[71]

R. Soloveitchik carefully chose the two terms "substance" and "accidents." "Accidents" are qualities of the object that are not essential, in contrast with form which is the essence. The medieval rationalists, with Maimonides foremost among them, classified the relationship between the components of the natural systems in terms of matter and form. Form expresses the stable element of existence in the natural world. In contrast, medieval theologians, such as those of the *kalām* school, used the terms "substance" and "accidents" to describe this relationship.[72] They did so because they negated the existence of a substantive and stable element in the reality (besides God), and asserted that all reality is directly dependent upon God. The rationalists were sharply critical of the approach of the theologians, which they deemed erroneous. The rationalists argued for the stability of the world after being created, which therefore possesses stable natural regularity. R. Soloveitchik deliberately characterized the relationship between mother and fetus in nonessential terms, since this is a relationship on the most basic and lowest level, one that is instinctive and animalistic. Qualitatively, the unity of these two lacks abstract value.

---

70 *Worship of the Heart*, 134-135.

71 *Worship of the Heart*, 135.

72 By "substance and accident," kalām philosophers actually meant "atom and accident," since they adopted the conception of atomism and adapted it to their theology. See, for example, Harry Austryn Wolfson, *The Philosophy of the kalam* (Cambridge, MA: Harvard University Press, 1976), 390. The meaning that interested R. Soloveitchik in this discussion is the negation of essentiality.

After the birth, the organic unity becomes one of "spiritual integration" and "ontic unity."[73] Instead of being weakened, the mother-child bond is intensified. The organic partnership becomes presence in the consciousness. The mother's existence is reflected in that of the child, with whom it is integrated in the consciousness: "the mother's life revolved around her child. She sees herself in him, she lives for him, and lets him not only share her personal existence but also absorb it."[74] R. Soloveitchik called this unity "community." The dialectic of which we spoke above is clearly revealed: integration within the other reveals selfhood. The lover who is present in his beloved discovers his own selfhood in the process. Self-nullification is the source of being. Love cannot be detached from existence; existence within another makes self-existence substantive and possessing value.

Love and Existence

In this discussion R. Soloveitchik turned love into a mirror of self-existence and existence with another. He refrained from entering the debate with the centrality of love in Christianity, as he did elsewhere.[75] For example, he argued in his lectures at the National Institute of Mental Health in New York that love cannot be set apart from the other emotions and afforded exclusivity.[76] The anti-Christian polemical context is evident in such an approach, but R. Soloveitchik did not draw such distinctions in his discussion of prayer. The consciousness of reading *Shema* does not fear love taken to an extreme. To the contrary, love is enrooted in the existence of selfhood and the other. Love is the foundation of existence. The discussion of the consciousness of *Shema* is also why R. Soloveitchik refrained from sweeping discussions of the love-fear dialectic, while such discussions filled many pages in *And from There You Shall Seek*. The love that is revealed in *Shema* is absolute. It is the bedrock of our shaky and dialectical existence. After defining love, R. Soloveitchik extended the concept to include love of God. He writes:

> In this sense we understand the love of God. The incessant pursuit of an
> allegedly ever-fugitive objective springs from a troubled and disquieted

---

73 *Worship of the Heart*, 135.
74 *Worship of the Heart*, 135.
75 Schwartz, *From Phenomenology to Existentialism*, 283-86. Christian thought devoted lengthy discussion to the relationship between self-love and love of God. See, for example, Avital Wohlman, *Loving God: Christian Love, Theology and Philosophy in Thomas Aquinas* [Hebrew] (Tel Aviv: Resling, 2005). R. Soloveitchik linked personality and selfhood with love of God.
76 Schwartz, *From Phenomenology to Existentialism*, 286-88.

personality. Man is restless and insecure because he himself cannot legitimize his ontic status, since he has none of his own. We long to anchor our existence in the absolute and unconditional, in Being as such.[77] We cannot love in our existential vacuum; we must obtain the unequivocal assurance that we exist.[78]

R. Soloveitchik then adopted Cartesian doubt regarding existence, but rejected the cognitive aspect of Descartes writings. For R. Soloveitchik, the true doubting of existence is formulated in existentialist thought. He asked: can we really see existence, in that it is fragmentary (finitude), dictated from the outset, and negates freedom? His answer is unequivocal: existence is not in doubt, because by the act of love for God man takes part in the divine existence, thereby extricating himself from doubt. The divine existence is absolute, and it gives existential confidence to man, who oscillates between the extremes. Confidence is acquired by means of activity, namely, the act of love. "Only by acting does one attain existence. And his action, his loving of God, signifies partaking of His Being."[79] R. Soloveitchik adopted the religious existentialist model, as can be found in the thought of Paul Tillich, Jacques Maritan, Gabriel Marcel, Emil Fackenheim (in his early writings), and others: the solution to existential problems is to be found in the religious experience.

Love's deep anchoring in ontology is apparently based on Scheler's essay "The Nature of Philosophy and the Moral Precondition of Philosophical Knowledge" that appeared in *On the Eternal in Man*. In this essay, Scheler argued that the goal of the ethical act is for consciousness to refrain from what is attributed to or intended for existence to engage in existence itself and in life itself (*das Sein für das Leben*). He maintained that the ethical act that accompanies philosophical cognition has three characteristics, each of which can be deemed an ethical act in itself:

(1) the spiritual man must love, with all his being, the absolute value and existence;

(2) he must rise above his natural selfhood and ego and repress them;

(3) he must exert self-control and curb his instincts.[80]

---

77 See *Lonely Man of Faith*, 56.
78 *Worship of the Heart*, 136.
79 *Worship of the Heart*, 136.
80 Scheler, *On the Eternal in Man*, 95.

Like any autonomous religious act, love relates to God, since the substantive focus of the religious conscious is only God. Scheler explained the first characteristic as follows:

> Love, which may be thought of as the heart and soul of the entire complex
> of acts, leads in the direction of the absolute. It thus takes us *beyond* objects
> existing only *relatively* to *our* being [*Gegenstände*].[81]

Love relates to the absolute experience, and as such pertains to the depths of the lover's true selfhood. For Scheler, the veracity of philosophical knowledge is dependent upon love. Penetration to substantiality and reality is made possible as a result of love.[82] Scheler, accordingly, concluded that love is the cognition of the absolute reality, on the one hand, and, on the other, knowledge of selfhood. In another place he observed that the divine will is anchored in love and, in great degree, subjugated to it. God desires what He loves, instead of loving what He desires because He wants it.[83] Love of God leads to imitation and participation in "an infinite activity of love." Man loves "in" God; the human personality and the divine "personality" merge in the act of love. Scheler asserts that religious thought replaced love *of* God with love *in* God ("*die Liebe* 'in' *Gott*").[84]

R. Soloveitchik adopted the anchoring of love in the absolute experience, both philosophically and stylistically. Love of God means implanting, as it were, our fragmentary and tenuous existence within God's eternal and infinite existence. Additionally, he took the notion of the divine will as giving purpose to the unity of existence as an indirect source of love, since unity leads to love. He also followed Scheler in arguing for the presence of the lover in the beloved.

R. Soloveitchik found an additional basis for anchoring fleeting and tenuous human existence in the abiding divine existence in the Scholastic doctrine of the spheres. He presented the Aristotelian and Peripatetic model, that the spheres' movement follows a circular route and is unending, since the sphere thirsts to imitate its specific separate intellect.[85]

---

81 Ibid., 95.
82 See William A. Sadler, *Existence and Love: A New Approach in Existential Phenomenology* (New York: Charles Scribner's Sons, 1969), 52.
83 Scheler, *On the Eternal in Man*, 225.
84 Ibid., 225; see also the essay: "Christian Love and the Twentieth Century," ibid., 367.
85 R. Soloveitchik presented this scientific teaching in his discussion of Maimonides' position in *Guide* 2:4. The notion of the spheres and the separate intellects has been the subject of scholarly inquiry. See Dov Schwartz, "The Separate Intellects and Maimonides' Argumentation (an Inquiry into Guide of the Perplexed II.2-12)," in *Beyond Rashi and*

This model viewed the structure of the universe as a series of hollow spheres made of transparent matter, concentric ("like layers of onions"), never coming into contact with one another (friction). Some spheres contain the stars and the planets. These orbs possess a soul, but not intellectual cognition. The model explains the movement of the spheres by means of the teleological principle that ruled Aristotelian physics: this movement is caused by the orbs' longing to be like the "separate intellects." Since they themselves lack intellect, they are similar in the perpetuality of their movement. The Aristotelian universe has intellect as its motive force. R. Soloveitchik was aware that this was an archaic scientific model, but he nevertheless drew from it the idea that the universe as a whole is infused by its search for fixed, eternal intellectual being. He took pains to find traces of this principle in classical Newtonian physics:

> What appears to us as a mechanical force, as a mathematical formula, might well be an expression of the quest for being, for self-realization. With inanimate things or even in the biological realm, in plants and in animals, which are unendowed with ethical awareness, the quest is to be accounted for as a quest devoid of intention and conscious effort. These things or organisms submit mechanically to the force. For them the drive is a fact, not an action. There is a quest on their part, but not conscious love.
>
> In the human world, however, this quest for God becomes a conscious effort, a meaningful movement towards the attainment of self-being, which is Divine Being. Man seeks himself by seeking his own personality and reality. He is bound to find God; love of God means love of Being. The lover, without the beloved, feels helpless, miserable, lonely. For in love there is mutual partaking of each other's existence. Desertion by the beloved is tantamount to loss of ontic worthiness or the frustration of one's cardinal desire, the desire to be—by denying it steadfastness and legitimacy.[86]

The underlying argument here is that love and the quest for sublime intellectual existence as teleological cause in Aristotelian physics was replaced by love and the desire for sublime and harmonious existence as mechanical cause (or "efficient" cause, in Aristotelian terminology) in classical Newtonian physics. The fundamentals of R. Soloveitchik's reasoning appear in the following table:

Maimonides: Theses in Medieval Jewish Thought, Literature and Exegesis, ed. Ephraim Kanarfogel and Moshe Sokolow (New York: Yeshiva University Press, 2010), 59-92.
86 *Worship of the Heart*, 138.

	Aristotelian physics	**classical physics**
type of love	rational	mechanical/natural
aim of love	intellectual beings	sublime existence
cause of love	teleological	effective

And now, to turn to the manifest arguments that R. Soloveitchik raises. The first chapter of *Worship of the Heart* offers an explanation for the activity of the universe in accordance with the principle of the quest for existence by means of love, that is, love of God. Moreover, this principle gradually developed into the identification of love and existence. "All things are directed, through their own inner necessity, toward God because God's cosmic will is engraved into their substances; only in Him do they exist."[87] The quest for existence is embedded in the cosmic regularity. According to R. Soloveitchik's explanation of the activity of the cosmos, the different levels of reality are distinguished by the following features:

(1) Awareness: on the lowest levels, the unconscious quest for existence is expressed in the mechanical and biological regularity that explains the activity of the inanimate and the vegetative. On the human level, the quest for existence is conscious: man is aware of the value of meaningful existence, and seeks it through the absolute divine existence[88]: "the quest for God is common to all things, either in the form of a mechanical force, or as a conscious desire for completeness of Being."[89]

(2) Activity: on the lowest levels, the quest for existence does not contribute to the refinement of nature. On the human level, the quest for existence is effected by means of action, that is, man takes

---

87 *Worship of the Heart*, 140.
88 The quest for meaningful existence characterizes man. Sin or error happen when man is unaware of this trait. R. Soloveitchik found the reasons for this in "short-sightedness, ignorance or sheer stupidity," and the mistaking of "finitude for infinity, vanity for absoluteness" (*Worship of the Heart*, 139). The style of his writing here is reminiscent of the causes of error listed by R. Saadiah Gaon in the beginning of *Beliefs and Opinions*, especially the third cause, of "the seeker who does not know what he is seeking" (Saadia Gaon, *Beliefs and Opinions*, "Introductory Treatise," 5). R. Soloveitchik mentions here, in the same context, a saying by "[a] Hasidic rabbi" (*Worship of the Heart*, 139), which might have added to emphasize the relevance of the explanation of error in all periods of Jewish history, whether in the Babylonian and Egyptian diasporas in the tenth century, or in Hasidism in the eighteenth century.
89 *Worship of the Heart*, 139.

action for the perfection of nature. This task is "paradoxical,"[90] and is inherent in man's dialectical nature.

(3) Relation and quality: on the lowest levels, this is the search for God; on the human level, this is love of God. The quest for existence is also a quest for love.

The quest for meaningful existence is not characteristic only of man's natural and instinctive inclinations. It also motivates engagement that is understanding ("intellectual exercise"), aesthetic ("beauty"), and hedonistic ("indulging in the lover's pleasures").[91] R. Soloveitchik casts this fact in a critical light. Those who indulge in intellectual, aesthetic, and hedonistic experiences erroneously think that they encapsulate reality. They delude themselves that these experiences will give them existential security. "All of them are seeking just one objective—Being."[92] Creative activity, however, and not only natural regularity, is based on the search for existence.

Love and existence are values for R. Soloveitchik. By inductive reasoning, then, the cosmic regularity, in its entirety, is driven by values. Ethics in its broad sense, the ethos, is the key to understanding existence.

> [...] the axiological experience is basically identical with the metaphysi-co-ontic consciousness. To experience a value, to undertake the great venture of realization and possession, translates itself into the metaphysical act of self-realization within the ontic dimension of attaining self-worth and existential dignity, of ascertaining my own status as a *being*.[93]

From Rationality to Totality

Now we can offer a phenomenological interpretation for the verse that begins the first passage of *Shema*. R. Soloveitchik writes of the verse "And thou shalt love thy God" that it "expresses the idea of perfecting an intelligent love, intentional in its grasp, clear and exact as to direction and means of execution."[94] This verse, then, relates to love as an intentional act that is directed to meaningful love, namely, the existence of God and

---

90 *Worship of the Heart*, 140.
91 *Worship of the Heart*, 138-39.
92 *Worship of the Heart*, 139.
93 *Worship of the Heart*, 138.
94 *Worship of the Heart*, 139.

existence in God. In short: this is an act whose object is God. R. Soloveitchik further states:

> Here we return to the role of Talmud, the content of Halakhah, which Maimonides introduced into the experience of the worship of the heart (*Sefer ha-Mitzvot*, Positive Commandment 5). The essence of the Halakhah exhausts itself in one theme: the guidance of man in his metaphysical quest of God, which is *eo ipso* a yearning for Being as such.[95]

R. Soloveitchik adopted the Maimonidean model that views halakhah as an educational tool, which prepares man for acquisition of metaphysical knowledge. In a number of works Maimonides formulated his opinion that the Torah is the best guidance for acquiring moral and rational virtues.[96] R. Soloveitchik focused on what is both means and goal, that is, Torah study and metaphysical truth. However, he understood "metaphysics" quite differently from Maimonides, in the process revealing his brilliant writing. In the Aristotelian source, metaphysics is the science of being, substance, and the first principles. In the Hellenistic and medieval periods, the vivid occupation with nonmaterial entities (separate intellects, angels) was included within the realm of the metaphysical.[97] R. Soloveitchik seemingly returned to the original sense of the term: Being and existence. He, however, did not address the reality with the tools of historical analysis, and rather gave it a phenomenological and existentialist interpretation. The consciousness act of love is also an act that seeks substantive existence—and this existence is realized in the existence of God. Using this interpretation of Maimonides, R. Soloveitchik could declare unequivocally that Judaism chronologically preceded existentialist philosophy, to which it was also qualitatively superior.[98]

We should note two conclusions that R. Soloveitchik drew from his perception of love as meaningful existence.

---

95 *Worship of the Heart*, 139.
96 See, for example, Maimonides, *Iggeret Teiman*, in *Iggerot ha-Rambam*, ed. Y. Shilat (Jerusalem: Maaliyot, 1987), 122-23 (in English translation: *Crisis and Leadership: Epistles of Maimonides*, trans. Abraham Halkin [Philadelphia: Jewish Publication Society of America, 1985], 99-100); *Guide of the Perplexed* 3:27 (trans. Pines: 510-12).
97 Aristotle's interpreters also examined his conception of the divine. See, for example, Koenraad Verrycken, "The Metaphysics of Ammonius Son of Hermeias," in *Aristotle Transformed: The Ancient Commentators and Their Influence*, ed. Richard Sorabji (Ithaca, NY: Cornell University Press, 1990), 215-216.
98 "Here, Judaism proclaimed to the world a philosophy of existentialism" (*Worship of the Heart*, 139).

(1) The place of halakhah: once again, we see the principle that infuses R. Soloveitchik's writings: the halakhah records and channels the predilections of the consciousness. When R. Soloveitchik instilled the intellective love of God in this opening verse, his intent was mainly to the mental effort required by Torah study. This study brings man to participate in the divine existence, and to attain certain and meaningful existence. Furthermore, both reading *Shema* and Torah study are included in "worship of the heart."[99]

(2) The polemical aspect: a polemical tone is typically present between the lines in R. Soloveitchik's phenomenological writings. He sought to demonstrate that Judaism is most suitable for the perfect religious consciousness. He related to the duality of the human experience: on the one hand, man belongs to the animate and natural world, while, on the other, he possesses consciousness.[100] The dualistic approaches emphasized one aspect, at the expense of the other. Paganism stressed the natural side, by its hedonistic approach, while Christianity favored the spiritual, by means of an ascetic approach that sought to downplay the material. Judaism united "the natural and intellectual aspects of the human being."[101] It gave meaning and content to the natural existence that is forced on man; it transformed the tragic to the heroic, and the meaningless to the sublime.[102]

R. Soloveitchik now presents his interpretation of the opening verse of the first passage of *Shema*:

> "And thou shalt love the Lord your God with all thy soul." The word "all"
> (*u-ve-khol*)[103] conveys a central thought. In his search for Being man

---

99   If *Shema* is examined solely on the basis of this first verse, as a rational declaration of faith, it might be assumed to remain beyond the realm of "worship of the heart." See Kaplan, "Review Essay," 88. However, the description of the experience of love blurs this distinction.

100   The terms that R. Soloveitchik used in this discussion of man's singularity ("conscious," "drive," and the like — *Worship of the Heart*, 140) are based on Scheler's terminology and discussions, but only generally. See, for example, Scheler, *Man's Place in Nature*, 40.

101   *Worship of the Heart*, 142.

102   *Worship of the Heart*, 141-142.

103   By including the Hebrew (in transliteration: *u-ve-khol*), R. Soloveitchik intentionally distanced himself from the literal meaning of the verse, which reads "*be-khol levavkha*" and not "*u-ve-khol levavkha*." He may have done this in order to emphasize that his object here is not *lev* [heart], but *nefesh* [soul]. It seems to me that R. Soloveitchik chose the soul, because it is the closest to the consciousness, while the heart (*levavkha*, "your heart") is perceived as a metaphor.

discovers his completeness. He is moved and guided by intelligent planning; he rids himself of ethical indifference. There are no more neutral
areas in his existence from which the halakhic ethical norm is barred. The
concrete person (not an abstract entity) commits himself totally to God-
Being. Through this commitment man finds the oneness of Being in which
he shares.[104]

We should first explore the meaning of the word *u-ve-khol* ([and] with all),
which R. Soloveitchik understood as completeness. There are two aspects
to this completeness.

(1) The totality of the halakhah[105]: the halakhah ("the halakhic ethical
    norm") relates to all areas of life, and therefore concurrently moti-
    vates the observant to perfection and reflects such perfection.
(2) Total commitment: completeness means commitment to two
    factors, which are actually one:
    (a) meaningful existence;
    (b) God. Meaningful existence is equivalent to "participation" in
        the divine existence.

This ends R. Soloveitchik's interpretation of the love of God in the
opening verse. The consciousness equation: existence = redemption of the
material = meaning = God, and the contrast between differentiated existence and existence in God, exhaust his commentary. Complete love is also
complete existence. Love of God means immersing human existence in that
of God.

This perception of love concludes R. Soloveitchik's commentary and
the original text of *Worship of the Heart*. From within it we can imagine the
interpretive method that he envisioned for reading *Shema* in its entirety.
The consciousness of reading *Shema* is composed of an experience that
is rooted in rationality, that is, cognition of the existence of God, and the
stormy landscape of the inclusion of human existence within the infinite
divine existence. Reading *Shema* begins with the cognitive and ends in
unbridled love.

---

104 *Worship of the Heart*, 141.
105 As usual, R. Soloveitchik viewed the halakhah as also including moral teachings and
     guidance, and therefore used ethical terminology.

The experience of love of God and immersion within His existence is not detached from the praxis. R. Soloveitchik was careful to preserve the objective halakhic dimension, even in the case of subjective experience. Reason leads to love, meaning *tikkun olam* (the mending of the world). By merging with the divine existence, man reveals his practical task, expressed in the halakhah.

The core *Worship of the Heart* ends by combining the subjective and the objective. "The way to the metaphysical ontic experience is via the ethico-halakhic domain. Existence is to be comprehended not only in contemplative noetic but also in halakhic categories."[106] The halakhic dimension of prayer concludes *Worship of the Heart*. The work began with the individual experience that R. Soloveitchik attempted to turn into the philosophy of prayer, and ends with halakhah, which is exoteric and suitable for all.

---

106 *Worship of the Heart*, 142.

Part II

"Reflections on the *Amidah*" in Perspective

Chapter 9

Prayer and Redemption

The essay "Reflections on the *Amidah*" contains, in nuclear form, many motifs that appear in detail in *Worship of the Heart*. After our analysis of this major essay on prayer, we can discuss the nuances in R. Soloveitchik's focused articles. "Reflections on the *Amidah*" is divided into three main topics:

(1) redemption of prayer, from the halakhic aspect;
(2) the philosophical and halakhic legitimacy of addressing God in prayer, and the order of the *Amidah* (the principle of preceding thanksgiving with hymn);
(3) the interpretation of the first blessings in the *Amidah*.[1]

In this section (Chapters Nine-Eleven) we will explore the central motifs of "Reflections on the *Amidah*" and their development in R. Soloveitchik's halakhic and philosophical works. In the current chapter we will discuss the first topic in "Reflections," on the connection between the *Amidah* and redemption, and continue with the meeting between the *Amidah* and redemption in R. Soloveitchik's other works. Chapter Ten will examine the conceptual and halakhic legitimacy of the *Amidah* as reflected in his halakhic thought, and Chapter Eleven will discuss R. Soloveitchik's commentary to the *Amidah*, as it appears in the concluding sections of "Reflections."

The *Amidah* was seen by R. Soloveitchik as a religious act of independent worth, while at the same time, also reflecting other religious values

---

1 "Reflections on the *Amidah*" was first published (in Hebrew) in 1978, as an article in *Ha-Darom*. It is unclear whether it was written at that time, or whether it dates from the middle of the 1940s, as does *And from There You Shall Seek*, which was also published in 1978. Kaplan attests that R. Soloveitchik referred to this article as "Reflections on the *Amidah* in Light of 'And from There You Shall Seek'" (see Kaplan, "Review Essay," 110 n. 51). We will return to this below, at the end of Chapter Eleven.

(the same could also be said about the idea of redemption). Furthermore, at times it is easier to draw conclusions regarding the nature of the *Amidah* in R. Soloveitchik's teachings from a discussion of general ideas it contains than from what he writes on the *Amidah* itself. The current chapter will examine the relation between the *Amidah* and redemption, which occupied R. Soloveitchik in different periods. The discussion will begin with Maimonides, the "redeemer" of prayer, and continue to redemptive prayer itself.

1. Introduction: The *Amidah* and Redemption

R. Soloveitchik's thought did not crystallize in a vacuum. When he studied in the universities of Warsaw and Berlin he was undoubtedly influenced by the intellectual trends of the time, just as when he was in the United States he absorbed the approaches that were prevalent among intellectuals and theologians there. The cultural climate left its imprint on his thought. At the beginning of our discussion, I will briefly relate to such influences.

The Messianic Dimension of Prayer

The conception of redemption in early twentieth-century Jewish thought was not absent from discussions of prayer. This notion underwent various changes until the personal, spiritual, and idealistic interpretation it received in R. Soloveitchik's formative period. Prayer as a spiritual act characteristic of both the individual and the community closely accorded with the interpretation of the messianic ideal. I will bring a few examples of this trend.

Walter Benjamin addressed the question of history in his reflections on prayer. The fragments that he wrote on this issue included a discussion of the relation between the *Amidah* and history, in which he viewed the former as an expression of memory. The *Amidah* directs modern man to the past, thereby redeeming the forgotten past. It enables man to stop during the course of time, and thus effects mending. Galili Shahar writes of this approach that

> for Benjamin, prayer embodies the concern for the welfare of the world, and thus the consciousness of cosmic responsibility. Consequently, tradition— specifically because of its imperfection and its broken forms, specifically because of its fragmentary nature and its alienness in the new world, specifically in the time of its decline—constitutes a "brake," and thus, its

power to upset and halt false narratives of progress, and to bring the present to a static state.[2]

The *Amidah* is capable of stopping the flow of time by means of messages from the past. It obligates modern man to decide for himself and take responsibility for himself and for history. This decision and responsibility are an expression of messianic redemption, into which Benjamin inserted his radical political views.

The question of redemption in Hermann Cohen's thought is a complex issue, focusing especially on the *Amidah* of the Days of Awe. Cohen argued that the prayers of these days of divine judgment and compassion focus on the redemption of the world. This, obviously, is not national redemption, but metahistorical redemption that is realized in history. Such redemption is, in great measure, the individual's becoming aware of his self ("the individual road to the I"),[3] and, we could say, the individual re-creation. Such a conception leads us to the prophet Ezekiel and his emphases on the personal. The *Amidah* prayers recited in the Days of Awe denote the transcendence of both the individual and the community, of the boundaries of individual personality and substantiality. Cohen wrote: "These messianic prayers are the climax [*Höhepunkt*] of Jewish prayer."[4]

Franz Rosenzweig wrote a long introduction to the third section of *Star of Redemption*, which he titled "On the Possibility of Entreating the Kingdom." He begins his discussion with individual prayer, which is primarily concerned with the possibility of speech. Individual prayer is spontaneous and lacks preestablished format. The transition from private to communal prayer reflects the individual's journey from standing before God to the redemption of the world and from the expectation of distant redemption that cannot be realized in the present to actual redemption. Communal chanted prayer contains an echo of eternity in terms of the future that is present in the here and now; consequently, prayer is redemptive. Only public prayer enables progress toward the total harmonization of man and the world. Prayer "must hasten the future, must turn eternity into the nighest, the Today. Such anticipation of the future into the moment would have to be a true conversion [*Umschaffung*]

---

2 Galili Shahar, *Fragments of Traditional Modernism and German-Jewish Literature* [Hebrew], vol. 16 of *Lecture Series of the Brown Chair for Prussian History, Bar-Ilan University* (Ramat Gan: Bar-Ilan University, 2011), 23.

3 Cohen, *Religion of Reason*, 188.

4 Ibid., 398.

of eternity into a Today."[5] Prayer in Rosenzweig's thought reflects the direction from revelation to redemption.[6] The step from individual to communal prayer makes possible the transition to redemption.

The approaches of Benjamin, Cohen, and Rosenzweig are a few examples of the dynamic nature of twentieth-century Jewish thought on the relation between prayer and redemption. The balance between individual and community and between present and future well-represented in prayer generated additional nuances in the conception of redemption.

Models of Redemption

R. Soloveitchik discussed both the *Amidah* and redemption in various contexts, viewing redemption as an important theological and consciousness milestone that could not be disregarded. There is a certain amount of tension between the traditional notion of redemption, with its general cosmic and social dimensions, and R. Soloveitchik's personal thought and specific philosophical interests, namely, the structure of the religious consciousness (the phenomenology of religion), religious existence in a modern and alienated world (existentialism), and halakhah's intrinsic suitability to these. The fact that redemption frequently appears in his essays points to the challenge that this religious concept posed to him.

A major way in which R. Soloveitchik approached the tension between the traditional cosmic and collective redemption and his individualistic thought was to develop a conception of personal redemption. That is, he moved the drama that played out beyond the personal realm and the consciousness inward, to the consciousness and concrete existence.[7] The traditional conceptions of redemption in the Prophets and in the apocalyptic and rabbinic literature presented the cosmic and national redemption, which, in turn, impacted on the individual. From many aspects, the rationalist literature that appeared in post-Geonic Jewish thought went in the opposite direction. It was concerned with personal perfection and intellectual communion with God, and only afterwards turned to national and cosmic consequences.

---

5 Franz Rosenzweig, *The Star of Redemption*, trans. William W. Hallo (New York: Holt, Rinehart and Winston, 1971), 289. Prayer in Rosenzweig's thought has been examined in various contexts. See, for example, Stéphane Mosès, *System and Revelation: The Philosophy of Franz Rosenzweig* (Detroit: Wayne State University Press, 1992), 156-159; Amir, *Faith out of Reason*, 197-213.

6 Rosenzweig, *Star of Redemption*, 294.

7 See Schwartz, *Faith at the Crossroads*, 193-221.

R. Soloveitchik began from the inner, that is, the existential, intimate personal event and proceeded from there to the community. Communal existence was of special concern to him, as a philosopher who was active in the American Jewish public sphere. In his thought, the movement was from the individual to the community. Personal existence occupied him more than communal existence, which was of greater concern to him than the national existence. Moreover, the terms that he applied to national existence drew upon personal and communal existence.[8] At the same time, he also adopted additional models, such as that of the future realized in the present and the naturalist messianic model. These models usually neutralize the messianic tensions that ensue from the traditional conceptions. As regards the connection between redemption and the *Amidah*, R. Soloveitchik also employed moderating and personal interpretations of the concept of redemption. I will examine two such interpretations.

(1) Redemption as exposure: (a) the redemption of the *Amidah*. This sort of redemption is concerned with movement from the edge to the center of the consciousness. The *Amidah* was at the edge of the consciousness, and now it has been redeemed and is at the center.

(2) Redemption as exposure: (b) authentic existence. This redemption is concerned with prayer as a means of redemption. Prayer reveals the basis of existence, and thereby also brings redemption.

2. The Model of the Redeemer

Messianic literature concentrated on the image of the redeemer because it was easy to focus the abstract idea of redemption on an actual messianic personification. The redeemer-Messiah reflects the redemption, just as the individual reflects the entire process. R. Soloveitchik enthusiastically supported shifting the messianic idea to this personification.[9] He also applied

---

8 This is especially evident in his homilies on Zionism. See Schwartz, *From Phenomenology to Existentialism*, 220-224.

9 R. Soloveitchik famously wrote in his Hebrew essay "On Love of the Torah and the Redemption of the Soul of the Current Generation": "The term 'messianism' is an alien shoot in my garden. I never used it. The application of this term could excise the personal motif from the belief in the Messiah, which is liable to undermine the entire building. […] A human being, despite his being a finite, limited, and conditioned creature, who is here today and in the grave tomorrow, is capable of ascending to the level of divine agency. The personal messianic aspect affords central standing to the idea of free choice, which gives man self-transcendent capability and the power to ascend to the infinite

redemption to the spiritual dimension of religious life, and for him, prayer, too, is in need of rèdemption. His discussion revolves around the great redeemer, who succeeded in rescuing prayer from its straits.

Redemption: A New Plane

The first part of "Reflections on the *Amidah*" concentrates on presenting Maimonides as the "redeemer of prayer." In the beginning of the essay, however, R. Soloveitchik prefaced his discussion of the messianic figure with a description of the redemption as a comprehensive event. Redemption can be understood as a characteristic, and at the same time, as a process. R. Soloveitchik was not interested in redemption as a process, as was, for example, R. Abraham Isaac Hakohen Kook, and limited himself to interpreting it as a feature of the existence. He wrote:

> Everything requires redemption: the historical community, the individual, nature, the world as whole—all cry out for redemption and repair. In similar fashion, man's thoughts, ideas, reflections, ideals and feelings must be redeemed. All these find themselves in narrow straits; they all cry out to God to be made explicit.
>
> Even the *Shekhinah*, the Divine Presence, as it were, is a captive of historical and metaphysical exile and hopes for redemption.[10]

Five planes of redemption are expressed, either by allusion or openly, in this passage: the personal, the social, the national, the cosmic, and the divine, described below in greater detail.

(1) In the personal plane ("the individual"), redemption means the soul's return to its source (in the Neoplatonic literature) or its personal perfection.
(2) In the social plane ("the historical community"), redemption is the wellbeing and mending of society.

---

and the eternal" (*In Aloneness, In Togetherness [Be-Sod ha-Yahid ve-ha-Yahad]: A Selection of Hebrew Writings*, ed. Pinchas H. Peli [Jerusalem: Orot, 1976], 404-405). As seen from this passage, for R. Soloveitchik, the emphasis on the personality is also the actualization of the messianic idea. On the personification of the messianic idea, see, for example, Dov Schwartz, *Messianism in Medieval Jewish Thought*, trans. Batya Stein (Boston: Academic Studies Press, 2017), 4-5. See also Aaron Lichtenstein, "A Review of the Intellectual Thought of R. J. B. Soloveitchik, may the memory of the righteous be for a blessing" [Hebrew], *Allon Shevut* 140-141 (1994): 11-12.
10 "Reflections on the *Amidah*," in *Worship of the Heart*, 144.

(3) In the national plane ("historical exile"), redemption means the return of the Jewish people to its land and the restoration of its religious and political standing.

(4) In the cosmic plane ("nature"), redemption reflects a change in the natural regularity (in the apocalyptic literature) or the imparting of meaning to the impermeable and inexplicable nature.

(5) In the deity plane ("the Divine Presence"), redemption expresses the divine mending after man's transgressions (midrash and Kabbalah).

R. Soloveitchik introduced a sixth plane of redemption: the realm of ideas, too, can be redeemed. He situated this innovation in the middle of his description of the other planes, presumably so as not to give inordinate prominence to his addition. Such a move can be explained in light of the special way of Torah study (*lomdut*) background of the Soloveitchik family, which placed creative thought on a pedestal, as R. Soloveitchik portrayed this in *Halakhic Man* and in *Mah Dodekh mi-Dod*. The fitting resolution of a series of questions exceeded the bounds of the local Talmudic meaning. The advancement of an idea from the fringe to the center, too, would be deemed "redemption."

We will now turn to the concept of the redeemed. R. Soloveitchik formulated this topic as follows:

> One halakhic concept that was sentenced to temporary isolation but was at last redeemed, is *avodah she-ba-lev* (service, or worship, of the heart). The concept of *avodah she-ba-lev* was coined by the Talmudic sages. The Tosafists, for example, cite a Rabbinic text on Deut. 11:13: "To serve Him with all your heart - what is the service of the heart? That is to say prayer" (*Ta'anit* 2a). But despite this derivation from a Biblical verse, prayer was regarded as a rabbinic commandment and did not occupy a central place in halakhic thought. Many discussed prayer, and many laws were formulated about it. Yet the central point, prayer as service of the heart, awaited its redeemer, who would highlight it and fill it with content.[11]

R. Soloveitchik began with the redemption of "worship of the heart" and ended with prayer. Redemption related generally to worship of the heart, but was realized specifically in prayer. As we have seen, prayer is only one

---

11 "Reflections on the *Amidah*," 145.

of the commandments included in "worship of the heart."[12] How is the idea in its entirely redeemed from within its single commandment? The two fundamental mandates of worship of the heart are Torah study and prayer. There are other relevant commands, as well, but these two are the most central. The redemption of prayer means presenting it as a Torah commandment. Such a presentation must be made by a Torah authority, and it itself constitutes Torah study. In light of the time-honored traditions that define the status of prayer as being *mi-divrei soferim* (the most authoritative level of Rabbinic law), such an innovation could not be suggested without dazzling scholarly deduction. Consequently, the idea of prayer is redeemed by the idea of Torah study. "Worship of the heart" is redeemed from it and by it. Once again, we hear an echo of the Brisk tradition, in which the creativity of study is effected within the intellectual process itself. It is the thought that creates, and as such, also redeems itself. In his eulogy for R. Zeev Soloveitchik, as well, R. Soloveitchik stated that the scholarly tradition of R. Hayyim of Brisk transformed prayer into a scholarly object.[13] Accordingly, prayer is redeemed by means of Torah study, whose very activity is redemptive.

From Redemption to Redeemer

After discussing the meaning of redemption as regards prayer, we will now turn to the personification of the idea. For R. Soloveitchik, Maimonides was the paradigm of the redeemer of ideas. What was the redemptive act of Maimonides? R. Soloveitchik gave a twofold answer to this: in the halakhic plane, Maimonides ruled that prayer is a Torah obligation, while in the philosophical plane, he presented prayer as the spiritual service of the Lord. R. Soloveitchik formulated this as follows:

> Rambam's contribution in the area of prayer is revolutionary in two respects. First of all, he determined as a matter of practical halakhah that prayer is a Biblical commandment—contrary to the virtual halakhic consensus, a view taken as almost obvious, that the obligation to pray every day is only rabbinic. Secondly, he held that prayer is identical with service of the heart, an idea that is, according to Rambam, all-encompassing and all-pervasive and which represents the essence of man's relationship with God.[14]

---

12 See above, Chapter Two.
13 See below, Chapter Ten.
14 "Reflections on the *Amidah*," 145-146.

We will now attempt to understand the meaning of redemption and redeemer, in order to deduce the nature of the Maimonidean revolution in the realm of prayer. To this end, we must return to R. Soloveitchik's discussion at the beginning of "Reflections on the *Amidah*" to determine the nature of redemption. He listed four traits.

(1) Redemption relates to a condition of distress.
(2) Redemption relates to all levels of existence, including deity.
(3) Redemption is concerned with "liberating."
(4) Redemption denotes movement from the fringe of the consciousness to its center ("from concealment to revelation").[15] The idea, trapped in the bonds of forgetfulness and anonymity, suddenly enters the general awareness and undergoes a process of redemption.

Thus, the redeemer struggles with suffering and necessity, on the one hand, and, on the other, with regularity. We can readily understand that R. Soloveitchik gave a clearly consciousness interpretation of redemption. The apocalyptic traditions have the redeemer doing battle with cosmic limitations and demonic evil, in order to free the elect. The national and social traditions present him as struggling against norms and conventions in order to establish proper values in society. And now, R. Soloveitchik brought a new tradition into being: the redeemer struggles against the relegating of an important religious idea to the fringes of the consciousness. We will return to these elements below, after clarifying the Maimonidean revolution in fashioning the standing of prayer in the consciousness.

The redeemer engages in a dual activity, one that is both halakhic and philosophical. Maimonides redeemed prayer halakhically, by determining that it is a Torah commandment, and even its gestures are, in part, of Torah standing.[16] The portrayal of Maimonides as the redeemer of prayer presents him as waging a hopeless battle. This depiction draws considerably from the standing of the hero in the Romantic literature. We also find echoes of the lost struggle of R. Eliezer ben Hyrcanus with the Rabbis

---

15 "Reflections on the *Amidah*," 145.
16 I will examine the various halakhic dimensions of prayer in the teachings of Maimonides below, in Chapter Ten. Cf. David Hartman, "Prayer in the Thought of Rabbi Soloveitchik—Study and Critique" [Hebrew], in Sagi, *Faith in Changing Times*, 213-14.

regarding the oven of Akhnai.[17] Maimonides, too, did not surrender to the "virtual halakhic consensus." He struggled against the consensus of the decisors (*poskim*) who preceded him and set forth a quite unique opinion, that prayer is a Torah obligation.

Maimonides redeemed prayer philosophically, as well. Redemption focuses on the presentation of the far-reaching and full meanings of the definition of prayer as the "service of the heart." R. Soloveitchik drew upon the final chapters of the *Guide of the Perplexed* to clarify the meaning of this "service."[18] Maimonides maintained that the goal of the Torah is the intellectual worship of the Lord. In this way he explained, for example, the sacrificial rite in *Guide* 3:32. This means that the act is the educational tool to achieve spiritual worship, which is, as was noted, intellectual contemplation. For R. Soloveitchik, prayer is the closest ritual expression to the abstract worship of the Lord. This is also Maimonides' position.[19]

The two redemptions are intertwined. If it had not been for this far-reaching halakhic innovation, placing prayer at the center of spiritual life would have been of no avail. The identification of prayer with worship of the heart appears in *midrashei ha-halakhah* and in the Talmuds, and was emphasized by the Tosafists, as well. "But despite this derivation from a Biblical verse, prayer was [still] regarded as a rabbinic commandment." Prayer "did not occupy a central place in halakhic thought."[20] If not for Maimonides situating abstract worship as the heart of the religious experience, his halakhic innovation would not have received its proper import.

R. Soloveitchik, however, did not define just what is revolutionary in the presentation of prayer as a Torah obligation. He described Maimonides' innovation as restorative. The latter did not offer a new model of redemption in his ruling, but rather restored prayer to the standing it had enjoyed in early times: "Rambam restored to prayer its crown, its preeminent position known to us from the days of the Patriarchs and prophets."[21]

---

17 This narrative ends with R. Eliezer's personal prayer, which harmed Rabban Gamaliel (BT Bava Metzia 59b).

18 Cf. above, Chapter Three. See also Marvin Fox, *Interpreting Maimonides: Studies in Methodology, Metaphysics, and Moral Philosophy* (Chicago: University of Chicago Press, 1990), 315-318; Ehud Benor, *Worship of the Heart: A Study of Maimonides' Philosophy of Religion* (Albany: State University of New York Press, 1995).

19 See, for example, *Guide of the Perplexed* 3:51.

20 "Reflections on the *Amidah*," 145.

21 "Reflections on the *Amidah*," 145. On restorative redemption, see Shalom Rosenberg, "The Return to the Garden of Eden: Reflections on the History of the Idea of Restorative Redemption in Medieval Jewish Philosophy" [Hebrew], in *The Messianic Idea in Jewish*

What, then, was lost in prayer over the ages? R. Soloveitchik was so convinced that this was clear and evident that he did not bother to formulate it. It seems to me that he meant that a person who stands in prayer, after the destruction of the Temple, does not take responsibility for standing before God. Relying on the work of the Rabbis, who ordered the prayers, makes this self-evident. In the Biblical period, in contrast, prayer did not rely on any authority. When the Patriarchs addressed the Lord in prayer, they took full responsibility for the perilous situation in which they placed themselves. At times, God did not pay heed to prayer.

When Maimonides determined that prayer is of Torah force, he returned responsibility to the worshiper. Now the worshiper can no longer rely on the authority of the Rabbis regarding the fateful decision to stand before God in prayer. From this aspect, Maimonides' redemption of prayer is retrospective: he restored the responsibility of standing before God. Although R. Soloveitchik did not explicitly state this conclusion, what he wrote leads to human autonomy and responsibility.

At this juncture, Maimonides' two redemptive actions meet. We could just as easily ask about the second action: what was new about Maimonides' connecting prayer to the idea of "worship of the heart," since the Rabbis had already spoken of this? R. Soloveitchik, however, cited the assertion in the *Guide* that the notion of "worship of the heart" means "setting thought to work on the first intelligible and in devoting oneself exclusively to this as far as this is within one's capacity."[22] Contemplative prayer leads to "devoting oneself." The phrase "devoting oneself to intelligibles [*hitbodedut ba-muskalot*]" was common in medieval Jewish rationalist thought.[23] R. Soloveitchik explained to the reader that even in the contemplative prayer model, Maimonides placed full responsibility on the shoulders of the worshiper. He stands alone, "devoting himself," in the presence of God. The ideal of perfection is personal for Maimonides: every individual is responsible for attaining individual intellectual communion with God. Once again, prayer reflects the step taken by man himself and for himself.

The figure of Maimonides is at work in both ways in which the messianic literature described the figure of the Messiah. The Messiah establishes the period, and he is also a product of the period, and therefore characterizes

---

Thought: A Study Conference in Honour of the Eightieth Birthday of Gershom Scholem, held 4-5 December 1977 (Jerusalem: Israel Academy of Sciences and Humanities, 1982), 37-86.

22 *Guide of the Perplexed* 3:51 (trans. Pines, 621).

23 See, for example, Idel, "*Hitbodedut* as Concentration."

it alone. On the one hand, Maimonides created the redemptive revolution. He determined that prayer is a Torah obligation, thereby teaching that it is the personality of the redeemer that effects the redemption. This image also suits the depiction of the tradition of Torah study as extremely creative, as participating with the Holy One, blessed be He, in creation.[24] On the other hand, Maimonides provided a powerful conceptual context for an element that already was present in the teachings of the early sages, that is, the service of the heart. Maimonides' activity led to Torah scholars directing their attention to prayer.

In either case, whether prayer is consciousness or an experience that awaits its redemption, Maimonides was its long-awaited redeemer. In order to understand the nature of this redemption, we must ask: what are the features of the religious experience to which prayer as worship of the heart gives orderly and balanced expression? R. Soloveitchik writes:

> What then is prayer? It is the expression of the soul that yearns for God via the medium of the word, through which the human being gives expression to the storminess of his soul and spirit.
>
> The Torah commands love and fear of God, total commitment (*hitmakrut*, devotion) to Him and cleaving unto Him. Antithetical, dynamic experiences which seek to erupt and reveal themselves must be integrated into the external, concrete realm through the forms of language and expression, by means of song, weeping and supplication.[25]

Prayer is the "external" and "concrete" expression of the subjective strata of the consciousness, according to the model that R. Soloveitchik constructed in his early essays. Prayer records movements between the poles, in accordance with the following various phases of the religious consciousness.

(1) Love and fear: on the one hand, the consciousness seeks closeness to God, while, on the other, it recoils from His greatness and manifestation.[26]

(2) Unification and communion: on the one hand, the consciousness seeks immersion within the divine entity, to the extent of "total commitment," while on the other, it desires communion, that is, closeness to God while maintaining individuality.[27]

---

24 See Schwartz, *Religion or Halakha*.
25 "Reflections on the *Amidah*," 146.
26 See Schwartz, *From Phenomenology to Existentialism*, chapter 2.
27 Ibid., chapters 6-7.

How, then, are we to understand redemption in light of the complex and dialectical structure of the subjective consciousness? R. Soloveitchik answers:

> When Rambam said that prayer is Biblically ordained and identical with the service of the heart, he thereby redeemed love, fear, and indeed our entire religious life from muteness. They were given a voice. The lover expresses his yearning, the trembler his fear, the wretched and dejected his helplessness, the perplexed his confusion, and the joyful his religious song—all within the framework of prayer.[28]

The opposing and dynamic tendencies of the consciousness are muted. In a certain sense, R. Soloveitchik portrayed the subjective consciousness as repressed, lacking expression. The *Amidah* enables the subjective inclinations to burst into the world beyond the consciousness. Consequently, redemption is primarily perceived as liberation. Maimonides liberated the religious sensibilities from their subjective straits and gave them orderly expression. "The act (*ma'aseh*) of prayer is formal, the recitation of a known, set text; but the *fulfillment* of prayer, its *kiyyum*, is subjective: it is the service of the heart."[29]

Now we have a better understanding of the meaning of the Maimonidean redemption, whose characteristics we listed above. Before the possibility of praying, the consciousness is in a state of distress. The subjective feelings and inclinations quest for freedom, that is, they seek expression in the world beyond the consciousness. As was noted above, in prayer the objective and subjective strata of the consciousness are in direct relationship with each other. The movement from the fringe to the center is made possible by the liberation—through expression—of the subjective dimensions of the consciousness. Now, the consciousness is fashioned in freedom. But this is not uncontrolled liberation. To the contrary: the liberation of the consciousness is effected with halakhic regulation, which provides a defined and measured framework for stormy emotions.

Legal Meaning

Maimonidean redemption preserves the framework and does not undermine it. Prayer is perceived as redemption, and the discussion of the

---

28 "Reflections on the *Amidah*," 147.
29 "Reflections on the *Amidah*," 147.

relationship between these two terms (prayer and redemption) is conducted exclusively in the plane of the consciousness.

R. Soloveitchik ascribed great importance to the Maimonidean conception of prayer. We will see below that he viewed Maimonides' ruling on prayer as the verbal expression of the Torah force as too narrow[30] and, in his classes, he also presented other liturgical components, such as the direction of prayer and the sanctity of the synagogue, as Torah-based obligations. R. Soloveitchik lost no time in asserting that Maimonides obligates women to pray, and that prayer is not a time-sensitive commandment.[31] He interpreted Maimonides' halakhic orientation as a messianic task, in the sense that the latter restored prayer to its source—the Torah mandate delivered at Mount Sinai and the prayer of the Patriarchs. Prayer returned to the domain and responsibility of the individual. Here we see R. Soloveitchik as the virtuoso who masterfully uses his analytical skills to elevate prayer to the highest sphere. Maimonides' messianism is presented as retrospective, that is, as a return to the source. Just as some apocalyptists thought that in the future man would return to the lost Paradise, Maimonides similarly redeemed prayer and the wealth of its accompanying gestures by restoring them to the revelational source—the Torah obligation—from which they presumably had been distanced. For R. Soloveitchik, the decisors of Jewish law had seemingly robbed prayer of its proper standing, which Maimonides restored in a daring stroke.

3. The Revelation of the Self

From the personal relation to prayer ("redeemer"), we will now move to the inner cohesion of this redemption and of prayer. We have seen that "Reflections on the *Amidah*" charted a clearly phenomenological context of relation between the elements of the *Amidah* and redemption. The consciousness was freed of its bonds by prayer. The relationship, however, between prayer and redemption would assume a different form in R. Soloveitchik's writings. In the article "Redemption, Prayer, Talmud Torah" (which was initially delivered as a lecture in 1973), he discussed the cohesiveness of redemption and prayer from a distinctly existentialist perspective. R. Soloveitchik's analysis moves between two stages. In the first stage, he sought to present prayer as a means of redemption. The second

---

30 See below, Chapter Ten.
31 Grodner, *On Prayer*, 9-10.

stage teaches that the commonality of redemption and prayer approaches identity. We will now turn to the existential expressions of the relation between prayer and redemption.

Dialogue: Two Aspects

Intersubjective communication, that is, the forging of an authentic connection between two subjects, is one of the features of the redeemed existence in R. Soloveitchik's existentialist thought. The existence of the redeemed people is the way in which it is possible to live a dignified life with existential loneliness. As was mentioned above,[32] dialogue expresses two existentialist characteristics in R. Soloveitchik's thought:

(1) the discovery of the other;
(2) the discovery of selfhood.

The second trait is presented at length in "Redemption, Prayer, Talmud Torah."[33] In that article R. Soloveitchik refrained from thoroughly discussing dialogue as intersubjective connection. The Other does not occupy a substantive place in the notion of redemption through prayer. R. Soloveitchik primarily presented dialogue as the exposure of one's self and as awareness of its authentic needs.[34] For him, the movement was dual: awareness of self-existence (inward movement) that enables addressing the other (outward movement). By means of speaking to the other, the speaker gains knowledge of himself. At times, addressing God as the ultimate Other leads to the discovery of one's own personality. The possibility of addressing the other exposes man to the very ability to speak and to communicate (which is a fundamental existential characteristic), and he thereby is transformed from object to subject. In great degree, awareness of selfhood expresses the overcoming of existential loneliness and alienation. The very possibility of formulating the subjective experiences is an expression

---

32 See above, Chapter Two.

33 David Hartman saw this approach as placing man at the center of prayer. The "anthropological" shift cannot be removed from the dialogue in which God participates. See Hartman, "Prayer in the Thought," 198.

34 The authentic needs are a component of the existential frame which must be exposed. R. Soloveitchik wrote: "Whoever permits his legitimate needs to go unsatisfied will never be sympathetic to the crying needs of others" ("Redemption, Prayer, Talmud Torah," *Tradition* 17, no. 2 [Spring 1978]: 65). See Seev Gasiet, *Menschliche Bedürfnisse: Eine theoretische Synthese* (Frankfurt: Campus Verlag, 1981).

of self-redemption. As we will see below, redemption is interpreted in
two ways:

(1) the discovery of one's personality; to be precise, of the existential
experiences that characterize it;
(2) the creation, or recreation, of the personality.

R. Soloveitchik used Platonic imagery to explain the meaning of
self-discovery. Before a person exposes his authentic existential frame, he
is like shadows or the faint reflection of ideas. Once he has revealed his
fundamental authentic dimension, he is like the substantive existence of
the world of ideas.[35]

R. Soloveitchik maintains that this process of discovery of selfhood
occurs by means of prayer (see below).

Prayer and Personality

The sources for the perception of prayer as a return to selfhood are to be
found mainly in existential thought.[36] The interpretation of such thought
as the exposure of the structure of the self was common in existentialist
psychotherapy. From a certain aspect, existentialist thinkers who were
therapists (Ludwig Binswanger, Henri Ellenberger, and others) viewed
treatment as the exposure of the existential infrastructure. This infrastructure
includes existential features such as finitude, anxiety, and inter-subjective
relationships. Rollo May portrayed existentialist therapists as engaged in
"analyzing the underlying assumptions about human nature and arriving
at a *structure* on which all specific therapeutic systems could be based."[37]

---

35 "Redemption, Prayer, Talmud Torah," 64.
36 See above, Chapter Two.
37 Rollo May, *The Discovery of Being: Writings in Existential Psychology* (New York and
London: Norton, 1983), 43. As May concluded: "Existentialism, in short, is the endeavor
to understand man by cutting below the cleavage between subject and object" (ibid.,
49); "Kierkegaard and the existential thinkers appealed to a reality *underlying both
subjectivity and objectivity*" (ibid., 53). Frederik Buytendijk presented the revealing of
the basic characteristics of existence as a central arena for what he called "phenomenological psychology." For example, he asserted that the discovery of existential anxiety requires self-awareness and reflection. See Frederik J. J. Buytendijk, "Husserl's
Phenomenology and Its Significance for Contemporary Psychology," in *Readings in
Existential Phenomenology*, ed. Nataniel Lawrence and Daniel O'Connor (Englewood
Cliffs, NJ: Prentice-Hall, 1967), 357. R. Soloveitchik, who was influenced by these thinkers,
also talked of the need to reveal the existential frame. For the dialogical dimension of

By the same coin, Hasidic thought, which stressed inner contemplation, contributed to the idea of discovering the self. The early Hasidim oscillated between maintaining one's identity in light of the ideal of self-annihilation and its absorption and dissolution. This oscillation itself directed attention to selfhood.[38] We will discuss the various sources of the combination of the construction and exposure of the self.

This conception, however, also has roots in modern Jewish thought. Prayer as addressing one's self appears in the thought of R. Samson Raphael Hirsch, who viewed prayer primarily as an educational act. The verb *hitpalel* (pray) is in the reflexive *hitpael* form, conveying the idea of prayer as a means of self-examination. The worshiper attempts

> to gain a true judgment about oneself, that is, about one's ego, about one's relationship to God and the world, and of God and the world to oneself It strives to infuse mind and heart with the power of such judgment as will direct both anew to active life—purified, subliminated, strengthened. The procedure of arousing such self-judgment is called "*tefillah*" [prayer].[39]

Prayer influences the personality, endowing it with sublime ideas about God and the world. To be more precise: the meaning of these ideas as they relate to self and personality is attained by means of prayer. But prayer is not only a means. R. Hirsch points out that *tefillah* is an approach on God and the world, particularly as related to the self.[40] He also explained the petitionary prayers in this spirit. Prayer teaches man to petition for his true needs ("to wish only that which is true" [*nur Wahres wünschen*]),[41] and thereby be aware of his selfhood. Additionally, prayer confronts man with his past, while he is naturally inclined to the future. Prayer is a sort of "repentance" and spiritual accounting, which makes a person face his past. It is a "reflection" and an "overall viewing [*Überblick*]" of life.[42]

---

prayer, see, for example, Ehrlich, *Nonverbal Language*, 219-221. Here, dialogue is an expression of an awareness of the self.

38 See, for example, Ron Margolin, *Human Temple: Religious Interiorization and the Structuring of Inner Life in Early Hasidism* [Hebrew] (Jerusalem: Magnes, 2005).

39 Hirsch, *Horeb*, para. 618 (In English translation: Samson Raphael Hirsch, *Horeb: A Philosophy of Jewish Laws and Observances*, trans. I. Grunfeld [New York: Soncino, 1981], 472) See also Isaac Heinemann, *Taamei ha-Mitzvot be-Sifrut Yisrael* [*The Reasons for the Commandments in Jewish Literature*] [Hebrew], vol. 2 (Jerusalem: Zionist Organization, 1956), 143-147.

40 Hirsch, *Horeb*, para. 620 (in English translation: Hirsch, *Horeb*, 473).

41 Ibid., para. 621 (in English translation: Hirsch, *Horeb*, 474).

42 Ibid., para. 623.

R. Hirsch's style is patently preachy. He discusses prayer as an expression of remorse for past sins and of God's involvement in man's personal life. The past is acknowledged by means of "*todah* and *vidui*, prayer of recognition (thanks) [*Erkenntnis (Dank)*] and in confession [*Bekenntnisgebet*]."[43] Nonetheless, his writing systematically constitutes prayer on discovery of the "I."

The conception of prayer as addressing one's self is not limited to the intimate personal plane. R. Hirsch asserts that the deluge of the individual's material world obscures the uniqueness of the Jewish people. And this is not all: the Jewish people's demeaning within its surroundings leads to despair and enslavement to the material world. Prayer is the remedy for such a blurring. It causes the individual to become aware of his true nature, in terms of both his personal identity and his national affiliation. This awareness comes about within a rational perception of Divine Providence.[44] R. Hirsch's approach is both moralistic and rational. Physical desires mask one's self, and prayer, as contemplation, reveals it.

Simply put, prayer is "inner Divine service."[45] R. Hirsch referred especially to the theological aspect, that is, man's relationship with God and the world. Man examines his relations with his surroundings. According to R. Hirsch, prayer is a departure from routine life in order to examine it from the outside, or more precisely, from within. The model of prayer as addressing the self, however, appears quite forcefully in his thought. In *Worship of the Heart*, as well, the experience of petition in prayer attests to the individual's emotional, consciousness, and existential maturity, and not to the bilateral aspect of dialogue.

The Argument

The following examination of "Redemption, Prayer, Talmud Torah" will explore the range of expressions of all the characteristic stages of redemption and their reflection in prayer. We must first, however, answer a number of questions raised by this conception: why is dialogue to be deemed redemption? Furthermore, how is the ability to use one's voice and words connected to the process of redemption? And finally, how is prayer incorporated in this

---

43 Ibid., para. 622 (in English translation: Hirsch, *Horeb*, 475).
44 Ibid., para. 620 (in English translation: Hirsch, *Horeb*, 473).
45 Ibid., para. 623 (in English translation: Hirsch, *Horeb*, 475) and para. 624 (in English translation: Hirsch, *Horeb*, 475-76).

redemption? The basis of all the questions that are posed in "Redemption, Prayer, Talmud Torah" can be presented in two arguments, with emphasis placed on the focal points of R. Soloveitchik's discussion:

Argument (1): Redemption

(1) The experience of suffering is the typical feature of human existence.
(2) Acknowledgement of the experience of suffering means the acknowledgement and adoption of the authentic self.[46]
(3) The awareness of the authentic self means redemptive existence. Therefore—
(4) Redemption is the acknowledgement of the authentic self.

Argument (2): Prayer

(5) The experience of suffering is the typical feature of human existence.
(6) This experience results from the disregard of existential needs.
(7) Prayer—mainly petitionary prayer—reflects existential needs.
(8) Suffering is acknowledged by means of prayer. Therefore—
(9) Prayer reveals the self and authentic existence.

The conclusion of each of the arguments is the following.

(10) Prayer and redemption are revealed to possess the identical meaning.

These arguments are anchored in the basic characteristics of human existence (suffering, dignity, authenticity, recreation of the self). Like the religious existentialists, R. Soloveitchik was of the opinion that theology facilitates a proper way of contending with life's problems. We will now examine the evolution of the ideas inherent in the central arguments of "Redemption, Prayer, Talmud Torah."

---

46 In R. Soloveitchik's terminology, "authenticity" means awareness of the true needs that characterize concrete existence. In this manner, man comes to know himself.

Redemption as Self-Discovery

At the beginning of the article R. Soloveitchik already set forth the argument that personal and communal redemption are characterized by dialogical and meaningful existence. He defined redemption in the following manner:

> Redemption involves a movement by an individual or a community from the periphery of history to its center; or, to employ a term from physics, redemption is a centripetal movement. To be on the periphery means to be a non-history-making entity, while movement toward the center renders the same entity history-making and history-conscious. Naturally the question arises: What is meant by a history-making people or community? A history-making people is one that leads a speaking, story-telling, communing free existence, while a non-history-making, non-history-involved group leads a non-communing and therefore a silent, unfree existence.[47]
>
> Redemption, we have stated, is identical with communing, or with the revelation of the word, i.e. the emergence of speech. When a people leaves a mute world and enters a world of sound, speech and song, it becomes a redeemed people, a free people. In other words, a mute life is identical with bondage; a speech-endowed life is a free life.[48]

The first passage defines redemption as a movement to self-consciousness. The individual and the community are aware of their selfhood. The second passage defines redemption as movement toward freedom by means of dialogue. But even the worth of such dialogue rests, first of all, in the freedom of the "I." Freedom, rather than limited to a characteristic or trait of the personality, is anchored in the ontological frame of selfhood.[49] Recognition of this fact, that is, exposure to selfhood, is redemption. In acoustic terms, R. Soloveitchik depicted redemption as an individual's movement from silence to voice, and from voice to dialogue; and simultaneously, also as an individual's latent movement to the community, and the community's movement into history.[50] These two movements are united by the dialogue

47 "Redemption, Prayer, Talmud Torah," 55.
48 "Redemption, Prayer, Talmud Torah," 56.
49 Paul Tillich adopted this approach. See, for example, David E. Roberts, "Tillich's Doctrine of Man," in *The Theology of Paul Tillich*, ed Charles W. Kegley and Robert W. Bretall (New York: Macmillan, 1964), 118.
50 This movement is not overtly expressed in the article. The relation between the individual and the community and people occupied R. Soloveitchik during different periods of his thought. Accordingly, this idea is present in "Redemption, Prayer, Talmud Torah,"

that reveals the self. Through dialogue, man becomes conscious of his true needs and his existential frame. R. Soloveitchik maintained that modern man often errs in his awareness of his self. "Man is surely aware of many needs, but the needs he is aware of are not always his own. At the very root of this failure to recognize one's truly worthwhile needs lies man's ability to misunderstand and misidentify himself, i.e. to lose himself."[51] Dialogue is seen as the very ability to express the true needs, and accordingly is also the realization of redemption. The redeemed individual finds himself and exposes his authentic existence. R. Soloveitchik, however, was not satisfied merely with exposing the self. He took an additional step and argued that the revealing of the "I" also means the creation of selfhood. Coming to know the true needs of existence leads to the *recreation* of the self. Man creates himself. R. Soloveitchik formulated the creative aspect of authentic existence in the following words:

> [Man's] first job is to create himself as a complete being. Man, the mute being, must search for speech and find it, all by himself. Man comes into our world as a hylic, amorphous being [...] It is up to man to objectify himself,[52] to impress form upon a latent formless personality and to move from the hylic, silent periphery toward the center of objective reality.[53]

After this brief clarification of the nature of redemption as revelation of personality and creation of the self, we can point to the sources that inspired this dual conception of existence and show how R. Soloveitchik adapted the philosophical and cultural traditions that influenced him. As usual, he did not conceive his ideas in a vacuum. In many instances he was influenced by the general intellectual climate, and not from any specific philosophical or theological approach. This analysis of the concept of redemption enables us to indicate a number of sources of inspiration, which, as a general rule, could not sprout within Orthodox Jewish thought, and which, in the end,

---

but only behind the scenes here. The article is largely focused on the experience of the individual.

51 "Redemption, Prayer, Talmud Torah," 62.

52 R. Soloveitchik used a reverse system of terminology: building the personality and coming to know the self is "to objectify oneself," where what is meant is the authentic existence, actually—subjective existence. This stylistic phenomenon is typical of R. Soloveitchik's writings over the course of time. He was not exacting as regards the consistency and cohesion of the terms he chose. Nonetheless, his ideas are clear. The movement here is from the hylic to the form and from the unreal to the substantial (self).

53 "Redemption, Prayer, Talmud Torah," 64.

became the key to understanding the meaning of prayer. R. Soloveitchik apparently blended together a few ideas:

First, authentic existence. R. Soloveitchik's notion of redemption as the exposure of existence is, first and foremost, Heideggerian. The task of revealing selfhood and authentic existence, anchored in Scriptural homily, is a religious version of Heidegger's approach. Traces of the conception of repetition and affirming of existence are evident also in Kierkegaard's thought,[54] in which the notion of selfhood as the object of the consciousness is central.[55] For Kierkegaard and Heidegger, however, authenticity means mainly to find the self, and not to create it.

Second, dialogue as revealing the self. Buberian dialogical thought discussed the meaning of dialogue in reference to selfhood. The assertion that the relation is primal necessarily has consequences for the discovery of the self from within this relation.[56] We already explained, however, that in "Redemption, Prayer, Talmud Torah" R. Soloveitchik did not discuss dialogue per se, but as a means for discovering the "I." Traces of the idea that the self is fashioned through dialogue can be seen in the writings of the "theologians of crisis," and their formulations are reflected in R. Soloveitchik's writings. Emil Brunner, for example, wrote that "the heart of the creaturely existence of man is freedom, selfhood, to be an 'I', a person. Only an 'I' can answer a 'Thou', only a Self which is self-determining can freely answer God."[57]

Third, the creation of self. R. Soloveitchik added the creative aspect of selfhood to Heidegger's awareness of authentic existence. Awareness of the true needs of existence is also the construction and formation of the self. R. Soloveitchik was influenced on this point by the concept of self-constitution in phenomenological thought, and mainly, by the psychotherapeutic ideas that were current in the United States in the middle of the twentieth century. As was noted, some of R. Soloveitchik's essays originated as lectures that he delivered at the National Institute of Mental Health in New York in the late 1950s. He was influenced by the cultural atmosphere, echoes of which (albeit not details) entered his preaching and thought. At the same time, he demanded "existential awareness" and

---

54 See, for example, Jacob Golomb, *In Search of Authenticity: From Kierkegaard to Camus* (New York: Routledge, 1995).

55 See Sagi, *Kierkegaard, Religion and Existence*, 7-12.

56 See, for example, Buber, *I and Thou*, 31-32.

57 Emil Brunner, *The Christian Doctrine of Creation and Redemption*, vol. II of *Dogmatics*, trans. Olive Wyon (Philadelphia: Westminster, 1952), 56.

"clear conception."[58] We already mentioned phenomenological and existentialist psychotherapy. Ludwig Binswanger argued that human existence fashions itself and the surrounding world. "Human existence not only contains numerous possibilities of modes of being, but is precisely rooted in this manifold potentiality of being."[59] Rollo May maintained that freedom is an expression of the consciousness of the "I."[60] He listed four levels or stages in the structure of the consciousness. The fourth and last consciousness level, which is not routinely experienced, is the consciousness of discovery. When a person suddenly discovers the solution to a problem that had troubled him for a long time, or experiences religious illumination in a dream or daydream, he discovers a new dimension of existence, of his existence. May called this level, which largely reflects authentic existence, the "creative consciousness of the self."[61] The motif of recreation of the self through its exposition appears in existentialist psychotherapy.

In order to explain the value of knowing one's self, R. Soloveitchik depicted the experience of anxiety from not knowing the self's true needs, in an autobiographical tone:

> Let me speak for myself: I know that I am perplexed that my fears are irrational, incoherent. At times I am given over to panic; I am afraid of death. At other times I am horrified by the thought of becoming, God forbid, incapacitated during my lifetime. One of my greatest fears is related to the observance of the Day of Atonement: I am fearful that I might be compelled, because of weakness or sickness, to desecrate this holiest of days. I don't know what to fear, what not to fear; I am utterly confused and ignorant..[62]

At times R. Soloveitchik would speak of himself in his existentialist writing, and, in great degree, we find a therapeutic dimension in his existentialist autobiographical writing.[63] The very act of writing balanced and regulated existential distresses (anxiety and finitude), albeit while not causing them to go away. Writing has independent worth. In this respect, R. Soloveitchik's style suits his content. Writing and speaking about authentic needs reflects the awareness of them, and therefore are a step in the direction of a life of

---

58 "Redemption, Prayer, Talmud Torah," 60, 67.
59 Cited in May, *Discovery of Being*, 124.
60 Rollo May, *Man's Search for Himself* (New York: Norton, 1953), 160.
61 May, *Man's Search for Himself*, 139-140. The third chapter of this book is dedicated to the creative consciousness, which May examined mainly from the moral aspect.
62 "Redemption, Prayer, Talmud Torah," 62-63.
63 Schwartz, *From Phenomenology to Existentialism*, xvii.

dignity and redemption. The fear of "desecrating" the Day of Atonement adds a religious dimension to the existential distresses. Clearly, then, for R. Soloveitchik the discovery and recreation of one's self are synonymous with redemption.

Redemption as a Process

As was his way, R. Soloveitchik grounded his interpretation of redemption in his preaching, and especially wrote about the redemptive process. Now Scriptural and midrashic passages become a tool employed by the new interpretation of redemption. He devoted especial attention to the exposition of a Zoharic passage that connected the Exile and the Redemption to the process of the voice emerging from the silence. This passage reads:

> Moses is voice, and speech, which is his word, was in exile; so he was "uncircumcised"—obstructed from expressing words [...] Come and see: As long as speech was in exile, voice withdrew from it, and the word was obstructed, voiceless. When Moses appeared, voice appeared. Moses was voice without word, which was in exile; as long as speech was in exile, Moses proceeded as speechless voice. And so it continued until they approached Mount Sinai and the Torah was given, whereupon voice united with speech, and then the word spoke.[64]

Based on the acoustic imagery of the *Zohar*, R. Soloveitchik set forth three stages in the process of redemption.

(1) "First it [the text] identifies bondage with the absence of both word and meaningful sound, with total silence."
(2) "The redemption begins with finding sound while the word is still absent."
(3) "Finally, with the finding of both sound and word, redemption attains it [*sic*] full realization."[65]

We will need the following distinction in order to clarify the process of redemption: R. Soloveitchik distinguished between external pain (sensation) and existential suffering (experience). Pain is a physiological

---

64 *Zohar* 2:25b (in English translation: *The Zohar*, trans. Daniel C. Matt, vol. 4 [Stanford, CA: Stanford University Press, 2007], 91-92). R. Soloveitchik completely ignored the symbolism of the *Zohar*, which described a process of emanation and crystallization, beginning with the voice (*Tiferet*), and proceeding to speech (*Malkhut*).
65 "Redemption, Prayer, Talmud Torah," 59.

response to injury. Suffering is an enrooted experience of a loss of existential confidence and dignity. At times suffering also expresses existential guilt. R. Soloveitchik frequently differentiated between an external phenomenon and the existential frame at its basis (fear-anxiety; vulnerability-finitude, and more). He applied the pain-suffering division to the exegetical realm: until the dialogue that Moses conducted with the Israelites, who groaned under the yoke of Pharaoh, the slaves did not discover the experience of suffering ("silence"). They sensed pain as a physical sensation, but they did not experience suffering. Once he addressed them as subjects, they discovered the experience. They cry out in their suffering ("voice"). At the Giving of the Torah at Mount Sinai, the awareness of the existential situation in which they find themselves is added ("word"). It was then that Moses and the people came to know the *meaning* of the experience of suffering, that is, its being anchored in the past (the covenant with the Patriarchs) and in the future (freedom and the legacy of the Land of Israel).[66]

> Even Moses, the Zohar emphasizes, who helped the people move from the silent periphery to the great center, did not acquire the word until he and the people reached Mount Sinai. Although Moses had the existential *awareness* of need, he had not as yet discovered the *logos* of need which would, in turn, have endowed him with the charisma of speech [...] Only at Sinai was the logos, both as word and as knowledge, revealed to him.[67]

Redemption is an experiential phenomenon, which is not exhausted in the external, physical dimension. It is the discovery of the existential experience of the "I" by means of dialogue.

R. Soloveitchik presented the halakhah as suited to life in accord with the deep dimensions of existence. Personal and existential redemption

---

66 In this respect R. Soloveitchik was inclined to the conception that existentialist thought is rational, in contrast with the view, among others, of William Barret, the author of *Irrational Man*. For the different opinions, see Herbert J. Paton, *In Defence of Reason* (London: Hutchinson's University Library, 1951), 213-228; William Barrett, *Irrational Man: A Study in Existential Philosophy* (Garden City, NY: Doubleday, 1958); Fernando Molina, *Existentialism as Philosophy* (Englewood Cliffs, NJ: Prentice-Hall, 1962); David E. Cooper, *Existentialism: A Reconstruction* (Oxford: Blackwell, 1990). See also Schwartz, *From Philosophy to Existentialism*, 260. Ernst Cassirer observed that the future as a theoretical concept is "a prerequisite of all man's higher cultural activities" (Ernst Cassirer, *An Essay on Man: An Introduction to a Philosophy of Human Culture* [Garden City, NY: Doubleday, 1953], 78). He also called it "symbolic future" and "prophetic' future," in that it speaks of a moral and religious ideal that cannot be deduced from past experience.

67 "Redemption, Prayer, Talmud Torah," 60.

is anchored in the halakhah, which records and regulates the existential frame. Repentance, *hatarat nedarim* ("the absolution of vows and oaths"), and *asmakhta* ("collateral security with condition of forfeiture beyond the amount secured"), which are clearly halakhic issues, point directly to the discovery of selfhood and, therefore, also to the expunging of past bonds of superficial and artificial existence. Now authenticity will replace the nonauthentic. In consequence, a person's repentance is accepted, his vow is absolved, and the irresponsible monetary agreement will be dissolved.[68] The halakhah is an expression of the discovery of authentic existence and the creation of the personality, in answer to its authentic needs and its fundamental existential characteristics, which it rivets with legal bonds. Conversely, the halakhah rejects shallow and nonauthentic existence. The most meaningful halakhic expression, however, of the exposure of the "I" and its renewed formation is undoubtedly prayer itself, which becomes an act of redemption.

Prayer as Self-Discovery

R. Soloveitchik bound together a few existential features in his interpretation of prayer: suffering, intersubjective communication ("communing"), meaning, dignity, and freedom. These characteristics connect with one another in redemption and in prayer. "The Halacha has viewed prayer and redemption as two inseparable ideas."[69] The two elements of redemption are authentic, subjective existence, on the one hand, and, on the other, gaining knowledge of this existence itself. Prayer is mainly awareness. It redeems, because it exposes the worshiper to his existential frame, and gives it a presence in the face of his fundamental needs.

How does prayer bring man to confront his authentic dimension? R. Soloveitchik specifically resorted to the utilitarian dimension of prayer, that is, prayer as petition and as the filling of need, in order to link it to authenticity: "through prayer man finds himself. Prayer enlightens man about his needs."[70] Petitionary prayer played an important role in the study of the consciousness of prayer, as we already saw in the analysis of *Worship of the Heart*.[71] Knowing one's true needs generates existential awareness.

---

68 "Redemption, Prayer, Talmud Torah," 63-64.
69 "Redemption, Prayer, Talmud Torah," 55. R. Soloveitchik referred to the juxtaposition of redemption and the *Amidah*.
70 "Redemption, Prayer, Talmud Torah," 66.
71 See above, Chapter Two.

The "superficial" utilitarian petition has its roots in the discovery of the authentic deep dimension of existence: utilitarian needs are merely an expression of authentic needs. The authentic need for meaningful existence, existential confidence, and overcoming finitude creates existential suffering. Unsurprisingly, the heart of the prayer service, the *Amidah*, consists mainly of petitions for a person's needs. R. Soloveitchik assumed that a petitioner is in existential distress. In short, prayer directs the worshiper to be aware of his true needs, and thereby to seek a dignified existence.[72]

Additionally, prayer is directly linked to speech and dialogue. It liberates man from silence. The very ability to speak and communicate reflects awareness of the basic existential dimension. Here, as well, prayer and redemption meet.

Prayer as Process

In "Redemption, Prayer, Talmud Torah," R. Soloveitchik did not limit himself to the philosophical cohesion of prayer and redemption. He also examined the mechanism of prayer as redemption, with personal redemption in this context meaning "liberation."[73] Redemption is depicted as a process of the transition from silence to the word, through the voice. R. Soloveitchik writes that the three stages of the formation of prayer parallel the stages of redemption. The multiplicity of meanings of the stages of prayer, however, is more complex and tortuous. The following table summarizes these three stages and their acoustic, liturgical, and philosophical expressions:

phase	meaning	acoustic expression	liturgical expression	philosophical expression
1	lack of knowledge about the true needs of the existence	silence	–	–
2	exposure to the true needs of the existence	cry [*tzeʻakah*]	*selichot*	concrete existence
3	observation and understanding of the true needs and the ways of satisfying them	word	wording of prayers (*seder tefillot*)	act of consciousness

---

72 "Redemption, Prayer, Talmud Torah," 67.
73 "Redemption, Prayer, Talmud Torah," 66.

The three stages denote a path of spiritual elevation ("when prayer rises from *tze'akah* to *tefillah*").[74] Now to turn to the process of the formation of prayer, and to explain its various expressions. We should make four comments regarding the two last stages:

First, the acoustic expression on the second and the third stages differs in form. The second stage is immediate, and to some degree, primitive and primal, as well. A person discovers the very existence of his true needs and confronts historical experiences by virtue of being imperfect and finite. In this stage a person is incapable of correctly defining these needs and the elements of the experience of suffering. The sudden discovery of a new existential dimension results in crying out. The third stage is reflective and exhibits maturity. It is the apex of prayer, because at this stage, the worshiper is aware of his true needs and of his substantive and authentic existence. Here, prayer is a contemplative and cognitive act. At this juncture, prayer reflects well-formed and fashioned selfhood. Accordingly, this stage is characterized by words, used in fluent, flowing sentences.

Our second comment regards the liturgical expression. Various types of prayer belong either to the second or the third stage. R. Soloveitchik stressed that halakhah relates not only to the mature stage, but also to the primal discovery, intuitive stage that is embodied in crying out. Halakhah records and balances the discovery stage as well, albeit only indirectly, by allusion. He included in the term "halakhah" both *minhag* [custom], which refers to the second stage, and definitive law, which refers to the third stage. He maintained that the diverse expressions of prayer are included in halakhah:

> *Tze'akah* is not only a phenomenological, but a Halachic-religious reality. *Tefillah*, though it represents a more advanced awareness, does not replace *tze'akah*, but co-exists with it. [...] In Halachic liturgy, prayer at the stage of *tze'akah* is called *selichot*. [...] While *tefillah* is a meditative-reflective act, *tze'akah* is immediate and compulsive.[75]

Selichot (penitential prayers, especially recited before and during the Days of Awe) are perceived as a spontaneous, and not institutionalized, manifestation of gaining awareness of the true needs of existence. Man cries out for forgiveness on the Days of Awe and fast days. Unlike fixed prayer, anchored

---

74 "Redemption, Prayer, Talmud Torah," 68.
75 "Redemption, Prayer, Talmud Torah," 67-68. The italicized words appear in Hebrew in the article.

in a long series of halakhot, the halakhah does not regulate the *selichot*, as it does other prayers. The backbone of the text of the *selichot*, namely, the Thirteen Attributes (*midot*) of God and the confessional (*vidui*), are taken from the second chapter of BT *Ta'anit*.[76] Versions of *selichot* were recited in the Temple in times of trouble, such as droughts. Upon the Destruction they were to be recited everywhere, to the *gevulin* (that is, outside of Jerusalem).[77] R. Soloveitchik sought to locate the recitation of the institutionalized *selichot* to the Rabbinic period. In the essay "Prayer, Confession, and Repentance" he argued that "the fixed order of *selichot* is not mentioned in the Talmudic literature, but *selichot* were clearly recited in the month of divine mercy, Elul."[78] The *selichot* range from extrahalakhic spontaneity to halakhic institutionalization. On the one hand, the *selichot* are not part of the prayers established by *anshei ha-knesset ha-gedolah* (the Men of the Great Assembly), and therefore "the halakhah is not occupied with this."[79] On the other hand, the framework of preceding the *selichot* with the recitation of *Ashrei* ("Happy are those…"—taken from Ps. 84, 144, 145), and concluding them with the recitation of the full *Kaddish* endows them with halakhic character. "The halakhah imparted a sort of ritual imprimatur to the order of *selichot*."[80] At any rate, the recitation of *selichot* and their text developed during the medieval period, when their praxis was formulated,[81] in contrast with the obligation of institutionalized prayer and its nuclear formulation. The complex standing of the *selichot* creates their relationship to halakhah. Despite the non-formalistic aspects of the *selichot*, they belong to the halakhah in its broad sense, where the second and third stages are combined. Institutionalized prayer, represented in the *Amidah*, presents the third (contemplative and reflective) stage of prayer.

Third, the philosophical expression differentiates between the objective and subjective domains. In the above passages R. Soloveitchik also

---

76 "Redemption, Prayer, Talmud Torah," 68. See also "Prayer, Confession, and Repentance," 100-101.

77 On *selichot* in the Temple and their closeness to the *Hosha'anot*, see Heinemann, *Prayer in the Talmud*, 150-154.

78 Rendered into English from the text in "Prayer, Confession, and Repentance," 99; the following cited passages were similarly translated from the Hebrew text. R. Soloveitchik also based this on *Seder Eliyahu Zuta* 23.

79 "Prayer, Confession, and Repentance," 106.

80 "Redemption, Prayer, Talmud Torah," 108.

81 See, for example, Shlomo Goldschmidt, *The Order of Selichot: According to the Custom of Poland and Most of the Communities in Eretz Israel* [Hebrew] (Jerusalem: Mossad Harav Kook, 1965), 8-9.

distinguished between crying out as an expression of consciousness ("phenomenological") and as substantive expression. This distinction offers us a glimpse into the manner in which R. Soloveitchik developed his thought. The study of the religious consciousness is concerned with the substantive dimension of the religious experience. The phenomenology of religion analyzes religious acts of consciousness. In his early articles R. Soloveitchik made efforts to include halakhic praxis within the context of consciousness. He argued in his essays from the 1940s that the halakhah is an objective expression of consciousness, while the other expressions of consciousness (emotions, cognitions, theological conceptions) are subjective.[82] In these writings R. Soloveitchik introduced the notion that the religious consciousness is not limited to its subjective dimensions. In order to correctly understand the structure of the consciousness in Judaism, an objective dimension—halakhah—must be added. R. Soloveitchik raised halakhah to the realm of consciousness or, from another perspective, lowered the consciousness to the halakhic praxis. Halakhah became an element of consciousness. In "Redemption, Prayer, Talmud Torah," R. Soloveitchik placed *selichot* as a facet of halakhah in the concrete plane and separated it from consciousness. In this essay he regarded substantive existence and consciousness as two realms that are complementary, but nevertheless very disparate. We now understand that the two halakhic expressions of prayer reflect the structure of consciousness, on the one hand, and, on the other, real existence. *Selichot* are a concrete and existential halakhic expression, which is completely separate from the essential religious consciousness. Fixed ("contemplative") prayer, in contrast, is clearly an act of consciousness. Here, the existential approach joins the phenomenological one.

Finally, we should mention the creative expression that relates to authenticity. The creative personality begins with an awareness of needs. Before the act of prayer, the personality is hylic and inauthentic. Reaching understanding of one's needs through prayer exposes the personality, which thereby shifts from blurred to authentic existence.

This enables us to precisely define the dialectical features of prayer (*tze'akah* vs. *tefillah*). R. Soloveitchik asserted that institutionalized prayer is the sublime, exalted development of the cry. He further maintained that the cry does not disappear in the exalted, institutionalized stage. Clearly, then, he viewed the dialectic of prayer as one of ups and downs.

---

82 See Schwartz, *Religion or Halakha*, 63-65.

The oscillation is between cry and contemplation. As we mentioned above, R. Soloveitchik presented the cry as an existential expression, while institutionalized prayer is an expression of consciousness. That is, prayer reflects both the concrete existence (the recitation of *selichot*) and the act of consciousness (institutionalized and contemplative prayer). Consequently, the religious consciousness and concrete existence are the focal points between which a person moves. Such a conception of the consciousness and existence is not common in R. Soloveitchik's thought. We learn from this that the parallel between prayer and redemption fashioned a fresh philosophical conception.

Torah and Prayer

R. Soloveitchik perceives prayer in his thought in its broad sense. We saw above that, along with its basic legal aspect, that is represented especially in the laws of the *Amidah* and reading *Shema*, that precedes it, prayer also comprises *selichot* and voluntary petitions. Such an expansion of the term "prayer" also includes Torah.[83] The Torah reading on Mondays and Thursdays, Sabbaths, *Roshei Hodashim*, festivals and the Days of Awe is conducted during the prayer service, and this fact reveals an additional dimension of the relation between redemption and prayer. Torah study is included in the redemptive activity: "by learning Torah man returns to his own self; man finds himself, and advances toward a charted, illuminated and speaking I-existence. Once he finds himself, he finds redemption."[84]

Once again, R. Soloveitchik used a Platonic motif to explore self-discovery in Torah study. Plato presented study as recollection: before the soul descended to the body it was brimming with knowledge, and study is simply its remembrance. R. Soloveitchik mentioned the well-known aggadah about the fetus studying Torah and forgetting it upon the birth.[85] He deduced from this that the Torah is enrooted in man's existential basis. When a person studies Torah, he actually comes to know his selfhood. R. Soloveitchik intentionally moved apart from the original Platonic theory, that is, the soul's preexistence, and thereby also rid his ideas of

---

83 The relation between prayer and Torah was discussed above, Chapter One.
84 "Redemption, Prayer, Talmud Torah," 69.
85 BY Niddah 30b; *Yalkut Shimoni*, Job, 916.

their mystical remnants.[86] The components of *Worship of the Heart*—prayer and Torah study—direct man inward, to his personality. R. Soloveitchik writes:

> Once man gains insight into his true self, by activating the intellect, he finds himself on the road towards discovering ultimate redemption. When man recognizes himself, he dissipates not only ignorance, but also the mist of anonymity. He is not unknown anymore: he knows himself, and finds freedom in his knowledge. He is aware of his needs because he prays; he is aware of his intellectual creative capacities because he studies. He is sure that the needs are his own, and that the intellectual capacities are a part of himself. This twofold knowledge is cathartic and redemptive.[87]

Evidently, Torah study is perceived as a means for self-knowledge, since study is an intellectual and creative action. Coming to know oneself is not a recollection of certain contents that had been forgotten, but rather an awareness of *lamdanut* and the faculty of reasoning in their own right. Torah study means renewal and creativity.[88] R. Soloveitchik already devoted the second half of *Halakhic Man* to this idea. For him, creative activity means self-awareness and the creation of the personality. In this sense, R. Soloveitchik's viewpoint did not change over the course of time.[89]

The various expressions of prayer include the different aspects of the "I"'s creativity by the exposure of its existential basis. Here, the expression is distinctly intellectual: the Torah reading, incorporated in the prayer service. *Selichot*, fixed prayer, and Torah reading express different dimensions of redemption by coming to know one's self. The conclusion is obvious: personal redemption, or salvation, is enrooted in prayer.

---

86 As was mentioned, R. Soloveitchik formulated his ideas in the exposition of a passage from the *Zohar*, *Va'era*, which he deliberately stripped of its mystical meanings. The question of R. Soloveitchik's attitude to mysticism is a complex one, and has already been discussed by many scholars.

87 "Redemption, Prayer, Talmud Torah," 70.

88 Cf. what R. Soloveitchik said in his lessons: "When the Torah is absorbed in a person and sanctifies him, it spreads light, and the gates of understanding are opened before him; he will possess, not only a store of information, he will also possess the power of innovation and creativity, comprehension, and profundity" (*Lessons in Memory of Father*, 22).

89 See Schwartz, *Religion or Halakha*, chapters 11, 12, and 13.

From Redemptive to Tragic

"Redemption, Prayer, Talmud Torah" ends with another facet of prayer, namely, sacrifice. In other words, prayer is perceived as absolute devotion to God. R. Soloveitchik indirectly relates to prayer here as a substitute for the sacrifices, which he developed into the offering of one's self. This approach seemingly is opposed to the conception that was formulated to this point in the essay, of prayer as self-discovery. David Hartman viewed this as "a sudden dialectical leap to the opposite pole," and further argued that "R. Soloveitchik offers no explanation for this surprising and extreme shift in his orientation."[90] This position was held also by Reuven Ziegler.[91] Lawrence Kaplan maintained that if we were to delete the fifth and last section of "Redemption, Prayer, Talmud Torah," it would not be missed.[92] R. Soloveitchik, on his part, thought of the two positions as "Judaic dialectic." On the one hand, these are two "irreconcilable aspects of prayer"; while on the other hand, the aspect of sacrifice is merely "another aspect,"[93] but not one that is contradictory or in opposition. Furthermore, R. Soloveitchik regarded the two aspects of prayer as consecutive stages in the self's journey to itself and from itself. He concluded the article as follows:

> Initially, prayer helps man discover himself, through understanding and affirmation of his need-awareness. Once the task of self-discovery is fulfilled, man is summoned to ascend the altar and return everything he has just acquired to God. Man who was told to create himself, objectify himself, and gain independence and freedom for himself, must return everything he considers his own to God.[94]

In the first stage, man discovers his self by means of prayer, and he is redeemed. In the second stage he forgoes selfhood and redemption in the presence of God. The redemptive is exchanged for the tragic, and then the tragic, for the redemptive, in cyclic fashion. It was not incidental that R. Soloveitchik mentioned Moses as a tragic figure who died before realizing his life's aim ("without permitting him to cross the Jordan"). Man consciously chooses to replace the redemptive with the tragic

---

90 Hartman, "Prayer in the Thought," 198-99.
91 Ziegler, *Majesty and Humanity*, 221.
92 In a personal letter.
93 "Redemption, Prayer, Talmud Torah," 70.
94 "Redemption, Prayer, Talmud Torah," 71-72.

("Moses complied, and willingly died the 'Death by Kiss'").[95] We learn that only one who knows the true needs of his self is capable of offering it to God, or in other words, to waive it. Total devotion to God is possible only when it comes from a profound understanding of the self. Without such an awareness, devotion loses its meaning, and becomes superficial emotion. The transition from prayer as self-exposure to prayer as sacrifice does not reflect an evolutionary process, but it does evince a continuous dialectic.

R. Soloveitchik mentioned Moses' request to enter the Land and the binding of Isaac as an expression of total devotion to God and the absolute obligation to accept the divine decree and command. He emphasized, however, that such devotion and obligation are incumbent on every person[96] and not only on the patriarchs and other paradigmatic figures. Prayer, then, expresses both the first stage of personal redemption, that is, the discovery of the self, and the second stage, the renunciation of redemption and absolute devotion. These two stages, however, are not separate from one another. To the contrary: this process is remarkable in its inner cohesion. Only one who has revealed his selfhood is capable of sacrificing it.

4. Additional Expressions

R. Soloveitchik examined the relation between redemption and prayer in additional works, as well, at times as part of an incisive discussion, and in other instances, only incidentally. I will concisely present two additional discussions, on issues that complete the ways in which R. Soloveitchik understood the connection between the two consciousness and halakhic actions.

The Adjoining of Redemption to the Amidah

R. Soloveitchik devoted considerable attention in his halakhic lessons to the adjoining of *Ge'ulah* (redemption) to the *Amidah*.[97] Redemption was perceived in these discussions as praise. It is not necessarily seen as a future event, but as any salvation of Israel. Consequently, the redemption from

---

95 "Redemption, Prayer, Talmud Torah," 71.

96 "Redemption, Prayer, Talmud Torah," 71.

97 See below, Chapter Ten. On the conjunction of redemption to the *Amidah*, see Israel M. Ta-Shma, "Three Topics in Prayer," in *Atara L'Haim: Studies in the Talmud and Medieval Rabbinic Literature in Honor of Professor Haim Zalman Dimitrovsky* [Hebrew], ed. Daniel Boyarin et al. (Jerusalem: Magnes, 2000), 555-562.

Egypt, too, is deemed to be a redemptive event. R. Soloveitchik accordingly interpreted redemption as "the praise included in the blessings of reading *Shema*."[98] Reading *Shema* mentions the Exodus, and therefore falls under the category of "redemption." The blessing that precedes the *Amidah* ("who redeemed Israel") concludes the section of redemption. In his lessons and essays, R. Soloveitchik took note of two paradoxes that prayer entails:

(1) praise of God, who possesses negative attributes and therefore cannot be lauded;

(2) petition for needs from God, who transcends the material sphere.

He therefore argued for the need for special permission (*mattir,* a "permitter," as he puts it) to resolve the paradox and enable prayer.[99] This led R. Soloveitchik to build a complex legal structure in which redemption and prayer merge: redemption is the "price" of the petition in the *Amidah*. The recitation of the passages of *Shema* make possible the *Amidah*. Reading *Shema* and the following blessing are a liturgical unit that begins and concludes with redemption. However, redemption itself, led by the act of praise, needs a *mattir*, namely, *Pesukei de-Zimrah*, the "verses of praise" that precede the passages of *Shema*.

The Babylonian Talmud calls the *Hashkivenu* ("Help us lie down") blessing that precedes the evening *Amidah* the "long redemption."[100] Following a ramified halakhic discussion, R. Soloveitchik explains:

> We should emphasize in explaining the long redemption that the blessing of redemption includes the acceptance of the yoke of heaven, and as we recite: "they willingly accepted His kingship," "the Lord shall reign for ever and ever"; and similarly in *Shaharit*: "Together they all gave thanks and proclaimed His kingship, saying: 'The Lord shall reign.'" In *Arvit* entrusting one's spirit and soul in the hands of the Holy One, blessed be He, constitutes a special *kiyyum* of the acceptance of the yoke of Heaven. Proof of this is provided by the obligation of reading the bedtime *Shema*, that consists mainly of accepting the yoke of Heaven shortly before sleeping and entrusting man's life in the Creator's hands. This is the precis of the verse from which this obligation is derived (Berakhot 4:2), "So tremble, and sin no more; ponder it

---

98 *Lessons in Memory*, vol. 2, 58.
99 An extensive discussion will be devoted to this issue in Chapter Ten, below.
100 BT Berakhot 4b; 9b.

on your bed, and be still" [Ps. 4:5]. That is, accept the yoke of Heaven before you fall asleep.[101]

In this passage, R. Soloveitchik once again raises the idea that recurs in his lessons: prayer expresses man's absolute dependence upon God. The idea of dependence, based on the religious philosophy of Friedrich Schleiermacher, becomes a key experience in the thought of R. Soloveitchik,[102] and it was in this spirit that he interpreted the acceptance of the yoke of Heaven. To support the idea that the acceptance of the yoke of Heaven is a component of redemption, R. Soloveitchik drew upon the practice of reading the bedtime *Shema*. Between the lines, he might have relied on the midrashic tradition that a person's soul flies away at night and is restored by God in the morning.[103] This tradition is an expression of the experience of absolute dependence on God. The connection between redemption, the *Amidah*, and the acceptance of the yoke of Heaven reflects the consciousness of such total dependence. And just as prayer is made possible by special divine lovingkindness,[104] so too, redemption is totally dependent on God and His will. Concisely stated, "the force of prayer is bound up in entrusting the spirit."[105]

Prayer and Mystical Redemption

In my study of *Halakhic Man*, I argued that R. Soloveitchik devoted this essay to a description of his learned family, and that he himself did not bond with its consciousness. *Halakhic Man* depicts the *yeshivah* head from the Brisk dynasty, his cognition, and his ethos. Additionally, in this work "halakhah" refers mainly to theoretical *lamdanut*, in the style of the Lithuanian *yeshivot*. At times in this work, R. Soloveitchik uses the concept of redemption of the halakhic man. He explained that "the ideal of the halakhic man is the redemption of the world not via a higher world but via the world itself, via the adaptation of empirical reality to the ideal patterns

---

101 *Lessons in Memory*, vol. 2, 65.
102 See above, Chapter Two.
103 See *Midrasch Tehillim (Schocher Tob)*, ed. Buber, 25:2; *Eliyahu Rabbah*, ed. Ish Shalom (Friedmann) (= *Seder Eliahu Rabba*), 8. Cf. *Tanhuma, Balak* 14; *Tanhuma*, ed. Buber, *Balak* 23:23.
104 See above, the preceding chapter.
105 *Lessons in Memory*, vol. 2, 65.

of Halakhah."[106] This line of reasoning is exemplified by an anecdote that is indirectly related to the Yom Kippur *Amidah* of *Ne'ilah*:

> I remember how once, on the Day of Atonement, I went outside into the synagogue courtyard with my father [R. Moses Soloveitchik], just before the *Ne'ilah* service. It had been a fresh, clear day, one of the fine, almost delicate days of summer's end, filled with sunshine and light. Evening was fast approaching, and an exquisite autumn sun was sinking in the west, beyond the trees of the cemetery, into a sea of purple and gold. R. Moses, a halakhic man par excellence, turned to me and said: "This sunset differs from ordinary sunsets for with it forgiveness is bestowed upon us for our sins" (the end of the day atones). The Day of Atonement and the forgiveness of sins merged and blended here with the splendor and beauty of the world and with the hidden lawfulness of the order of creation and the whole was transformed into one living, holy, cosmic phenomenon.[107]

R. Soloveitchik would use a poetical style to portray the one-dimensional cognition of the halakhic man that, for him, corresponds to Hermann Cohen's structure of scientific cognition.[108] The rhetorical style cloaks the scientific cognition, in which there is no room for uncontrolled emotion. And now, for an analysis of the anecdote itself. Obviously, this account presents the halakhic cognition as it is formed. The cosmic event—sunset—receives its true meaning in light of the dimension of forgiveness that it contains. The halakhic perspective of sunset is equivalent to the world's mending and sanctification. From this respect, applying halakhic categories to the cosmic event is interpreted as redemption in quasi-apocalyptic dimensions. The concrete sensory event (the sunset) leads to the following two occurrences:

(1) the perception of the sunset as an experience, that is, as halakhic regularity perceived and ordered in halakhic categories (the "space" and "time" of halakhah);
(2) the creation of an analytic structure: a forgiving sunset (on Yom Kippur) and a sunset that does not exculpate (that of an ordinary day).

---

106 *Halakhic Man*, 37-38.
107 *Halakhic Man*, 38.
108 See Schwartz, *Religion or Halakha*.

Constructing the halakhic model of the sunset as atoning in the cognition of the halakhic man is equated with redemption. R. Soloveitchik concluded the vignette with the sanctification of the universe ("one living, holy, cosmic phenomenon"), to hint that the realization of the halakhic cognition replaces the cosmic-apocalyptic redemption, which is based on the formation in the distant future of a new universe.[109] The future vision of the prophets seemingly refers to the actualization of the halakhic cognition in the external world.

In a certain respect, this interpretation greatly exceeds Maimonides' naturalistic messianism, for example, since the latter argues for external, social, and political changes that will characterize redemption. In the understanding of *Halakhic Man*, in contrast, redemption occurs within cognitive halakhic strata, and is concerned with the perception of the cosmic event through the "forms of sensibility" of the halakhah, and its halakhic categorization. This redemption is distinctly cognitive, even though it has external consequences (the phase of the *Bewusstsein*, in Hermann Cohen's terminology).

The sunset is the time of the *Ne'ilah* prayer ("the closing of the gates of Heaven").[110] Here, too, R. Soloveitchik alludes that the prayer experience on this most holy day is linked to redemption; for the halakhic man, both of these experiences are anchored in the Torah study (*lomdut*) experience, that is concerned with the arousal to engage in the construction of the halakhic cognition and consciousness.

5. Summary

The nature of prayer is seen to have different aspects, in light of its identifications with redemption. Alternatively, the idea of redemption in R. Soloveitchik's writings is formulated from within an understanding of the standing of prayer. Yet, we still have not exhausted all the meanings that R. Soloveitchik found in the connection between exile, redemption,

---

109 Once again, aesthetic-poetic content and style are presented in stark contrast to the content that exchanges the cosmic vision with normative regularity. The halakhic cognition becomes aware of the vision to the extent that it is perceived within the frame of clearly halakhic-legal categories. Cf. Zachary Braiterman, "Joseph Soloveitchik and Immanuel Kant's Mitzvah-Aesthetic," *AJS Review* 25 (2000-2001): 8-9.

110 PT Berakhot 4:1, 7c. Both *Rishonim* and *Ahronim* discussed this. See, for example, Rashi on BT Taanit 26a, s.v., *Ne'ilat She'arim*.

and prayer.[111] Now, I will offer a few conclusions that emerge from the relation between these issues.

Tradition

For R. Soloveitchik, redemption is not necessarily a future event, but one that occurs in the present. By the same coin, redemption need not be a collective event. It might be an intimate occurrence that takes place in the inner layers of one's personality and the creation of the self. And finally, redemption is not necessarily an apocalyptic event, but one that happens in the present world. Man is redeemed when he creates himself, and prayer plays a significant role in the discovery of one's personality and in the formation of the self.[112] From this respect, R. Soloveitchik's thought is one link in the continuum of Jewish thought from the beginning of the twentieth century. Furthermore, prayer itself presumably undergoes a redemptive process in the person of Maimonides. This homiletical and symbolic move is intended to strengthen the image of the *Amidah* as redemptive activity. R. Soloveitchik, however, was not only a modern Jewish thinker, his thought also accords with early Jewish thought. Ezra Fleischer wrote on the *Amidah* prayer:

> The eschatological position that emerges from the *Amidah* is totally exceptional. The relatively minor place afforded in this context to the rebuilding of the Temple, the renewal of the sacrificial rite, and the image of the Messiah-king cannot but teach something about what the early legislators sought to state in this document. The *Amidah* is definitely thought to be a still hesitant first step on the way to the formulation of a new messianic doctrine in Israel. At any rate, what the *Amidah* delineates here reveals the path in which the post-Destruction sages sought to lead the people in its belief in this realm. The evolutionary, restrained nature of the program of redemption (which was actually charted out in the tempestuous, despair-laden days following the Destruction) teaches that the Rabbis did not want to instill in the people excessive expectations for the imminent, apocalyptic Redemption. Despite their maintaining and strengthening the belief in the Redemption, they afforded it the serene countenance of balance

---

111 See below, Chapter Twelve, in which the issue is discussed in relation to the synagogue.
112 Just as redemption shifts in R. Soloveitchik's writings from the general to the individual, so, too, prayer moves from the community to the individual, See Schwartz, *Faith at the Crossroads*, 193-221.

and natural means. They also desired to strengthen Israel's belonging in the present and to teach them to esteem their simple involvement in it. A nation that prays for salvation from tribulations, from sickness, and from poverty, and petitions for rain in anticipation of a rich harvest, lives in a concrete reality, and not in messianic illusions.[113]

In our analysis of *Worship of the Heart* we realized that R. Soloveitchik gave himself over to the stormy and spirited experience of the *Amidah*, to the extent of blurring the boundaries between the subjective and objective consciousnesses.[114] Intent and act were intermingled, and direct causality replaced reconstruction in the description of the relationship between the subjective and the objective consciousness. This dedication to the experiential did in no way come at the expense of the conception of personal redemption. R. Soloveitchik did not succumb to the temptation of fiery and unbridled public messianism. To the contrary: redemption was channeled inward, to the innermost strata of the religious consciousness. In prayer a person discovers his personality, ascends the rungs of the religious consciousness to communion with God, is absorbed in dialogue with himself and with his God, and attains spiritual redemption. All of these achievements pertain to the religious consciousness, and have no substantive connection to messianic activity beyond the consciousness, nor to the formation of a distinct messianic approach.

Redemption: Assuaging Tensions(?)

The connection between the *Amidah* and redemption attests, once again, to the general nature of R. Soloveitchik's thought. He was engaged with the consciousness's tensions and the basic features of existence. R. Soloveitchik saw it as his primary mission to reveal those tensions and traits. He was less concerned with the solution to existential problems.

---

113 Fleischer, "The *Shemone Esre*," 207 (republished in Mack, *Studies*, 185). See the studies by Reuven Kimelman: "The Literary Structure of the Amidah and the Rhetoric of Redemption," in *The Echoes of Many Texts: Reflections on Jewish and Christian Traditions: Essays in Honor of Lou H. Silberman*, ed. William G. Dever and J. Edward Wright, vol. 313 of *Brown Judaic Studies* (Atlanta: Scholars Press, 1997), 171-230; idem, "The Messiah of the Amidah: A Study in Comparative Messianism," *Journal of Biblical Literature* 116 (1997): 313-20.

114 As was explained above, *Worship of the Heart* is primarily a phenomenological work, and therefore, by definition, is concerned with the religious consciousness.

The main task he set for himself in his writings can be formulated in two ways:

(1) the very awareness of the consciousness and existential tensions;
(2) the balancing and regulation of those tensions.

On rare occasions R. Soloveitchik added the disappearance of these tensions in the higher experiential phases (this approach appears mainly in *And from There You Shall Seek*). The uniting chord that runs through the various periods of his thought is that the halakhah is the linchpin of the different tasks that he took upon himself. The halakhah confronts man with his consciousness and his existence, balances the consciousness and existential inclinations, and, infrequently, also leads to the unity of the consciousness.

At times R. Soloveitchik argued that the very awareness of fundamental streams of consciousness and existence, too, constitutes redemption. In most instances, he does not accept the claims of some religious existentialist thinkers that theology solves existential problems and assuages the tensions that ensue from them. He definitely, however, saw the advantage possessed by theology— to be precise, by halakhah—in its approach to these issues. He never tired of asserting that the halakhah enables a life of awareness. Accordingly, prayer as redemption is, first and foremost, a matter of awareness and cognition. The halakhah does not cloak these tensions; to the contrary - it emphasizes and highlights them. Thus, the halakhah confronts man with his concrete existence, and this encounter is an expression of redemption.

Redemption and the Amidah

R. Soloveitchik's conception of the *Amidah* as redemption is, without question, remarkable in the Orthodox Jewish world. The characterization of something as "original" is both shopworn and pretentious, and so I will not use it regarding this conception. Various aspects of this notion appear in liberal Jewish thought of the nineteenth and twentieth centuries. The application, however, of personal and phenomenological models of the *Amidah* as redemption are innovative in the twentieth-century Orthodox landscape.

The personal and spiritual perception of redemption is what enabled R. Soloveitchik to connect prayer and redemption. Now, redemption became the transition from object to subject, gaining an awareness of the features of existence and the existential experience, liberation from silence and muteness, and communication with the other. Such a conception of redemption is comfortable with the presentation of prayer as a personal and spiritual religious act. R. Soloveitchik marginalized the consciousness of the collective apocalyptic and public approaches to redemption, since such positions had no place in the consciousness and existential orientation of his thought. This enabled him to reveal a new redemptive world, one that did not necessarily follow from the literal interpretation of the sources. R. Soloveitchik, on the other hand, possessed the faculty of theological flexibility, namely, homiletical ability. The breadth of his homiletical powers enabled him to open a new world to redemption, one that was inward-oriented and personal.

At the same time, the *Amidah* was given a new character. The traditional paean to God gave way to the processes of coming to know and exposure to selfhood and the foundation of one's existence. The utilitarian petitions in the *Amidah*, also gave way to dialogue, freedom, and the quest for meaning. Routine public prayer became a collection of individuals who reveal their existential experiences. The prayer community became one that is experiential and existential. In all these aspects, R. Soloveitchik found no contradiction between tradition and innovation. Finally, it should be recalled that R. Soloveitchik also concerned himself with the communal aspect (that is, public prayer) and the synagogue as an expression of the oscillation between exile and redemption.[115]

---

115 See below, Chapter Twelve.

Chapter 10

Covering the Profound: The Legal-Halakhic Dimension of the *Amidah*

Further issues discussed in "Reflections on the *Amidah*" are the legitimization of prayer and the order of the *Amidah* (praise and petition). On the question of legitimacy, R. Soloveitchik introduced a key concept in his halakhic discussions of the *Amidah*: the *mattir*. In order to pray to the Holy One, blessed be He, permission is required. R. Soloveitchik brought a series of consciousness reasons that enable the very standing (*amidah*) before God. On the question of the order of the *Amidah*, R. Soloveitchik derived the precedence of praise to petition from an analysis of the situation of standing before God. For him, standing before God in prayer is supported by the Maimonidean approach that prayer is a Torah commandment. We need R. Soloveitchik's halakhic lessons in order to fully understand these issues. An analysis of the permission to stand before God, especially, will lead us to the halakhic realm in R. Soloveitchik's thought, which employs methodologies different from those of the areas we have already examined.

The philosophical and experiential dimension of prayer unquestionably occupied R. Soloveitchik. This said and done, he revealed great interest—perhaps the greatest interest—in a formal halakhic and *lomdut* (Lithuanian traditional yeshivot analytical Torah study) examination of prayer, that is, the very fact of this being a clearly halakhic and practical issue.[1] R. Soloveitchik enlisted his analytical, halakhic-scholarly cognitive ability to formulate insights on the obligation of reciting prayer, its wording,

---

1 R. Shagar was critical of the excessive formalism of R. Soloveitchik's analytical Torah study lessons on prayer. See Shimon Gershon Rosenberg-Shagar, *In His Torah He Meditates: The Study of Talmud as a Quest for God* [Hebrew] (Allon Shevut: Institute for Rav Shagar's Writings, 2009), 74-79.

styles, and gestures. He freely engaged in an examination of the many liturgical gestures and the textual and ideational meaning of *piyyutim* and *selichot*. We saw some expressions of this inquiry above, in the analysis of the original chapters of *Worship of the Heart*. R. Soloveitchik presented the halakhic discussion as an important source for understanding the workings of the religious consciousness.[2] In the current chapter, we will examine other instances in R. Soloveitchik's writings in which he relates to the formal and legal dimension of the *Amidah*.

The general coloration of the halakhic and Talmudic classes related to prayer that R. Soloveitchik taught is clearly phenomenological. I refer mainly to the text of *Lessons in Memory of Father, My Teacher... R. Moses Halevi Soloveitchik.* These halakhic lessons assume the basis for a complex and ramified consciousness of prayer. Just as the primary aim of the original chapters of *Worship of the Heart* was to describe the religious consciousness by means of prayer, so, too, in between the lines, the *Lessons* reveal a profound interest in the workings of the religious consciousness. This consciousness is not without oscillations and tensions. R. Soloveitchik, however, did not chart an explicit outline of the religious consciousness. The structure of the consciousness of prayer takes shape from an attentive reading of the hidden messages that are concealed within the formulations of his formal halakhic novella (*hiddush*). The reader must be attentive to the clearly religious-phenomenological aspects that emerge from the Talmudic and halakhic discussions. In the preceding chapters I devoted extensive discussions to the genesis of the structure of the consciousness of prayer. The current chapter will focus on the general *lomdut* attitude to prayer in R. Soloveitchik's writings.

1. Basic Assumptions

Before discussing R. Soloveitchik's lessons on prayer, we should mention a few basic assumptions that characterize his approach to its halakhic-scholarly cognitive (*lamdani*) dimension. We will relate mainly to ideas and not to style, since his *Lessons* and public lectures underwent editing.

Prayer and the Analytical Method of Torah Study

R. Soloveitchik's treatment of prayer is most formal and legalistic in his discussion of the attitude to prayer of the *lamdanim*—the Torah scholars and

---

2 See above, Chapter Seven.

yeshivah heads following the Brisk method of Torah scholarship. Many of these Torah scholars neglected tractates such as Berakhot and Ta'anit, which discuss prayer in all its manifestations, and these tractates were absent from study routine of many yeshivot. Since prayer was not perceived as a topic for analytical Torah study and as an intellectual challenge in the study regime of the Ashkenazi, and especially Lithuanian, yeshivot,[3] R. Soloveitchik felt the necessity of emphasizing the ongoing analytic occupation with prayer. In his well-known eulogy for his uncle, R. Zeev Soloveitchik, he depicted the boundless creative dimension of the analytical Torah scholar, who is the ideal type of *Halakhic Man*. He related to R. Hayyim Soloveitchik (the "Brisker")'s revolution in the analytical Torah study attitude to prayer as follows:

> Prayer suddenly ceased to be a technical layman (whether or not one must repeat [incorrectly recited] prayers or not) or Hasidic pietist and enthusiastic (the quest for allusions and *yihudim* [the effecting of mystical unions]) topic, and it entered the system of halakhic ideas born out of powerful postulative activity.[4] A broad field of halakhic thought, the most subtle of abstraction, precise definition, and meticulous formulation is spread out before us. The multitude of blessing and prayer formulas reflects a fundamental change in halakhic concepts. And once again, new categories, terms heard by no ear before, sprang forth from the kiln of the halakhah—the *ma'aseh* of prayer and the *kiyyum* of prayer, *kiyyum* in action, and *kiyyum* in the heart, the intent of prayer is the intrinsic body of prayer, unlike the intent of commandments which is merely an external manifestation,[5] the *heftza* [legal object] of obligation, permission, and free-will offering, communal prayer and individual prayer as two specific subjects. The matter of the omission of *Ya'aleh ve-yavo* in the *Amidah* of *Rosh Hodesh* is no less important than the question of *shi'buda de-Orayta* [whether this is a Torah obligation].

---

3 See, for example, Mordechai Breuer, *Oholei Torah (The Tents of Torah): The Yeshiva, Its Structure and History* [Hebrew] (Jerusalem: Zalman Shazar Center, 2014), 88-89.

4 Just as the postulate in Kantian thought is an idea which has meaning and a basis only within the context of ethics and teleology, so, too, halakhic creative activity has a system of ideas that ensue from it, only within which it has meaning and purpose. The "postulative" activity of prayer acquires meaning solely within the halakhic context, to remove it from activity in the sensory world or from mysticism. Ideas have a complex relation to postulates in Kantian thought, and R. Soloveitchik was inclined to an idealistic interpretation, following Hermann Cohen. See Lewis W. Beck, *A Commentary on Kant's Critique of Practical Reason* (Chicago: University of Chicago Press, 1963), 264-265.

5 R. Soloveitchik is referring to the causal relation between the subjective and objective strata of prayer, and to the very mandate of the subjective dimension.

One belongs to the ideational system of the laws of prayer, while the other is from the system of [halakhic] civil law.[6]

In R. Hayyim Soloveitchik's halakhic thought, prayer became a halakhic object is all ways, an object whose quantitative dimension was reduced to the infinitesimal by the analytical Torah scholar, and which was recreated in his cognitive world as pure quality by means of the methodology of *hilukim* (ideal legal constructs). This process expresses tremendous freedom, but is still conducted in accordance with given rules: prayer is perceived in the analytical Torah scholar's cognition as an independent issue, as something that corresponds to the system of principles and laws that were formulated in Maimonides' *Mishneh Torah* or in other sources. Prayer itself is not dependent on the world beyond cognition. R. Soloveitchik used the term "halakhic idea" to express the cognitive process, and for this creativity, "new categories" and "terms heard by no ear before." I already devoted an extensive discussion to R. Soloveitchik's use of Hermann Cohen's thought in order to describe the inner cognitive creative process.[7]

The analytical process of Torah study gives prominence to formal treatments of prayer. Prayer is now classified within the creative halakhic system, no less than legal issues deemed complex or complicated. The halakhic man, who is defined as the Brisk *lamdan*, is related to the issue of intent ("*kiyyum* in the heart"). R. Soloveitchik already explained that there is no difference, in terms of their halakhic standing, between the question of intent in prayer and any issue in civil or personal-status law. For the analytical Torah scholar, both are simply inner cognitive creations, and the only experience they entail is an intellectual one. It is only when the analytical Torah scholar finishes creating the halakhic object that he turns to the extra-cognitive reality to ensure that this creation was not a figment of his imagination (the "consciousness" phase). If the cognition corresponds to the sensory world, then the analytical Torah scholar undergoes an uplifting experience.[8] Again, such an experience is characteristic of every halakhic creativity, and prayer has no special standing in this respect.

At the beginning of this passage, R. Soloveitchik highlighted the metamorphosis that prayer underwent among the analytical Torah scholars.

---

6 Joseph B. Soloveitchik, "*Kol Dodi mi-Dod*," in Joseph B. Soloveitchik, *Words of Thought and Appreciation* [Hebrew] (Jerusalem: Eliner Library, World Zionist Organization, 1982), 79-80. See Cherlow, *Joined Together*, 103.

7 See Schwartz, *Religion or Halakha*.

8 Ibid., chapter 10 (246-266).

A person could think that the practical and mystical dimensions of prayer are added to the creative *lomdut* dimension. This, however, was not the case for the analytical Torah scholars of the classical Brisk mold. Once R. Hayyim Soloveitchik began to relate to prayer creatively, as an analytical Torah scholar, prayer "ceased" to be a source for the praxis and the ecstatic religious experience. Now prayer is a halakhic object, and nothing more.[9] We can easily understand that the formal dimension of the *Amidah* reached an extreme among the analytical Torah scholars of the Soloveitchik family. This is not the formalism of laws and halakhot, but of a legal framework. The other, transcendental, dimensions transform the *Amidah* into a mirror of the religious life that completely disappears when this prayer is an object of analytical Torah study creativity. R. Soloveitchik adopted this framework formalistically; contentually, however, I intend to show that profound phenomenological philosophical considerations drove his halakhic thought.

Family Tradition

In a series of lessons in which prayer played a major role, R. Soloveitchik mentioned his commitment to the family tradition of *lamdanut*. He wrote:

> In my opinion, "most of one's knowledge"[10] is to be understood in the sense of "the principles of his knowledge." Father, my teacher, of blessed memory [= R. Moses Soloveitchik] set me on my feet, gave me the key to Torah scholarship and to the Oral Law; he showed me the way and gave me the method to understand and become wise, to learn and to teach.[11] Whether I learned from him five hundred pages of Talmud or six hundred—the number is of no consequence. What is important, and determines the relationship of teacher to pupil, is the imparting of the method and approach, and showing the way [...] This is as clear as the noonday sun. The interpretation of the term "most of one's knowledge" is what we call *lomdut*—how to conduct halakhic

---

9 See above, n. 1. I heard from Lawrence Kaplan that R. Soloveitchik used the verse from Psalms (114:8): "who turned the rock into a pool of water, the flinty rock into a fountain," to portray his *lomdut* analyses of the tractate of Berakhot.

10 BT Bava Metzia 33a. R. Soloveitchik referred to Maimonides, *Mishneh Torah, Hilkhot Talmud Torah* (Laws of Torah Study) 5:9.

11 The specific lesson is concerned with the blessings of the Torah, and the halakhic literature already mentions that the blessings of *Ahavah rabbah* ("great love") or *Ahavat olam* ("eternal love") are in part related to blessings of the Torah. See Rashi on BT Berakhot 11b; *Machsor Vitry*, ed. S. Hurwitz (Nuremberg: Bulka, 1923), 5, and others.

discussions, to deliberate on the words of the Rabbis and the *Rishonim*, and to collect pearls and gems from them.[12]

Accordingly, R. Soloveitchik understood the special qualities of studying Torah at night as *lomdut* and as halakhic creativity. Torah study in the day-time gives "a collection of information and Torah knowledge, to understand in order to observe and to do";[13] study at night affords analytical ability and creativity (*lomdut*). When engaged in the dimension of prayer related to analytical Torah study, R. Soloveitchik devoted himself totally to it. Torah study and Torah creativity were clearly the supreme value for him, to which prayer is totally subservient. "Over a lengthy period," R. Aaron Lichtenstein writes, "at least until the end of the 1950s, the Rov [= R. Soloveitchik] had no qualms about praying privately, in order to free time for study."[14]

In his published halakhic lessons, R. Soloveitchik referred to prayer as a pure halakhic object, to which he often applied the Brisk method of study. In these lessons, *Mishneh Torah* was frequently the source paralleling *das Faktum der Wissenschaft* in Hermann Cohen's thought,[15] that is, a system of laws by which cognition creates halakhic objects from the start. Unlike his teachers, R. Soloveitchik could not completely divorce himself from the religious experience of consciousness. Even when he delved into the depths of the halakhic analysis of prayer, he was not detached from its conscious-ness dimension. We can discover the tempests of consciousness that were shunted aside in favor of the creativity of *lamdanut* only by listening to the deep nuances of this virtuoso halakhic discussion.

The Amidah *and Innovation*

R. Soloveitchik did not completely identify with the approach of the Brisk rabbis who preceded him. As we already noted, he advocated the pluralism of cognitions.[16] For him, halakhic cognition is not the only creative

---

12 *Lessons in Memory of Father*, vol. 2, 22.

13 *Lessons in Memory of Father*, vol. 2, 22. See Yochanan Silman, "The Torah of Israel in Light of Its New Interpretations: A Phenomenological Clarification," *PAAJR* 57 (1990/1991): Hebrew section, 60-61; Schwartz, *Religion or Halakha*, 269-271.

14 Aaron Lichtenstein, "Prayer in the Teaching of G[aon], R. Y. D. Soloveitchik, of Blessed Memory" [Hebrew], *Shanah be-Shanah* (1999): 288.

15 Schwartz, *Religion or Halakha*, 113-114, and more.

16 Schwartz, *Religion or Halakha*, 111, 198-201. See Jonathan Sacks, "Rabbi J. B. Soloveitchik's Early Epistemology: A Review of *The Halakhic Mind*," *Tradition* 23, no. 3 (1988): 75-87.

cognition, rather, there is epistemological pluralism (scientific cognition, mythic cognition, religious cognition, etc.). This enables us to understand how R. Soloveitchik could give lessons based on the analytical Torah study (Brisk) methodology, while also expressing independent religious phenomenological thought, which takes into account relation to the transcendental, and accordingly defines *homo religiosus*. Projecting this insight to prayer enables us to understand that R. Soloveitchik opposed the collapse of the other dimensions (praxis, objectivity, mysticism, contemplation, and the like) when confronted by the dimension of analytical Torah study. He was of the opinion that prayer could be seen as the mirror of stormy religious life, together with the halakhic creativity of analytical Torah study. The harmonization of these cognitive realms was not always his goal. That is, when he taught a lesson in yeshivah style, he maintained the style, formulation, and content of the creativity of analytical Torah study; when he delivered sermons on the weekly Torah portion or at certain events, their style and character suited a broader public (and at times here, he combined philosophical and theological notions with halakhic *lomdut*, such as in his expositions on repentance); and when he engaged in philosophical thought, he examined the features of the religious experience in the theoretical manner employed by phenomenologists.

In his halakhic lessons, extensively documented by a number of students, R. Soloveitchik usually did not incorporate any abstract idea in his analytical Torah study. Even if he did mention philosophical or theological notions, they were always in the service of the analytical Torah study. He therefore refrained from the poetic emotional formulations distinctly present in his philosophical essays, sermons, and eulogies. In many respects, this continues the study tradition of many Jewish sages in different periods, who unequivocally distinguished between halakhic creativity and philosophical idea. Nahmanides, R. Solomon ben Abraham Adret (*Rashba*), R. Yom Tov ben Abraham Ishbili (*Ritba*), R. Nissim ben Reuben Gerondi (*Ran*), and other medieval scholars composed numerous novellae, that bear almost no trace of their stimulating and ramified philosophical or Kabbalistic thought. This division is characteristic of many yeshivah heads in recent generations, from whose recorded lessons their ideational sermonizing is totally absent. R. Soloveitchik, too, refrained from abstract ideational and philosophical discussion in his analytical Torah study pursuits. His special touch is obviously evident here and there in the voicing of a philosophical thought, in the incidental mention of the *Guide of the Perplexed*, or in some restrained pen strokes in which he expresses emotions. His formal style, however, does not significantly deviate from the novellae literature and lessons of yeshivah heads that come mainly from the ultra-Orthodox world. Every lesson and every topic within it immediately begins with a quotation on which the discussion will be based, and this opening lacks rhetoric or poetical style. The analytical Torah study lesson used *lomdut* terminology, and keeps its distance from stylistic innovation.

I still maintain that the analytical discussions on Torah study and halakhah that R. Soloveitchik formulated in a dry and informative style, at least in the lessons meant for the public at large,[17] exhibit inklings and allusions with significant philosophical consequences. Furthermore, these implications constitute the basis for the discussion that he conducted in his philosophical writings. To some degree, traces of the religious consciousness that R. Soloveitchik describes with methods taken from the phenomenology of religion, are evident in these lessons. The mark of these methods seems to extend considerably beyond the formality of the Brisk method, and even beyond its adaptation to neo-Kantian models, as some scholars have sought to demonstrate.[18]

---

17 See Shlomo Zeev Pick, "Rabbi Soloveitchik and the Academic Study of Talmud and Its Implications" [Hebrew], in *Rabbi in the New World: The Influence of Rabbi J. B. Soloveitchik on Culture, Education and Jewish Thought*, ed. Avinoam Rosenak and Naftali Rothenberg (Jerusalem: Van Leer Institute and Magnes, 2010), 285. Although at times Pick included *Lessons in Memory of Father* among R. Soloveitchik's classes to the public at large, they seem to occupy a middle position: stylistically, they are closer to the classic model of halakhic novellae that are free of theoretical idea and thought, but nevertheless frequently contain philosophical allusions. Cf. the introduction to the 2002 republication of *Lessons in Memory of Father*, vol. 1, 7-9; Aviad Hacohen, "The Legal Methodology of Rabbi Soloveitchik: What's New?" [Hebrew], in Rosenak and Rothenberg, *Rabbi in the New World*, 318. Note should be taken of the differing views on the question of the extent to which *Lessons* is reflective of R. Soloveitchik's method of study. See Elyakim Krumbein, "From Reb Haim of Brisk and Rav Joseph B. Soloveitchik to 'Shiurim of Rav Aharon Lichtenstein'—the Growth of a Learning Tradition" [Hebrew], *Netuim* 9 (2002): 51-94; Avraham Walfish, "The *Brisker* Method and Close Reading—A Response to Rav Elyakim Krumbein" [Hebrew], *Netuim* 11-12 (2004): 95-137; Lawrence Kaplan, "Exposition as High Art; Review Essay," *Hakirah* 15 (2013): 91-92.

18 See Avinoam Rosenak, "Philosophy and Halakhic Thought: A Reading of the Talmud Lessons of Rabbi J. B. Soloveitchik in Light of Neo-Kantian Models" [Hebrew], in Sagi, *Faith in Changing Times*, 275-306. This influence is not expressed in the relation between source or principle and details, but rather in his general methodological approach (see below). I am convinced that, for R. Soloveitchik, the neo-Kantian approach was the proper scientific or philosophical way to explain and characterize the Brisk method of study. See, for example, Shlomo H. Pick (ed.), *Mo'adei haRav: Public Lectures on the Festivals... in Light of the Teachings of the Rav* [Hebrew] (Ramat Gan: Bar-Ilan University, 2003), 30-31; Jeffrey R. Woolf, "In Search of the Rav: The Life and

In the following sections I will examine some philosophical and consciousness aspects of prayer that emerge from R. Soloveitchik's analytical Torah study lessons. I will attempt to show that the *lamdani* discussions hint at deep and tempestuous inclinations that are not immediately evident in a first reading. Our discussion will focus on a series of lessons on prayer that appear in the second volume of *Lessons in Memory of Father*.

2. The Character of the Halakhic Discussion

R. Soloveitchik strove to include prayer in the analytical Torah study agenda. We will now examine the methodology of his lessons on prayer in two levels.

(1) In the formal legal plane, I will attempt to show his effective use of Hermann Cohen's cognitive approach to describe halakhic thought.[19]

(2) In the content plane, I will argue that the phenomenological conception of religious consciousness assumed legal standing in R. Soloveitchik's lessons. That is, he had no qualms about turning an abstract element of consciousness into a factor on which weighty halakhic considerations were dependent. In this way, the Brisk method now revolved around a philosophical idea.

R. Soloveitchik's methodology will be extensively examined in our discussion of his lesson on the blessings of the Torah. We will follow this with the idea of permission to pray in "Reflections on the *Amidah*" and in *Lessons in Memory of Father*. Finally, we will explore additional lessons to determine the presence of the dual methodology: the analytic and the phenomenological.

Kiyyum and Quality

The affinity, to the point of identification, between prayer and Torah study is an important motif that appears from time to time in R. Soloveitchik's

Thought of Rabbi Joseph Soloveitchik in Recent Scholarship," *BDD: Journal of Torah and Scholarship* 18 (2007): 5-28, especially 20-21.

19 Rosenak, "Philosophy and Halakhic Thought," showed this in a certain way, but, as was noted, my methodology is different.

philosophical and homiletical thought.[20] These two major norms are encompassed in the commandment of "worship of the heart."[21] As we already explained, the structure of such commandments differs from that of other commandments. In this commandment, the relation between the subjective and objective dimensions of the consciousness is causal and substantive, unlike other commandments in which this relation is reconstructive. The notion of the affinity between prayer and Torah study, however, appears in R. Soloveitchik's halakhic thought as well and we will examine a few developments of this idea. R. Soloveitchik's lesson on the blessings of the Torah, which begins the second volume of *Lessons in Memory of Father*, was intended to prove that the principle of the merging of prayer and Torah study clarifies a number of difficulties and halakhot. These blessings themselves represent the encounter between prayer and Torah study, and R. Soloveitchik wanted to show that this meeting expresses the substantive relation between the two religious actions. After an examination of the sources, he made two statements.

(1) The synagogue is the place of prayer, and from this respect, prayer in the study hall (*beit midrash*) has no special worth. Prayer "must be conducted only in the synagogue, which has been designated for this purpose, and not in another place, although it has twice the sanctity."

(2) The sanctity of the study hall also encompasses prayer, and from this respect, study hall prayer is of special worth. "The study hall is holy, not only for the commandment of Torah and its study, but also for the commandment of prayer—and this is on a higher level than the sanctity of the synagogue."[22]

These statements are dialectical and generate inner tension regarding the worth of prayer in the study hall. R. Soloveitchik, therefore, distinguished

---

20 See, for example, the essay "Redemption, Prayer, Talmud Torah," which was discussed above, in Chapter Nine.

21 R. Soloveitchik's central source is *Sefer ha-Mitzvot* of Maimonides, Positive Commandment 5 (*Sefer Hamitzvot: Book of Commandments* [Hebrew], ed. Joseph Kafih [Jerusalem: Mossad Harav Kook, 1971], 60-61; English translation: Maimonides, *The Commandments*, trans. Charles B. Chavel, part 1, *The Positive Commandments*, 8-9). See, for example, *Lessons in Memory of Father*, vol. 2, 13-14.

22 *Lessons in Memory of Father*, vol. 2, 12. Much has been written on the connection between Torah study and prayer. See, e.g., *Maharal, Netivot Olam, Netiv ha-Avodah* 2. On prayer and the study hall, see also Heinemann, *Prayer in the Talmud*, 251-275.

between the intrinsic worth of prayer (statement (1)) and that of prayer in relation to Torah study (statement (2)); or, in another formulation, between the *kiyyum* of prayer and its quality. Taken by itself, the place of prayer is in the synagogue. In terms of the fulfillment of the commandment, there is no difference between prayer in the synagogue and that in the study hall. The commandment of prayer, however, is to be fulfilled in its proper place, namely, the synagogue. In terms of the worth of Torah study, on the other hand, prayer is of greater quality when it is conducted in the place of study, that is, the study hall. Generally speaking, "the sanctification of prayer that is incorporated in the context of Torah [study] is of greater worth than [that in a place] set aside [*haktza'ah*] for prayer alone."[23] Now the "object" of prayer undergoes an analytical process, regarding both fulfillment and quality.

I showed in *Religion or Halakha* that such a model of thought can be explained by means of Hermann Cohen's cognitive idealism.[24] For Cohen, the phases of cognition are the following.

(1) Sensation and the meeting with the sensory-quality world (*Wahrnehmung*) present cognition with stimulation, problem, and demand.

(2) Experience, that is, the rules of mathematical-physical science or "the fact of science" intrude into philosophical thought. Philosophy is aware of a phenomenon that exists within the given (Newtonian) scientific regularity, and seeks to reveal its conditions of possibility.[25]

---

23 *Lessons in Memory of Father*, vol. 2, 12. This is much clearer, albeit less polished, in another summation of the same lesson: "Shall we say that because the study hall possesses greater sanctity, that praying in the study hall is more greatly enhanced [*hidur*]? Certainly not! On the contrary, praying in a place that is dedicated and designated for prayer is more greatly enhanced [...] [On the other hand,] the designation for prayer in the study hall is greater than the designation for prayer in the synagogue. The study hall is designated not only for Torah study, it is also designated for prayer. The synagogue is designated for prayer, while the study hall is designated both for prayer and for Torah study. The designation [*hakza'ah*] for prayer in the study hall is greater than the designation for prayer in the synagogue, because the study hall is deemed 'the gates that are distinguished through halakhah' [BT Berakhot 8a]" (Grodner, *On Prayer*, 52).

24 Schwartz, *Religion or Halakha*, 113-114. See also Lawrence Kaplan, "Rabbi Joseph B. Soloveitchik's Philosophy of Halakhah," *Jewish Law Annual* 7 (1987): 139-197, in particular, 148.

25 In epistemology, "experience" is the system of Newtonian laws formulated in physics books. In his *Ethics of Pure Will*, Cohen applied this model to ethics. In place of the

(3) The creative process begins with the goal of cognizing the object:
   (a) the differential quantitative limitation of the object to the infinitesimal;
   (b) the intellective creation of the scientific objects by rational judgments (objectivization), from the first judgment (infinitesimal) to the appearance of the object itself as pure quality within in the cognition ("the judgment of the beginning creates").[26]

The above describes the development of the "naïve" stage of cognition.

(4) Critical examination, conducted to find out whether the inner cognitive analytic creation actually corresponds to the sensory-quality reality. This is the critical phase of reason, when consciousness comes into being. The process begins with a judgment of possibility analogous to the judgment of the beginning in the "naïve" stage,[27] and concludes with the judgment of necessity.

A similar methodological process occurred in the discussion of the proper place of prayer. The phases of this process are the following.

(1) Prayer is found in specific locations (synagogue, study hall).
(2) This meeting arouses the study of authoritative sources (the discursive unit in BT Berakhot 8a; *Mishneh Torah, Hilkhot Tefillah* [Laws of Prayer] 8:3, and more).
(3) The creative process begins.
   (a) The mind is detached from concrete prayer and transitions to methodical reasoning.
   (b) Prayer in the specific locations is recreated as a cognitive halakhic object by means of the distinction between prayer in itself (whose place is the synagogue) and prayer in the study hall (the qualitative nature of prayer). This reconstruction is conducted while resolving contradictory or opposing sources.

Newtonian system we find various sets of laws, such as Roman law. Ethical rules are built from the origin (Schwartz, *Religion or Halakha*, 207-210). This approach brings the cognitive model closer to the halakhic one.

26 Hermann Cohen, *Logik der reinen Erkenntnis* (Berlin: Bruno Cassirer, 1922), 587.
27 See Cohen, *Logik der reinen Erkenntnis*, 454.

(4) The resulting conceptions are examined while facing concrete reality: is the new understanding, namely, the principle of the preference of study hall prayer, possible for actual halakhic fulfillment?

Essential Consciousness

R. Soloveitchik would now concentrate on the essence of prayer, and not on its praxis. He was interested in the essence of prayer, which led him to include it in Torah study. We will now see how the essential aspects of the relation between prayer and Torah study appear in his thought.[28] R. Soloveitchik showed the similarity between Torah study and prayer by making the obligation to pray a component of inner, subjective consciousness (the "worship of the heart"). But his aim was more far-reaching. He postulated the cohesiveness of prayer and Torah study in terms of their structure, goal, and function. In other words, he sought to show that prayer and Torah study are two normative and applied aspects of the same expression of religious consciousness, even though their worth is not equal, as we shall see below. R. Soloveitchik wrote, as an analytical Torah study scholar would, about this component of the consciousness:

> The *kiyyum* of the other commandments does not entail *avodah she-be-lev*, except, perhaps, in a general sense [*kiyyum klali*], but not as a component of that commandment per se. The one who studies Torah worships the Holy One, blessed be He, with all his heart and with all his soul, and this is the *kiyyum* of *avodah she-be-lev* for him, just as the one who prays. Consequently, Torah [study] and prayer merge into a single point and the *kiyyum* of the single commandment of *avodah she-be-lev*.[29]

R. Soloveitchik based the affinity between these two religious acts on various arguments, some of which he stated outright, while others emerge from his halakhic discussions. These arguments are the following.

(1) Torah study and prayer demonstrate that man accept the yoke of Heaven.
    Explanation: Torah study is based on the acceptance of certain principles and the adoption of time-honored tradition; this fact requires the one engaged in such study to accept the yoke of

---

28 Kaplan, "Review Essay," 92-93.
29 *Lessons in Memory of Father*, vol. 2, 13-14.

Heaven ("the very study and the act of transmission from father to son, from teacher to student, and from one person to his fellow is a magnificent demonstration of subjugation to the Holy One, blessed be He, and His Torah, and this acceptance comprises the *kiyyum* of *avodah she-be-lev*").[30] Obviously, prayer entails the acceptance of the yoke of Heaven.

(2) Torah study and prayer are a petition for man's needs.

Explanation: Torah study is a "silent and comprehensive petition."[31] The emphasis placed on the worth of nocturnal Torah study is reminiscent of the natural tendency, imprinted in the sources and customs, to cry, bemoan, and request, specifically at night.[32] In any event, R. Soloveitchik was cautious when making this statement and used the wording "apparently [*ka-nir'eh*]."[33] Prayer includes requests for man's needs.

(3) Torah study and prayer include praise of the Lord.

Explanation: Torah study comprises song and praise to God, since such extolment is grounded in knowledge of the divine attributes and imitation of His ways ("the foundation of halakhic morality, and the lamp that lights man's way in all his acts and deeds");[34]

---

30 *Lessons in Memory of Father*, vol. 2, 14.

31 *Lessons in Memory of Father*, vol. 2, 15.

32 *Lessons in Memory of Father*, vol. 2, 14. R. Soloveitchik emphasized this again (18-22), where he distinguished between the intellectual aspect of Torah study ("a collection of data") and that of "worship of the heart," namely, personality change (see below, the fourth argument). He added that the distinction between day and night is valid only for the latter. In terms of acquiring information, there is no difference between day and night.

33 *Lessons in Memory of Father*, vol. 2, 14.

34 *Lessons in Memory of Father*, vol. 2, 14. R. Soloveitchik noted the moral and practical aspect of *imitatio dei*. He based this on *Guide of the Perplexed*, and mainly on the concept of action-attributes. See, for example, Lawrence V. Berman, "Ibn Bajjah and Maimonides" [Hebrew], PhD dissertation, Hebrew University, 1959, 24, 38; Shalom Rosenberg, "'And Walk in His Ways'" [Hebrew], in *Israeli Philosophy*, ed. Moshe Hallamish and Asa Kasher (Tel Aviv: Papyrus, 1983), 72-91, and especially, 76-77; Gerald J. Blidstein, *Political Concepts in Maimonidean Halakha* [Hebrew] (Ramat Gan: Bar-Ilan University, 1983), 40; Lawrence V. Berman, "Maimonides on Political Leadership," in *Kinship and Consent: The Jewish Political Tradition and Its Contemporary Uses*, ed. Daniel J. Elazar (Ramat Gan: Turtledove, 1981), 115-116; Abraham Melamed, "Maimonides on the Political Nature of Man: Needs and Obligations" [Hebrew], in Idel, Dimant, and Rosenberg, *Tribute to Sara*, 328-30; Howard T. Kreisel, *Maimonides' Political Thought: Studies in Ethics, Law, and the Human Ideal* (Albany: State University of New York Press, 1999), 130; Dov Schwartz, *Contradiction and Concealment in Medieval Jewish Thought* [Hebrew] (Ramat Gan: Bar-Ilan University, 2002), 72-73.

Torah study engages in *in imitatio dei*. Prayer includes praise and paean.

(4) Torah study and prayer effect personality change.

Explanation: Torah study leads to renewal and change in the character and traits of the one engaged in it ("following study, we find a change in the person and a renewal of personality. The spiritual force in man expands, and its ethical power is prominent").[35] R. Soloveitchik's discussion teaches that the blessings of the Torah add prayer to the factors effecting this renewal.

(5) Torah study and prayer deepen the selection of Israel and its sanctity.[36]

Explanation: the study of Torah reveals that the Torah is uniquely suitable for the Jewish people and unveils the story of their being chosen by God. The blessings of the Torah, speaking of chosenness, emphasize this unique nature and also reflect this special relation.

These arguments are merely associative ideational moves that are formulated in the style of *lomdut*, and that seek points of similarity between Torah study and prayer. They represent, however, a much deeper phase of consciousness. R. Soloveitchik set forth a one-directional transformation of two intentional religious acts: prayer is transformed into Torah study. In other words, Torah study has the same accomplishments or consequences as prayer. The points of similarity enable him to present Torah study as including the accomplishments and experiences of prayer. He did not, however, present the opposite direction. Prayer does not leave the same impression as Torah study. Or, to reformulate this: the merging of Torah study and prayer is not the unification of two equal

---

35 *Lessons in Memory of Father*, vol. 2, 20. See Schwartz, *Religion or Halakha*, chapter 13. R. Soloveitchik presented this approach as interpretation of the "three crowns" of the Torah, the priesthood, and kingship (M Avot 4:13; *Avot de-Rabbi Nathan*, Version A, 1:41; *Mekhilta de-Rabbi Simeon bar Yohai* 19:6, and others). He linked kingship and the priesthood with prophecy, which is concerned with the renewal of the personality; consequently, Torah study is also connected with such renewal.

36 R. Soloveitchik wrote that "in truth, there are not many sanctities. There is only the sanctity of Israel on different levels" (*Lessons in Memory of Father*, 21). In his thought he sought to remove sanctity from its usual transcendental meaning (beyond the cognitive or beyond the consciousness), and to view it solely as a characteristic of material activity. See Schwartz, *Religion or Halakha*, 162-163; *From Phenomenology to Existentialism*, 295-296 and the index, s.v. "Holiness."

factors; at most, prayer is subsumed under the category of Torah study. Such inclusion is possible because both religious acts are the "worship of the heart." And R. Soloveitchik already established: "Torah study contains the *kiyyum* of prayer."[37]

R. Soloveitchik formulated a dual division, actually a hierarchy of the realization of the merging of Torah study and prayer. One realization (*kiyyum*) of this merging is prayer in the study hall. Prayer has a special, qualitative, value when it is recited in the study hall. Even though the synagogue is the natural venue of prayer, it assumes special meaning in the study hall. A second actualization is the conducting of prayer specifically where a person learns, namely, in *his* study hall. We learn from what R. Soloveitchik writes that such *kiyyum* is of greater quality than prayer in a study hall that is not one's own. "There is a special *kiyyum* of the combining in *avodah she-be-lev* of Torah with *avodah she-be-lev* by prayer. The halakhah that both are to be conducted in the same place was accepted within the context of this *kiyyum*."[38] We, therefore, learn that R. Soloveitchik established the following hierarchy:

(1) prayer in a synagogue;
(2) prayer in a study hall;
(3) prayer in the worshiper's regular study hall.

This is not an actual hierarchy, but a casuistic structure of "three *dinim* [categories]," that is, a division of the same topic into three aspects, each of which has its own legal significance. Prayer in a synagogue is the optimal option in terms of prayer in its own respect, that is, as regards the very obligation to pray ("the *kiyyum* of prayer"). However, from the aspect of the importance of Torah study, the optimal choice is prayer in a study hall ("the quality of prayer"). And in terms of one's personality and the religious consciousness, the best choice is "prayer in a place of Torah," in one's regular study hall.

Thus, the merging of the two religious acts, to be more precise, the elevation of prayer to the level and surroundings of Torah study, in an important value in R. Soloveitchik's halakhic thought. The blessings of the Torah

---

37 *Lessons in Memory of Father*, vol. 2, 14.
38 *Lessons in Memory of Father*, 17. See Aharon Lichtenstein, "Eulogy" [Hebrew], *Mesorah 9: Eulogies for Our Master, the Gaon, R. J. B. Soloveitchik, May the Memory of the Righteous Be for a Blessing for the World to Come* (February 1994): 29-31.

faithfully express the unifying aspect of these two acts. These blessings also reflect the dominance of Torah study. In his lessons he called Torah study "the shining and most brilliant crown,"[39] and added: "Torah study is the most sublime prayer that an Israelite can perform."[40] He further strengthened the merging of these two values in his theoretical thought.

An additional story in the structure of the consciousness of prayer is the search for the foundations of the dialogic situation in which man stands before his God. The following discussion is devoted to this situation and to its very legitimacy—issues that troubled R. Soloveitchik.

3. The Permission to Pray

We have so far presented in detail R. Soloveitchik's methodology in his arguments that reflect traditional analytical Torah scholarship, on the one hand, and, on the other, the consciousness-philosophical element as a consideration within this same body of traditional scholarship. The element of consciousness was undoubtedly the most innovative in the corpus of the many such scholarly lessons that have been published in the past generation, and therefore I will concentrate on this aspect below. As was noted, the second part of "Reflections on the *Amidah*" is concerned with the questions of the legitimacy of prayer,[41] and R. Soloveitchik employed his explanation of this issue as a halakhic tool to contend with questions and contradictions regarding prayer. I will now discuss the place of the *mattir*—the permission to pray—in R. Soloveitchik's thought. The discussion has two parts:

(1) The *mattir* in the essay "Reflections on the *Amidah*."
(2) The *mattir* in his halakhic lessons.

---

39 *Lessons in Memory of Father*, 21.
40 *Lessons in Memory of Father*, 15.
41 R. Soloveitchik wrote in a few places of the theologically and morally problematic nature of prayer, while nonetheless mentioning the consideration shown the religious consciousness and its profound aspiration to praise God. See, for example, "Ha-Berakhot be-Yahadut" [The Blessings in Judaism], in *Yemei Zikaron* [Memorial Days], trans. Moshe Kroneh (Jerusalem: Elinor Library, 1996), 34; "Prayer, Confession, and Repentance," 102-105. In another place Grodner writes in his name: "Man is not worthy to stand before the Holy One, blessed He, in prayer. Prayer is a prideful act of man" (Grodner, *On Prayer*, 21).

Prayer and Prophecy

Maimonides' revolutionary approach stating that a person stands before God, praises Him, and petitions for his needs by force of Torah law needs to be explained, since standing before God is paradoxical. Such a clarification is especially imperative for petitionary prayer. "Can man attain a foothold within Divine transcendence? Can he shower Him with a plethora of insignificant matters?"[42] This question, however, is valid not only for inconsequential mundane needs, it also is relevant for paeans. Two elements of the consciousness of God do not allow the situation of prayer.

(1) The divine fullness. Since God is infinite and encompasses all, there is no place for the finite and limited to stand before Him.

(2) Otherness (transcendence). Since God is completely different from anything familiar, nothing can bridge the chasm between creature and Creator.

Accordingly, man's status before God is absurd. Since we are concerned with an issue that is of a halakhic nature, for prayer is a clearly halakhic obligation, then this situation becomes, not only paradoxical—it is also forbidden. What, then, permits us to pray? Special license is needed to enable the fulfillment of the halakhah. R. Soloveitchik presented this problem within a comparison with prophecy. We should examine this passage in its entirety:

> Of course, the experience of fear and trembling, which is an integral part of religious life, complicates the problem of prayer and turns it into a riddle. On the one hand, it is impossible for man to come close to God. The more he approaches God, the more man negates his finite human status. Finitude is swallowed up by infinity and perishes in its labyrinth. Man at times flees from God and hides from Him, lest he be engulfed: "And Moses hid his face, for he feared to look upon God" (Ex. 3:6). Man's selfhood and self-confidence are annulled in confrontation with the greatness of God and His majesty. If so, the question arises: How can prayer take place? Prayer is standing before God, in the presence of the *Shekhinah*; but how can man find himself in the presence of God without losing his individual existence?

---

42 That is, everyday needs; from "Reflections on the *Amidah*," 150.

God, the awesome and terrifying sovereign,[43] negates all being, annihilates all otherness, and turns all else into nothingness.[44] When Moses pleaded with God to be shown His Glory, he received but a curt reply: "You cannot see My Face, for no man can see Me and live" (Ex. 33:20). When God speaks to him, the prophet recoils and collapses in trembling. Daniel attests to such a psychological state, and Rambam incorporated the latter's description into his code: "When any of them prophesy, their limbs tremble, their physical powers are attenuated, they lose control of their senses, and thus their minds are free to comprehend what they see, as it states concerning Abraham 'and a great dark dread fell over him' (Gen. 15:12). Similarly, Daniel (10:8) states: 'My appearance was horribly changed and I retained no strength'" (*Hilkhot Yesodei ha-Torah* 7:2).[45]

The starting point is the pole of personal self-negation in the presence of God. The experience of drawing inward and of nullity before God makes standing in prayer impossible, and some factor has to be found to enable prayer. The task of finding "a basis for permitting flesh and blood to approach his Creator"[46] is imposed on the halakhah.

The pole of self-negation in this passage by R. Soloveitchik is represented by the prophets. Moses, Daniel, and other prophets attest to this drawing inward that characterizes the prophetic experience. This is understandable: Maimonides ruled that prayer is a Torah mandate. R. Soloveitchik consequently confronted it with the prophet's self-negation. He therefore also mentioned Moses, the bringer of the Torah, as fleeing from God. The paradox inherent in the question of the legitimacy of prayer arises within the Torah itself: the prophet (Moses) obligates others to pray, when he himself is denied standing before God.

The comparison of prayer with prophecy is complex and problematic. R. Soloveitchik emphasized in several places in his writings that prayer is the continuation of prophecy. He further clarified that the distinction between them lies in the exchange of speakers: in prophecy God speaks and man hears, while in prayer, it is man who speaks and God who hears. It seems, however, from the passage cited above that the prophets failed and were unsuccessful in overcoming the dialectic typical of standing before

---

43 The divine name *Elohim* carries a meaning of authority, and therefore the court is called by this name, as well. R. Judah Halevi argued that this is the plural of *Eyal*, that is, "power" (*Kuzari* 4:1).
44 See BT Kiddushin 80a.
45 "Reflections on the *Amidah*," 149-150.
46 "Reflections on the *Amidah*," 150.

God. The prophet completely negates himself and cannot express himself. R. Soloveitchik, therefore, stressed at the end of this passage that the prophet Daniel had his outstanding characteristic (*hod*, meaning "majesty")[47] shattered and became a nullifying factor when facing God.

In the end, the prophet expresses human needs before God, but not in a balanced manner. Nullification is the dominant factor in prophecy. Trembling limbs are integral to prophecy. The prophet stands before God in a position of inferiority. Prayer, in contrast, succeeds in overcoming the dominance of fear and self-negation. The worshiper stands before God self-assured. He combines the great self-negation before God with petitionary prayer, which highlights selfhood and its personal needs.

The worshiper acquires the right to prayer thanks to a special permission. In the face of the nullification of the experience of God, the worshiper retains his identity and his awareness of his needs following a string of permissions which we shall discuss below. This, then, is R. Soloveitchik's implicit question: How did prayer succeed, where prophecy failed? The dialectic scene in this passage only intensifies in light of the fact that prayer is not the exact continuation of prophecy, as R. Soloveitchik attempted to argue in various places. In between the lines, he hints that the halakhah is superior to prophecy, since the former found the balance between the polar experiences of God, while prophecy is bound to only a single pole, that of self-negation and withdrawal within oneself in the face of the divine.

Now we must find, from the halakhic aspect, permission that will enable prayer. This license provides a basis for the self-assurance of standing before God, which the prophets lack. In "Reflections on the *Amidah*" R. Soloveitchik offers four such *mattirim*. The first three are explicit, while there is only an allusion to the fourth toward the end of the essay.

(1) The religious necessity for prayer is anchored in the human structure, and as such is a given (consciousness).
(2) Historical precedent: the Patriarchs and the prophets prayed (the tradition of prophecy).
(3) The sacrifices constitute standing before God (halakhah).[48]
(4) The miracle: God effects phenomena that are incomprehensible in the regular order of nature (theology).[49]

---

47 Following Dan. 10:8. Intriguingly, *Malbim* (R. Meir Loeb ben Jehiel Michael Malbim) understood this as "the power of the intellect."

48 "Reflections on the *Amidah*," 150-151.

49 Ibid. 179-80. R. Soloveitchik did not explicitly present this as a *mattir*, but after he raised the problem of the absurdity of prayer, he wrote: "The answer, that the essence of prayer

These four considerations grant release from the prohibition to pray, which follows from the absurdity of the prayer situation. The first permission sharpens the latent distinction between prophecy and prayer, and highlights the superiority of the latter. R. Soloveitchik writes:

> Prayer is a vital necessity for the religious individual. He cannot conceal his thoughts and his feelings, his vacillations and his struggles, his yearnings and his wishes, his despair and his bitterness—in a word, the great wealth stored away in his religious consciousness[50]—in the depths of his soul. Suppressing liturgical expression is simply impossible: prayer is a necessity. Vital, vibrant religiosity cannot sustain itself without prayer. In sum, prayer is justified because it is impossible to exist without it.[51]

The permission to pray is inherent in the structure of the religious consciousness. Just as the nullifying divine is a component built into this consciousness, and there can be no such consciousness without this nullification, so, too, prayer is an act of consciousness without which the religious consciousness cannot exist. Prayer is a necessity. R. Soloveitchik did not speak in this manner regarding prophecy. Prophecy is the perfection of

---

[…] is an opaque riddle. We do not comprehend the mystery of sacrifice-prayer, and the idea of restoration is also opaque and not understood - how can man appear before God and how can one imagine standing before Him—remains in full force. Therefore, from the outset, we are compelled to say about the whole subject of prayer that it is miraculous from beginning to end" (179-180). Actually, R. Soloveitchik's argument here is that prayer is hidden and incomprehensible. This is also shown by the word "miraculous." The assertion that the question of the possibility of prayer remains unanswered contains the argument that there is a *mattir*, which we cannot identify. It therefore seems that R. Soloveitchik presented the *mattir* as a miracle; and miracles are rooted in history and the Jewish sources.

50 In "Reflections on the *Amidah*," 146, R. Soloveitchik writes that prayer is an expression of "antithetical, dynamic experiences," that is, of "love and fear," and of "total commitment to Him and cleaving unto Him." This means that prayer becomes a mental necessity, since *homo religiosus*, by definition, finds himself in a situation of contrasts. This condition oppresses him, since the sense of simultaneous attraction and repulsion weighs heavy on the soul. Prayer as expression enables the religious individual to bear these contrasts.
  Incidentally, one of the contrasts mentioned by R. Soloveitchik is the distinction between "total commitment" and "cleaving." He himself might have come to the distinction drawn by Gershom Scholem between assimilation in God and presence within Him while preserving one's personality. He ascribed *devekut* to Hasidism, but not assimilation. The English version of the essay, "*Devekut*, or Communion with God," was first published a the end of the 1940s (in *Review of Religion* 14 [1949/1950]: 115-139) and was reprinted two decades later, in the collection *The Messianic Idea and Other Essays* (New York: Schocken, 1971), 203-227.
51 "Reflections on the *Amidah*," 150.

the consciousness, since it places the supreme aim before it, but prophecy is not a necessity for the consciousness. If we return to R. Soloveitchik's classic distinction between prophecy and prayer, we can formulate this as follows: the monologue with God is necessary for the consciousness, while the dialogue is not. The religious consciousness is conditional upon prayer, while prophecy simply serves it as an end and goal.

R. Soloveitchik labored to blur and moderate the distinction between prophecy and prayer. Accordingly, the second permission shows the Patriarchs, Moses, and the prophets engaged in the tradition of prayer. This second permission reinforces the first. The prophets, too, needed prayer. The Patriarchs, Moses, and the prophets were "conversing with Him as a man would with a friend," but this was after they "fell before God in supplication."[52] Even a prophet needs prayer in order to stand before God.

The third permission is clearly halakhic. The sacrifice draws man closer to God and enables him to stand before Him.[53] Thus, the halakhah is the dominant factor in the permission to pray, and in this case, prophecy is shunted aside to the edge of the consciousness. R. Soloveitchik softened the distinction by attempting to unite the second and third permissions. "Prayer is justified by both factors, historical precedent and the ceremonial law of the Temple cult."[54]

We see that R. Soloveitchik attempted to create a complementary structure of permissions to pray in "Reflections on the *Amidah*." He wanted to paint a moderate and harmonious picture of prophecy, prayer, and halakhah. He was not successful in this endeavor. There is an underlying tension between prophecy, on the one hand, and prayer and the halakhah, on the other. This tension is ever-present between the lines, and cannot be missed in a close reading. In any event, the question of permission to pray often occupied R. Soloveitchik in his writings.

---

52 "Reflections on the *Amidah*," 150-151.

53 According to the prayer of Solomon, the Temple was primarily a place of prayer. Ron Margolin wrote: "According to this conception, prayer is the fundamental action undertaken in the Temple, although in practice prayer is adjunctive to the offering of sacrifices" (*Inner Religion*, 102).

54 "Reflections on the *Amidah*," 151. R. Soloveitchik thereby sought to resolve the two opinions: that the Patriarchs established the prayers, and that the prayers were instituted to replace the daily sacrifices (BT Berakhot 26b). The first view reflects the second permission (historical tradition), and the second, the third permission (sacrifices). R. Soloveitchik implicitly intended to argue that the passage in the Talmud did not relate to the source of prayer itself, but to the permission to pray. Each opinion reflects a different permission.

Prayer as Divine Lovingkindness

We will now turn to the halakhic aspect of *Lessons in Memory of Father*. We should take note of an insight that characterizes the halakhic discussion of prayer. R. Soloveitchik maintained that, fundamentally, prayer is patently divine lovingkindness. From the outset, man, on his own, cannot pray. The act of prayer is not self-understood. To the contrary, it is silence in the face of the divine that is self-understood. He gives two reasons for this in these lessons.

(1) Praise: God is above any possible praise. The negation of the divine attributes expresses total perfection, and therefore praise is actually denigrating, as was discussed above (see the *Hallel* texts).
(2) Petition for needs: God's exaltation precludes any possibility of petition for one's everyday needs, and, in effect, denigrates it.

Consequently, R. Soloveitchik coined the concept of *mattir* or *heter* (permission) to pray: divine lovingkindness enables prayer, as there exist defined and explicit legal boundaries attesting to such a possibility. R. Soloveitchik wrote in his *Lessons*:

> For how can man, who is short-lived and sated with trouble,[55] approach the King in petition and supplication? Prayer in its entirely is a gift of the Holy One, blessed be He, to flesh and blood in His great lovingkindness, and this is the greatest lovingkindness that the Creator gives the creature. Consequently, the halakhah determined that this permission [*heter*] is dependent solely upon the format of prayer and its halakhot. It is forbidden to cry out to the Lord without using the form and format of prayer.[56]

As we saw above, the *mattirim* are an important consideration in R. Soloveitchik's lessons. R. Aharon Lichtenstein stressed the absurdity of asking for one's needs in R. Soloveitchik's conception of prayer and described the place of the *mattir* in this philosophy as follows:

> But according to the Rav, a person may indeed approach God and present his requests. Human beings who dwell in this physical world have all kinds of deficiencies, wants and aspirations, and as a result they sometimes choose to knock on the gates of Heaven, to break through the barricades, and to

---

55 Following Job 14:1.
56 *Lessons in Memory of Father*, vol. 2, 49.

present themselves before God asking that He answer their requests. Would we dare to act in this way before a king of flesh and blood? Would we shout, demand, request and plead? Where do we find such audacity? How do we allow ourselves such "chutzpa" in our relationship with God? This led the Rav to speak at length of the necessity for the existence of "permission" (a "*mattir*") for tefilla, something that would serve as a license of sorts, and in this regard he pointed towards a number of halakhot.[57]

R. Soloveitchik stated that, in the final analysis, man is permitted to make personal requests after completing the *Amidah*. In this manner the personal petition joins the set text of the *Amidah*; and each requires a halakhic *mattir*.[58] He generalized: "The very nature of all prayer requires a special *mattir*."[59] He set forth a clear statement of consciousness: the consciousness act of prayer is the result of patent divine lovingkindness, God's gift to mortals. Accordingly, the consciousness of the worshiper is bound up with what Schleiermacher called the "feeling of absolute dependence."[60] Prayer reflects man's dependence on divine lovingkindness and his own absolute nullity in the face of the perfection of omnipotent God. After God has made prayer possible, the dialectic between man's total insignificance and his standing before God in prayer becomes a reality. Without the *mattir*, however, such movement would be impossible.

Once again, we see that R. Soloveitchik's halakhic lessons, the majority of which are worded in a formal halakhic style, transform the act of consciousness into a clearly legal consideration. The license to pray, grounded in profound theological considerations, becomes a tool in analytical Torah study. We will now continue to observe the appearances of the *mattir* to pray in R. Soloveitchiks lessons.

Praise and Paean

Following Jewish liturgical tradition, R. Soloveitchik viewed praise as an outstanding expression of prayer, and in his halakhic lessons, too, he attempted to find subterranean streams of the consciousness of praise. He examined the analytical aspects of laudatory prayer relating to Torah

---

57 "Prayer in the Teachings of Rav Soloveitchik ZT"L," summarized by Aviad Hacohen, part 2, in *The Israel Koschitzky Virtual Beit Midrash*, accessed September 6, 2018, http://etzion.org.il/vbm/english/archive/ralpray2.htm. See also passim.

58 *Lessons in Memory of Father*, vol. 2, 49-51.

59 *Lessons in Memory of Father*, vol. 2, 52.

60 See Chapter Two, above.

study in his lesson on *Pesukei de-Zimrah*,[61] which follows the lesson on the blessings of the Torah. Deep and tempestuous consciousness processes recorded, balanced, and channeled by halakhah are evident between the lines in his formulation of these aspects.

The starting point of the lesson is the distinction between the reading of texts that are concerned with praise (*Pesukei de-Zimrah*) and their recitation as *Hallel*. The reading of the texts is "the praise of the Omnipresent [*Makom*]," while their recitation as *Hallel* is an autonomous concept, "as praise to the Creator."[62] Accordingly, the *Hallel* paean is preceded by the blessing for a commandment ("… who has sanctified through His commandments, and commanded the reading of *Hallel*"), while *Pesukei de-Zimrah* is not preceded by such a blessing, but only by *Barukh she-amar* ("Blessed is He who spoke," which is not a blessing for a commandment). R. Soloveitchik attempted to contend with the basis for this distinction through a precise normative separation between the reading of the verses of praise for the sake of praise and their recitation in *Hallel*. The difficulty lies in the similarity between the two. Both *Pesukei de-Zimrah* and *Hallel* include entire chapters from the book of Psalms. The difference is that *Hallel* has a distinct social and communal character, while *Pesukei de-Zimrah* lacks such nature. R. Soloveitchik framed this argument as follows.

(1) The chapters in *Pesukei de-Zimrah* are regarded as a collection of verses, while in *Hallel* they are considered *parshiyot* (integral units of the text).

(2) Verses are not repeated in *Pesukei de-Zimrah*, but they are in *Hallel*.[63]

Consequently—

---

61 R. Soloveitchik argued in "Reflections on the *Amidah*" that *Pesukei de-Zimrah* expresses the aesthetic cosmic experience, while the blessing of *Gevurot* reflects the moral cosmic experience. "Those who arranged the prayer introduced the cosmic-majestic element into the *Pesukei de-Zimrah* […] but not into the *Amidah* prayer" ("Reflections on the *Amidah*," 158). See below, Chapter Eleven.

62 *Lessons in Memory of Father*, vol. 2, 23.

63 Maimonides mentions the multiplicity of practices (*minhagim*) regarding the recitation of *Hallel*. See Isadore Twersky, *Introduction to the Mishneh Torah of Maimonides* [Hebrew edition], trans. M. B. Lerner (Jerusalem: Magnes, 1991), 94. See also Shmuel Sprecher, "*Hallel*: Things as They Are" [Hebrew], in Boyarin et al., *Atara L'Haim*, 221-231.

(3) In *Pesukei de-Zimrah* there is no "special connection to the public,"[64] while such a bond exists in regard to *Hallel*.

This discussion introduces an exacting examination of the boundaries, possibilities, and ways of praising God. R. Soloveitchik distinguished between the public, ceremonial, and institutionalized aspect of praise and the personal, intimate dimension. The latter is expressed in the fact that one of the laws, as set forth by Maimonides in *Mishneh Torah*, is that each worshiper reads *Pesukei de-Zimrah* by himself, while the *shaliah tzibbur* (prayer leader) commences with the *Kaddish* preceding *Barkhu*.[65] This arrangement lays down different levels of praise. Some praise is personal ("as verses"), while other is communal ("as [whole] *parshiyot*," suitable for public reading).

R. Soloveitchik proceeded from his discussion of the ceremonial dimension of praise to an examination of its consciousness dimension. He highlighted the contrast within and paradox of the obligation to praise God. On the one hand, man naturally desires to laud God. Thanksgiving for and submission to God's bounty and power are natural inclinations of consciousness. On the other hand, man is inherently finite and base, and therefore is incapable of praising the absolute divine perfection. The presumption to praise God is theologically worthless, and even borders on impudence and brazenness of character. As R. Soloveitchik shows in his phenomenological writings, the halakhah records the tensions in the consciousness and channels them. The consciousness of praise, as well, is explained in such a manner.

The basic assumption of the halakhah regarding the objective dimension of the consciousness is that man is incapable of extolling God because of His sublimeness and perfection, as we discussed extensively above. Accordingly, voluntary praise of God is forbidden, and could even be viewed as defiance. In order not to ignore the natural inclination of the consciousness to offer praise, there is a need for a *mattir*, an explicit halakhic

---

64 *Lessons in Memory of Father*, vol. 2, 24. On *Pesukei de-Zimrah*, see Israel M. Ta-Shma, "*Pesukei de-Zimrah* and Its Standing in the Prayer Service" [Hebrew], in *Studies in Memory of Professor Ze'ev Falk*, ed. Michael Corinaldi et al. (Jerusalem: Schechter Institute of Jewish Studies, 2005), 269-275. In his philosophical talks, R. Soloveitchik would distinguish between *Pesukei de-Zimrah*, which reveals the miraculous character of the natural order, and *Hallel*, which reflects manifest divine miracles (as is often reflected in the Biblical miracles). Possibly, then, *Pesukei de-Zimrah* reflects a higher degree of spiritual abstraction than *Hallel*.

65 *Lessons in Memory of Father*, vol. 2, 23, based on Maimonides, *Mishneh Torah, Hilkhot Tefilah ve-Nesiat Kapayim* (Laws of Prayer and the Priestly Blessing) 9:1.

directive with specific boundaries that will abrogate the prohibition in special circumstances and, in its stead, allow praise.

We presented above three *mattirim* that are listed expressly in "Reflections on the *Amidah*," and an additional one to which the essay alludes. R. Soloveitchik's discussion of the very possibility of laudatory prayer contains at least two additional *mattirim*.

(1) The first *mattir* is related to the situation when official thanksgiving is "a commandment in its own right, or ensues from another commandment, as on Hanukkah or a Festival."[66] In such a case the obligation (*hovat gavra*—a personal obligation) enables the act of praise. There is no need for any special act or initiative by the worshiper to authorize the praise. The *mattir* is inherent in the duty to recite *Hallel*.

(2) The second *mattir* appears in the situation when thanksgiving verses are read within the context of formal Torah readings. In this case, praise is facilitated by the authority of Torah study, whose substantive influence on prayer was shown above. Unlike the preceding *mattir*, action, namely, the act of Torah study, is needed here to enable the praise. *Pesukei de-Zimrah* is included in this *mattir*.

The book *The Soul of the Rav* adds a few more *mattirim*.

(3) Tradition of praising: Ps. 145 and the introductory phrase before the *Hallel*, "Happy [*Ashrei*, which gives its name to the entire passage] are those who dwell in your house" (Ps. 84:5), that are recited before the *Amidah* in the morning *Shaharit* and afternoon *Minhah* services, function as permission. "It seems that the verse in *Ashrei* that serves as the *mattir* is the verse: 'One generation shall laud Your works to another' (Ps. 145:4). That is, our fathers and our father's fathers acted in this manner, and we follow in their footsteps."[67] In other words, the tradition provides a special permission to pray. As noted before, tradition was also the second *mattir* mentioned in "Reflections on the *Amidah*."

(4) Tradition of religious poetry. The authority of King David enables prayer for later generations.

---

66 *Lessons in Memory of Father*, vol. 2, 25.
67 Schachter, *The Soul of the Rav*, 109.

Accordingly, the recitation of *Barukh she-Amar* was instituted before commencing the recitation of *Pesukei de-Zimrah*, for it is a *mattir*, and this is *reshut* (like the recitation [in prayer during the Days of Awe] of the secret of the wise and the discerning [*mi-sod hakhamim u-nevonim*]),[68] [thereby] saying, with the poetry of Your servant David we will laud, praise, and aggrandize You. We hereby rely upon King David, who composed these chapters of Psalms that we are about to recite now.[69]

(5) *In imitatio dei*: "For we are permitted to plumb the depths of the attributes of the Lord so that we will know how to act in His ways, by force of the commandment to be similar to Him."[70] That is to say, concern with the divine attributes with the aim of imitating them grants permission to pray. The intellectual engagement with these attributes is insufficient. The ethical behavioral goal of imitating divine conduct is what makes prayer possible.

Yemei Zikaron adds yet another *mattir*:

(6) Theurgy: R. Soloveitchik made use of a Kabbalistic illustration, that of the male and female dimension of the Godhead. The two dimensions are disjoined, and only human praise can bring them together. Just as man needs God, so, too, does God need man, and this fact makes it possible to address Him.[71] If we transfer this symbolic language to modern terminology, we can say that the high value given to dialogue enables addressing God in praise. Dialogue is so significant that even God needs it.[72]

Finally, R. Soloveitchik adds a last *mattir* in a lesson on the juxtaposition of redemption and the *Amidah*:

(7) Praise: based on the principle that praise comes before prayer, reciting *Pesukei de-Zimrah* and reading *Shema* comprise a *mattir*.

68 The opening of the repetition of the *Amidot* for the Days of Awe, which is interpreted here as a *mattir*.
69 Schachter, *The Soul of the Rav*, 110.
70 Ibid., 109.
71 "*Ha-Berakhot be-Yahadut*," 34-37.
72 Following BT Berakhot 32a; *Lessons in Memory of Father*, vol. 2, 55.

From many aspects, all the *mattirim* have a common basis. For R. Soloveitchik, the *mattirim* are the reason for preserving the number and the traditional wording of the *Amidah* prayers every day. The halakhah is decisive on this point: "No Jew has the right to add to the three prayers ordained by the sages of Israel; we have no license to compose new prayers."[73] The *mattirim* and the maintenance of the framework of the prayers are an expression of the objective consciousness whose existence R. Soloveitchik posited in various works. We can easily understand that the halakhic ("objective") dimension of consciousness balances the natural stormy inclination, which seeks to praise the Creator without limit, and anchors it in fixed frameworks.

As in other writings by R. Soloveitchik that were written in different periods of his life, the halakhah has a dual role here.

(1) Recording: the halakhah records the opposing directions of success and failure. Success is reflected in the recital of praise while failure comes forth in the admission of limits in human language and knowledge.

(2) Channeling: the halakhah inserts the refinement of modesty in communal aspirations in two ways:

(a) hindering voluntary praise and limiting it to the explicit obligation (such as *Hallel*);

(b) the recitation of *Kaddish*, which admits the inability to praise God.

In the lesson on *Pesukei de-Zimrah*, R. Soloveitchik showed that opposing inclinations of consciousness are recorded in *Pesukei de-Zimrah*, while the *Hallel* presents a special halakhic obligation. In this lesson he presented the dialectical dimension of consciousness as a process that begins with daring and courage and ends in submission and cessation. It starts with initiative and activism and concludes in a passive withdrawal inwards. Once again, we have a dialectical consciousness.

How does this play out? *Pesukei de-Zimrah* is a private recitation of praise that reaches the conclusion that the consciousness surrenders, and seemingly gives over to God the possibility of praise. This conclusion directly ensues from the *Yishtabah* and *Kaddish* prayers that precede *Barkhu* and that expropriate praise from the consciousness. "The song is Yours,

---

73 "Reflections on the *Amidah*," 152.

as is the praise."[74] According to these prayers, after reciting the laudatory *Pesukei de-Zimrah* the worshiper admits that this attempt to praise God was a complete failure. "We stand and proclaim that all our labor was in vain."[75] To a certain extent, this model appears in the article "Redemption, Prayer, Talmud Torah." The redemption, attained through prayer, comes crashing down after man willingly foregoes it. The halakhah, therefore, records the ascents and descents of the turbulent and effervescent religious consciousness and gives them allotted and fixed expression.

4. Other Aspects of Consciousness

As was noted, a careful reading of R. Soloveitchik's lessons brings to light a gradual unfolding of the consciousness of prayer and its different elements. This consciousness is built, layer after layer, out of his halakhic discussions, the lion's share of which are of a completely legal nature. The consciousness layers are constructed one over the other, they come from different directions and from diverse issues. We will continue to examine the different phenomenological aspects that drive R. Soloveitchik's *lomdut* and halakhic considerations for questions pertaining to prayer in *Lessons in Memory of Father*.

Prayer and Community

One important role of halakhah is to regulate consciousness. The *Kaddish* that is recited before *Barkhu* is the halakhic factor that transforms the individual worshipers into a public (*metzaref*, "joiner").[76] Since worshipers do not all come at the same time or leave the synagogue together, a legal element is needed that will turn latecomers and early leavers into one community ("transforming it into a 'public'").[77] This element, as noted, is the *Kaddish*, whose fundamental message is that the exaltation of God's name depends on nothing but God's name. The worshiper is passiveand praise, as it were, is self-generated. As R. Soloveitchik writes:

> In the *Kaddish* we do not say that we magnify and sanctify the Holy One, blessed be He, as we say in the *Kedushah* of the *Shemoneh Esreh*, rather that

---

74 *Lessons in Memory of Father*, vol. 2, 27.
75 *Lessons in Memory of Father*, vol. 2, 28.
76 See Schachter, *The Soul of the Rav*, 116.
77 *halot shem tzibbur*, literally, "applying [to it] the name or concept of public"; based on the halakhic term *halot shem*.

> He is magnified and sanctified *qua* Himself [...] By means of [the *Kaddish*]
> we say to the Holy One, blessed be He, that we are not permitted to utter
> even a single sound of praise and acclaim, but we pray to You, that Your
> Name be magnified and sanctified.[78]

Consequently, the theological failure to praise God unites the worshipers. Giving over praise to God Himself is a constitutive characteristic of the community. It is the negation, the withdrawal into one's self, and the shock delivered to the consciousness that become a powerful uniting factor of the collective consciousness. The recitation of the *Kaddish* is the legal element that reflects this social and public cohesion. Now, the society is based on humility and an awareness of the limitations of the consciousness. *Hallel*, in contrast, is a stable obligation of praise. Here the halakhah is regulated and balanced, and allows *Hallel* only within fixed and limiting boundaries.

The link of prayer and community finds additional expression in the connection between the communal and national dimensions. R. Soloveitchik was exacting in his reading of Maimonides' directive stating that a synagogue must have two arks containing Torah scrolls, one in the regular Torah ark that faces east, and the other, where the prayer leader (*shaliah tzibbur*) stands. The first ark is seen as a necessary component of the sanctity of the synagogue (it "completes"), while the second is an expression of the fact that the portable temple (*mishkan*) stood in the midst of the Israelite camp.[79] This extraordinary understanding implies that the synagogue also functions as the image and representation of the center of the Israelite nation and its beating heart, as the venue around which the nation's spiritual and religious life are conducted. Accordingly, the prayer community represents the nation in its entirety. Moreover, the leader's praying before the Ark shows that the Torah scroll, too, is a "joiner"[80] (see below).

R. Soloveitchik further concluded from Maimonides' wording that the latter derived the need for a quorum of ten for the recitation of *Kaddish* from the word "community" (*eidah*, Num 14:27 and BT Megillah 23b),[81] for Maimonides viewed ten as representing all Israel. That is, every *devar*

---

78 *Lessons in Memory of Father*, vol. 2, 30.

79 *Lessons in Memory of Father*, vol. 2, 32. See Itzhak Hamitovsky, "From Chest (*tevah*) to Ark (*aron*): The Evolving Character of the Ark of Scrolls in the Periods of the Mishnah and the Talmud" [Hebrew], *Kenishta* 3 (2007): 99-128.

80 *Lessons in Memory of Father*, vol. 2, 40.

81 *Mishneh Torah, Hilkhot Tefilah* 8:5.

she-be-kedushah (literally, "act of sanctification"), such as *Kaddish*, should be conducted in the presence of the entire Jewish people; since, however, this is not possible, then ten "are called a community in microcosm, that symbolizes the presence of the entire community of the congregation of Israel."[82] This explanation of Maimonides' thought is reinforced by the presentation of prayer as a sacrifice. R. Soloveitchik showed at length that the fixed prayers are a substitute for the *tamid* daily sacrifices, which are an offering of the public. Such a sacrifice is offered by all Israel, and not merely by ten, nonetheless, if a person recites one of the fixed prayers in a *minyan* of ten, this is deemed as if he offered a sacrifice. Consequently, ten who prayed together are "transforming it into 'all Israel'"[83]—ten worshipers represent the entire Israelite nation.

R. Soloveitchik then distinguished the perspective of the worshiper from that of God. For the worshipers, the following principles are true.

(a) The principle of prayer as *tamid* sacrifice does not apply to each *minyan* of worshipers, since a single *tamid* is offered for the entire nation.

(b) Individual prayer has no significance in terms of offering a sacrifice, since the *tamid* is always a public offering.

He therefore asserted that the comparison between prayer and sacrifices was not drawn from the perspective of the worshiper but from that of the recipient of the prayer, God. He receives the prayer of ten, and also that of the individual, as if it were the sacrifice of the nation as a whole. For man, prayer is not a sacrifice, but it is for God because God joins all the prayers together into a single one, and this single prayer becomes the substitute for the *tamid* sacrifice (offered by the public). "We do not have here the combination of action and deed, but rather that of placation and acceptance."[84] The prayers of the individuals and communities join together into a single homogeneous prayer, which, for God, is a temporary substitute for the *tamid* sacrifice. We could say that the prayer of the individual is accepted because it joins together with the homogenous prayer of all Israel.

---

82 *Lessons in Memory of Father*, vol. 2, 34.
83 *Lessons in Memory of Father*, vol. 2, 36.
84 *Lessons in Memory of Father*, vol. 2, 38.

As noted, Maimonides has the prayer leader standing before the Ark, which R. Soloveitchik explains declaring that the Torah scroll joins the prayer of the specific community to that of all Israel. According to him, the quality of the prayer varies from place to place and from one community to another. That is, the principle of *metzaref* does not mean simply that God receives the aggregate of the communal prayers as a single prayer, rather, the prayer of a specific community becomes the prayer of all Israel. R. Soloveitchik writes:

> Prayer before a Torah scroll is obligatory, because the scroll joins together this public and the act of its prayer to all Israel. By the connection to it, and due to the halakhah of "that I may be sanctified in the midst of the Israelite people" (Lev. 22.32), that adds, according to Maimonides, that all [prayer] among ten represents the entire Jewish people,[85] this public prayer is connected with the entire public of worshipers everywhere; they merge into a single prayer, not only in terms of its placation and acceptance, but also as regards the very act and *heftza* [legal object] of the prayer.[86]

The joining together of prayer and the Torah scroll transforms the prayer into one of the entire nation. Once again, we see R. Soloveitchik's characteristic approach to the consciousness of prayer, namely, the merging of prayer and Torah study. Torah study imparts a special quality to prayer and elevates it. Thus, the prayer community reflects the national dimension of the prayer, and the traits that characterize both the individual and the community (self-affirmation versus humility and modesty), as well, are a reflection of all Israel. For R. Soloveitchik, the separate communities that gather in synagogues are the delegates of the entire Jewish people. The consciousness of prayer is anchored in the consciousness of the Israelite nation.

Prayer and the Consciousness of Finitude

In the last part of the lesson on *Pesukei de-Zimrah*, R. Soloveitchik distinguished between two practical, or functional, dimensions of prayer (*kiyyumim*): sacrifice and the request for divine compassion. We briefly discussed above the connection between sacrifice and prayer and the meaning of public sacrifice. Now we will examine the conception of prayer

---

85 R. Soloveitchik refers here to the idea of mission, which he develops in his essay "The Synagogue as an Institution and as an Idea" (see Chapter Twelve, below).
86 *Lessons in Memory of Father*, vol. 2, 41.

as a request for divine compassion, even though this was not the focus of R. Soloveitchik's analysis. He wrote:

> The request for divine compassion, that ensues from the consciousness of hardship and weariness in man, the feeling that he is poor and hapless [*halkhah*],[87] weak, unable to save himself, to solve his problems, or to meet his needs, either spiritual or material; the knowledge that even if he dwells in the palaces of kings, his life is suspended over emptiness.[88] [...] This idea of complete hope in the Holy One, blessed be He, is rooted in the awareness that if, Heaven forbid, He will not come to man's aid, he is lost forever, comprises one element of prayer.[89]

This passage does not necessarily portray a psychological feeling (despite the use of the word "sense"), but rather a subjective consciousness and existential trait, recorded and balanced by the halakhah. This is not a fear of some external stimulus, as threatening as it may be. R. Soloveitchik is concerned here with "the awareness," in his language, that man is a finite creature, that he develops the consciousness of finitude and that after he has finished his life he is "lost forever." Only reliance upon the infinite God and His lovingkindness gives man security. In other words, the consciousness of divine compassion of prayer balances the consciousness of insecurity and finitude.[90]

Finitude and the anxiety it causes are common motifs in R. Soloveitchik's thought. By perceiving prayer as a request for divine compassion, R. Soloveitchik explicitly explained that prayer is a matter of the consciousness ("the consciousness of hardship and weariness in man"). Prayer records the consciousness of God that makes it possible to endure finitude, and prayer also balances the consciousness of finitude by linking it with absolute trust in God. R. Soloveitchik presented prayer as the religious answer to existential questions.

---

87 Ps. 10, 8, 14. This might be connected to *helkaim* (the helpless—v. 10). R. David Kimhi interprets v. 10 thus: "the *helekh*, this is the pauper" (David Kimhi, *The Complete Commentary on Psalms* [Hebrew], ed. Avraham Darom [Jerusalem: Mossad Harav Kook, 1979], 31); he offers a similar interpretation on v. 8.

88 Following Job 26:7.

89 *Lessons in Memory of Father*, vol. 2, 35.

90 See Schwartz, *From Phenomenology to Existentialism*, 241-257. In his *Lessons*, R. Soloveitchik related to finitude as consciousness, that is, as a type of cognition and experience. The content of this cognition and experience is that man, as subject, is finite and needs divine compassion in order to overcome finitude and to live with it.

The conception of the *Amidah* as compassion also emerges from the halakhic discussion of the juxtaposition of redemption and the *Amidah*.[91] R. Soloveitchik argued that, in contrast with blessings and other obligations such as *Hallel*, which are imposed on a person (*hovat gavra*), the *Amidah* has independent standing. It is a religious act of autonomous value independent of a person's situation and religious history ("*heftza shel tefillah*"— the body of prayer).[92] R. Soloveitchik clearly expressed this principle:

> There is a *heftza* of the *Amidah* that is formulated in its blessings that is not dependent on the obligations incumbent on the person [*gavra*]. Its permissibility ensues from its being compassion in its own right, for even if a person has already fulfilled his obligation, the situation [lit., "applying"] of prayer as compassion has not expired. To the contrary, the obligation incumbent on the person ensues from the fact that it [i.e., the obligation] exists as the *heftza* of prayer in the reality.[93]

If there were not a special law that a person must pray three times a day and no more, prayer would be continuous and uninterrupted.[94] Prayer is not included in what R. Soloveitchik called "obligatory consciousness." Prayer "need not be performed in order to fulfill one's obligation."[95] Other obligations, such as the commandments to recite grace after meals or the *Hallel*, are obligations incumbent on a person, and as soon as he has fulfilled them, he is not permitted to recite the blessing for them yet again. In contrast, prayer is a value that is not dependent upon man's actions. The legal expression for this is *tefillat nedavah* (freewill prayer), which has no allotted time.

As a "*heftza* of compassion [*rahamim*]," prayer is not time-dependent. This principle enables the resolution of additional halakhot. First, women are required to pray, even though they are exempt from time-dependent commandments. Second, it is possible to compensate for a missed prayer, because prayer has intrinsic value; otherwise, it would not be possible to complete a prayer after its time had passed. "The same reasoning that obligates women applies to the matter of compensation for a missed prayer."[96] We learn from

---

91 This halakhah appears numerous times in BT and PT Berakhot. See, e.g., PT Berakhot 1:5, 2d; BT Berakhot 4b.

92 *Lessons in Memory of Father*, vol. 2, 46.

93 *Lessons in Memory of Father*, vol. 2, 47.

94 Mention should be made of the approach of R. Abraham Isaac Hakohen Kook, who states that prayer is similar to the constant speech of the soul.

95 *Lessons in Memory of Father*, vol. 2, 46.

96 *Lessons in Memory of Father*, vol. 2, 48.

these discussions that presenting prayer as a consciousness act of compassion facilitates a complete legal understanding. The phenomenological and philosophical meaning was used by R. Soloveitchik to resolve interpretive and halakhic problems.[97] Other Torah scholars, as well, made use of such distinctions, but R. Soloveitchik's terminology and style show that he was unwilling to completely detach his legal-halakhic activity from his philosophical concerns.

5. Prayer as a Torah Obligation

The attempt to determine the value which Torah gives to the components and details of prayer is one of the major features of R. Soloveitchik's developing the concept of prayer. In the preceding chapter we discussed the importance that he ascribed to Maimonides' approach stating that prayer is a positive Torah commandment. The stumbling block in the way of R. Soloveitchik's understanding is the fact that institutionalized prayer, with its texts, times, and gestures, wasmainly established by the Rabbis. R. Soloveitchik, accordingly, sought to connect the gestures and styles of prayer to a Torah obligation, even though its text is rabbinic in origin. This direction is evident in both his writings and the lessons that he delivered.

The Structure of the Amidah

R. Soloveitchik wrote the following about the *Amidah* in "Reflections on the *Amidah*":

> Rambam stated as a matter of law that, although the formula and times for prayer are rabbinic in origin, the threefold structure of prayer is Biblical. The first three benedictions comprise praise (*shevah*); the middle benedictions comprise supplication and petition; and the last three benedictions comprise acknowledgement and thanksgiving. Rambam writes: "Rather this commandment obligates each person to offer supplication and prayer every day and utter praises of the Holy One, blessed be He; then petition for all his needs with requests and supplications; and finally give praise and thanks to God for the goodness that He has bestowed on him. [He is to do this] each day according to his own ability" (*Hilkhot Tefillah* 1:2).[98]

The Rabbis based the sections of the *Amidah* on various Scriptural verses. Since the formula of the *Amidah* was determined by the Rabbis, it seems

---

97 It should be noted again that R. Shagar (above, n. 1) opposed this.
98 "Reflections on the *Amidah*," 148.

reasonable that this action consisted of general Scriptural support. From time to time the Rabbis would anchor their laws and enactments in Scriptural passages. R. Soloveitchik, however, stated that "for Rambam, these *derashot* (rabbinic deductions of laws from of biblical texts) provide a full-fledged proof that the principles of prayer are derived from the Torah, rather than the Torah verses constituting a mere prop or support (*asmakhta*)."[99] We find such reasoning in R. Soloveitchik's explanation of *Mishneh Torah, Hilkhot Avel* (Laws of Mourning) 1:14. On the one hand, Maimonides sets forth the commandments that he defines as rabbinic (visiting the sick, consoling mourners, and the like), while, on the other hand, he subsumes them under the biblical "Love your fellow as yourself" (Lev. 19:18). R. Soloveitchik wrote in his *Lessons* on the honoring of Sabbath and deriving pleasure from this holy day:

> These commandments "from their words" [i.e., rabbinic commandments] are special certain commandments, each with its special *kiyyum* and act, each with its special preferences. When a person visits a sick person, then he fulfills the commandment of visiting the sick, and when he consoles mourners, he has [performed] the commandment of consoling, and not the commandment of visiting; and when he brings joy to the groom and bride, he has performed the specific commandment of causing the groom and bride to rejoice, which does not unite with consoling mourners, and similarly regarding all such. The author of *Halakhot Gedolot* counted many of these commandments among the 613 as separate commandments. The one who does these things aids his fellow and helps him, and thereby fulfills the commandment from the Torah of "Love your fellow as yourself." With regard, however, to the commandment of "Love…," all these acts do not comprise a special independent commandment. These are not different matters [lit., concepts]: a person does not fulfill the commandment of visiting the sick, nor of consoling mourners, nor of bringing the bride [under the wedding canopy], but rather the commandment of love and assistance [the other].[100]

R. Soloveitchik maintained that each rabbinic commandment of this type has both an individual and a general dimension. The individual dimension is rabbinic, while the general dimension is provided by Torah law. Such a model appears, in a different style, in the obligation of prayer. The formula of the set order of prayers is of rabbinic composition, but its obligation comes from the Torah. The content, which is a matter for individuals, is

---

99 "Reflections on the *Amidah*," 149.
100 *Lessons in Memory of Father*, vol. 1, 71-72.

an enactment devised by the Rabbis, but its structure, which is the general frame (praise and petition) is derived from the Torah. Presumably, the essence of prayer is human, but the mold in which it was cast is divine. In order to clarify this, R. Soloveitchik discussed the *mattir* at length.[101] The possibility of man addressing God is something new, and therefore, the protocol of this address is most important (praise preceding petition). This protocol, therefore, is a Torah obligation.

The Direction of the Amidah

To now, we have spoken mainly of a few expressions of prayer in R. Soloveitchik's writing and in his lessons that were recorded by R. Soloveitchik himself and edited by his sons-in-law R. Prof. Isadore Twersky and R. Dr. Aaron Lichtenstein. The editors took care to impart to *Lessons in Memory of Father* a style tending more to novellae and less to philosophical and theoretical writing. We will now examine another composition that reinforces R. Soloveitchik's image as an interpreter of prayer.

After R. Soloveitchik's death, several volumes of his lessons appeared, not published by his family, one devoted entirely to prayer (*Al ha-Tefillah*). We have already noted the parallels between this and other essays published by the Soloveitchik family and the Toras HoRav Foundation. "Reflections on the *Amidah*" contain detailed summaries of R. Soloveitchik's lessons on the relevant topics as well as theoretical lectures. We will examine a few unconventional conceptions that were raised and highlighted in "Reflections on the *Amidah*," which contributed to the philosophical climate created by R. Soloveitchik. From the summaries of his lessons we can infer how R. Soloveitchik was perceived by his audience on the consciousness and laws of prayer.

As was noted above, R. Soloveitchik ascribed great importance to the Maimonidean idea that prayer is a Torah obligation. Furthermore, based on a passage in Maimonides' *Sefer ha-Mitzvot*, R. Soloveitchik asserts that prayer facing the Temple is of Torah force. Maimonides' well-known view that prayer is a Torah obligation is based on the dictum of R. Eliezer ben Yose ha-Gelili:

> Whence do we learn that Prayer is obligatory? From the verse, "Thou shalt fear the Lord thy God; and Him shall thou serve." The Sages also say: "*Serve*

---

101 See above.

Him through the Torah, and *serve* Him in His Sanctuary", which means that we should aspire to pray either in the Temple or towards it, as Solomon clearly said.[102]

According to *Al ha-Tefillah*," R. Soloveitchik derived that "what Maimonides writes, both in *Mishneh Torah*[103] and in *Sefer ha-Mitzvot*, shows that the obligation to pray facing the Temple is a Torah commandment."[104] This approach also appears in chapter 6 of *Worship of the Heart*.[105]

The Sanctity of the Synagogue

An additional example is R. Soloveitchik's statement arguing that, for Maimonides, the sanctity of the synagogue is also of Torah force.[106] Support for his approach is only found in a few words in *Sefer ha-Mitzvot*, where Maimoides writes, "We are forbidden to break down houses of worship of the Lord."[107] This is not a routine statement, since the prevalent interpretation of these words is that this phrase referred to different parts of the Temple, as Maimonides himself specified in the continuation of the commandment ("such as pulling down any part of the Sanctuary, or the Altar, or the like"). For R. Soloveitchik, this expression certainly

---

102 *Sefer ha-Mitzvot*, Positive Commandment 5 (English translation: Maimonides, *The Commandments*, trans. Chavel, vol. 2: *The Positive Commandments*, 8). This commandment in *Sefer ha-Mitzvot* is also the source for the inclusion of prayer and Torah study in "worship of the heart."

103 Reliance on *Sefer ha-Mitzvot* is the very aim of the book, to list the commandments of the Torah (and assuming that Maimonides did not include aspects of Rabbinical dicta in his listing of the commandments). Maimonides states in the latter: "All pray facing the Sanctuary [*Miqdash*], wherever it might be" (*Hilkhot Tefilah* 1:3; English translation: *The Code of Maimonides*, book 2: *The Book of Love*, trans. Menachem Killner [New Haven: Yale University Press, 2004], 17). He added that until Ezra's ordinances people prayed facing the Sanctuary. A few commentators interpreted this as a Torah commandment.

104 Grodner, *On Prayer*, 5.

105 *Worship of the Heart*, 100.

106 "According to Maimonides, the sanctity of the synagogue is by Torah law" (Grodner, *On Prayer*, 138).

107 Negative Commandment 65 (English translation: Maimonides, *The Commandments*, trans. Chavel, vol. 2: *The Negative Commandments*, 64. In *Hilkhot Yesodei ha-Torah* Maimonides mentions only the altar, the *Heikhal*, and the *Azarah*, but not the houses of worship of the Lord. And similarly in *Hilkhot Beit ha-Behirah* (Laws of the Temple) 1:17, as Joseph Kafih mentions in his translation (Maimonides, *Sefer Hamitsvot: Book of Commandments* [Jerusalem: Mossad Harav Kook, 1971], 115 n. 46).

included study halls ("houses of worship of the Lord"), since for him, Torah study and prayer are intertwined, and in some senses, Torah study and the study hall are perceived as superior to prayer and synagogues.[108] Relying on this passage by Maimonides, then, he states in *On Prayer* that "this shows that a house of worship of the Lord, that is, the synagogue, has Temple sanctity like the *Heikhal* [the Sanctuary] and the Altar."[109] R. Soloveitchik wrote in a letter that Maimonides "seemed to agree [...] that at least on a rabbinic level [*de-rabbanan*], the monetary sanctity has devolved upon the very structure of the synagogue."[110]

Ascribed to R. Soloveitchik, then, was the aim of elevating the legal standing of prayer. This led to some unconventional assertions, stating that the direction and the place of prayer acquire the standing of Torah obligations.[111]

The Elevation of the Amidah

The intellectual climate that R. Soloveitchik created in his halakhic lessons regarding the centrality of prayer in analytical Torah study is reflected in the following details.

First, R. Soloveitchik's interpretation of Maimonides highlights the quest for the source. R. Solovetchik sought to include in his lessons as many aspects of prayer as possible under the category of "Torah obligation." Maimonides' opinion lent itself to such a move, since he declared that the obligation of prayer is derived from the Torah. R. Soloveitchik was not deterred by the obstacles in the way of his approach. For example, the claim that synagogue sanctity is derived from the Torah is not free of difficulties. Even if we were to argue that the obligation of prayer comes from the Torah, we still did not find that public prayer has roots in the Torah itself. According to R. Soloveitchik, the Torah obligation refers to this stipulation:

---

108 My friend R. Dr. Shlomo Pick showed me that in the responsa *Heikhal Yitzhak* (*Orah Hayyim* 12:2) and *Helkat Yaakov* (*Orah Hayyim* 37:2) the decisors considered the question as to whether synagogue sanctity is of Torah or rabbinical force. Blidstein evidently doubts this (Blidstein, *Prayer in Maimonidean Halakha*, 199-200). In any event, Maimonides explicitly includes synagogues in his list of commandments at the beginning of *Mishneh Torah*.

109 Grodner, *On Prayer*, 138.

110 *Community, Covenant and Commitment*, 317.

111 An examination that I conducted with the rabbis Ezra Bick and Binyamin Tabory revealed that students of R. Soloveitchik confirm this direction in his interpretation of Maimonides.

since the public decided to pray, even though there is no Torah obligation to pray in public, then this venue has a sanctity derived from the Torah. R. Soloveitchik would probably have grounded such a move in the distinction between *hiyuv ha-mitzvah* [obligation] and *kiyyum ha-mitzvah* [realization]. The sanctity of the synagogue belongs to *kiyyum ha-mitzvah*. This means that there is no obligation of public prayer, but if, in practice, the public made such a decision, and further decided that such prayer will be conducted in a permanent place (the synagogue), then the sanctity of this place is regarded as coming from the Torah.[112]

Second, R. Soloveitchik was also engaged in a more general quest for a source. At times in his classes on prayer, he attempted to base his novellae on Scripture itself. The verse became the key to the division between the various legal aspects (*heftza gavra, maaseh kiyyum,* and the like). R. Soloveitchik stripped from the *asmakhta* the sense of illustration and mnemonic aid and turned it into an actual source of the law. This fact too reveals his aim to discard the idea that the *Amidah* is a late development (that is, devised in the late Biblical period) and restore its standing as an actual Torah obligation. R. Soloveitchik's leading students apparently did not regard these new interpretations as a quasi-Torah enactment, but as an actual Torah obligation. This direction also spread to *minhagim*. At this juncture we should cite R. Shlomo Zeev Pick on rabbinical obligation (*hiyuv mi-de-rabbanan*):

> The Rav proposed new explanations for customs relating to *Orach Chayyim* and *Yoreh De'ah* that accorded with the explanations and distinctions that he offered in the framework of his *shiurim* or *derashot*. He did not like to say that a custom or rabbinic law was "merely a custom" or "merely a prohibition." As a rule, anything enacted or instituted by the Rabbis has an "address" in the Torah, that is, it can be classified under some Torah commandment or law. The Sages did not create new categories, but rather they made use of existing categories, adding enactments, decrees, prohibitions, and even customs into the existing framework of the Torah's commandments and laws.[113]

The third and last quest concerns the center of consciousness. R. Soloveitchik enhanced the importance of prayer as a commandment of rich subjective-consciousness content by infusing the halakhic discussion with consciousness

---

112 As was noted by my son-in-law, R. Baruch Weintraub.
113 *Moadei HaRav: Public Lectures on the Festivals,* ed. Shlomo H. Pick (Brooklyn, NY: Ktav, 2016), p. 34.

aspects. At times, and following their editing, his public lectures created the impression that he was exclusively focusedon the legal dimensions. But not even the most precise editing can obfuscate the rich depth of consciousness analysis. This train of thought is also evident in what was written by R. Soloveitchik's student R. Shalom Carmy:

> In the Rav's halakhic studies, he reveals a special attraction to those commandments which can be defined both as active commandments, that is, norms of conduct, and as subjective actions that are realized when interiorized. In such cases, "*maaseh ha-mitzvah*" is externalized, while "*kiyyum ha-mitzvah*," its achievement, in internalized. The nature of the intent required for such commandments is dependent upon the reciprocal action between the objective and subjective dimensions.[114]

R. Carmy correctly indicated a methodical direction in R. Soloveitchik's writings, namely, the emphasis on commandments that have deep underlying consciousness dimension. From this aspect, prayer is a prime example of an objective dimension of consciousness that documents and regulates concealed but vital consciousness streams. R. Soloveitchik translated this concept into the language of Torah study and anchored it in his interpretation of Maimonides. Thus we can understand his tendency to present prayer and its components as Torah obligations and to lead it from the periphery to the center of Torah scholarship.

6. Summary

The difference between the teachings of halakhists from the Soloveitchik family and those of R. Soloveitchik's studies is evident. The values and ideas that emerge from the analytical Torah discussion of the classic halakhist are meaningful, but only within the halakhic world. The analytical Torah scholar puts forth an idea, but it does not occupy him apart from his study. That is, this scholar may use an idea to resolve a question and create a halakhic object using his analytical cognition and the accepted methods of Torah study. However, this idea, a halakhic "postulate" or halakhic "regulative idea" lacks meaning beyond this framework. R. Soloveitchik

---

114 Shlomo Carmy, "Introduction," to *Worship of the Heart* [Hebrew] (Alon Shvut: Toras HoRav Foundation, 2006), 11.

objected to this characterization of halakhic man, as I showed at length elsewhere.[115]

However in his halakhic lessons he used ideas that find expression outside the legal system as well. He had no qualms about using terminology that alludes, between the lines, to religious and existential phenomenological thought. At times, the dry halakhic discussion cloaks effervescent consciousness and existential depths..

Formally, R. Soloveitchik preserved the structure and style of the extant analytical Torah writings from the Soloveitchik line of scholars and from other traditions of Torah novellae. Indirectly, however, he was of the opinion that the power of the idea emerging within the context of the analytical Torah exploration is not limited to the resolution of a theoretical knot or the creation of a new halakhic object, one that is free of problems. For him, this idea was valid also for a philosophical or theological worldview, and sometimes even ensued directly from such a worldview. The following are some additional examples of such ideas:

(1) merging of Torah study and prayer, inclusion of prayer in Torah study;
(2) emphasis on an extra value of prayer in its relation to Torah study;
(3) antithetical consciousness of praise to God;
(4) social element of the consciousness formulated as a result of the theological failure;
(5) relation between prayer, community and nationality;
(6) prayer as an independent value and not a consequence of the usual legal obligation.

These ideas are at the basis of the subjective dimension of the consciousness of prayer and clarify the processes of its formation. We discussed them at length in the preceding chapter. The consciousness of prayer became a hidden but important key for understanding the legal status that prayer actually has. Moreover, R. Soloveitchik stated during the course of his discussions that the halakhah organizes the subjective inclinations of the consciousness and creates a balance within the consciousness by means of defined legal statements. Formally he did not significantly digress from the halakhist writing style. But his lessons establish a new genre in contentual terms.[116]

---

115 Schwartz, *Religion or Halakha*.
116 On the nature of *Lessons in Memory of Father*, see above.

The philosophical and consciousness foundation only becomes stronger in the light of R. Soloveitchik's inclination to include the *Amidah* and its components within the realm of Torah obligations (following the view of Maimonides). Not only did he include issues relating to *Amidah* in his *lomdut* lessons (unlike the prevalent trends in many yeshivot); his lessons revolved around Maimonides view, which he extended to encompass additional aspects. R. Soloveitchik exhibited tremendous halakhic flexibility in order to overcome what he perceived as the fundamental paradox characterizing Maimonides' view: the content of the *Amidah* is rabbinic, but its gestures are dictated by the Torah.

R. Soloveitchik's lessons clarify the very permission to pray (the *mattir*). In this respect, the second part of "Reflections on the *Amidah*" is a precis of a course of his detailed halakhic discussion. R. Soloveitchik's phenomenological approach in this essay corresponds to his thinking recorded in his halakhic lessons, and especially to that in *Lessons in Memory of Father*.

Chapter 11

Interpretation of the *Amidah* Prayer

From time to time, R. Soloveitchik engaged in interpretation of liturgical texts. This commentary applied the phenomenological principles that he advanced in his various essays on specific prayers, and in the interpretation he offered, which is clearly phenomenological, the liturgical text reflects the processes and experiences of the consciousness. An examination of the text's meanings reveals the consciousness of prayer. The third, and in fact, major part of "Reflections on the *Amidah*" is devoted to interpretation of prayer, and especially, of the blessings of the *Amidah*. R. Soloveitchik sought to recreate the consciousness that emerges from the prayerbook of Simeon ha-Pakuli, who established, and reestablished, the *Amidah* blessings.[1] Accordingly, he explored the phenomenological meanings of these blessings, mainly, those of the weekday *Amidah*. In a certain sense, this section completes *Worship of the Heart*, in which R. Soloveitchik began to interpret the blessings and especially the first passage of the *Shema*.[2] In this chapter we will continue to examine R. Soloveitchik's phenomenological hermeneutics, as recorded in "Reflections on the *Amidah*."

1. The Hymnal Blessings: (1) Introduction

Phenomenologists of religion such as Gerardus van der Leeuw distinguish between prayer and praise. While prayer focuses on the image of man and his needs, praise and paean are directed to the divine. While prayer has man confront himself and his personality, a principle held in extremely

---

1 On the structure of the *Amidah* and the various theories regarding its formulation, see, for example, Tzvee Zahavy, *Studies in Jewish Prayer* (Lanham, MD: University Press of America, 1990), 87-93; Fleischer, "The *Shemone Esre*," 182-187 (in Mack's edition: Mack, *Studies*, 160-165).

2 See above, Chapter Eight.

high regard by phenomenologists and existentialists, with praise man encounters God, who is external to him. Praise is simply the affirmation of the divine power before which man stands. Deep religious emotional motivation requires praise and paean. Conversely, they reflect the negation of the personality in face of the divine.[3]

Maimonides rules that hymnal prayer is a Torah obligation, along with the other parts of the *Amidah* (petition, thanksgiving). R. Soloveitchik maintains that preceding petition with praise, which is usually supported by Rabbinic teachings, affirms standing before God. For him, one of Maimonides' revolutionary actions regarding prayer is his determination that the precedence given to praise is no less than a Torah obligation. R. Soloveitchik, however, diluted this praise with well-concealed fear, both in the opening of the *Amidah* and in the hymnal blessings themselves. We will begin our discussion with the introduction to the *Amidah*.

The Primacy of Love

R. Soloveitchik set forth the foundations for a phenomenological interpretation of the *Amidah* in the section "The First Blessing: Avot" of "Reflections on the *Amidah*." The structure of the opening text of the *Amidah* reflects opposing orientations. On the one hand, the *Amidah* begins with praise. The three hymnal blessings represent a dialogue and an outpouring of the worshiper's heart. The worshiper stands before God and praises Him. On the other hand, the line that precedes the *Amidah*: "O Lord, open my lips, and let my mouth declare Your praise" (Ps. 51:17) conveys the worshiper's silence and trembling. The contrast between the silence and the outburst attests to a dialectic of consciousness.

Now, for an extensive examination of the elements of this dialectic. In the order of the *Amidah*, the hymnal blessings precede the petitionary ones. R. Soloveitchik went so far as to state that, according to Maimonides, this order originates in the Torah.[4] He explained the precedence of praise within the dialectical religious experience. R. Soloveitchik never tired of describing the religious experience in the style of Rudolf Otto, which we have already discussed at length. In "Reflections on the *Amidah*" he noted that the religious experience is dialectical in the following respects:

---

3 Gerardus van der Leeuw, *Religion in Essence and Manifestation: A Study in Phenomenology*, trans. John E. Turner (New York: Harper & Row, 1963), vol. 2, 430.

4 "Reflections on the *Amidah*," 148-149.

(1) the consciousness of the one undergoing the experience (reverence and love, withdrawal and yearnings);[5]

(2) the consciousness of God (King and Father, dispassionate and supportive, antagonistic and friend);[6]

(3) the consciousness of the experience (revelational and cosmic).[7]

R. Soloveitchik, however, indicated that the starting point is the pole of proximity to God and the primal sensation of consciousness is love and longing for Him. R. Soloveitchik explained beginning the *Amidah* with praise and its preceding petition in the following manner:

> Man experiences God's sublimity and grandeur, His infinity, omnipotence and omniscience,[8] His disclosure in the world through the cosmic drama, through the experience of God's mightiness and majesty,[9] for the universe and all that fills it demonstrate all these. "The heavens tell God's Glory, and the firmament proclaims His handiwork" (Ps. 19:1).
>
> Awareness of God as Creator of the world and of man is a firm principle of Judaism. The Torah opens with "in the beginning," with the world's genesis. From the cosmic experience there is born, as we noted, a love directed toward God. Love of God is thus based on man's relationship to the majestic reality on which the Holy One, blessed be He, has imprinted His seal.[10]

R. Soloveitchik began *And From There You Shall Seek*, as well, with the consciousness seeking God, while the pole of chaotic revelation is uncovered only following the experience of the scientific conquest of the world, that

---

5 "Man fears God and reveres Him, but also loves Him. Man withdraws from Him but also longs for Him; his soul yearns for the living God" ("Reflections on the *Amidah*," 152).

6 "In such a state of mind, he envisions God not only as a lofty and exalted King—standing apart, distinct from all other reality—but as a merciful Father, the source of his being" ("Reflections on the *Amidah*," 152).

7 "Awareness of God as Creator of the world and of man is a firm principle of Judaism" ("Reflections on the *Amidah*," 153). Understandably, R. Soloveitchik did not refer here to the revelational experience. Rather, he wanted to emphasize the pole of closeness as the background for hymnal prayer. The initial revelation, in contrast, is traumatic, as R. Soloveitchik showed at length in *And From There You Shall Seek*.

8 The attributes of omnipotence and omniscience reflect an experience of cognition, knowledge, and analysis, while His revelation is also indicative of a sensory experience.

9 Alluding to the attributes of God. Strict law, *Din* ("mightiness"), is indicative of God's indifferent and unyielding aspect, while *Tiferet* ("majesty") is taken to mean the balance between it and His compassionate and friendly side.

10 "Reflections on the *Amidah*," 153.

parallels the cosmic experience.[11] R. Soloveitchik uses Ps. 42:2 ("Like a hind yearning for water brooks, my soul yearns for You, O God") as a motto for *And From There You Shall Seek*. In the beginning of that work, he describes the relationship between the beloved and her lover. "The Shulammite, blackened by the sun,[12] yearns for her heart's chosen one."[13] R. Soloveitchik also opened his commentary to the *Amidah* with the primacy of the consciousness of love and nearness. The religious experience starts with the pole of yearning. Moreover, R. Soloveitchik rejects fear as the starting point of this experience. "Man does not begin with trembling, but by approaching with love, by singing a hymn about the wonders of creation."[14]

Flinching

Immediately following this, however, R. Soloveitchik presented a completely different position regarding the experiential starting point. The beginning is no longer love and longing but the experience of the silent self turning inward in the presence of God. The text under analysis is the opening of the *Amidah*. The worshiper asks that God help him to pray ("O Lord, open my lips"). The interpreters of the prayerbook viewed this opening verse as an expression of a lack of perfection[15] and of a sensation of sin.[16] The unspoken question is, why is there a need for preceding a canonical text that was formulated by the early sages with an introductory text? R. Soloveitchik writes:

> every individual who [...] seeks to initiate the prayer with fearful supplication and petition: his initial, immediate reaction is expressed in paralyzing

---

11 See Schwartz, *From Phenomenology to Existentialism*, chapter 1.

12 Following Song 1:6.

13 *And From There You Shall Seek*, trans. Naomi Goldblum (Jersey City, NJ: Toras HoRav Foundation, 2008), 1.

14 "Reflections on the *Amidah*," 154.

15 R. Samson Raphael Hirsch wrote: "*Adonai*—Every individual addressing God by this Name, acknowledges Him therewith as the Lord, and views himself as God's servant" (*The Hirsch Siddur: The Order of Prayers for the Whole Year* [Jerusalem: Feldheim, 1972], 130). R. Hanokh Zundel of Bialystok wrote in his prayerbook commentary *Etz Yosef* on the opening verse: "For we pray in it for the Lord, may He be blessed, that he open our lips so that we can utter His praises with intent" (*Siddur Otzar ha-Tefilot* [Vilna, 1915], fol. 154b). That is, proper intent is a difficult task posed before the worshiper, who, consequently, asks for assistance.

16 R. Aryeh Leib Godron wrote in his *Iyyun Tefilah* commentary that since prayer is in place of the sacrifices, which were canceled due to sin, then the worshiper requests: "Permit me to open my lips before You" (*Siddur Otzar ha-Tefilot*, fol. 154b).

fear and shuddering dread. How is it possible to set up a dialogue between man and his Creator, he asks himself. As his lips move with trepidation and trembling,[17] he expresses his frailty and nothingness, beginning the *Amidah* as follows: "God, open my lips, let my mouth utter Your praise" (Ps. 51:17). In other words: I do not know how to move my lips, how to find the right words to express the thoughts in my heart.[18]

R. Soloveitchik wanted to explain to the reader that the constitution of the consciousness, with its poles, results from analysis. The actual process of consciousness, however, is dialectical by definition, as evident at every stage of its development. Even in the place where the initial orientation of the consciousness is love and longing, fear and anxiety are present under the surface, and vice versa. Even though the consciousness is predominantly drawn to longing, fear does not disappear. The movement toward God includes inherent recoil. R. Soloveitchik formulated this thought by declaring: "'I am ignorant, I know nothing.'"[19] "Nonetheless, within the space of a single phrase comes *Avot*, the first benediction of the *Amidah*," in which "the Holy One, blessed be He, revealed Himself to Abraham, not as King but as Father."[20] The opening to the *Amidah* expresses the contrasts within the religious consciousness that are present even when its inclinations are seemingly evident and explicit.

2. The Hymnal Blessings: (2) Two Models

The tension of the opening to the *Amidah* is indeed indicative of what is to follow. As I clarified a number of times, R. Soloveitchik undertook the theological and apologetical task of showing that religious consciousness in Judaism is more complex and dialecticalthan others. In *And From There You Shall Seek*, he took pains to reveal, layers within layers, the contrasting and polar nature of Jewish religious consciousness. Additionally, what seems like mending the breach bears within it a new split.

In this spirit, the discussion of the hymnal blessings concurrently reflects two dialectical models. In one model, inherent tension arises in the first blessing, that of *Avot* (the "depth" model), while this tension is resolved

---

17 Following I Sam. 11:13.
18 "Reflections on the *Amidah*," 154-155.
19 Following Ps. 92:7.
20 "Reflections on the *Amidah*," 155.

in the next two blessings, *Gevurot* and *Kedushah*.[21] This latent tension bubbles under the surface. In the second model, this tension is obvious (the "surface" model) and is not fed from subterranean currents. The blessing of *Avot* reflects a certain state of consciousness, and *Gevurot* shows the opposing state. This tension is assuaged in the blessing of *Kedushah*.[22]

The hymnal prayers, therefore, reflect the fundamental dynamics of R. Soloveitchik's thought, oscillating between the tensions in plain sight and those under the surface. We will begin with an analysis of the first model, which describes the depth dimensions of consciousness.

Avot: *Fundamental Tension*

The blessing that begins the *Amidah* is presumably concerned with the pole of the quest and longing for God, accompanied by the consciousness of the beneficent God. R. Soloveitchik started the discussion of this blessing with an emphasis on divine lovingkindness, unequivocally declaring: "*Avot* contains two elements: that of paternal lovingkindness and the appeal to historical precedent."[23] He explained in a long discussion that the opening lines of various blessings reflect intricate dialectical knowledge of the different poles. After affirming the relations between God and all the Patriarchs, *Avot* continues with "the great, mighty, and awe-inspiring God," and these three divine attributes give added depth to the stormy consciousness. R. Soloveitchik labored strenuously to reflect the primacy of the longing for God and love of Him; and now, this primacy is itself based on polar divine models, as he portrays in the "Prayer and Life" section of "Reflections on the *Amidah*" (164). He attempted to cloak this oscillation by maintaining that, in actuality, by mentioning these three attributes, "one praises God" for the three; but as we will see below, avoidance and fear are concealed in these praises.[24]

R. Soloveitchik proposes the following structure: the first blessing (*Avot*) is the blessing of lovingkindness. However, it fosters a dialectical understanding of God, whose attributes are lovingkindness ("great"), fear ("mighty"), and substantive separateness ("and awe-inspiring"). In terms of the divine attributes, the first blessing includes the two following parts:

21 This model appears in "Reflections on the *Amidah*," 155-163.
22 "Reflections on the *Amidah*," 163-164.
23 That is, generational continuity began with the Patriarchs ("Reflections on the *Amidah*," 155).
24 "Reflections on the *Amidah*," 156.

Avot blessing		
divine attributes	**Meaning**	**expressed in separate blessing**
great	lovingkindness (greatness expresses lovingkindness)	*Avot*
mighty	fear (might expresses strict law and fear)	*Gevurot*
awe-inspiring	separation ("awe-inspiring" expresses isolation)	*Kedushah*

That is, the models of flinching from God and of total divine indifference are at play within the lovingkindness model. R. Soloveitchik's discussions contain a trace of the Kabbalistic notion that the divine *sefirot* contain dimensions of other *sefirot*. Each *sefirah* contains aspects of other *sefirot*. Many Kabbalists spoke of the aspects of *Hesed she be Hesed, Din she-be-Hesed, Tiferet she-be-Hesed*, and so on (*she-be* meaning "which is in"). Such a discourse appears in Zoharic deliberations, in the Kabbalistic doctrine of sabbatical years (*shemittot*), and other discussions. In this spirit, R. Soloveitchik presented the blessing of *Hesed* (lovingkindness) as including aspects of *Din* and *kedushah*. We understand from this that the solemn opening of the *Amidah*, one that contains infinite love of God and the sense of majesty in light of the divine support, is actually replete with tensions and oscillations. The love expressed in the blessing of *Avot* cloaks a maelstrom of anxiety, fear, and a sense of self-annulment before a concealed God.

Thus, the nuclei of the second and third blessings of the *Amidah* are already found in first blessing. In many respects, the blessing of *Avot* is the key to understanding the experiences entailed in the following blessings. Now, we will examine the structure of consciousness reflected in the last two blessings of praise.

Gevurot: *Ethics*

The sense of solemnity connects lovingkindness to the cosmic experience of God's *gevurah* (might). We do not, however, have here uninterrupted continuity, but oscillation that finds its resolution. R. Soloveitchik set forth the following model: the tension that erupts in the aspect of *gevurah* or fear of the blessing of *Hesed* is resolved when we proceed to the blessing of *Gevurot*. To find proof for his model, R. Soloveitchik analyzed the cosmic experience and found that it contained two modes and, in effect, two experiences.

(1) The aesthetic and the maaesthetic[25] cosmic experience: man stands before the physical universe. Feelings of impotence accompany this stance in two dimensions:

    (a) The intellectual dimension: a total lack of understanding in the face of impermeable nature (the consciousness of God as Creator);

    (b) The dimension of freedom: self-annulment and powerlessness in the face of a threatening and invasive universe (the consciousness of God as omnipotent).

(2) The moral cosmic experience: the universe is seen to be a moral one. Cosmic physical regularity unites with moral regularity. This is an axiom, a given, and not a logical conclusion from some argument. "We do not understand how the laws of nature relate to the absolute ethical laws of God. But the bond exists."[26]

These modes clarify the process that consciousness undergoes, beginning with tension and ending in resolution. In the first stage, when the might aspect of lovingkindness in the blessing of *Avot* ("the mighty") is prevalent, the worshiper stands before the aesthetic cosmic experience. *Hesed* does not succeed in obscuring the anxiety caused by this experience. R. Soloveitchik writes:

> Man cognizes God in the world not only as abundant in *hesed* but also as *gibbor*, omnipotent. No action lies beyond His capacity. In this experience of Divine mightiness is embedded also man's sense of frailty and helplessness, and from this sensibility there emerges a recognition of utter exhaustion. Man cannot be his own master; he cannot nourish his personality on his own and preserve his independence. He is not free, nor is he able to plan, initiate and execute through his own powers. He requires God's assistance, blessing and supervision. A feeling of waiting for God suffuses the human being. The Divine attribute *gibbor* implies to him that none of his human achievements are the fruit of his thought and action, but only the product of the Divine act and might. Pride recedes, humility grows. At first man approaches with joy and wholeness of soul, a cleaving unto God who calls out to him from the hidden recesses.[27] This optimistic stance gives way to

---

25 R. Soloveitchik used this term to convey the experience of dignity and majesty.

26 "Reflections on the *Amidah*," 251. See, for example, Yoram Hazony, "The Rav's Bombshell," *Commentary*, April 2012, 54.

27 Meaning that the blessing of *Avot*, which begins the *Amidah*, is concerned with perfection and optimism.

the cry of one who feels frail and miserable and whose eyes are lifted to "deliverance and rescue from another place" [Esther 4:14].[28]

In this passage R. Soloveitchik stressed the loss of freedom in the aesthetic cosmic experience. The latent *gevurah* in the blessing of *Avot* presents man as an empty vessel. For R. Soloveitchik, powerlessness leads man to a sort of quietist sentiment. He puts all his trust in God and loses his independence and autonomous standing. If the tension of *Avot* would have sufficed for the redactors of the *Amidah*, then the experience would have been limited to a lack of initiative and a turning inward. The tension between *Hesed* and *Gevurah-she-be-Hesed* may be destructive. They, accordingly, concealed this tension in another divine attribute, *gibbor*—"mighty." How, then, is the ruinous dimension of the dialectic to be avoided?

R. Soloveitchik gives a decisive answer: the redactors of the *Amidah* restored man's freedom and initiative in the second blessing (*Gevurot*). This blessing transports the worshiper to the moral cosmic experience and saves him from powerlessness. The dialectic of this oscillation is resolved in terms of the divine consciousness, as well: the blessing of *Gevurot* portrays God from the aspect of the intensity of His action on behalf of man ("Who sustains the living with *hesed*, resurrects the dead with abundant mercy..."), and not from the aspect of His being the Creator of the cosmic laws of nature. The experience passes from the cosmic impermeability to the cosmic good, and from the consciousness of God the Creator to the God of lovingkindness. How does *Gevurot* reflect the moral experience of the good? R. Soloveitchik explains:

> God's might is not concentrated only in the dynamic that governs the cosmic process, but extends into the realm of the moral as well. Mightiness is modeled on *hesed*.[29] God saves those who cannot be delivered and redeemed on their own. All God's deeds, all His acts, even in the realm of nature, are imprinted with an ethical seal. The causal-cosmic process is nothing but an exalted ethical drama, which is rooted in the Divine will that is beyond our grasp. [...] The dynamic and the beautiful of [sic] are not the context for this prayer. The ear of the individual at prayer is bent to receive the whisperings of the moral law that is active within the beauty, the moral might found within the splendor of power. The heart of the person at prayer senses the miracle of a moral vision embroidered in the cosmic veil, and he recounts it in his prayer.[30]

---

28 "Reflections on the *Amidah*," 156-57.
29 See BT Yoma 69a; Sanhedrin 96b, 104b, and others.
30 "Reflections on the *Amidah*," 157-58.

The element of morality becomes the content of the cosmic aesthetic factor. In other words, the inner good drives the cosmic experience. In the blessing of *Gevurot*, the divine might is revealed as lovingkindness, and God's lovingkindness is seen as might. We could say that the *Gevurah* in *Hesed* (*Avot*) is transformed into the *Hesed* in *Gevurah* (*Gevurot*). The divine attributes and man's sensibility undergo a metamorphosis.[31] Once man is cognizant of the "real" inner nature of reality, then the conflict between *hesed* and *gevurah* becomes the metamorphosis of *hesed* in *gevurah* and *gevurah* in *hesed*. Terror becomes love, and aversion becomes the quest for closeness; determinism and the lack of initiative become choice and the acceptance out of free will, of divine regularity and morality. The worshiper understands that the terrifying cosmic experience is actually the experience of the moral good, that is, God's concern for his wellbeing: "aesthetic-ecstatic contemplation turns into an ethical demand—a command to act."[32]

R. Soloveitchik anchored the metamorphosis of these attributes and experiences into each other inside human consciousness in a number of terminologies and sources.

(1) Kabbalistic terminology: the consciousness passes from *Gevurah* in *Hesed* (*Avot*) to *Hesed* in *Gevurah* (*Gevurot*).

(2) Interpretation of Ps. 104: the entire psalm is itself an aesthetic cosmic experience. Its ending, however, is moral-cosmic ("May sinners disappear from the earth").

(3) The Maimonidean doctrine of divine attributes: the aesthetic cosmic experience is reflected in the negative attributes, and the moral experience, in the attributes of Divine action.[33]

---

31 Such model already exists in *And From There You Shall Seek*. R. Soloveitchik argued there that love is transformed into fear, and fear, into love. See Schwartz, *From Phenomenology to Existentialism*, 65-88.

32 "Reflections on the *Amidah*," 159. On "the dependence of action," that is, the conception that the divine command is a condition for realizing moral life, see Daniel Statman, "The Moral Views of Soloveitchik," in Sagi, *Faith in Changing Times*, 254.

33 R. Soloveitchik understood the Maimonidean conception of attributes of Divine action as "moral principles, imposing upon man an ethical obligation, and compelling him to mend his ways according to the ethical-halakhic imperative which derives from observing the world" ("Reflections on the *Amidah*," 159). Thus, the attributes of action are elements of the ethical legal rules that are derived from the universe in some way. These attributes are also the motivating factor for *in imitatio dei*. R. Soloveitchik wrote: "We would not have been permitted the most sublime praise of the Deity, if this praise did not obligate us to follow in His ways and to imitate Him" (159). He did not understand the action attributes as objects, that is, the existents, as Maimonides does understand

In the blessing of *Gevurot*, God's mightiness is manifest as lovingkind-ness. When aesthetic might becomes moral might, then the initial tension is resolved.

R. Soloveitchik's discussion has manifold contexts. As usual, he learned about the religious consciousness from different and polar sources (Kabbalah, Bible interpretation, and Maimonidean rationalism). The coherent consciousness of prayer is built from sources that are different from one another, and even of opposing nature. The process that the con-sciousness undergoes from the first to the second blessing can be portrayed in the following table:

from *Avot* to *Gevurot* (the experience of *gevurah*)					
blessing	Wording	experience	Divine model	Kabbalistic symbol	state of consciousness
Avot	the mighty	aesthetic	Creator	*Gevurah* in *Hesed*	tension
Gevurot	He sustains the living with loving kindness, and with great compassion revives the dead.…	moral	Good	*Hesed* in *Gevurah*	resolution of tension

Now, to return to a brief depiction of the stormy moves of the conscious-ness in the first two blessings of the *Amidah*, in the following four stages.

(1) Love: the blessing of *Avot* is concerned with love. The beginning of the *Amidah* entails the experience of love.

(2) Hidden anxiety: lovingkindness is seen to be bubbling with sub-terranean anxiety (*gevurah* in *hesed—gibbor*).

(3) Revealed anxiety: the aesthetic cosmic experience that was con-cealed in the preceding aspect now becomes manifest, and a con-sciousness rift comes into being ("You are eternally mighty, Lord").

(4) Love: the aesthetic cosmic experience becomes moral or is exposed to morality. The anxiety is revealed as love. The tension is resolved, and the rift is mended ("who resurrects the dead").[34]

---

them in *Guide of the Perplexed* 1:54. On the distinction between the negative attributes and the attributes of action in Maimonides' thought, see Schwartz, *Contradiction and Concealment*, 73. On R. Soloveitchik's approach regarding the latter, see Harvey, "Notes on Rabbi Soloveitchik," 96; Kaplan, "Maimonides and Soloveitchik."

34 On the meaning of resurrection, see also Harry (Menahem Tzvi) Fox, "A Concealed Polemic in Prayer" [Hebrew], in Corinaldi et al., *Studies in Memory*, 123-164.

This enables us to understand the ending of the *Gevurot* blessing, that is, the resurrection of the dead. This ending reveals, definitively, that the moral cosmic experience is one of love and *hesed*: "the greatest of all kindnesses, the singular ethical act, is resurrection of the dead."[35] R. Soloveitchik explained that kindness to the dead is a model of pure ethical behavior, or at the least borders on such behavior ("the most miraculous and majestic ethical act").[36] The purity of the act ensues from the total passivity of the dead; they are expressionless. The initiative for kindness comes exclusively from God.

Sanctity: Commitment

A process similar to the transition from the experience of "the mighty" to the blessing of *Gevurot* occurs in the progression from the experience of "the awe-inspiring" (*nora*) to the blessing of *Kedushah* (sanctity).

To return to the blessing of *Avot*: R. Soloveitchik explained that the adjective "awe-inspiring" in this blessing is "the pole opposite to that expressed in *Avot*."[37] This reveals the tempestuous process experienced by the consciousness in the blessing of *Avot*. The blessing is totally focused on the appearance of the personal God who is beneficent and returns love. And yet, the descriptions of God that appear in the blessing gradually fashion a model of a completely indifferent God. Such a Deity negates any reality outside Him. Consciousness, therefore, goes through three stages:

(1) The phase of love and the model of the good God ("great" [*gadol*]);
(2) the phase of dread and the model of the Creator ("mighty" [*gibbor*]);
(3) the phase of total disconnection and the model of the indifferent and annihilating God ("awe-inspiring").

It should be recalled that these descriptions appear in a blessing that is all love and kindness. That is, two parallel processes are at work in the hymnal blessings. One process is the longing for a beneficent and protecting God, while the other consists of regression and decline toward total separation from God. Consciousness concurrently moves between two parallel

---

35 "Reflections on the *Amidah*," 159.
36 "Reflections on the *Amidah*," 160.
37 "Reflections on the *Amidah*," 160.

divine models: one is an affirmative model, a God who supports man and treats him kindly, while the other is annihilating.

The negating model turns God into a separate Deity completely lacking in personality. This enables us to understand why R. Soloveitchik returned to a question that troubled him for many years: the possibility of praying. How is it possible to say "You"[38] to the indifferent and annihilating God? How is prayer possible in the setting of standing before Him? As R. Soloveitchik puts this: "From this perspective it is impossible to approach God at all."[39] The attribute of "awe-inspiring" rules out any possibility of standing before God. Prayer is therefore the tension between the actual situation and its impossibility.

Again, the discussion of the blessing of *Kedushah* presents it as resolving the tension. This blessing speaks of the negation and sacrifice of the self. R. Soloveitchik placed great emphasis on the conception of the Temple offering as self-sacrifice. The offering symbolizes the sacrifice of one's personality. "The fundamental correlative[40] of the external action is a spiritual action of self-sacrifice. The blood sprinkled on the altar, the fat and limbs consumed by fire - these represent the blood and fat of the owner of the sacrifice."[41] Prayer as a substitute for the sacrifices in the Temple also reflects self-sacrifice. What has sacrifice to do with the blessing of *Kedushah*? R. Soloveitchik writes:

> Build an altar. Arrange the wood. Kindle the fire. Take the knife[42] to slaughter your existence for Me. This is the command of the awesome God who suddenly appears out of an absolute separation. This approach is the very foundation of prayer. Man hands himself over to God.[43]

---

38 Following the text of the blessing, which begins: "You are holy and Your name is holy." See Mirsky, "The Origin," 38.

39 "Reflections on the *Amidah*," 160.

40 Again, R. Soloveitchik writes of the conception of reconstruction. The subjective dimension is "correlated" to the objective one, but without any causal relationship between them. This fact adds force to the conjecture that "Reflections on the *Amidah*" was written in the middle of the 1940s, along with *And From There You Shall Seek* and *The Halakhic Mind*.

41 "Reflections on the *Amidah*," 161. R. Soloveitchik ascribed this notion mainly to Maimonides. He also discussed the concept of the scapegoat, which led him to mention R. Abraham Ibn Ezra. See Dov Schwartz, *Amulets, Properties and Rationalism in Medieval Jewish Thought* [Hebrew] (Ramat Gan: Bar-Ilan University Press, 2004), 35-66.

42 Following Gen. 22:9-10.

43 This wording is reminiscent of the discussions by *Maharal* on the relation between sacrifice and prayer. In each, he writes, "Man offers himself over to the Lord, may He

He approaches the awesome God, expressing this movement in sacrifice and binding of oneself.[44]

R. Soloveitchik hinted at the resolution of the tension inherent in the act of prayer. A self-affirming person negates himself before God, like a reed standing in the windthat will eventually break it. The standing before God of a self-affirming person is paradoxical. As R. Soloveitchik puts this, "God will not tolerate the arrogant man."[45] On the other hand, a self-abnegating individual, who modestly turns inwards and sacrifices his personality to God, is the one who communes with Him. If a worshiper is cognizant of the fact that his entire selfhood is merely divine tension, he is not in conflict with the divine presence, but rather merges with it. The traumatic negation of one's self becomes a willing sacrifice. The worshiper chooses the negation of self and total commitment to his God. Thus, in the final analysis, the blessing of *Kedushah*, as well, ends with love.

The Second Model: On the Surface

To this point, R. Soloveitchik saw only a single consciousness stream (the concealed, subterranean tension and its resolution) in the complex consciousness process of the blessings of praise. This, however, was not all for him. He added an additional stream, one that expresses an overt typological process. This process is detailed in a presumed summation of the first, "depth" model.[46] I will first cite this passage in its entirety before analyzing the second model and its meanings:

> The three opening benedictions thus place in relief three fundamental motifs pertaining to the structure of prayer and its essence. First, man yearns for God and discovers Him via that which surrounds him. God is the God of *hesed* who permeates all, and makes the creature a partner in his Being. In Him we find a refuge and stronghold, a protective fortress.[47] We approach Him calmly and confidently. The motto is "Divine *hesed* everlasting," (Ps. 103:17) from the

---

be blessed [...] and this is called *avodah* [divine service], because the slave [*eved*]—he and his property—is acquired for his master, all for his master" (*Netivot Olam, Netiv ha-Avodah* 1, 77a).

44 "Reflections on the *Amidah*," 163. On the versions of the traditions of the relationship between prayer and sacrifice, see, for example, Blidstein, *Prayer in Maimonidean Halakha*, 69-74.
45 "Reflections on the *Amidah*," 162.
46 "Reflections on the *Amidah*," 163.
47 Following Ps. 144:2; see also Ps. 18:3.

beginning to the end of the generations.[48] The God of Abraham participates in the sorrow of the miserable, impoverished human being. He responds to his entreaty and hears his cry. Unto Him do we pray.

Studies in the psychology of religion that report on the benefit of prayer as a source of consolation and relief for the weary,[49] reflect the belief that the God of *hesed* receives our prayer with love and favor.

The situation is altered when we move from *Avot* to *Gevurot*. Here prayer changes direction. At the outset, in the benediction of *Avot* the praying individual did not feel confusion, need or inadequacy. At this first stage he lacked nothing; he had more than enough. He was close to God and was nourished by a perfect existence, devoid of deficiency or flaw.

In the second benediction, a new motif wells up. The human being discovers his emptiness, and begins to understand that he has no standing at all. He can be rescued only through God's *hesed*, to which he has no right. Here is an introduction[50] to the prayer of supplication and vigorous entreaty. God is mighty and omnipotent, whereas man is weak and miserable, incapable of earning his bread[51] and fulfilling his needs. Man flees toward God, seeks protection beneath His wings,[52] and presents before Him his supplication, like a slave or maidservant before a master.[53] Man is ready to entreat and plead for undeserved *hesed* from the All-powerful. "You are mighty forever, O God." The "You" excludes everything. Only *You* are high, not *I*: "Who is like You, master of mightiness." In the first benediction man is aware of his greatness and singularity—he was created in the Divine image, and therefore can approach God; the second benediction expresses man's self-abnegation, his feeling of weakness and his recognition of his own nothingness.

The third benediction commands both the person who believes in his worth and importance and the one who negates his own self to offer up their entire being to God. When man appears before the great God, the God of

---

48   See Deut. 11:12; M Makkot 3:15, and others.
49   See Isa. 28:12. R. Soloveitchik's style here might be influenced by Nathan Alterman's poem *Shir ha-Emek* (*Song of the Valley*; 1934), which begins: "Rest for the weary and repose for the laborer." This style appears in a lengthy critical note at the beginning of *Halakhic Man*. Here, it is used with no apparent critical nuance. At any rate, R. Soloveitchik did not rescind his view of the destructiveness of the unrestrained consciousness of *hesed*.
50   That is, R. Soloveitchik refers to the beginning of the blessing of *Gevurot* (see the detailed discussion, below).
51   Following Prov. 30:8.
52   Following Ruth 2:12.
53   Following Ps. 123:2.

hesed, he is joyful and happy.[54] When he encounters the mighty God, he is filled with dread. When he praises the awesomeness of God, he is prepared to surrender everything to Him.[55]

From the formal aspect, this passage is a summary of the preceding discussion. R. Soloveitchik, however, chose tortuous language where a simpler style and approach were possible. He apparently did so to indicate the richness of the overt and covert processes of consciousness. According to the typological dynamic set forth in this section, the eighth in 'Reflections on the *Amidah*," the three blessings represent two types of people:

(1) The person who undergoes different experiences. The experience is: love (*Avot*), turning inward (*Gevurot*), and willing self-abnegation in the encounter with God (*Kedushah*).[56] Such a personality experiences tension, resolved on a superficial level, that is, without subterranean tensions as were presented in the previous discussion.

(2) The one who is subject to a dominant experience: for some individuals, their central experience is love (*Avot*), while others experience a turning inward (*Gevurot*). Each of these types find perfection in communion (*Kedushah*).

In the following discussion I will examine the two character types that R. Soloveitchik portrays in his summation.

The First Type

We will begin with the type whose consciousness undergoes various experiences. The first experience is expressed in *Avot*, which is the blessing of *hesed*. Here, R. Soloveitchik completely disregards the subterranean inner tension in the first blessing. There is no tension between the "great," the "mighty," and the "awe-inspiring." Now, "God is the God of *hesed* who permeates all,[57] and makes the creature a partner

---

54 Following Esther 5:9.

55 "Reflections on the *Amidah*," 163-64.

56 I will use this term in our discussion for the sake of convenience, and because of the connotation it bears. This state of consciousness, however, could be more precisely defined as "self-projection," or as a state of total commitment to God. On the comparison of the sacrifice to prayer in terms of absolute commitment in the thought of R. Samson Raphael Hirsch, see Heinemann, *Taamei ha-Mitzvot*, vol. 2, 145.

57 An allusion to the Zoharic idea that God's presence "fills all the worlds" (*memale kol almin*), as opposed to the God's aspect of indifference (*sovev kol almin*).

in his Being."⁵⁸ At the same time, consciousness responds accordingly: "In Him we find a refuge and stronghold, a protective fortress.⁵⁹ We approach Him calmly and confidently."⁶⁰ The first stage is entirely placid and has no inner tensions. This is the stage of perfection. "At this first stage he [the worshiper] lacked nothing."⁶¹ The contradiction is first revealed in the second stage. Now the consciousness encounters God's might. This stage is depicted in R. Soloveitchik's writing as a fall, as crashing to the earth. In his words: "The human being discovers his emptiness."⁶²

R. Soloveitchik relates primarily to the moral cosmic experience. In the first blessing, man is cognizant of God's kindnesses; in the second, he discovers, to his horror, that these kindnesses are "the bread of charity" (*nahama de-khisufa*—literally, "the bread of shame"). He benefits from such kindnesses without justification—and this fact reveals his shaky and tenuous existence. The second stage is therefore an experience of nullity and negation. The personality totally loses its self-esteem. The *hesed* in the blessing of *Avot* becomes an annihilating factor in *Gevurot*.

Furthermore, R. Soloveitchik previously wondered how the worshiper could say "Thou" (or "You"). Now, he interprets the "You" in the beginning of *Gevurot* as the negation of the "I." In other words, "You" is not a personal address. Although formulated in the second person, the meaning of this address is the negation of the self (not "I"). In R. Soloveitchik's language: "The 'You' excludes everything. Only *You* are high, not *I*."⁶³

The third stage is the consciousness of the communion in the blessing of *Kedushah*, which R. Soloveitchik saw no need to discuss a second time. The *hesed-gevurah* tension ends with self-projection. The consciousness experiences total commitment to God.

The conscious processes inherent in the first typological category— the person who undergoes different experiences—can be summed up in the three sentences: "When man appears before the great God, the God of *hesed*, he is joyful and happy. When he encounters the mighty God, he is filled with dread. When he praises the awesomeness of God, he is prepared

---

58 "Reflections on the *Amidah*," 163.
59 Following Ps. 144:2.
60 "Reflections on the *Amidah*," 163.
61 "Reflections on the *Amidah*," 163.
62 "Reflections on the *Amidah*," 163. In *And From There You Shall Seek*, the experience of the fall is mainly expressed in the arbitrariness of revelation (*And From There You Shall Seek*, 29-37); see also above.
63 "Reflections on the *Amidah*," 164.

to surrender everything to Him."[64] From a certain aspect, this is a process of kindness and love: in the first blessing the *hesed* ensues from the yearning for God; in the second, it is revealed as gratuitous kindness; and in the third, the worshiper chooses to adopt the gratuitous kindness and offer himself to God.

The Second Type

Those of the second typological category are one-dimensional individuals, who cannot grasp complexity. Some experience divine *hesed* without the sensation of emptiness and the crisis of receiving charity. Their consciousness of God is limited to the beneficent and kind God. In general, their entire religious consciousness is reflected solely in the blessing of *Avot*. Others experience man's nullity without the spiritual elevation and closeness imparted by divine *hesed*. Their consciousness of God includes solely the negating and annihilating God who shows them overwhelming kindness. Their whole religious consciousness is reflected only in the blessing of *Gevurot*. The two hymnal blessings do not, therefore, denote an experiential process, but rather the experiences of two different subtypes. Each finds its balance in the experience of communion and the surrendering of his personality to God. "The third benediction commands both the person who believes in his worth and importance and the one who negates his own self to offer up their entire being to God."[65]

We learn that one-dimensional individuals become whole in sanctity (which is also the literal translation of the name of the third blessing). Both—one with a consciousness of lovingkindness and the other with a consciousness of might—reach the apex of their religious consciousness by means of communion with God, personal sacrifice, and complete commitment to Him.

More than any other blessing, *Kedushah* clarifies the role of prayer as taking the place of the lost sacrifices. A person consciously, and with prior preparation, sacrifices his personality. The blessing of *Kedushah* reflects the overall flow of the laudatory blessings and their aim. The blessings of praise manifest a process within consciousness which culminates with the

---

64 "Reflections on the *Amidah*," 164.
65 "Reflections on the *Amidah*," 164.

sacrifice of the self. In this respect, these blessings advance the consciousness to the realm of the transcendental.

3. The Hymnal Blessings: (3) The Sacrifice of the Self

The hymnal blessings enabled R. Soloveitchik to engage in a thorough discussion of the relation between prayer and sacrifice, and of that between the two and consciousness of *avodah she-be-lev*. Prayer represents the innermost strata of the personality, and in this respect it expresses the "worship of the heart." The simplistic approach that sees prayer as a substitute for the sacrifices opens the way to outstanding consciousness and interpretive insights that R. Soloveitchik described at length. He explored two such understandings in the continuation of his discussion of the hymnal blessings: sacrifice and dependence. These insights set the stage for a homogeneous interpretation of the blessings of praise and a new understanding of the relations between them. We will begin with an analysis of the different meanings of sacrifice and their interpretive consequences.

Outer and Inner

Man oscillates between two existential planes: the outer material and social reality and the inner spiritual world. The halakhah, correspondingly, expresses a comprehensive obligation that relates to all the details and events of these two existential planes. It is directed to all the details of man's material and social world and also speaks to his inner world. The whole religious consciousness is deployed in these two realms. While the physical act is fixed and realized in defined periods of time, man's inner world is uninterrupted and continuous. Consequently, the outer world must be an expression of the inner one. R. Soloveitchik refers to *Guide of the Perplexed* 3:51, in which Maimonides presents the perfect man as one who acts in the material world but whose mind is directed to acquiring intelligibles and attaining knowledge.[66] R. Soloveitchik presented prayer both as the link connecting the two existential planes and as a reflection of inner existence. Now we understand why prayer is one of the central expressions of "worship of the heart." R. Soloveitchik writes:

---

66 "Reflections on the *Amidah*," 182 n. 16. In Chapter Two (above) we noted the affinity to model R. Bahya presents in *Duties of the Heart*.

> The first stage in the service of the heart is the integration of halakhic-religious value into the human being's life in all areas, from the lowest instinctual level to the apex of spiritual being. Prayer is not merely an additional stage in the worship of the heart, but, as we have stressed, the mirror that reflects the soul of the worshipper who is totally and perpetually committed to God. Prayer is a kind of information center which reports occurrences in the depth of the love-sick soul.[67]

In other words, prayer extends from the outer reality to the inner. It is a reflection of full halakhic life, from the material to the spiritual aspect. It expresses the correlation between the different aspects, as well as being the voice of the soul. It is the yardstick for the spiritualization of religious life. Accordingly, prayer as a ritual, without relation to the totality of a person's ethical and religious life, is worthless.

Sacrifice occupies the same place in religious life. It is an expression of the sacrifice of one's personality, that is, the turn of man's inner dimensions to God.[68] Accordingly, there is no meaning to a sacrifice without connection to the aggregate of moral and religious life. R. Soloveitchik consequently argued that the criticism of sacrifices leveled by the prophets related to the conception of the sacrifice as a ritual divorced from life. The prophets demanded that the sacrifice be regarded as worship of the heart, which is an indication of the overall moral and religious state of the one bringing it. "Worship in the Temple and worship of the heart are both rooted in man's existence as a singular being endowed with identity and continuity."[69] R. Soloveitchik formulated this approach within the context of his frequent critique of the Christian flesh-spirit dichotomy. He maintained that the prophets did not voice a sweeping rejection of the sacrifices, as secular and Christian historiography seeks to argue. The Gospels, especially Paul's Letter to the Hebrews, are critical of the sacrifices, to which they give allegorical meaning. From then on, the Church Fathers, beginning with Justin Martyr, reiterate their criticism of the sacrificial rite in the name of the prophets.[70] According to R. Soloveitchik, the prophets negated the value of an actual sacrifice when it was separate and divorced from the offering of the soul.

---

67 Following Song 2:5; "Reflections on the *Amidah*," 165.

68 This style is also found in the discussion of R. Samson Raphael Hirsch, who stated in his prayerbook that the *Amidah*, with its three sections, parallels the three parts of the daily *Tamid* sacrifices (Hirsch, *The Hirsch Siddur*, 127).

69 "Reflections on the *Amidah*," 168.

70 See, for example, Justin Martyr, *Dialogue with Trypho*, trans. Thomas B. Falls; ed. Michael Slusser (Washington, DC: Catholic University of America Press, 2003), 28:5 (p. 44); 41:2 (p. 63).

The Sacrifice: Two Meanings

Thus, the sacrifice and prayer are a mirror of the inner processes that occur within an individual's personality. R. Soloveitchik alluded to R. Judah Halevi's notion of prayer in order to express this view. For Halevi, prayer is an expression of the fact that the perfect man finds himself in a constant two-directional process: on the one hand, he is purified of sins that adhered to him in the past, while on the other, he prepares for the future.[71] The various prayers are symptomatic of this constant movement. Each prayer contains purification of the past and preparation for the future. This approach is formulated in R. Soloveitchik's writing as follows: "This prayer [...] expresses the aggregate of his [Abraham's] past deeds and served as an impulse towards future elevation."[72]

R. Soloveitchik sought to delineate an additional meaning of the sacrifice and self-sacrifice. To this point he had adopted the classical meaning: the waiver of one's personality. The beast that is offered is merely an expression of the personality that retreats in the encounter with God; the sacrifice reflects the total renunciation of self before God. Now, the sacrifice also becomes the way is which life is conducted in accordance with the halakhah. Sacrificing is renunciation; this time, however, this waiver is not of the self, but of freedom.[73] The fact that the Jew regularly lives a life based on constant compliance and discipline transforms his life into a sacrifice. Sacrificing, in the second sense, is merely observance of the commandments, which demands self-control and limits freedom. R. Soloveitchik writes:

> the Jew's [...] table, his bed, his place of business, his abode—all become altars upon which man offers himself up daily. Man makes his person holy through daily self-control, by renouncing acts of pleasure and satisfaction, by undertaking preoccupations that cause pain and anguish, in order to attain a moral ideal.[74]

---

71 See Judah Halevi, *Kuzari* 3:5; Isaac Heinemann, *The Reasons for the Commandments in Jewish Thought: From the Bible to the Renaissance*, trans. Leonard Levin (Boston: Academic Studies Press, 2008), 67-68, 142-143; Eliezer Schweid, "Prayer in the Thought of Yehudah Halevi," in *Prayer in Judaism: Continuity and Change*, ed. Gabriel H. Cohn and Harold Fisch (Northvale, NJ: Jason Aronson, 1996), 109-117, at 115-116. This experiential and educational approach stands alongside the magical conception of the commandments that was adopted by R. Judah Halevi.

72 "Reflections on the *Amidah*," 168.

73 The waiver of freedom is not in the Kantian sense of freedom as willing subjection to imperative, but in that as the possibility of choosing evil, as well ("negative" freedom), that is, the lack of any compulsion.

74 "Reflections on the *Amidah*," 169.

Not only extreme asceticism is self-sacrifice. The regulation of religious and ethical life, too, counts as a sacrifice.

Interpretive Consequences: (1) Avot-Kedushah

The new sense of sacrifice, as the regulation of religious life, has far-ranging consequences for the interpretation of the hymnal blessings. The character of the Patriarch Abraham begins and ends the section "Prayer and the Gesture of Surrender" of "Reflections on the *Amidah*" (168-71). Therefore, an examination of this character clarifies the direct connection between the blessings of *Avot* and *Kedushah*. R. Soloveitchik joined together bits of Biblical and midrashic notions in order to form the character of Abraham the worshiper, from which we learn about the consciousness of prayer. He writes at the beginning of this section:

> Abraham, the first to discover the constancy of man's service to God,[75] offered the morning service (*shaharit*),[76] but he was occupied with the worship of God day and night,[77] whether sitting at the entrance to his tent at noon[78] or looking up at the blue, star-seeded sky, raising his eyes to wondrous heights[79] as he sought the way up to God;[80] while engaged in dealings with others, in speaking and acting.[81]

---

75 *Maharal* explained that prayer reflects constant communion with God. This clarifies the need to set a place for prayer. See *Netivot Olam, Netiv ha-Avodah* 4, 86a-b.

76 Following BT 26b; *Gen. Rabbah* 68:9; *Tanhuma* (Buber's edition), *Miketz* 11.

77 This apparently reflects a tradition mentioned in many rabbinic sources that Abraham observed the entire Torah. See, for example, M Kiddushin 4:14; PT Kiddushin 4:12, 65a; BT Yoma 28b; *Tanhuma* (Buber's edition), *Behar* 3. See also Marc (Menachem) Hirshman, *Mikra and Midrash: A Comparison of Rabbinics and Patristics* [Hebrew] (Tel Aviv: Hakibbutz Hameuchad, 1996), 42-43.

78 Following Gen. 18:1.

79 A description of the cosmic experience in a liturgical context appears in *And From There You Shall Seek*: "the Jew is enthusiastic about each and every phenomenon! For the Jew there is no such thing as routine. Everything is a wondrous miracle. He is excited by everything, from the novel and unknown to the everyday and the ordinary. In everything he sees the glory of God; over everything he utters a benediction. The beloved goes out always—at each dawn with the radiance of the morning star, and at every twilight with the winking of the evening star, when her drowsy eyelids droop each night and when she opens her eyes every morning—to greet her ruddy lover who peers out from the radiant dawn and the starlight, and from tiredness and rest!" (21).

80 See Ex. 19:22; 20:18.

81 "Reflections on the *Amidah*," 168.

And he writes at the end of the section:

> Abraham renounced many things. He rejected the instincts that impelled
> him to rebellion,[82] he continued to wait for his relationship to be fulfilled
> in spite of the smug mocking[83] that jeered at him and his obstacle-strewn
> way of life. He triumphed: "You are holy and Your Name is holy." Before You
> human prominence must bend,[84] You shake the foundations of the world.
> And yet, "the holy praise You each day." Reality is sanctified through the
> self-sacrifice of man, as he is offered up on the altar before God.[85]

Now, for a detailed examination of the three stages of the interpretive path
taken by R. Soloveitchik for the hymnal blessings, and especially the blessing of *Kedushah*. The key to this interpretation is the conception of prayer
as sacrifice, described in the following three stages.

(1) *Avot*: since, for example, the moderate and rich in *hesed* life that
Abraham chose for himself comprises self-sacrifice, then the *Avot*
blessing, too, entails such sacrificing. This path taken by Abraham
is the background for the "prayer of [all] the Patriarchs."[86]

(2) *Kedushah*: the blessing of *Kedushah*, as self-sacrifice, relates to both
the dialectical process of surrendering the self to God and to life regulated by the halakhah. Both senses of self-sacrifice are included in
the blessing. "You are holy and Your Name is holy" reflects the sense
of self-abnegation, and "holy ones daily," that of halakhic regulation.

(3) Unity: as we noted, the blessing of *Kedushah* includes both
senses of self-sacrifice. The interpretive consequence of the

---

82 The rabbinic literature links Abraham's struggle with the evil inclination to the tests he
   underwent, mainly to the binding of Isaac.

83 Following Ps. 123:4. On the scoffers, see Rashi to Gen. 21:7 and 25:19. See what
   R. Soloveitchik writes about the two types of scoffers in "The Revolving Sword and
   the Two Cherubim," in *The Rav Speaks: Five Addresses on Israel, History, and the
   Jewish People*, trans. S. M. Lehman and A. H. Rabinowitz (Brooklyn, NY: Toras HoRav
   Foundation, 2002), 89-94.

84 Following Isa. 2:12.

85 "Reflections on the *Amidah*," 171. The ending of the passage alludes to two senses of
   sacrificing: the negation of the self and life regulated by the halakhah; see also below.

86 "Reflections on the *Amidah*," 168. On the midrashic image of Abraham the worshiper,
   see Noam Zohar, "The Figure of Abraham and the Voice of Sarah in Genesis Rabbah"
   [Hebrew], in *The Faith of Abraham: In the Light of Interpretation throughout the Ages*,
   ed. Moshe Hallamish, Hannah Kasher, and Yohanan Silman (Ramat Gan: Bar-Ilan
   University Press, 2002), 80-82.

consciousness of the hymnal prayers, according to the sense of the regulation of halakhic life, is that the blessing of *Kedushah* refers back to *Avot* and reveals its meaning. Accordingly, the blessings of *Avot* and *Kedushah* are a single homogeneous unit. The mention of Abraham's name in the context of *Kedushah* teaches that, from the outset, the two senses of self-sacrifice apply to him. What previously seemed to be a stormy process is now seen to be a unified process, one that was planned from the beginning.

The dual interpretation of sacrifice and self-sacrifice enabled R. Soloveitchik to present the first and third of the hymnal blessings as a consolidated consciousness unit. The self-sacrifice in life that is conducted in accordance with the halakhah makes it possible to connect a life that is moderate, social, and infused with lovingkindness together with self-sacrifice.

Interpretive Consequences: (2) Gevurot-Kedushah

What of the relation between the second and third of the hymnal blessings? The next interpretive move clarifies that the blessings of *Gevurot* and *Kedushah*, too, are a homogeneous unit. Self-sacrifice is interpreted here in the sense of self-abnegation, and not that of regulation. R. Soloveitchik linked the act of prayer in general to the consciousness of absolute dependence upon God ("total dependence"),[87] as we discussed above.[88] It should be recalled that such dependence does not allow actual dialogue, in which two speakers autonomously express themselves. The blessing of *Gevurot* reflects man's absolute need for God.

Full dependence leaves man powerless to such a degree that he is even incapable of properly expressing his needs.[89] Man "requires Divine assistance not only for his sustenance but also in order to recognize his

---

87 "Reflections on the *Amidah*," 171.

88 See above, Chapter Two.

89 We have already seen that the personal expression of human needs is born out of an awareness of the concrete existence, which, in turn, is triggered by the signs of an "authentic" existence (see above, Chapter Nine). R. Soloveitchik writes here in a clearly phenomenological style, and the perception of needs as authentic existence is absent from his writings, but his description closely resembles this model.

deficiencies and to arrange his words."[90] Now R. Soloveitchik charts out a new interpretive direction, which leads from the introduction to the *Amidah* ("O God, open my lips") through the blessing of *Avot* to that of *Kedushah*, and even beyond to the *Tahanun* supplicatory prayer (*nefilat appayim*, "falling on one's face") that follows the conclusion of the *Amidah*. As we observed, R. Soloveitchik bases this on the sense of surrendering the self to God: "To him all commit their souls and offer up all they have."[91]

Finally, the question arises: what is the dominant sense of this sacrificing: regulation or self-abnegation? To which was R. Soloveitchik himself inclined?

R. Soloveitchik did not expressly raise this question, but he unequivocally declared that the framework of the *Amidah* suits self-abnegation. He argued that "this institution of *Tahanun* or *nefilat appayim* stresses the annihilation of man's being. Man lowers himself to the dust[92] and negates his existence."[93] Thus, the *Amidah* begins with the silence characteristic of the abnegation of selfhood, and its conclusion ushers in the "falling on one's face," to firmly ground man's absolute reliance on God. R. Soloveitchik mentions the prayer versions that precede *nefilat appayim* with *vidduy* (confession). *Vidduy* consists of detailing a person's sins. Presenting the individual as a sinner is the last stage in crushing the fragments of his personality and self-affirmation. The *Amidah* opens with man's cessation ("O God, open my lips") and ends with the loss of his firm standing on the earth (the supplication of *Tahanun* and falling on one's face). The blessings of the *Amidah* do not blur this framework, which consists entirely of surrendering one's self to God.

The sense of negation of personality enabled R. Soloveitchik to present the two hymnal blessings of *Gevurot* and *Kedushah* as a homogeneous unit. In consequence, his interpretation of prayer placed the hymnal blessings in two parallel homogeneous streams, that create a single interpretive canvas built of two sheets. The dual interpretation for self-sacrifice and the sacrifice produced a complex and intricate consciousness structure, one based in its entirety on the worshiper's sacrifice of his personality.

---

90 See, for example Prov. 16:1; "Reflections on the *Amidah*," 172.
91 "Reflections on the *Amidah*," 171.
92 See Micah 1:10.
93 "Reflections on the *Amidah*," 172. R. Soloveitchik here uses the image of falling, and, we may reasonably assume, has in mind many of the Kabbalistic meanings given to this image. See, for example. Hallamish, *Kabbalah in Liturgy*, 474-85.

These two integrated flows are presented in the following table:

self-sacrifice as regulation	self-sacrifice as self-abnegation
	(1) Opening ("O Lord, open my lips")
(2) *Avot* blessing	
	(3) *Gevurot* blessing
(4) *Kedushah* blessing	(4) *Kedushah* blessing
	(5) *nefilat apayim*[94]

During the course of the hymnal blessings a person slowly learns that standing before God is primarily self-abnegation. The impression left by the confident mention of the magnificent tradition of the Patriarchs is already fractured in *Avot* and fades away completely in the other blessings. While in the blessing of *Hesed* the man is aware of his own worth and proudly speaks of it as God's gift, being, with the blessing of *Gevurot* this firm foundation crumbles, and in *Kedushah* it disintegrates completely.[95] The dimension of halakhic regulation is walled up against the mysticism of assimilation in the divine, but it does not alter the framework of self-sacrifice.

4. The Petitional Blessings: From Materiality to Abnegation

R. Soloveitchik explained in the first interpretive discussion in "Reflections on the *Amidah*" that the central concern of the hymnal blessings is the waiver of the self. The conception of sanctity as self-abnegation is the framework of the entire *Amidah*. Petition is possible after the drawing inward and negation of the self in the encounter with God. Consequently, the petitionary blessings emerge from self-sacrifice. Nor are the thanksgiving blessings a foreign object here: to the contrary, they are anchored in the petitionary blessings. In contrast with the detailed phenomenological interpretation that he gave the first three blessings, R. Soloveitchik only generally explained the petitionary and thanksgiving blessings. He elected not to delve into the depths of meaning of each individual blessing.

---

94 Continuing his discussion in "Reflections on the *Amidah*," R. Soloveitchik added the petitionary prayers to the consciousness of self-abnegation. See below.

95 We should recall the replication of the consciousness model that was formulated in *And From There You Shall Seek*, namely, the confirmation and subsequent collapse of the consciousness in the second stage (the consciousness of revelation).

Once Again: Against Pantheism and Mysticism

R. Soloveitchik explained that the petitionary blessings are the body and heart of the *Amidah*. Unlike the hymnal blessings, which proceed from halakhic regulation to self-abnegation, all the petitionary prayers are anchored in the material reality. Man requests wisdom, health, livelihood, and the like. The *Rosh Hodesh* and *Mussaf* prayers recited during festivals also include appeals for liberation from the Exile ("But because of our sins we were exiled from our land"), which are material requests (wishing for return to the Land of Israel). This appeal appears in the hymnal section of these *Amidot*, even though it contains a trace of sadness ("a mute sadness")[96] for the Exile. It is well known that halakhah forbids being sad on the Sabbath, because this would detract from Sabbath pleasure.

Turning to the worldly rules out pantheism, as R. Soloveitchik writes.

> There is no prayer without petition and supplication. Halakhah opposed all those outlooks which derive from pantheistic mysticism[97] and which aim to excise entreaty from prayer and to establish worship exclusively on an aesthetic-ecstatic[98] basis of the hymn.[99]

We saw above that the belief in the unity of God expressed in reading *Shema* rejects pantheism,[100] which is not allowed for completely different reasons. There can be two ways in which God is equated with the world: either the world is spiritual, and materiality is an illusion, or God is material.

Mystical pantheism is based on the first alternative. Pantheism presents the world as divinity, as a spiritual reality, and therefore negates the standing and worth of materiality. As we saw above, trends in Christian mysticism used the terminology of prayer to express states of assimilation in God.[101] R. Soloveitchik might have alluded to *Shirei ha-Yihud* that were composed by the pietists in Ashkenaz, and which contain traces of

---

96 "Reflections on the *Amidah*," 173.
97 See, for example, Yossef Schwartz, *"To Thee Is Silence Praise": Meister Eckhart's Reading in Maimonides' Guide of the Perplexed* [Hebrew] (Tel Aviv: Am Oved, 2002), 271-74.
98 The hymn was written in meter and rhyme, and therefore is an "aesthetic" work. The petitional prayers, in contrast, do not exhibit such stylistic composition. "Aesthetics" refers also to the hymn's literary environment, namely, the mystical literature, as we shall see below.
99 "Reflections on the *Amidah*," 173.
100 See above, Chapter Eight.
101 See above, Introduction. See also Nelson Pike, *Mystic Union: An Essay in the Phenomenology of Mysticism* (Ithaca, NY: Cornell University Press, 1992).

the conception of divine immanence.[102] The term "hymns," however, seems to allude mainly to the *piyyutim* in the *Heikhalot* literature, some of which became an integral part of the fixed prayers of many communities (*Ha-Aderet ve-ha-Emunah*, *Mi k-Elohenu*, and *Aleinu le-Shabe'ah*).

R. Soloveitchik presented the hymn as a product of pantheistic mysticism. Jewish prayer includes hymns, but it mainly relates to material life and its needs. R. Soloveitchik argued that "Halakhah [...] is displeased by the ecstatic separation of soul from body during prayer."[103] He might have referred here to the penetration of the *Heikhalot* literature hymns into prayer.[104] This literature of *Yordei ha-Merkabah* (those are occupied with the Heavenly Chariot) centered around one's ecstatic ascent to the upper *Heikhalot* (the heavenly "chambers"). According to R. Soloveitchik, the halakhists ensured that the hymns would influence the worshiper's experience of exaltation and the internalization of praise to God; however, they had reservations regarding the mystical and ecstatic background of the hymns' source.

R. Soloveitchik did not limit his critique to pantheistic mysticism. He completely removed prayer from the realm of mysticism. He writes:

> Halakhah observes scrupulously the principle of exotericism. The community as a whole cannot escape the bounds of corporeality and its petty needs. Any attempt to require all members of the community to achieve such liberation entails greater loss than benefit.[105] [...] The hymn, embroidered with aesthetic experience is confined to the private domain of the elite. It is pleasing only to mystics, who are characteristically anti-social.[106]

---

102 For example, "Who surround all and fills all / And since all has been created, You are in all" (Abraham Meir Habermann, *Shirei ha-Yihud ve-ha-Kavod* [Hebrew] [Jerusalem: Mossad Harav Kook, 1948], 26, l. 49); "For You are present [*ve-hoveh*] in all/ All is Yours and all is from You" (Habermann, *Shirei ha-Yihud ve-ha-Kavod*, 28, l. 66).

103 "Reflections on the *Amidah*," 173.

104 These hymns were collected and interpreted by Meir Bar-Ilan, *The Mysteries of Jewish Prayer and Hekhalot* [Hebrew] (Ramat Gan: Bar-Ilan University Press, 1987). Gershom Scholem's *Jewish Gnosticism, Merkabah Mysticism and Talmudic Tradition*, first published in 1960 (New York: Jewish Theological Seminary of America), drew attention to the *Heikhalot* literature. Previously, in 1941, he published *Major Trends in Jewish Mysticism* (Jerusalem: Schocken), in which a chapter is devoted to the *Heikhalot*. Jellenik and Wertheimer published parts of this literature in their midrashic collections.

105 Following M Avot 5:11-12; *Avot de-Rabbi Nathan*, Version B, chapter 45.

106 R. Soloveitchik's style might be somewhat ironic. This wording (*she-hitztaynu be-anti-sotzialiyut*), however, might also be understood in the spirit of the Passover Haggadah: *shehayu Yisrael metzuyanim sham*, in the sense of being unique or conspicuous in their uniqueness.

Their mode of existence is esoteric; they are spiritually fastidious.[107] Halakhah cannot be confined within the domain of the spiritual nobility. Only petition can bring prayer to the public domain.[108]

Mysticism, by its very definition, is directed to "the elite"[109] and is not meant for all. As was mentioned above, the question of esotericism and exotericism was important for R. Soloveitchik. He stressed in various works that the Jewish religious consciousness is, first and foremost, a halakhic consciousness, and the halakhah is meant for the entire public.[110] Accordingly, the hymnal blessings are a minority in the *Amidah*, and even these blessings lack hymnal style.

R. Soloveitchik was forced to emphasize the centrality of petition, because the halakhah is the foundation of his thought. Nonetheless, most of the discussion in which he interprets the *Amidah* is, surprisingly, devoted to the hymnal blessings. The length of the discussion of the petitionary blessings is less than a quarter of that of the hymnal blessings. This means that the experience of praise, which, from the outset, is characteristic of an elite public, occupied R. Soloveitchik to a much greater degree than the general experience of entreaty. He did not, in advance, limit the tempestuous experience of praise to individuals, but the complex movements that occur in different dimensions of the consciousness generally typify the *homo religiosus*. In this respect, R. Soloveitchik oscillated between the experiences characteristic of outstanding individuals and those common to the broad public. He also emphasized that "it is impossible to recite the middle benedictions without the first three."[111] That is, the experience of praise facilitates entreaty and becomes the essential condition of a request.

The centrality of the hymns can be explained in an additional way, in light of the parallel to *And From There You Shall Seek*. Both compositions were meant to denote the oscillations of the consciousness, that is, the different states between which the consciousness swings. *And From There You Shall Seek* describes the journey taken by the consciousness, while *Worship of the Heart* bases its depiction on the *Amidah*. More than anything, the hymnal blessings express the movement of the consciousness, because, at

---

107 Following BT Pesahim 113b; *Kallah Rabbati* 9:6.
108 "Reflections on the *Amidah*," 174.
109 The sources state that the elite are "few" (BT Sukkah 48b; Sanhedrin 97b).
110 See above, Chapter Six.
111 "Reflections on the *Amidah*," 175.

the same time, they contain apex and nadir, esotericism and exotericism, closeness and distance.

Petition and Self-Abnegation

After R. Soloveitchik discussed the petitionary blessings in a negative fashion, namely, by rejecting mysticism, he turned to explicate them in a positive way. His approach is unequivocal: the petitionary blessings are intended to create the consciousness of man's dependence upon God.

R. Soloveitchik presented a concealed dichotomy between the hymnal and petitionary blessings. Praise encourages an (ecstatic) separation of the soul from the body, while petition is directed mostly to physicality. Praise is rooted in esotericism, and petition, in exotericism. Praise is meant mainly for the perfect, while petition is for sinners. He accordingly determined that "the vigor and power of prayer derive from petition."[112] Nonetheless, R. Soloveitchik sought to fracture this dichotomy and present a picture of the *Amidah* as uniform. He noted the parallel between the prayer of Solomon upon the completion of the Temple and the installation of the Ark and the *Amidah*.[113] The Bible describes this prayer as "supplication" (I Kings 8:54). This is the parallel:

> The *Amidah* is based on these words enunciated by Solomon. The *Amidah* deals with the needs of this world: bodily health,[114] fertility of the earth,[115] sustenance, political needs of the nation in the land, ingathering of the exiles,[116]

---

112 "Reflections on the *Amidah*," 173.

113 This parallel is alluded to in PT Berakhot 1:5, 3c, which discusses the genuflections in the *Amidah*. During the course of the discussion, the Talmud states: "R. Simon in the name of R. Joshua ben Levi [said]: Once the king bows down deeply, he does not get up until he completes his entire prayer. What is the reason? 'When Solomon finished offering to the Lord all this prayer and supplication' [I Kings 8:54]." And similarly in *Gen. Rabbah* 39:3. However, the statement at the beginning of the next cited passage, that the *Amidah* was based on the prayer of Solomon, does not appear in the sources.

114 The blessing of healing, which ends with "Healer of the sick of His people Israel," parallels the line "In any plague and in any disease" in the prayer of Solomon (I Kings 8:37).

115 The blessing for prosperous years, which ends with "who blesses the years," corresponds to the lines "Should the heavens be shut up and there be no rain" (I Kings 8:35), "and send down rain upon the land" (v. 36), and "if there is a famine in the land, if there is pestilence, blight, mildew, locusts or caterpillars" (v. 37).

116 The blessing for the ingathering of the exiles, which ends with "who gathers the dispersed of His people Israel," corresponds to I Kings 8:46-53 (captivity in an enemy land,

restoration of judicial autonomy,[117] the perpetuation of Israel's sages,[118] the building of Jerusalem,[119] the restoration of Davidic kingship,[120] and the like form the background of prayer in all its diversity. The very gesture of falling before God and acknowledging His unlimited sovereignty and man's utter impotence, constitutes an act of sacrifice. Service of the heart is expressed in the middle benedictions.[121]

The omission of the blessings of repentance ("who desires repentance") and forgiveness ("the gracious One who repeatedly forgives") is striking, even though sin and forgiveness are mentioned at length in the prayer of Solomon. R. Soloveitchik focuses on the material and political needs to show that petition is located in the earthly plane. Repentance, atonement, and purification reflect ascent above the material sphere. He consequently stressed the aspects of economic and political beseeching.

At the end of the passage, however, R. Soloveitchik connected the petitionary blessings with the consciousness of self-abnegation. Although the worshiper addresses the material, the result of petitionary blessings is not self-consciousness. The request for health, livelihood, and the like is not connected to the worshiper's awareness of his needs, his self-cognizance, or his facing his own self. In fact, the entreaty leads to a sense of dependence ("unlimited sovereignty" and "utter impotence") and to sacrificing one's personality. "Worship of the heart" is perceived at the end of this passage as the subjective dimension of the consciousness. It should be recalled that "worship of the heart" also includes communion with God, Torah study, and the like. The "earthly" petitionary blessings are presented as the direct continuation of the hymnal blessings in terms of the consciousness of self-sacrifice, that is, the subjective dimensions of "worship of the heart."

---

and the mention of the Exodus from Egypt as an allusion to the return to the Land of Israel. For understandable reasons, Solomon's prayer in I Kings does not take actual exile into account. It speaks mainly about concern for those in captivity in an enemy land. Consequently, there are no parallels to the other blessings for political needs). See also I Kings 8:34: "and restore them to the land that You gave to their fathers."

117 The blessing of justice, which ends with "who loves righteousness and justice."
118 The blessing of the righteous, which ends with "who is the support and trust of the righteous."
119 The blessing that ends with "who builds Jerusalem."
120 The blessing of the offshoot of David, which ends with "who makes the glory of salvation flourish."
121 "Reflections on the *Amidah*," 175.

In interpretive terms, the petitionary blessings join the series of sacrificing as abnegation. The motif of self-sacrifice connects the hymnal and petitionary blessings and links both with the *nefilat appayim* that comes after the conclusion of the *Amidah*, apparently leading to a homogeneous picture. The consciousness of the *Amidah* is that of sacrificing in both its channels, self-sacrifice as regulation and as surrender. R. Soloveitchik succeeded in revealing the uniform consciousness within the different blessings. Actually, this uniformity encapsulates contrasts, and the worshiper oscillates between an awareness of his selfhood and physicality and self-abnegation before God.

The Prayer of One Who Walks in a Dangerous Place

Ezra Fleischer demonstrated at length that the prayer of one who walks in a dangerous place is based on national needs and characteristics.[122] R. Soloveitchik, in contrast, accentuates the negation of the detailing of the individual's needs. He chose to quote the *baraita* (external mishnah) in BT Berakhot 29b that sets forth a fourfold disagreement on the texts of the prayer recited in a dangerous place:

> Our masters taught: One who passes through a place infested with wild beasts and robbers says a short *tefilah*. And what is a short *tefilah*?
>
> R. Eliezer says: Do Your will in Heaven above, grant peace of mind to those who fear You below, and do what is good in Your eyes. Blessed are You, who hears prayer.
>
> R. Joshua says, Hear the supplication of Your people Israel and speedily fulfill their request. Blessed are You, who hears prayer.
>
> R. Eleazar son of R. Zadok says, Hear the cry of Your people Israel and speedily fulfill their request. Blessed are You, who hears prayer.[123]
>
> Others say, The needs of Your people Israel are many and they have no patience. May it be Your will, O Lord our God, to give each one his sustenance and to each body what it lacks. Blessed are You, who hears prayer.[124]
>
> R. Huna says, The law follows the others.

---

122 Fleischer, "The *Shemone Esre*," 206-8 (in Mack's edition: Mack, *Studies*, 184-86).

123 R. Soloveitchik did not cite this view. T Berakhot 3:7 (Lieberman's edition: 13) adds the view of R. Yose: "Hear the prayer of Your people Israel and speedily fulfill their request. Blessed is the One who hears prayer."

124 R. Soloveitchik claims in *Lessons in Memory of Father* (vol. 2, 50-51) that R. Eliezer was the most stringent, and "the others" were the most lenient. This explanation also appears in "Reflections on the *Amidah*," 176.

In practice, R. Soloveitchik constitutes the disagreement between the Tannaim in the *baraita* on two questions:

(1) Is it permitted to mention the nation's needs? R. Eliezer forbids this mention, while R. Joshua, R. Eleazar son of R. Zadok, and "others" permit it.

(2) If it is indeed permitted to mention the needs of the Jewish people, is it also allowed to generally mention the individual needs? (R. Joshua and R. Eleazar son of R. Zadok prohibit this mention, and "others" permit it.)

In any event, R. Soloveitchik maintains that the Tannaim totally forbade detailing individual needs. He asked: why did the Sages offer various liturgical versions for the *tefilah* in a dangerous place, when such versions do not fulfill the obligation of prayer? Why should not the one in danger pray spontaneously, saying whatever he thinks? He answers:

> If the praying individual is unable to present before God the entire order of prayer in its authentic form—to arrange God's praise and beg leave to approach Him boldly, to mention the merits of the Patriarchs and God's graciously attending to the deficiencies of every creature—then he is not permitted to petition for his needs.[125]

R. Soloveitchik understood the aim of the Tannaim's versions as negating and as restricting: the Rabbis specifically suggested the text of an abbreviated prayer, so that a person in a dangerous place would not pray for his private needs. This is not allowed because he has not properly preceded the prayer with the hymnal blessings. Since these blessings are a sort of *mattir* for the petitionary blessings, a person may not submit a request for his needs without this necessary preamble. The Rabbis most likely feared that a dangerous situation would invite a person to ask for his personal needs and thereby be insolent. Accordingly, they took pains to anchor these liturgical versions in halakhic norms. R. Soloveitchik seemingly argued that the Tannaim not only desired to offer prayer versions for a worshiper in a time

---

125 "Reflections on the *Amidah*," 176. In *Lessons in Memory of Father* (vol. 2, 50), R. Soloveitchik writes: "Since the worshiper does not employ the wording of the *Amidah* and does not recite eighteen benedictions, then he obviously is forbidden to engage in supplication and petition. Even R. Eliezer, who is of the opinion that a person should ask for his needs before the *Amidah*, permitted this only if one immediately prays afterward, since the *Amidah* retroactively permits. If, however, the fixed *Shemoneh Esreh* prayer [= the *Amidah*] is lacking, there is nothing to permit (*mattir*) petition."

of danger but also wanted to erect a barrier against a descent to versions containing a request for his own needs.

Thus R. Soloveitchik once again buttressed the conception of the unity of the *Amidah* as an interpretive principle. The petitionary blessings are totally dependent upon the hymnal blessings. Commentators and scholars spoke about the unity of the *Amidah* in this respect. Joseph Heinemann wrote that

> most of the Eighteen Benedictions (which the Rabbis of the *Misnah* and the *Talmud* refer to as the *Tefillah*, the "Prayer" *par excellence*), are petitionary in content. To be sure, each of these petitionary prayers concludes with a eulogy formula, and is thereby infused with elements of thanksgiving and praise to him who satisfies the needs of all his creatures. (For example, the petition "Heal us, O Lord, and we shall be healed", concludes by praising him "who heals the stricken of his people Israel".) So, too, it was ordained that the Eighteen Benedictions [...] open with prayers of praise, which are to be recited before the petitionary prayers, and close with prayers of thanksgiving, which are to be read after them. Nonetheless, the primary purpose of the weekday *Tefillah* is unquestionably to petition for Israel's necessities out of the firm conviction that the Lord will hear these supplications and respond favorably to them.[126]

Heinemann locates the praise within the petition and thereby presents the mutual incorporation of praise and petition. For him, as well, petition is not divorced from praise. Heinemann, however, maintained that the Rabbis were not concerned by what he termed the "philosophical" problem[127] of the very act of prayer, that is, the absurdity of troubling God for a person's everyday needs. In any event, Heinemann, too, offered as unified as possible an interpretation of the *Amidah* structure. R. Soloveitchik, on the other hand, used the principle of petition to highlight dependence and the sacrifice of personality.

Petition: A Comparative Aspect

R. Soloveitchik related to the central standing of the petitionary blessings in various writings, thereby following thinkers such as R. Joseph Albo.[128] In each composition of his, however, he offered a different aspect of this centrality. Lawrence Kaplan suggested the following comparative theory.[129]

---

126 Heinemann, *Prayer in the Talmud*, 18.
127 Ibid., 19.
128 See Dror Erlich, "Dualism as a Stylistic Characteristic in the Discussion of Prayer by R. Joseph Albo" [Hebrew], *Kenishta* 3 (2007): 23.
129 In a personal letter to me.

(1) In *Worship of the Heart*, the petitionary blessings create a community between man and his God.
(2) In "Redemption, Prayer, Talmud Torah," these blessings bring the worshiper to an awareness of his values and existence.
(3) In "Reflections on the *Amidah*," the petitionary blessings expose the worshiper as a psycho-physical being, who, unlike the notions of the mystics, is conscious of his physicality and its needs, as well as man's absolute dependence on God.

The common element of the petitionary blessings that underlies this theory is the retreat in man's status when faced by himself and by God. This regression exists regardless of which approach we adopt: either the religious phenomenological approach, that is, man's nullity in the face of divine fullness, or the existential approach, namely, existential distress. Now we will reexamine the meaning of the petitionary blessings in these works.

(1) In *Worship of the Heart*, the petitionary blessings are connected with the depth crisis of existence.[130]
(2) In "Redemption, Prayer, Talmud Torah," as Kaplan indicated, the focus is coming to know human needs.
(3) In "Reflections on the *Amidah*," the petitionary blessings express absolute dependence upon and self-abnegation before God.

We learn that the centrality of the petitionary blessings ensues from an awareness of human existence as limited and from the acceptance of these limitations. Connection with God on the one hand and awareness of selfhood, on the other were meant to contend with the human condition. The subject, his consciousness, and his existence are the key to the standing of the petitionary blessings.

5. The Thanksgiving Blessings: The Return

After the reader has internalized the unity of the hymnal and petitionary blessings, R. Soloveitchik turns to the thanksgiving blessings. Here, too, he wanted to interpret the blessings as a combination of praise and self-sacrifice. Such an incorporation returns the thanksgiving blessings to the

---

130 See above, Chapter Four.

hymnal blessings that begin the *Amidah*, thereby presenting the *Amidah* as a homogeneous unit.

Reversal: (1) From the Objective to the Subjective

The Temple service is the source of the *Avodah* blessing, which ends with "who restores His Presence to Zion." This blessing was originally recited after the sprinkling of the blood in the course of the daily *Tamid* sacrifice. After the destruction of the Temple, when the sacrificial rite was canceled, the text "who restores His Presence to Zion" was established as a prayer for the return of this rite.[131] R. Soloveitchik viewed the fact that this blessing endures, even though the Temple has been destroyed, as the triumph of the subjective.[132] As we mentioned, he constructed the subjective consciousness on the objective one. The stability of the objective dimension is the reason for this division of the consciousness. The halakhah, from the aspect of action, is not fluid, and it fences and balances the effervescent subjective dimension. We saw above that the standing of prayer eroded one of the solid foundations of this structure, namely, reconstruction. This standing also led to a "reversal," as regards the derivation of the objective from the subjective. At this juncture R. Soloveitchik took an additional step in fracturing the firm structure that he presented in *The Halakhic Mind*. Now, prayer effects a change in the focus of consciousness. The subjective "spiritual act"[133] is stable, while the action is fluid. The halakhah ordering that sacrifice be followed with a prayer cannot be fulfilled at present; however, the subjective dimension of surrendering the self remains in force. The blessing of *Avodah* is founded on the subjective dimension of consciousness.

R. Soloveitchik ascribed the stability of the subjective dimension of consciousness to the new conception of sacrifice as the sacrifice of the self. While the objective side is limited to the actions comprising the sacrifice (slaughtering, receiving the blood, carrying the portions, sprinkling the blood), self-sacrifice is the subjective aspect. R. Soloveitchik based his conception on differing expositions cited by *Tosafot*. BT Menakhot 110a states: "This refers to the altar where Michael, the great prince, stands and offers up on it a sacrifice." *Tosafot* cite "differing expositions: one says,

---

131 See, for example, Moshe Weinfeld, "Biblical Roots," 553-54 (in Mack's edition: Mack, *Studies*, 41-42).
132 See above, Chapters Six and Seven.
133 "Reflections on the *Amidah*," 178.

The souls of the righteous; and another says, Fiery sheep," which the Tosafists connect with the blessing of *Avodah*. For R. Soloveitchik, these expositions are complementary. The "fiery sheep" reflect the objective dimension, that is, the historic sacrifice that involved actual animals, and "the souls of the righteous" refer to the subjective side, namely, the surrendering of one's self.

> According to the first interpretation, the phrase *ve-ishei Yisrael* (the burnt offerings of Israel) [in the *Avodah* blessing][134] does not refer to the physical fire on the altar but to a celestial, transcendent offering, and the sacrifice is the soul, the individual personal being of man. This sacrifice continues to exist today; it did not come to an end with the cessation of the daily offerings.[135]

Thus, the *Amidah*, as "worship of the heart," is capable of changing the set structure of religious consciousness.

Reversal: (2) From Assimilation to Personality

R. Soloveitchik argued at the beginning of the last section of "Reflections on the *Amidah*"[136] that the hymnal and thanksgiving blessings have the following chiastic structure:[137]

blessings of praise	blessings of thanksgiving	reasoning
Avot	*Shalom*	lovingkindness
Gevurot	Thanksgiving	dependence
Kedushah	*Avodah*	self-sacrifice

In this structure, the blessing of *Avodah* is parallel to that of *Kedushah*, and both are concerned with the same matter: communion with God. Such communion, however, which is analogous to the surrender of the personality, might only move in a single direction. An individual who has reached the experience of *Kedushah* and *Avodah* must completely negate his own self.

---

134 On the version of the blessing, see Ezra Fleischer, "On the *Avodah* Blessing" [Hebrew], *Sinai* 60 (1967): 269-275; idem, "Fragments of Prayer Collections from the Land of Israel in the Genizah" [Hebrew], *Kobez al Yad* 13 (1996): 116.

135 "Reflections on the *Amidah*," 178.

136 "Reflections on the *Amidah*," 179.

137 This structure appears in the discussion by Ziegler, *Majesty and Humanity*, 228.

R. Soloveitchik accordingly emphasized that communion with God paradoxicallty generates self-affirmation. He observed that the movement between communion and personality is maintained even when the worshiper is lost in the heights of the communion experience. He writes about the blessing of *Avodah*:

> His [the Jew's] soul is bound up in a great, profound, world-embracing request. He asks God to accept the great sacrifice he has just offered, to accept his being that is returned to God, cleaving unto the Infinite and connecting itself to the Divine throne. God is "satisfied" with this offering. He receives it and restores it to the one who has offered it. The praying individual annuls himself in order to acquire himself. From his prayer man emerges firm, elevated and sublime, having found his redemption in self-loss and self-recovery.[138]

The beginning of this passage, "his soul is bound up in a great, profound, world-embracing request," is a paraphrase of Esther's request, "let my life be granted me as my wish."[139] R. Soloveitchik seems to argue that the worshiper wishes to sacrifice his soul to God, as in the blessing of *Avodah*. However, the Biblical source, at which R. Soloveitchik hints here, also demonstrates Esther's desire for self-preservation. Esther begs for her people's life, which is antithetical to the preceding assumption of self-sacrifice. Accordingly, R. Soloveitchik incorporated both meanings, in a manner reminiscent of the "ladder of ascension."[140] A person sacrifices his soul to God, and in this act he rediscovers his personality. The experiential intensity of self-sacrifice paradoxically reveals the personality of the sacrificer. Self-abnegation is also self-affirmation.

We learn from the end of this passage that redemption is dialectic: it combines surrendering one's self to God and the rediscovery of self. The oscillation between losing and uncovering the soul, and especially its rediscovery, does not appear in R. Soloveitchik's earlier discussions. This motif made its way into R. Soloveitchik's writings towards the end of his discussion of the blessing of *Avodah*, and in some respects this is a surprising shift. We can offer an explanation that suits R. Soloveitchik's religious phenomenological path: the more consciousness advances toward perfection by means of prayer, the more complex it becomes. This dialectic deepens

---

138 "Reflections on the *Amidah*," 179.
139 Esther 7:3.
140 On the motif of the ladder of ascension, which is concerned with both ascent and descent, see Altmann, *Studies in Religious Philosophy*, 41-72.

as consciousness approaches redemption. The more a person negates himself, the more he reveals himself, due to divine grace. God "receives it [the offering] and restores it to the one who has offered it." Thus, redemption also fluctuates.[141]

Why did R. Soloveitchik add the revelation of the self here, of all places? And how does this revelation fit into the phenomenological explanation of the *Amidah*? The parallelism between the blessings of *Kedushah* and *Avodah* is most probably at the basis of the motif of self-discovery in the wake of self-abnegation. We explained above that sacrifice has two meanings: the negation of the self and halakhic regulation.

The second sense, life in accordance with the halakhah, includes self-sacrifice, but the one who observes the halakhah is aware of his self. The one who follows the halakhah waives a substantive dimension of his freedom—and this is, indeed, a sacrifice—but he does not lose his selfhood. R. Soloveitchik himself emphasizes[142] that when a person takes the Four Species on Sukkot or puts on *tefilin*, he does not imagine that he is bound, with his blood pouring out, as if he were sacrificed.

This parallel reveals two meanings in *Avodah*, as well: self-abnegation (surrender to God) and self-discovery (regulation). R. Soloveitchik connected the two ideas: the negation of the self leads to its discovery, by means of halakhic observance. The combination of the two aspects of sacrifice in a process of assimilation and a return to the self is manifest in the blessing of *Avodah*—to be more precise, in the parallel between the blessings of *Kedushah* and *Avodah*. The former expresses uncompromising communion with God. The blessing of *Avodah*, in contrast, also contains an aspect of national life and its regulation. The blessing of *Kedushah* is totally focused on God and His praise, while the thanksgiving in *Avodah* also contains petitionary elements. The wording of the blessing reveals this insight ("Find favor, Lord our God, in Your people Israel and their prayer").

R. Soloveitchik believed that his composition on the consciousness of prayer should end with the return to the self, and not with its negation. Unlike *And From There You Shall Seek*, for example, which ends the description of the stages of the consciousness with communion (at least in the overt stratum), "Reflections on the *Amidah*" ends with the idea of return: "the binding of man and his demise together with his return to

---

141 See above, Chapter Nine.
142 "Reflections on the *Amidah*," 161.

existence and being."[143] The flow of ideas in "Reflections on the *Amidah*" joins the direction of *And From There You Shall Seek*. The latter strives for the consciousness of self-sacrifice and communion with the divine, but the end of the discussion changes its direction.

Thanksgiving

In a chiastic structure, the blessing of thanksgiving (*Modim*—"We thank") is parallel to the blessing of *Gevurot*. Both express the feeling of dependence. Giving thanks to God means dependence upon His kindnesses. R. Soloveitchik explains:

> Following the acceptance of his request that his sacrifice be accepted, man thanks God for its fulfillment.[144] He adopts the optimistic position that God has hearkened to his prayer. As God has accepted his great sacrifice, surely, his prayer shall emerge into the light.[145]

R. Soloveitchik interpreted *Modim* as thanksgiving, even though many understood it as a theological and dogmatic statement.[146] In the continuation of his discussion, however, he stated that the thanksgiving and trust become "complete certitude."[147] This certitude is grounded in the conception of prayer as a dialogue between man and his God: the worshiper, in his monologue, is persuaded that God listens to his petition.

We see that the chiastic structure is the key to understanding the process of consciousness. In the end, the feeling of dependence is revealed as the experience of the beneficent God who showers His kindnesses on man. The transformation of the consciousness in the *Amidah* is expressed also in the blessing of thanksgiving: "God's might [*gevurotav*] appears in His mercy."[148] Just as the blessing of *Gevurot* expresses the transformation of the consciousness in which lovingkindness (*hesed*) becomes might (*gevurah*), as was noted above, a similar process also occurs in the blessing of thanksgiving.

---

143 "Reflections on the *Amidah*," 180.
144 That is, the fulfillment of the request.
145 "Reflections on the *Amidah*," 180.
146 At times thanksgiving is also perceived as the experience of God. See Max Kadushin, *The Rabbinic Mind* (New York: Jewish Theological Seminary of America, 1952), 344-46.
147 "Reflections on the *Amidah*," 180.
148 "Reflections on the *Amidah*," 180.

Shalom—Peace

The blessing of peace [*Shalom*] denotes the return to kindness (the blessing of *Avot*). The ending of the *Amidah* revolves around serenity and calm. R. Soloveitchik presented the *Amidah* as a tempest of overt and covert movements. The worshiper is tossed between opposing emotions and inclinations, and ending in such a condition would induce a pessimistic atmosphere. The composers of the *Amidah*, however, wanted to chart a situation, in which the tensions would be resolved. R. Soloveitchik ends "Reflections on the *Amidah*" with the following:

> The praying individual lies down in green pastures [Ps. 23:2], cleansing himself before God like a son before his father.[149] His tempest-tossed, riven soul finds happiness and serenity, all fear being forgotten. Dread has disappeared; the awesome mystery[150] is past. In their place is a welling up of joy and a yearning for communion with the source of being. Man does not flee from God, but rather races toward Him[151] and resides in the bosom of the *Shekhinah*. All is blanketed in the serenity of peace and quiet.[152] Over all, there flows the blessing of the Infinite; the *hesed* of God descends "like the dew on Mount Hermon" (Ps. 133:3). The word [should be: world] is illuminated with the precious light that flows from the Infinite.[153]

Again, as in *And From There You Shall Seek*, R. Soloveitchik wanted to end "Reflections on the *Amidah*" with a resolution of this tension, and pointed to the uniformity of consciousness. *Amidah* comes full circle and returns to *hesed*, so that its end expresses a stage of communion and attainment of the goal. The reader who is familiar with the preceding pages of "Reflections on the *Amidah*," however will know that immediately after serenity, the worshiper plunges into *nefilat appayim*. The surrender to God does not leave the consciousness free of tensions. Furthermore, the blessing of

---

149 This intimate description of the son-father relationship is very different from the Biblical idea of covenant, which also frequently appears in R. Soloveitchik's thought. See, for example, Alon Goshen-Gottstein, "God and Israel as Father and Son in Tannaitic Literature" [Hebrew], PhD dissertation, Hebrew University, 1987, 248-55.

150 That is, God's concealment.

151 R. Soloveitchik used the word of "racing" as racing to God, and not as an escape. Apparently, we see here traces of R. Solomon Ibn Gabirol's lines in *Keter Malkhut*: "I flee from You to You."

152 Following Ezek. 16:49.

153 "Reflections on the *Amidah*," 181.

Shalom is depicted as a return to the blessing of *Avot*: but this blessing itself, concerned with an abundance of kindness, is based on latent streams of absolute dependence and the sacrificing of one's self, which are presented by means of the divine attributes in the beginning of the blessing ("the great, mighty, and awe-inspiring").

In any event, R. Soloveitchik sought to create the impression that the *Amidah* ends with infinite *hesed*. He chose to finish with the Kabbalistic terminology of *Ein-Sof* ("the Infinite," which also appears as *Al-Sof*). His motive is clear: R. Soloveitchik wanted to declare that the "awesome mystery" of the past had not vanished. In Kabbalistic literature, *Ein-Sof* denotes the impervious aspect of God that is not involved in the *Sefirot* and the material world and is decidedly indifferent to the worshiper, his personality, and his desires. R. Soloveitchik just declared that the model of the concealed God ("the awesome mystery") belongs to the vanished past. However, in order to express God's abundant lovingkindness, he chose another, more powerful model of the concealed God: the Infinite. In the Kabbalistic literature, even when *hesed* emanates from the upper strata of the Godhead, the source—the Infinite—remains completely indifferent to the worshiper's desires for communion. Even though the one experiencing this process returns to *hesed*, the sanctity and self-sacrifice remain in force and continue to bubble and flow torrentially below the surface.

Now we can determine the consciousness and interpretive framework of the *Amidah*, according to R. Soloveitchik:

(1) Beginning with self-abnegation ("O Lord, open my lips") and ending with self-abnegation (*nefilat appayim*).
(2) Beginning with *hesed* (*Avot*) and ending with *hesed* (*Shalom*).
(3) Beginning with covert *Din* ("mighty, and awe-inspiring" in *Avot*) and ending with overt strict law (the Infinite, *nefilat appayim*).

6. Summary

R. Soloveitchik's phenomenological interpretation of the *Amidah* uncovers varied dimensions and processes of consciousness in the liturgical text, which the scholarly research of prayer may help to clarify. In this section I will examine these positions and attempt to understand the direction and interpretive patterns in R. Soloveitchik's commentary on the blessings of the *Amidah*.

Tense Unity

The starting point of R. Soloveitchik's interpretation of the blessings of the weekday *Amidah* is paradoxical. The style of the *Amidah* attests that it is meant for all. We saw that R. Soloveitchik ascribed great importance to the exotericism of the *Amidah*. Both the plural language of the blessings and their content are directed to the public. Ezra Fleischer added in his extensive article on the *Amidah* that it is "the prayer for the mending of the nation."[154] He further wrote:

> The content of the prayer [= the *Amidah*] is focused on the absolute in the national sphere, and it is only by merit of being part of the nation that the individual has any place in it; the mending of the nation is obviously also his mending. Accordingly, the prayer should be recited by the public, that is, by Israel who, for this purpose, become a single brotherhood in which their personal uniqueness is negated. An individual who is incapable of standing in the prayer of the public joins himself from afar to this brotherhood, by directing his own prayer to the prayer of the public.[155]

R. Soloveitchik was well aware of the *Amidah*'s relation to the public. He preferred, however, to interpret the blessings of the *Amidah* as reflecting dramas of the consciousness and storms of the personality. After the feeling of exaltation of the blessing of *Geulah* ("who redeemed Israel"), the worshiper immediately experiences the nadir of helplessness before God, and he therefore requests aid in praying ("O Lord, open my lips").[156] And from the exaltation of *hesed*, love, and the capacity for speech (*Avot*), he plunges into the God of indifference ("mighty, and awe-inspiring"), where he experiences silence and the paralysis of his personality. From here, the dialectic path continues in different ways through the other blessings of the *Amidah*. R. Soloveitchik wanted to present the prayer experience as a range of processes taking place within human consciousness: a dialectical structure that reaches its resolution and balance alongside unabated tension. This tension occurs in the subjective strata of consciousness, but it is also evident in the oscillation between the public nature of the *Amidah* and the personal consciousness of the worshiper.[157] At any rate, for R. Soloveitchik

---

154 Fleischer, "The *Shemone Esre*," 202 (In Mack's edition: Mack, *Studies*, 180).
155 Fleischer, "The *Shemone Esre*," 202-3 (in Mack's edition: Mack, *Studies*, 180-81).
156 See also what R. Soloveitchik wrote in *Koren Mesorat Harav Siddur*, ed. Arnold Lustiger (New York: OU Press, 2011), 510.
157 See also Blidstein, *Political Concepts*, 153-54.

the main element of the *Amidah* consists of the individual standing before God. The shift to the individual personality is additionally expressed in R. Soloveitchik's almost complete disregard of the messianic dimension in the *Amidah*.[158] We have already spoken of his reason: for the subjective consciousness, the sacrifice and the *Amidah* are one and the same, even if the sacrificial rite is not conducted normatively in the realm beyond the consciousness. In the personal plane, personal redemption consists of communion, as is expressed in the blessing of *Shalom* that ends the *Amidah*. The *Amidah* ends with redemption, that is, the redemption of the individual. Moreover, the end of the *Amidah* is immediately followed by the fall, that is, the confession and *nefilat appayim*, which reflect the return to the divisive and partial reality of sin.

Consider yet another substantive oscillation: R. Soloveitchik's commentary was meant to denote the processes and agitation characteristic of the consciousness, from self-affirmation to surrendering the self to God. On the other hand, he wanted to maintain the unity of the text. R. Soloveitchik strove to show that, despite the oscillations, the flow is unified, and the states of consciousness are anchored one in the other and create a uniform textual and consciousness context. Again, Fleischer wrote:

> The *Amidah* is not a bundle of sorts of prayers that were composed in different places and at different times; nor is it a mechanical copying, divorced from any reality and any guiding intent, of Biblical or other prayer models. It rather is a literary work that was composed all at once and in a single place, by a body aware of its desires and its role.[159]

R. Soloveitchik thus presented a model of the unity of opposites as an interpretive key to the uniform texts of prayer.

Patterns

From a certain aspect, the dynamics of R. Soloveitchik's phenomenological interpretation can be compared to the Kabbalistic doctrine of *kavvanot* (mystical intents). According to this doctrine, the worshiper experiences the tempests of contrasts and reconciliations, ascents and descents, transitions from one blessing to another, each expressing a certain *Sefirah* or

---

158 See, for example, Eliezer Schweid, *The Siddur of Prayer: Philosophy, Poetry and Mystery*, translated by Gershon Greenberg (Boston: Academic Studies Press, 2015), chapters 12-13.

159 Fleischer, "The *Shemone Esre*," 206 (in Mack's edition: Mack, *Studies*, 184).

combination of *Sefirot* in the passage from the *Amidah* to *Tahanun*. Each of these changes reflects a different station in the worshiper's journey. These shifts turn the *Amidah* into a rich and tension-laden experience, which mirrors the changes in the divine world. In R. Soloveitchik's thought, the *Amidah* reflects the events in the world of consciousness. The consciousness experiences states of love and fear, attraction and aversion, discovery and disappearance, and the like, that become most complex situations.

Again, similar to the Kabbalah, where each level latently includes all the others, and the divine influence becomes a lively drama, so, too, the consciousness of prayer is composed of numerous tensions, each of which contains a series of other tensions, both hidden and revealed. These Kabbalistic models might have been in the background of the phenomenological description of the consciousness of prayer, even though R. Soloveitchik usually objected to mysticism, which he preferred to use only for ornamental purposes and as a hermeneutical tool. The patterns of the Kabbalists, however, are present in his discussions. Additionally, the interpretive discussion of the blessings of the *Amidah* partially revolved around the divine attributes ("great," "mighty," "awe-inspiring"), which may hint at a connection with the Kabbalistic literature. This is indirectly supported by R. Soloveitchik's ending this work with the attribute of "Infinite."

Self-Sacrifice

The motif of R. Soloveitchik's interpretation of prayer is a sense of sacrifice. Prayer is a substitute for sacrifice in the objective realm. In the subjective-consciousness realm, however, prayer and sacrifice are one and the same. The worshiper sacrifices his selfhood. R. Soloveitchik's son-in-law, R. Aharon Lichtenstein, said in a conversation with R. Haim Sabato:

> We—and by "we" I mean to some degree students of Rav Soloveitchik, though I also include those who subscribe to culture and modern Torah culture—tend to glorify sacrifice, giving, and the tragic aspect of life. We do not say that a person is God-fearing only when things are going well for him.[160]

This relates to the central place, which the motif of suffering occupied in R. Soloveitchik's writings, in particular in his earlier works. But it also expresses the ethos of self-sacrifice, of the surrender of one's personality to God, and the ideal of communion with God in his intimate circle.

---

160 Sabato, *Seeking His Presence*, 75.

However, R. Soloveitchik also emphasized the parallel element: the return to life. The conception of sacrifice as the regulation of halakhic life already alludes to this new emphasis.

R. Lichtenstein unquestionably voiced the dominant position. R. Soloveitchik saw absolute sacrifice, the self's complete communion with God, as the goal of prayer. The tensions of life in accordance with halakhah are meant to give expression to the ramification of religious life. This complexity does not obscure the motif of sacrifice as the summit of the religious experience. This principle became an interpretive tool for understanding the intents of the *Amidah*.

And From There You Shall Seek *and "Reflections on the* Amidah"

Since this discussion in this chapter concludes our analysis of "Reflections on the *Amidah*," we should note, once again, the background of this work, as reflected in R. Soloveitchik's works from the presumed time of its composition. As was mentioned above, "Reflections on the *Amidah*" is in many respects congruent with *And From There You Shall Seek*. The quest for the perfect religious experience, devoid of tension, on the one hand, and, on the other, the latent tensions that are present and ever-stirring in the covert stratum guide the description of the religious consciousness in both of these works. The framework of a phenomenological discussion, too, is common to both, and is especially evident in his interpretation of the *Amidah*. Nor does his florid Hebrew style allow any doubt regarding the shared nature of these two compositions. In sum, I wish to present different aspects of the two works that have the same root:

(1) Extent: *And From There You Shall Seek* is of broad scope, and offers a detailed and precise phenomenological description of the subjective and objective consciousness, while "Reflections on the *Amidah*" limits the discussion to a general portrayal.

(2) Depth: *And From There You Shall Seek* describes dense and convoluted consciousness processes, with varied allusions to subterranean consciousness streams. Such an intricate depiction is no longer prevalent in "Reflections on the *Amidah*." Again, the subterranean oscillations are portrayed in only general fashion in the latter.

(3) Extremity: *And From There You Shall Seek* extends to all the extremities of the religious consciousness, and therefore reaches

its extreme aspects. An example of this is the arbitrariness of revelation, which is extensively described in the context of the revelational consciousness. "Reflections on the *Amidah*" also portrays
ascents and descents, but in quite moderate style and content.

(4) Rhetoric: *And From There You Shall Seek* intends, both implicitly
and openly, to prove that Jewish religious consciousness is more
intricate and tense, but also more balanced, because of its regulation by halakhah. For the most part, the alluded and explicit
polemical goal is the general (Christian) religious consciousness,
as set forth in the phenomenological studies of religion. This
polemical element is secondary in "Reflections on the *Amidah*."

Despite the distinctions between these two works, they are not mutu-
ally contradictory and, instead, they merge into one another, as we showed
above. These perceptions are meant to show how R. Soloveitchik adapted the
rich diversity of ideas in *And From There You Shall Seek* to the defined and
limited context of "Reflections on the *Amidah*." In the former, he attempted
to demonstrate how different branches of the halakhah record and balance
the tempests of the consciousness. In "Reflections on the *Amidah*," he did
so for only a single halakhic branch, namely, prayer. The focus on the consciousness in *And From There You Shall Seek* laid the groundwork for his
exposition on prayer.

Both *And From There You Shall Seek* and "Reflections on the *Amidah*"
were originally published in Hebrew in the same issue of the journal
Ha-Darom. Although we do not possess direct testimony regarding the
time of the writing of *And From There You Shall Seek*, we may reasonably
assume that both were written in the middle of the 1940s. In that period
R. Soloveitchik explored the substantive elements of the Jewish religious
consciousness and sought to show that this consciousness is complex and
dialectic, but also balanced. The need to outline such consciousness is
the task of *The Halakhic Mind*, that was also written in the same period,
but published only about eight years after *And From There You Shall
Seek*. The consciousness of prayer is an important expression of religious
consciousness, and R. Soloveitchik interpreted the *Amidah* as part of the
same task.

Part III

Community

Chapter 12

Synagogue and Community

In the preceding chapters we engaged in a detailed analysis of *And From There You Shall Seek* and "Reflections on the *Amidah*." These are phenomenological works intensively examine the weaving of the consciousness of prayer and its unique elements as compared with Jewish religious consciousness as a whole. References to prayer frequently appear in many other works by R. Soloveitchik and are too numerous for a detailed survey here. A few of them, however, provide new and fascinating perspectives on prayer. I will now examine additional aspects of R. Soloveitchik's philosophy of prayer, although they are not dominant in the totality of his thought, at least not on the basis of his published writings. I will begin with the place of the synagogue and end with observations on prayer as dialogue. As we will see, the relation of prayer to loneliness is the connecting link between these two issues.

1. The Synagogue

For R. Soloveitchik, loneliness is an experience anchored in concrete human existence. The redemption of loneliness by means of prayer is expressed in R. Soloveitchik's thought in two ways: (1) exposure to God and an awareness of selfhood; and (2) exposure to God and an awareness of the Other. The first way was formulated in the essay "The Synagogue as an Institution and as an Idea," and the second, in *The Lonely Man of Faith*. In each, prayer expresses the overcoming of loneliness.

The Mirror of the Period

In R. Soloveitchik's theoretical essays published to the present, he relates more to prayer, and less to the synagogue. This institution is an important component of the consciousness of prayer. Why, then, did he prefer to publish compositions that are more oriented to prayer itself? We have seen that R. Soloveitchik viewed the analysis of the religious experience as a mission. He said in one of his documented talks:

> Prayer in Judaism is the most exalted religious experience—as a dialogue between the lonely man and the one God who is isolated in His world. Prayer is a dialogue between man and the Omnipresent [*Makom*].
>
> It is true that public prayer occupies very great place for us. In essence, however, private prayer is the foundation and cardinal. It ensues from within the individual's inner, true need that is of tremendous force. The correct expression of prayer is the words of the prophet Isaiah (45:23): "To Me every knee shall bend, every tongue swear loyalty."[1]

R. Soloveitchik thought it important to reveal the essential consciousness elements of prayer, based on the intimate dialogue between man and his God. Although the public realm and the community are important in determining the contents and the venue (the synagogue) of prayers, the essence of prayer pertains to the individual.

But R. Soloveitchik, as a key figure in American Orthodoxy, had to relate to the synagogue and its important role in American Judaism. At times, the influence of Jewish religious streams is measured in accordance with their synagogues and their impact.[2] Within Orthodoxy, the synagogue continues to fill the role of the *shtiebel* (prayer house).[3] Since Orthodox Jews are not mobile on the Sabbath, the synagogue is also a neighborhood institution. R. Soloveitchik developed his discussion of the synagogue with young people's alienation from this institution. "The Synagogue as an

---

1 "On the Religious Definition of Man," in *Ha-Adam ve-Olamo*, 23.

2 See, for example, the works by Liebman: Charles S. Liebman, "Orthodoxy in American Jewish Life," *American Jewish Yearbook* 66 (1965): 31, 34-36, 47-48; idem, "A Sociological Analysis of Contemporary Orthodoxy," in *Understanding American Judaism: Toward the Description of a Modern Religion*, ed. Jacob Neusner (New York: Ktav, 1975), vol. 2: *Reform, Orthodoxy, Conservatism, and Reconstructionism*, 144. See also the articles in the first volume of this important collection (*The Rabbi and the Synagogue*): Wolfe Kelman, "The Synagogue in America," 69-89; Marshall Sklare, "The Sociology of the American Synagogue," 91-102; Abraham Feldman, "The Changing Functions of the Synagogue and the Rabbi," 103-112. Note should be taken of the discussions regarding the original function of the synagogue. According to one view, the synagogue was originally the venue for religious Jewish culture and leisure time activities, while others question this. On the issue as a whole, see Gerald J. Blidstein, "From the Home to the Synagogue—On the Innovations of the Post-Talmudic Synagogue," in *Ta Shma: Studies in Judaica in Memory of Israel M. Ta-Shma* [Hebrew], ed. Avraham Reiner et al. (Alon Shevut: Tevunot, 2011), vol. 2, 105-34.

3 See, for example, Michael Berenbaum, *After Tragedy and Triumph: Essays in Modern Jewish Thought and the American Experience* (Cambridge: Cambridge University Press, 1990), 167-68.

Institution and as an Idea" was delivered as a sermon or lecture in 1972 in honor of R. Joseph H. Lookstein, but was published only in 1980.

To explain Jewish attitudes to synagogue, R. Soloveitchik alluded to the phenomenological division between subjective and objective consciousness. In the middle of the 1940s, he explained the two World Wars in light of this approach. R. Soloveitchik's insight regarding the history of the twentieth century and its horrors was directly based on this phenomenological conception and colored by the Orthodox dimension of his own thought. As R. Soloveitchik explained, man's behavior is undermined and loses direction as a consequence of his domination by subjective consciousness. The subjective dimension is chaotic, fluid, stormy, and lacks balance. Only objective consciousness is capable of regulating the subjective dimension. When R. Soloveitchik used concepts of religious phenomenology, he identified the objective dimension with action (commandments), and when he referred to phenomenology in general, he identified this dimension with rationality.

R. Soloveitchik argued that the synagogue had been slowly shunted aside from the center of life of American Jewry. He listed three reasons for this shift. The institution of the synagogue was not popular, first and foremost, due to "an upsurge of shallow, amorphous emotionalism, which rejects religious institutionalism and objectivism."[4] Here he added a new feature to objective religious consciousness, beyond action and rationality: objective consciousness is institutional. Rebellion against the establishment is a result of domination by subjectivism. The synagogue is a direct expression of the religious establishment.

The second reason that he gave for the decline of the synagogue is commitment to the State of Israel. This related directly to the economic aspect as a reflection of that commitment. Lack of financial support for a synagogue lowers its standing and thrusts it to the fringes of the consciousness. The shift in donations relates, in practice, to the objective plane; but this plane reflects changes in the subjective consciousness. In the heady days between the Six-Day War and the Yom Kippur War, the State of Israel was a focus for identification by American Jewry. Deep identification with Israel was characteristic of American Jewry until the late 1980s. This stance is intriguing, in light of R. Soloveitchik's attitude to the State of Israel, as was

---

4 "The Synagogue as an Institution and as an Idea," in *Rabbi Joseph H. Lookstein Memorial Volume*, ed. Leo Landman (Hoboken, NJ: Ktav, 1980), 321-39, at 321. R. Soloveitchik wrote that subjectivism came to dominate in a "frightening" manner. That is, the opposition to the synagogue is an expression of a more general mood, and from this respect, opposition to the establishment is linked to the historical events of the twentieth century.

noted above.[5] Now prayer is the arena. If we read between the lines, joining the State of Israel and religious Zionism with the prayers was deleterious to the standing of the Jewish house of worship in the United States.

The third reason for the sorry state of the synagogue is the fact that congregational rabbis were not attuned to the young, the generation that would continue Judaism. The figure of the rabbi was central to the influence wielded by synagogues as community centers for American Jewry. "The young man of today is volatile, very excitable, his emotionalism is not deep-rooted. He would like to attend a service which is more fervent and less fixed. He would also like to see the synagogue become a house of study rather than just a house of prayer."[6] He first characterized the young as suffering from superficial sentimentality. At the end of this passage, he altered his assessment, and added that they seek knowledge and desire to study.

From many aspects, the first and third reasons can be viewed as complementary. The subjectivism that took control of culture and religion did not pass over the young. To the contrary: the young person in America is immersed in the surrounding culture and, in consequence, dominated by subjective consciousness. Congregational rabbis did not read the signs correctly and chose to ignore the trend that swept away the young.

We may, therefore, assume that R. Soloveitchik did not intend to equate the synagogue with the study hall when he presented the former as a center of Torah. He probably thought that synagogue rabbis must expand the areas of synagogue activity, so that the young would receive a response to the fluid subjectivism that so influenced their lives. The task imposed on the rabbis was twofold.

(1) Awareness: this task was imposed on the rabbi himself: to be aware of the wave of subjectivism.
(2) Education: this assignment relates to the rabbi as he stands before the youth, and it, too, is twofold:
   (i) to explain to young people the need for objective consciousness.

---

5 R. Soloveitchik did not hesitate to harshly criticize Israel's attitude to religion and tradition. This passage, which speaks of the harm suffered by synagogues in the Diaspora, also indirectly expressed the negative sides of the State of Israel, albeit—this time—through no fault of its own. In any event, this critical tone is characteristic of his attitude to Israel.

6 "Synagogue as an Institution," 322.

(ii) to explain the correct relation—in most instances, reconstructive—between the subjective and objective dimensions of
consciousness.

The three causes listed by R. Soloveitchik for the "unpopularity" of
the synagogue are anchored in the period and its characteristics. The synagogue is the focal point of the community, and the rabbi is its driving force.
The decline of the synagogue reflects the rabbi's weakness. R. Soloveitchik
described the rabbi's struggle against the declining prestige of the synagogue as "heroic efforts."[7] The status of the synagogue was fractured, and
R. Soloveitchik hinted that the standing of the rabbis, as well, was no longer
the same. Therefore, he attempted to provide what was missing and offer
rabbis and educators tools for coping with the subjectivism of the young
generation.

An examination of R. Soloveitchik's possible responses to the decline
of the synagogue points to action in the philosophical rather than the
concrete realm given that, as R. Soloveitchik explains, the synagogue had
been a communal institution.[8] Even Jews who were not fully observant
came to the synagogue. This state of affairs, however, existed only in the
past. In the reality of American Jewry in the 1970s, the synagogue was
no longer able to function as a communal institution. This was the given
situation. The restoration of the synagogue could take place only in the
realm of ideas.

---

7 "Synagogue as an Institution," 323. R. Soloveitchik writes in "Abraham the Hebrew": "if
there is a group that has earned the right to utter this blessing with joy and pride, it is
our comrades in Israel whose heroism has found expression not only within the framework of their private lives, but also in their struggle for heroic national existence, and in
their demand that the State should conduct itself heroically not only on the battlefield
but also in its daily life. Our colleagues are not powerful. Their representation in the
Knesset is very limited. Their financial resources are meager, their relations with the
press poor. Yet they are carrying on a proud struggle to transform Eretz Yisrael from an
affluent secular State into a sacred, heroic country. What is our greatest achievement?
The struggle itself! Through it the essence of Judaism and Jewish historical existence is
expressed" ("Abraham the Hebrew," in *The Rav Speaks: Five Addresses on Israel, History,
and the Jewish People* [New York: Toras HoRav Foundation, 2002], 105-106). Manifest
in this passage is the romantic motif of the hero who struggles with the fate, a struggle that becomes existential and acquires intrinsic worth. The struggle for meaningful
existence is not dependent on its results or the chances of its success. Furthermore, the
very willingness to engage in a hopeless struggle makes this struggle meaningful. Prayer
attests to such willingness. Consequently, in "Abraham the Hebrew" prayer is linked to
the heroic struggle.
8 "Synagogue as an Institution," 322-23.

Let us delve deeper into R. Soloveitchik's idea. The institutional nature of the synagogue expresses the objective consciousness plane of prayer in general, and especially, of public prayer. The objective dimension is the great balancer and most important regulator of the tempestuous religious emotions that find their outlet in prayer. And yet, the struggle for the objective dimension failed and, in order to restore it, we must turn to the subjective, fluid dimension. Moreover, R. Soloveitchik states that the struggle is to be waged in the subjective realm because of its dominance, and even exclusivity, in the young person's mind. R. Soloveitchik hoped that upon the restoration of the subjective realm, the objective could be similarly revived.

The tactic for this struggle is to explain that prayer in general, and specifically the synagogue, are suitable for the subjective human consciousness and reflect its fundamental paradoxical nature—in short, it is a question of meaning. "We simply did not explain to the young people what *tefilah* is and what *bet ha-kneset*, the house dedicated to prayer, means, and how deeply rooted these ideas are in our philosophy of man and his destiny."[9] Prayer expresses the individual's essential experience.

R. Soloveitchik began with the synagogue as an institution, and we already explained the importance of such a discussion on the background of the reality in the United States. We learn from his discussion, however, that in practice, he returned to describing the synagogue primarily in relation to prayer. The synagogue becomes a mirror of the state of prayer and, in a certain sense, the pretext for returning to scrutinize the consciousness of prayer. If the importance of prayer and its place in consciousness is explained to the young person, it will finally be possible to resolve the institutional issue, namely, to prevent the decline of the synagogue.

R. Soloveitchik directed his comments especially to young Americans. As mentioned, the orally delivered address was the basis for the 1970s article. For the young religious Israeli, who saw the synagogue as necessary, these were years replete with ideology and ideological activity. Bnei Akiva and Gush Emunim channeled ideological activity to the intensive development of settlements on both sides of the Green Line (that is, pre-1967 Israel and the territories that came under its control in the Six-Day War). Religious young people felt that they were fashioning the character of Israeli society. In many respects, the young people who settled in Judea, Samaria, and the Gaza Strip were the creators of a pioneering mythos, which religious Zionism had lacked for too many long years. This youth would

---

9 "Synagogue as an Institution," 323.

fall under the sway of pronounced subjectivism only in the late 1980s, not before.[10] Accordingly, R. Soloveitchik related to the alienation and subjectivism of the American young people, and viewed bringing prayer closer to their consciousness as a special mission.

Exile as Experience: (1) Historical Exile

R. Soloveitchik's central argument is that prayer enables the individual to contend with the problem of alienation. Alienation, or "exile" in his words, characterizes human existence in its entirely. "Judaism says that not only the Jew is in exile, but that man as such, man in general, leads an exilic existence."[11] The discussions returns us, yet again, to the messianic arena, whose relation to prayer occupied us above.[12] R. Soloveitchik listed two modes of exile:

1. Historical exile: this experience is uniquely characteristic of the Jewish people. Just as R. Soloveitchik undertook in his various writings to explain the structure of the singular Jewish religious consciousness, he similarly strove to argue that the characteristically Jewish alienation—exile—is not congruous with the usual human alienation. The historical exile is the exile from the Land of Israel.

2. Existential exile: alienation and being incomplete. In other words, man, by his very being, is vulnerable and lacking. Existential exile is symbolized by the exile from the Garden of Eden. This primordial place expresses the state of perfection, and the forced departure from it, alienation and a lack of perfection.

While man as such experiences the exile from the Garden of Eden, the Jew experiences both the exile from Eden and from the Land of Israel. Historical exile is an additional stratum above the existential exile.

---

10 See, for example, Dov Schwartz, "Religious Zionism and the Struggle against the Evacuation of the Settlements: Theological and Cultural Aspects", in *Religious Zionism Post Disengagement: Future Directions*, ed. Cahim I. Waxman (New York: Yeshiva University Press, 2008), 93-115 .

11 "Synagogue as an Institution," 325. R. Soloveitchik used the motif of the expulsion from the Garden of Eden to claim that alienation is characteristic of human existence. Adam's natural place was in the Garden, and when he was cast forth from it he became a "homeless being." See Rosenberg, "Return."

12 See above, Chapter Nine.

In this first stage, R. Soloveitchik discusses the historical exile experience limited to Jews and Judaism. He writes:

> Exile, as a historical experience, is known only to the Jew. No other nation has ever led an exilic existence [...] It is very hard to guess how they managed to do it, but somehow they did manage to preserve their historical identity as a people and to maintain a very strong sentimental relationship to a land from which they were exiled nineteen hundred years ago. That we have maintained such a relationship, or rather commitment, is best proven by the State of Israel. Without that strange commitment, a nineteen-hundred-year-old commitment, to a land from which we were exiled, the State of Israel would never have come into existence.[13]

A number of features turned exile into a uniquely Jewish experience. Jewish nationalism accordingly differs from its European or American counterparts.[14] Some nations experienced repression and servitude on their land, but not removal from it. R. Soloveitchik identified the experience of exile with the preservation of historical memory and the refusal to assimilate to surrounding cultures. He wanted to highlight the importance of tradition. Additionally, the State of Israel is the result of the consciousness of exile. Together with the second reason for the decline in the standing of the synagogue, this shows that the State of Israel, which has the synagogues to thank for its establishment, undermined the same institutions to which it owes its existence. The lesson to be learned from this is that the State of Israel subverts the foundations of Jewish diasporic existence. R. Soloveitchik states this outright in the beginning of his article: commitment to the State of Israel overshadowed the commitment to the synagogue. His reserved and skeptical attitude toward the State of Israel, manifest in the Zionist sermons he delivered at Mizrachi conferences in the United States, continued in "The Synagogue as an Institution and as an Idea." This attitude necessitates the revival of the consciousness of prayer as a suitable expression for indecision and doubts.

In R. Soloveitchik's analysis, the Jew developed two responses to exile:

1. The cognitive, dogmatic, and emotional response: Jewish diasporic existence is characterized by the messianic idea. The anticipation

---

13 "Synagogue as an Institution," 324-25.

14 See Dov Schwartz, *Land of Israel in Religious Zionist Thought* [Hebrew] (Tel Aviv: Am Oved, 1997), 11-12. On conceptions of exile in Jewish thought, see Arnold M. Eisen, *Galut: Jewish Reflection on Homelessness and Homecoming* (Bloomington: Indiana University Press, 1986).

of redemption ("a messianic vision")[15] is present in this existence, in different periods and in changing cultures.

2. The practical response: the prayers. The exile experience necessitates prayer, mainly the prayer for a return to the Land of Israel.

Prayer is the response to the historical exile of the nation. R. Soloveitchik wrote as follows on the attitude of institutionalized prayer to the messianic mental charge characteristic of exile:

> As an exile the Jew prayed; his homelessness cried out of his very being. If you analyze the *shemoneh 'esreh*, six of the eighteen or nineteen benedictions are concerned with one burning passion, with one strong desire, the termination of the exile.[16]

In this passage R. Soloveitchik presented the consciousness of exile. Its subjective dimension is sentiment: commitment, longing, dreaming. The hope to be extricated from exile is a component of the exiled subject. The objective dimension of exile is prayer. In "Reflections on the *Amidah*" and *And From There You Shall Seek* prayer was presented as a commandment for the subjective dimension of the consciousness. R. Soloveitchik sought to show that the boundaries between the subjective and the objective are blurred in prayer, and that this imperative enters the emotional and mental dimension. However, R. Soloveitchik indirectly returns here to the structure of consciousness recorded in *The Halakhic Mind*. Prayer expresses action. The role of prayer in relation to the historical exile is to express the hope for national redemption. In between the lines, we can also understand its role in regulating and balancing the fiery messianic sentiments.

Exile as Experience: (2) Existential Exile

Historical exile is the unique experience of the Jewish people. This experience creates an effervescent messianic consciousness, and prayer is the expression that balances and regulates this consciousness. The Jew, however, undergoes a double experience of exile, since exile is a basis feature of human existence. Man as such experiences exile. In the

---

15 "Synagogue as an Institution," 325.
16 "Synagogue as an Institution," 325.

fourth, fifth, and sixth sections of "The Synagogue as an Institution and as an Idea" R. Soloveitchik set forth two human types who experience existential exile:

(1) The "small man"[17]: this is the ordinary individual, in whose life existential anxiety is dominant. This type experiences anxiety immediately, since for him, the fears of annihilation are not hidden in the fog. Exile is a situation of anxiety and rootlessness, while redemption means overcoming them.

(2) The "great man": this type is characterized by a higher level of self-affirmation and self-fashioning. He controls many systems, as a sort of "king," in traditional terminology. Anxiety is not a dominant factor in his life. Exile, for him, is a state of unease, boredom, and frustration. Redemption is a life of tranquility.

R. Soloveitchik was not unequivocal in his definition of these types, at times viewing them as distinct and at times as two aspects of the same person. For R. Soloveitchik, Kohelet expresses a defined type, the "great man,"[18] while "King Solomon" and "modern man"[19] represent the oscillation between the two poles. Prayer reflects exile as well as a victory over it.

The "Small Man"

We will now examine the traits of the individual whose basic existential experience is the anxiety of exile (the "small man"), and, specifically, the characteristics of the Jew. R. Soloveitchik explained that the uniquely Jewish experience of historical exile is built on the existential human experience as an additional layer. He described existential exile as follows:

> Man is homeless because he was expelled from his Paradisiacal home, and he, like the historical Jew with regard to the Promised Land, has never forgotten that once upon a time, many millennia ago, he lived in Paradise. Of course, he lost it; however, he has not forgotten it. Man's home has been, and still is, the Paradise upon which God showers so much beauty and grace. Outside of Paradise, man finds himself lost in the vast spaces and boundless

---

17 "Synagogue as an Institution," 327.

18 "Synagogue as an Institution," 326. In *Lonely Man of Faith*, 32, R. Soloveitchik implies that Kohelet represents Adam the first, that is, "majestic man."

19 "Synagogue as an Institution," 327.

distances of an unknown, strange, and frightening world, which is at best indifferent and at worst hostile toward man.[20]

He used the motif of exile to denote a lengthy list of existential traits: alienation, anxiety, a lack of perfection, and vulnerability. He expressly declared that we must draw upon existentialist philosophy in order to understand existential exile. R. Soloveitchik succinctly defined such philosophy: "In fact, existentialism is nothing but an attempt on the part of man to understand himself and his fellow man, and inject a little bit of rationality[21] into his existential awareness, because the awareness is quite often fraught with tragic absurdities."[22]

Existentialist philosophy asked: What is man? R. Soloveitchik argued that the answer is not anchored in the intellectual plane, as Aristotle or the medieval rationalists had thought. Man is not defined as one who acquires of knowledge. Nor is the answer moored in the realm of scientific achievements. Likewise, man is not defined as manipulator and ruler of nature. Existentialist philosophy defined man as an alienated being. He is detached from his natural place and alienated from its current place, which is always deficient and partial. By his very definition, man lives in exile. In his apologetic manner, R. Soloveitchik maintained that

> [t]his question, which modern philosophy asks, has been answered by Judaism a long time ago. The Psalmist already declared: "*ger anokhi ba-aretz*[23] [...] *toshav ke-khol avotai*". I am a stranger, I am a homeless being,

---

20 "Synagogue as an Institution," 326. In the essay "Sacred and Profane," which was first published in 1945, the image of the homeless man expresses the lack of tradition. The past and the people of the past are not present in this man, and his consciousness of place and time is fragmentary and detached. "The man of the street has no personal relationship with, no consciousness of continuity and interdependency between the glorious periods of antiquity and the emerging present" (English translation: "Sacred and Profane," in *Shiurei HaRav: A Conspectus of the Public Lectures of Rabbi Joseph B. Soloveitchik*, ed. Joseph Epstein [Hoboken, NJ: Ktav, 1994], 22); "The timeless wanderer has no *sdeh ahuzah* [Leviticus 26:16] or *kivrot avotav* [II Chronicles 35:24]" (24-25). This approach is characteristic of R. Soloveitchik's phenomenological thought from that period, when he discussed at length the substantive features of the tradition. Here, in contrast, "homeless" expresses concrete alienation.

21 This implies that R. Soloveitchik thought that existentialism is fundamentally rational, and that its primary aim is to cast existential characteristics in rational molds (see above, Chapter Nine, n. 66). R. Soloveitchik also expressed this position in other writings. See Schwartz, *From Phenomenology to Existentialism*, 260.

22 "Synagogue as an Institution," 326. This sentence concludes the paragraph. It shows that R. Soloveitchik believed that existential exile and its sources in existential philosophy deserve a discussion of their own.

23 Ps. 119:19.

I am in exile, even though *"toshav ke-khol avotai,"* I have lived so many years on this globe.[24]

In other words, just as Judaism addresses the fundamental traits of the Jew, it also relates to man's basic characteristics as such. Judaism primarily defined man as being in exile.

This teaches that man, in his very being, is an anxious creature, lacking in confidence and detached. R. Soloveitchik presented King Solomon as an extremely self-affirming individual.[25] The image of Solomon is a metaphor for a "scientist" who conquers new worlds. But Solomon surrounds himself with mighty men "because of terror by night" (Song 3:8). The conquest of nature does not eclipse man's fundamental alienation and vulnerability. R. Soloveitchik asserts here that detachment and alienation—the "exile"—are the cause of the existential anxiety symbolized by the terror by night. In *Out of the Whirlwind*, another work I examined, R. Soloveitchik suggests existential psychotherapy for the treatment of such anxiety.[26] According to *Out of the Whirlwind*, the main cause of existential anxiety is the imperfection of human existence. In contrast, philosophers such as Paul Tillich, for example, argued that the leading cause of anxiety is non-being. He coined the term "ontology of anxiety," which he discussed at length in his magnum opus *Systematic Theology*. I have devoted an extensive discussion to this term.[27] At times Tillich formulated his views in focused fashion in his shorter essays. In such a work he defined the nature of anxiety as "the state in which a being is aware of its possible nonbeing";[28] and likewise: "Anxiety is the existential awareness of nonbeing."[29] He wrote that "being has nonbeing 'within' itself."[30] This awareness of nonbeing does not ensue from the experience of the death of a friend or relative, for instance, but from the impression that this experience leaves on the "latent awareness," that the one who undergoes the experience will also die in the future. And this awareness leads to anxiety.[31] Tillich then distinguished between fear

24 "Synagogue as an Institution," 326. The verse in Psalms is concerned with prayer, being an alien (*gerut*), and residency (*toshavut*): "Hear my prayer, O Lord; give ear to my cry; do not disregard my tears; for like all my forbears I am an alien, resident with you."
25 "Synagogue as an Institution," 326.
26 See Schwartz, *From Phenomenology to Existentialism*, chap. 9.
27 See Schwartz, *From Phenomenology to Existentialism*, 243-246. Prof. Lawrence Kaplan told me that he heard from R. Zeev Gothold that R. Soloveitchik engaged in intensive reading of Tillich and Niebuhr.
28 Paul Tillich, *The Courage to Be* (New Haven: Yale University Press, 1952), 35.
29 Tillich, *The Courage to Be*, 35.
30 Ibid., 34.
31 Ibid., 35.

and anxiety. Fear is directed to an object while anxiety has no object. Tlllich maintained "in a paradoxical phrase" that "its [anxiety's] object is the negation of every object."[32] Fear and anxiety are anchored in each other.

While *Out of the Whirlwind* maintains that imperfection is the cause of anxiety, "The Synagogue as an Institution" marks a return to Tillich's approach, albeit not a full one. He presented anxiety as lack of confidence, and fear as "a degenerative disease."[33] That is, man's basic apprehension is of nonbeing. This apprehension is accompanied by the fear of tribulations that cause man to lose his vitality and humanity. In any event, degenerative disease is merely an example. R. Soloveitchik's intent was to discuss foundational anxiety, which is not directed to any specific traumatic event, but rather relates to a lack of existential confidence: "human beings are frightened."[34] He continued by relating that as a child he asked his teacher and mother about the meaning of "the terror in the night."[35] Neither gave him an informative answer. The appearance of existential anxiety in childhood shows that anxiety does not result solely from analysis or knowledge of illnesses and sick individuals. It characterizes man from the time that he begins to think. At the end of his autobiographical anecdote, however, the child overcame his fear by means of a twofold action:

(1) "She told me, 'Read *Shema*,[36] and go to bed.'"
(2) "When she tucked me in, I forgot the dread in the night."[37]

R. Soloveitchik hinted in this account that overcoming existential anxiety entails action by the person himself and by the Other. In this instance, the person's action is represented by means of prayer (reading *Shema*), and that of another (the mother), by a gesture (covering).[38] Tillich wrote at length about the proper "courage" to confront anxiety. R. Soloveitchik, in contrast, proposed prayer as a response to existential exile.

---

32 Ibid., 36.
33 "Synagogue as an Institution," 328.
34 "Synagogue as an Institution," 328.
35 "Synagogue as an Institution," 327.
36 That is, *keriat shema al ha-mitah* [reading *Shema* before going to sleep at night]. It is noteworthy that Song 3:8 contains an expanded version of *keriat shema al ha-mitah* (both the Ashkenaz and Sefard versions).
37 "Synagogue as an Institution," 327.
38 In a certain sense, a person is to be both active and passive. The mother herself is the source of activity (the request to read *Shema*) and passivity (she covers the child). The protection, therefore, is a result of opposing movements, and thereby suits a prevalent pattern in R. Soloveitchik's thought.

When R. Soloveitchik posited prayer as a response to historical exile, he hinted at its being a balancing factor, while in his discussion of existential exile, he pointed out that the main task of prayer is to document anxiety and overcome it through love of God. Prayer reflects a process of existential redemption. R. Soloveitchik writes:

> Our evening and morning prayers reflect our fright in the night and our joy in the morning. In the evening we recite the blessing *Barukh Hashem le-olam Amen ve-Amen*,[39] whose central phrase is *Be-yadkha afkid ruhi*, "I entrust my spirit to Thee." Man surrenders his total existence to God. Man is ready to bring the supreme sacrifice. The fear in the night manifests itself in the recital. The Jew accepts God's inscrutable will. He does not know whether God's grace will be bestowed upon him and that he indeed will rise from his slumber. When he does rise in the morning, he recites with a happy mind the prayer *Elokai neshamah she-natatah bi*.[40] Man is a happy and surprised person. There is an element of excitement and wonder in that blessing. God bestowed a precious gift upon him—a new life. He praises the Almighty for every heartbeat and every activity he can engage in. The terror in the night, *pahad ba-leilot*, turns into a great ecstasy, *Ahavah rabbah*.[41]

That is, the action of prayer is twofold:

(1) The evening prayer (*Arvit*) prayer makes man aware of existential anxiety. Now, this anxiety is no longer a repressed and

---

39 Naphtali Wieder, "Chapters in the History of Prayer and Benedictions" [Hebrew], *Sinai* 77 (1975): 127-133; reprinted in Wieder, *The Formation of Jewish Liturgy in the East and the West* (Jerusalem: Ben-Zvi Institute for the Study of Jewish Communities in the East, 1998), 166-172.

40 The model set forth by the Rabbis consisted of *keriat shema al ha-mitah* vs. *Elohai neshamah* (see BT Berakhot 60b; *Derekh Eretz Rabbah*, chapter 11. R. Soloveitchik mentioned *keriat shema al ha-mitah* in the autobiographical narrative that preceded this discussion. He creates a movement from the *Arvit* prayer (the blessing "Blessed are You forever, *Amen ve-Amen*") to *keriat shema al ha-mitah*, awakening in the morning (*Elohai neshamah*), and the second blessing of *Shema* (*Ahavah rabbah*). R. Soloveitchik did not include the *Shema* of *Arvit* and of *Shaharit*, apparently because of their dogmatic coloration, which is not related to the experience of anxiety and the emotional metamorphosis that overcomes it.

41 "Synagogue as an Institution," 328. On the conclusion of the blessing (*Ahavah rabbah* and *Ahavat olam*), see Avigdor Aptowitzer, "*Ahavah Rabbah ve-Ahavat Olam*" [Hebrew], *Hazofeh Quartalis Hebraica* 10 (1926): 37-38. Aptowitzer interpreted the textual differences in the light of exile and redemption. See also Aaron Wertheim, *Law and Custom in Hasidism*, trans. Shmuel Himelsten (Hoboken, NJ: Ktav, 1992), 172 and n. 13.

covert factor, but rather an existential characteristic that must be acknowledged, affirmed, and embraced. Man accepts "God's inscrutable will." The meaning if this process is the adoption of existential exile.

(2) The morning prayer (*Shaharit*) prayer effects an emotional and existential change in a person. Fear becomes wonder, and anxiety turns into joy. This process means the attainment of existential redemption.

These two phases do not occur concurrently. In the first phase, a person adopts anxiety by surrendering his selfhood to God. This step is expressed in the *Arvit* prayer, that is, this phase happens before sleep. An emotional revolution occurs in the second stage, when the individual discovers that the process that began with the embracing of anxiety ends upon awakening in the morning, namely, the return to life. At this point, his feelings and his existential condition change. This stage is expressed in the *Shaharit* prayer and begins with rising in the morning to *Ahavah rabbah* ("great love"). Prayer denotes the existential state (anxiety), and its overcoming by means of an emotional and existential change (love).

How is existential exile to be mastered? When R. Soloveitchik described the state of fear, he implicitly answered this question. He argued that "some people know how to sublimate their fright into creativity," and that "the American Jew does not know how to handle old age. He cannot sublimate old age to wisdom, to dignity, or to creative efforts."[42]

The preceding discussion enables us to indicate two phases, or strata, of existential redemption.

(1) Existential characteristics: creative and intellectual activity and dignity. Now, the existential anxiety is channeled to self-realization.

(2) Religious characteristics: love of God to the extent of ecstasy. From this point on, the existential anxiety is directed to surrendering one's self to God.

These features relate to those who experience anxiety and detachment. R. Soloveitchik called such a type the "small men."

---

42 "Synagogue as an Institution," 328.

The Great Type

We will now analyze the second type and its relation to prayer. Some individuals experience exile out of self-affirmation. These are the "great men." The Biblical character of Kohelet is the model for such an experience. R. Soloveitchik portrayed Kohelet as one who strives to overcome the absurd in existence and to repress the existential crisis. In *Out of the Whirlwind*, Kohelet is a paradigm of hubris, pride that does not allow a true understanding of the existential crisis.[43] He spends his time in a never-ending quest for experience and conquest. In "The Synagogue as an Institution," R. Soloveitchik presented Kohelet as one who experiences exile in two planes.

(1) An absence of purpose and meaning ("Why is man restless? What is he looking for?").

(2) Distance from God, due to hubris ("Man's restlessness is man's questing for God, sometimes knowingly, consciously, intentionally, and other times unconsciously and unintentionally. Man searches for God even when he, driven by pride and impudence, tries to move away from God").[44]

As in *Out of the Whirlwind*, here too R. Soloveitchik hints thatthe proud and conquering type is incapable of attaining redemption. His prayer has the intent of "fulfillment and total realization," but "from time to time the quest is misunderstood by man."[45] Kohelet wants to conquer all fields: science, the aesthetic realm, and pleasure. He strives to control all and also harnesses prayer to this end. His prayer is directed to the attainment of these unobtainable goals, since man cannot have it all. R. Soloveitchik emphasizes that such a man is unaware of the fact that his endless search is merely an expression of seeking God. The "great man" searches for the divine, but the sin of hubris does not enable a true return to the elusive God.

What, then, is to be gained by the prayer of the "great man"? What does it contribute to his personality? The type whose personality is expressed

---

43 See Schwartz, *From Phenomenology to Existentialism*, 250-252.

44 "Synagogue as an Institution," 329.

45 "Synagogue as an Institution," 329. This passage seemingly describes both human types, but it is clear from the continuation: "He may erroneously think that what he is searching for is another field, another million dollars, another luxury" (329), that R. Soloveitchik is referring to the "great man."

in the Biblical Kohelet knows why he prays, at least on the conscious level: he prays to attain his incessant conquests. His prayer, however, also has a covert level: he—unwittingly—seeks God. The question arises: is there any objective personality advantage to such prayer? R. Soloveitchik answers in the affirmative. Prayer makes life possible for such a type with his problematic personality. He writes:

> In prayer, both great man and small man find their home. Through prayer great man finds home, peace, and serenity, and through prayer small man liberates himself from his fright, the dread in the night.[46]

Prayer redeems the anxiety of the average person, as we discussed at length above. R. Soloveitchik adds here that prayer enables serene existence for the type who possesses excessive self-affirmation. To be precise, R. Soloveitchik compared, but also implicitly distinguished between, the activity of the two types. They both experience liberation from existential anxiety by the discovery of identity and affiliation in the house of worship. The difference between the two, however, is measureless: the small man is redeemed by prayer and finds a solution to his existential problems. The great man, in contrast, is not redeemed. For him, prayer is an island of calm in the tempestuous sea of restless aspirations and conquests. He was freed from his anxiety, but he did not fully comprehend the motive for his endless searching. He still is unaware that he actually seeks God. Liberation from anxiety does not mean coming to know one's self.

Prayer is seen to have utilitarian benefit. R. Soloveitchik, however, states that this benefit is relative. Only feeling at home in the synagogue redeems a person, including modern man. Prayer itself is a relative home; prayer in the synagogue is the perfect home. When R. Soloveitchik wrote immediately following this that "the modern Jew does not know how to pray,"[47] he meant that the synagogue is an element of prayer itself. The consciousness of prayer is not complete without the synagogue.

Interim Summary: Prayer and the Existential Condition

We can now summarize in the following table the philosophical structure of existential exile and redemption for the two types, the small and the great, and their relation to prayer:

---

46 "Synagogue as an Institution," 329.
47 "Synagogue as an Institution," 329.

existential exile and redemption

starting point	central existential characteristic	meaning of exile	redemptive action	meaning of redemption	prayer
inferiority	anxiety	alienation, detachment	1. embrace of anxiety 2. emotional and existential metamorphosis	1. creative activity and existential respect 2. love of God	1. *Arvit* 2. *Shaharit*
greatness (Kohelet)	self-affirmation	1. lack of meaning 2. divine concealment	endless search and conquest	not attained	– (not detailed)

The table shows the disproportionality between the small and great personalities. The person who experiences "smallness" has a good chance of being redeemed. He is more open, and his narrow horizons can be expanded. The "great man," in contrast, misunderstands his quest,[48] because he denies his self and its search for God; consequently, prayer does not redeem him, albeit bringing him peace.

To this point, R. Soloveitchik discussed the relevance of prayer for the existential condition of modern man. He showed how prayer influences different types and fashions their variegated existence. Prayer enables quality, or redeemed, existence. He still did not specifically clarify the central place of the synagoguein this redeemed existence.

Home

The synagogue offers two benefits to modern man.

(1) It is a home.
(2) It is a home of mission.

To begin with the first benefit: R. Soloveitchik argued that prayer is an expression of "returning home."[49] So far, he considered prayer and its qualities, but not the synagogue. Now he bases his discussion on the motif of home in general, and especially the synagogue, in his attempt to determine

---

48 See above, n. 42.
49 "Synagogue as an Institution," 330.

its relevance for modern man. In order to understand the meaning of the synagogue as a return, we must once again list the many existential achievements of prayer:

(1) becoming aware of existential anxiety;
(2) embracing this existential anxiety;
(3) overcoming existential anxiety;
(4) existential metamorphosis (from anxiety to joy);
(5) an expression of creativity and action;
(6) peace and serenity.

R. Soloveitchik presented the factor common to all these achievements. The principle that prayer is returning home becomes evident in an analysis of the standing of the synagogue. This is attested by a story he brought about Eastern European Jews who would travel about during the week in order to earn their living. On Sabbath eve they would gather in the synagogue, dressed in their Sabbath finery, and begin by reciting Ps. 107, about those who travel on the sea and in the wilderness.[50] R. Soloveitchik used the concrete and metaphoric meaning of home:

> Bayit in Hebrew has a double connotation. Bayit means a house, the physical structure, four walls, a roof, and floor, and bayit means a home. We err when we translate bet ha-kneset as "the house of prayer." This rendition is not true.[51] There is no need for a house of prayer, because I can pray to God and I can kneel to Him and have a rendezvous with Him anywhere on the globe, even on the outskirts of the universe. I am confronted with God everywhere. Bet ha-kneset is not a house but a home of prayer. The structure is symbolic. Bet ha-kneset, if understood as a house of prayer, is an institution; however, if translated into a home of prayer, it turns into an exalted idea, namely, the house of man, of homeless man, which is at the same time the home of God, meonah Elohay kedem [Deut. 33:27].[52]

The concept of bayit has an extensive presence in various direct and indirect sources that R. Soloveitchik possibly used. The notion that connects the image of the home with the consciousness and the personality

---

50 "Synagogue as an Institution," 330.
51 R. Soloveitchik was forceful in his negation of what he viewed as a misunderstanding.
52 "Synagogue as an Institution," 330-31.

has deep cultural roots in twentieth-century thought.[53] We will offer a few examples.

Heidegger was a key figure in the conception of the home as identity, and R. Soloveitchik was familiar with his thought. Heidegger viewed "being-at-home" and, alternately, "homelessness," as concepts central to his thought. Homelessness expresses the following states.

(1) Alienation. The lack of a home is not merely detachment. For Heidegger, homelessness expresses alienation from the world. The world is not man's home, in the bourgeoisie and usual sense.

(2) Lack of authenticity. Heidegger identified the state of "home" as serenity and self-assurance. A person is aware of being outside his home. Being at home, for Heidegger, means being oneself, since the home expresses authenticity.

(3) Anxiety. Being outside the home causes dread. This anxiety ensues from a lack of meaning. Heidegger argued that "in anxiety one feels *uncanny* [*unheimlich*]."[54]

Heidegger's thought in his later writings is characterized by the desire to return home. For him, the lack of home expresses existential anxiety. A homeless individual is one who lives in an artificial and meaningless world.

Other philosophers were also concerned with home and homelessness. Freud wrote "*Das Unheimliche*," where he argued that the sense of home and intimacy contain dimensions of foreignness that both threaten and attract.[55]

Gaston Bachelard offered a phenomenological analysis of architecture, and asserted that the geographical expanse is an expansion of the

---

53 On this issue in the Jewish and Israeli discourse, see Zali Gurevitch, *On Israeli and Jewish Place* [Hebrew] (Tel Aviv: Am Oved, 2007); Haviva Pedaya, *Expanses: An Essay on the Theological and Political Unconsciousness* (Tel Aviv: Hakibbutz Hameuchad, 2011).

54 Martin Heidegger, *Being and Time*, trans. John Macquarrie and Edward Robinson (New York: Harper and Row, 1962), 233. Heidegger's *unheimlich* was translated as "uncanny." The translators' note adds: "it means more literally 'unhomelike.'" See, for example, W. B. Macomber, *The Anatomy of Disillusion: Martin Heidegger's Notion of Truth* (Evanston, IL: Northwestern University Press, 1967), 83-84.

55 See Sigmund Freud, "The Uncanny," in *The Standard Edition of the Complete Psychological Works of Sigmund Freud*, trans. James Strachey, vol. 17: *An Infantile Neurosis and Other Works* (London: Hogarth Press, 1955), 218-233.

personal expanse. For Bachelard, the home is merely a poetic image. He attempted to describe the subjective consciousness that created the poetics of the home. "Our house," he wrote, "is our first universe, a real cosmos in every sense of the word."[56] Additionally, "the house is one of the greatest powers of integration for the thoughts, memories and dreams of mankind."[57]

Derrida's thought contains an important development of the motif of home, albeit one not included among R. Soloveitchik's sources. According to Derrida, the normative system of accepting guests into a person's home denotes a series of laws and conventions, while, on the other hand, the guest threatens to take control of it:

> ...the stranger, here the awaited guest, is not only someone to whom you say "come," but "enter," enter without waiting, make a pause in our home without waiting, hurry up and come in, "come inside," "come within me," not only toward me, but within me: occupy me, take place in me, which means, by the same token, also take my place, don't content yourself with coming to meet me or "into my home."[58]

Derrida's approach goes beyond the influence of the threatening stranger suggested by by Sartre. In any event, the home is the basis of the transcendental law (the "metaphysical," in Derrida's terminology) of hospitality, Jewish and Christian law (for example), and the immanent law in which the stranger comes to dominate the self.[59] It is noteworthy that the influential book *The Homeless Mind*, which is concerned with the anxiety and fear that modernity engenders in man, was published in the same year "The Synagogue as an Institution" was written.[60]

R. Soloveitchik maintained that the home primarily represents a state of belonging and security, while homelessness means solitude and detachment. The home expresses the existence of communication and relation between subjects. This is a redeeming existence. The lack of home means silence and separation, that is, existential exile.

---

56 Gaston Bachelard, *The Poetics of Space: The Classic Look at How We Experience Intimate Places*, trans. Maria Jolas (Boston: Beacon Press, 1994), 4.

57 Bachelard, *The Poetics of Space*, 6.

58 Jacques Derrida, *Of Hospitality: Anne Dufourmantelle Invites Jacques Derrida to Respond*, trans. Rachel Bowlby (Stanford, CA: Stanford University Press), 123.

59 "To give the new arrival all of one's home and oneself" (Deridda, *Of Hospitality*, 77).

60 Peter Berger, Brigitte Berger, and Hansfried Kellner, *The Homeless Mind: Modernization and Consciousness* (New York: Random House, 1973).

As in "Reflections on the *Amidah*," in "The Synagogue as an Institution" R. Soloveitchik also derived the essential nature of prayer as a whole from the prayer of Solomon.[61] King Solomon mentioned the prayer "Whenever one man commits an offense against another" (I Kings 8:31). R. Soloveitchik stated: "If you lose a friend, you become a homeless being."[62] The person who experiences friendship has a symbolic home, while one who lost a friend is "homeless." As was mentioned, the article "The Synagogue as an Institution" is based on a lecture given in 1973. In *The Lonely Man of Faith* R. Soloveitchik already discussed the question of intersubjective relation, that is, the relation to the Other as a unique being.[63] Here, he uses such an approach to observe that the lack of relation means that the subject feels homeless.

R. Soloveitchik further asserted that the Temple is the ultimate home. The Temple is not only a home for the nation but also a substitute for the individual's lost home. According to Solomon's prayer, one who feels homeless finds his home in the Temple. This means that prayer in the Temple restores a person's home to him. Consequently, exile made the entire Jewish people homeless, detached, lonesome, and lacking existential confidence.

R. Soloveitchik further argued in a letter he wrote that the synagogue, as home, is also an expression of simplicity and directness. He related to the difference between the Christian church and the Jewish synagogue:

> The holiness of the synagogue, like the sanctity of the home, finds expression in our respect for its privacy and exclusiveness. To be dedicated to a plurality of cultic modes is a pure paradox. This paradox becomes more striking when we consider the discrepancy between the Jewish service and the Christian form of worship. The Christian Orthodox church sees in the act of worship a sacramental mysterious performance, which is fraught with otherworldliness and beatitude, and is rooted in the miracle of transubstantiation. The whole organization of the service and the arrangement of its surroundings, like the passive role of the audience, the soft music of the organ, the stained glass window and the Gothic style of the architecture, serve one purpose, namely the intensification of a feeling of super-naturalness, strangeness and meta-rationality. In contrast to this, the Jewish service is distinguished by its simplicity. It asserts itself in a dialogue between God and man on the level

61 See above, Chapter Eleven.
62 "Synagogue as an Institution," 331.
63 See Schwartz, *From Phenomenology to Existentialism*, chapter 11.

of this-worldliness and concreteness. It is conducted in an atmosphere of rationality, familiarity, and naturalness.[64]

This letter is of a public nature and directed to non-Jews, as well. R. Soloveitchik sharply contrasted the church, with its characteristically transcendent orientation, with the synagogue that transfers the dialogue between God and man to this world. The home does not only express privacy, as was stated at the beginning of this passage, but also directness and a familiar and intimate atmosphere that inspires confidence. The divine presence and the dialogue with it are concrete. In the typical style of *Halakhic Man*, the church seeks to elevate man to God, while the synagogue, in its aspect as home, brings God down to man.

The Synagogue as Return

Thus, the synagogue is the way to overcome the existential crisis whose features were listed above. For R. Soloveitchik, the synagogue symbolizes not only the spatial home. It also represents man's original state, in which he encounters God. Exile is the situation where man is distanced from his home and environment. Prayer in a synagogue returns man to his home; in the synagogue, a person feels at home.[65] The synagogue, as home, is a double metaphor:

(1) The Jew's natural home is the Land of Israel, and the Temple is the natural venue of his encounter with God. The synagogue is a metaphor for the national home.
(2) Exile is a state in which a person is alienated from his self, while redemption is the return to the self. The synagogue is a metaphor for selfhood.

The return to the self is also an encounter with God. God does not need a geographical expanse. For R. Soloveitchik,

God does not need a home for Himself. God feigned homelessness in order to induce man to build a home for man. And whatever name is assigned to this home is to be understood in terms of human, not divine, homelessness.

---

64 "On Depiction of Human Images on Stained Glass Windows in an Interfaith Chapel," in *Community, Covenant and Commitment*, 9.
65 R. Soloveitchik briefly discussed the relation between prayer and place in *Abraham's Journey*, 63.

> It is the home of God, because it is the home of man. God comes to that
> house in order to keep His appointment with man.[66]

God meets man at home, in the synagogue. Prayer is a return to the self,
and man's "original" natural state is standing before God. The idea of
the synagogue as an expression of one's self is the subjective dimension of the
laws of the synagogue.[67]

Further on the question of sources: R. Soloveitchik, apparently, incorporated the Kierkegaardian notion of repetition, of which he was especially
enamored, in his conception of prayer. Already in the middle of the 1940s,
he spoke of the idea of return as a central religious category.[68] According
to Kierkegaard, the return to one's self means overcoming alienation. The
return to concreteness is not a move to the past or to the historical or
chronological source (with the irony in this concept), but to the self that
contains both past and future.[69] A return to the original condition in its
entirety is not possible, just as Job, for example, did not return to his original situation.[70] Repetition incorporates the current substantiality with the
past, thus, its results are likely to be more productive. By the same coin,
prayer is a return to the home, albeit not the national home. Prayer is both
a return to the source, to the self, and an encounter with God. This return
includes new religious heights. When a person returns to his original self,
he also meets God in it; consequently, this is an old-new situation.

At this point we should draw a comparison with "Redemption, Prayer,
Talmud Torah."[71] In both articles, written at about the same time, prayer
expresses the redemption of the self. In each, prayer confronts the worshiper
with his identity and personality, and, in other words, brings a person to over-
come his existential alienation and anxiety and to find meaning in his life.
The difference between the two is that in "Redemption, Prayer, Talmud
Torah," R. Soloveitchik presented prayer as the discovery of the self, while in
"Synagogue as an Institution," it is a return to the self. He continued in the latter:

> In a word, man—be he an individual, be he a community, is homeless
> because he is vulnerable. He is terrorized by the fright in the night. He needs

---

66 "Synagogue as an Institution," 331.
67 "Synagogue as an Institution," 330-331.
68 *The Halakhic Mind*, 49.
69 See Sagi, *Kierkegaard, Religion and Existence*, 20.
70 See Gregor Malantschuk's analysis in his *Kierkegaard's Thought*, ed. and trans. Howard
    V. Hong and Edna H. Hong (Princeton, NJ: Princeton University Press, 1971), 232-33.
71 See above, Chapter Nine.

a home that will give him security, at least a sense of security, and shelter. "He will come to this house and He will spread out his hands: (I Kings 8:38). That is exactly the idea of *bet ha-keneset*. As we said above, *bet ha-keneset* is the home of God because it is the home of man.[72]

Prayer is a return home, in the sense of leaving exile, and the synagogue is a symbol of this return. R. Soloveitchik emphasized that this also holds true in the social, communal, and national planes. When the Jewish people returns to its land, this is obviously a restorative action. But life in the era of redemption, which is also the modern era, cannot be identical to life thousands of years ago. Thus, the synagogue reflects both the return of the self along with a fresh start, effecting its elevation.

To conclude, the synagogue offers modern man a home, a place of identity, which expresses the return to his self and an encounter with God. It enables man to be reconciled with himself, gives him a sense of belonging, and allows him to overcome his existential distresses.

The Synagogue as Representation

The other benefit of the synagogue is inherent in the concept of *shelihut* (halakhic agency). The community of worshipers represents the entire Jewish people, in all times. The synagogue becomes an institution of ahistorical national agency. From time to time R. Soloveitchik examined the issue of agency in his writings, and devoted to it the article "*Shelihut*" in the book *Yemei Zikaron*; this essay was originally the aggadic part of a lesson in memory of his father, R. Moshe Soloveitchik. "Synagogue as an Institution" and "*Shelihut*" are concerned with two types of agency.

(1) Human agency: man appoints his fellow as agent. Such a type of agency is discussed in the classic halakhic literature.
(2) Divine agency: God appoints man as His agent. This sort of agency appears in the homiletical and philosophical literature.

The first distinction between "Synagogue as an Institution" and "*Shelihut*" pertains to human agency:

> In the *sugyot* [discursive units] of agency in *Hoshen Mishpat* and *Even ha Ezer*, the *sholeah* [the sender] does not accompany the *shaluah* [the agent].

---

72 "Synagogue as an Institution," 332.

Immediately following his appointment, he, the agent, becomes the representative of the sender, and he does everything from his own mind, without the aid or presence of the sender.[73]

The idea [of *shelihut*] belongs not only to the juridic, formalistic realm, but it also has a personalistic note, which sometimes extends into the metaphysical [...] The alter ego, the *shaliah* [agent], actually undergoes a miraculous metamorphosis and turns into the *meshale-ah* [= *sholeʾah*, above]. He enacts the part of the latter. He impersonates the latter, like an artist on a theatrical stage, but with one distinction. While the artist, the actor, impersonates a certain character in the drama in an artistic, fictional manner, the *shaliah*, according to [Judaism, impersonates the *meshale-ah* in an existential, personalistic way. The very phrase *sheluho shel adam kemoto* [one's emissary is as oneself][74] says that the *shaliah* assumes the identity of the *meshale-ah*. There is a personal union of *shaliah* and *meshale-ah*.[75]

The central topic in *"Shelihut"* is divine agency. The article's basic assumption is that man as such is the agent of divine Providence. Therefore, he is born and acts in a specific period and not in others.[76] In contrast, in "Synagogue as an Institution," the worshiper is the agent of the Jewish people.[77] R. Soloveitchik drew upon the Kabbalistic notion that *Knesset Yisrael* (the divine being that represents Israel) is a given entity, and is more than the sum of its parts.[78] In other words, he did not hesitate to shift the concept of agency to the philosophical realm. He also, however, gave expression to this idea in his halakhic lessons.[79] He therefore instilled in

---

73 *"Shelihut,"* in *Yemei Zikaron*, 14.

74 This rule first appears in M Berahot 5:5, regarding the *shaliah tzibbur* (the leader of communal prayer; literally, the "agent of the congregation"). See also T Taanit 3:2; BT Hagigah 10b; Nedarim 72b; Kiddushin 41b; Bava Metzia 96a.

75 "Synagogue as an Institution," 333.

76 *"Shelihut,"* in *Yemei Zikaron*, 11.

77 It is noteworthy in this context that ethnic heritage and identity comprise an essential component of the intersubjective correlation. R. Soloveitchik took note of the halakhic rule that agency does not apply to a non-Jew, as the Talmud establishes: "Just as you are Israelites [*bnei berit* literally, members of the Covenant], so must your agents be Israelites" (BT Gittin 23b; Kiddushin 41b; Bava Metzia 71b). This is because shared "destiny" and "historical memories" are necessary to effect the existential correlation ("Synagogue as an Institution," 334).

78 "Synagogue as an Institution," 337.

79 See above, Chapter Ten. In *Lessons in Memory of Father*, the idea of national representation is treated as a halakhic consideration parallel to the *Tamid* daily sacrifice, which shows that the Kabbalistic motif was taken in a metaphorical, and not ontic, sense.

human agency what he would later include in divine agency: unlike the formalistic followers of the halakhah, the *shaliah* does not part ways with the *meshale-ah*. Agency is the union of the two, the agent and the one who appoints him. R. Soloveitchik stressed that this combination is "existential." Indeed, the existentialist literature contains many descriptions of the Other as one who invades the domain of the subject. In this respect, the nonformalistic conception of agency records the relation between subjects and gives it orderly expression.

Both "*Shelihut*" and "Synagogue as an Institution" mention divine agency. In the former, this is the main, and even sole, topic, while the latter speaks of it only briefly.[80] In "*Shelihut*" R. Soloveitchik states that God, as the appointer of the agent, constantly accompanies the latter, in contrast to human agency.[81] In "Synagogue as an Institution" human and divine agency unite in that the sender is present in the agent. "He [God] moves along with the prophet and acts and speaks through him."[82] As the latter article has it, divine agency is a specific instance of agency in general, one that is concerned with existential union and presence. R. Soloveitchik is forced to argue thus, since he speaks of human agency in this article. The thesis of this article is that a *minyan* in the synagogue represents all Israel, which is present in this quorum. Moreover, it is not only the current Israelite community that is represented by the *minyan*, but rather the national entity in all times. Such an argument is valid only if the presence of the sender with the agent is assumed as a basic characteristic of every agency.

Summary

We learn from R. Soloveitchik's analyses that the synagogue offers the common basis for the many benefits of prayer. He asserts that prayer speaks to modern man by directly relating to his existential needs, but this relation is individual. It is expressed in a certain way regarding the average person (the "small man"), and in another way for the self-affirming individual (the "great man"). Prayer redeems a series of distresses experienced by modern man. The deep meaning, of all these individual troubles, however, is the lack of a home, which is provided by the synagogue. That is, the importance of the synagogue, in relation to the individual, is achieved with a

---

80 "Synagogue as an Institution," 335.
81 "*Shelihut*," in *Yemei Zikaron*, 14.
82 "Synagogue as an Institution," 335.

true understanding of the meaning of this distress and of the meaning of existential redemption. Detachment, anxiety, and alienation derive directly from the lack of home, and they can be overcome by finding home, namely, the synagogue.

From this respect, the synagogue expresses the deep dimension of the consciousness of prayer. The construction of the consciousness—the consciousness of prayer, which was described in detail in the preceding chapters, presumably was a sort of interim stratum that ensues from the deep stratum (the synagogue). Such an approach is obviously of an apologetic nature, with the aim of implanting the synagogue in the consciousness of modern man. The synagogue offers a return home, and thereby enables one to properly contend with the modern condition. Herein lies the advantage of the synagogue for man as such. The synagogue, however, also provides a benefit in the national plane. Prayer in a *minyan* represents, in the deepest sense, the nation. The synagogue is a return to both the individual and national home. Consequently, this institution offers affiliation to the detached individual, and to the exiled community, identification with the entirety of the nation.

2. Communication and Community

We already noted that *The Lonely Man of Faith* is concerned with the loneliness caused by the absurdity of intersubjective relation. Man as subject is exposed to another subject by virtue of divine grace, which in the course of the essay becomes a norm. Clearly, the intersubjective connection is possible only because God joins the "I" and the "Thou." In *The Lonely Man of Faith* R. Soloveitchik once again set forth the model of the change of direction between prophecy and prayer: in prophecy, it is God who initiates the community of I, Thou, and Him, while in prayer, man begins to create this community.[83] In *The Lonely Man of Faith* R. Soloveitchik devotes a focused discussion, possibly the most exhaustive in all his writings, to prayer as a dialogic situation. Until that essay, he was concerned, at most, with the *consciousness* of dialogue. He considered mainly man's turn to God and analyzed the correlation between the two participants in the dialogue. As we showed in the current chapter, R. Soloveitchik spoke of the dimension of affiliation and the national representation of dialogue, but not of its concrete and intersubjective standing. *Worship of the Heart* did not relate

---

83 See above, Chapter Two.

to concrete dialogue, and it is therefore fitting to focus on intersubjectivity in order to end these discussions with the standing of prayer in *The Lonely Man of Faith*.

The key concept of the discussion of prayer as actual dialogue is "covenant" (*berit*). R. Soloveitchik used this term to comprehensively denote the mutual encounter between man and his God.[84] The covenant that reflects dialogue[85] is not limited to any given generation, but rather unites the tradition of all generations.[86] It also constitutes the conception of community, and as such extends to all realms of life. According to this understanding, the standing of prophecy is clearly that of a covenant. Can this be said of prayer as well? R. Soloveitchik undertook to present the standing of prayer as such, giving aspects in which prayer can be understood as covenant: confrontation, community, and norm. We will now examine his arguments.

Confrontation

In prayer, as in prophecy, man stands before his God. R. Soloveitchik distinguished between the cosmic experience and that of prayer. He wrote:

> Prayer likewise is unimaginable without having man stand before and address himself to God in a manner reminiscent of the prophet's dialogue with God. The cosmic drama, notwithstanding its grandeur and splendor, no matter how distinctly it reflects the image of the Creator and no matter how beautifully it tells His glory, cannot provoke man to prayer.[87]

The cosmic experience is ecstatic and subjective; in most instances, it has no balancing objective expression. It is oscillatory, with a sensation of drawing near and moving away.[88] The experience of prayer, despite taking place

---

84 David Hartman wrote extensively on the concept of covenant (*berit*) in R. Soloveitchik's thought. See, for example, David Hartman, *Love and Terror in the God Encounter: The Theological Legacy of Rabbi Joseph B. Soloveitchik* (Woodstock, VT: Jewish Lights, 2001), 111. See also David Hartman, *A Living Covenant: The Innovative Spirit in Traditional Judaism* (New York: Free Press, 1985), 21-41.

85 See below.

86 See, for example, *Festival of Freedom*, 21.

87 *Lonely Man of Faith*, 55.

88 *Lonely Man of Faith*, 48. R. Soloveitchik expresses the fluidity of the cosmic experience when he speaks of Ps. 19:2 ("The heavens declare the glory of God"): "Yet, let me ask, what kind of tale do the heavens tell? Is it a personal tale addressed to someone, or is it a tale which is not intended for any audience? Do the heavens sing the glory of the Creator without troubling themselves to find out whether someone is listening to this great song, or are they really interested in man, the listener? [...] We may conclude that

in the subjective plane (covenantal standing), has an objective expression: the recitation of texts. R. Soloveitchik emphasized that the objective dimension does not exhaust prayer. "The latter [prayer] transcends the bounds of liturgical worship and must not be reduced to its external-technical aspects such as praise, thanksgiving, or even petition."[89] He then differentiated between the two experiences by distinguishing between hymn and prayer. The cosmic experience is followed by the composition of songs of praise,[90] while the experience of prayer creates measured and considered texts. The cosmic experience is a monologue, and that of prayer, a dialogue.

R. Soloveitchik was inclined to emphasize the weakness of the cosmic experience as compared to the force of the prayer experience. He implied that the cosmic experience is tainted with "fleeting, amorphous subjectivity."[91] Additionally, the composers of the *Amidah* text kept the cosmic experience away from it. The title *melekh ha-olam* (King of the Universe) is absent from the *Amidah*. Presumably, the composers of this prayer feared two threats to its standing:

(1) The cosmic experience could harm its balancing objectivity.[92] At times, R. Soloveitchik drew on Kabbalah in his various writings, as has been discussed by many scholars.[93] In numerous places, however, he patently objected to mysticism and the spirit of mysticism. Therefore, he took care to distance the encounter with God from mysticism. This situation includes both prayer and prophecy, and is *"toto genere* different from the mystical experience."[94]

the message of the heavens is at best an equivocal one" (*Lonely Man of Faith*, 47-48). In contrast, in *Halakhic Man*, the verse is understood as referring to the normative message and therefore is presented in a positive light. See *Halakhic Man*, 64.

89 *Lonely Man of Faith*, 55.
90 On the cosmic experience as the source of poetry, see, for example, Karl Erich Grözinger, *Musik und Gesang in der Theologie der frühen jüdischen Literatur: Talmud, Midrasch, Mystik* (Tubingen: Mohr Siebeck, 1982), 27-55. The second part of Grözinger's book examines hymns in early mystical literature.
91 *Lonely Man of Faith*, 56.
92 *Lonely Man of Faith*, 56 n.
93 See Rivka Horowitz, "Rav Soloveitchik's Attitude to the Religious Experience and to Mysticism" [Hebrew], in Sagi, *Faith in Changing Times*, 45-74; Lawrence Kaplan, "Kabbalistic Motifs in Rav Soloveitchik's Thought: Meaningful or Ornamental?" [Hebrew], in Sagi, *Faith in Changing Times*, 75-93; Schwartz, *Religion or Halakha*, chapter 7.
94 *Lonely Man of Faith*, 54. Once again, R. Soloveitchik drew a distinction between prophecy and mysticism, also regarding the moral and normative message of the experience (ibid., 61). See also below.

The encounter with God is covenantal, because it is balanced, and man does not lose his personality,[95] nor does the singing of hymns exhibit a surfeit of uncontrolled creativity.

(2) The cosmic experience does not enable dialogue. The dialogical dimension is preserved by God not appearing as King. This is because dialogue cannot be conducted with a king, since his greatness and the fear he engenders do not allow for an exchange between speakers. The sovereign may be praised, with paeans to his majesty and splendor (hymn), but he is not a conversant whom one can face in prayer.

We are seemingly left with the question of whether praise is inherent in the *Amidah*. The first three are blessings of praise. Is the beginning of the *Amidah* not a sort of cosmic experience ("acquires [and creates] all," "sustains the living," "revives the dead," and the like)? R. Soloveitchik particularly noted that the praise of the *Amidah* is primarily the recollection of the Patriarchs—in other words, the covenant. "The fact that we commence the recital of the 'Eighteen Benedictions' by addressing ourselves to the God of Abraham, Isaac, and Jacob is indicative of the covenantal relationship."[96] That is, he related solely to the blessing of *Avot*, and probably thought that it set the pattern for the two other blessings (*Gevurot* and *Kedushah*), as well. The praise in the *Amidah* relates to the covenant, and the covenant is, first and foremost, dialogue. As it were, God is so praiseworthy because of His entry into a covenant with mere mortals. This is a sort of surrender and an expression of divine kindness, which itself is outstanding praise.

The Lonely Man of Faith discusses two figures, majestic man and the man of faith. The former is portrayed as one who frequently undergoes a cosmic experience and considers it the peak of his religiosity. R. Soloveitchik writes:

> Majestic man, even when he belongs to the group of *homines religiosi* and feels a distinct need for transcendental experiences, is gratified by his encounter with God within the framework of the cosmic drama. Since majestic man is incapable of breaking out of the cosmic cycle, he cannot interpret his transcendental adventure in anything but cosmic categories.[97]

---

95 The cosmic experience is "indirect and impersonal" (*Lonely Man of Faith*, 54).
96 *Lonely Man of Faith*, 56 n.
97 *Lonely Man of Faith*, 50.

Although R. Soloveitchik asserted that both models are pleasing to God, it is clear from an analysis of the covenant that majestic man is exposed to the dangers of the cosmic experience, namely, obscuring the objective dimension of the experience. Furthermore, R. Soloveitchik was of the opinion that majestic man and the man of faith are two poles of the same individual,[98] and that these types reflect the fundamental dialectic of religious existence. Consequently, in the oscillation between the cosmic and covenant experiences, prayer is to be found at the covenant pole.

In a certain sense, the covenant not only leads to dialoguebut is also identical to it. In other words, the mutual address, the encounter, is the covenant itself. R. Soloveitchik states: "Covenantal prophecy and prayer blossomed forth the very instant Abraham met God and became involved in a strange colloquy."[99] Thus, prayer definitely has the standing of covenant and itself is dialogue, which is covenant. Dialogue is the subjective dimension of prayer, and the essence of prayer is the encounter with God. The worshiper moves between the institutionalized prayer (the covenant) and spontaneous praise. He fluctuates between the fixed text, which expresses the continuity of tradition, and the hymns that burst forth. He shifts between dialogue and monologue. Prayer is the dialogue of covenant.

Community

If prayer were a conversation only between man and his God, we would return to R. Soloveitchik's phenomenological model in *Worship of the Heart*. Such a model, examining consciousness and experience, does not go beyond the individual and God. We saw that R. Soloveitchik's use of the term "community" includes only man and God.[100] In *The Lonely Man of Faith*, he stressed that the dialogue between man and God is not complete. Dialogue must also be conducted with one's fellow, that is, the Other, who in this case is a concrete worshiper. The worshiper must be open to the world around him. R. Soloveitchik used the images of two Adams to convey this approach: Adam the first, who represents majestic man, and Adam the second, who represents the man of faith. The most characteristic representative of Adam the first is the mathematical scientist who whisks us away from the array of tangible things. Adam the second

---

98 *Lonely Man of Faith*, 84-85.
99 *Lonely Man of Faith*, 57-58.
100 See above, Chapter Five.

turns to the qualitative world out of curiosity rather than out of an attempt to impose mathematical-physical models on it. His dominant feature is loneliness. Adam the second is lonely because he is a unique creature. R. Soloveitchik wrote:

> The foundation of efficacious and noble prayer is human solidarity and sym-
> pathy or the covenantal awareness of existential togetherness, of sharing and
> experiencing the travail and suffering of those for whom majestic Adam the
> first has no concern. Only Adam the second knows the art of praying since
> he confronts God with the petition of the many. The fenced-in egocentric
> and ego-oriented Adam the first is ineligible to join the covenantal prayer
> community of which God is a fellow member. If God abandons His tran-
> scendal numinous solitude, He wills man to do likewise and to step out of
> his isolation and aloneness.[101]

Majestic man is "fenced-in" within himself,[102] while the man of faith (that is, Adam the second) is open to his fellow man. The common existential-ist terminology used by R. Soloveitchik is especially characteristic of *The Lonely Man of Faith*. Openness to the world is a fundamental existentialist principle.[103]

R. Soloveitchik's discussion is anchored in the existentialist discourse. Heidegger rejected idealism as centered within itself and argued that the liberation of the self means being open to the world. Buber criticized Heidegger and maintained that

> human life possesses absolute meaning through transcending in practice its
> own conditioned nature, that is, through man's seeing that which he con-
> fronts, and with which he can enter into a real relation of being to being,
> as not less real than himself, and through taking it not less seriously than
> himself.[104]

---

101 *Lonely Man of Faith*, 59-60.
102 "Fenced-in" here does not mean that majestic man is not a social type. To the contrary,
     he is involved in society, due both to his psychological need for company and the effi-
     caciousness and utility he finds in social relations. He does not, however, open up as a
     subject to his fellow.
103 See, for example, Avi Sagi, *Living with the Other: The Ethic of Inner Retreat*, trans. Batya
     Stein (Cham, Switzerland: Springer, 2018), 55-77.
104 Martin Buber, "What Is Man?," in *Between Man and Man*, trans. Ronald Gregor-Smith
     (London: Routledge, 2002), 198-199. Buber formulated the idea of openness to the
     other in his socialist thought.

Buber claimed that Heidegger's doctrine does not assume a priori openness to the other, that is, dialogue. Such a doctrine, in fact, is "monologic." For Buber, Heidegger did not succeed in breaching the barrier of existential loneliness, not in regard to the Other, and certainly not in regard to God.[105] In *The Lonely Man of Faith*, R. Soloveitchik added to Buber's approach the Kierkegaardian motif of impossibility of self-transcendence, that is, going forth to the other without the divine presence.[106] Adam the first discovered Eve due to divine grace, and he succeeds in creating a covenantal community through divine intervention. This community, however, is not limited to man and God, as was noted above. The covenant is conditional upon openness to the Other.

We should also mention another matter: Buber, Rosenzweig, and R. Soloveitchik hold that God's address to man is out of His kindness and love, and it enables man to act in a similar manner to others. Yet, unlike Buber and Rosenzweig (for whom the divine address means only divine love),[107] R. Soloveitchik maintained that this address imposes obligatory moral and normative tasks on man (see below).[108]

An additional term (that is based on Heideggerian elements) is "covenant of fate,"[109] implicit in what R. Soloveitchik wrote. He states that Job "failed to understand the covenantal nature of the prayer community in which destinies are dovetailed."[110] The covenant of fate is the fundamental characteristic of Jewish national existence.[111] The conception of prayer as covenant makes an important contribution to our understanding of the "covenant of fate." Addressing the Other is a fundamental condition for the Jewish existence,

---

105 See George Kovacs, *The Question of God in Heidegger's Phenomenology* (Evanston, IL: Northwestern University Press, 1990), 235.

106 Kierkegaard developed this idea mainly in *Works of Love*.

107 See, for example, Nahum N. Glatzer, "The Concept of Language in the Thought of Franz Rosenzweig," in *The Philosophy of Franz Rosenzweig*, ed. Paul Mendes-Flohr (Hanover: University Press of New England, 1988), 176-77.

108 *Lonely Man of Faith*, 61.

109 Fate is parallel to existence that lacks meaning, while destiny corresponds to a meaningful existence. See Avi Schweitzer [Sagi], "The Loneliness of the Man of Faith in the Philosophy of Soloveitchik: A Dialectic of Fate and Mission" [Hebrew], *Daat* 2-3 (1978-1979): 249.

110 *Lonely Man of Faith*, 60.

111 On the sources of the national context, see Gerald Blidstein, "On the Jewish People in the Writings of Rabbi Joseph B. Soloveitchik" [Hebrew], in Sagi, *Faith in Changing Times*, 168-71 ("Appendix: On the Sources of the Terms 'Fate' and 'Destiny'"); see also Dov Schwartz, *Challenge and Crisis*, 297-301; Schwartz, *From Phenomenology to Existentialism*, 210.

and prayer reflects this orientation. The Jewish community is, by definition, a prayer community. The Jewish fate is intertwined with communality.

Norm

The covenant ceremony includes actual normative commitments (in R. Soloveitchik's terminology, "kerygma"). In regard to these commitments, R. Soloveitchik used the terms "moral," "ethical," and "normative."[112] He went from the general social sphere to a more limited one:

(1) the faith community, committed to living a moral life ("the universal faith community");[113]
(2) the "Halakhic community"[114] is a particular example of the faith community;
(3) the prayer community is one expression of the halakhic community.

The movement from the general sphere to the particular reflects the relation between *The Lonely Man of Faith* to R. Soloveitchik's thought as a whole, which is centered around the halakhah. Furthermore, he patently strove to forge such a relation in *The Lonely Man of Faith*. To a certain degree, this work is exceptional in R. Soloveitchik's thought, since it lacks the openly, emphasized apologetic dimension characteristic of his works. R. Soloveitchik's writings present the halakhah as the ideal objective expression of the subjective consciousness, on the one hand, and, on the other, as the element best suited to, and as answering, modern man's existential distresses. *The Lonely Man of Faith* speaks of phenomena, some of which precede the halakhah. It ranges from a typological reading of the first chapters of Genesis to prophecy and the prayer that was instituted by the Men of the Great Assembly. Rabbinic halakhah appears only in motifs such as the normative dimension of the covenant and the presentation of the halakhah as the Jewish version of the moral norm. This enables us to understand the acceptance of the norm in the covenant ceremony. R. Soloveitchik took pains to connect the covenant ceremony and dialogue with the halakhah and the halakhic community, and not only to the moral norm.[115] The first

---

112 *Lonely Man of Faith*, 61.
113 *Lonely Man of Faith*, 63.
114 *Lonely Man of Faith*, 63.
115 This is an expression of what Yehoyada Amir termed a "cultural agent." See Yehoyada Amir, "Rabbi Soloveitchik as a Cultural Agent: A Critical Reading of *The Lonely Man*

glimmerings of this polemic are only latent in *The Lonely Man of Faith*, as we shall see below.

To return to the hierarchy of the three communities: the movement from the faith community to the prayer community teaches that communality and norm are intertwined. The personal experience lacks an objective norm that can be analyzed, while the communal experience facilitates the existence of the norm. Furthermore, the limited communality movement from faith to halakhah intensifies the commitment from one to the general moral norm to obligation to the specific halakhic norm. The following are the meanings of communality and normativity for the conception of prayer.

(1) Scope: prayer is not an esoteric experience. Once again, R. Soloveitchik contrasted covenant (prophecy and prayer) with mysticism. He wrote:

> In contradistinction to the mystical experience of intuition, illumination, or union which rarely results in the formulation of a practical message, prophecy [...] is inseparable from its normative content.[116] [...] If we were to eliminate the norm from the prophetic God-man encounter, confining the latter to its apocalyptic aspects, then the whole prophetic drama would be acted out by a limited number of privileged individuals to the exclusion of the rest of the people. Such a prospect, turning the prophetic colloquy into an esoteric-egotistic affair, would be immoral from the viewpoint of Halakhic Judaism, which is exoterically-minded and democratic to its very core.[117]

---

of Faith" [Hebrew], in Rosenak and Rothenberg, *Rabbi in the New World*, 240. In any event, R. Soloveitchik clearly viewed prayer as a universal expression of covenantal man, and Jewish prayer as a particular instance of the moral community. It is noteworthy that he leveled veiled morality-based criticism of *homo religiosus*. See *Halakhic Man*, 40-41.

116 *Lonely Man of Faith*, 61.

117 *Lonely Man of Faith*, 64. R. Soloveitchik advanced various reasons in his writings for rejecting esotericism. In *The Lonely Man of Faith* he did so because esotericism is rooted in a tendency to the transcendent, and such an inclination is not suitable for the present, but rather for the messianic future (see Schwartz, *Religion or Halakha*, 171-178). In *And From There You Shall Seek* he argued that esotericism is suitable for natural religiosity, which demands knowledge of the sciences (Schwartz, *From Phenomenology to Existentialism*, 83-87). Both works reject esotericism because it is not appropriate for the religious consciousness. However, here R. Soloveitchik presented a clearly moral argument: esotericism repels the multitudes from the prophetic experience, specifically, and from the dialogical experience in general.

(2) Continuity: prayer is not divorced from the individual's way of life. It is a component of the worshiper's halakhic behavior. Consequently, R. Soloveitchik emphasized the emergence of the prayer community from the halakhic community. He wrote:

> The Halakhah has never looked upon prayer as a separate magical gesture in which man may engage without integrating it into the total pattern of his life.[118] [...] Prayer [...] is not a separate entity, but the sublime prologue to Halakhic action.[119]

(3) Mending: this meaning ensues from continuity. Prayer requires repentance. Dialogue with God demands intimacy. Sin does not permit an intimate situation, because it raises a barrier between man and his God:

> Who is qualified to engage God in the prayer colloquy? Clearly, the person who is ready to cleanse himself of imperfection and evil. Any kind of injustice, corruption, cruelty, or the like desecrates the very essence of the prayer adventure, since it encases man in an ugly little world into which God is unwilling to enter.[120]

R. Soloveitchik wanted to stress that prayer is reflective, but not autonomous. It mirrors the worshiper's moral and halakhic life, but does not claim any place for itself. This approach has a polemical core. In the Introduction (above), we noted the important place of prayer in the phenomenological conception of religion. R. Soloveitchik's sources afforded prayer a standing superior to that of other ritual acts and other expressions of inner religion. He was influenced by the terminology and content of the discussions of Friedrich Heiler and other phenomenologists, but opposed the separation of prayer from the other components of the religious consciousness. Prayer is intertwined with halakhah and is common to all observant Jews. The prayer community is a reflection of the halakhic community. Without commitment to the norm, which is bound up with the dialogical standing of prayer, prayer would go beyond its dimensions and become an independent institution, one limited to exceptional individuals, similar to mystical and magical activity.

By introducing the normative element into the covenant, R. Soloveitchik returned the innovative discussion of dialogue and the Other to the traditional

---

118 *Lonely Man of Faith*, 65.
119 *Lonely Man of Faith*, 66.
120 *Lonely Man of Faith*, 65.

stream of ideas that characterized the different periods of his thought. Dialogue reflects the subjective and experiential dimension of prayer, one that is fluid and could easily cross over into mysticism and destructiveness. The normative characteristic of the covenant balances and tones down the dialogue experience. From this aspect, the dialogical conception is a branch of the consciousness conception of prayer.

Summary

Prayer is an experience. It reflects the religious consciousnes turning to God and its relation to Him. In his writings R. Soloveitchik related to the experience of prayer from the consciousness aspect, that is, he focused on the personality and its connection to God. In *The Lonely Man of Faith* he examined this experience mainly from an existentialist perspective, which is a refreshing departure, as an additional layer of his thought. Prayer is also a product of community, the "prayer community." Here, the community is not only between man and God; it also includes the other. In this respect, the discussion in *The Lonely Man of Faith* is singular; weaving the question of the Other into the consciousness of prayer is untypical of R. Soloveitchik's areas of interest.

The singular discussion in this work does not cloak the traditional patterns of R. Soloveitchik's thought. This is exemplified by the fact that three features of the prayer community are indirectly based on the distinction between the cosmic and covenantal experiences, as follows.

(1) The cosmic experience is one of self-negation before God,[121] while the covenantal experience consists of standing before and confronting God.

(2) The cosmic experience is personal, while the covenantal experience is of communal significance.

(3) The cosmic experience is one of devotion, but not of subordination and limitation. To the contrary, at times it is antinomistic. The covenantal experience, in contrast, is one of acceptance of the law, from choice and freely.

---

121 The fact that this experience is characteristic of the majestic man is representative of R. Soloveitchik's dialectical thought. The experience of self-abnegation contains no ongoing commitment or responsibility. This is an experience of mood that facilitates the continuation of routine activity when this state has passed.

R. Soloveitchik patently sought to define the covenantal experience typical of prayer as in opposition to the cosmic experience. His attitude to the latter resembles, in great degree, that to Kabbalah as a branch of mysticism. He viewed the cosmic experience as representative of prevalent, and almost necessary, religiosity, but also of potentially dangerous religiosity which is to be treated with caution.

The Lonely Man of Faith contains an extremely focused discussion of prayer as intersubjective dialogue. R. Soloveitchik highlighted the dual dialogue in prayer: on the one hand, man turns to God and confronts him directly, even if He does not respond; while, on the other, man addresses the Other as a member of the community. Moreover, he mentioned the confrontation with God first, and the address to the Other and openness to the community only afterwards. It seems that he did not give precedence to God out of respect, but as a substantive stipulation. R. Soloveitchik truly believed that only addressing God enables addressing the Other. In other words, only opening oneself to God will lead to openness to the Other. Again, we have the motif of divine lovingkindness, this time hidden. Intriguingly, the discussion of prayer as a dialogue both with God (text) and with the Other (*minyan* and prayer community) is almost completely absent from all the works written by R. Soloveitchik himself, at least those already published. At most, prayer appears as dialogue with God alone. Thus, R. Soloveitchik thought that his first task, namely, the presentation of prayer as confrontation with God, had not yet been completed. Consequently, he did not relate to the second task of openness to the Other.

The consciousness and existential meanings of prayer are anchored in its status as a halakhic obligation. Such standing is parallel to existentialist thought that endows meaningless existence with meaning. The halakhah transforms an outpouring of an individual soul into a meaningful event.

The action of the halakhah has a dual consequence. On the one hand, it organizes the personality's chaotic inclinations and gives them a goal and a purpose, molding them into an experience. On the other hand, the halakhah infuses the experience of prayer with meaning.

Summary
The Consciousness of Prayer

Prayer was one of R. Soloveitchik's major interests. He left hardly any topic pertaining to prayer untouched, subjecting them to analytical, homiletical, and philosophical inquiry. His thought contains sweeping halakhic and analytical discussions of prayer, holidays, and the Days of Awe, studies of the standing of the synagogue, and more. Nor did he overlook the gestures accompanying prayer, whose meaning he examined in depth. The wealth of works on his personal practices which were published posthumously are replete with his references to prayer. It was to be expected that he would devote an independent composition to prayer, and such a work, albeit not complete, was published after his death. R. Soloveitchik presented prayer as a window to the religious consciousness and as its reflection. At times the careful reader of R. Soloveitchik's writings has difficulty in shaking off the feeling that prayer is merely a pretext to explore the religious consciousness. At times the realms of his interest appear to be the same substantive elements that create religion and the religious experience. Or, possibly, prayer is not an "excuse," but a powerful tool, one of unparalleled import, that facilitates our penetration to the depths of the religious consciousness.

The Task

Prayer as praxis has received different meanings, and the act of prayer came to mirror the religious consciousness and life as a whole. More precisely, the act of prayer has been transformed into the apex of the religious experience. Although this experience is primarily characteristic of the individual, R. Soloveitchik also included the public for apologetic purposes (the discussion in his "The Synagogue as an Institution and as an Idea"). Not only did he relate to prayer in the broadest and most substantive sense that could be ascribed to it, he also took various aspects of prayer to an extreme; all this in order to afford it center stage in Jewish thought.

For R. Soloveitchik, moving prayer from the fringes to the center lay in the sphere of the consciousness. The task that he set for himself was therefore phenomenological. First, he described the consciousness of prayer. When he summarized laudatory prayer, he wrote:

> Studies in the psychology of religion that report on the benefit of prayer as a source of consolation and relief for the weary, reflect the belief that the God of *hesed* receives our prayer with love and favor.[1]

R. Soloveitchik was interested in the way in which consciousness perceives the act of prayer. Second, prayer becomes a subjective and objective act of consciousness in his writings. But unlikeother commandments where the subjective is reconstructed from the objective, the structure of prayer is twofold.

(1) The reconstruction completely disappears. Now, the subjective is the cause of the objective.
(2) The subjective is changed into the objective. The divine command relates directly to the subjective dimension.

R. Soloveitchik wrote that prayer is "like a mirror reflecting the image of the person who worships God with heart and soul, is shot through with perplexity, for worship itself is rooted in the human dialectical consciousness."[2] Intent makes the subjective mandatory and not merely possible. The experience is an obligation, and not a possibility. Prayer is seen to be an expression of rationality, on the one hand, and, on the other, of the mystic; an expression of belief and theological statements, on the one hand, and, on the other, of emotion and dialogue.

Although R. Soloveitchik devoted much attention to the consciousness conception of prayer in most of his writings, this did not suffice for him. Along with the consciousness aspects, prayer also reflects fundamental existential characteristics, such as dialogue, freedom, anxiety, suffering, dignity, and authenticity. Prayer became the factor that makes man aware of these existential elements. Prayer makes possible intersubjective communication with God. Thanks to prayer, man acquires a consciousness of community with Him. Prayer becomes redemptive action, which relates to the inner strata of reality and personality. In this chapter I shall attempt to portray the intuitions and inner orientations of R. Soloveitchik's

---

1 "Reflections on the *Amidah*," 163.
2 "Reflections on the *Amidah*," 148.

conception of prayer. Already clear, however, R. Soloveitchik was interested in prayer as dialogue inasmuch as this dialogue was conducted between man and his God. The confrontation between the worshiper and God that occurs in prayer is at the center of R. Soloveitchik's inquiry, as we see from his published writings. Prayer has an aspect of dialogue with the Other. The *minyan* (prayer quorum) and the community are an island of discourse in individual life. But they do not occupy a significant space in R. Soloveitchik's thought. Even when he spoke of discourse with the other in the context of prayer (*The Lonely Man of Faith*), he emphasized divine kindness that develops into a moral and normative task, which facilitates addressing the Other. God imparts *hesed* and the commandment, but does not necessarily engage in actual dialogue. In the final analysis, the arena of R. Soloveitchik's interest is consciousness, that is, the standing of consciousness before God.

Prayer came to mirror the influence of general culture and religious philosophical thought on R. Soloveitchik. As we saw above in Chapter Ten, signs of the central place of prayer are to be found also in R. Soloveitchik's philosophical thought. He frequently had to employ unconventional halakhic insights in order to enhance the standing of prayer in the Jewish consciousness. Moreover, R. Soloveitchik transformed Maimonides into a key figure who redeemed prayer from its shift to the margins of the halakhic norm. R. Soloveitchik often took pains to present most of the laws of prayer as Torah obligations, even granting the status of Torah law to its gestures.

The Center of Consciousness

R. Soloveitchik anchored the most important messages of his thought in the issue of prayer. Despite his incessant emphases that prayer is only one of the objective commandments and the subjective consciousness experiences, he did so, apparently, to curb himself. Apparently, he felt the animated movement in his thought and personal ethos that moved prayer from the edge of the consciousness to its center. This movement is especially evident in the sphere of halakhah and the analytic study of Torah, but its various expressions also appear in his philosophical thought. To give just a single example: since the Psalms of King David and the verses from the Book of Daniel entered the set prayers, R. Soloveitchik had no qualms about enhancing the standing of the Psalmist and of Daniel, stating unequivocally that they were prophets.[3]

---

3 Grodner, *On Prayer*, 36; "Reflections on the *Amidah*," 150.

In this spirit, prayer supports the status of the synagogue as the center of Jewish life. R. Soloveitchik voiced his opinion that Jewish prayer is simply an expression of natural emotions, with a vast chasm separating these feelings from the ceremonial.[4] Therefore, he unhesitatingly showed forgiveness and understanding for improper behavior in the synagogue. For R. Soloveitchik, everyday actions and a purely social atmosphere, which halakhic norms would ban from the synagogue, assert the synagogue's standing as a natural venue for the worshiper. Reuven Grodner writes, in R. Soloveitchik's name:

> This is the Jewish story. The Jew always felt at ease in the study hall. This was not the case in the place of worship of non-Jews, in contrast. Reform Jews, for example, are critical of behavior in the Orthodox synagogues and of Jews talking during the middle of the service, walking about in the synagogue, and the like. While it is forbidden to talk in the repetition of the *Amidah* and the Torah reading, we can understand that they are the ones about whom it is said, "Even the sparrow has found a home, and the swallow a nest for herself" (Ps. 84:4). The synagogue is their home, and they feel at home in it. This is not like entering a temple, in which people feel like strangers. "Near Your altar, O Lord of hosts" (loc. cit.)—where there is an altar, which that is my home.[5]

According to these words, which were recorded by one of R. Soloveitchik's listeners and should thus be regarded with caution, improper behavior does not desecrate prayer and attests instead to a homely atmosphere. Obviously, R. Soloveitchik would not legitimize such conduct. The contrary is the case. But he did not refrain from exploring its consciousness and existential roots. And at times the boundaries between the synagogue and prayer are blurred, as is patent in "The Synagogue as an Institution and as an Idea."

Flexibility

In terms of methodology, R. Soloveitchik presented prayer as a special realm in the background of his thought from several aspects. First, he moderated the rigid consciousness ties that he had established in his phenomenological thought. As we mentioned above, the subjective dimension of prayer directly fashions the objective dimension. Second, while in most of his writings the phenomenological and existentialist approaches coexist

---

4   See, for example, his short article, "The Prayer of Jews" [Hebrew], *Maayanot* 8 (1964): 9-11.
5   Grodner, *On Prayer*, 32.

without friction, he maintained in his discussion of prayer that phenomenology is insufficient for explaining the participation of the public at large in such an experience. The existential frame, therefore, contributes to the clarification of the activity of prayer as a whole. In his explication of the *Amidah* R. Soloveitchik used both the existential crisis and the structure of religious consciousness to explain the complete prayer experience (see *Worship of the Heart*). In order to shed light on the standing of the synagogue, he, once again, made use of the consciousness model (the messianic idea as a subjective dimension, and prayer as an objective one) along with the existential model (existential exile).

After *And From There You Shall Seek* R. Soloveitchik abandoned the "naïve" notion that consciousness is capable of reaching a state of communion with God without fluctuations. Yet, the singular nature, of the conception of prayer caused him to return to this naïveté. R. Soloveitchik hinted that prayer expressed the realization of religious consciousness: petitionary blessings reflect existential distress and the blessings of praise and thanksgiving, the formative stages of this consciousness. The consciousness advances from one of contrasts (praise) to the united consciousness of love and communion alone (thanksgiving). At any rate, the consciousness of prayer records and channels religious life in its entirety. It would seem that only a deep appreciation of the prayer experience could bring about such a rethinking. Prayer is unique in that it caused R. Soloveitchik to ignore, to some extent, the definitive statements he had made in his various writings, and to adopt a fresh approach.

Sources

In the Introduction above, we mentioned the philosophical traditions that left their mark on R. Soloveitchik's thought. For the most part, the methodologies that he adopted in his analyses are based on a limited range of such philosophies. His responses to modernism and to the problems raised by religion in the modern period were formulated within an extremely limited philosophical expanse. R. Soloveitchik paid no attention to postmodernist approaches that began to emerge in the United States during the 1970s. The writings of French intellectuals such as Sartre and Levinas, for example, did not directly concern him. He was active in the expanse of cognitive idealism, of a few methods of the phenomenology of religion, and of some basic assumptions from existentialist thought. Some of the philosophical approaches that he listed in his book *The Halakhic Mind* did not penetrate into the philosophical sphere in which he composed his works.

The central methodology of *Worship of the Heart* and indeed of most of R. Soloveitchik's works is based on the phenomenology of religion. R. Soloveitchik's curiosity was substantive. He sought to enter the depths and roots of the consciousness of prayer. For him, "prayer is an art, not just a mechanical performance. It is an attitude, a state of mind, a mood. It is a great and exciting experience, an adventure."[6] Declarations such as this were the thin shell covering an astute phenomenological analysis.

The phenomenological approach is esoteric for the average reader. The modern reader who seeks to understand Maimonides' *Guide for the Perplexed* must have some knowledge of Aristotelian scientific principles, which are not readily accessible to the contemporary reader. Likewise, comprehending *Worship of the Heart* requires an awareness of the religious phenomenological approaches of Max Scheler, even though this is *terra incognita* for the modern reader, whether in the original German or in English translation. The English-speaking scholarly world has yet to reveal any special interest in Scheler's religious philosophical thought. As I showed elsewhere, one must be familiar with the cognitive approach of Hermann Cohen in order to fully grasp *Halakhic Man*.[7] The terminology that R. Soloveitchik used in *Worship of the Heart* and in his other writings on prayer, together with an analysis of the ideas he set forth, lead inevitably to the centrality of the religious phenomenological method in his writings. Indeed, R. Soloveitchik devoted intellectual efforts to clarify the phenomenological method he used for the interpretation of prayer.

R. Soloveitchik's religious phenomenology is based on an analysis of liturgical and midrashic texts and on the deciphering of the subjective structure of religious law (halakhah). Unlike his methodology, R. Soloveitchik's sources were undoubtedly numerous and diverse. His intimate knowledge of the rabbinic literature gave his ideas preeminently Jewish roots. Nonetheless, some sources carry greater weight in his discussions, both contentually and methodologically. The Hasidic conception of prayer, for instance, left a certain mark on his thought. Hasidism's view of prayer as a supreme religious value suffices to understand its centrality in R. Soloveitchik's thought. Many scholars, including myself, have studied his Hasidic education in his youth. The disparity between the Hasidic notion of prayer and R. Soloveitchik's thought, too,

---

6 *Abraham's Journey*, 188.
7 Schwartz, *Religion or Halakha*. Cohen's major philosophical works are still not translated to English.

is considerable. As one example, in the early days of Hasidism, prayer was seen as competing with Torah study; for some Hasidic masters, it even exceeded the latter.[8] R. Soloveitchik, in contrast, almost completely refrained from comparing the value of prayer with that of study. His response was rather characteristic of the analytical method of Brisk: he applied to prayer the analytical rules of *lamdanut* that are characteristic of the Talmudic passages learned in *yeshivot*, and he turned prayer into an object of such study. In his *hiddushim* (novel interpretations) he strove to formulate the elements common to prayer and Torah study. Furthermore, he describes prayer as a stage of self-annihilation in the face of divine might, or one in which the worshiper seeks communion with God and His infinite love. The simultaneous portrayal, of closeness and distance or the dialectic between them is characteristic of the phenomenology of religion, d not of the Hasidic corpus. The diversity of R. Soloveitchik's sources therefore enables us to understand his wide-ranging and rich style. His direct sources, however, are usually philosophical ones.

Intuition

The primary goal of the discussions of prayer in the current book is to enter R. Soloveitchik's philosophical intuition, that is, to attempt to uncover the message that he took pains to express by analyzing his modes of expression. Like every great individual, R. Soloveitchik had characteristic ways of expressing himself that strove to represent personal momentum and dynamics. The revealed and concealed dialogue that he conducted with philosophical approaches, too, was meant to formulate directions and leanings that could not necessarily be formulated positively.

We may state that R. Soloveitchik's basic philosophical intuition consisted of the confirmation and formulation of the exceptional standing of prayer. Every commandment is an expression of seething subjective and existential consciousness currents. Prayer, however, is a sweeping expression, that unites the complete range of the worshiper's consciousness and existential biography. This expression allows the outburst of subjectivity to dominate *ma'aseh ha-mitzvah* (the execution of the commandment) and to undermine the precise bounds typical of other commandments. This subjectivity is based on standing before God, dialogue, an awareness

---

8 See, for example, Jacobs, *Hasidic Prayer*, 17-20.

of one's personality, existential distress, and other complex consciousness and existential states.

R. Soloveitchik struggled with the question of the proper methodological way to express this effervescent mood. At times he tended to prefer the existential statement, but in the final analysis both the phenomenological and the existential statements desperately strive to pour the fluid subjectivity into the objective vessels that characterize the halakhah. *Worship of the Heart* contains these different modes of expression, and R. Soloveitchik's complementary articles, too, join the effort to give voice to the subjective charge in prayer.

Innovation

From time to time, critics argued that *Worship of the Heart*, R. Soloveitchik's major work on prayer, contains nothing not already present in his other compositions. Scholars are wont to blithely offer a presumably definitive opinion on questions of originality and eclecticism. Without attempting to draw a distinction between formal and contentual innovation, I will limit myself to summarizing in a few sentences the content of R. Soloveitchik's book.

According to *Worship of the Heart*, there are two phases to the religious consciousness, which are preceded by the stage of crisis. After a person experiences existential crisis, he discovers the divine. In this stage of consciousness he stands before the fearful and silent God (the "exalted"). The next stage of consciousness is standing before the beneficent God, who joins with man to form a community of friendship and love. These phases of consciousness are described in aesthetic terms. A person senses his God. The transition of the consciousness from the intimidating God to the loving One occurs when a person, of his own free will, accepts the daunting God, who then becomes loving. This consciousness process is recorded by means of prayer. The *Amidah* prayer channels the stages of consciousness: the petitional blessings (crisis), the blessings of praise (the "exalted"), and the thanksgiving blessings (the beneficent God).

The consciousness function of prayer is presented in light of R. Soloveitchik's phenomenological approach in his compositions from the middle of the 1940s (*And From There You Shall Seek* and *The Halakhic Mind*). In other words, the two-phase (or three-phase, if we count the consciousness of crisis that precedes the consciousness of the threatening and beneficent God) structure represents the subjective consciousness, and prayer expresses the objective consciousness. The commandment of prayer, however, extends into the subjective dimension of the consciousness. R. Soloveitchik steadfastly maintained that intent is an integral component of prayer itself.

In prayer and reading *Shema* the subjective overcomes the objective and fashions it. In a certain sense, the attempt to reconstruct the consciousness of reading *Shema* and prayer is reflective of its collapse and disappearance, since in fulfilling these commandments the subjective is not reconstructed at all—rather, it is the very essence of the commandment. Paradoxically, this fact is revealed by means of reconstructive methodology: the breaking of the frameworks that led to prayer emerges from what I called "reverse reconstruction." In matters of worship of the heart, R. Soloveitchik desired to reconstruct the expressions of the halakhic praxis within the subjective consciousness. For instance, he sought the halakhic aspects of the unity of God within the philosophical foundation. These developments shattered the existing frameworks. In *The Halakhic Mind* R. Soloveitchik attempted to bolster the objective consciousness, namely, observance of the commandments and their norms, and to constitute the absolute autonomy of this consciousness. In *Worship of the Heart*, R. Soloveitchik showed that some commandments are above the inflexible framework. Prayer, reading *Shema*, and Torah study—commandments that constitute the "worship of the heart"—blur the sharp boundaries between the subjective and the objective. The result is a vibrant and unbridled consciousness.

The consciousness of prayer knows no bounds. In his consciousness analyses R. Soloveitchik frequently refrained from either mystical or rational displays (in the limited medieval-period sense). In contrast, the mystical and rationalist elements are present in the consciousness of prayer, since this consciousness embraces all possible intentional acts.

Moreover, the consciousness of prayer is dialectical. The oscillation within the consciousness of the worshiper is evident in its different stages; but these are not the sole expression of this dialectic. An additional example is the movement between prayer as uncovering the self and prayer as the negation of the self. This means that the command relating to the subjective dimension is based on this dimension's dialectical structure.

Thus, R. Soloveitchik presented a distinctly phenomenological religious theory of prayer, several typical features of which are new additions to the background of his thought, that is, Modern Orthodoxy and religious Zionism in the middle of the twentieth century. The consciousness models of prayer are characterized by a pronounced dialectical dimension, and thereby do not diverge from the general direction of his thought. The foundations of these models, however, rest on unconventional phenomenological thinking. Obviously, R. Soloveitchik did not succeed in weaving the chapters of *Worship of the Heart* into a methodical presentation, nor did he always manage to tie up all the loose ends. His statements are not always consistent with one another, and I do not think that editing could have definitely resolved them. But his lengthy discussions sketch an outline of a cogent religious phenomenological theory, which in many respects is also unique in the perspective of the Orthodox thought that preceded him.

Statement

R. Soloveitchik's conception of prayer reflects complex efforts that are anchored in various philosophical traditions, to express a personal truth. We spoke above of the intuition underlying his idea of prayer. I would now like to address R. Soloveitchik's thought as a whole, based on my discussions in the current book. I want to focus on the statement, or message, that an outstanding thinker like R. Soloveitchik endeavored to express in different periods of his philosophical development. I assume that a profound author such as R. Soloveitchik would labor his entire life on the formulation of the statements, messages, or intuitions that he would want to express in his writings, but it is doubtful whether his surroundings or personality would give him free reign to do so. R. Soloveitchik himself had no qualms about attempting to characterize tendencies and directions of his character that are present in his thought, as well. For example, we find the following admission: "I certainly possess a spiritual inclination to elegy, to religious melancholy." He wrote about the impression left by the spiritual atmosphere of the Days of Awe: "A wave of paradoxical sadness mingled with silent joy floods my consciousness, and I feel myself released and redeemed."[9] This melancholy bent contributes greatly to understanding R. Soloveitchik's existentialist thought. He endeavored, both in the writings published during his lifetime and in those released only posthumously, to formulate the outline of a tortured religious consciousness, to describe the adaptation of this consciousness to Judaism, and even to encourage this

---

9 "Days of Repentance and Sanctity," [Hebrew], in *Divrei Hashkafah*, trans. Moshe Kroneh (Jerusalem: Elinor Library, 1995), 113. Kaplan told me that the poetic style of this essay substantially differs from that of the other compositions in this collection, which are transcriptions of talks, thus indicating that R. Soloveitchik wrote it himself, with the intent of future publication.

adaptation. Along with this, he wrote that during prayer he felt closeness to God, with His hand, as it were, on his shoulder.[10] The personal stories that were inserted in his writings, a bit here and a bit there, have been the subjects of scholarly examination. Our concern here is not the statement that is influenced by R. Soloveitchik's personality, but that which is part and parcel of his thought.

From the formal aspect, the halakhah is at the core of R. Soloveitchik's thought. R. Soloveitchik, however, wanted to express in many ways the intuition that in human consciousness and existence, nothing is as it seems upon initial thought or superficially. Even what seems constant and unequivocal conceals opposing subterranean ferments. No subjective statements—no matter how authoritative—are to be accepted at face value. This intuition is the source of the unrest, suffering, personality tempests, and man's helpless standing before the Source, that is, God. R. Soloveitchik desperately sought to depict this fundamental fluidity.

He strove for unity. He hoped to safely reach shore. His thought cries out for a state of communion with God. By the same coin, his fundamental intuition was that the objective sources do indeed lead to the coveted repose in the bosom of God. He also wanted to believe that the liturgical and halakhic texts support this sure path. Aware that these sources suit religious consciousness, he felt that they must include textual and behavioral expressions of stormy and opposing inclinations.

R. Soloveitchik apparently felt that, as a believer, an additional, weighty task was incumbent upon him: to persuade, and be persuaded, that the halakhah is the perfect way to exist with the oppressive intuition. The intellectual paths he travelled in his search for this persuasion were as vast as the sea. The halakhah is a collection of routine and individual acts. R. Soloveitchik assayed to argue that small everyday actions express fateful consciousness and psychological upheavals. Soaring upwards and diving to the depths, ebb and flow, self-affirmation and self-denial; all these are bound together by routine, drab deeds. Taken from the other direction, an analysis of the routine reveals the gales and gusts that storm within the depths of the consciousness. This agitation is at the core of R. Soloveitchik's approach to halakhic and philosophical sources: the halakhot and the rites are the tip of the iceberg of the personality; but they are also the implements for reaching the profound. The consciousness, gestures, and institutions of prayer are merely the means to uncover its most hidden penchants.

---

10 *Abraham's Journey*, 165.

R. Soloveitchik did not make life easy for his students and scholars of his thought. He wanted to show in his writings that activity was the remedy for this chaotic and anchorless intuition. Halakhah is the only stable factor in human life. However, by definition, the steady and the fluid sides clash. The balance between them also contains, within itself, ferment and contrast, leading us once again to the initial intuition. R. Soloveitchik nonetheless believed that the halakhah is the best way to contend with a fluid, effervescent, and changing world such as that of personality and consciousness. Prayer is a central expression of the direction of R. Soloveitchik's thought.

Scope

This book engaged mainly in an analysis of the works composed by R. Soloveitchik himself, and we hardly touched upon those written by others. His many talks, however, which were recorded and transcribed in various venues make many references to prayer. For instance, he devoted a good number of pages to an analysis of the first three blessings of the *Amidah*. He barely related in his writings to what he published or prepared for publication on the *Kedushah* that appears in the prayer leader's repetition of the *Amidah* between the second and third blessings. He did, however, relate to the *Kedushah* in his talks.[11] He likewise interpreted the fourth *Amidah* blessing in a talk devoted to the *Havinenu* (abridged *Amidah*) prayer.[12] He likewise devoted extensive treatment to the prayers recited during holidays and the Days of Awe in his sermons, lessons, and lectures.[13] Additionally, his interpretations on the *kinot* (laments) for Tisha be-Av have already been published;[14] these commentaries largely reflect R. Soloveitchik's interpretive and expositional methods regarding prayer.

The goal we set for ourselves in this book was to determine the philosophical foundation of the writings formulated by R. Soloveitchik. We strove to understand the basic intuitions of the conception, philosophy, and hermeneutics of prayer in his thought. Although he painted a very expansive landscape, this does not excuse us from the labor of exploring its rich hues and colors.

---

11 See "*Ha-Berakhot be-Yahadut,*" in *Yemei Zikaron*, 55-57.

12 See "The *Havinenu* Prayer" [Hebrew], in *Ha-Adam ve-Olamo*, 85-102.

13 See, for example "*Iyyunim be-Malkhuyot, Zikhronot ve-Shofarot*" [Hebrew], in *Yemei Zikaron*, 153-164.

14 *The Lord Is Righteous in All His Ways: Reflections on the Tish'ah be-Av Kinot*, ed. J. J. Schachter (Jersey City, NJ: Toras HoRav Foundation, 2006).

Bibliography

(A) The Writings of Rav Soloveitchik

Soloveitchik, Joseph Dov. *Ish ha-Halakhah: Galui ve-Nistar* [Halakhic Man: Revealed and Concealed]. Jerusalem: World Zionist Organization, 1979.

———. *The Halakhic Mind: An Essay on Jewish Tradition and Modern Thought*. New York. Seth Press, 1986.

———. *Divrei Hashkafah* [On Worldview], translated by Moshe Kroneh. Jerusalem: Elinor Library, 1994.

———. *Ha-Adam ve-Olamo* [Man and His World] [Hebrew]. Jerusalem: Elinor Library, 1998.

———. "*Ha-Berakhot be-Yahadut*" [The Blessings in Judaism]. In *Yemei Zikaron* [Memorial Days], translated by Moshe Kroneh. Jerusalem: Elinor Library, 1996.

Soloveitchik, Joseph B. "*Devekut*, or Communion with God." *Review of Religion* 14 [1949/1950]: 115-139.

———. "The Prayer of Jews" [Hebrew], *Maayanot* 8 (1964): 9-11.

———. "*Devekut*, or Communion with God." In Joseph B. Soloveitchik, *The Messianic Idea and Other Essays*, 203-227. New York: Schocken, 1971.

———. *In Aloneness, In Togetherness* [*Be-Sod ha-Yahid ve-ha-Yahad*]: *A Selection of Hebrew Writings*, edited by Pinchas H. Peli. Jerusalem: Orot, 1976.

———. "Catharsis." *Tradition* 17, no. 2 (Spring 1978):38-54

———. "The Community," *Tradition* 17, no. 2 (Spring 1978): 7-24.

———. "Redemption, Prayer, Talmud Torah." *Tradition* 17, no. 2 (1978): 55-72.

———. *Reflections of the Rav: Lessons in Jewish Thought Adapted from Lectures of Rabbi Joseph B. Soloveitchik*, edited by Abraham R. Besdin. Jerusalem: World Zionist Organization, 1979.

———. "The Synagogue as an Institution and as an Idea." In *Rabbi Joseph H. Lookstein Memorial Volume*, edited by Leo Landman, 321-39. Hoboken, NJ: Ktav, 1980.

———. "*Kol Dodi mi-Dod*," in Joseph B. Soloveitchik, *Words of Thought and Appreciation* [Hebrew], 79-80. Jerusalem: Elinor Library, World Zionist Organization, 1982.

———. *Halakhic Man*, translated by Lawrence Kaplan. Philadelphia: Jewish Publication Society of America, 1983.

———. "*Kol Dodi Dofek*: It Is the Voice of My Beloved That Knocketh," translated by Lawrence Kaplan. In *Theological and Halakhic Reflections on the Holocaust*, edited by Bernhard Rosenberg, 53. New York: Ktav, 1992.

———. "Sacred and Profane." In *Shiurei HaRav: A Conspectus of the Public Lectures of Rabbi Joseph B. Soloveitchik*, edited by Joseph Epstein, 4-32 Hoboken, NJ: Ktav, 1994.

———. *Lonely Man of Faith*. Northvale, NJ: Jason Aronson, 1997.

————. *Family Redeemed*, edited by David Schatz and Joel B. Wolowelsky. N.p.: Toras HoRav Foundation, 2000.

————. ("Abraham the Hebrew." *The Rav Speaks: Five Addresses on Israel, History, and the Jewish People*, translated by S. M. Lehman and A. H. Rabinowitz, 105-106. Brooklyn, NY: Toras HoRav Foundation, 2002.

————. "The Revolving Sword and the Two Cherubim." In *The Rav Speaks: Five Addresses on Israel, History, and the Jewish People*, translated by S. M. Lehman and A. H. Rabinowitz, 89-94. Brooklyn, NY: Toras HoRav Foundation, 2002.

————. *Out of the Whirlwind: Essays on Mourning, Suffering and the Human Condition*, edited by David Schatz, Joel B. Wolowelsky, and Reuven Ziegler. Hoboken, NJ: Toras HoRav Foundation, 2003.

————. *Worship of the Heart: Essays on Jewish Prayer*, edited by Shalom Carmy. New York: Toras HoRav Foundation, 2003.

————. *Community, Covenant and Commitment: Selected Letters and Communications*, edited by Nathaniel Helfgot. Jersey City, NJ: Toras HoRav Foundation, 2005.

————. *The Emergence of Ethical Man*, edited by Michael S. Berger. Jersey City, NJ: Toras HoRav Foundation, 2005.

————. *Festival of Freedom* [Hebrew]. Alon Shvut: Toras HoRav Foundation, 2006.

————. *The Lord Is Righteous in All His Ways: Reflections on the Tish'ah be-Av Kinot*, edited by J. J. Schachter. Jersey City, NJ: Toras HoRav Foundation, 2006.

————. *Abraham's Journey: Reflections of the Life of the Founding Patriarch*, edited by David Shatz, Joel B. Wolowelsky, and Reuven Ziegler. Jersey City, NJ: Toras HoRav Foundation, 2008.

————. *And From There You Shall Seek*, translated by Naomi Goldblum. Jersey City, NJ: Toras HoRav Foundation, 2008.

————. "Final Exam in Jewish Philosophy of Dr. Joseph Soloveitchik," edited Nathaniel Helfgot. *Text and Texture*, October 21, 2009. Accessed August 29, 2018. http://text.rcarabbis.org/final-exam-in-jewish-philosophy-of-dr-joseph-soloveitchik-1936.

————. "Joyfully Shall You Draw Water" [Hebrew]. *Ma'ayanotekha: Quarterly for Habad Thought* 30 (2011): 21-24.

————. *Koren Mesorat Harav Siddur*, edited by Arnold Lustiger. New York: OU Press, 2011.

————. "Prayer in the Teachings of Rav Soloveitchik ZT"L," summarized by Aviad Hacohen, part 2. In *The Israel Koschitzky Virtual Beit Midrash*. Accessed September 6, 2018. http://etzion.org.il/vbm/english/archive/ralpray2.htm.

Solowiejczyk, Josef. *Das reine Denken und die Seinskonsitutierung bei Hermann Cohen*. Berlin: Reither & Reichard, 1933.

(B) General

Abraham ben Moses ben Maimon. *Sefer ha-Maspik Le'Ovdey Hashem: Kitab Kifayat al-'Abidin* [Hebrew], part 2, vol. 2, edited by Nissim Dana. Ramat Gan: Bar-Ilan University, 1989.

Adler, Eli. *Tefilat Yesharim* [Hebrew]. Atzmonah: n.p., 2003.

Altmann, Alexander. *Studies in Religious Philosophy and Mysticism*. London: Routledge & Kegan Paul, 1969.

Alston, William P. "Religion." In *The Encyclopedia of Philosophy*, edited by Paul Edwards, vols. 7-8, 141-142. New York: Macmillan, 1967.

Amaru, Joshua. "Prayer and the Beauty of God: Rav Soloveitchik on Prayer and Aesthetics." *The Torah u-Madda Journal* 13 (2005): 148-176.

Amir, Yehoyada. *Reason out of Faith: The Philosophy of Franz Rosenzweig* [Hebrew]. Tel Aviv: Am Oved, 2004.

―――. "Rabbi Soloveitchik as a Cultural Agent: A Critical Reading of *The Lonely Man of Faith*" [Hebrew]. In *Rabbi in the New World: The Influence of Rabbi J. B. Soloveitchik on Culture, Education and Jewish Thought*, edited by Avinoam Rosenak and Naftali Rothenberg, 223-244 Jerusalem: Van Leer Institute and Magnes, 2010.

Aptowitzer, Avigdor. "*Ahavah Rabbah ve-Ahavat Olam*" [Hebrew]. *Hazofeh Quartalis Hebraica* 10 (1926): 37-38.

Bachelard, Gaston. *The Poetics of Space: The Classic Look at How We Experience Intimate Places*, translated by Maria Jolas. Boston: Penguin Classics, 1994.

Ballan, Joseph. "Dialogic Monologue: Hermann Cohen's Philosophy of Prayer." *Journal for Jewish Thought* 1 (2010): 1-11.

Bar-Ilan, Meir. *The Mysteries of Jewish Prayer and Hekhalot* [Hebrew]. Ramat Gan: Bar-Ilan University Press, 1987.

Barrett, William. *Irrational Man: A Study in Existential Philosophy*. Garden City, NY: Doubleday, 1958.

Barth, Karl. *Dogmatics in Outline*, translated by G. T. Thomson. New York: Harper & Row, 1959.

―――. *The Doctrine of Reconciliation*. Vol. IV, part 1 of *Church Dogmatics*. London: SCM Press, 1965.

Beck, Louis White. *A Commentary on Kant's Critique of Practical Reason*. Chicago: University of Chicago Press, 1963.

Ben-Or, Assael. *Gershonides' Numeration of Commandments* [Hebrew]. Jerusalem: Keren Or, 2003.

Benor, Ehud. *Worship of the Heart: A Study in Maimonides' Philosophy of Religion*. Albany: State University of New York Press, 1995.

Berenbaum, Michael. *After Tragedy and Triumph: Modern Jewish Thought and the American Experience*. Cambridge: Cambridge University Press, 1990.

Berger, Peter, Brigitte Berger, and Hansfried Kellner, *The Homeless Mind: Modernization and Consciousness*. New York: Random House, 1973.

Bergman, Shmuel Hugo. *Dialogical Philosophy: From Kierkegaard to Buber*, translated by Arnold A. Gerstain. Albany: SUNY Press, 1991.

Berkovits, Eliezer. "Expectations from Prayer." In *Sefer Aviad: Collection of Articles in Memory of Dr. Isaiah Wolfsberg-Aviad* [Hebrew], edited by Yitzhak Raphael, 179-184. Jerusalem: Mossad Harav Kook, 1986.

Berman, Lawrence V. "Ibn Bajjah and Maimonides" [Hebrew]. PhD dissertation, Hebrew University, 1959.

———. "Maimonides on Political Leadership." In *Kinship and Consent: The Jewish Political Tradition and Its Contemporary Uses*, edited by Daniel J. Elazar, 115-116. Ramat Gan: Turtledove, 1981.

Bernet, Rudolf, Iso Kern, and Eduard Marbach, *An Introduction to Husserlian Phenomenology*. Evanston, IL: Northwestern University Press, 1993.

Bettis, Joseph Dabney, ed. *Phenomenology of Religion*. London: SCM Press, 1969.

Blank, Sheldon H. "Some Observations Concerning Biblical Prayer." *HUCA* 32 (1961): 75-90.

Blidstein, Gerald J. *Political Concepts in Maimonidean Halakha* [Hebrew]. Ramat Gan: Bar-Ilan University, 1983.

———. *Prayer in Maimonidean Halakha* [Hebrew]. Jerusalem: Bialik Institute, 1994.

———. "On the Jewish People in the Writings of Rabbi Joseph B. Soloveitchik" [Hebrew]. In *Faith in Changing Times: On the Teachings of Rabbi Joseph Dov Soloveitchik* [Hebrew], edited by Avi Sagi, 168-71. Jerusalem: World Zionist Organization, 1996. ("Appendix: On the Sources of the Terms 'Fate' and 'Destiny.'")

———. "From the Home to the Synagogue—On the Innovations of the Post-Talmudic Synagogue." In *Ta Shma: Studies in Judaica in Memory of Israel M. Ta-Shma* [Hebrew], edited by Avraham Reiner et al., vol. 2, 105-34. Alon Shevut: Tevunot, 2011.

———. *Society and Self on the Writings of Rabbi Joseph B. Soloveitchik*. New York: KTAV Publishing House, 2012.

Blumenthal, David R. *Philosophic Mysticism*. Ramat Gan: Bar Ilan University Press, 2006.

Boyarin, Daniel. "*Ha-Shir ve-ha-Shevah*: Ambiguity and Poetics in the Fixed Prayers" [Hebrew]. *Eshel Beer-Sheva* 3 (1986): 91-99.

Braiterman, Zachary. "Joseph Soloveitchik and Immanuel Kant's Mitzvah-Aesthetic." *AJS Review* 25 (2000/2001): 1-24.

Breuer, Mordechai. *Oholei Torah (The Tents of Torah): The Yeshiva, Its Structure and History* [Hebrew]. Jerusalem: Zalman Shazar Center, 2014.

Breuer, Zeev Zekharya. "The Structure of the *Yozer* Benediction" [Hebrew]. In *Proceedings of the Tenth World Congress of Jewish Studies*, division C, vol. i: *Jewish Thought and Literature*, 261-68. Jerusalem: World Union of Jewish Studies, 1990.

Brill, Alan. "Elements of Dialectic Theology in Rabbi Soloveitchik's View of Torah Study." In *Study and Knowledge in Jewish Thought*, edited by Howard Kreisel, 265-296. Beer Sheva: Ben Gurion University of the Negev Press, 2006.

Brunner, Emil. *Man in Revolt: A Christian Anthropology*, translated by Olive Wyon. New York: Scribner's, 1939.

———. *The Christian Doctrine of Creation and Redemption*, vol. II of *Dogmatics*, translated by Olive Wyon. Philadelphia: Westminster, 1952.

———. *The Divine Imperative: A Study in Christian Ethics*, translated by Olive Wyon. Cambridge: Lutterworth Press, 2002.

Buber, Martin. *I and Thou*, translated by Ronald Gregor Smith. New York: Scribner, 2000.

———. "What Is Man?" In *Between Man and Man*, translated by Ronald Gregor-Smith, 140-185. London: Routledge, 2002.

Burke, Edmund. *A Philosophical Enquiry into the Origin of Our Ideas of the Sublime and the Beautiful*. Oxford: Oxford University Press, 1990.

Buytendijk, Frederik J. J. "Husserl's Phenomenology and Its Significance for Contemporary Psychology." In *Readings in Existential Phenomenology*, ed. Nataniel Lawrence and Daniel O'Connor, 352-364. Englewood Cliffs, NJ: Prentice-Hall, 1967.

Cameron, J. M. "John Henry Newman and the Tractarian Movement." In *Nineteenth Century Religious Thought in the West*, vol. 2, edited by N. Smart, J. Clayton, P. Sherry, and S. T. Katz, 69-109. Cambridge: Cambridge University Press, 1985.

Carmy, Shlomo. "Introduction," to *Worship of the Heart* [Hebrew]. Alon Shvut: Toras HoRav Foundation, 2006.

Carr, David T. *Phenomenology and the Problem of History: A Study of Husserl's Transcendental Philosophy*. Evanston, IL: Northwestern University Press, 1974.

Cassirer, Ernst. *An Essay on Man: An Introduction to a Philosophy of Human Culture*. Garden City, NY: Doubleday, 1953.

Cherlow, Yuval. *Joined Together in Your Hand: From Dialectics to Harmony in the Thought of Rabbi Joseph Dov Halevi Soloveitchik* [Hebrew]. Alon Shvut: Tevunot, 1999.

Cohen, Hermann. *Ästhetik des reinen Gefühls*. Berlin: Bruno Kassirer, 1922.

———. *Logik der reinen Erkenntnis*. Berlin: Bruno Kassirer, 1922.

———. *Jüdische Schriften*. Berlin: Schwetschke, 1924.

———. *Religion of Reason: Out of the Sources of Judaism*, translated by Simon Kaplan. New York: Ungar, 1972.

———. *Ethics of Maimonides*, translated by Almut Sh. Bruckstein. Madison, WI: University of Wisconsin Press, 2004.

Cohen, Naomi. "On the Original Nature of the Prayerbook of Rabbi Saadia Gaon" [Hebrew]. *Sinai* 95 (1984): 350-360.

Collinson, Diane "Aesthetic Experience." In *Philosophical Aesthetics: An Introduction*, edited by Oswald Hanfling. Oxford: Blackwell, 1992.

Cooper, David. *Existentialism: A Reconstruction*. Oxford: Blackwell, 1990.

Cumming, Robert. "Existence and Communication." *Ethics* 65 (1955): 79-101.

D'Ancona, Cristina. "Greek into Arabic: Neoplatonism in Translation." In *The Cambridge Companion to Arabic Philosophy*, edited by Peter Adamson and Richard C. Taylor, 24-26. Cambridge: Cambridge University Press, 2005.

Dan, Yoseph. "*Hekhalot Rabbati* and the Legend of the Ten Martyrs" [Hebrew]. *Eshel Beer-Sheva* 2 (1980): 63-80.

Derrida, Jacques. *Of Hospitality: Anne Dufourmantelle Invites Jacques Derrida to Respond*, translated by Rachel Bowlby. Stanford, CA: Stanford University Press.

Dreyfus, Hubert L. "Husserl's Perceptual Noema." In *Husserl, Intentionality and Cognitive Science*, edited by H. L. Dreyfus and H. Hall, 97-123, Cambridge, MA: MIT Press, 1984.

Efros, Israel. *Medieval Jewish Philosophy: Systems and Problems* [Hebrew]. Tel Aviv: Dvir, 1965.

Ehrlich, Uri. *The Nonverbal Language of Prayer: A New Approach to Jewish Liturgy*, translated by Dena Ordan. Tubingen: Mohr Siebeck, 2004.

Eisen, Robert. *Galut: Modern Jewish Reflection on Homelessness and Homecoming.* Bloomington: Indiana University Press, 1986.

Elbaum, Jacob. *Repentance and Self-Flagellation in the Writings of the Sages of Germany and Poland 1348-1648* [Hebrew]. Jerusalem: Magnes, 1993.

Elbogen, Ismar. *Jewish Liturgy: A Comprehensive History*, translated by Raymond P. Scheindlin. Philadelphia: Jewish Publication Society, 1993.

Erlich, Dror. "Dualism as a Stylistic Characteristic in the Discussion of Prayer by R. Joseph Albo" [Hebrew]. *Kenishta* 3 (2007): 23.

Faur, José. "Delocutive Expressions in the Hebrew Liturgy." *The Journal of the Ancient Near Eastern Society* 16-17 (1984-1985): 41-54.

Feldman, Abraham. "The Changing Functions of the Synagogue and the Rabbi." In *Understanding American Judaism: Toward the Description of a Modern Religion*, vol. 1: *The Rabbi and the Synagogue*, edited by Jacob Neusner, 103-112. New York: Ktav, 1975.

Fleischer, Ezra. "On the *Avodah* Blessing" [Hebrew]. *Sinai* 60 (1967): 269-275.

———."The Diffusion of the *Qedushshot* of the *'Amida* and the *Jozer* in the Palestinian Jewish Ritual" [Hebrew]. *Tarbiz* 38, no. 3 (1969): 226.

———. "Fragments of Prayer Collections from the Land of Israel in the Genizah" [Hebrew]. *Kobez al Yad* 13 (1996): 116.

———. "Towards a Clarification of the Expression '*Poreis 'al Shema*'" [Hebrew]. *Tarbiz* 41 (1972): 133-144. Also included in *Studies in Jewish Liturgy: A Reader* [Hebrew], edited by Hananel Mack, 79-90. Vol. 6 of *Likkutei Tarbiz.* Jerusalem: Magnes, 2003.

———. "The *Shemone Esre*—Its Character, Internal Order, Content and Goals" [Hebrew]. *Tarbiz* 62 (1993): 179-223. Also included in *Studies in Jewish Liturgy: A Reader* [Hebrew], edited by Hananel Mack, 157-201. Vol. 6 of *Likkutei Tarbiz.* Jerusalem: Magnes, 2003.

Fox, Harry (Menahem Tzvi). "A Concealed Polemic in Prayer" [Hebrew]. In *Studies in Memory of Professor Ze'ev Falk*, edited by Michael Corinaldi et al., 123-64. Jerusalem: Schechter Institute of Jewish Studies, 2005.

Fox, Marvin. *Interpreting Maimonides: Studies in Methodology, Metaphysics, and Moral Philosophy.* Chicago: University of Chicago Press, 1990.

———. "The Rav as a Maspid." *Tradition* 30 (1996): 164-181.

Freud, Sigmund. "The Uncanny." In *The Standard Edition of the Complete Psychological Works of Sigmund Freud*, translated by James Strachey, vol. 17: *An Infantile Neurosis and Other Works.* London: Hogarth Press, 1955.

Frimer, Norman E., and Dov Schwartz, *The Life and Thought of Shem Tov Ibn Shaprut* [Hebrew]. Jerusalem: Ben-Zvi Institute, 1992.

Gasiet, Seev. *Menschliche Bedürfnisse: Eine theoretische Synthese.* Frankfurt: Campus Verlag, 1981.

Gerrish, Brian A. "Friedrich Schleiermacher." In *Nineteenth Century Religious Thought in the West*, edited by Ninian Smart et al., 123-156 Cambridge: Cambridge University Press, 1985.

Gilath, Itzchak D. *Studies in the Development of the Halakhah* [Hebrew]. Ramat Gan: Bar-Ilan University, 1992.

Goldman, Eliezer. "The Worship Peculiar to Those Who Have Apprehended True Reality" [Hebrew]. *Bar-Ilan* 6 (1968): 287-313.

———. *Expositions and Inquiries: Jewish Thought in Past and Present*, edited by Daniel Statman and Abraham Sagi [Hebrew]. Jerusalem: Magnes, 1997.

———. "Religion and Halakha in the Teaching of Rabbi J. B. Soloveitchik" [Hebrew]. *Daat* 42 (1999): 125-136.

Glatzer, Nahum N. "The Concept of Language in the Thought of Franz Rosenzweig." In *The Philosophy of Franz Rosenzweig*, edited by Paul Mendes-Flohr, 172-184. Hanover: University Press of New England, 1988.

Goldschmidt, Shlomo. *The Order of Selichot: According to the Custom of Poland and Most of the Communities in Eretz Israel* [Hebrew]. Jerusalem: Mossad Harav Kook, 1965.

Golomb, Jacob. *In Search of Authenticity: From Kierkegaard to Camus*. New York: Routledge, 1995.

Gopin, Mendi. *Davening with the Rav: My Rabbi and My Rebbe*. Jersey City, NJ: Ktav Publishing House, 2006.

Goshen-Gottstein, Alon. "God and Israel as Father and Son in Tannaitic Literature" [Hebrew]. PhD dissertation, Hebrew University, 1987.

Greenberg, Moshe. "On the Refinement of the Conception of Prayer in Hebrew Scriptures." *AJS Review* 1 (1976): 57-92.

———. *Lectures about Prayer* [Hebrew]. Jerusalem: Akademon, 1985.

Grodner, Reuven. *On Prayer: The Classes of Rabbi Joseph Dov Soloveitchik* [Hebrew]. Jerusalem: OU Press, 2011.

Groll, Meshullam. *Selected Writings* [Hebrew], vol. 1. Tel Aviv: Sifriat Poalim, 1956.

Grözinger, Karl Erich. *Musik und Gesang in der Theologie der frühen jüdischen Literatur: Talmud, Midrasch, Mystik*. Tübingen: Mohr Siebeck, 1982.

———. "Sprache und Identität: Das Hebräische und die Juden." In *Sprache und Identität im Judentum*, edited by K. E. Grözinger, 75-90. Wiesbaden: Otto Harrassowitz Verlag, 1998.

Gruenwald, I. "The Song of the Angels, the *Qedushah* and the Composition of the *Hekhalot* Literature" [Hebrew], in *Jerusalem in the Second Temple Period: Abraham Schalit Memorial Volume*, edited by A. Oppenheimer, U. Rappaport, and M. Stern, 476-79. Jerusalem: Yad Izhak Ben-Zvi and Ministry of Defence, 1980.

Gurevitch, Zali. *On Israeli and Jewish Place* [Hebrew]. Tel Aviv: Am Oved, 2007.

Gurfinkel, Eli. "The Influence of Ideological Changes on the Text of the Declaration of Faith (*ani maamin*)" [Hebrew]. *Kenishta* 4 (2010): 80-81.

Habermann, Abraham Meir. *Shirei ha-Yihud ve-ha-Kavod* [Hebrew]. Jerusalem: Mossad Harav Kook, 1948.

Hacohen, Aviad. "The Legal Methodology of Rabbi Soloveitchik: What's New?" [Hebrew]. In *Rabbi in the New World: The Influence of Rabbi J. B. Soloveitchik on Culture, Education and Jewish Thought*, edited by Avinoam Rosenak and Naftali Rothenberg, 299-322. Jerusalem: Van Leer Institute and Magnes, 2010.

Hadad, Eliezer. *The Torah and Nature in Maimonides' Writings* [Hebrew]. Jerusalem: Magnes, 2011.

Halkin, Abraam S. "The Ban on the Study of Philosophy" [Hebrew]. *P'raqim: Yearbook of the Schocken Institute* 1 (1967-1968): 53-55.

Hallamish, Moshe. *Kabbalah in Liturgy, Halakhah, and Customs* [Hebrew]. Ramat Gan: Bar-Ilan University Press, 2000.

Hamitovsky, Itzhak. "From Chest (*tevah*) to Ark (*aron*): The Evolving Character of the Ark of Scrolls in the Periods of the Mishnah and the Talmud" [Hebrew]. *Kenishta* 3 (2007): 99-128.

Hanfling, Oswald, ed. *Philosophical Aesthetics: An Introduction.*Oxford: Blackwell Publishers, 1992.

Hartman, David. *A Living Covenant: The Innovative Spirit in Traditional Judaism.* New York: Free Press, 1985.

———. "Prayer in the Thought of Rabbi Soloveitchik—Study and Critique" [Hebrew]. In *Faith in Changing Times: On the Teachings of Rabbi Joseph Dov Soloveitchik* [Hebrew], edited by Avi Sagi, 213-14. Jerusalem: World Zionist Organization, 1996.

———. *Love and Terror in the God Encounter: The Theological Legacy of Rabbi Joseph B. Soloveitchik.* Woodstock, VT: Jewish Lights, 2001.

Harvey, Steven. "Avicenna and Maimonides on Prayer and Intellectual Worship," in *Exchange and Transmission across Cultural Boundaries*, edited by Haggai Ben-Shammai, Shaul Shaked, and Sarah Stroumsa, 82-105 Jerusalem: Israel Academy of Sciences and Humanities, 2013.

Harvey, Warren Zev. "Judah Halevi's Synthaesthetic Theory of Prophecy and a Note on the Zohar." In *Rivkah Shatz-Uffenheimer Memorial Volume* [Hebrew], vol. 1, edited by Rachel Elior and Joseph Dan, 141-155. Vol. 12 of *Jerusalem Studies in Jewish Thought.* Jerusalem, Mandel Institute for Jewish Studies, 1996.

Harvey, Zeev. "Notes on Rabbi Soloveitchik and Maimonidean Philosophy." In *Faith in Changing Times: On the Teachings of Rabbi Joseph Dov Soloveitchik* [Hebrew], edited by Avi Sagi, 95-107. Jerusalem: World Zionist Organization, 1996.

Hazony, Yoram. "The Rav's Bombshell." *Commentary*, April 2012, 54.

Heidegger, Martin. *Being and Time*, translated by John Macquarrie and Edward Robinson. New York: Harper & Row, 1962.

Heiler, Friedrich. *Das Gebet: Eine Religionsgeschichtliche und Religionspsychologische Untersuchung.* Munich: Verlag von Ernst Reinhardt, 1921.

———. *Prayer: A Study in the History and Psychology of Religion*, translated by S. McComb. New York: Oxford University Press, 1958.

Heinemann, Isaac. *Taamei ha-Mitzvot be-Sifrut Yisrael* [*The Reasons for the Commandments in Jewish Literature*] [Hebrew], vol. 2. Jerusalem: Zionist Organization, 1956.

———. *The Reasons for the Commandments in Jewish Thought: From the Bible to the Renaissance*, translated by Leonard Levin. Boston: Academic Studies Press, 2008.

Heinemann, Joseph. *Prayer in the Talmud: Forms and Patterns*, translated by Richard S. Sarason. Vol. 9 of *Studia Judaica.* Berlin: De Gruyter, 1977.

———. "*Qedushah* and Proclamation of 'Kingship' in the Reading of the *Shema*' and in the '*Amidah*" [Hebrew]. In *Studies in Jewish Liturgy*, edited by Avigdor Shinan, 12-21. Jerusalem: Magnes, 1981.

————. *Studies in Jewish Liturgy* [Hebrew], edited by Avigdor Shinan. Jerusalem: Magnes, 1981.

Heschel, Abraham Joshua. *God in Search of Man: A Philosophy of Judaism*. New York: Farrar, Straus and Giroux, 1978.

Hirsch, Samson Raphael. *Horeb: A Philosophy of Jewish Laws and Observances*, translated by I. Grunfeld. New York: Soncino, 1981.

The Hirsch Siddur: The Order of Prayers for the Whole Year. Jerusalem: Feldheim, 1972.

Hirshman, Marc (Menachem). *Mikra and Midrash: A Comparison of Rabbinics and Patristics* [Hebrew]. Tel Aviv: Hakibbutz Hameuchad, 1996.

Hoffman, Lawrence A. *Beyond the Text: A Holistic Approach to Liturgy*. Bloomington: Indiana University Press, 1987.

Holzhey, Helmut, Gabriel Motzkin, and Hartwig Wiedebach, eds. *"Religion der Vernunft aus den Quellen des Judentums". Tradition und Ursprungsdenken in Hermann Cohens Spätwerk*. Hildesheim: Olms, 2000.

Horowitz, Rivka. "Rav Soloveitchik's Attitude to the Religious Experience and to Mysticism" [Hebrew]. In *Faith in Changing Times: On the Teachings of Rabbi Joseph Dov Soloveitchik* [Hebrew], edited by Avi Sagi, 45-74. Jerusalem: World Zionist Organization, 1996.

Husserl, Edmund. *Cartesian Meditations: An Introduction to Phenomenology*, translated by Dorion Cairns. The Hague: Martinus Nijhoff, 1982.

Idel, Moshe. "*Hitbodedut* as Concentration in Jewish Philosophy" [Hebrew]. In *Shlomo Pines Jubilee Volume*, edited by Moshe Idel, Warren Zev Harvey, and Eliezer Schweid, vol. 7 of *Jerusalem Studies in Jewish Thought* (1988), 39-60.

————. *Maïmonide et la mystique juive*, translated by Charles Mopsik. Paris: Cerf, 1991.

————. *Hasidism: Between Ecstasy and Magic*. Albany: SUNY Press, 1995.

Ilan, Nahem. "Between Halakhic Codification and Ethical Commentary: Rabbi Israel Israeli of Toledo and Intention of Prayer." In *Esoteric and Exoteric Aspects in Judeo-Arabic Culture*, edited by Benjamin H. Hary and Haggai Ben-Shammai, 131-173. Leiden: Brill, 2006.

Ish-Shalom, Benjamin. "R. Kook, Spinoza and Goethe: Modern and Traditional Elements in the Thought of R. Kook" [Hebrew]. In *Rivkah Shatz-Uffenheimer Memorial Volume*, vol. 2, ed. Rachel Elior and Joseph Dan, 525-556. Vol. 12 of *Jerusalem Studies in Jewish Thought*. Jerusalem, Mandel Institute for Jewish Studies, 1996.

Jacobs, Louis. *Hasidic Prayer*. New York: Schocken, 1973.

Jospe, Raphael. "Maimonides and *Shi'ur Komah*" [Hebrew]. In *Tribute to Sara: Studies in Jewish Philosophy and Kabbala Presented to Professor Sara O. Heller Wilensky*, edited by Moshe Idel, Devora Dimant, and Shalom Rosenberg, 195-209. Jerusalem: Magnes, 1994.

Justin Martyr. *Dialogue with Trypho*, translated by Thomas B. Falls; edited by Michael Slusser. Washington, DC: Catholic University of America Press, 2003.

Kadari, Adiel. "Liturgical Recitation as a Ritual of Study" [Hebrew]. In *Study and Knowledge in Jewish Thought*, edited by Howard Kreisel, vol. 2, 21-35. Beer Sheva: Ben-Gurion University of the Negev Press, 2006.

Kadushin, Max. *The Rabbinic Mind*. New York: Jewish Theological Seminary of America, 1952.

Kaelin, Eugene Francis. *An Existentialist Aesthetic*. Madison: University of Wisconsin Press, 1962.

Kainz, Friedrich. *Aesthetics the Science*, translated and introduction by Herbert M. Schueller. Detroit: Wayne State University Press, 1962.

Kaminka, Aharon. "Judea and Greece in Rhetorical and Ethical Writings" [Hebrew]. *Knesset* 4 (1939): 345-364.

Kanarfogel, Ephraim. *"Peering through the Lattices": Mystical, Magical, and Pietist Dimensions in the Tosafist Period*. Detroit: Wayne State University Press, 2000.

———. "Did the Tosafists Embrace the Concept of Anthropomorphism?" In *Ta Shma: Studies in Judaica in Memory of Israel M. Ta-Shma* [Hebrew], edited by Avraham Reiner et al., 671-703. Alon Shevut: Tevunot, 2011.

Kant, Immanuel. *Critique of Judgment*, translated by J. H. Bernard. New York: Hafner, 1972.

Kaplan, Lawrence. "Rabbi Joseph B. Soloveitchik's Philosophy of Halakha." *The Jewish Law Annual* 7 (1987): 139-197.

———. "Kabbalistic Motifs in Rav Soloveitchik's Thought: Meaningful or Ornamental?" [Hebrew]. In *Faith in Changing Times: On the Teachings of Rabbi Joseph Dov Soloveitchik* [Hebrew], edited by Avi Sagi, 75-93. Jerusalem: World Zionist Organization, 1996.

———. "Maimonides and Soloveitchik on the Knowledge and Imitation of God." In *Moses Maimonides (1138-1204): His Religious, Scientific and Philosophical Wirkungsgeschichte in Different Cultural Contexts*, edited by G. Hasselhof and O. Fraisse, 491-523.Würzburg: Ergon, 2004.

———. "Review Essay: Worship of the Heart." *Ḥakirah: The Flatbush Journal of Jewish Law and Thought* 5 (2007): 79-114.

———. "Exposition as High Art; Review Essay." *Hakirah* 15 (2013): 91-92.

———. *Between Philosophy and Halakhah: Rabbi Joseph B. Soloveitchik's Lectures on the "Guide of the Perplexed."* Jerusalem: Urim, 2016.

Kaufmann, David. *Mekhkarim ba-Sifrut ha-Ivrit shel Yemei ha-Bainayim* [Studies in Medieval Hebrew Literature] [Hebrew], translated by Ysrael Eldad. Jerusalem: Mossad Harav Kook, 1962.

Kaufmann, Fritz. "Cassirer, Neo-Kantianism, and Phenomenology." In *The Philosophy of Ernst Cassirer*, edited by P. A. Schilpp, 801-854. Evanston, IL: Library of Living Philosophy, 1949.

Keck, David. *Angels and Angelology in the Middle Ages*. Oxford: Oxford University Press, 1998.

Kellner, Menachem. *Dogma in Medieval Jewish Thought: From Maimonides to Abravanel*. Oxford: Littman Library, 1986.

———. *Maimonides on Human Perfection*. Atlanta: Scholars Press, 1990.

———. *Must a Jew Believe Anything?* . Portland, OR: The Littman Library of Jewish Civilization, 1999.

———. *Maimonides' Confrontation with Mysticism*. Portland, OR: The Littman Library of Jewish Civilization, 2006.

Kelman, Wolfe. "The Synagogue in America." In *Understanding American Judaism: Toward the Description of a Modern Religion*, vol. 1: *The Rabbi and the Synagogue*, edited by Jacob Neusner, 69-89. New York: Ktav, 1975.

Kierkegaard, Søren. *Either/Or: A Fragment of Life*, vol. 1, translated by David F. Swenson and Lillian Marvin Swenson. Princeton: Princeton University Press, 1949.

———. *Kierkegaard's Journals & Papers*, edited by Howard V. Hong and Edna H. Hong. Bloomington: Indiana University Press, 1970.

Kimelman, Reuven. "The Literary Structure of the Amidah and the Rhetoric of Redemption." In *Echoes of Many Texts: Reflections on Jewish and Christian Traditions, Essays in Honor of Lou H. Silberman*, edited by William G. Dever & J. Edward Wright, 171-230. Vol. 313 of *Brown Judaic Studies*. Atlanta: Scholars Press, 1977.

———. "The Messiah of the Amidah: A Study in Comparative Messianism." *Journal of Biblical Literature* 116 (1997): 313-320.

———. "The *Shema'* Liturgy: From Covenant Ceremony to Coronation" [Hebrew]. *Kenishta* 1 (2001): 9-105.

. *Mystical Meaning of Lekha Dodi and Kabbalat Shabbat* [Hebrew]. Jerusalem: Magnes, 2003.

Kimhi, David. *The Complete Commentary on Psalms* [Hebrew], edited by Avraham Darom. Jerusalem. Mossad Harav Kook, 1979.

Klausner, Joseph. "Judea and Greece: Two Opposites?" *Festschrift Armand Kaminka zum siebzigsten Geburtstage*, edited by S. Rappaport and M. Zikier, Hebrew volume, 49-58. Vienna: Verlag des Wiener Maimonides-Instituts, 1937.

Knohl, Israel. "A Parsha Concerned with Accepting the Kingdom of Heaven" [Hebrew]. *Tarbiz* 53 (1984): 11-31.

Kohler, Kaufmann. *Jewish Theology Systematically and Historically Considered*. New York: MacMillan, 1968.

Kolender, Aaron. *Transcendental Beauty* [Hebrew]. Jerusalem: Bialik Institute, 2001.

Kovacs, Georges. *The Question of God in Heidegger's Phenomenology*. Evanston, IL: Northwestern University Press, 1990.

Kreisel, Howard. *Maimonides' Political Thought: Studies in Ethics, Law, and the Human Ideal*. Albany: State University of New York Press, 1999.

Kristensen, W. Brede "The Phenomenology of Religion." In *Phenomenology of Religion*, ed. Joseph D. Bettis, 36-51. New York: Harper & Row, 1969.

Krumbein, Elyakim. "From Reb Haim of Brisk and Rav Joseph B. Soloveitchik to 'Shiurim of Rav Aharon Lichtenstein'—the Growth of a Learning Tradition" [Hebrew]. *Netuim* 9 (2002): 51-94.

———. "The Importance of the Book *Avodah She-ba-Lev* by R. J. B. Soloveitchik" [Hebrew]. *Akdamot* 18 (2007): 141-163.

Lasker, Arnold A., and Daniel J. Lasker. "The Jewish Prayer for Rain in Babylonia." *Journal for the Study of Judaism* 15 (1984): 124-144.

———. "The Jewish Prayer for Rain in the Post-Talmudic Diaspora." *AJS Review* 9 (l984): 141-174.

Lasker, Daniel J. "Definitions of 'One' and Divine Unity" [Hebrew]. In *Studies in Jewish Thought*, edited by Sara O. Heller-Willenski and Moshe Idel, 51-61. Jerusalem: Magnes, 1989.

Laycock, Steven W. "God as the Ideal: The All-of-Monads and the All-Consciousness." In *Phenomenology of the Truth Proper to Religion*, edited by Daniel Guerrière, 247-272. Albany, NY: State University of New York Press, 1990,

Lee, Jonathan Scott. "Omnipresence and Eidetic Causation in Plotinus." In *The Structure of Being: A Neoplatonic Approach*, edited by R. Baine Harris, 90-103. Norfolk, VA: International Society for Neoplatonic Studies, 1982.

Leeuw, Gerardus van der. *Religion in Essence and Manifestation: A Study in Phenomenology*, trans. John E. Turner. New York: Harper & Row, 1963.

LeFevre, Perry D. *Understandings of Prayer*. Philadelphia: The Westminster Press, 1981.

Levinger, Jacob S. *Maimonides' Techniques of Codification* [Hebrew]. Jerusalem: Magnes, 1965.

Lichtenstein, Aaron. "Eulogy" [Hebrew]. *Mesorah 9: Eulogies for Our Master, the Gaon, R. J. B. Soloveitchik, May the Memory of the Righteous Be for a Blessing for the World to Come* (February 1994): 29-31.

———. "A Review of the Intellectual Thought of R. J. B. Soloveitchik, may the memory of the righteous be for a blessing" [Hebrew]. *Allon Shevut* 140-141 (1994): 11-12.

———. "Prayer in the Teaching of G[aon], R. Y. D. Soloveitchik, of Blessed Memory" [Hebrew]. *Shanah be-Shanah* (1999): 288.

Liebman, Charles. "Orthodoxy in American Jewish Life." *American Jewish Yearbook* 66 (1965): 21-92.

———. "A Sociological Analysis of Contemporary Orthodoxy." In *Understanding American Judaism: Toward the Description of a Modern Religion*, vol. 2: *Reform, Orthodoxy, Conservatism, and Reconstructionism*, edited by Jacob Neusner, 285-304. New York: Ktav, 1975.

Lobel, Diana. *A Sufi-Jewish Dialogue: Philosophy and Mysticism in Baḥya Ibn Paqūda's "Duties of the Heart."* Philadelphia: University of Pennsylvania Press, 2007.

Lorand, Ruth. *Philosophical Reflection on Beauty* [Hebrew]. Haifa: Haifa University Press, 2007.

Luz, Ehud. "The Dialectic Element in R. Soloveitchik's Works" [Hebrew]. *Daat* 9 (1982): 75-89.

Machsor Vitry, edited by S. Hurwitz. Nuremberg: Bulka, 1923.

Macomber, William B. *The Anatomy of Disillusion: Martin Heidegger's Notion of Truth*. Evanston, IL: Northwestern University Press, 1967.

Macquarrie, John. *Studies in Christian Existentialism*. Montreal: McGill University, 1965.

Maharal (Judah Loew ben Bezalel). *Netivot Olam*. Jerusalem, 1972.

Maimonides. *Iggeret Teiman*, in *Iggerot ha-Rambam*, edited by Y. Shilat, 122-23. Jerusalem: Maaliyot, 1987.

———. *The Code of Maimonides*, book 3: *The Book of Seasons*, translated by Solomon Gandz and Hyman Klein. New Haven: Yale University Press, 1961.

———. *Mishneh Torah: The Book of Knowledge by Maimonides*, translated by Moses Hyamson. Jerusalem: Boys' Town Jerusalem, 1962.

———. *The Commandments: Sefer Ha-Mitzvoth of Maimonides*, translated by Charles B. Chavel. London and New York: Soncino, 1967.

————. *Sefer Hamitzvot: Book of Commandments* [Hebrew], ed. Joseph Kafih. Jerusalem: Mossad Harav Kook, 1971.

————. *Crisis and Leadership: Epistles of Maimonides*, translated by Abraham Halkin. Philadelphia: Jewish Publication Society of America, 1985.

————. *The Code of Maimonides*, book 2: *The Book of Love*, translated by. Menachem Kellner. New Haven, Yale University Press, 2004.

Malantschuk, Gregor. *Kierkegaard's Thought*. Translated by Howard V. Hong and Edna H. Hong. Princeton, NJ: Princeton University Press, 1971.

Mantel, Hayyim Dov. *The Men of the Great Synagogue* [Hebrew]. Tel Aviv: Dvir, 1981.

Margolin, Ron. *Inner Religion: The Phenomenology of Inner Religious Life and Its Manifestation in Jewish Sources (from the Bible to Hasidic Texts)* [Hebrew]. Ramat Gan: Bar-Ilan University Press, 2002.

————. *Inner Temple: Religious Interiorization and the Structuring of Inner Life in Early Hasidism* [Hebrew]. Jerusalem: Magnes, 2005.

Mauss, Marcel. *On Prayer*, translated by S. Leslie. Oxford: Berghahn, 2003.

May, Rollo. *Man's Search for Himself*. New York: Norton , 1953.

————. *The Discovery of Being: Writings in Existential Psychology*. New York and London: Norton, 1983.

Melamed, Abraham. "Maimonides on the Political Nature of Man: Needs and Obligations" [Hebrew]. In In *Tribute to Sara: Studies in Jewish Philosophy and Kabbala Presented to Professor Sara O. Heller Wilensky*, edited by Moshe Idel, Devora Dimant, and Shalom Rosenberg, 328-30. Jerusalem: Magnes, 1994.

Minkovitz, Moshe. "Variant Customs and Traditions for the Recitation of *Shema*" [Hebrew]. *Sinai* 93 (1983): 119-122.

Mirsky, Aaron. "The Origin of 'The Eighteen Benedictions' of the Daily Prayer" [Hebrew]. *Tarbiz* 33 (1963): 28-39. Also included in *Studies in Jewish Liturgy: A Reader* [Hebrew], edited by Hananel Mack, 64-73. Vol. 6 of *Likkutei Tarbiz*. Jerusalem: Magnes, 2003.

Molina, Fernando R. *Existentialism as Philosophy*. Eaglewood Cliffs, NJ: Prentice-Hall, 1962.

Moore, George Foot. *Judaism in the First Centuries of the Christian Era: The Age of the Tannaim*. New York: Schocken, 1971 [1927].

Morgan, Michael L. *Dilemmas in Modern Jewish Thought: The Dialectics of Revelation and History*. Bloomington: Indiana University Press, 1992.

Morgan, Robert. "Ernst Troeltsch and the Dialectical Theology." In *Ernst Troeltsch and the Future of Theology*, edited by John P. Clayton, 33-77. Cambridge: Cambridge University Press, 1976.

Mosès, Stéphane. *System and Revelation: The Philosophy of Franz Rosenzweig*. Detroit: Wayne University Press, 1992.

Mukarovsky, Jan. *Aesthetic Function, Norm and Value as Social Facts*, translated Mark E. Suino. Ann Arbor, MI: University of Michigan, 1970.

Munk, Reinier. *The Rationale of Halakhic Man: Joseph B. Soloveitchik's Conception of Jewish Thought*. Amsterdam: Brill, 1996.

Nachum, Doron. "The Social Constitution of the Selfhood: The Theory of Intersubjectivity in Alfred Schutz's Thought (1899-1959)" [Hebrew], PhD diss., Bar-Ilan University, 2011.

Neher, André. *Le Puits de l'exil: Tradition et modernité: la pensée du Maharal de Prague, 1512-1609*. Paris: Cerf, 1991.

Neusner, Jacob, ed. *Understanding American Judaism*. New York: Ktav Publishing House, 1975.

Newman, John Henry. *An Essay in the Aid of a Grammar of Assent*. London: Longmans, Green, and Co., 1903.

Niebuhr, Rynhold. *The Nature and Destiny of Man*. Louisville, KY: Westminster John Knox Press, 1996.

Nuriel, Abraham, *Concealed and Revealed in Medieval Jewish Philosophy* [Hebrew] Jerusalem: Magnes, 2000.

Oron, Michal. "*Merkavah* Texts and the Legend of the Ten Martyrs" [Hebrew]. *Eshel Beer-Sheva* 2 (1980): 81-95.

Otto, Rudolf. *The Idea of the Holy*, translated by J. W. Harvey. Oxford: Oxford University Press, 1950.

Pascal, Blaise. *Pensees*. Accessed August 17, 2018. www.ccel.org/ccel/pascal/pensees.pdf.

———. *Thoughts and Minor Works*, translated by W. F. Trotter. New York: Collier, 1910.

Paton, Herbert James. *In Defence of Reason*. London: Hutchinson's University Library, 1951.

Pedaya, Haviva. *Expanses: An Essay on the Theological and Political Unconsciousness*. Tel Aviv: Hakibbutz Hameuchad, 2011.

Peli, Pinchas H. "The Uses of Hermeneutics ('Derush') in the Philosophy of J. B. Soloveitchik—Method or Essence?" [Hebrew]. *Daat* 4 (1980): 111-128.

Pfuetze, Paul F. *Self, Society, Existence: Human Nature and Dialogue in the Thought of George Herbert Mead and Martin Buber*. New York: Harper & Row, 1961.

Pick, Shlomo H., ed. *Mo'adei haRav: Public Lectures on the Festivals… in Light of the Teachings of the Rav* [Hebrew]. Ramat Gan: Bar-Ilan University, 2003. 2nd edition Brooklyn, NY: Ktav, 2016.

Pick, Shlomo Zeev. "Rabbi Soloveitchik and the Academic Study of Talmud and Its Implications" [Hebrew]. In *Rabbi in the New World: The Influence of Rabbi J. B. Soloveitchik on Culture, Education and Jewish Thought*, edited by Avinoam Rosenak and Naftali Rothenberg, 281-298 Jerusalem: Van Leer Institute and Magnes, 2010.

Pickering, W. S. F. "Introduction" to Marcel Mauss, *On Prayer*, translated by. S. Leslie. New York: Durkheim, 2003.

Pike, Nelson. *Mystic Union: An Essay in the Phenomenology of Mysticism*. Ithaca, NY: Cornell University Press, 1992.

Pines, Shlomo. "Nachmanides on Adam in the Garden of Eden in the Context of Other Interpretations of Genesis, Chapters 2 and 3" [Hebrew]. In *Exile and Diaspora: Studies in the History of the Jewish People Presented to Professor Haim Beinart*, edited by Aharon Mirsky, Avraham Grossman, and Yosef Kaplan, 159-164 Jerusalem: Ben-Zvi Institute, 1988.

Poma, Andrea. *Yearning for Form and Other Essays on Hermann Cohen's Thought*. Dordrecht: Springer, 2006.

Rashba. *Sifrei ha-Rashba*, edited by Menahem Mendel Gerlitz. Jerusalem: Oraysoh, 1986.

Ratshabi, Shalom. *Between Destiny and Faith: The Jewish Theological Discourse in the United States* [Hebrew]. Tel Aviv: Am Oved, 2003.

Ravizki, Aviezer. "Possible and Contingent Existence in Exegesis of Maimonides in the 13th Century" [Hebrew]. *Daat* 2-3 (1978-79): 67-97.

Reif, Stefan C. *Judaism and Jewish Prayer: New Perspectives on Jewish Liturgical History.* Cambridge: Cambridge University Press, 1993.

Roberts, David E. "Tillich's Doctrine of Man." In *The Theology of Paul Tillich*, edited by Charles W. Kegley and Robert W. Bretall, 108-130. New York: MacMillan, 1964.

Rotenstreich, Nathan. *Jewish Thought in the Modern Period* [Hebrew]. Tel Aviv: Am Oved, 1966.

Rosenak, Avinoam. "Philosophy and Halakhic Thought: A Reading of the Talmud Lessons of Rabbi J. B. Soloveitchik in Light of Neo-Kantian Models" [Hebrew]. In *Faith in Changing Times: On the Teachings of Rabbi Joseph Dov Soloveitchik* [Hebrew], edited by Avi Sagi, 275-306. Jerusalem: World Zionist Organization, 1996.

Rosenberg, Shalom. "Prayer and Jewish Thought: Approaches and Problems (A Survey)." In *Prayer in Judaism: Continuity and Change*, edited by G. Cohn and H. Fisch, 69-107. Northvail, NJ: Jason Arondon, 1996.

———— "The Return to the Garden of Eden: Reflections on the History of the Idea of Restorative Redemption in Medieval Jewish Philosophy" [Hebrew]. In *The Messianic Idea in Jewish Thought: A Study Conference in Honour of the Eightieth Birthday of Gershom Scholem, held 4-5 December 1977*), 37-86. Jerusalem: Israel Academy of Sciences and Humanities, 1982.

————. "And Walk in His Ways." In *Israeli Philosophy* [Hebrew], edited by Moshe Halamish and Asa Kasher, 72-91. Tel Aviv: Papyrus, 1983.

Rosenberg-Shagar, Shimon Gershon. *In His Torah He Meditates: The Study of Talmud as a Quest for God* [Hebrew]. Allon Shevut: Institute for Rav Shagar's Writings, 2009.

Rosenzweig, Franz. *The Star of Redemption*, translated by William W. Hallo. New York: Holt, Rinehart and Winston, 1971.

Rynhold, Daniel. *Two Models of Jewish Philosophy: Justifying One's Practices.* Oxford: Oxford University Press, 2004.

————. "Letting the Facts Get in the Way of a Good Thesis: On Interpreting Rabbi Soloveitchik's Philosophical Method." *Torah u-Madda Journal* 16 (2012-13): 52-77.

Saadia Gaon. *The Book of Beliefs and Opinions*, translated by Samuel Rosenblatt. New Haven: Yale University Press, 1948.

Sabato, Haim. *Seeking His Presence: Conversations with Rabbi Aharon Lichtenstein*, translated by Binyamin Shalom. Tel Aviv: Yedioth Books, 2016.

Sacks, Jonathan. "Rabbi J. B. Soloveitchik's Early Epistemology: A Review of *The Halakhic Mind*." *Tradition* 23, no. 3 (1988): 75-87.

Sadler, William Alan. *Existence and Love: A New Approach in Existential Phenomenology.* New York: Charles Scribner's Sons, 1969.

Sagi, Abraham. *Kierkegaard, Religion and Existence: The Voyage of the Self*, translated by Batya Stein. Amsterdam: Rodopi, 2000.

Sagi, Avi. "The Loneliness of the Man of Faith in the Philosophy of Soloveitchik" [Hebrew]. *Daat* 2-3 (1978): 247-257.

———. *A Challenge: Returning to Tradition* [Hebrew]. Jerusalem: Shalom Hartman Institute, 2003.

———. *Facing Others and Otherness: The Ethics of Inner Retreat* [Hebrew]. Tel Aviv: Hakibbutz Hameuchad, 2013.

———. *Prayer After the Death of God: A Phenomenological Study of Hebrew Literature*, translated by Batya Stein. Boston: Academic Studies Press, 2016.

———. *Living with Others: The Ethics of Inner Retreat*. New York: Springer, 2019.

Schachter, Zvi (Herschel). *The Soul of the Rav* [Hebrew]. Jerusalem: Reshit Yerushalayim, 1999.

———. *From the Pearls of the Rav* [Hebrew]. Jerusalem: Beit Midrash of Flatbush, 2001.

———. *The Words of the Rav* [Hebrew]. Jerusalem: Mesorah, 2010.

Schatz, David. "Science and Religious Consciousness in Rav Soloveitchik's Thought" [Hebrew]. In *Faith in Changing Times: On the Teachings of Rabbi Joseph Dov Soloveitchik* [Hebrew], edited by Avi Sagi, 307-44. Jerusalem: World Zionist Organization, 1996.

Schatz-Uffenheimer, Rivka. *Hasidism as Mysticism: Quietist Elements in Eighteenth-Century Hasidic Thought*, translated by Jonathan Chipman. Princeton: Princeton University Press, 1993.

Scharlemann, Robert P. *Reflection and Doubt in the Thought of Paul Tillich*. New Haven, CT: Yale University Press, 1969.

Schechter, Solomon. *Aspects of Rabbinic Theology*. New York: Schocken, 1961 [1901].

Scheler, Max. *Man's Place in Nature*, translated by H. Meyerhoff. Boston: Beacon Press, 1961.

———. *On the Eternal in Man*, translated by B. Noble. Hamden, CT: Archon, 1972.

Schleiermacher, Friedrich. *The Christian Faith*, edited by H. R. Mackintosh and James S. Stewart. London: Bloomsbury Publishing, 1999.

Scholem, Gershom. *Major Trends in Jewish Mysticism*. New York: Schocken, 1941.

———. *Jewish Gnosticism, Merkabah Mysticism and Talmudic Tradition*. New York: Schocken, 1960.

———. *The Messianic Idea in Judaism and Other Essays*. New York: Schocken, 1971.

Schopenhauer, Arthur. *Complete Essays of Schopenhauer*, translated by T. Bailey Saunders. New York: Willey, 1942.

———. *The World as Will and Representation*, translated by E. F. J. Payne. New York: Dover, 1969.

Schurmann, Reiner. "The One: Substance or Function?" In *Neoplatonism and Nature: Studies in Plotinus' Enneads*, edited by M. E. Wagner, 157-177. Albany, NY: State University of New York Press, 2002.

Schwartz, Dov. "Ethics and Asceticism in the Neoplatonic School of the Fourteenth Century" [Hebrew]. In *Between Religion and Ethics*, edited by Avi Sagi and Daniel Statman, 185-208. Ramat Gan: Bar-Ilan University Press, 1993.

———. "*Maamar Magen David* by ibn Bilia" [Hebrew]. *Kobez al Yad* 12/22 (1994): 196-197.

———. "On the Study of Jewish Homiletics" [Hebrew]. *Peamim* 59 (1994): 149-153.

————. *Land of Israel in Religious Zionist Thought* [Hebrew]. Tel Aviv: Am Oved, 1997.

————. *Religious Zionism between Logic and Messianism* [Hebrew]. Tel Aviv: Am Oved, 1999.

————. *Challenge and Crisis in Rabbi Kook's Circle* [Hebrew]. Tel Aviv: Am Oved, 2001.

————. *Contradiction and Concealment in Medieval Jewish Thought* [Hebrew]. Ramat Gan: Bar-Ilan University, 2002.

————. *Faith at the Crossroads: A Theological Profile of Religious Zionism*, translated by Batya Stein. Leiden: Brill, 2002.

————. *Amulets, Properties and Rationalism in Medieval Jewish Thought* [Hebrew]. Ramat Gan: Bar-Ilan University Press, 2004.

————. *Central Problems in Medieval Jewish Philosophy*. Vol. 26 of *Brill Reference Library of Judaism*. Leiden: Brill, 2005.

————. *Messianism in Medieval Jewish Thought*. Ramat Gan: Bar-Ilan University Press, 2006.

————. *Religion or Halakha*, translated by Batya Stein. Leiden: Brill, 2007.

————. *Halakhic Man: Religion or Halakha?* [Hebrew]. Ramat Gan: Bar-Ilan University Press, 2008.

————. "Personality and Psychology," *The Review of Rabbinic Judaism* 12 (2009): 273-284.

————. "R. Soloveitchik as a Maimonidean: The Unity of Cognition." In *Maimonides and Mysticism: Presented to Moshe Hallamish on the Occasion of His Retirement* [Hebrew], edited by Abraham Elqayam and Dov Schwartz, 301-321. Ramat Gan: Bar-Ilan University Press, 2009.

————. *Habad's Thought from Beginning to End* [Hebrew]. Ramat Gan: Bar-Ilan University Press, 2010.

————. "Psychological Dimensions of Mosaic Prophecy—Imagination and Intellect" [Hebrew]. In *Moses the Man—Master of the Prophets: In the Light of Interpretation throughout the Ages*, edited by Moshe Hallamish, Hannah Kaser, and Hanokh Ben-Pazi, 251-283. Ramat Gan: Bar-Ilan University Press, 2010.

————. ""Religious Zionism and the Struggle against the Evacuation of the Settlements: Theological and Cultural Aspects", in *Religious Zionism Post Disengagement: Future Directions*, edited by Cahim I. Waxman, 93-115. New York: Yeshiva University Press, 2008.

————. "The Separate Intellects and Maimonides' Argumentation (an Inquiry into Guide of the Perplexed II.2-12)." In *Beyond Rashi and Maimonides: Theses in Medieval Jewish Thought, Literature and Exegesis*, edited by E. Kanarfogel and M. Sokolow, 59-92. New York: Ktav, 2010.

————. "The Sermons of R. Ephraim ben Gershon: Sources and Character" [Hebrew]. In *Alei Sefer* 21 (2010): 91-98.

————. *From Phenomenology to Existentialism*, translated by Batya Stein. Leiden: Brill, 2012.

————. *Messianism in Medieval Jewish Thought*, translated by Batya Stein. Boston: Academic Studies Press, 2017.

Schwartz, Yossef. *"To Thee Is Silence Praise": Meister Eckhart's Reading in Maimonides' Guide of the Perplexed* [Hebrew]. Tel Aviv: Am Oved, 2002.

Schwarz, Michael, ed. *The Guide of the Perplexed.* Tel Aviv: Tel Aviv University Press, 2002.

Schweid, Eliezer. "Prayer in the Thought of Yehudah Halevi." In *Prayer in Judaism: Continuity and Change,* edited by Gabriel H. Cohn and Harold Fisch, 109-117. Northvale, NJ: Jason Aronson, 1996.

———. *A History of Modern Religious Philosophy,* part IV [Hebrew]. Tel Aviv: Am Oved, 2006.

———. *The Siddur: Philosophy, Poetry and Mystery* [Hebrew]. Tel Aviv: Miskal, 2009.

———. *A History of Modern Jewish Philosophy,* vol. II: *The Birth of Jewish Historical Studies and the Modern Jewish Religious Movements,* translated by Leonard Levin. Leiden: Brill, 2015.

———. *The Siddur of Prayer: Philosophy, Poetry and Mystery,* translated by Gershon Greenberg. Boston: Academic Studies Press, 2015.

Shahar, Galili. *Fragments of Traditional Modernism and German-Jewish Literature* [Hebrew]. Vol. 16 of *Lecture Series of the Brown Chair for Prussian History, Bar-Ilan University.* Ramat Gan: Bar-Ilan University, 2011.

Sharpe, Eric John. *Comparative Religion: A History.* London: Duckworth, 1975.

Siddur ha-Gra [Prayerbook of the Vilna Gaon], edited by Naphtali Hertz Ha-Levi. Jerusalem, 1895.

Siddur im DEH (Prayerbook of the *Admor ha-Zaken*) [Hebrew]. Brooklyn, NY: 2002.

Siddur Otzar ha-Tefilot. Vilna, 1925.

Silman, Yochanan. "The Torah of Israel in Light of Its New Interpretations: A Phenomenological Clarification." *PAAJR* 57 (1990/1991): Hebrew section, 60-61.

Sklare, Marshall. "The Sociology of the American Synagogue." In *Understanding American Judaism: Toward the Description of a Modern Religion,* vol. 1: *The Rabbi and the Synagogue,* edited by Jacob Neusner, 91-102. New York: Ktav, 1975.

Sokolow, Moshe. *Tefilat Rav: Educating for Prayer, Utilizing the Writings of Rabbi Joseph B. Soloveitchik (the Rav); Curricular and Instructional Guidelines. The Azrieli Papers.* New York: Azrieli Graduate School of Jewish Education & Administration, Yeshiva University, 2006.

Solomon, Robert C. *From Hegel to Existentialism.* Oxford: Oxford University Press, 1987.

Spiegelberg, Herbert. *The Phenomenological Movement: A Historical Introduction.* The Hague: Martinus Nijhoff, 1965.

Sprecher, Shmuel. "*Hallel*: Things as They Are" [Hebrew]. In *Atara L'Haim: Studies in the Talmud and Medieval Rabbinic Literature in Honor of Professor Haim Zalman Dimitrovsky* [Hebrew], edited by Daniel Boyarin et al., 221-231. Jerusalem: Magnes, 2000.

Statman, Daniel. "The Moral Views of Soloveitchik." In *Faith in Changing Times: On the Teachings of Rabbi Joseph Dov Soloveitchik* [Hebrew], edited by Avi Sagi, 249-264 Jerusalem: World Zionist Organization, 1996.

Strauss, Leo. "How to Begin to Study the *Guide of the Perplexed.*" Introductory essay to *The Guide of the Perplexed,* translated by Shlomo Pines. Chicago: University of Chicago Press, 1963), xlvii-xlix.

Svendsen, Lars. *A Philosophy of Boredom*, translated by John Irons. London: Reaktion Books, 2005.

Ta-Shma, Israel M. "Ashkenazi Hasidism in Spain: R. Jonah Gerondi—the Man and His Work" [Hebrew], in *Exile and Diaspora, Exile and Diaspora: Studies in the History of the Jewish People Presented to Professor Haim Beinart*, edited by Aharon Mirsky, Avraham Grossman, and Yosef Kaplan, 177-178. Jerusalem: Ben-Zvi Institute, 1988.

———. *Talmudic Commentary in Europe and North Africa: Literary History*, part 2: *1200-1400* [Hebrew]. Jerusalem, Magnes, 2000.

———. "Three Topics in Prayer." In *Atara L'Haim: Studies in the Talmud and Medieval Rabbinic Literature in Honor of Professor Haim Zalman Dimitrovsky* [Hebrew], edited by Daniel Boyarin et al., 555-562. Jerusalem: Magnes, 2000.

———. "Standing and Sitting While Reading the *Shema* '" [Hebrew]. *Kenishta: Studies of the Synagogue World* 1 (2001): 53-61.

———. "*Pesukei de-Zimrah* and Its Standing in the Prayer Service" [Hebrew]. In *Studies in Memory of Professor Ze'ev Falk*, edited by Michael Corinaldi et al., 269-275. Jerusalem: Schechter Institute of Jewish Studies, 2005.

Tabory, Joseph. *Jewish Prayer and the Yearly Cycle: A List of Articles*. Supplement to *Kiryat Sefer* 64 [Hebrew]. Jerusalem, 1992-1993.

Targin, Eli, and Michael Rubinstein. *Prayer as Encounter: The Laws of Prayer—A Journey from the Halakhah to the Soul* [Hebrew]. Jerusalem: Merkaz Halakhah and Sifriyat Bet-El, 2011.

Tillich, Paul. *Systematic Theology*. Chicago: The University of Chicago Press, 1951.

———. *The Courage to Be*. New Haven: Yale University Press, 1952.

Twersky, Isadore. *Introduction to the Code of Maimonides (Mishneh Torah)*. New Haven: Yale University Press, 1980.

———. *Introduction to the Mishneh Torah of Maimonides* [Hebrew edition], translated by M. B. Lerner. Jerusalem: Magnes, 1991.

Underhill, Evelyn. *Worship*. New York: Harper & Brothers, 1957.

Urbach, Ephraim E. "The Role of the Ten Commandments in Jewish Worship." In *Collected Writings in Jewish Studies*, ed. Robert Brody and Moshe D. Herr. Jerusalem: Magness, 1999.

Verrycken, Koenraad. "The Metaphysics of Ammonius Son of Hermeias." In *Aristotle Transformed: The Ancient Commentators and Their Influence*, edited by Richard Sorabji, 215-216. Ithaca, NY: Cornell University Press, 1990.

Walfish, Avraham. "The *Brisker* Method and Close Reading—A Response to Rav Elyakim Krumbein" [Hebrew]. *Netuim* 11-12 (2004): 95-137.

Wieder, Naphtali. "Chapters in the History of Prayer and Benedictions" [Hebrew]. *Sinai* 77 (1975): 127-133. Also included in Naphtali Wieder, *The Formation of Jewish Liturgy in the East and the West*, 166-172. Jerusalem: Ben-Zvi Institute for the Study of Jewish Communities in the East, 1998.

Weinfeld, Moshe. "The Biblical Roots of the Standing Prayer on the Sabbaths and Festivals" [Hebrew]. *Tarbiz* 65 (1996): 547-548. Also included in *Studies in Jewish Liturgy: A Reader*

[Hebrew], edited by Hananel Mack, 35-36. Vol. 6 of *Likkutei Tarbiz*. Jerusalem: Magnes, 2003.

———. *Decalogue and the Recitation of "Shema": The Development of Confessions* [Hebrew]. Tel Aviv: Hakibbutz Hameuchad, 2001.

Wertheim, Aaron. *Law and Custom in Hasidism*, translated by Shmuel Himelsten. Hoboken, NJ: Ktav, 1992.

Wohlman, Avital. *Loving God: Christian Love, Theology and Philosophy in Thomas Aquinas* [Hebrew]. Tel Aviv: Resling, 2005.

Wolfsberg-Aviad, Isaiah. *Thoughts on the Philosophy of History* [Hebrew]. Jerusalem: Mossad Harav Kook, 1958.

Wolfson, Harry Austryn. "Notes on Proofs of the Existence of God in Jewish Philosophy." *HUCA* 1 (1924): 584-596.

———. "The Double Faith Theory in Clement, Saadia, Averroes and St. Thomas, and Its Origin in Aristotle and the Stoics." *Jewish Quarterly Review* 32 (1942-1943): 213-264.

———. *The Philosophy of the Kalam*. Cambridge, MA: Harvard University Press, 1976.

Woolf, Jeffrey. "In Search of the Rav: The Life and Thought of Rabbi Joseph Soloveitchik in Recent Scholarship." *BDD: Journal of Torah and Scholarship* 18 (2007): 5-28.

———. "Time Awareness as a Source of Spirituality in the Thought of Rabbi Joseph B. Soloveitchik." *Modern Judaism* 32, no. 1 (2012): 54-75.

Yalom, Irvin D. *Existential Psychotherapy*. New York: Basic Books, 1980.

Yerushalmi, Yosef Hayim. *Zakhor: Jewish History and Jewish Memory* [Hebrew]. Tel Aviv: Am Oved, 1988. English edition: Seattle: University of Washington Press, 1996.

Zahavy, Tzvee. *Studies in Jewish Prayer*. Lanham, MD: University Press of America, 1990.

Zahavy, Tzvi. *God's Favorite Prayers*. Teaneck, NJ: Talmudic Books, 2011.

———. "*Kavvanah* (Concentration) for Prayer in the Mishnah and Talmud." In *New Perspectives on Ancient Judaism*, vol. I, edited by J. Neusner et al., 37-48. Lanham: University Press of America, 1987.

———. *The Mishnaic Law of Blessings and Prayers: Tractate Berakhot*. Atlanta: Scholars Press, 1987.

Ziegler, Reuven, *Majesty and Humanity: The Thought of Rabbi Joseph B. Soloveitchik*. Jerusalem: Urim Publications, 2012.

Zohar, Noam. "The Figure of Abraham and the Voice of Sarah in Genesis Rabbah" [Hebrew]. In *The Faith of Abraham: In the Light of Interpretation throughout the Ages*, ed. Moshe Hallamish, Hannah Kasher, and Yohanan Silman, 80-82. Ramat Gan: Bar-Ilan University Press, 2002.

The Zohar, translated by Daniel C. Matt. Stanford, CA: Stanford University Press, 2007.

CPSIA information can be obtained
at www.ICGtesting.com
Printed in the USA
BVHW040557081219
565982BV00005B/64/P